TO THE
WARRIOR
HIS ARMS

TO THE WARRIOR HIS ARMS

The story of the Royal Army Ordnance Corps

by

Brigadier Frank Steer MBE

Pen & Sword

MILITARY

First published in Great Britain in 2005 by
Pen & Sword Military
an imprint of
Pen & Sword Books Ltd
47 Church Street
Barnsley
South Yorkshire
S70 2AS

ISBN 1 84415 329 0

A CIP catalogue record for this book is
available from the British Library

Printed and bound in England
by CPI UK.

Pen & Sword Books Ltd incorporates the Imprints of Pen & Sword Aviation,
Pen & Sword Maritime, Pen & Sword Military, Wharncliffe Local history,
Pen & Sword Select, Pen & Sword Military Classics and Leo Cooper.

For a complete list of Pen & Sword titles please contact
PEN & SWORD BOOKS LIMITED
47 Church Street, Barnsley, South Yorkshire, S70 2AS, England
E-mail: enquiries@pen-and-sword.co.uk
Website: www.pen-and-sword.co.uk

Contents

BUCKINGHAM PALACE

My late grandfather, His Majesty King George VI., and my mother, Her Majesty Queen Elizabeth II, were the Colonels-in-Chief of the Royal Army Ordnance Corps for the seventy-five years of its existence from November 1918 to April 1993. It was a matter of great pride for them both, and when the opportunity came for me to continue that relationship with the Patronage of the Royal Army Ordnance Corps Charitable Trust I was both delighted and honoured to accept.

This book tells the story of those seventy-five years. It reflects the enormous contribution the RAOC made to the Army and the tremendous legacy it passed on in 1993 to the fledgling Royal Logistic Corps. It was a legacy that encompassed not only a record of military and sporting excellence, but also commercial managerial experience gained from years of supplying the Army from industry. From providing units for special forces to undertaking bomb disposal throughout the world; from providing units in close support of warfighting operations to delivering support in depth for the prosecution of hostilities; from being there to support the whole range of Army peacetime activities to meeting a plethora of short notice requirements for Ordnance support; from an active programme of unit sport to winning many, and varied, Combined Service and Army sporting trophies; from the management of major installations covering the full range of logistic disciplines to introducing major, leading edge Information Technology systems; the RAOC was at the forefront of so much. Wherever the Army was, the RAOC was always there. And so often it delivered so much against considerable opposition.

It is a proud record, and one which we should not forget. This book is a tribute to the people who have created the RAOC's history and an inspiration to those who follow in their footsteps.

Anne

Preface

by

Major General D F E Botting CB CBE

Director General of Ordnance Services   1990 – 1993
Representative Colonel Commandant 1993
President RAOC Charitable Trust

This is the story of the Royal Army Ordnance Corps, a famous Corps that with its predecessors has for centuries served the country and the Army with courage and professionalism. It is a story about the spirit, initiative and achievements, in many fields, of its members and why we are proud to have served in the RAOC.

The RAOC was taken from the Order of Battle of the British Army on 5 April 1993. Its functions were brought together with those of the Postal and Courier Service of the Royal Engineers, the Royal Corps of Transport, the Royal Pioneer Corps and the Army Catering Corps to form The Royal Logistic Corps.

The RAOC has been extremely well served by its historians who have covered the history of Ordnance in its various guises since the dawn of British Military time. The three volume work by Major General A Forbes, published in 1929, starts in medieval times and concludes in 1918 with the end of the First World War.   The period 1918 to 1945 was covered by Brigadier A H Fernyhough's work and the period from 1945 to 1982 by Major General L T H Phelps and published in 1991.   All these histories are of the highest standard and remain the definitive work for their period. This latest work by Brigadier F R Steer, bringing the story of the RAOC up to the date of its amalgamation, continues the high standard and completes an excellent quartet.   The Trustees and I are most grateful to Frank Steer for undertaking this mammoth task with such enthusiasm and skill.

So well had our history been recorded that only the last ten years, to 1993, remained to be written. However in order to put the last ten years in context a longer period needed to be covered. This story starts with a brief summary of our history up to 1918 and then concentrates on the Royal Years 1918 – 1993. It is not a rewrite of our previous histories, indeed they provide the basis for much of the story together with new material, mostly from individual contributions.

The history of the RAOC records a constant cycle of change. Changes in responsibilities and to whom responsible; reorganizations, cuts in manpower and funding and under investment in logistic facilities and information technology. Many of the changes were not properly implemented, others not given a chance to prove their effectiveness, many tried to solve yesterday's problem rather than tomorrow's. The reorganization, the Logistic Support Review, which led to amalgamation, was part of this cycle of change. A period of poor equipment availability brought about by twenty years of running on old equipment alongside new, thus increasing the range of equipment and the number of variants of those types, trebled the spares support needed and coupled with several reorganizations of the Field Force, changes in the equipment mix and severe cuts in the funding of spares, seriously distorted the provision model The demand led system, as the RAOC always feared, could not cope.

As this equipment crisis came to a head the Wall in Germany came down and everything changed. The resultant reorganization of the Army – Options for Change – together with the consequent redundancies and the amalgamation, created a life changing event for many in the RAOC. The performance of the Corps in these last years which covered the Gulf War and the clear up, Options for Change, the closure of BAOR Depots and the withdrawal and disposal of equipment and stock from Belgium and Germany, and the amalgamation, whilst – at the same time – providing an unbroken supply system, are a fitting finale to its outstanding history. The reader might reasonably wonder why a Corps that could jump through so many hoops at the same time was amalgamated.

Throughout its history, despite constant under resourcing and many dubious and wasteful changes and reorganizations, the RAOC and its predecessors continued to provide a supply system day in and day out, around the clock, around the world in peace and war. Despite under investment, the Corps continued to innovate and to develop new systems and facilities across all its many functions. Always with enthusiasm and a positive attitude and an indomitable spirit that shone through whatever difficulties were added to managing the supply system that were put in its way, be it clearing up, closing down or changing around. The RAOC and its predecessors and its civilian staff have served the Army and the Nation marvellously.

Sua Tela Tonanti

Acknowledgements

The simple logistics of the task dictated the way this book would be written, and its style. Wherever the Army was deployed so would be the RAOC, providing the essential logistic support to allow warlike operations to take place as well as underpinning peacetime activity. To include everything in detail would have produced a book so large as to make it unmanageable and the task, therefore, involved deciding what to leave out rather than what to put in. What was important was to tell of the life of the RAOC and life in the RAOC; to give a flavour of what the RAOC and the men and women in it gave to the Army and the Nation. That was my guiding theme; only the reader will judge if I have accurately reflected it.

The three authors who preceded me in writing the history of the RAOC undertook a huge amount of detailed and very comprehensive research in compiling their histories of the RAOC for the periods they covered. In the case of the second two their texts were well fleshed out by the experience they were able to bring from their service in the RAOC covering almost entirely the period covered by their books. As a repository for facts they were outstanding and were of great help to me in creating my chronology of events. They, however, covered their histories by theatre which meant the reader changing timings each time they changed the place in which events were occurring. I chose to run everything concurrently, to take the horizontal approach across time rather than the vertical approach by function or location. In this way I have tried to represent just how much was going on at the same time across the world that affected the RAOC. It provided me with an amazing insight into a huge amount of simultaneous activity and a sense of wonder that so much was achieved whilst at the same time retaining the capacity and making the time to enjoy life. I hope I have been able to communicate that.

Where I have shown prices they are at the value of the day, then following in brackets is the value at 2005 prices. This I have derived from a most useful piece of software which provides a handy guide to values to which I hope the modern reader will be able to relate.

I must record my thanks to the trustees of the RAOC Charitable Trust who accepted my ground rules for agreeing to write this book: that there should be but one author, not a committee; and that the book should be written in such a way and with such a flavour as to appeal to the largest possible readership. They agreed and left me alone to get on with it and for the privilege of their trust in me I am more grateful than I can say. However, it would have been impertinent to proceed unilaterally and without consultation so I created my own small editorial committee comprising Major General David Botting, CB, CBE, Major General David Burden CB, CBE and Major General Peter Chambers CBE who read every chapter as it was completed, who confirmed that the style and content were on track, and who offered guidance and encouragement throughout the considerable challenge of pulling all this together. Major (Retd) Robin McDermott, who entered the RAOC the same day as me, and was best man at my wedding, also took a long hard and detailed look at a large part of the manuscript, and his telling comments were most helpful. Colonel Peter Walton undertook a great deal of research for me, and without his support and wise counsel this work would have been so much harder. It would also be wrong to omit mention of the contribution of Colonel Terry Byrd OBE. There is no proper record of the history of Information Technology in the RAOC, despite the major impact it had. His memory provided it, and helped me enormously in reflecting its importance. Gareth Mears, the archivist at the RLC Museum has been universally helpful. No request was ever too much for him and his willing and friendly help has been of enormous value. Finally, but by no means least, Kathy Ford, whose late father, Brian Ford, retired in 1983 as an RSM in the RAOC, helped with some of the typing and proved much faster and better at it than I could ever have been and researched a number of photographs for me. To them all my gratitude is immense.

To achieve what I was seeking I consulted as widely as I could, both the written word and interviews with as many as were prepared to be interviewed. Those sources are recorded below, and I am inordinately grateful to those, or their relatives, who took the time to write or to talk, to dig for information or to offer guidance, for they provided me with a feeling, I suppose of comradeship, that I hope I have been able to impart. It matters not if I did not use their material directly; it was the flavour that the sum total of it all gave me that mattered as much as the individual stories. Wherever possible the rank on discharge is shown, thereby offering an indication of the spread of support provided: Allured RK, Corporal; Anthony SE, Private; Aram GD, Lance Corporal; Alderman F, Sergeant; Avery D, Lieutenant Colonel; Baker BM, Private; Baldwin A, Sergeant; Barratt KH, Sergeant; Bateman C, Corporal; Bates SH; Bell J; Bennett SE, Major; Berragan GB, Major General; Berresford K, Brigadier; Biggs BR, Brigadier; Birch WH, WOI; Birt LJ, Captain; Blundell JE, Private; Bomford PR, Major; Botting DFE, Major General; Bowden RB, Colonel; Bradley D, Conductor; Breadmore WJ, Major; Bretherton T, Lieutenant; Broadbent MH, Staff Sergeant; Broweleit H, Hon Colonel; Brown EH, Brigadier; Bulcock R, Private(?); Burden DL; Major General; Burrows CH, Sergeant; Bye DF, Sergeant; Bye G, Corporal; Byrd T, Colonel; Cantrell F, Lieutenant Colonel; Carman RT, Lieutenant Colonel; Chambers J, Sergeant; Chambers PA, Major General; Child FW, Corporal; Clark F, Staff Sergeant (?); Clews H, Staff Sergeant; Cluderay CA, Private; Comerford M, WOI; Connolly M, Lieutenant Colonel; Cook JFG, Colonel; Cooper FJ, Sergeant; Cooper Sir Henry, Lance Corporal; Cowdry DFA, Brigadier; Crago B, WOI; Craven A, Corporal; Crowther AW; Cruickshank JM, Corporal; Crump LA, Sergeant; Davies RJ, Corporal; Davison MJ, Lieutenant Colonel; Dawson CH, Colonel; Doudie W; Dowle WH, Private; Dukes RS, WOI; Dymock J, Corporal; Edwards TJ, Private; Eyles CH, Sergeant; Fairhead D; Fletcher V; Ford WV, Lieutenant Colonel; Forshaw L, WOII; Fox BA, Colonel; Frere JSB, Lieutenant Colonel; Fuller CM, Lieutenant Colonel; Gallacher TM, Corporal; Gilbertson MA, Brigadier; Glen BR, WOI; Goodeve RCE, Captain; Goodwin FS, Brigadier; Goozee PK, Brigadier; Gosling R, Corporal; Govier E; Grassby C, Lieutenant; Gray HJ, Sub-Conductor; Green Mr and Mrs K; Greenberg B, Private; Griffiths DL, Staff Sergeant; Grimes G; Hall GA, Private; Hall DS, Colonel; Hall J, Private; Halsey DHJ, Colonel; Hampson P, Second Lieutenant; Harvey M, Staff Sergeant; Hendy CMG, Colonel; Hewitt CA, Brigadier; Hocking WJ, Captain; Holland GC, Staff Sergeant; Hossack AP, Private; Howe L, Private; Howden E, Corporal; Husband NA, Private; Istead PWE, Major General; Jackson JA, Brigadier; Jackson Sir William, General; Jarvis REH, WOII; Jeans FCJ, Sergeant; Jennings GB, WOII; Johnson DW, Private; Jones G, WOII; Kay DW; Kerr J S, Major General; Kirby RHT Brigadier; Laceby AJ, Lieutenant Colonel; Lambert AH, Corporal; Lampard NA, Lieutenant Colonel; Lee B, Corporal; Lindsay P, Lance Corporal; Luscombe AT, Corporal; Manners CC, Corporal; Mathams MA, Colonel; Maxwell D; Mayfield TW, Corporal; McChrystal J; McConnell WJ, WOI; McHardy KC, Corporal; McNicoll F, Private; Midgley A; Morris K Sergeant; Morton CJ, Major; Moss KH, Sergeant; Mountford AH, Lieutenant Colonel; Mullins, K, Brigadier; Murdoch IAB, Corporal; Murray MA, Corporal; Naden E, Sergeant (Acting); Nunn J, Pte(W); Oakland J, Private; O'Dea M, Colonel; Owen DG; Padmore LA, Lance Corporal; Parkes GL, Lance Corporal; Peacock RL; Peaker MG, Group Captain; Pemberton R, Private; Pennington I, WOI; Perkins GA, WOI; Phelps LTH, Major General; Philips J, Corporal REME; Pittam CC, Lieutenant Colonel; Pole WM, Major; Poulter TW, Conductor; Pursglove, D, Private; Ranson RV, Brigadier; Rees DL, WOII; Rendell R, Private; Roberts D; Robertson W, Lance Corporal; Rook R, Brigadier; Rowell AS, Lance Corporal;

Ruddy K, Corporal; Saunders K; Scott G, Lieutenant Colonel; Searle R; Sharland JFF, Brigadier; Sharman W, WOI; Sharpe LC, Colonel; Shepherd J, Lance Corporal; Sinclair-Lee R, Captain; Simpson AF, Staff Sergeant; Skinner JH, Brigadier; Slade CE; Smart JH, WO; Smellie NA, Lieutenant Colonel; Smith AC, Colonel; Smith J, Corporal; Smith RPB, Colonel; Smith WA; Snape D; Sparrow REL, Lance Corporal; Spiller J; Stevens RT, WOI; Stafford GH, Major; Stone M, Colonel; Storey C; Swindley RA, Lieutenant Colonel; Tattersall JR, Captain; Tarran J, Sergeant; Taylor A, Lieutenant Colonel; Thomas COS, Lieutenant Colonel; Thomas DJ, Private; Titley FA, Private; Turner JA, Brigadier; Wales JK, Private; Walton P, Colonel; Waller A; Warden G, WOI (Sub Conductor); Watt DC, Colonel; Weaver GR, Lance Corporal; Webster CA, Lieutenant; Webster GFA, Captain; Welch ACD, Brigadier; White RJ, Conductor; Whitehouse J, WOI; Willox R, Lieutenant Colonel; Wilson R, Private; Wintle K; Wood MD, Major General; Wood LJR, Corporal; Worth I, Private.

In the background a great deal of work had to be undertaken to get the administration of creating the book and to distribute it to members of the RAOC Association and the Officers' Club. The secretary of the RAOC Charitable Trust, Lieutenant Colonel (Retd) Dennis Irvine was always there when needed, and was, as ever, utterly reliable. It is always handy having a friend you know you can trust when the pressure is on.

I am enormously grateful to the proof reading team that assembled at Deepcut to check the edited proofs of the book and to offer me their insight, wisdom, memories and guidance. All retired, they were Brigadier Gordon Dennison, Brigadier Mike Owen, Brigadier Mike Roycroft, Colonel Baz Dickson, Lieutenant Colonel Bill Masterton, Lieutenant Colonel Dennis Irvine, Lieutenant Colonel Tony Camfield, Major Bob McLagan, Major Tim Lill and Major Bob Corbey. They found and corrected the errors I would have missed, having become too closely involved with the script.

I am honoured that Her Royal Highness the Princess Royal agreed to write the foreword. She is Patron of the Royal Army Ordnance Corps Charitable Trust, carrying on a link with the Royal Household that the RAOC has been privileged to enjoy since its creation in November 1918. It is a link that is a matter of great pride for the RAOC and all who served in it over the seventy-five years of its existence, and her gracious support for this venture is a further cementing of an important and much treasured association.

Finally, no expressions of gratitude would be complete without mention of my wife, Virginia, who followed me through thirty-four houses and brought up five children during thirty-two of the thirty three years I served with the RAOC and RLC; and then endured with considerable patience the three years it took me to write this book to say nothing of the effort involved in scanning almost every picture.

I have tried to reflect accurately what happened. If there are errors, inconsistencies or omissions they are mine and mine alone. I apologise for them and take full responsibility for them.

Brigadier F R Steer MBE
Paddock Wood
Kent
October 2005

Glossary

A Vehicle	Armoured Vehicle
AA	Anti-aircraft
AAC	Army Air Corps
AAD	Advanced Ammunition Depot
ABOD	Advanced Base Ordnance Depot
ACC	Army Catering Corps
ACDS(L)	Assistant Chief of the Defence Staff (Logistics)
ACE	Allied Command Central Europe
Ack-ack	Anti-aircraft fire (slang)
ADGB	Air Defence of Great Britain
ADP1	Automated Data Processing Installation
ADMS	Assistant Director of Medical Services
ADOC	Armoured Division Ordnance Company
ADOS	Assistant Director Of Ordnance Services
ADP	Automated Data Processing
AE	Ammunition Examiner
AER	Army Emergency Reserve
AFG 1098	Unit equipment for its own general administration
AFHQ	Allied Forces Headquarters
AFS	Army Fire Service
AGC	Adjutant General's Corps
AIDU	Ammunition Inspection and Disposal Unit
AMF(L)	Allied Command Europe Mobile Force (Land)
AOC	Army Ordnance Corps
AOD	Advanced Ordnance Depot
AOD	Army Ordnance Department
AOER	Army Officers Emergency Reserve
AOS	Army Ordnance Services
AOW	Advanced Ordnance Workshop
APFC	Airportable Fuel Container
APR	Adjustable Pallet Racking
APTC	Army Physical Training Corps
ARH	Ammunition Rail Head
ARMDU	Armaments Research and Development Unit
ASA	Army School of Ammunition
ASC	Army Service Corps

ASCT	Army School of Clerical Training
ASDN	Army Supply Data Network
ASMT	Army School of Motor Transport
AT	Ammunition Technician
ATAF	Allied Tactical Air Force
ATO	Ammunition Technical Officer
ATS	Auxiliary Territorial Service
AVP	Army Vehicle Park
B Vehicle	Soft skinned vehicle
BAD	Base Ammunition Depot
BAOR	British Army of the Rhine
BATUS	British Army Training Unit Suffield
BCOF	British Commonwealth Occupation Force
BCR	Battle Casualty Replacement
BEF	British Expeditionary Force
BFAP	British Forces Arabian Peninsula
BFES	British Forces Education Service
BFI	Bulk Fuel Installation
BFME	British Forces Middle East
BFSU	British Forces Support Unit
BFT	Basic Fitness Test
BIT	Bomb Intelligence Team
BL	Breech Loading
BLT	British Liaison Team
BMA	Brigade Maintenance Area
BMP	Beach Maintenance Pack
Bn	Battalion
BOD	Base Ordnance Depot
BOO	Brigade Ordnance Officer
BOW	Base Ordnance Workshop
BOWO	Brigade Ordnance Warrant Officer
BRITFORLEB	British Force in the Lebanon
BVD	Base Vehicle Depot
C Sups	Combat Supplies (Ammunition, Rations, POL)
C Vehicle	Plant or materials handling vehicle
CAD	Central Ammunition Depot
CATO	Chief Ammunition Technical Officer
CCK	Commonwealth Contingent Korea
CCRAOC	Corps Commander RAOC
CDS	Chief of the Defence Staff
CENTO	Central Treaty Organisation
CEPS	Central European Pipeline System
CGS	Chief of the General Staff
CiCC	Commanders in Chief Committee
CICP	Central Inventory Control Point

CIGS	Chief of the Imperial General Staff
CILSA	Chief Inspector of Land Service Ammunition
CIOO	Chief Inspecting Ordnance Officer
CLA	Chemical Laboratory Assistant
CMG	Composite Maintenance Group
CO	Commanding Officer
COD	Central Ordnance Depot
COFFER	Computerised Office and Field Force Electronic Record
COME	Chief Ordnance Mechanical Engineer
COMP	Corps Ordnance Maintenance Park
COO	Chief Ordnance Officer
COSLOG	Chief of Staff the Logistic Executive
COSSEC	Combined Chiefs of Staff Committee
CRP	Complete Round Proof
CRPAT	Complete Round Proof Assessment Team
CSA	Corps Support Area
CSDW	Computer Systems Development Wing
CSM	Company Sergeant Major
CSS	Combat Service Support
CT	Communist Terrorist
CVD	Central Vehicle Depot(s)
CVHQ	Central Vehicle Headquarters
D Log IS (A)	Director of Logistic Information Services (Army)
D Sup(A)	Director of Supply (Army)
DAA	Divisional Administrative Area
DAA&QMG	Deputy Assistant Adjutant & Quartermaster General
DADOS	Deputy Director General of Ordnance Services
DAM	Directorate of Artillery and Mechanisation
DAQMG	Deputy Assistant Quartermaster General
DBD	Director/Directorate of Base Depots
DCAO	Deputy Chief Administrative Officer
DCOS	Deputy Chief of Staff
DCT	Directorate of Clothing and Textiles
DDOS	Deputy Director of Ordnance Services
DDOS(P)	Deputy Director of Ordnance Services (Provision)
DEOS	Director of Equipment and Ordnance Stores
DES	Director of Equipment Support
DG Log Sp (A)	Director General Logistic Support (Army)
DGAE	Director General of Army Equipment
DGEME	Director General of Electrical and Mechanical Engineers
DGES(A)	Director General Equipment Support (Army)
DGLP(A)	Director General of Logistic Planning (Army)
DGMP	Director General of Munitions Production
DGOS	Director General of Ordnance Services
DLSA	Director/Directorate of Land Service Ammunition

DOS	Director of Ordnance Services
DOWO	Divisional Ordnance Warrant Officer
DP	Distribution Point
DPM	Disruptive Pattern Material
DSA	Divisional Support Area
DSCS	Director/ Directorate of Supply Computer Services
DSM	Director/Directorate of Supply Management
DSM(A)	Directorate of Supply Management (Army)
DSP(A)	Director of Support Planning (Army)
E Man	Equipment Management
EAAOC	East Africa Army Ordnance Corps
EADCU	Enemy Ammunition Depot Clearance Unit
EALF	East African Land Forces
EFI	Expeditionary Forces Institute
EOD	Explosive Ordnance Disposal
ESH	Explosive Store House
FAD	Forward Ammunition Depot
FAMTO	First Aid Motor Transport Outfit
FARELF	Far East Land Forces
FATSO	First Aid Technical Stores Outfit
FFMA	Forward Force Maintenance Area
FLT	Fork Lift Truck
FMA	Forward Maintenance Area
FMB	Forward Mounting Base
FOD	Forward Ordnance Depot/Detachment
FOWO	Force Ordnance Warrant Officer
FSD	Forward Stores Depot
FTS	Field Trailer Section
FVRDE	Fighting Vehicles Research and Development Establishment
G4	Logistics Staff
GC	George Cross
GHQ	General Headquarters
GM	George Medal
GM	Guided Missile
GOC	General Officer Commanding
GS	General Service
GT	General Transport
HE	High Explosive
HMG	Her Majesty's Government
HMSO	Her Majesty's Stationery Office
IAOC	Indian Army Ordnance Corps
ICP	Inventory Control Point
IED	Improvised Explosive Device
IEDD	Improvised Explosive Device Disposal
IOM	Inspector of Ordnance Machinery

IOO	Inspecting Ordnance Officer
IRA	Irish Republican Army
ISDW	Inventory Systems Development Wing
IT	Information Technology
JIC	Joint Intelligence Committee
JSU	Joint Supply Unit
KD	Khaki Drill
LAD	Light Aid Detachment
LCT	Landing Craft Tank
LE(A)	Logistic Executive (Army)
LEC	Locally Engaged Civilians
LofC	Line of Communication
LRS	Local Resources Section
LSG	Logistic Support Group
LSL	Landing Ship Logistic
LSR	Logistic Support Review
LST	Landing Ship Tank
M&RO	Manning and Record Office
MA	Military Assistant
MBE	Member of the Most Excellent Order of the British Empire
MBSTD	Main Base Stores Transit Depot
MBT	Main Battle Tank
MEC	Middle East Command
MEF	Middle East Forces
MELF	Middle East Land Forces
MEXE	Military Engineering Experimental Establishment
MGO	Master General of the Ordnance
MHE	Materials Handling Equipment
MHEU	Materials Handling Experimental Unit
MHPEU	Materials Handling and Packaging Experimental Unit
MHTU	Materials Handling Trials Unit
MiD	Mention in Despatches
MINIS	Ministers' Information System
MIO	Military Intelligence Officer
MLBU	Mobile Laundry and Bath Unit
MMC	Materiel Mounting Centre
MOD	Ministry of Defence
MOR	Malay Other Rank
MPAT	Missile Proof Assessment Team
MQES	Married Quarters Exchange Shop
MRE	Meals Ready to Eat
MSM	Meritorious Service Medal
MSO	Mixed Services Organisation
MT	Motor Transport
MTI	Military Training Instructor

NAAFI	Navy Army and Air Force Institute
NATO	North Atlantic Treaty Organisation
NBC	Nuclear Biological and Chemical
NCO	Non Commissioned Officer
NCR	National Cash Register
NEARELF	Near East Land Forces
NICRA	Northern Ireland Catholic Rights Association
NMS	New Management Strategy
NORTHAG	Northern Army Group
NSE	National Support Element
NSN	NATO Stock Number
NTM	Notice To Move
O Group	Orders Group, key individuals in a unit whom the commander assembles to give orders
OBD	Ordnance Beach Detachment
OBE	Officer of the Most Excellent Order of the British Empire
OC	Officer Commanding
OCD	Ordnance Composite Depot
OFP	Ordnance Field Park
OLIVER	On Line Verification
OMC	Ordnance Maintenance Company
OME	Ordnance Mechanical Engineer
OMP	Ordnance Maintenance Park
OMW	Ordnance Mobile Workshop
ORBAT	Order Of Battle
Ordnance Stores	Name used for complete range of Technical, MT and General Stores
ORP	Operational Ration Pack
OSP	Ordnance Sub Park
OSU	Ordnance Support Unit
PAD	Port Ammunition Detachment
PAF	Provision Action Figure
PC&A	Provision Control & Accounts
PLOD	Pipeline Over The Desert
PLUTO	Pipeline Under The Ocean
POD	Port Ordnance Detachment
PoE	Port of Entry
POL	Petroleum, Oils and Lubricants
POME	Principal Ordnance Mechanical Engineer
POO	Principal Ordnance Officer
POW	Prisoner of War
PPQ	Primary Packaged Quantity
PUE	Pre-Stocked Unit Equipment
PWO	Prince Of Wales Own Regiment Of Yorkshire
QM	Quartermaster
QMG	Quartermaster General

QMS	Quartermaster Sergeant Major
RA	Royal Artillery
RAAOC	Royal Australian Army Ordnance Corps
RAC	Royal Armoured Corps
RAEC	Royal Army Educational Corps
RAF	Royal Air Force
RAMC	Royal Army Medical Corps
RAOC	Royal Army Ordnance Corps
RAPC	Royal Army Pay Corps
RAR	Royal Australian Regiment
RARDE	Royal Armaments Research and Development Establishment
RASC	Royal Army Service Corps
RAVC	Royal Army Veterinary Corps
RCIED	Radio Controlled Improvised Explosive Device
RCT	Royal Corps of Transport
RCZ	Rear Combat Zone
RE	Royal Engineers
RFA	Royal Fleet Auxiliary
RHA	Royal Horse Artillery
RIC	Royal Irish Constabulary
RIH	Royal Irish Hussars
RLC	Royal Logistic Corps
RM	Royal Marine(s)
RMA	Rear Maintenance Area
RMA	Royal Military Academy
RMN	Royal Malaysian Navy
RN	Royal Navy
ROF	Royal Ordnance Factory
ROLAND	Revised On Line Ammunition Network Development
RP	Replenishment Park
RPC	Royal Pioneer Corps
RQMS	Regimental Quartermaster Sergeant
RSD	Returned Stores Depot
RSG	Returned Stores Group
RSM	Regimental Sergeant Major
RSSD	Returned Stores Sub Depot
RTR	Royal Tank Regiment
RUC	Royal Ulster Constabulary
RUR	Royal Ulster Rifles
RVD	Rear Vehicle Depot
SACEUR	Supreme Allied Commander Europe
SAF	Singapore Armed Forces
SALOME	System for Accounting Location and On line Management of Equipments
SAS	Special Air Service

SATO	Senior Ammunition Technical Officer
SBA	Sovereign Base Area
SCAO	Standing Committee on Army Organisation
SCARAB	Scales and Related Applicability Base
SD	Service Dress
SEAC	South East Asia Command
SEATO	South East Asia Treaty Organisation
SHAPE	Supreme Headquarters Allied Powers Europe
SITREP	Situation Report
SLR	Self Loading Rifle
SNCO	Senior Non Commissioned Officer
SO	Staff Officer
SQMS	Staff Quartermaster Sergeant
SSM	Staff Sergeant Major
STUFT	Shipping Taken Up From Trade
T&AVR	Territorial and Army Volunteer Reserve
TA	Territorial Army
TAF	Tactical Air Force
TAIS	Transportable ADP Inventory System
TDU	Theatre Drawdown Unit
TEZ	Total Exclusion Zone
TLC	Tank Landing Craft
TSSD	Technical Stores Sub Depot
TSW	Tactical Supply Wing RAF
UBRE	Unit Bulk Refuelling Equipment
UDR	Ulster Defence Regiment
UKLF	United Kingdom Land Forces
UKMF(L)	United Kingdom Mobile Force (Land)
ULS	Unit Load Specification
UNFICYP	United Nations Force in Cyprus
UNIFIL	United Nations Force in the Lebanon
USAS	Unit Supply ADP System
USMC	United States Marine Corps
VAOS	Vocabulary of Army Ordnance Stores
VC	Victoria Cross
VITAL	Visibility In Transit Asset Logging
VQMG	Vice Quartermaster General
VS	Vehicle Specialist
WAAOC	West African Army Ordnance Corps
WEU	Western European Union
WIS	Weapons Intelligence Section
WRAC	Women's Royal Army Corps
WRVS	Women's Royal Voluntary Service
XP	Exchange Point

Chapter One

In the Beginning...

Ordnance: A branch of government service dealing with military stores and materials (Middle English, variant of Ordinance). *Concise Oxford Dictionary*

Since before the existence of any form of real control of the Armed Forces of the Crown there has been a department with responsibilities for Ordnance, a word that really made its first appearance in the parlance of military administration in England early in the fifteenth century. However, the functions of providing, supplying and maintaining warlike capability goes back into time immemorial, a date set in common law as 1189; but the role of the supplier went back even further than that into the very earliest beginnings of any military force that might be described as 'national'.

It appears probable that an official with the responsibilities associated with the centralized control of weapons and ancillaries was conducting his business at the time of the Norman Conquest in 1066. The record would indicate that he carried out his duties in a Roman castle beside what is now the River Thames, converted by William the Conqueror into a defensive structure dominated by a tower; a white tower.

The Tower of London viewed from the River Thames, with the White Tower prominent.

Some form of central control of weapons and the associated stores was always considered essential. Not only were they the means of waging war and hence important for the security of the state, they were also the means of equipping rebellion, and hence a potential danger to the security of the state, and to its rulers. However, the 'word' made its first appearance in 1414 when Nicholas Merbury was invited to take charge as 'Master of our Works, Engines, Cannon and other kinds of Ordnance for war'. One John Louth was appointed as his clerk and with these two there began a chain of Masters and Clerks of Ordnance at the Tower of London. The derivation of the word probably lies with an ancient Ordinance regulating the dimensions of cannon; and there were other Ordinances related to the design, manufacture, shape and size of military equipment. Such was a view expressed by Lord

Coke, a much-respected man of the law during the reign of Queen Elizabeth I.

John Louth was directed by a Royal Warrant of 1418 to work with John Bennet of Maidstone to produce warlike material. Bennet was a stonemason and the task required him to provide cannon balls of various dimensions, as well as shields, tampons, cannon carriages and gunpowder, among other things. The thought that John Louth may have had a conflict of interest with his public service responsibilities as the Clerk to the Master of the Ordnance does not appear to have been a hindrance.

Little appears then to be known about the office, which saw a revival during the reign of Henry VIII. His time as Sovereign saw the advent of the legitimized piracy undertaken by such as Hawkins and Drake. The Privy Council supervised the work of the Ordnance, and its earliest dealings in its resurrected state were with the Brethren of Trinity House, an ancient Guild of Mariners responsible for equipping and arming warships. In those early days the office was not the tight knit structure it was to become for there were Masters of Ordnance in different places addressing the wide range of issues required for warlike operations, and especially for the Navy. There was, of course, always a central figure in all this, providing an oversight. It was an important post and the incumbents were carefully selected from among the great men of the nation; such men as the Earl of Warwick and the Earl of Essex.

In those early days the main function of the office required the issuing of Royal Warrants to provide money for the provision of munitions, and it is here we see the first origins of the word 'imprest', a term known to just about every modern soldier. On 12 March 1546 a Mr Peckham was instructed to deliver 'in prest' to Francis Fleming, Lieutenant of the Ordnance, 'for the emption *(sic)* of certain things wanted in the Tower...'.

Robert Devereux, Earl of Essex 1566 - 1601.

There is also a reference in 1518 to the duties in the field of the Master of the Ordnance, together with his clerks. He was responsible for the provision of the ammunition and all the ancillaries required by the guns and the gunners. He also had to undertake reconnaissance of the area in which the artillery was to be used to make sure the ground was suitable for the positioning of the artillery. He had to ensure that there were sufficient craftsmen available to effect repairs when necessary, and that ammunition was issued as required by the gunners. In the process of issuing, however, he was to ensure that his clerks retrieved the 'bill' for the munitions demanded so that due account could be rendered to the sovereign and due account could be taken of the Master of the Ordnance's stewardship. The interesting point here is that issues, including ammunition, were made on repayment and no exception was made for being involved in active service. Clearly, this was an indication to commanders that they should take responsibility for their stewardship and not to be profligate.

It was in 1598 that the department was restructured along lines that would prevail largely unchanged for some 250 years, to the time of the Crimea. Prior to that the processes and systems in place for the control of funds and stores had leant themselves relatively easily to corruption and fraud. This had come to a head with the defeat of the Armada in 1588, where there were massive opportunities for officers and clerks to enrich themselves at the expense of the state, and it was something of which they were not slow to take advantage.

The new structure saw the appointment of a Great Master of the Ordnance who was responsible for the support of naval and land forces. Assisting him was a treasurer, known as a lieutenant. He also had a surveyor, responsible for the quality and quantity of the stores purchased, while there was a storekeeper whose job was to take charge of the stock. Stock control was exercised and issues undertaken by the Clerk of the Deliveries, whilst the Clerk of the Ordnance took responsibility for the

2

finance. The first task of the incumbents of this newly structured department was to conduct a massive stock take of the total stock throughout the land of powder, shot and other munitions. All this was occurring as the infantryman's weapons of war moved away from the bow and the pike, to be replaced by firearms, although the transition would take some time.

At the Restoration of the Monarchy in 1660 the pay of an infantry soldier was 8d (£3.25) per day. However, apart from expenditure in wartime on such things as camp equipment, a regiment had to support itself from the soldiers' daily pay. The Master General of the Ordnance provided, on repayment, muskets and ammunition and the regiment purchased all its other needs as and where it could and very much at the individual whim of commanding officers who held the purse strings. Indeed, the business of repayment so permeated the system of military administration that when hospitals came into being in war, the costs of the patients were charged to their parent regiments and this included not just those who fell sick, but also those wounded in battle. Units also had to make good any deficiencies due to loss or to wear and tear. And the only one to suffer was the soldier whose paltry 8d a day was used for every need under the sun, including as a source of funds to pay pensions to the widows of officers killed in battle, and it paid the fee charged by the Ordnance for the delivery of muskets and ammunition. The system, if system it could be called, was ripe for mismanagement and fraud, and it is no surprise that both were endemic.

But it was in 1660 that we see the first Master General of the Ordnance, as opposed simply to 'Master'. With this appointment, attempts were made to eradicate a number of long-standing abuses, placing officials on salaries and removing the perquisites that had provided their source of income and had hence led to graft. The responsibilities of the office were also extended to cover all forts, seeking to use the same systems in use for the control of weapons to eliminate the maladministration of fortifications. His responsibilities were extended yet further in 1682 when he assumed responsibility for training the master gunners and gunners in all garrisons. This centralized a devolved responsibility that had been placed with the governors of castles and forts since feudal times.

Further recognition of the importance of the office and its works came with a Royal Warrant of 1683 which delineated in very great detail the organization, the structure, the duties of individuals and the salary scales of all those employed in the department, from the Master General at £1,500 (£155,000) per year to the labourer at £26 (£2,750) per year; a considerable disparity and reflecting a senior public service salary out of kilter with that one might expect in modern times. The principle of a Board of Management remained, with the Master General chairing it and with the purpose of the Board being to decide what stocks had to be replenished and to submit the necessary estimates to Parliament. The five members also had other duties, along exactly the same lines as those outlined for the Elizabethan structure, the execution of which they were bound to record daily in a journal. In addition to the principal officers there were a number of craftsmen and artisans charged with the production, repair and maintenance of equipment.

King James II.

James II, arguably not the greatest monarch to grace the throne of England, actually took great interest in the Board of Ordnance, and took steps to strengthen the working practices and procedures that had been introduced with the 1683 Warrant; and the department undertook the additional responsibility for the 'Office of Tents and Toyles'. If the procedures used appear overly bureaucratic, this was deliberate. No one was trusted, neither their honesty nor their political integrity, and this drove the essentially inquisitorial nature of the procedures, set in place for the control of stores and, especially, the control of weapons and munitions.

Nonetheless, graft and mismanagement continued to be rife. However, given the essentially dishonest nature of the public service in those days the department worked reasonably well. With its work now stretched to include the provision of barracks and barrack accoutrements, such as blankets, the Board of Ordnance and those who worked for it gradually assumed more and more of a grip on the supply issues facing the Army. However, its main work remained the furnishing of armaments for fortresses and ships and in providing the wherewithal during periods of conflict for an effective siege train; including engineering and artillery stores and expertise. Depots existed at the time in such places as Chatham, Portsmouth, Tilbury, Sheerness and Plymouth, demonstrating the influence and importance of sea warfare on the provision of stocks. The army was served from depots in, for example, St James' Park, Windsor and Woolwich. The disparity in importance and stock levels is demonstrated by the difference in salaries of the storekeepers – £120 (£12,500) at Plymouth and £20 (£2,250) at St James' Park.

From the very earliest times there was no distinction between the Ordnance soldier and the Ordnance civilian. It was a link that, whilst it fluctuated from time to time, remained, nonetheless, a feature of the Ordnance that the ties were generally close and unwavering. So it was that these two Corps of Ordnance grew from different origins to the rest of the army and pursued, in many cases, a different ethos. Promotion, for example, was based on seniority and merit, at least in principle. Certainly, they did not suffer the problems associated with purchase of commissions. The men were clothed from central pools, there was far less opportunity for graft in the officer corps and men were generally better paid than their colleagues in the Army.

On 14 January 1707 the Duke of Marlborough, one of the few logistically 'aware' generals ever to grace the ranks of the British Army, saw to the introduction of a Royal Warrant whose transition through the bureaucracy he had overseen. It formed the basis of the equipment and clothing regulations which transcended the formation of the RAOC in 1918 and which continued in principle through the life of the Corps. Its effect was to establish a Board of General Officers, who were all colonels of regiments, to supervise the provision of clothing for regiments by individual commanding officers.

They ensured the right clothing was purchased to the authorized patterns and that the money existed to pay for it and that it met the needs of the regiment in peace and in its preparedness for war. Once made, and prior to issue, it was inspected by the Board to ensure that it was of an appropriate quality and matched the pattern. And Marlborough insisted that the quality had to be of a high order to withstand the rigours of campaigning.

The system was, of course, open to abuse. The generals were subject to the blandishments of fellow officers to see things 'their' way, and contractors would constantly beat a path to their door seeking favours. However, despite these shortcomings, and occasional 'weaknesses' by Board members, there was at least a system in place with the purpose of seeing that soldiers were well clothed and equipped and, in large part, it worked well. Further warrants later in the eighteenth century tightened up the process by instituting further checks at regimental level, all designed to ensure contractual compliance and quality.

In 1793 a major change took place in the organization and control of the British Army. There had been a growing acceptance, publicly and politically, of the need for a standing army – to police the growing empire and to provide a means of policing the burgeoning inner cities as the march of the industrial revolution drew people from the land into the factories. The office of the Commander-in-Chief was established, placing under his hand the responsibility for discipline, quartering, movements, appointments and promotions. There was a Secretary at War who was responsible for finance, but his post only came into effect when the country was physically at war.

The two principal staff officers working for the C-in-C were the Adjutant General for clothing and regimental equipment whilst the Quartermaster General had responsibility for camp and field equipment. The flaws here are obvious, with compartmentalization rife, and the resource provider, the financier, being a parliamentary official and not on the staff of the C-in-C. The Board of General Officers, still in existence almost a century after it had been instigated by the Duke of Marlborough, worked in the Adjutant General's department.

The huge expansion in military effort caused by the Napoleonic Wars, and the subsequent seesaw effect of the forty years' of peace that followed, had a major impact on the logistic support of the Army. Resources to make the 'system' work simply did not exist and abuses were common; and then the 'peace dividend' that followed gave no incentive whatsoever to correct the abuses and put in place a system that learned from the lessons and sought to ensure there would be no repeat.

The same period saw the Board of Ordnance identifying failings and seeking to put its house in order. Instant dismissal followed any suggestion of an untoward relationship with a contractor. Inspection regimes for ammunition, undertaken by civilians, were found to be very poor and the responsibility was transferred to uniformed officers of the artillery. Another shift was that the relatively small collection of artillery sub-units had now formed into a large regiment of several battalions; and a corps of Royal Military Artificers was started from among the Department of Ordnance – to become in 1813 the Royal Sappers and Miners, the forerunners of the Royal Engineers. Given this expansion of its responsibilities the department changed its structure to reflect this, effectively splitting into two. On the one hand the Lieutenant General dealt with armaments and the Surveyor General provided munitions, and saw to their storage as well as the equipping of forts and barracks. The Master General himself was a very senior member of the establishment, and a Cabinet Minister. He was a man of very considerable power and influence.

One thing that the Napoleonic Wars generated was a plethora of separate logistic functions with parallel roles, caused in part by failings in one part of the system leading to compensating, and often conflicting, organizations emerging elsewhere. It also brought into sharp focus the differences in the efficiency and effectiveness of the Commissariat, a branch of the Treasury, and the Department of Ordnance which, whilst far from perfect, was, very much better run. The Department of Ordnance realized that to be effective in its support of operations in the field it needed to be self sufficient. Accordingly, in 1792 an Artillery officer had been appointed as Director General of the Ordnance Field Train with the express purpose of providing supply support to the artillery and to the engineers. The Train was a logistic department instructed in the handling of munitions and in established methods of supply. It moved and issued Ordnance stores in the field and supervised the movement of guns, other than those of the Royal Horse Artillery, and pontoons for bridging. The Train existed in cadre form in peacetime and was expanded rapidly in crisis by recruiting from Ordnance storekeepers or elsewhere. Except for its small headquarters at Woolwich, its members were civilians who wore uniform when mustered for operations, and it was that of the Royal Artillery with different buttons. The blue jacket and scarlet facings continued in use in mess kit and formal dress until the demise of the RAOC in 1993. It also boasted its own independent medical department.

The first recruits to the Field Train joined in 1793. Between 1795 and 1815 the Train served in thirty expeditions and campaigns including Egypt in 1801, the Peninsula War, and North America and at Waterloo, and its members were awarded prize money in the same way as soldiers.

The Army relied upon the Royal Wagon Train, which it created specifically for the task; and had its own medical department. Like the Field Train it also provided its own camp equipment. It was to be the Army that disbanded the military transport corps in 1830 as a savings measure and would go to the Crimea in 1854 without a military transportation system of any sort. Throughout that period the Field Train remained in being.

Following the Napoleonic Wars new organizations and structures for the supply of the Army in peace and in war were suggested, implemented, abandoned, changed and adjusted. The key feature of all this was the desire to save money at any cost and had little to do with the effective support of the Army either at home or abroad. It was even suggested that the Ordnance Department should take over complete control of the provision of all logistic support to the Army. The Duke of Wellington, however, was quite clear on the issue: it was impossible for one organization to manage the hugely complex business of supporting an Army at war and supplying it with its needs.

The Duke of Wellington was Master General from 1818 to 1827, a period during which there was vitality in the department driven entirely by his personality and his understanding of the importance of the proper organization of logistic support for the Army. Regrettably, when the Iron Duke left the post, the department drifted once more, a cause entirely attributable to lack of leadership by the incumbents of the post of Master General. In fairness, there was a concentration on the political nature of the post, leaving much of the day-to-day work of the department to paid officials. And there was a distinct lack of military experience not only among the Master Generals, but also on the staff of the department. Indeed, there was never an Artillery or an Engineer officer there.

Arthur Wellesley, 1st Duke of Wellington, Master General of the Ordnance 1819 - 1827.

The forty years leading up to the Crimean War were characterized by increasing bureaucracy, dispersion of effort, split responsibilities and lack of focus. It is important, perhaps, to remember that, even at this stage in our history, the Army was still viewed with suspicion and there was a positive disinclination, politically and socially, properly to support a standing army.

The Crimean War, between 1854 and 1856 was not, in military terms, a major event. Indeed, under normal circumstances it would have been considered a sideshow. It was little more than a prolonged siege of Sevastopol, preceded by a few low intensity battles that caught the imagination of the time. Balaclava, The Thin Red Line, The Heights of Inkerman became bywords in the lingua franca in public houses and drawing rooms in the United Kingdom. They were names brought to the attention of the public by William Russell, the *Times* correspondent; but it was the same reporting that led to the stories of the disastrous logistic difficulties that so plagued the campaign.

There is no surprise that it was disastrous. Control, focus, organization, doctrine, and communications – all were absent and in large measure. The Ordnance actually did quite a good job, and looked after the needs of the gunners and sappers well. This was because the Ordnance retained the Field Train's capability in cadre form and it went to the Crimea, manned by volunteers from the Ordnance Storekeepers' department. Sergeants of the Royal Artillery were appointed as Sergeant Conductors to serve under Field Train Officers.

Ordnance soldiers were also far better off than their Army counterparts, so much so that there were complaints about preferential treatment. However, whilst it looked to the needs of its two Corps, the artillery and the engineers, it was far less assiduous about the provisions it was expected to make for the Army. A great deal went astray due to mismanagement and poor control and despite any good it may have done regarding the provision of the two corps for which the department was directly responsible, it became the victim of the reported failures in the other parts of its area of responsibility. And this was all swept up in the general malaise that was so fully brought to the attention of the British public through the newspapers.

The movements plan for the delivery of stores was so badly judged that items required for winter arrived with the spring. The Admiralty was unable to provide the necessary shipping, and those stores that did arrive in the Crimea could not be effectively distributed due to the lack of any transport system

Balaclava Harbour.

for the Army. All the lessons that the Duke of Wellington had sought to impart in the early part of the century, and which he had enshrined to some extent in field service regulations, had been forgotten or discarded. Just as the deployment was announced it was decided to limit the functions of the Ordnance and leave everything else to the Commissariat, which had only the experience of working in peacetime upon which to base its activity. And the peacetime bureaucracy, with which it went about its business, was not conducive to the conduct of warlike operations.

The difficulties in the theatre were exacerbated by the system in the UK for the provision of stores and supplies. The Quartermaster General saw only to the business of camp equipment, the Commissariat for special clothing and the medical department for medical supplies, whilst boots were not apparently anyone's responsibility. Indeed, one consignment was returned from the Crimea as no one could be found to take responsibility for it.

The road from Balaclava to the area of operations did not make the logistic support of the fighting troops any easier.

There was no focus. The Master General, Lord Raglan, was removed from his post to command the Army in the Crimea, and was not replaced. The post of Lieutenant General that had been discontinued was reinstated to compensate for the absence of the Master General, but his duties were never clearly delineated and, consequently, never fully addressed. The principal civilian in the department also went off to the war, leaving only the Clerk to the Board. In short, at the time of greatest need the department ceased to be in any sense effective.

Here lies the real importance of the Crimea, for it highlighted huge shortcomings in the support of the Army, and provided the basis for reform that would stand the Army in good stead for the wars that were to come at the turn of the century. It would see to the development of a system of logistic support that would lead eventually to the formation of an Army Ordnance Corps and Army Ordnance Department, and eventually the RAOC. The reforms that led to this were focussed across over half a century of improving the administration of Army stores.

However, the immediate aftermath was a huge series of reforms that saw the demise of the ancient office of the Ordnance, and with it the Field Train. Swept up in the blood letting was the disbandment of an effective, uniformed, cohesive supply management organization for a crucial element of the inventory. It was a model of how a supply system should work, incorporating transport and supply, but it was seen as part of a flawed system and had to go. All support issues were focussed under a Secretary of State at War. It was basically a sound structure, a drawing together of functions that would lead to a more focussed approach. However, there was one intrinsic weakness; the loss of the close link between the user and the provider. Now the only link was between the C-in-C and the Secretary of State. With this went any sense of responsibility in the Army for the efficiency and effectiveness of its administration, and senior officers had no financial control function.

The benefit, of course, was that what regimental commanders had been able to deny their soldiers under the old system could not be denied by the state. Thus the lot of the individual soldier and his equipment saw a significant improvement; as indeed did his welfare provision. The price was massive centralization of administration in London, and a burgeoning bureaucracy as the fledgling organization sought to cope with an army where there were no scales and every commanding officer seemed to have differing aspirations for his regiment and his soldiers. And, whilst the centre struggled under a mass of detail, the Army gradually grew more and more detached from the realities of the cost and importance of its own administration.

From this the 1860s saw the introduction of the much maligned Control System. Born of the need for delegated control to fight the battle in Ireland, it was a system of delegation to the Districts in which the Army in the UK was organized. It meant the creation of a senior finance post in the district and was designed to ensure that senior officers took professional and budgetary interest in the administration of their commands. It did not work and led to antipathy between the military and the civilian components of the District HQs. Neither was it popular in the centre where protectionism abounded.

Following Cardswell's reforms which commenced in 1870, a new organization for the Army was introduced. Key in this was the placing under the direct control of the Secretary of State at War of the C-in-C, with direct responsibility for the Army, a Financial Director and a Surveyor General for Ordnance, thereby greatly easing his span of management. The latter post was responsible for everything to do with supply services, which included the Ordnance Factories. With the revival of the old title of the Surveyor General came two appointments on his staff of the Director of Supplies and Transport, and the Director of Artillery and Stores.

Meanwhile, the Control System staggered on, and eventually died in 1876. It foundered on the rock of interdepartmental squabbling at District level and lack of direction from a disinterested Centre. The Army no longer shared responsibility for its supply services. The Commissariat and Transport Departments and the Ordnance Store Department, previously called the Military Store Department split away and were administered by their own chief at the War Office in London where the supply services were coordinated by the Surveyor General of Ordnance. However, the benefit was that, as a result of the Control System, books of scales and regulations had been drawn up, thereby allowing Ordnance Officers to conduct business locally and to approved levels.

There was one positive outcome of the changes which would lead ultimately to the formation of an Ordnance Corps. From the residue of the Control System those officers who had been employed on stores duties were formed into the Ordnance Store Department. However, the Transport and Distribution arm which had been such a feature of the old Ordnance Field Train was not included.

A serious shortcoming of the new structures was that the functions of administration and command were now once again separated. The Army failed to realize the potential power it had for its own destiny, had it grasped the delegated authority that had been a feature of the Control System. However, the realization suddenly dawned that whilst commanders no longer had any responsibility for administration in peace it was a responsibility they had to assume in war. And the day war breaks out is no time to change the system of command and control. Somehow that which happened in war had to form the basis of the organizational structure in peace.

The Arms of the Board of Ordnance. Its shield would form the basis of the RAOC's cap badge when it formed.

To redress this the only real solution was to entrust the Army in peace with that for which it would have responsibility in war. However, to do that would mean placing under the control of the Army the Ordnance Store Department and its vast inventory, including ammunition. Government reluctance to entrust these resources to a standing army was a feature of history, and to make such a transition would require not just a major shift in policy, but also an almost seismic change in attitude. Therefore, the decision was only partially taken in 1881, when the responsibility for Commissariat and Transport was passed to the C-in-C. The Ordnance Store Corps was formed, creating the second part of what would eventually become the RAOC, but which was only placed under the C-in-C's control for disciplinary purposes. The supply system of the Army was still not a cohesive whole, still lacked a focus, and was still serving more than one master each with different priorities.

It was not until 1887, during yet another reform of War Office structures and organization, that finally, almost inevitably, the Army was granted responsibility for its own weapons, munitions and critical stores. However, the outcome was less than perfect. The original plan had been that the Surveyor General, to whom the direct responsibility was to be passed, would be a soldier of some distinction. Indeed, in terms of qualification, experience and competence the incumbent was to be modelled on the Master Generals of old. However, whilst this was seen to work the first time, subsequent holders of the post were political appointees. Constant changes of appointee and lack of military knowledge denuded the post of its value and effectiveness. Financial and political considerations overrode the military aspects of the function.

Although the Army had control of its own stocks and supplies, the responsibility to procure them was left with the Financial Secretary in the War Office. He exercised his responsibilities through a Director of Contracts, who undertook all procurement, and a Director General with responsibility for the Ordnance Factories. The C-in-C's part in supplying the Army not only brought him control of the stocks and the staff to look after them, he also became responsible for Ordnance soldiers' training and discipline, their housing and welfare, their feeding and equipment. Now the Army had to take an interest in economical use of resources.

It was the South African war that was to have a major effect on the future Royal Army Ordnance

AOC soldiers maintaining a 110 Ton Railway Gun.

Corps. Prior to that there had been companies of the Ordnance Store Corps in garrisons throughout the country, and they had deployed on operations. Some supported the Zulu war and others were in Egypt, and there were detachments throughout the world. However, in 1893 a new organization for war was developed. This was borne of a growing concern in the War Office that some form of major mobilization may one day be necessary, and the Ordnance Companies were far too large and unwieldy. Thus it was that the five companies in existence were made ten, and based on an establishment of fifty men. When on active service they were to be called Depot Units.

There were further developments in 1894 when the importance of the service provided by Ordnance Services was greatly enhanced by the assumption of a range of new duties. There was to be a new title. The Army Ordnance Corps was formed. A key difference was that its formation saw the absorption of the Corps of Armourers and the Armament Artificers into the new Corps. At the same time the Inspectors of Ordnance Machinery were transferred from the Royal Artillery into the Army Ordnance Department and re-titled Ordnance Mechanical Engineers. These moves provided the basis of what would become the mechanical engineering element of the RAOC.

So in 1899, when numbers 1, 2, 3, 4, 5, 9 and 11 Companies of the AOC sailed for the South African war, to be joined shortly afterwards by numbers 6 and 10 Companies, the fledgling Corps was going to war for the first time. Subsequently, there was further inflation in strength as in 1900 a further eight companies were formed, and then four more in 1902, to relieve the deployed units. The impact was the creation of a powerful Ordnance esprit de corps. Previously lacking due to the disparate and non-regimental nature of many of the undertakings on which individuals

The Ordnance Store Corps, Woolwich, Tug of War Team 1896.

The Ordnance Staff in Aldershot in May 1897.

had been employed, it would not be amiss to refer to the war in South Africa as building the soul of what one day would become the RAOC. A memorial to the fallen was erected at Woolwich, and a magazine was launched – both seminal events in the founding of the fledgling Corps, and helping the binding process that would carry it through the war to come in Europe and on beyond it.

A key lesson from the campaign was the difficulty of obtaining manpower for the AOC, and this was taken into account when the Esher Committee made its post war recommendations for the organization and structure of the Army. It was a wide-ranging report, its recommendations not appreciated by all. However, it quite correctly saw the future of logistics for the Army lying with the Quartermaster General and was successful in seeing the transfer of the AOC to QMG's area of responsibility. This would focus the management of logistics, and the provision of resources to manage it, under one guiding hand. This made the QMG responsible for holding and issuing all military stores in peace and in war and a Director of Equipment and Ordnance Stores would undertake that task for him, based at the War Office.

It wasn't perfect, for there was still a separate Commissary and Transport branch, initially responsible for both foodstuffs and clothing, although the latter was transferred to the DEOS within

Part of No 4 Coy AOC Red Barracks, Woolwich 1898.

two years and there was a further amalgamation of transport and food supply. There was also the potential for confusion in the minds of the untutored, for there were now an Army Ordnance Department and an Army Ordnance Corps which had no relationship with the Master General of the Ordnance, whose post continued to be responsible for the provision of munitions and weapons. However, despite the imperfections it was a great step forward in that the Army now had a logistics focus in the QMG although, with one exception, he would never be a logistician, and the handling of stocks was spread only between two organizations. This was a significant improvement on the disparate nature of logistic systems and the spread of responsibilities that had created the fragmentation from which the logistic ills of the Army had resulted over the centuries.

After the South African war, the size of the Corps continued to rise. This was a feature not only of its increased responsibilities, but the fact that they were spread far and wide throughout the Army, at home and abroad. In 1907 the AOC was established for 237 officers, 140 warrant officers, 898 sergeants and 1,338 other ranks, this representing a six-fold increase in Ordnance manpower since 1880.

The last reorganization, the one that would lead the AOC and the AOD into the Great War, took place in 1912. It was due to the finalization of plans to send an expeditionary force to continental Europe, an undertaking quite different to the colonial adventures to which the Army and the Corps had become used. The plans foresaw a massive concentration of force on the other side of the Channel. With speed being of the essence it was planned to put Ordnance in early and this would be impossible if a large part of the Corps was abroad in the colonies. And it was not simply concentration of numbers that was required, but concentration of skills and competencies as well and with each unit capable of operating independently if need be. One key addition was that of the armourers who had previously not deployed with companies, but had operated independently. Nine companies were created, each with two officers and 165 soldiers, and the range of trades included clerks, foremen, saddlers, wheelers and carpenters, tent menders, smiths and hammer men – and the mysterious and quaintly named 'painters and miscellaneous' of which there were four.

There were thirty officers and 1,360 men deployed to France in August 1914, at the start of the Great War. At the end there were 800 officers and 38,000 men. And during the First World War, a war that saw huge armies raised, vast new ranges of equipment provided, masses of ammunition stockpiled, the Corps and the department faced huge challenges.

The conflict started with no clear concept, doctrine or plan for Ordnance support in war. It is hard

The AOC was stationed all over the world, supporting the Army wherever it was, like the AOC detachment in Tientsin, China, in the winter of 1911.

to gauge why, but it seems most likely that the cause lay with a failure of the Army to realize the implications of supplying the huge amounts of equipment that would be required for an army fighting a modern, high intensity, equipment intensive war. The concept at the time was that a formation requiring clothing, weapons, equipment and stores to replace losses would be withdrawn from the line and re-equipped in the rear areas. There was no system of forward re-supply of the range of stores provided by Ordnance Services. Only food, fodder and ammunition had a practised forward delivery system provided by the Army Service Corps. And after a long fight to establish the posts, there was just one Ordnance Officer established for Divisional Headquarters, together with one clerk. It was not long before it became obvious that the system, if it could ever have been called that, would be unable to cope.

On the bright side, Brigadier Hugh Perry was deployed early as the Director of Ordnance Services at the General Headquarters of the British Expeditionary Force. He was followed fairly soon in the deployment by four companies of the AOC setting up the first BEF depot, in Le Havre. Planning was plagued by a lack of information. There were two departments responsible for the war

Brigadier Hugh Perry.

reserves; QMG and MGO. Whilst the Chief Ordnance Officer knew the contents of the QMG's war reserves schedule he was never made privy to that of the MGO. Consequently, he had no idea what weapons, ammunition and associated stores he might expect to see delivered and to store or move forward. Requests to obtain a copy of the MGO's schedule were rejected, for reasons that remain unknown. The outcome of these major shortcomings in the provision for Ordnance support was that the BEF on its retreat from Mons, the battles on the Marne and the Aisne and the race for the sea, to the first battle of Ypres, was not good. It was hindered further by the need to move the depots in the channel ports further south to the Loire in the face of the German advance that threatened their existence.

General Harold Parsons took over as DOS from Brigadier Perry on 9 October 1914, a post he was to hold until the end of the war.

As the war settled down into static trench warfare a system began to be developed for the forward supply of Ordnance stores. There was still an inexplicable resistance to developing a cohesive, all-embracing logistic system for the forward delivery of all stocks. Indeed, the senior ASC officer in the BEF wrote to his superiors in London of 'this bugbear of Ordnance Stores'. He saw his role as forward supply of ASC provisioned stocks only, and was reluctant to help in any way. Nonetheless, a system was put in place, based around the Deputy Assistant

Major General Parsons and officers of Ordnance Branch HQ BEF, a picture taken in 1918.

Director of Ordnance Services at Divisional Headquarters.

At this stage in its history the Corps was also responsible for the repair and maintenance of vehicles and equipment. There was an almost inevitable division of responsibility, with the ASC providing the vehicle and its components, and carrying out light repairs forward. Heavy repair took place in Ordnance workshops at the rear. However, there was a natural desire by the ASC to hang on to its vehicles and to keep as many as far forward as possible. The result was that those vehicles that eventually made their way back to Ordnance Workshops had been cannibalized beyond recognition for every useable spare and were little more than shells, requiring a complete rebuild which was expensive in time, spares and manpower.

The ASC was responsible for supplying spares for all levels of repair, and it was concentrating on the forward repair requirement to keep as much transport on the roads as it could. The outcome was a lack of focus on the Ordnance requirements for base repair, and vehicles awaiting repair for want of parts. Any process whereby repair parts are provided by a separate organization to that responsible for undertaking the repair is doomed to inefficiency if not outright failure, and this was no exception. The remedy, in January 1915, was to pass the responsibility for all MT repair to the ASC. The Ordnance was then left with the responsibility for repair of guns and associated stores. The advantage was that it allowed the Corps to concentrate its repair effort on battle-winning equipment, but nonetheless left the Army with a duplicated repair capability and two spares purchasing and supply systems.

The war was a major test for all branches of the Corps and Department. The increasing range and complexity of equipment and the repair burden it brought with it was a constant tax on resources, as was the handling of a vast range of stores and the associated problems. By the time of the Armistice the Corps had handled 25.5 million tons of stores, and 70 per cent of the queries dealt with by the QMG's department were related to Ordnance matters. Over 5 million tons were ammunition, which was consumed in vast quantities once British industry had come to terms with the impact of surging to meet the requirements of a war, the intensity and consumption of which had simply not been predicted. As an example, the Passchendaele operation in 1917 consumed 465,000 tons of ammunition with a value of £84 million (£2.6 billion).

The entrance to a large shell dump in a forward area.

A light railway dump at St Eloi, August 1917.

Once the front settled down, ammunition re-supply was effected from a base depot in Boulogne, which was the port of entry. From there two trains re-supplied railheads at Arques and Aire and from the railheads mechanized transport took stocks forward to the exchange points where they were transferred onto the horse-drawn carts that re-supplied the forward areas. With some variations, due to fluctuations in force levels, it was a system that was to remain, in principle, throughout the war. The supply, up to the point of transfer to horse-drawn transport, was the responsibility of the DDOS at GHQ, under orders from the QMG. From there responsibility transferred to the ASC.

One of the key lessons of the war was the need for technical training of those whose responsibility was the care of ammunition. This rationale was developed at a time when ammunition storage was undertaken with no scientific basis at all. Indeed, one small bomb dropped by a German aircraft on the depot at Audruicq in July 1916 destroyed the complete depot. It held 9,000 tons, with over 100 pre-loaded vehicles, and it was these that acted like a massive fuze, carrying the fire throughout the depot. One oblong crater was sixty feet deep.

Salvage also became recognized as an important task. A controller of salvage was appointed at GHQ, and a small crew was established down to Divisional level in order to glean what they could. The bulk, some 90 per cent of that collected, was Ordnance material, yet it never occurred to the staff that the task should be made the responsibility of the DOS. And it never was for the whole of the war.

As the war developed, as the level of equipment and its complexity increased, as the requirement for increased levels of equipment grew larger almost daily, there were an inevitable series of reorganizations throughout the four years of the conflict. The great flaw was that the office of the DOS was never a part of GHQ. There was a plethora of staff officers in the AG's and QMG'S departments in GHQ. Most of the questions they had related to Ordnance work, each branch had to keep duplicate records and the duplication of effort led not only to a waste of valuable manpower but also to breakdowns in communication and a less effective service. It was a situation, a most unsatisfactory situation, that was to prevail beyond the armistice.

It is important to mention, of course, that the Corps served all over the world, supporting the Army in all theatres; Palestine, Gallipoli, Mesopotamia, East Africa, Italy, Russia and Siberia. And the issues facing the Army in Europe were replicated to different degrees and in different ways.

As it all drew to a close the problems of the Army Ordnance Corps grew, with the need to

The size of just part of the salvage problem; empty ammunition boxes.

demobilize huge armies and to recover as much as possible from the carnage. However, as this monumental task began, the diary of Major General Sir Charles Matthew, General Parson's successor as DOS, records a dinner with the King who informed him that in recognition of its excellent work during the war the Army Ordnance Corps was to be conferred with the title 'Royal'.

Army Order 363/1918 was published on 27 November 1918:

> Whereas we deem it expedient to alter in certain respects the conditions under which the officers employed upon Ordnance duties of our Army are at present serving; OUR WILL AND PLEASURE IS that the officers of our Army Ordnance Department shall be in future amalgamated with, and form part of, our Army Ordnance Corps.
>
> The officers of our Army Ordnance Corps shall continue to be subject in all respects to the provisions laid down for the Army Ordnance Department in the Warrant of her late Majesty Queen Victoria dated 16 June 1896, as amended by subsequent warrants.
>
> IT IS OUR FURTHER WILL AND PLEASURE that in recognition of the splendid work which it has performed during the present war, Our Army Ordnance Corps shall be styled Our 'Royal Army Ordnance Corps' and shall take precedence in our Army immediately before our Royal Army Veterinary Corps.
>
> Given at Our Court of St James's, this 25th day of November, 1918, in the 9th Year of Our Reign

> *By His Majesty's Command*

It was, however, given the status of a non-combatant Corps. And the birth of the RAOC came at a time when the Corps was about to endure what was, arguably, its most difficult task of the entire conflict – put simply, staying behind to clear up when everyone else was packing up and going home. It was a birth fraught with difficulty.

Chapter Two

The Aftermath of War
1920 – 1926

I hope that we may say that thus, this fateful morning, came an end to all wars.

David Lloyd George 11 November 1918

The guns fell silent. In London maroons were fired, there was dancing in the streets, factories closed, church bells rang, there was an air of expectation, of the end of something awful and the prospect of a new beginning.

In France and Belgium men sat in trenches listening to a quiet they could barely believe, staring wordlessly into a half distance as they reflected on the enormity of what had happened. From having risked violent injury or death one minute they were suddenly faced with the prospect of peace and the chance to return to a life that some of them had left as much as four years previously when the British Expeditionary Force marched off to war in August 1914. God knew few enough of those were left alive, and of the tens of thousands who had followed so many too had perished or carried irredeemable scars. To a man Lloyd George's prayer, that this would see an end to all wars, would have struck a chord for those, that is, who bothered to read of it.

And so far as the soldiers were concerned the war ended on 11 November 1918. It was difficult to explain that this was, in fact, simply an armistice and that there was a need to remain vigilant until a final treaty was signed, properly to draw hostilities to a close. Despite this, the process of demobilization began, adding further to the 'end of the war' feeling, and the demeanour of the average soldier was not improved by the 'rules' that were applied to it. Rather than proceed on the basis of first in first out, those who had served longest found themselves superseded in the race for civilian life by men with less service, but who were required for industries judged important to national reconstitution, such as coal mining.

It was the corps providing the range of logistic support that would be kept back to do the clearing up, like the RAOC, where the anger and bitterness over the rules was most keenly felt. It did not help that many of the RAOC soldiers were, by the end of the war, artisans, from those industries where the burgeoning Trades Union movement was making itself felt. Gone was the spirit of the BEF of 1914, rather there were too many who saw the recently successful Russian Revolution as a model upon which to build a society. It was Marx himself, after all, who had envisaged a western capitalist society falling to the lure of Communism rather than the essentially agrarian Russian state with its widely dispersed population. Post-war Britain seemed to many to be a perfect breeding ground, and there was something of a spirit of revolution in some areas of the country and, indeed, the Army.

There were protests at the iniquity of the demobilization planning, and in the Ordnance Workshops in Calais in January 1919 the soldiers refused to work until there was some rearrangement of the rules. This, coupled with similar events elsewhere, led to a change such that length of service became the predominant factor in determining discharge dates. However, this sudden change in priorities for discharge brought its own problems as new surges of work appeared from nowhere, further to stretch an already overstretched, and disgruntled, RAOC. As an example, there were in March 1919 some 4,000 soldiers in France due for discharge who simply could not be released due to the pressure of work.

It was an unhappy time, and it was into this that the Royal Army Ordnance Corps was born. It was faced with a huge task as the vast armies wound down, as the nation and its politicians began to come to terms with a post-war world with new political imperatives which would drive the foreign and domestic policies that would determine the future direction of the Army and, with it, the RAOC. From the Army's perspective this meant maintaining a British Army of the Rhine with a strength of 45,000 and that would remain in place until 1930, enforcing the terms of the armistice once the Treaty of Versailles was signed. There was also an expedition to support the anti-Bolshevik armies in Russia operating from Archangel, and another, with the same purpose, that entered Russia from Vladivostok.

There was another, and semi-permanent, addition to the Army's responsibilities, caused by the collapse of the Ottoman Empire and the Government's determination to control as much as possible of the residue. In addition, therefore, to keeping a watchful eye on Atatürk, the occupation of Mesopotamia, Palestine, Cyprus and Egypt had also to be undertaken, to say nothing of staffing a plethora of detachments all over the world.

These were tasks added to the enormous burdens caused by the two traditional trouble spots for the British Army – Ireland and India, with 60,000 men in India and, by November 1919, the Army in Ireland was almost 40,000 strong. The RAOC was going to have to play its part supporting these deployments and the home base while, at the same time, disposing of the flotsam and jetsam thrown up by the draw down of the post-war Army. It all added up to a widely dispersed Army some 484,000 strong in need of Ordnance services.

Meanwhile, at home there was a General Election. It was long overdue, the onset of the war in 1914 having permitted the existing Government to extend its period in office to the end of hostilities, which meant it had been in power since December 1910 – some eight years. It took place on 14 December 1918, although the result was not announced until 28 December to give time for the postal votes of soldiers to be counted. That said, only one in four submitted a vote, so the Army's impact on the outcome was negligible. Lloyd George won at the head of a coalition of which a major component was the Conservative Party, and which saw the political death of his own party, the Liberals.

One key aspect of the election campaign was that a number of politicians appealed to the public desire for some sort of 'revenge' against the Germans for having inflicted four years of war on Europe. This forced statements on the hustings that the full cost of the war would be sought in the peace negotiations, and the public desire for vengeance was fuelled further by campaigns in the press appealing to popular sentiment, often using casualty lists as a major influence on opinion. The impact of this on the British position in negotiating the Treaty of Versailles is hard to judge, but it was the penal nature of the terms of the Treaty that fuelled German discontent and was to be the foundation that would lead within twenty years to the return of war, and this time on a truly global scale.

The RAOC was supporting an Army that had returned, in part, to its imperial policing role, but within which there was a move, in thinking at least, to mechanization. There were those who saw events in Flanders as an aberration, and believed that the day of the tank had come and gone. However, there were others who foresaw a different future; speed, pace, aggression, attacking the enemy's command

From its very inception shooting was a major part of RAOC life, as witness the Corps' contingent at Bisley in July 1919.

structure rather than battering his front line, ground-air cooperation and integration of all arms in every aspect of warfare.

All this was against the background of a reduction in defence expenditure by the Treasury from £502 million (£13.2 billion) to £135 million (£3.5 billion) and, of the £135 million, £75 million (£2 billion) was to be spent between the RAF and the Army. This massive cut was accompanied by a Ten Year Rule which offered the assumption that the British Armed Services would not be engaged in any great war during the next ten years. Therefore, no expeditionary force would be required and the main function of the Army and Air Force would be to garrison India, Egypt and all territories under British control, and to provide whatever support the civil authority at home required. It was a rule that was to be renewed every year up until 1932, the year before Hitler came to power in Germany, and it was to have a huge impact on the effectiveness of the British Army, which lived in virtual penury for twelve years. The key impact was to inhibit the development of mechanized theory, doctrine, equipment and training and therefore limit the effectiveness of the Army when the real test came.

For the RAOC the myriad of tasks it was asked to undertake grew at a time when its own numbers were shrinking. Such was the imperative to get men out of uniform and back to rebuild a battered British industrial base that there was no coordination with the needs of the RAOC or the support requirements of the Army. Instead there was a rather unseemly rush through the door, leaving those behind with a monumental task that had them facing in several directions at once.

In 1920 the QMG who, at the time, was Lieutenant General Sir Travers Clarke KCMG, CB, and he controlled Ordnance Services. He had been the QMG in France for much of the war and had a good grasp of the problems faced by the Corps, and of its capabilities. He was a friend of the RAOC, and presented a sports trophy which was competed annually, initially with a shooting competition and then with an athletics competition, that endured for the remaining life of the RAOC. Directly responsible for the Corps was the Director of Equipment and Ordnance Stores. Sir Harold Parsons KCMG, CB had a small staff of eleven officers grouped under different ADEOS, and there were three QMG branches, 7, 8 and 9, responsible for clothing, personnel and stores respectively.

Lieutenant General Sir Travers Clarke.

19

There was also an Inspector of Army Ordnance Services, whose responsibility lay directly to the QMG; effectively a spy on his own Corps. At Woolwich there was another Major General, the Principal Ordnance Officer, and he controlled the storekeeping activities of the Arsenal and the Dockyard as well as the main storekeeping depots at Didcot, Chilwell, Georgetown and Aintree. There was also a Chief Inspector of Stores and Clothing based at Woolwich, and the School of Instruction was there too. The RAOC actually controlled the manufacture of clothing and the whole affair, including the inspectors, was housed at Pimlico, with a Chief Ordnance Officer.

There were 1,365 officers in the RAOC in January 1920, and they came in four categories. Directing Staff officers filled the senior posts. They were all transferees into the Corps from other arms, bringing with them what was considered to be an 'essential' user experience. Regardless of the rank of other Ordnance officers in headquarters or in an installation, a Directing Staff Officer was always in command. They were distinguished by 'class' as well as rank, with an Ordnance Officer 1st Class being a colonel and 4th Class being a captain. As an incentive to join the RAOC a subaltern would receive a captain's pay and a bonus of 5s (£6) per day Corps pay. It was an inducement worth having, but some would argue well-earned after a Corps attachment followed by the rigours of the Ordnance Officers' course, the syllabus of which included mathematics, physics, chemistry, metallurgy, weapons, optics, organization, stores accounting and the practicalities of ammunition management. It lasted one year. Completion of the course resulted in the post-nominal letter 'o' in the Army list and it qualified the student as an Inspecting Ordnance Officer. This was the precursor to the Ammunition Technical Officer, and qualified the officer to undertake inspection, proof and repair of ammunition held by the RAOC, as well as unit stocks.

The course was held at the Artillery College Woolwich, the establishment that was the precursor to the Royal Military College of Science at Shrivenham. It was the start of a long association between the RAOC and the scientific academic community in the Army, especially the ammunition fraternity.

The workshop branch officers ran the workshops, and advised Directing Staff officers on workshop issues. They too were graded by class as well as rank, but one down from their Directing Staff officer counterparts. An Inspector of Ordnance Machinery (IOM) 1st Class was only a lieutenant colonel. Recruiting for the Workshop Branch was mainly by direct recruiting from civilian industry.

Officers commissioned from warrant rank formed a large part of the officer corps in the RAOC, from its very beginning. They were entitled in 1920 as Commissaries of Ordnance, with the exception of those commissioned into the Workshops Branch where they were known as Assistant Inspectors of Armourers. There were also a number of temporary officers who were employed to fill the gap between the future peace establishment of the Corps and the additional burdens imposed by the immediate post-war RAOC task.

The training of officers also included a wide range of technical training associated with the care of stores entrusted to the RAOC and the repair and maintenance of equipment. Of particular note was the six months spent by selected officers at the London School of Economics in training on administration. A key advantage to the course was the contact it brought with future decision makers in government and the Civil Service.

The officers of the RAOC formed a dinner club, which held its first gathering at the Hyde Park Hotel on Friday 9 July 1920 at '1945 pm' (sic) at a cost of £2.10s.0d (£58). The RAOC officers' club still meets annually, even since the demise of the Corps. It dines rather better and at less cost.

Regimental Sergeant Major Tom Payne.

Soldiers were divided into three branches: Stores, Armament Artificer and Armourer branches. Stores branch encompassed some twenty trades. These included storemen and clerks as well as a wide range of artisans; such trades as welder and blacksmith. Some of the storemen and clerks trained as laboratory technicians, the precursors to the Ammunition Technician trade. However, in those days it was only considered a subsidiary trade. Armourers joined as boy soldiers, and Armament Artificers came from other regiments and corps on transfer, or joined from civilian life, having previously gained the necessary qualifications. Regimental Duties were undertaken by tradesmen who had an aptitude for such work, and the only non-tradesman in this area of employment was the Regimental Sergeant Major at the Depot.

RSM Tom Payne was one such. An RSM in the AOC before the Great War, his was the very sort of example that was passed on to the fledgling Corps as it began to grow. One who had passed through his hands described him as a man firm without being overbearing, kindly yet strict, an iron hand in a buckskin glove. No one ever attempted to take advantage of his apparent leniency; no one had the courage to try. He had left the Army at the end of his service in 1907. However, with the advent of hostilities he was not the sort of man to stand idly by. He spent his war training others and then ended it in the Ordnance depot in Cologne, where his maturity and his gentle but firm manner continued to be an inspiration to all. He was a fatherly man of huge integrity. He set an example for others who would follow, and was a role model for anyone fortunate enough to come within his sphere of influence.

The ranks and appointments of RAOC soldiers conformed to the rest of the Army, with one exception. The appointment of Conductor was afforded to a very few highly qualified WOs1 and ranked them in order of precedence as the most senior warrant officer appointment in the Army. It continued to do so for the life of the RAOC and is carried on in the Royal Logistic Corps. Bill Newby was a Conductor. He was one of the warrant officers in the RAOC support element for the British Force in Siberia, sent to provide support to the anti-Bolshevik forces seeking to turn back the tide of revolution in Russia. The port of entry for the force was Vladivostok. The British Mission withdrew from the operation early in 1920, and in his final report the Commander wrote that he wished to make special mention of Captain Edwards and the then Sub-Conductor Newby. He recorded:

> ...had it not been for the grit and the manner of these representatives of the Ordnance we should have broken down several times as the Russian workmen, sometimes numbering 200, would refuse to handle the stores saying they would not send up ammunition to kill their brothers, and it was only by the personality of Captain Edwards and Sub-Conductor Newby that they were enticed to work again. That is only one of the many difficulties they overcame.

Bill Newby retired as a Conductor and died in August 1925. His son, Tom, joined the RAOC as a drummer boy at the age of fifteen and went on to serve his Sovereign, his Country and his Corps as a soldier, a commissioned officer, eventually a major, and then as a retired officer for fifty years. It remains a proud and distinguished family record, and was not untypical of long and distinguished service by so many of all ranks over the years.

Officers and soldiers were spread throughout the Army. There were seven Home Command HQs, at each of which there was an ADOS with a small staff. The Company organization of the war disappeared to be replaced by sections in stations. Their size varied, between a few officers and men to several hundred for the larger garrisons such as Aldershot. Overseas there was an ADOS and staff at each HQ. Depots were manned initially by Ordnance Companies, and workshops were set up by combining existing Field Force units into something more static. Ordnance sections and detachments were to be found in such places as Basra in Iraq, Danzig in Poland, Jamaica, Ludd in Palestine, Ballincollig in Ireland – and many more. It seems that a major part of life for soldiers in Palestine was to take advantage of the weather to learn tennis with a view to taking on the officers' and the sergeants'

A worldwide presence. This picture, taken in 1930, shows the RAOC detachment in Shanghai.

Top row (reading from left to right): –Ptes. Hocknell, Stevens, Wells, House, Clifton, O'Reilly, Thomas, Richardson, Tucker, Sands, Fagan, Bayly and McGrory.

Centre row: –Ptes. Mathews, Osborne and Williamson, Lce. Cpls. Filer and Dawber, Cpls. Moran and Turner, Sgt. McCarthy, Cpls. Littlewood, Ackerman and Reece, Lce. Cpls. and Underwood, Ptes. Kemp and Hicks.

Front row: –Sgts. Griffiths, Pinson and Paston, S. Sgt. Bastin, Sub-Condr. Smoker, Condr. Speller, Capt. W. H. Genders, O.O., Capt. J. P. Wills, M.C., D.A.D.O.S., Lieut. G. W S.M. Vigus, S. Sgts. McDonald, Richardson and Price, Sgts. Wright and Byer.

messes and with no intention whatsoever of losing to them. There remains, regrettably, no record of the eventual outcome. However the balance of probability lies with success having gone to the officers, who are known to have beaten the sergeants' mess nine games to seven – a change for the officers to beat the sergeants' mess at anything

It was February 1920 that also saw the birth of the *RAOC Gazette*, the last *AOC Gazette* having been published in 1914, with the inevitable cessation of production during the Great War. One of its first campaigns was to open a memorial fund for Corps victims of the war – a precursor to what would become the RAOC Aid Society. A statement explaining the objects of the fund was issued by the DEOS and circulated widely. It was intended not only to raise money to benefit children, up to the age of 16, of all ranks of the RAOC who lost their lives during the Great War, but also to provide a permanent

memorial to record the service given to the Corps. They were seeking £10,000 (£230,000) to set up a bursary system that would produce a fixed income made up partly of the interest on the sums raised and partly of the capital which would be completely absorbed. This income would be made available for the education or the technical or business training of each child. The fund was to be administered on a thoroughly democratic basis, the needs and merits of each case being considered, without regard to the rank of the parent.

In considering the permanent memorial, it was thought it might take the form of a brass or a shrine with an urn containing a vellum scroll bearing the names of the officers, WOs, NCOs and men who lost their lives. Any small balance that might be left would be credited to the Corps Charitable Fund. There were other initiatives, many of them local, to provide benevolence in the wake of the war. The depot at Chittening near Bristol, for example, set up a local 'Mutual Aid' Society. For a subscription of 4d (£0.40) weekly, 10s (£12) sick benefit was paid, and at Christmas there was a sharing out of the balance.

Major W J Asser.

The *Gazette* in those early days was laid out in a style that prevailed largely unaltered through the whole of its life with its mix of editorial, main articles of general interest and unit news. Its first editor was Major J W Asser, who undertook a virtually unbroken reign of nineteen years in the post. Reports from units contained the same mix of personal information, sporting prowess, exercises and visits that remained the stuff of the *Gazette* throughout. Indeed, aside from the style of the prose, it would be hard to distinguish unit news in 1920 from that of 1990. However, in those early days the *Gazette* was also used to pass information, almost like a Corps Orders Bulletin, on such issues as pay, conditions of service, ammunition inspection and disposal and training, and civilian job opportunities and preparedness for them. It was also used to serialize the work of the then Colonel Forbes on the history of the Ordnance service, later to be enshrined in his three-volume book. Furthermore, on a range of issues there were political views expressed which ran counter to a modern view of the place of the armed forces in a modern, democratic society. The *Gazette* remained, nonetheless, a tremendous binding agent, drawing together a Corps spread in penny packets throughout the Army and providing the basis of the *esprit de corps* that would carry the RAOC through the difficult times ahead as it supported the Army wherever it was sent. It never seemed to lose its sense of what really was relevant to soldiers and officers. There was, for example, even guidance on the costs of running a small, light car, set at £157 12s 4d (£4,000) per year, equating to some 7d (£0.70) per mile.

One of the main operational theatres at the forming of the RAOC, then as in 1993, was Ireland. In this case it was the entire island, as opposed to the Six Counties with which so many were to become familiar in the years to come. The process that led to the creation of the state of Eire and the province of Ulster began on 23 December 1920 when the Government of Ireland Act established separate parliaments for the six counties in the north and the twenty-six in the rest of Ireland. The plan was for elections to be held between January 1921 and March 1922, with the imposition of martial law being seen as a guarantor of peace. It was a major commitment, with fifty-one infantry battalions stationed there in June 1921, a force of 50,000 men all to be supported by the RAOC from its static installations. The main concentrations were in Dublin and the Curragh, but there were small detachments deployed all over the country to meet the needs of isolated bodies of troops. One early task was to issue a uniform to the reinforcements for the much-depleted Royal Irish Constabulary. The mix of khaki service dress jackets and black trousers combined with a black RIC forage cap created a name that was to go down notoriously in modern Irish history – the Black and Tans.

Major General Sir John Steevens.

Ireland then was a home station and was treated differently for those aspects of military life that related to the 'troubles'. However, for much of the activity, especially repair and depot work, it was no different from the rest of the United Kingdom base, and was not without its problems.

However, despite their difficult circumstances, the importance of sport was never forgotten, and sporting activities were as much a regular feature of RAOC life on operational stations as they were at home. At a football match in Phoenix Park, for example, 14 Company from the Curragh played 15 Company from Dublin, and there were upwards of 9,000 spectators. The result, on a windy and rainy day, was a three all draw and a night out in Dublin for the soldiers from the Curragh. It is perhaps interesting to note the venue, currently the home of Irish national sporting activity, and that is a feature

The RAF and RAOC teams leave the pitch at the Oval at the end of the RAF innings.

of much of the post-war sporting activity; the use of sporting venues that are now national institutions. For example, the annual cricket match between the RAOC and the RAF took place at the Oval, and was won by the RAF. The game between the RAOC and the RASC at Lords was drawn. The golfing fraternity acquitted itself rather better, winning the Army Golf Challenge Cup in 1921.

The support that could be provided by the Corps at the time, at home or overseas, at peace or on operations, was limited by three key factors. There was the post-war parsimony caused by the Treasury cuts. The Army was on operations yet scales of equipment were at peacetime rates and hence often inadequate, even if budget restrictions had permitted the scales to be held complete, and the accounting system used was pedestrian, to say the least, and hardly conducive to speedy response to operational needs.

Provision was annualized, requiring frenetic periods of activity at the turn of the financial year with the balance of the year spent resolving the problems created by an annual attempt to predict the future. The demanding accounting procedures required a mass of documentation and supporting signatures, the whole process requiring an army of clerks to cross-reference the paperwork. It was an auditor's dream, a logistician's nightmare and, because it was entirely paper-based, the account always lagged behind reality. The contents of the storehouse could not at any stage have borne any real resemblance to the account.

It was not helped by the fact that a system of cost accounting was imposed upon the stores accounting and provisioning system. A Corps of Military Accountants had been formed to manage it, and they were distributed among units to operate the system. In simple terms it was intended to change the balance of the account not to reflect the cost of the commodity, but the aggregated cost of commodities by unit to provide, for example, the 'cost' of an infantry battalion. It involved a major pricing exercise and imposed yet another layer of bureaucracy on the Corps, further slowing down the speed and effectiveness of the support process. The impact of this was felt very keenly in Ireland, and so a special case was made for the theatre. There was a concession in February 1920 that allowed a speedier response to be offered by the 450 or so Ordnance personnel distributed throughout the island, principally in the two sections, formerly 14 and 15 Companies, in the Curragh and Dublin.

The RAOC and RASC teams at Lords.

When the truce came about in July 1921 a civil war followed between the Provisional Government of the Irish Free State and the Irish Republican Army, the latter being made an illegal body by its own government. It was a war that would go on until May 1923, and, paradoxically, the new Irish government turned to the British government for assistance. From the time of the truce up to the withdrawal of the British Army northwards into the Six Counties in December 1922, weapons, transport and clothing valued at £458,000 (£17 million) were donated to the Irish authorities.

It was not a happy withdrawal, for the blood letting that took place between Irish men and women transcended anything that had taken place during the post-war policing of the island by the British. However, one of the 'Irish' casualties was Field Marshal Sir Henry Wilson, an Irishman by birth and a former Chief of the Imperial General Staff. He was murdered by the IRA on the steps of his London home having been elected as an MP in the elections for the government of the North of Ireland. Other 'casualties' of the political changes were the disbanded Irish regiments with proud histories stretching back over the centuries. The 88th Connaught Rangers and the 94th, who featured in so many of the actions of the Peninsular War under the command of that other great Irish Peer, Wellington, as well as the Leinsters and the Munsters and the Dublin Fusiliers.

Amidst all this sadness the RAOC packed its bags and quietly, behind the scenes, received all the surplus equipment and stores, checked them and moved it all either to the depot they were to use in the North, in Carrickfergus Castle, or across the water to the UK mainland. The depot in Carrickfergus became a detachment of No. 10 Section in Burscough near Liverpool, retaining in the new Northern Ireland District a DADOS and an IOM.

In the rest of the home commands life was beset by the problems of managing the equipment and stores of an Army reducing in size and with a consummate lack of interest in getting the 'books' right before disappearing back into civilian life while, at the same time, trying to reorganize and restructure itself and to recruit for the tasks to come. A campaign was mounted to try and attract the right recruits in the right numbers and of the right quality. It met with mixed success in the early stages, but a focus on junior soldiers properly trained with an eye to a long-term future in the RAOC bore fruit. And it wasn't simply the Regular Army that was beset by problems of organization, training and quality of tradesmen and soldiers. The TA too was adjusting to the new peacetime structures and forming Divisional Ordnance Companies in the districts into which the country was being divided to support the TA divisions being formed on a regional basis. The first to 'appear' in public was 53 West Lancashire Divisional Ordnance Company, successfully claiming the first article by a Territorial Ordnance Company in the Corps' *Gazette* in October 1921 after forming in February of that year. It was followed swiftly by 44, 48, 49, 50 and 56 Divisional Ordnance Companies

While all this was going on major changes were taking place in the UK affecting the regimental side of Corps life. RAOC Headquarters was moved from Red Barracks, Woolwich, to Hilsea Barracks in Portsmouth, with the move taking place at the end of 1921. It was a barracks large enough to accommodate not just the soldiers, but also the School of Instruction and the RAOC Records Office. Work would be needed to bring it up to a suitable standard, but it was to provide the

Married quarters were available at Hilsea for those who needed them.

Corps with a home for some time to come. The war memorial, for which the committee had been formed in 1920, was erected there and unveiled on 11 November 1922.

On the same day the church was named St Barbara's after the RAOC's patron saint. Her association with Ordnance and firearms was born of the manner of her martyrdom. Following her persistent refusal to renounce her Christian faith, her father had reported her to the Roman authorities. Despite being tortured by them she continued to refuse to recant and was eventually returned to her father for execution. He beheaded her personally, and the legend says that as she died at his hand the heavens opened and he was struck down by a bolt of lightning and consumed by fire. The legend concerning the manner of her father's death and the association of lightning and thunderbolts with the instruments of war once gunpowder appeared on the scene, has associated her with ordnance and the artillery ever since, and has done so in many nations.

The RAOC needed a band. That was clear, and in April 1922 it was formed under WOI R T Stevens, formerly the bandmaster of the 3rd Battalion Rifle Brigade. It was he who suggested the *Village Blacksmith* as the future Corps' march. He saw it as a traditional air relating to the Corps' role and to its artisans, with the words drawn from Longfellow's poem, and which, in his view had enough musical potential to be turned into a march. The martial nature or otherwise of the RAOC March has been a debate often heard raging in messes and barrack rooms throughout the Corps, usually after a parade when one had been forced to march to it. Nonetheless, it remained the RAOC March to the end.

Equally fiery can be the debate about the village wherein lay the smithy and upon which the poem is based. There are villages in Kent, Northamptonshire and Sussex that lay claim to the honour. Perhaps the most likely, however, is one where a powerful belief lies locally – Figheldean in Wiltshire. Whether founded on fact or fiction, the smithy at Figheldean was overshadowed by a large chestnut tree, the village church did stand across the street and in the surrounding houses there must have been many children who lingered on their way to and from school to watch the mighty man with the sinewy hands knocking sparks off inoffensive lumps of metal. As to it being the village wherein lay the Corps' smithy it is sufficient unto the day; and if there is opinion to the contrary it is quite reasonable to argue that Figheldean will do very nicely indeed.

The band was available just in time for the visit to Hilsea of the Colonel-in-Chief, His Royal Highness the Duke of York. The QMG, Lieutenant General Sir Travers Clarke, the Colonel Commandant, Major General Sir John Steevens, the DEOS, Major General Sir Harold Parsons and the Mayor of Portsmouth and other dignitaries welcomed him. In his speech following the parade the man who would be the future King, unbeknown at that time, made reference to his pleasure at having been granted permission by the King to accept the appointment of Colonel-in-Chief of the RAOC. He couched his words in the first person plural, referring to 'we' and its possessive 'our' and won hearts throughout. He welcomed the Corps to its new home and

The Hilsea Memorial unveiled 11 November 1922.

reassured those present that they would, in these new surroundings:

> …continue to maintain that high standard of efficiency which has always been the hallmark of the Royal Army Ordnance Corps.

His visit and the speech cemented a relationship with the royal household that would eventually become a relationship with the sovereign; and which would carry on for the remaining life of the RAOC. It was a relationship treasured by the Corps and one of which it was justly proud. It spent the whole of its time seeking to ensure that the maintenance of high standards, referred to by its Colonel-in-Chief so soon after its birth, never wavered.

Given the close association that built from the outset between the Duke and the RAOC it is no surprise that the wedding of His Royal Highness to Lady Elizabeth Bowes-Lyon just one year almost to the day from his Hilsea visit was extensively covered in the Corps' *Gazette*. Five officers and ten soldiers represented the RAOC at the wedding.

HRH The Duke of York inspects the guard of honour at Hilsea on 2 May 1922.

The Corps had adopted the motto of the Board of Ordnance, whose arms appeared in the centre of the RAOC cap badge. *Sua Tela Tonanti* has never received a satisfactory translation. That which appeals to soldiers does not apparently appeal to classicists. However, 'To the Warrior his Arms' or 'To the Thunderer His Weapons' are accepted as being as close as one might get. The 'Warrior' would seem to have more of an affinity with the soldiers and on balance remains therefore the most appropriate translation.

It was also 1922 that saw the first RAOC officer to make an attempt on Everest. Captain George Finch, with Captain Bruce and a Gurkha NCO climbed to within 2,000 feet of the summit. George Finch had left the service a little while before his attempt on the mountain, and his effort is no less superhuman for the equipment he had to ward off the cold and the oxygen deprivation. It demonstrated a spirit of great adventure, and stories like his were often used in the *Gazette* as part of the 'binding agent' that was drawing the RAOC together.

Meanwhile, the focus on sporting prowess continued undiminished. Its role as a training medium and as a valuable builder of *esprit de corps* was very much recognized, and perhaps never more so than in shooting, which was clearly something considered to be very important. Probably not surprising, given the recent end to hostilities, and the freshness in the minds of many of the need for prowess in skill at arms. In 1921 an ex-AOC armourer, Sergeant Cunningham, won the King's Prize at Bisley aged sixty-two, setting an example that many would seek to emulate in the years following his feat. For example the Travers Clarke annual shooting competition was won in 1921 by the Depot, and throughout the RAOC there were local and regional competitions both within the Corps and with other units at which the RAOC was well represented.

The RAOC was also represented widely overseas, stretched as thinly as the rest of the Army that it served. Paradoxically, that other great drain on military manpower, India, was not a problem for the

Corps because of the existence of the Indian Army Ordnance Corps. There were, of course, liaison visits and other attachments, and Major General Sir Hugh Perry took up the post of DEOS India immediately after the war, taking with him a number of RAOC staff. It was not, however, a drain of Corps resources. The HQ was at Simla and there were small detachments in such places as Madras Arsenal and Ishapore in Bengal.

Much closer to home was the Army of Occupation in Germany. In theory it was an operational theatre, with the British Army of the Rhine in place to ensure that a beaten enemy adhered to the terms of the Treaty of Versailles. However, so far as the Treasury was concerned it was a static command and Ordnance services had to treat it as such. It was a command whose requirements would fluctuate considerably as the reduction in force levels and the state of the country changed in the post-war period. At the outset, in 1920, there were 134,000 troops of which 38,000 were British soldiers, 71,000 Indians and a Chinese Labour Corps of 25,000. The programme of clearing up was huge, and by the end of 1920 something like 0.5 million tons of stores had been returned to the UK. Life, however, was good for an RAOC soldier living in Germany. He was paid in sterling and there were 1,000 Marks to the £ sterling. He had good married quarters and generally speaking there was little acrimony with the German population in the British Zone. In the immediate post-war period the

British were in the north of Germany, with workshops and depots at Nippes and Cologne and an ammunition depot at Longerich. There was also a detachment at Danzig (Gdansk) in what is now Poland, where two officers and eleven soldiers provided Ordnance support for the plebiscite area. There were a number of units in the plebiscite area and despite their small numbers the first reports from the Detachment speak of the desire to get the depot running properly and to take on just about everybody at pretty much any sport there was, including football and boxing.

In addition to the main depots in Germany there were IOMs scattered about the country. For example, there were three in Berlin, two of whom were Lieutenant Colonel P G Davies and Lieutenant Colonel A I Allan, with similar representation in places such as Breslau, Königsberg, Münster, Düsseldorf and Hanover. In particular Lieutenant Colonel Allen had expertise in ammunition. Their main task appears to have been supervision of the destruction of warlike stores and weapons following the provisions of the Treaty of Versailles.

This advertisement of 1922 attempted to ease the overstretch by encouraging young men to join the RAOC.

Despite the peace in Europe between the Allies and Germany, other parts of Europe were less stable. There was tension in the south-east between Greece and Turkey. Despite the drive for economy and the need to rebuild its national commercial base, the British Government felt, some would argue almost inevitably, a need to be involved in policing the situation and in keeping the warring factions apart. Its aim, of course, was to be on hand to pick up any worthwhile pieces of the Turkish Empire as it collapsed. Consequently, the Army of the Black Sea was deployed to keep the peace in a neutral zone that had been established around what was then known as Constantinople; modern day Istanbul.

There were 150 RAOC deployed to support the operation, commanded by Major M Meares. Their welcome at Kilia, where they were to establish a depot, was not auspicious and did not bode well for a successful outcome. They were not expected, and spent their first night in a local hospital. In the morning they woke to find that their 'depot' comprised lines of tents on a half-finished road, perched on a site quite close to the beach. Stores had to be brought in over the beach, they were often mixed up with RE and NAAFI stores and had to be sorted, and there was rarely, if ever, any warning of an impending receipt. The confusion thus created was exacerbated by a regular flow of urgent demands from the Army in Chanak, just across the straights from the depot.

The depot account stood no chance of ever providing an accurate record of the quantities and locations of stocks held. This was a huge problem with the depot staff seeking to provide the best possible service under difficult conditions. However, a great deal of time was wasted because of the insistence that peacetime accounting rules had to be applied and this inevitably detracted from the effort that could be applied to meeting operational needs. The sort of example quoted by depot staff includes such things as Courts of Enquiry into trivial matters such as the loss of soap valued at 8s 6d (£13) and the accompanying wealth of administration and paperwork. Bad for the service levels and bad for morale.

The movements plan, if plan it could be called, also presented its problems. Ships arrived that had been loaded in a hurry with loads configured to suit the situation in the UK and with no account being taken of the requirements of the depot in the theatre. The inevitable result was a chaotic, unsorted jumble of stores on the beach with little clue as to what was there, who required it and the priority at which, once found, it was required. The 150 RAOC were woefully inadequate in numbers to meet the task, and it was some time before a miscellaneous heap of stores reached the account and became assets that could be used.

In the end the anticipated fighting did not occur and the system was never fully tested, so no significant lessons were taken on board. One outcome, however, of the Chanak affair was to end the career of Lloyd George who had, unwisely, taken the Greek side when the balance of national and international opinion had favoured the Turks. Coupled with the failure of a major international conference he had sought to dominate in September 1922, Chanak was the straw that broke his political back. For the Army, it was the last time it would find itself facing the possibility of serious war fighting until 1939. Regrettably, the lessons learned from the lamentable performance of the system of logistic support were not retained and in the years to come peacetime parsimony would restrict the ability of professionals to prepare the necessary stocks and systems to sustain intense conflict.

In the Middle East the RAOC found itself supporting the Army in Mesopotamia (modern day Iraq) and in Egypt. A rebellion in Iraq in July 1919 had been quelled by the dispatch in August of the 6th Division. Control was established by the end of the year. The British force was eventually distributed throughout the country in a number of districts, commanded by a General Headquarters at Baghdad. The Line of Communication, some 600 miles from Baghdad to Mosul was constantly raided. The RAOC representation comprised six under strength companies and two mobile workshops, a total of some 350 officers and men. They were widely dispersed to ensure local support was immediately available and to compensate for the disruption caused by Arab raids on the LofC.

By 1922 the Kingdom of Iraq was beginning to emerge from the chaos, and an Iraqi army began to

build. By 1923 it was felt that the situation had stabilized sufficiently to allow the RAF to take over responsibility for defence under the terms of the treaty that had been negotiated on the formation of the fledgling state. The outcome was a massive draw down in the RAOC strength. Those left were attached to the RAF stores organization with the depot at Magill being named Ordnance Group RAF, to be subsequently known locally as 'O' Squadron. It was not to be the last time the RAOC worked closely alongside the RAF.

Not far away in Egypt there was an Egyptian Expeditionary Force of some two divisions. Stationed principally in Egypt, there were also detachments in Palestine, Khartoum and Cyprus. There was the normal

Local labour was employed in the Ordnance Depot Basra in clothing repair. A portent, perhaps, of another time when the RAOC would help to try to bring peace and stability in Iraq.

HQ staff at GHQ in Cairo, with an ADOS. By the mid 1920s there was a depot at Alexandria, including a clothing depot, and at Cairo. Ammunition was stored at Cairo, and there was a small outpost on Cyprus. RAOC units were involved not simply in their routine duties but also as fighting units to help contribute to local defence. Despite the difficulties, however, every effort was made to maintain normalcy. For example, the Sergeants' Mess in Cairo had a very pleasant outing in May 1920 when a party of over 100, including women and children, went to the Barrage. They chartered a boat for the voyage up and down the Nile and lunch and tea were served on the lawn at the Barrage. There were races for the children at which everyone got a prize and it was a very happy but tired party that arrived back in Cairo at 7 pm that evening. And more similar events were planned.

Of all the theatres the Far East was the most benign. There was a small depot in Colombo, modern day Sri Lanka, and in Malaya there was a depot on a small island on the southern tip of the peninsula, called Singapore. China was a separate command with Ordnance depots at Hong Kong and Tientsin, some 1,000 miles apart. Peking (Beijing) boasted a small sub-depot for ammunition and defence stores, manned by two RAOC soldiers.

A major event in the life of the RAOC was the creation of the Old Comrades Association. There had been all kinds of indicators that it was needed, if for no other reason than to add to the *esprit de corps* created by such things as the *RAOC Gazette* and the various RAOC-wide sporting competitions. The indications were clear, if in nothing other than the various reunion dinners that were being held by people who had served together in the Great War. Indeed, it was the Great War that was the catalyst, but it took the initiative of one man, Captain F H S Brehaut MM, some time after it formed, to actually get the Association off the ground. Advertising by every means at his disposal, he organized a gathering on 16 May 1923 in London that was very well attended. In particular, it was supported by the RAOC hierarchy with Major General Parsons and Major General Sir C M Mayhew together with a number of colonels and lieutenant colonels. There were 200 attendees in all and the agreed outcome was the launch of an Association with an annual subscription of 2s 6d (£5.25). In his absence, due to illness, General Sir John Steevens KCB KCMG was made its first president, with Major General Parsons as the vice.

Work started at once on building the Association, but by July there were only 137 members with donations to the tune of £39 19s (£1,650), but it was a start. Following some hard work by the committee the first social function, in the Harrods Restaurant on 24 November 1923, saw 280

Association members sit down to the first annual dinner. The Colonel-in-Chief sent a telegram of congratulation and it was clear from the number of apologies that by the end of the year the Association was off to a very good start. The first two branches were in Woolwich and Manchester, with the indefatigable Captain Brehaut responsible for setting up the Manchester branch.

In 1923 the top management structure that had been put in place for the RAOC in the immediate post-war period was adjusted to align itself better with the more stable situation now prevailing in peacetime Britain. They were essentially cosmetic changes which did not alter the fundamental fact that Ordnance was a QMG service and did not make any inroads into the difficulties caused by the separation of QMG and MGO's responsibilities or their means of conducting business. At this stage the RAOC's principal depots were Bramley for ammunition; Chilwell for surpluses, general stores and some clothing; Hereford for ammunition; Pimlico as a clothing factory and depot; the Royal Arsenal at Woolwich for gun stores and ammunition; and Weedon for small arms. In addition to the organizational changes, another inevitable feature of military life was the tendency to change names at regular intervals. For example, in 1924 the title of the IOM changed to Ordnance Mechanical Engineer (OME). It didn't make a jot of difference to the job, nor was it any more or any less descriptive of the task performed by these individuals. Much more important was the decision by the Treasury to reduce officers' pay by as much as £1 2s 0d (£38) in every £100 (£3,500) of salary. Recruiting the quality of officer required to manage an increasingly complex inventory with engineering effort and spares support was not made any easier. The insouciant disregard for morale and the future effectiveness of the Army with which the measure was passed is hard to believe, and the effect easy to imagine.

On 15 November 1924 the RAOC Old Comrades Club held its annual dinner; its second.

The Army of Occupation in Germany went through some major adjustments late in 1925. Under the terms of the peace treaty the British Army had to transfer its sphere of influence from the area of Cologne to what was known as the Wiesbaden Bridgehead, wedged in between a French Corps on the right and left and abutting a demilitarized zone to its east. The move presented a challenge of the sort the Corps was used to and would find inflicted on it many more times in the future. The move was in the middle of winter, arranged at two weeks notice and with virtually no transport. The British Army of the Rhine in the twenties was a far different organization to that with which so many post-Second World War BAOR soldiers would become familiar. It was a static garrison organization with its supporting infrastructure, including transport, cut to the bare minimum. The task was undertaken by train and by barge, on time and in good order, with surpluses being sold off to civilians before the move was finally complete. Inevitably the accommodation to which they moved required a great deal of work to be brought up even to minimum standards, and again, by dint of a great deal of hard work, this was achieved, although not for six or seven months.

On Friday 13 February 1925 the RAOC lost one of its great servants. Major General Sir Harold Parsons had only retired some eighteen months earlier. However, the strain he had suffered providing Ordnance support on Flanders for almost the whole of the war and then as DEOS in the tumultuous post-war period had taken its toll. He had served thirty years with Ordnance, in the South African war

The funeral of General Parsons was a magnificent affair...

and as the officer responsible, for five years, for the RAOC records office before the Great War. He knew the Corps for which he was responsible inside out, and he gave it his all. The retirement he had so richly deserved was short lived. He was buried in the military cemetery in Aldershot, with honours appropriate to a man of his stature and integrity, and as one who was responsible for creating the foundations upon which the strength of the RAOC was being built in those early days.

In the same year the RAOC was dealt another blow with the untimely death of the Colonel Commandant, Major General Sir John Steevens. The correspondence between Lady Steevens and the Principal Ordnance Officer was probably typical of its time, but will appear phlegmatic, to say the least, to a modern reader. Her telegram read:

Director Ordnance, War Office, London.   12 June 1925

Regret inform you that Sir John Steevens died this morning. Funeral Monday four-thirty afternoon at Uplowman. Writing.

From:- Lady Steevens

The response, by letter, was hardly effusive:

WAR OFFICE   15 June 1925

Dear Lady Steevens

I was deeply grieved on receiving your telegram announcing the death of Sir John.
He laid the foundation of the RAOC as it exists today, and by his death we lose the help and counsel of a sincere friend of the whole Corps.
I write to express to you, on behalf of the whole of the RAOC, our deepest sympathy at your sad loss.

Yours sincerely

R K Scott, Major General POO

... at which the RAOC was well represented.

In 1926 the country was beset by the huge political, social and economic problems associated with the onset of the Great Depression and the General Strike. In May of that year the RAOC deployed twenty-five men to Hyde Park to establish a field depot, the function of which was to equip and sustain the thousands of Special Constables being recruited to police the General Strike. Stores were delivered from Pimlico, Didcot and Weedon and, since the Special Constables had not been recruited at this

The RAOC General Strike party, May 1926.

stage, they could not provide working parties to help a very small RAOC detachment in the unloading and sorting of the loads. True to their traditions of getting on with the job, the Hyde Park party turned to and undertook the work themselves. However, many of those who volunteered to join the Specials were ex-RAOC and it was not long before these Ordnance Specials were bringing their expertise to bear not only in the Field Store in Hyde Park, but also in the control of stocks once they were in the hand of the Specials. Another source of labour showed up in the form of sixty ex-Artists Rifles and another sixty ex-London Scottish all of them anxious to help.

One impact of the General Strike was to delay the final of the Army Billiards Championship. Sergeant. W F Scully, from the Depot at Hilsea, eventually won it. The final game at Messrs Thureston's was reached after games against soldiers and officers across a range of regiments and corps. In the final he met Bandsman Kelly of the 13th/18th Hussars, a previous winner of the tournament, but Sergeant Scully reached his total of 1,000 when his opponent was still on 977.

Later that same year, in December, the situation in China destabilized, civil war broke out and the threat to British nationals increased markedly. The British government reinforced the region, and in particular Hong Kong and Shanghai, in the latter case for the defence of the international settlements in the city. The

Sergeant W F
Scully RAOC.

Shanghai force would eventually muster 16,000 men, with an RAOC contingent of four officers, two warrant officers and thirty-nine soldiers commanded by Major A G B Stewart.

So it was, strike breaking in London, embattled in Shanghai and supporting the Army everywhere else and with a new home and a new organizational structure in the War Office, that the RAOC moved on from a period of retrenchment and winding down. The future brought with it the constant drives for further and further economy, whilst at the same time far-sighted officers in the Army were continuing to talk and to write of a new kind of warfare, of fast action, swift, coordinated attack and mobile defence. The views of men like Basil Liddell-Hart and J F C Fuller were beginning to make themselves felt. These new concepts would create not only their own logistic challenges affecting systems and methods, but would bring with them the burdens associated with mechanization and an increasingly equipment intensive form of warfare.

Meanwhile, in Europe, in the heart of Germany, something was stirring; something that would change the world.

Chapter Three

Mechanization and the MGO 1927 – 1937

The problem of maintenance and repair...forms the foundation of all tactical efficiency.

Major General J F C Fuller

More damaging than the General Strike was the national miners' strike that followed it in the first half of 1927. In fact, in many ways the General Strike delivered benefits. It rallied large sections of the population to supporting the community and created, paradoxically, a spirit of cooperation. Rather than mark a high point of socialism and a move towards communism in the wake of the Russian revolution it was, in fact, the death knell of extreme left wing politics in any great strength across the United Kingdom.

However, the miners' strike was a classic of its kind. The downturn in heavy industry and alternative sources of coal brought in from elsewhere in the world created a reduction in the requirement for British coal, and cheaper sources meant a reduction in price. This translated into reductions in wages and the resultant strike. The damage lay in the support by the Tory government for the employers, as they withdrew from pay and conditions of work agreements that had been settled with the unions. Public opinion was generally sympathetic to the miners' cause, and the Government's line was unpopular, leading to a significant decline in its support.

The economy was perceived, nonetheless, to be strong, despite the ravages of the two strikes. There was no warning at this stage of the effects of the economic depression that lay a few short years away. With hindsight the weakened economies in Europe and a perceptible decline in growth and productivity in the US were indicators of trouble to come, but lay unseen; an economic iceberg with its bulk largely below the surface.

Despite the apparent strength of the economy the Armed Forces continued to suffer financially under the Ten Year Rule, which limited investment in manpower, facilities and future equipment programmes. This was at a time when the many-headed hydra of mechanization was rearing its head. Men like Fuller and Liddell-Hart were preaching the philosophy and practice of the use of mechanized forces and, despite lack of funding, it was clear that the drive to mechanization was to be a major feature of the coming decade. It was obviously a subject the discussion of which permeated throughout the Army. Extensive and detailed articles and essays appeared on a regular basis in the Corps' *Gazette*, written by bright far-sighted RAOC officers who would make their contribution to developing the organizations and practices that would support the new, fast moving, mechanized forces that would eventually emerge from the theory.

In practical terms Fuller, then a Colonel, was Military Assistant to the CIGS in 1927, and was given the task of creating an Experimental Mechanized Force. It was based on two battalions of the Royal Tank Corps, an infantry machine-gun battalion, two regiments of artillery and some engineers. Most of the equipment was a mix of what was available and there was no attempt to even consider any of the support implications. It was at best an ad hoc arrangement that never stood the test of time, with the whole idea being abandoned and the unit disbanded in 1928. At the heart of its failure were the mixed views and opinions held in British military circles. There was a conflict between those who saw mechanization simply as a means of doing on wheels that which had previously been undertaken on foot or on horseback, and those who saw the opportunity for a new form of warfare where tracked vehicles, well armed and fast, would change the face of the battlefield. To pursue the latter route cost more money, of which there was little, and required industrial capacity with specialist designers and industrial facilities of which there were precious few.

However, those who aspired to the conspiracy theory saw the abolition in 1928 of the lance as a weapon of war as just one more of the undesirable effects of this quite unnecessary trend towards mechanization.

Within the Corps, 1927 saw the retitling of the RAOC Old Comrades Association to RAOC Association in order to open it up not only to Old Comrades, but to serving members of the Corps. It was the model that has continued until the present day. By then it had, since its inception, placed over 100 men in employment and provided support to fifty-eight cases of former members of the RAOC in need. By now branches had been formed at Bramley, Tidworth, Aldershot, Liverpool, Didcot, York, Stirling and Dover and the membership had grown to over 1,800.

It was also the year in which the *Daily Telegraph*, on 10 April, was able to report the victory of the RAOC over 1 Brigade Royal Horse Artillery by two goals to one in the Army Football Cup. It is perhaps a measure of the huge interest in Army sport that, not only was the game reported extensively in the national press, but 30,000 spectators turned up to the stadium in Aldershot to witness the match, and King George V sent his apologies for not being able to attend due to illness. It was the gunners' first time in the final. The RAOC had been there the previous year and been

Above: St Barbara's Church at Hilsea in 1928.

Left: Inside St Barbara's Church at Hilsea in 1928.

By 1928 the RAOC band was a major feature of Corps life.

beaten, but had been determined to get back to the final and to prevail – which it did.

In March 1928 the depot in Aden was handed over to the RAF. Conductor F W Hall, a man typical of his breed with a long and devoted service to the RAOC, was awarded the MBE for his work in ensuring a smooth transition. He had seen service in South Africa, France during the First World War, Italy and Egypt prior to his Aden tour. He was ideally suited to take the place of the Ordnance Officer when the incumbent fell ill and had to be repatriated.

The General Election of 1929 was an inconclusive affair. Labour won with a small majority, but there were sufficient Liberal seats to hold the balance of power. Furthermore, the Conservatives held the greater slice of the national vote. It was far from satisfactory, and Labour hardly had a mandate to rule. It was a time when strong leadership would be required as the financial realities of the world's economic situation began to have their effect, and as a wind of change was beginning to blow through the European political scene. As it was, however, the United Kingdom drifted almost aimlessly into crisis.

On the surface all was well. Peace was in the ascendancy, The Kellogg Peace Pact had been signed and the issue of German reparations had been reviewed. This would see the evacuation of the Rhineland by 30 June 1930. The French, deeply concerned about their security, began to promote a plan for European union, for a United States of Europe. Reaction was varied, with the British finding it difficult to reconcile such a theme with their own global interests. The feeling was that there was peace, that everyone was committed to peace and that there was nothing on the horizon that might alter that. The status quo seemed, certainly to the British Government, the most attractive option.

However, as the Army toyed with the tactical implications of the new ranges of equipment being considered, other minds were turning to the means whereby such forces could be supported if they were to be used to best effect. *The Times* of 27 February 1929 reported an RUSI address by Colonel D C Cameron of the RASC. The summary of his thesis was that armoured forces could not operate effectively given the current support system, with its large depots, its massive quantities of munitions and its huge volumes of equipment. Were this to remain the case, then the scope of operations for the new flexible, fast and aggressive forces being postulated lay within a few short miles of the logistic base to which the mechanized formations would be glued.

Something new had to be developed. Something that would provide fuel and ammunition when and where it was needed, and that would ensure the necessary repair effort with associated spare parts was also available in a timely manner. Cameron was conscious that changes in industry and a more flexible approach to manufacturing and the support of the commercial mechanized fleet would aid a similar upsurge in the military requirement.

The first essay in the Corps' *Gazette* came also to the view that support units could not burden the operational commander with the need to ensure their protection. They would have to be capable of looking after themselves without external support. The converse was also judged to be true, in that vehicle crews would have to understand the basics of the mechanics' trade such that they could render mechanical 'first aid' in the event of breakdown. The first hint of an integrated system of logistics began to emerge, as the point was made that the RASC was responsible for supplying the fuel upon which the vehicles depended, and the consequent suggestion, more 'wouldn't be a good idea ', that a single entity should be responsible for the total logistic support of the force.

In that same year a group of OMEs attended the first of a series of courses on mechanization. They were based at the Military College of Science, and the instructor was an officer in the Royal Artillery from the Mechanical Traction Branch. It was a great success, and marked the start of a series that would follow. The spread of knowledge was also being passed on to the Army, pursuing the theme that regimental officers and soldiers needed also to have a sound mechanical knowledge. For example, the first two regiments to be equipped with armoured cars were the 11th Hussars and the 12th Lancers, and lectures were given by OMEs on the inspection and repair of vehicles. This was in the absence of any formal training courses.

These thoughts and developments were emerging at a time when there remained a split in the logistic support arrangements for the Army that was, to say the least, inconvenient. The RASC was, in the immediate post-war period, the sole user of the 2,000 or so wheeled vehicles in the Army. Hence, they had their own repair organization and supply system for spare parts, and had retained it throughout the 1920s. The QMG provided its vehicles. As mechanization increased and MT vehicles began to be issued to units, the realization grew that there were too many logistic systems in one Army. For example, units with MT vehicles and AFVs would have two cap badges repairing them with spares from two different sources of supply; and this was to say nothing of the split responsibilities for such things as ammunition, fuel, food, tentage, clothing and other stores. The complications were extended with the Royal Engineers retaining responsibility for repair of their own equipment, and the same was also true of the Royal Signals with their technical equipment.

Studies were undertaken into the best way to organize the logistics to support the new mechanized Army. The recommendations were similar to the recommendations of so many other studies that would follow over the years. They suggested that all motor vehicles should be provisioned by the MGO; that the RAOC should become a corps of mechanical engineers; and that all other stores and supplies, not related to MT or other vehicles, should be provisioned by the RASC. It was a 'cap badge' oriented proposal for what should have been a functional breakdown of responsibility based on a coherent analysis of the need, but it was at least a start in the thought process if nothing else, for little that was practical came of it.

Possibly it was too soon, too advanced before the impact of mechanization and equipment intensive combat had been fully understood. The only real outcome of the studies was a reorganization of the War Office which took effect in January 1928. The MGO took over the responsibility for the provision of all wheeled vehicles from the QMG, except for those held by the RASC and by medical units. The RAOC was moved from the QMG's area to the MGO's and undertook responsibility for the management and repair of these vehicles. It meant that there was only one repair agency at unit level, the RAOC, with resources emanating from one source; the MGO. However, it did nothing to rationalize the issues surrounding duplication of logistic systems in the wider Army. Specifically, it placed control of different parts of the Army's MT fleet with the MGO and the QMG. It did, however, give birth to the terms 'A' Vehicle for armoured vehicles and 'B' Vehicle for soft skinned, wheeled vehicles; terms that would become very familiar to generations of soldiers.

Mechanization, the most profound impact on the means of providing logistic support for the British Army since the transition to the use of firearms, began to take effect with a logistic system that was conceptually flawed from the outset. The MGO, Lieutenant General Sir Webb Gilman, did write an open letter expressing his delight that the Ordnance Corps was once again back with the Ordnance, but the question has to remain as to what was in a name. The real damage was that it detached the RAOC from the Army it served, for the MGO's reach did not extend down into the Field Army. Anything the RAOC might do to redress that would be in spite of the higher organization of the Army and not because of it.

A key issue was representation in the Field Army. There were Ordnance officers on the staff, but there were no units dedicated to formations other than in the Territorial Divisions where there were Ordnance Companies. These units, however, performed their duties only at Annual Camp and were largely restricted to the handling of the stores needed for the camp. It was hardly a test of supply in contact with the enemy. When a regular formation was deployed the Ordnance support was allocated from the most appropriate unit and put together for the operation. Experience of the formation's requirements was limited and effective support took some time to achieve. As the impact of mechanization began to bite the RAOC attached tradesmen to units, particularly in the RAC, to assist unit tradesmen in repair and maintenance, but this was an ad hoc arrangement with the tradesmen concerned not included in the official unit establishment. Spares for repair activity were not held in the workshop, but separately with the store holding unit, the Ordnance Field Park, assembled for the operation and operating at corps level. It was a mobile unit – but it could be expected to cover an area of 40,000 square feet when parked and occupy one mile and 700 yards of road when on the move. It was intended that it should hold not only spares but also a range of replacement vehicles, although none of these would be fighting vehicles. In 1931, however, the concept was new and no scalings had been assessed against which to stock the unit when it formed and deployed.

Almost as an aside, yet another study removed from the MGO his role in personnel management of the RAOC, shortly after he had received it from the QMG, and handed it back to the Army. In 1929 the Corps was brought into line with other Arms and Services when this task was transferred to the Adjutant General. There was a one-year trial of the arrangement, whereupon a new branch was formed to manage officers' careers. It was called AG9.

At the beginning AG9 controlled MGO8, the Branch responsible for the career management of the 7,000 civilians who worked for Ordnance services. A year later, in 1930, the Corps' trade groups were reorganized. A two-branch structure was retained; Store Branch (clerks, storemen, ammunition examiners) and Workshop Branch (armament artificers, armourers and artisans). This removed artisans from the Store Branch and placed soldiers' trade structures in a corresponding situation to the officers'.

At about the same time a DDOS was established to supervise and administer all Central Ordnance Depots and the Central Provision Office. This small reorganization of the higher echelons of the RAOC focussed the control of inventory and its storage in the hands of one man. However, this one man served many masters: DOS for Vote 7 (Clothing) and Vote 8 (General Stores), the Director of Artillery and of Mechanization for Vote 9 (Warlike and MT stores) and the Director of Movement and Quartering for Vote 5. His was a responsible post with complex management responsibilities. He prepared contracts and demands, managed War Reserves and worked directly with Contracts Branches.

Within the RAOC, if perhaps not in the Army at large, the problem of mechanization was being addressed seriously. In 1929, for instance, a new type of workshop was developed and exercised. It was mobile and self-contained with a number of sections that could be detached to support elements of a formation. Recovery was one of its tasks, and it was established accordingly. During its major test exercise it was located in Blackdown Barracks as an independent unit serving all those other units, of all sides, involved in a major mechanized manoeuvre, but repairing only 'B' Vehicles, which limited the breadth of experience that could be gained. One of the key lessons learned, however, was the lack of experience in addressing battlefield damage repair.

The exercise also stressed the need to repair as far forward as possible. From the requirement had grown the idea of Light Aid Detachments capable of being attached to mechanized units to provide local repair effort to a relatively sophisticated level. In peace they remained part of the parent workshop, only detaching when required and tailored to suit the force or unit they were to support.

A Scammel recovery vehicle on exercise on Salisbury Plain.

In 1928 a new 'B' Vehicle depot was opened at Farnborough, to sweep up the arrival of MT spares transferred from the RASC for that part of the MT fleet that was being passed into the responsibility of the RAOC. It wasn't entirely satisfactory and was only kept as a depot until a proper MT spares storage focus could be found. Eventually, it was decided that Chilwell should be the spot. It had been an ammunition depot from 1919 until 1925, whereupon it was closed down. It had been looked over on a few occasions as a potential depot, but would not be taken into use until 1935. In the meantime Farnborough carried on as the RAOC's principal depot for the handling of vehicle spares. It was an ad hoc arrangement, and nothing more so than the storage media. For the first few years after the war the storage bins were empty ammunition boxes, but work went ahead to design something more useful. The outcome was the range of three types of adjustable binning, Nos. 1, 2 and 3, that would grace many an Ordnance installation and QM's store for decades to come. And it wasn't just the physical storage media that was developed, there were also advances in accounting and handling of information as Ordnance officers tried to come to grips with the maintenance of an account, commercial part numbers, scalings, accuracy of holdings and the need for an audit trail.

In the background the debate continued, following the inadequate outcome of the 1928 changes, as to the optimum organization for the support of the Army, as mechanization began to spread its tentacles throughout. The RASC continued to press for control of the maintenance and repair of their fleet. They based this on the view that it was an essential prerequisite to the effective supply of their commodities to the Army. This argument was unconvincing, but even more unconvincing was the offering that repair of transport vehicles was in some way different from the repair of anything else. The RAOC argument was that repair was repair, and the provision of spares was best undertaken by just one agency. At the same time there was the anomaly of the RAOC providing a range of general stores whilst the RASC provided accommodation stores. Obvious though these shortcomings were, the issues were not considered sufficiently important to warrant serious attention, and the opposing camps could not mount sufficient clout to sway the arguments. Consequently, nothing was done.

Throughout the UK there were Command depots and workshops providing local support. Catterick was the jewel in the crown, with the camp growing from a couple of sheds in 1926 to an extensive garrison rebuilt to replace the loss of the Curragh in Ireland and to be a centre for mechanized training. New workshops were constructed at Kinnegar in Northern Ireland and Chatham, and there were enlargements at Bovington and Hilsea. Another new depot was built at Ashford in Kent to absorb increased stock requirements in that area. Compensating reductions were made elsewhere in areas of lower activity, such as Pembroke Dock.

At the end of 1928 the winter in Europe was severe, sufficient to freeze the Rhine. However, it was also time to go. The mandate to occupy the Rhineland was coming to an end as a result of the Young Plan and the revision of the policy on German reparations. It would take six months to achieve, based on a plan developed by the Rhineland Evacuation Committee working from the War Office. The six months was later shortened to three, with volume of work undiminished. The RAOC contingent undertook the complete operation of selecting stocks for return to the UK, selling off surplus vehicles and equipment and disposing of unwanted stocks by sale or by destruction. They also planned the transport for the move, principally by barge to Rotterdam where stocks, including ammunition, were cross-loaded under RAOC supervision onto ships for the journey across the North Sea. The evacuation was completed on time and below budget.

In August 1929 there was unrest in Palestine, with fighting between Jews and Arabs and a number of deaths. With no troops in the country, the swiftest response was from Cairo and an infantry advance party was flown in, perhaps the first use of the speed afforded by air transport rapidly to deploy troops. It was a portent for the future that passed unnoticed. An infantry brigade followed more slowly, by rail, together with a squadron of armoured cars and supporting units. SQMS Hewitt went as the BOWO, and he set himself up in a railway carriage to conduct his business. Just as he was beginning to work out the size of his dependency, its dispersion and its requirements, the first stocks arrived unannounced from Cairo. It was Cairo's assessment of his anticipated requirements, and it gave him an initial holding, at least of ammunition and clothing, with which to support the Force.

The military situation in Palestine, however, calmed very quickly and was to remain so for some time to come. It was the last operational deployment for some time and the Corps was able to turn to its peacetime role of supporting an Army that maintained the home base and policed the empire.

On 17 January 1930 Major General A Forbes CB CMG died. He was the author of the three volume history of the RAOC, charting the Corps' existence through from its inception to 1918. He was an officer with a distinguished record of service. He had retired in October 1926 and was wintering with his wife in the South of France when he died suddenly and unexpectedly. The RAOC owes him a debt, not simply for the comprehensive history from which it can chart its origins, but also for the vision and drive he brought to the work of the Corps.

In Germany, as the forces of occupation departed, the economy, no longer underpinned by the advantages it had gained from post-war foreign loans, began to collapse. Brüning, the German Chancellor, had to cope with civil unrest and had to rule by decree. The ground was being laid for the ascendancy of a nationalist focus and, in the September 1930 elections, the National Socialists raised their share of the seats in the Reichstag from twelve to 107. Further south in Italy, in May of that year, Mussolini had already affirmed that in his view 'right unaccompanied by might was an empty word'.

It was May 1930 when the extent of the financial crisis facing the United Kingdom was made clear in a report to Parliament. It was a particular blow as the general feeling in the Nation had been that the UK was insulated from the economic woes that had been affecting the rest of the developed world. It was a naïve view, as the prospect put before the Government was a deficit of £120 million (£6 billion) requiring taxation of £24 million (£1.2 billion) with reductions of £96 million (£4.5 billion) in public expenditure. Two thirds of the reductions were to be found in benefit reductions. It was to be the first of a series of crises that would lead in August 1931 to the collapse of MacDonald's Government and its replacement by a National Government, but with MacDonald still at its head as Prime Minister, the King having refused his resignation while accepting that of his Labour cabinet.

However, this did not solve the financial crisis and its impact on the political map of the UK was to split the Labour Party, damage the Liberals and enhance the position of the Conservatives. Within a year it had been decided that the situation in Europe warranted abandoning the Ten Year Rule. This was a paradox for, setting aside the difficulties at home, the pervading atmosphere was hopeful that there would be international peace, and indeed a disarmament conference opened in Geneva in February 1932. It was perhaps significant that Germany, America and Russia were unable to agree the agenda. However, these international political events were well reported in the Corps' *Gazette*, showing it to be in many ways an organ for informing officers and soldiers of wider events outside the day-to-day life of the RAOC, but which affected them either personally or professionally.

In the meantime, from a practical viewpoint, a time of national, political and economic crisis was not the ideal moment to tell the Army that it was to equip and train for modern warfare. International peace movements, political uncertainty and financial limitations are not good bedfellows for a rearmament programme, especially since the public service pay cuts in Snowden's budget of 10 September 1931 saw 10 per cent shaved off armed forces' pay, bringing it down to 1925 levels with a saving to the exchequer of £2.2 million (£115 million), and there were a number of other similar public service cuts. Despite this, and almost paradoxically, the unemployment that accompanied the Great Depression saw an influx of highly skilled tradesmen and engineers into the RAOC, especially the engineering disciplines. It was an influx of quality that was to stand the RAOC and the Army in good

In 1931 soldiers were still wearing the uniform and accoutrements of the First World War; Here the retiring DOS, Major General C D R Watts, makes a final inspection of a parade at Didcot.

stead up to and through the challenges of the war no one knew was yet to come. And the RAOC was going to need all the help it could find, for the Army was the poor relation in the rearmament programme that had, as its priorities, the air defence of Great Britain, the protection of overseas trade routes and the creation of a regular expeditionary force of five divisions, for a war of limited liability or of a colonial type. There was still no suggestion that planning was under way for a major equipment-intensive ground war.

The worsening of the financial crisis as the Nation entered the Great Depression in 1931 did not help the Army's situation as it embarked on its programme of mechanization. The result was, typically, a compromise. Instead of an effective medium tank upon which a concept for armoured warfare could be built, the outcome was a light tank armed only with a machine gun. It allowed the cavalry to undertake its traditional role, and could be used in policing tasks when there was unrest in some part of the Empire. It was not a weapons' platform that would make any contribution to the kind of armoured warfare being preached by Fuller and Liddell-Hart, and which was being put into practice in Germany.

As part of the drive for economy the Government also introduced a 'buy British' campaign. It was promoted in the Corps' *Gazette* and soldiers were encouraged, as part of their patriotic duty, to pursue it whenever and wherever they could.

For the RAOC there was a massive task ahead in receiving, storing and issuing the new equipment, to say nothing of scaling and provisioning spares, developing repair policy and ensuring the right tradesmen were in place to maintain and repair the new equipment. As was so often the case, the headline news produced a huge amount of 'behind the scenes' effort that was unpredicted and unrecognized. The scale of the task for the ADGB involved conversion of 470 3-inch guns on a lorry mounting, the receipt and distribution of over 1,200 40-mm, 3.7-inch and 4.5-inch anti-aircraft guns, searchlights, locating equipment, predictors and other stores. Depots had to be constructed and the staff of the newly formed Anti-Aircraft Command was established for a DDOS.

One by-product of the rearmament programme was to change the role of the TA. It was no longer required to reinforce the Expeditionary Force in a continental war, but to assist in anti-aircraft defence and with law and order issues in support of the civil authority.

But perhaps some could see the potential for future conflict on a grand scale for, as Snowden was presenting his budget, there was a signal of impending international unrest, to add to the messages coming from Germany and Italy. The Japanese staging of the Mukden Incident and its invasion of Manchuria was the first assault on the League of Nations' system of collective security and the first dent in the Kellogg Pact. One of the outcomes of this invasion was a Japanese attempt in January 1932 to take the port of Shanghai. In the city was an international force, with the British element supported by an Ordnance Detachment. The depot lay near where much of the fighting took place, with the span of the 'front line' being eloquently described in the Corps' *Gazette* as occupying a space equivalent to that lying between Oxford Street and the Thames. The British contingent, which had been there since the international force deployed in 1927, comprised two infantry battalions, an RASC MT company, a 150-bed hospital and the RAOC detachment which was by now two officers and thirty-seven soldiers. The Ordnance Depot was compactly sited in a disused garage on three floors, part of which was used for billets and the Sergeants' Mess. There were also nine Russian labourers, two Sikh watchmen and some Chinese carpenters, sail makers and casual workers. It was a one-year unaccompanied posting for most people, although there were one or two family billets.

They were subjected to collateral fire emanating from the Sino-Japanese fighting, including aircraft cannon, and lived under these circumstances for a month. The working day was twelve hours, for each of the seven days in a week. Captain Townsend, the DADOS, was injured about half way through the siege when a 'blind' Japanese shell exploded as he was trying to render it safe. As an officer who had completed the one-year Ordnance Officers' course, he was qualified as an IOO to undertake such work and appears to be the first RAOC officer injured undertaking Explosive Ordnance Disposal duties. Reports of the fighting suggest huge damage to the civilian infrastructure and heavy casualties. Mercifully, that was not the case in the small British garrison, despite its proximity to the fighting.

Arrangements were made to evacuate the wives and families of officers and soldiers on the ships *Neuralia* and *Lancashire*. It was an offer that was refused en bloc. Captain Graham did apply for such a passage for his wife, but was informed in no uncertain terms that should he continue to pursue the arrangement she would 'see the brigadier first'. It was a wise Captain Graham who beat a well-judged retreat.

There is an innate ability in the British soldier, especially in the midst of adversity, to find the vaguely ridiculous and make capital from it. In this case, in the midst of an absolute chaos of bloodletting locally, it was the arrival, assembly and onward dispersal to deserving soldiers of 2,000 iron bedsteads with associated mattresses.

Sport, of course, was a major feature of life, even in far-flung garrisons and under fire. In March 1931 the RAOC detachment in Shanghai had five football matches in hand and lay only six points behind the leaders in the military league, but their chief opponents, belonging to infantry and artillery units, were formidable. It was, however, some consolation to know that the RAOC team was miles ahead of any other 'minor unit' team. Three of the team played for the Army against the Interport trial team, whilst two others were selected as reserve. Of those selected for the team, Corporal Sansom

Captain Graham RAOC and a sandbagged sentry in Shanghai in 1931, bearing in mind that the RAOC was non-combatant.

played on two occasions with great success. The success of the men's team led to the spread of a 'football fever' amongst the ladies. From being great supporters of their menfolk on the touchline, a match was arranged for them on Boxing Day 1930 against a team of 'old crocks', who were handicapped by being compelled to walk and to kick only with the left foot. Mrs Larmour, the wife of the ADOS, Colonel Larmour, kicked off. The ball was quickly passed to Mrs Sparey who, with a view to settling a domestic difference, promptly landed the ball square in her husband's face. Mrs Richardson, giving a hefty kick, sent her shoe following the ball, and Mrs Fettis cuddled the opposing goalkeeper while Mrs Mitchell scored a goal. The ladies won, inevitably, by three goals to one, a result hardly in doubt when the referee gave the ladies a penalty kick on the grounds that the linesman was offside.

Another unusual match was held later in the season between a team representing the RAOC and the South Wales Borderers. The conditions were that each team was to have a minimum of 220 years' service (exclusive of boy service), and that no member was to have less than twelve years' service. Quality football was not a feature of the game, but this was more than rectified by the fun that ensued, both for the players and the barracking spectators. The result was a defeat for the RAOC by three goals to nil.

Shanghai was actually something of a focus for unusual sporting occasions. There was, for example, in 1930, a Polo match with a team of RAOC soldiers versus the Transport Drivers and Grooms of the 2nd Battalion the Green Howards. During the first chukka the pace was slow, and although the RAOC team were better mounted and displayed better hitting ability, they failed to score. The rest of the match was considerably faster. The Green Howards' back attacked the RAOC goal with a fine shot, but it was well saved by Lance Corporal Filer who then got a good run up the field. He was crossed in front of goal and a forty yard penalty was awarded. Lance Sergeant Mathew took the hit, but failed to score and the game ended goalless. The return match took place on 18 September. In this game the RAOC's opponents showed better form and improved mounts, which evened the odds, but another draw resulted, this time by one goal each. One outcome of the example set by these young soldiers was a move within a couple of years to develop a RAOC Polo Team, but the officers who tried to make it work met with less success, both organizationally and in sporting prowess, than the young soldiers in Shanghai whose example they sought to emulate.

Typical of RAOC sportsmen, and just to prove the officers also made their contribution, was Captain G T W Horne. Apart from serving on numerous management and referees' committees, and representing the Army FA for a number of years on the Hampshire FA Council, he successfully captained teams that won the Army Cup and Hampshire Senior Cup in successive years. An unfortunate accident in the Aldershot Command Gymnasium had removed his services as a half-back during the previous two seasons, but he accompanied the team to every game, home or away, wet or fine, and his ability to size up any soccer situation made him a very useful critic to have in a dressing room at half-time. And his activities were not confined to soccer alone. He could more than hold his own in any branch of athletics. On the track his stamina made him a very useful half-miler to have in relay teams, at tennis he was streets ahead of most people and the Depot cricket team could always rely on him for a good knock and some sound 'keeping'. He also turned out for the hockey team, and sensible men would prefer to be on Captain Horne's side in a rugger game.

Meanwhile, the War Department realized it was due to lose, in 1937, the lease on the building housing the Royal Army Clothing Department in Grosvenor Road, Pimlico in London. This forced a decision on the future of the department and with it the future of the clothing factory and therefore internal manufacture of clothing by the RAOC. A review in 1932 that showed a £25,000 (£1.4 million) annual saving in the cost of service dress from private industry was the death knell of the factory and RAOC clothing manufacture. Pimlico could not be retained sensibly as a stores depot alone, and so the decision was to rescind the lease early and leave. On 23 September 1933 the Royal Army Clothing Department ceased to exist, and with it the role of the RAOC as a clothing manufacturer. The Clothing and General Stores provision branches went to Didcot whilst some other functions were transferred to Woolwich, splitting the management of clothing for the Army. It also led, arguably, to an excessive reliance on trade, in a notoriously unreliable element of British manufacturing industry, for a key part of soldiers' equipment, for in those days service dress was the uniform with which they went to war.

In 1932 the RAOC decided to issue a record of the RAOC's march, with a new march, *Sua Tela Tonanti*, written by the Bandmaster, on the reverse side. A minimum order quantity of 350 was required to make it economically viable and the number was very quickly reached. The price was 2s 6d (£7) a copy, reduced to 2s (£6) for orders of four or more. The HMV record company recorded it. Regrettably, postage costs rendered it uneconomic to send copies abroad, which limited both its appeal and the number of copies that might be sold. In the end some 750 were taken up.

In August the RAOC lost its Colonel Commandant. Major General Sir Charles Mayhew KCMG, CB, DSO was typical of senior Corps officers at the time. Commissioned into the infantry he had transferred to the RAOC in mid career, rising to senior rank in a life of service during which he had brought his own brand of leadership, understanding and vision to the work of the RAOC. His sudden death was a shock and he was sadly missed.

Major General Sir Charles Massey Mayhew KCMG CBE DSO.

Training in mechanized warfare carried on, and gradually the RAOC built its concepts for the support of mechanized forces. In September 1932 1 Tank Brigade with three battalions exercised on Salisbury Plain. It was supported by an Ordnance Mobile Workshop, which was fully self-contained. It was a deployment from which many lessons were learned. In particular, and following erudite essays on the subject, it was clear that there was a need for a separate recovery organization within the Workshop Branch. It had to be well organized with properly trained soldiers skilled in the arts of vehicle recovery and possessed of the necessary military skills to survive as they sought to recover vital armoured assets at some risk and potentially under fire. And this for a 'non-combatant' corps.

On 30 January 1933 Hitler became Chancellor of Germany. The Disarmament Conference, which had faltered and stuttered on for just over a year, by March 1933 was faced with a proposal that would reduce the size of the French Army and place it in parity with that of Germany. Then, in May, Hitler appeared to assuage the fears of the international community with a number of speeches seemingly aimed at conciliation. He even suggested that Germany would disarm and disband its military forces if other nations would do the same in order to avoid the 'madness' of a European War. There was great hope, therefore, when the Conference met again in October 1933 and the British proposed a five year pact with international supervision of arms to be followed by disarmament bringing all nations onto parity with Germany. Hitler, sensing a trap, telegraphed his representative in Geneva and on 14 October 1933 offered notice that Germany intended to resign from the League of Nations. It was a huge gamble, inviting the ire and possible hostile action of at least, so he felt, Britain and France. Nothing happened; he had won the first of a series of diplomatic victories on the road to Armageddon.

Under the terms of the Versailles Treaty there was to be a plebiscite on the Saar regarding its return, or not, to Germany. It had been, since 1919, a territory administered by the League of Nations. The plebiscite was to be held on 13 January 1934, and an international force was deployed on 21 December

1933 to oversee it. The British contribution was commanded by a major general and comprised HQ 13 Infantry Brigade with two battalions, a detachment of armoured cars from the 12th Lancers and administrative support. The RAOC sent Lieutenant B D Jones as DADOS SAAR Force, and he was accompanied by twelve soldiers from Catterick. The 12th Lancers had a small LAD from Tidworth, commanded by Lieutenant G E Butler.

They deployed via Calais, accompanying the stores, and were installed in the Artillery Barracks in Saarbrücken with all stores issued or put to stock as appropriate by 24 December 1933, in time to enjoy a Christmas away from home as best they could. As was so often the case, the level of stocks taken was parsimonious and allowed only a basic quality of life. It was not until the standard of living of other contingents was observed by the soldiers and by the press that a sensible level of mess and accommodation stores was permitted and a reasonable life was possible. The plebiscite was undertaken, the vote was for a return to German autonomy and SAAR Force was withdrawn by the end of February.

In Singapore the decision, taken in the late twenties, to build a large naval base, began to become a reality. The initiative was underway by early 1933 when it was decided to complete the work by 1937. So far as the Army was concerned this meant a garrison of two battalions with the appropriate support. The RAOC depot in Singapore was inadequate, and a new site was planned at Alexandra. The reserves included a number of weapons, including artillery and there was, almost inevitably, one spare gun barrel, in this case for a 15-inch coastal battery gun. Subsequently, when motor vehicles replaced horse-drawn transport in 1937 a workshop was built, again at Alexandra.

The Army estimates for 1934 were increased with a view to remedying some of the shortcomings left over from the Ten Year Rule, and to address some of the new issues facing the Army. However, the RAOC view on the £1.65 million (£90 million) addition was scornful to say the least. There was enough just to cover some works projects and the provision of some warlike stores. In the latter case this was mainly for some half-tracked and some logistic vehicles. It also made provision for the establishment of 1 Tank Brigade, but that was really only the reshuffling of tank battalions and did not provide the additional mechanized forces, such as artillery, that would make it a truly effective fighting formation. The parliamentary announcement also saw notice given of the demise of the Lewis Gun as the infantry light machine gun within the foreseeable future, but gave no indication of its likely replacement.

It was in 1934 that the CIGS, Sir Archibald Montgomerie-Massingberd offered his view on Army sport. 'Physical fitness', he said, 'is one of the soldier's chief attributes, and if organized games seem to play a disproportionate part in his life as compared with the civilian's, the results prove the soundness of the policy.' It was a view the RAOC took to its heart, not only with its various internal competitions but also the successes it achieved in Army-wide events. And it was not simply in the 'traditional' team sports they competed and excelled, but also those less well known. The Hilsea Fencing team for example, drawn from all ranks of the Depot, acquitted themselves nobly in a range of competitions, and in field sports the events undertaken stretched, among others, to pole vaulting. The records, for example, of the 1933

An important feature in RAOC sport has always been the Annual Travers Clarke athletic tournament, here meeting in 1933.

cricket season showed few fixtures unfulfilled or of matches that were not played to a finish, with generally successful results and always, most importantly, enjoyable. There were certain performances that merited a special mention. The RAOC marksmen in Malta had, by now, won the Collingwood Cup eighteen times, and within that for the past thirteen years without a break. With them were the rifle teams from Didcot, winners of the Sheppard Cup, and Corps Headquarters coming runners-up in the inter-departmental competition at the Southern Command Meeting. The combined team of Didcot, Hilsea and Tidworth then made runners-up in a field of sixteen teams at the Southern Command inter-unit meeting.

Tennis brought forward the names of three players who had earned distinction for themselves and for the RAOC. Two of them were Sub-Conductor Pearce and AQMS Reid whose brilliant success in the Army Tennis Championships was received with great delight. In addition, AQMS Reid in partnership with Mr Fox, an ex-gunner, won three important cups in open tournaments whilst Sub-Conductor Pearce's long and successful record in big military tournaments since 1918 had been an inspiration

Typical of unit involvement in shooting, the team from No 1 Section in Aldershot won the Battersby Challenge Cup in 1934.

to Corps' sportsmen. Additionally, still with tennis, Armourer Staff Sergeant Parr, attached to the Small Arms School at Netheravon, in combination with Sergeant Major Frosdick of the school, won both the open and the unit doubles in the Salisbury Plain area tournament at Bulford.

A significant event for the RAOC in 1934 was the selection of Major (Brevet Lieutenant Colonel) L H Williams as the COO of a depot yet to be founded, but which was to replace Farnborough for storage of MT spares. He was told to inspect the site at Chilwell. His initial thoughts were that the site would only be used for the storage of 'B' vehicle spares and that 'A' vehicles would remain at Woolwich. He felt it would be more efficient to have the two centres and less confusing or demanding for units trying to work out from where they should source particular items.

In setting up the plan for the depot, a number of visits were made, not only to other depots but to manufacturing industry as well. And these visits were not simply to benchmark structures and handling methods, but also accounting systems. There was apparently no centralized and agreed accounting system onto which the new depot could blister its procedures.

Virtually every shed required refurbishment and there was a great deal of demolition, and disruption as railway track was laid. As this was going on Lieutenant Colonel Williams continued to visit motor firms and to apply the lessons he learned from them to the plan he had made and was refining for the construction of the depot. He worked hard and well,

Sub-Conductor W Pearce.

AQMS
A R Reid.

for it was as early as 1 May 1935 that the advance party arrived. Chilwell was once more an Ordnance Depot. By then it had been decided that the logic for two separate sites for 'A' and 'B' vehicles was flawed, and the move of both vehicle types to Chilwell was planned to cover two phases, with the 'B' vehicles moving first. The vehicle reception station was opened during the summer training period when most vehicles would be out with units, and the workshop was in place in time to start inspecting and repairing them when they returned and before being put back to stock. It was farsighted and intelligent planning.

Despite a lack of initiative from on high exercises continued to attempt to improve the UK's posture for war, like this one of a forward engineering workshop at Vernham Dean in 1935.

Recovery training was given a lot of emphasis. Here a bogey is removed from a tank transporter...

The move was, however, time consuming, coinciding as it did with the rearmament programme and the development of mechanized forces. The Depot was receiving large volumes of stock from trade as well as completing the transfer from the other two depots. The last of these moves did not take place until July 1936. The incentive to complete the work and develop a fully functioning depot came from a realization beginning to grow in the minds of many, that war in Europe might now be a possibility. It provided a focus for all those involved in the planning and building.

In 1935 there was an earthquake in Quetta in India (now in Pakistan), and the Ordnance detachment there was hit quite badly with the loss of Captain and Mrs Robinson in the Alexander Hotel and Sub-Conductor Austen in his collapsed house. Mrs Austen was also injured, although the two Austen children escaped unhurt. The interesting thing about the Quetta earthquake was the involvement of the RAOC in providing humanitarian help to the afflicted military and civilian population, and the fact that much of the re-supply to initiate and sustain the humanitarian aid, and for casualty evacuation, was by air. A portent of things to come.

The invasion in 1935 by Italy of Abyssinia had made many realize not that war was possible, but possibly inevitable. Unfortunately this did not seem to be a view shared by the Government, at least not publicly in either its utterances or its actions. The impact of the invasion was reflected in a reinforcement of Egypt, which included RAOC, but there was no overt military activity.

...and then refitted

In the same year, Army estimates were increased by £4 million (£210 million) to just under £50 million (£2.6 billion). Whilst much of the money was to be spent on remedying the ills of under investment in previous years, a goodly chunk was to go on mechanization and improving the operational capability of the Army. The result was an increase in depot workload and in repair effort. This included the necessary training load.

...to allow the transporter to move off with its vital load.

No 4 Section at Didcot on parade in 1934.

Didcot was the source for the Army of non-technical items encompassing a whole range of general stores. There was a high level of activity throughout the late thirties, as the depot supported almost the whole rearmament programme. Improvements in procedures were constantly sought and in 1934 half the depot's holdings were put onto the National Cash Register accounting system as the old ledger and tally systems could not cope with volume. There had been a six-fold increase in the twenty or so years since 1913. Chilwell also started to use machine accounting as well, and Sub-Conductor A J Hunt ran the first course for the first women employees in March 1936. However, although work on machine accounting went ahead in both Didcot and Chilwell, both depots moved to the Visidex system of hand posting. It seems the audit trail was easier.

In addition to building a depot layout that worked and creating efficient internal procedures, Chilwell had to make known to the rest of the Army what it was doing and what the effect was on them. They were advised that the MT sections on Command Depots were essentially detachments of the central organization in Chilwell. The aim was an over-the-counter service to units at the Command Depots. Makers' parts lists were provided to units to ease the demand process, and lists of proprietary items such as distributors and carburettors supplemented them. It all gave units a complete schedule of their spares needs, and the associated tools. The use of makers' parts lists for units to demand spares was new. However, it obviated the need to create Army part numbers for those items that would always remain peculiar to a particular vehicle type. A combined catalogue and commonality list, it was at the time a revolutionary concept, pioneered by Captain E Tankard and Sub-Conductor Hunt.

One of the early problems Lieutenant Colonel Williams identified in his work was that the system of provisioning was inadequate. In particular centralized provisioning separated the account from the storehouse by too great a distance. His view was that provisioning should be split into two parts. That related to the depot should be in the depot and that relating to new vehicles and equipments was best done in the War Office.

Neither were provision branches equipped to work out the scales of spares required to support equipment. As a result a Scales Branch was created, employing specialist staff, to build the initial scalings for vehicles being introduced into service.

Much of the work being undertaken in Chilwell was visionary, and gave a lead not only for other depots to follow, but also for commercial industry to learn from. It was in many ways a model and it would set the pattern for many of the depot processes and procedures that would stand the RAOC as a whole in good stead in the testing times to come.

During 1935 the Corps' Bandmaster, Mr R T Stevens achieved the unique record of having attended three jubilee celebrations. He was present at the Silver Jubilee of Queen Victoria, while a band boy in the Kings Shropshire Light Infantry, and again at her Diamond Jubilee while in the same regiment as its Bugle Major. Then, in 1935, as the RAOC bandmaster, he was at the Silver Jubilee of King George V.

Among the many sporting activities throughout the Corps that were initiated by the presentation of a cup bestowed by a senior officer was the Watts Cup for tennis. Typical of the broad appeal of these competitions was the doubles meeting between Conductors Gillow and Mitchell and SQMS Hartridge and Staff Sergeant Mockford during the finals held on the courts of the Hilsea Headquarters Officers' Mess in July 1935. Mitchell and Gillow won, and on receiving the prize Conductor Mitchell closed the event by thanking Major General Watts and his wife for spending the day with the Corps. The gathering was typical of events throughout the family of the RAOC, a family that was growing stronger and more resilient given the interest shown, and demonstrated for all to see in the RAOC, by senior officers, including the Colonel-in-Chief, and the support constantly there from the Sergeants' Mess.

Bandmaster R T Stevens.

That this percolated throughout the Corps is evinced by Private Barrett who was the Salisbury Plain Open Singles Champion in 1935. He went on to come fourth in the Army Championships that year.

In 1936 trouble flared again in Palestine. The Arabs united and declared a General Strike, which was unpopular and led to violence. In May the first reinforcements to the two battalions in Palestine were sent from Egypt – 1st Battalion the Royal Scots Fusiliers and C Company 6th Battalion Royal Tank Corps. The 6th Battalion LAD was, however, to be left behind in Egypt and a special LAD was created and dispatched with the Force. It comprised an OC, one senior NCO, twelve soldiers, an 8-ton breakdown lorry and trailer, a machinery wagon, a 3-ton stores wagon, an Austin 7 and a motorcycle. Given the 300-mile LofC back to Egypt the OC LAD was granted local purchase powers of up to £5 (£275) per item, which he found most useful. Active service was declared on 21 May, and it is believed the LAD was the first of its kind in the RAOC to see active service. Replenishment from Egypt took four to five days initially, with demands being placed over the RAF radio system. However, this time later extended as congestion and sabotage on the communications links back to Cairo slowed things down. One lesson that came clear was a lack of military training among the RAOC soldiers. Their musketry and weapon handling skills were below par, and in one case non-existent, and with the interdiction of the LofC there was a clear need for all soldiers to be capable of being just that; soldiers, even in a 'non-combatant' corps. The problem was resolved locally, with on-the-spot training, but perhaps it hid a wider difficulty.

However, it is hard to believe, given the involvement of the RAOC in shooting by men such as Corporal Sankey. The then Private Sankey was posted to Egypt in 1926 where he began to build his reputation. He took life seriously, being a staunch teetotaller and non-smoker, and he worked hard at practicing his shooting. His record in the Egypt

Private Barratt RAOC, winner Salisbury Plain open singles 1935.

The Ordnance Depot in Basra 1936 – a glimpse of things to come?

Command Shooting Competition is a proud testament to his commitment. – 1926, winner; 1926, best Private in Egypt Command; 1927, runner up; 1927, best Lance Corporal in Egypt Command; 1928, runner up; 1928, best Lance Corporal in Egypt Command; 1929, runner up; 1929, best Lance Corporal in Egypt Command; 1930, runner up; 1931, best Corporal in Egypt Command; 1927 and 1930, winner of Snipers' Match (Juniors). In addition Sankey was twice awarded the 'Osmond Cup ', 1926 and 1929, and in 1926 he was also the winner of the 'Sergeants' Mess Cup'. He also represented the RAOC in all the victorious inter-Corps shoots in Egypt.

At the end of June a larger combined force was sent to Palestine from Egypt, followed by a division from UK. There would eventually be a corps of two divisions with the 1st Division arriving in September from the UK fully equipped and with over 700 vehicles. From Egypt came the 5th Division. The Force ADOS was Lieutenant Colonel G W Palmer and the COME was Lieutenant Colonel D White. The workshop capability was raised from the LAD to an OMW with a warrant officer and twenty soldiers plus a wider range of repair capability. However, no Ordnance Field Park was established for the Force, so the OMW commander was burdened with the question of stores to the exclusion of everything else. Certainly, he had no time for technical input to his work. Recovery was a major task and had to cover many hundreds of miles. Lack of experience with MT in the units deployed gave rise to a lot of accidents and recovery resources were very stretched. The arrival of 1st Division eased that

The training continued, with this Field Workshop on exercise at Tilshead in 1936.

A truck shot up and burnt out in Palestine.

problem, but the workload on the RAOC detachment, with no Ordnance Field Park, in receiving the Division's vehicles was considerable.

A Forward Ordnance Depot eventually went to the theatre with twenty soldiers and they were based at Sarafand. There was also a Depot with a Vehicle Reception Park at Haifa, and staff were also sent out for that. It was decided that the original party that set up the Haifa installation would be replaced, and a detachment was sent out from the UK. However, the loss of continuity was found to be a failing and the switch was regretted. And then, just as all the issues were being made, the situation was judged to have stabilized and the decision was taken to downsize the force. So, just as stocks were going out to units they were coming in from others. The problem was compounded by the fact that the ADOS took the line that supporting the force was more important than ensuring correct accounting procedures were adhered to. A laudable sentiment, but it added yet further to an already heavy workload for a small staff faced with balancing the books.

Many lessons came out of the Palestine affair, but like so many lessons on so many deployments they were lost in the post operational fog. The extent to which they were applied was to be tested just a few years hence.

On 10 April 1936 Mr Tom Payne, the first Regimental Sergeant Major of the RAOC, passed peacefully away. It was Good Friday, and he died at home in Tiverton, at the age of seventy-two, after an illness extending over several months. A measure of his importance in the life of the RAOC was the attendance of Major General J Baker, CB, CBE, the representative Colonel Commandant, RAOC, at his funeral. He had been one of that essential group of high grade senior warrant officers whose personality was stamped into the very soul of the RAOC, and there were many who read of his death and remembered the debt they owed him.

In 1936 the transfer of 'A' vehicles from Woolwich to Chilwell began, eventually to be completed in 1938. In the same year the idea of a Ministry of Supply was floated. The Warrenden Committee was established to consider the problems of coordination of how arms might best be supplied. There was no coordination of planning for the use of the nation's industrial base. The Directorates of Artillery and Mechanization, the Royal Ordnance Factories and the Army Contracts Department all had a

The RAOC Detachment in Tientsin, China. Captain Lancelot Cutforth, a future DOS, is in the centre and Conductor Timmins is on his right.

finger in the pie. One outcome of the deliberations to address the problem was the creation of the post of DG Munitions Production with a seat on the Army Council. The first incumbent was an Engineer Admiral, and his job was to accelerate the supply of MGO's stated requirements. The Directorate of Army Contracts and the ROFs were transferred from MGO's area of responsibility to DGMP, and new directorates were established in DGMP for industrial planning and progress.

This dismembered the MGO's department and by the end of 1937 his appointment disappeared and he was merged with DGMP. It is difficult to see what had been gained with this reshuffle, other than to make the Army responsible for its own ammunition and other procurement. The Royal Navy and the RAF objected strongly to the Ministry of Supply concept and won. In the end it became an agency for the Army with some responsibility for common user stores. The loss of an inter-service focus devalued the concept.

One effect, with the disappearance of the MGO, was to return the Corps once more to the QMG as one of the services for which he was responsible. The DOS took responsibility for provision, storage and issue of all Ordnance stores whilst the Ministry of Supply undertook design, production and inspection. All the changes finally occurred during the summer of 1939, with work towards the final goal under way in 1937. From the RAOC's position this would see a Controller of Ordnance Services appointed to deal with broad policy and planning. Beneath him a DOS and a POME were appointed, both in the rank of major general. The DOS had two deputies, a DDOS(MT) and a DDOS(A), for ammunition, warlike and technical stores. However, the Director of Supplies and Transport continued with responsibility for MT driven by the RASC, thus preserving the flawed split in the logistic system that reached down into operational units. Branches of the Directorate of Artillery and Munitions moved to DOS' area of responsibility

There were at this time concerns about career structures. The DOS, Major General Basil Hill, proposed to the MGO, before the transfer of responsibility back to the QMG, a number of improvements in career prospects for OMEs, stressing the importance of recruiting the right quality of officer into the RAOC, and retaining them. The impact of mechanization and the development of wireless communications in the field required more and more engineers to deal with the problems of repair and recovery. A new approach was needed, and there was already a view, by no means new in 1937, that a separate corps of qualified engineers was what was needed. However, General Hill took the view that an improvement in what they had stood a better chance of success than taking a revolutionary approach, especially with a Government that still did not see a major war in Europe as a possibility.

Major General Basil Hill DSO.

Within existing rules OMEs could not reach the higher ranks. Only a few made the rank of colonel and the DOS wanted the whole thing opened up with full career prospects available for all. He asked for some specialist posts to be created for OMEs with special pay, and for the appointment of a major general as the POME, together with some other enhancements. A War Office committee reviewed the position and judged the DOS to be right: that there was a need for some adjustment given the additional work being brought about by increasing mechanization. There was, however, to be no change in the non-combatant status of the RAOC. This was based on the logic that the Corps' role did not bring officers, or soldiers, into touch with fighting troops and there were no opportunities for them to command troops of all arms. So, it was judged, the Corps that supplied the Army right down into the Field Force was not a combatant service.

Fighting, of course, was not the issue. One only had to look at the Bisley results to see the military competence, and view the essays on mechanization to realize the understanding of the impact of modern logistic problems on the future operational doctrine of the Army. The real issue was not to do with any of these things, but it meant that an RAOC officer could not, like the RAMC, be employed outside his discipline. This meant there would be no places at Staff College and no wider employment on the staff. Hence, the Army was just not aware of the wider logistic implications of developments in technology at a time when it was becoming increasingly important. DOS' proposals were rejected on the basis that they would conflict with the conditions of service in the RAF Equipment Branch, although the relevance of that comparison is hard to discern. Direct entry to Sandhurst or Woolwich was denied, and although there were some pay enhancements, they were not much despite the fact that the RASC had many of these benefits. The manning situation was getting worse, to the point of being critical, and the DOS knew he had to do something in the absence of any support from the military hierarchy. A man with nine England rugby caps to his name, he was not one to be put off lightly. However, it was to be well into 1938 before he was to prevail, and the war clouds were gathering.

There were also concerns about the manning of the technical trades in the RAOC, and efforts were made to attract recruits through advertising in the *Gazette*. Of interest is the fact that the RAOC felt it had to redress the problems of its technical capability through its own efforts. Equally interesting are the rates of pay being offered. For a WOI the daily rate was 14s (£35), for a sergeant it was 8s 3d (£21) and a private was ranged between 2s (£5) and 5s 7d (£14). The top range of the privates' pay equated to the starting rate for a corporal.

In November 1936 Germany, Italy and Japan drew closer together, bound by the Berlin-Rome Axis. There was also a German-Japanese Anti-Commintern Pact and both these treaties were merged on 6 November 1937 forming a single triangular pact. Italy then left the League of Nations, following the example of the Japanese and the Germans several years earlier. With this, and with bitter fighting in Spain, the British Prime Minister, Neville Chamberlain, set about acting as his own Foreign Secretary, almost sidelining the Foreign Office and pursuing his own brand of foreign policy. It was a policy of appeasement, and it would fail.

The Country entered the two years leading up to the Second World War with foreign policy beginning to see a divide along partisan class lines. The bestialities that Hitler had started to inflict on minority groups in Germany and the bestialities being wrought, one side against the other, in the Spanish Civil War both polarized opinion on the right and the left of British politics, although at that stage in Britain's history they were terms hardly known and rarely, if ever, used. The mood of the Nation was further disturbed by the abdication of the King on 10 December 1936, and the country began 1937 in a state of political and constitutional disruption.

Behind the scenes the RAOC continued to prepare for a war no one would admit lay just over the horizon. A small moment in history, perhaps, was the arrival of the first Bren guns in COD Weedon, a weapon that would replace the Lewis gun and continue in service in the Army for several decades to come. Behind the scenes the RAOC was also continuing to excel on the sports field. The RAOC Boys' football team won the final of the Boys' Army Cup against the 2nd Battalion the East Yorkshire Regiment by six goals to nil.

New types of ammunition were coming into service, and Bramley was proving not to be big enough. More depots were needed, and Brigadier Verschoyle-Campbell and Colonel Stokes studied the possibility of underground storage. Work on developing a site at Corsham as an underground depot began in 1936, with £1 million (£48 million) as initial funding. The outcome would be a unique depot dug into the caverns beneath the chalk hills around the small town just to the east of Bath.

The fighting dress of the Army came under scrutiny. Service dress was no longer considered to be relevant. A new pattern was developed, based on the ski suit, and denim was the material selected. It was intended that it be used in place of overalls on active service, but it was decided after trials in 1938 to adopt it for all troops, although for the infantry it was to be made in serge. All these increases in clothing scales rendered Didcot too small as the Army's main clothing depot. A new site was required and after extensive reconnaissance a disused pickle factory at Branston near Burton-on-Trent was chosen. Conversion and preparation of the site for use as a depot cost £500,000 (£23.5 million).

King George VI had succeeded his brother late in 1936, following Edward's abdication. Very shortly afterwards he afforded the RAOC the honour of confirming that, as Sovereign, he would also remain the Corps' Colonel-in-Chief. In June 1937 he held a gathering of Old Comrades at Buckingham Palace. His message to former servicemen of his Corps was personal and to the point, reflecting his own individual feeling for those who had served their country in times of crisis:

I am very pleased to see so many Old Comrades here to day. I appreciate your having come, both men and women, in such large numbers, many of you from long distances, and I hope that you will take away lasting memories of this great gathering. I am happy to think that, as Patron, I am in the future to be associated with the work of some of those Bodies which make up the great Brotherhood of Ex-Service Men. Being one of that Brotherhood myself, I have always followed their progress with real interest and sympathy. I have especially welcomed the inter-change of visits between the Ex-Service Men of other countries and ourselves. Those of us who have seen war know what a great calamity it is for victors and vanquished alike, and if, with the united weight of our experience, we can convince the world of this fact, then I feel we can render no greater service to the human race.

A display by 140 apprentice armourers from Hilsea for the 1937 Tidworth Tattoo.

Some among you have not known the tragedy of War, and, I pray God, never will. For you, too, there is a task to perform. It is not only in times of common danger that we need the fellow feeling so lavishly outpoured during those dark years. The spirit of unselfishness and sympathy is just as necessary now for the welfare of mankind in our daily life, and it is up to you, and to all of us, to see that this spirit is never allowed to fade. These are not easy tasks, but we must all do our best to carry them out; and by setting this example to our fellow men we shall win honour and glory for the proud name of Ex-Service Man.

The Queen and I wish every one of you prosperity and happiness. For us this gathering will always remain one of the great outstanding events of our Coronation Year.

And with that the Nation, the Army and the RAOC moved on into the last two years before the outbreak of the next European war.

Chapter Four

Descent into War 1938 – 1942

I believe it is peace for our time. *Neville Chamberlain, 1 October 1938*

It is evil things that we shall be fighting against, brute force, bad faith, injustice, oppression and persecution. And against them I am certain that right will prevail.

Neville Chamberlain 3 September 1939

It was still believed possible for there to be peace. There appeared to be three options – perhaps the League of Nations might do something, or there might be an anti-Axis alliance or perhaps it would just be best to find some way of appeasing the dictators. However, all of them meant surrendering in some way to the bully – never a satisfactory means of conducting business. As to choices, the League had proved to be without substance and an alliance would also be ineffective without the USA as a member, and the American Neutrality Act of 1935, together with the natural US predilection for non-involvement, put paid to that.

On the face of it the policy of appeasement seemed to make most sense and offer the greatest chance of success. Certainly, that had been Eden's opinion in 1936, and when Chamberlain came to power his view was that he should seek to institute a general scheme of appeasement. In this he had the support of the bulk of the British press and a large section of the population. It was a view he would retain until March 1939 when the inevitable would cause him to shift his position.

It should have been clear to him a year earlier, with the invasion on 11 March 1938 by the Nazis of Austria, especially when the protest from Downing Street elicited a response that Austria was no business of Britain's. Inevitably there were disagreements on how to react to the situation caused by the invasion, but it was Churchill who pointed out the true and full impact. Czechoslovakia was now exposed, Germany now controlled road, rail and river communications in south-eastern Europe and was now in reach of the rich oil and mineral deposits of the region. It was the first stage of an unstoppable German expansion unless something was done.

But, even then, Chamberlain was not to be diverted from his appeasement policy, refusing to offer any confirmation of support for Czechoslovakia in the event she might suffer a similar fate. He felt there were sufficient guarantees in place to ensure her security. However, this was to forget the strategic importance of the country borne of its geographical location, its natural resources and its relationship with France and Russia that worked against Germany. When the time came the interests of the Sudeten Germans, 3.2 million people in a nation of 14 million, would prevail. Even so, in spite of his belief in the potential to avert war, much had happened in the preceding year to strengthen and restructure the Army with the speeding up of mechanization a major feature. During 1937 there had been considerable advances: infantry brigades had been organized on a three-battalion basis; there had been only one Bren gun per battalion, but mass production had allowed regular units to reach the planned allocation of fifty-two per battalion; the anti-tank rifle would be issued in time for the 1938 training season; the Mobile Division had been reorganized and would consist of two brigades of mechanized cavalry, each with three light tank regiments, and a tank brigade; and the first mechanized cavalry brigade in Aldershot was just receiving its vehicles at the end of the year. However, it is worth noting that, in all this reorganization, the means of providing logistic support was not considered – there were no intrinsic logistic units in the Mobile Division. Despite the thought-provoking essays produced by RAOC officers and warrant officers and Lieutenant Colonel G C Shaw's book *Supply In Modern War*, the forward support of mechanized forces was not addressed in any sense in the Army's Order of Battle. A change was instituted in 1938 when a section of an OFP was allocated to the Mobile Division. However, it would only be successful in providing support if a doctrine of forward support with both engineering and spares was implemented and it had yet to be developed.

The growing Army imposed a huge load on the RAOC, and COD Weedon had much to do with the issues of small arms as new weapons came on stream. But the greatest load fell on Chilwell. Built as the centre for MT receipt, storage and issue, it was ideally located in the epicentre of the British motor industry. It was a major task for there had been no time to develop standard vehicles for the Army with the clouds of war gathering with such great speed. It was the farsightedness of Leslie Williams that made Chilwell the success it became in handling in a structured and efficient manner the disparity of spares, vehicles and engineering work that came its way. It was considered by the motor industry to be a model of its type in process, procedure and in systems.

Leslie Williams would eventually become Major General Sir Leslie H Williams KBE CB MC.

March of 1938 also saw the introduction of the 1937 Pattern Web Equipment, to replace the 1908 version that was still in use thirty years after its introduction into service. It was an advance, but many would find its buckles a nightmare to polish, and the nooks and crannies in it so difficult to blanco to the satisfaction of an eagle-eyed drill sergeant.

Despite the obvious international political difficulties, life continued as normal in many ways and every effort was made to preserve the peacetime norms of sporting activity and social life. On 2 April 1938 Hilsea won the Boys' Army Football Cup for the seventh year in succession, beating the Cameron Highlanders with the only goal of the match scored just four minutes before the final whistle. General Hill was present, and his wife was delighted to be able to present the cup to the RAOC team. And on 30 April the

'37 Pattern webbing, although the soldier demonstrating it for the *RAOC Gazette* was clearly yet to receive his new battledress.

RAOC association held its annual dinner in London. The ticket price was just 5s 0d (£12), but that did not include wines.

Meanwhile, the Germans, had a clear, almost transparent, agenda. On 19 May two Sudeten Germans were shot, and the incident coincided with German troop movements in the area. However, Hitler's obvious plan to overpower Czechoslovakia was foiled by unexpected and firm diplomatic pressure by the British and the French. It was sufficient to dissuade Hitler and his generals, but it angered him and the die was cast. At the end of May 1938 Hitler ordered his staff to resolve the Sudeten German question. It was a question that had not been asked, but it suited him to seek an answer. He wished it done by 1 October that year. The political wrangling and the military posturing carried on through the summer. However, Czechoslovakia's fate was sealed by the fact that neither the British nor the French wanted war, and if a small mid-European country was to be sacrificed so be it.

On 23 September Chamberlain sent Hitler a telegram asking to see him 'in view of the increasing critical situation' over Czechoslovakia. Hitler was staggered and agreed. Chamberlain went to Berchtesgarten on 15 September, a dignified, elderly man in a sombre suit seeking peace in his time. It was an image that endeared him to a large part of the British population, and that scared the Czechs terribly.

The negotiations seeking to resolve the Sudeten issue went on over the next two weeks. German intransigence and Franco-British appeasement policy brought Europe to the brink of war. The fleet was mobilized, the auxiliary air force called up, trenches were dug and gas mask drill practised. However, just as the invasion seemed inevitable, Hitler asked Chamberlain to intercede once more to seek a resolution, despite having overturned previous solutions he had negotiated.

On 29 September Chamberlain flew to Munich to meet Hitler at his request. By 2.30 pm on 30 September 1938 Czechoslovakia had been betrayed and handed to Hitler; Britain and

Issues being made to a TA Searchlight Unit in 1938.

France had been sidelined politically and militarily; Poland was now exposed given that the Danzig issue was not significantly different to the Sudeten issue and Russia, not included in any of these negotiations, had been marginalized.

The crisis had its effect on the RAOC, and that is reflected in many of the articles in the Corps' *Gazette* at the end of 1938. The TA was embodied and this entailed the issue of large quantities of mobilization equipment, such as camp stores and, at the other extreme, anti-aircraft ammunition. The crisis ended peacefully, but the exercise had taught many lessons, not least of which was the effect of the bad weather on ammunition packaging in field storage, to which less attention had been paid than might be considered necessary.

It also uncovered the fact that there was no reserve of clothing or equipment to meet any possible requirement for an increase in the size of the TA, and consequently additional funding was authorized. Also approved was an increase in holdings of accommodation stores, overturning earlier Treasury barriers when the DOS had tried to do this before the crisis.

There was also a restructuring of the TA, with the need for Light Aid Detachments and Divisional Workshops becoming rapidly more and more apparent. Divisional Ordnance Companies were renamed Divisional Ordnance and established to provide both a spares and a workshop capability. However, they had little chance to train, as the TA during the 1930s was very much the poor relation.

Really the only opportunity to train in any sense lay with the workshop elements, as they were often able to provide repair support to their parent divisions on annual camp.

Importantly for the RAOC, the shortcomings in its own doctrine were pointed up. The Ordnance Manual (War) had last been revised in 1931 and was seriously behind the many developments in process and in organization that had taken place in the intervening years. It had to include methods for operating base ordnance depots, organizing OFPs and structuring field workshops. Colonel R F Johnson undertook the task, and he had it finished just in time for mobilization in 1939.

Another feature of the Corps' *Gazette* at the end of 1938, the last New Year before the war, was the last appearance of the cartoon figure of a pretty lady who, for years, had wished officers and soldiers a happy New Year. It is not known upon whom she was modelled or if she was just a figment of a cartoonist's imagination, but she seemed to encapsulate something special in someone's mind and she too became a victim of the war that was to engulf Europe in just eight months time.

Whoever she was she was clearly the apple of someone's eye.

After Munich the War Office opened a register called the Army Officers Emergency Reserve. The RAOC recognized the need to have qualified people with MT and engineering skills, and the motor industry agreed to help. The outcome was the formation of RAOC (AOER). It was headed up by the President of the Society of Motor Manufacturers and Traders, W E Rootes, later Lord Rootes. It was given War Office recognition and a secretary was appointed. Names were put forward from the motor trade, the individuals were screened and only those who would make good officers were recommended for appointment. The creation of the Corps' emergency reserve made a huge difference with build up of COD Chilwell and the rapid expansion needed to make it all work.

Although something of a paradox, given the semi-official government policy of appeasement, re-armament was hastened as the decade neared its end, albeit with the Treasury maintaining its normal restraints. In this process of rearmament the Army, less capital-equipment intensive than the other two services, was relatively neglected. An Army of five divisions in 1938 had just two of them fully equipped. However, this was but part of the problem. The issue was less that it was ill equipped, but rather that there was no doctrine or training for mechanized warfare. The Army existed, even at this late stage, to be a force only for home defence or for imperial policing. It was neither configured nor prepared to mount expeditionary operations in any strength, and certainly not to become involved in a major European war. And neither was the RAOC in a strong position, with no regular field force units in direct support of the Army and, until Colonel Johnson's work on the war manual was complete, not much idea as to how to support formations on operations, especially mechanized mobile operations.

The disparity in defence spending was huge. In 1938 Germany was disbursing £1.71 billion (£80 billion), one quarter of national income, on building its armed forces. In the UK it was £358 million (£14 billion), just 7 per cent of national income, although more than that being spent by France. To help defray some of the costs, income tax in the April 1938 budget was raised from 5s in the £1 to 5s 6d.

The winter of 1938/1939 was very cold, so cold that the idea that denim could be the working dress for the Army had to be abandoned. It had been, in any event, only an attempt to find a cheap way out of the problem of replacing Service Dress. Serge was to be issued to all troops, and denim was to be used only for fatigues. Battledress was born as the standard uniform for the British Army.

As 1939 dawned more and more measures began to be put in place that would prepare the nation for a war, the likelihood of which many politicians were still not acknowledging, least of all the Prime Minister. In January a reserved occupations list was commenced which, once complete, would allow direction of manpower.

But some manpower was going in a different direction. Early 1939 saw the eventual retirement of Mr Richard T Stevens. He had been the Corps' bandmaster for seventeen years when he retired in 1939, having seen fifty years service with the Army. It was a remarkable record, and he made a major contribution to the musical heritage of the RAOC, not least of which was that, while under his tutelage, the RAOC band was, in 1938, at last officially recognized after twenty years in the wilderness, operating on a manpower black economy. The reason for the change of heart was the need to encourage recruiting.

On 15 March 1939 Hitler took Czechoslovakia. He capitalized on internal wrangling in the country and eventually brought the President to Berlin. Here he was bullied and cajoled into signing a treaty creating the German Protectorate of Bohemia-Moravia. By the next morning the Gestapo were in Prague; the country had been surrendered by the large nations of Europe as a pawn in an attempt to avert a war that was, in any case, inevitable.

It all added yet further impetus to the need to provide something with which to counter Germany's investment in the size of its armed forces and its obvious political

Left: This recruiting poster was offering a career, with a salary for a private soldier set between 14s (£34) and 40s3d (£95) per week.

Below: The new bandmaster was H C Jarman, seen here with the band in 1939.

and military agenda. The UK's budget of April 1939 sought to wrest yet more money from a population already heavily burdened with taxes, in order to find additional moneys to fund the cost of rearmament. This time the better off were singled out with increased surtax rates and death duties on larger estates. April 1939 also saw the completion of the work to create a Ministry of Supply with Chamberlain giving it the final seal of approval. Indeed, April was a momentous month. It also saw a huge change in the acceptance of the true function of the Army. Hore-Belisha made it clear that the defence of Britain had to be understood to involve the defence of France. The consequence was that the British Army had to be capable of fighting a continental war of attrition, mechanized and mobile, at high intensity.

A BEF was to be prepared, comprising nineteen infantry and two cavalry divisions. The Army was to be raised to thirty-two divisions, of which six were regular, and the decisions to do this were made on 29 March and 21 April 1939 respectively. The bulk of the warlike stores for this rearmament programme passed though Woolwich Arsenal and the dockyard. Items making up the work load included the fitting of pneumatic tyres to all types of field artillery, the distribution of 6-pounder guns for coastal defence, initial issues of the new 3-inch mortar, and the 2-pounder gun for use in the tank and anti-tank roles, the dispatch of heavy guns to Malaya and the distribution of those 18-pounder guns that had been converted to 25/18-pounder. Communications equipment was also high on the list of stores handled. Woolwich's capacity, however, was limited and it was clear that its days as a major centre of RAOC activity as a COD were numbered.

The invasion of Czechoslovakia forced a powerful swing in British foreign policy and, with the obvious threat to Poland's security, Chamberlain announced in the House, quite unexpectedly and with no apparent consultation, that the Government would feel bound at once to lend the Polish Government 'all support in their power' in the event of any action that threatened Polish independence. Having just two weeks earlier

Militiaman Horace Hannaford – was he the tallest? A special uniform was on order for him.

rejected support for one country he pledged unconditional support for another. Chamberlain hoped it would be a deterrent to Hitler, but it was extraordinarily rash.

On 26 April 1939 Chamberlain announced a measure for military conscription involving the call-up of all men aged twenty to twenty-one for six months military training. In all 170,000 men answered the call, and the RAOC allocation was 3,900. Clearly, such a swift political measure, translating as it did into so many people arriving at the 'barrack gate', imposed a considerable load on the RAOC, and not just for the 3,900 men it had to call its own. Issues of clothing and equipment were made swiftly and effectively, although uniform was in such short supply that on duty they wore the new battle dress since it was all that was available. The last in were the first to use it.

Those who came to the RAOC were absorbed quickly. The riding instructions were clear – they were to concentrate on training for their military duties and could not, for example, be used on fatigues. They were paid 1s 6d (£4) per day, about half the pay of a regular private soldier, but with many less compulsory deductions. At the end of their six months they returned to civilian life, but the things they had learned in their brief acquaintance with the RAOC were to stand them, the Corps, the Army and the Nation, in good stead when they flocked to the colours in September 1939.

On 1 May 1939 two things happened. Arborfield was opened as a training establishment for apprentice mechanics and tradesmen. This was one of many results of a review of Army training and training establishments designed to cater for the rapid expansion of the Army. The month also marked the retirement of Major John Asser as editor of the *Gazette*. It was a post he had held since the formation of the RAOC and he had been a major force in forging the new Corps together by the spirit he engendered through the pages of the *Gazette*.

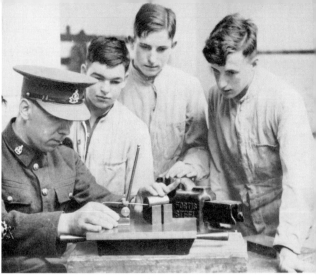

RAOC Apprentices under training in 1939 – in this case working on a scribing block.

Fred McNicol remembers the campaign by the government asking people to join one or other of the Services. In Birmingham the Motor Traders' Association decided to form a territorial unit of the RAOC and it was based at Lombard House in Great Charles Street in the city centre. Most of the volunteers worked in the motor trade. Over 150 worked at the Dunlop Tyre Company and the unit used to drill on their sports field. The unit was called 5 Ordnance Field Park and 14 Army Field Workshop RAOC. They were not to know it at that time but 14 Field Workshop was to reach Berlin in 1945, although by then no longer part of the RAOC. They had no equipment, no barracks, nothing, and Fred felt very strongly that the country was unprepared for what was to come. The OFP was tasked to send detachments around the country to garages to assess cars as to their fitness for sale to the military. The maximum paid was £50 (£2,500) for the best car, and garages either had to sell the car or it was commandeered. A vehicle park was established at Newbury on the racecourse, and units arranged collection.

The Travers Clarke athletics meeting took place on 3 June at Hilsea. Only six stations were able to compete due to the frenetic activity across the Corps, and Hilsea won. During the competition the RAOC record for the pole vault was taken by Sergeant Chapman from Hilsea.

Hitler was committed to using the Danzig question as an excuse for crushing Poland. He wanted Lebensraum, or living space, as well as food supplies for the eastern part of Germany. During August the hate campaign against the Poles was intensified in the German press and in speeches. It was a repeat

5 Ordnance Field Park and 14 Army Field Workshop RAOC.

performance of the build up to the occupation of Czechoslovakia, and it was obvious to all that the writing was on the wall. On 24 August the United Kingdom enacted the Emergency Powers Act calling up service reserves and alerting the ARP services.

Then, on 29 August, came the Russo-German non-aggression pact. France and Great Britain had been trying all summer to woo Russia to their cause, but were less than effective in doing so. Then Hitler sent Ribbentrop to talk to Stalin and the issue was sealed. Russia was not in the Allied camp and the declaration of the pact caused horror in the rest of Europe. Hitler now had the clearance he needed to take Poland without interference from the east. By this time in the UK just four of the nineteen divisions planned for the BEF were ready.

There was one small contribution from the RAOC, at Didcot, to improving the nation's posture for war. 'S' shed was finished just before the outbreak, providing six acres of covered storage accommodation for clothing.

On 1 September 1939, one month after it completed its annual camp, 48th Division Company RAOC, based at Yeomanry House, Reading, was mobilized. It was one of the sixteen Ordnance units scheduled for training that year, a number of which were still on their annual camp when mobilization was ordered. They assembled in Newbury, and the Ordnance Depot that kitted out the Ordnance Company was established on Newbury Racecourse.

On 3 September war was declared. Chamberlain reformed his cabinet, and brought Churchill in as First Lord of the Admiralty. On Newbury racecourse George Critchell and his comrades in 48th Division Company, cheered when they heard Chamberlain's announcement in the House. Early that same morning German Forces had invaded Poland. It was the start of a war that broke out with the combatants ill matched. Germany had 106 fully equipped divisions compared with the few properly equipped divisions that could be found by the British, where the focus for Army re-equipping was still very much on anti-aircraft artillery. However, Britain had used the year since Munich wisely and greatly strengthened the RAF, not just with numbers but also with quality. And the first war budget, in September, raised income tax from 5s 6d to 7s 6d in the pound to help foot the bill.

As the nation went to war the strength of the RAOC was 727 officers and 5,292 soldiers; wholly inadequate for the tasks with which they were faced even then and which subsequently they would have to face. The Corps was, however, ably assisted by the women of the Auxiliary Territorial Service, a proportion of which was attached to RAOC units. It was a proportion that would grow and their contribution to the effectiveness of the RAOC during the war was without measure.

The tank situation at the commencement of hostilities was not good. Prevarication about doctrine and the use of armour, coupled with Treasury parsimony, meant that the majority of Army tanks were light and virtually useless on a modern battlefield. The few medium tanks were under-armoured, slow and unreliable. The gun with which they were fitted, the 2-pounder, was every bit as good as the German 37-mm, but the problem lay with the doctrine for the use of armour that laid too much emphasis on speed and not enough on armament and armour and the cooperation of all arms on the battlefield. Damaged tanks in need of repair were going to feature high on the RAOC's list of priorities in the years to come.

The flood of volunteers for the RAOC appeared at Hilsea Barracks on every bus from Portsmouth railway station, causing major problems for the one captain and one staff sergeant who were available to receive them. This was the outcome of a decision by the Government to draft all volunteers into administrative corps, where the lack of a weapon and uniform would not prevent them training for their primary task. Military training had to wait anyway, as most experienced soldiers were being deployed elsewhere and the few left had enough to do just administering the flood. Within two weeks 6,000 had passed through the barracks and were being accommodated in schools throughout Portsmouth and Cosham. This would prove to be a problem throughout the RAOC as the willing amateurs arrived just as the professionals were off to war. This created difficulties for the Command

Depots from which the mobilization stocks were issued, as many of their regulars and any experienced reservists left to join field force units. One man, however, made life easy for the 'system'. His Majesty the King, the RAOC's Colonel-in-Chief, signed promptly for his issue pistol and cleared the account quickly; leadership by example.

Forming four training battalions at different locations throughout the country and pulling in older reservists to undertake the training met the training requirement. Most of these instructors were old, and a bit rusty, but the rudiments could, nonetheless, be instilled into the recruits. It was a start. Clearly the result would not be a fully trained soldier, and there were complaints about the 'product' of the training organization. Well, of course, it wasn't an 'organization' at that stage, and the situation was not helped by the lack of a training focus in the Ordnance Directorate at the War Office. This was not remedied until the arrival of Lieutenant Colonel F G Coleman in the Directorate. His arrival created a huge improvement, but he was too late to recover the existing situation; that had to be left to units.

The country really was not prepared for war on the scale that was to come. Whilst the BEF was fully mechanized, it was very much on paper rather than a complete reality. The modern

The King's voucher.

vehicles and equipment it possessed were only at the level of initial issues, and there was little, if anything, in reserve. Industry was behind in production and would remain so for some time to come. Production was barely enough to equip the four divisions of the BEF, let alone the rest of the Army back home in Great Britain.

There were also issues to be faced elsewhere in the world. The Italian conquest of Ethiopia had changed the balance in East Africa, with Italian colonial borders now pressing up against the Sudan and Kenya. Tanganyika and Kenya could no longer enjoy the peacetime status they had enjoyed in the inter-war period. In September 1939 an ADOS was appointed and the East African Army Ordnance Corps was created. Its strength at the outset was four officers, two warrant officers, three sergeants, fourteen Asians and thirty-eight Africans. The site of the first AOD was Nanyuki, a place well known to generations of post-war LRS members as they supported infantry training exercises.

Back in Europe the deployment of the BEF did not go well. The DOS of the BEF was not made privy to the plan for logistic support and consequently was unable to influence it. It is hard to say, but perhaps he may have been able to suggest the right ports were used to reduce the length of the LofC, to improve the time taken to meet demands for stores. He might also have pointed out that it was not sound planning to have soldiers appearing at one port, vehicles at another and stores, unaccompanied, at a third. But he was not invited, so he couldn't.

The initial plan for the base and the LofC called for one Base Ordnance Depot, one Advanced Ordnance Depot, two Base Ammunition Depots, one Base Ordnance Workshop, one Advanced Ordnance Workshop and four Port Workshop Detachments.

Storage and workshop accommodation were underestimated for the BOD and BOW, both based in Nantes. There was a conflict with the French authorities over priorities. They behaved perfectly amicably, but inevitably they considered their own needs first. Consequently, some of what was offered was less than satisfactory: part of a bottle factory with the floor covered in broken glass and a tram depot subsequently taken back as it was needed to repair trams. The main body of 2 BOW arrived on 14 September to find a garage with only 5,000 square feet as its sole working accommodation. It estimated a need for 135,000 square feet. DOS made his views very clear. He pointed out not only that the mechanized force deployed was heavily dependent on repair effort to maintain its effectiveness, but also that once operations commenced he would need to increase six-fold his repair accommodation requirements. Finally, he warned that, given the lack of accommodation, there was a risk of the total breakdown of the Ordnance repair

No 3 Port Workshop Detachment, Cherbourg October 1939. A Morris Commercial 6x4 Machine Lorry is manned by Staff Sergeant D McGilveray, Private R M Woodward and Sergeant WG Comber MM.

effort. He suggested that to avoid this the French should be invited to provide two full engineering works with a capacity of 0.5 million square feet between them. It worked, almost, and by 4 October he had 250,000 square feet he could use.

The BOD had, by the end of November, acquired 566,000 square feet of covered accommodation in Nantes. However, it was spread among twenty-eight buildings throughout the town and was difficult to administer.

Two BADs were established, one near Nantes and the other just east of Brest. Neither was a satisfactory site, both being damp and with roads that were inadequate for the weight of traffic. And the general policy was to hold ammunition in wooded areas for concealment, despite the difficulties of accessibility and handling without effective cross-country MHE. The planned capacity of a BAD was 21,000 tons. To deliver stocks forward to the fighting formations a mobile reserve was established on trains, on a scale of one day's supply for one corps. Each corps had an Ammunition Railhead manned by teams found from the BADs. The assumption was that the BEF would hold a prepared defensive position on the Belgian border and, to meet replenishment times, nine days' stock would be held at ARHs and on rail. The weakness in the plan lay in the attempt to provide standard loading of the trains, since ammunition expenditure would not be standard – even the equipment firing it was not standard, so how it was expected that consumption would be mirrored, formation by formation, it is hard to see. Replenishment by standard trains under these conditions was wasteful, and meeting actual expenditure from a distant BAD would be time consuming and, usually, late.

But these difficulties were small beside the problems faced by the DOS with the shortage of stores. The major problem of accommodation stores was resolved in part by local purchase. However, such was the speed with which the BEF had mobilized that many units arrived with serious deficiencies, having been told it would all be waiting for them on 'the other side'; this in an environment where there was insufficient stock of essential items to provide maintenance stocks let alone filling gaps in initial issue scales. And to resolve this, the DOS had a staff of sixty-six men of whom forty-four were either reservists or militia – all inexperienced.

Then in October 1939 it was decided to open a second BOD, and to take advantage of the Navy's command of the channel to base it around Le Havre. The COO of the BOD, Colonel W W Richards, was a man of some initiative and, dissatisfied with what he had been allocated by the local authorities,

Colonel W W Richards would go on to be a significant force in the development of the RAOC, and would rise to the rank of Major General as shown in this photograph.

made personal contact with the president of the Compagnie Générale Transatlantique and acquired some of the best storage in Le Havre. The provision of the extra depot allowed a balanced distribution of work between them and permitted 1 BOD to concentrate on holding warlike and technical stores. They were crucial and the failure of the Treasury to fund wartime scales until February 1939, and the failure of British industry to surge to meet the requirement, meant they had to be carefully controlled.

MT spares were also a problem. Mechanization was new, and there was no real experience upon which to base provision for replenishment. The situation was made worse by the fact that there were a large number of impressed non-standard vehicles issued to units, for which no provision for support was made. And then there was the driving – many of the BEF's drivers had little experience and the accident rate was astronomical, with a major impact on overall vehicle and spares availability.

Meanwhile, on 24 November the RAOC Officers' Club held its annual dinner in Aldershot. Guests were afterwards invited to the local Conservative Club where they were treated to a musical evening.

The BEF deployed initially with four divisions in two corps. By 27 September there were 152,000 Army personnel in France, sustained by, inter alia, 36,000 tons of ammunition, 21,500 vehicles and 60,000 tons of frozen meat. It was planned to have an Army HQ in place once the troop numbers warranted it, but when the Germans attacked on 10 May 1940 this had still not been implemented and GHQ had to do both jobs. GHQ was spread through a number of villages around Arras. It was unsatisfactory for it separated functions and made communications difficult. Ordnance Branch was in the village of Barley collocated with Q Maintenance, the branch responsible for dealing with Ordnance stores and ammunition. It was helpful that many of the officers in Q (Maint) were RAOC as it injected an element of realism into the decision making. Throughout the formations the RAOC representation allowed for the stores and the workshop elements to be reflected. There was a disparity in rank between engineers and supply officers, and although this had been allowed to work in peacetime, it was soon found to cause confusion on operations and was discontinued.

Four Army Field Workshops were sent to France at the start of the campaign. Others followed as more divisions deployed. However, the state of military training among all ranks was poor. Fred McNicol and his friends in 14 Field Workshop, the Motor Trade Association workshop from Birmingham, were amongst them. Fred does not think any of them had ever fired a rifle – he certainly hadn't. The workshops were large and unwieldy, and occupied large areas and considerable lengths of road when on the move. Furthermore, there was no doctrine as to their use, and no direction on the policy for forward repair. Any forward repair component was structured and deployed on the initiative of the workshop commander in consultation with the staff of the division they were supporting. It was completely ad hoc.

There were no divisional Ordnance Field Parks. They were established one per corps, and broken down into four sections; one reserve, one for corps troops and one for each division in the corps. They were fully mobile and each section could operate independently if necessary, although centralized control was the norm. Army Field Workshops existed on a scale of one per division. There were also GHQ workshops and two anti-aircraft brigade workshops. Formation workshops did not have an attached stores section and relied upon the supporting OFP for the provision of spare parts. Importantly, none of these units existed in the Regular Army in peace. A number were TA units that had to be made up to war establishment on mobilization. Others had to be created from scratch from a mix of regular soldiers, reservists, militia and volunteers who were recruited early in the war.

There was still no proper system of delivery forward for Ordnance Stores. A lesson learned from the First War, it had been forgotten in the inter-war period. Consequently all demands were sent forward on RASC ration trucks, and a great deal went astray. Eventually, the obvious was realized and DADOS was given RASC trucks he could use for the forward delivery of stores. But it should have never been necessary, for one of the clear lessons of the First World War was the need for dedicated RAOC transport. As with so many lessons it was forgotten or ignored.

The deployment of a third corps into the BEF increased the ammunition requirement. Additionally, there was an over-production of ammunition in the UK with insufficient storage available. Consequently, some of that over-capacity was shoved out to Europe just to make room in the UK Base. By May 1940 there were four BADs in France, together with 22 BAD near St Malo to hold small stocks coming through the port and 21 BAD for chemical ammunition in case the Germans resorted to its use.

The RAOC had problems, as already mentioned, with the training of tradesmen. And nowhere was it worse than in the ammunition depots, and it grew yet worse as the requirements of the BEF increased. Fortunately Lieutenant Colonel Temple Morris was a DAQMG dealing with ammunition at GHQ and he was formerly Officer Commanding the ammunition school at Bramley. His technical knowledge was a great boon in making the best of the assets they had in France for the storage and handling of ammunition. Unfortunately, he was evacuated, sick, in March 1940. Fortunately his successor was Lieutenant Colonel Lonsdale who, although not an ammunition specialist, was a hugely talented man. The early work he undertook in France was to guide the organization of ammunition management and re-supply for the rest of the war; and beyond.

The February 1940 edition of the *Gazette* contained the important news that the Corps' March had been written in a pianoforte version in response the requests by the many new units being formed for a version they could use. The *Gazette* re-told the story of the march's history and the Longfellow poem was reproduced as well. It may perhaps be considered trite to view this as important news, but it was a manifestation of an *esprit de corps* that would prove vital in the dark years ahead.

However, despite all the preparations for war nothing happened once Poland had been overrun. The armies in France sat and trained and waited, right through the winter and into the spring of 1940. It was a merciful interlude as it allowed the fledgling RAOC units, created to support formations with which they had previously had no contact, to settle and become effective. They were also encouraged to play sport and many inter-unit competitions were run.

Such was the level of inactivity that it imbued a feeling in some that the anticipated battle might never happen and that German expansionism had been curbed. Indeed, on 4 April Chamberlain made a speech, with some confidence, making the point that Hitler's failure, thus far, to attack France and the UK meant he had missed an opportunity that was now closed to him. Despite this the budget that April provided for £2,667 million (£10,000 million) of expenditure, of which £2,000 million (£7,500 million) was for the war effort. Then, on 9 April, Germany invaded Denmark.

In mid April troops were landed in Norway to counter the

Early in 1940 the adjutant of 3 Training Battalion RAOC was 6'8" tall, which made it difficult for him to communicate with Boy Kenneth Fee who was just 4'5" tall.

German invasion there. It was a short-notice half hearted affair, and the lack of operational planning led inevitably to a concomitant paucity of logistic planning. The problem was exacerbated by constant changes of objective that took no account of the logistic implications. Frankly, the RAOC had neither the manpower, the stocks nor the means to provide the support it would have wished. In the Trondheim area there was an ADOS, Lieutenant Colonel W T Cobb, and he was supported by Captain Downer and three soldiers. This was the total RAOC commitment to support the divisional deployment through Aandalsnes, near Trondheim, to the area of operations. The second area of operations had its port of entry at Namsos, north of Trondheim. Here the ADOS was Lieutenant Colonel L E Cutforth.

In both cases stores either did not arrive, or were largely destroyed by the German Air Force, which had complete air superiority. There were insufficient vehicles to carry anything forward to the fighting troops and a lack of manpower to establish dumps and control stocks. It was a disaster. In the end it became clear that the force could not be supported and it was evacuated on 1 and 3 May.

The evacuation put a huge dent in public confidence leading to a debate in the House on 7 and 8 May. A vote of censure was moved and, although the Government won, forty Conservatives voted against it. Chamberlain considered resigning so that a national government could be formed. Then on 10 May the Germans attacked the Low Countries and it was clear the Government could not survive in its current form. A national government it would have to be, but the Labour Party would not accept Chamberlain as Prime Minister. It was to be Churchill who was a popular choice in the country and one supported by Labour, and that swung the balance in his favour.

In Norway another, separate, force had been sent to capture Narvik and had succeeded in doing so. Here the ADOS was Lieutenant Colonel T H Clarke, and a composite depot was established, called

Detachment BOD, commanded by Lieutenant Colonel St J C Hooley. There was a sub-depot for clothing and general stores, another for warlike and technical stores and an ammunition sub-depot. It was established on an island some twenty miles north-west of Narvik. It was cold, with temperatures of almost zero degrees Fahrenheit. A major problem was that when stores arrived they were packed and documented in a manner that was wholly unsuitable for an operational theatre. The contents could not be identified until the boxes had been opened, and the boxes were too heavy and bulky to be handled without MHE, of which there was none. There was a lack of essential documents and stencilling was inadequate. Furthermore the administrative load involved in transmitting demands to the UK was prohibitive, and they were burdens imposed by the communications staff, not by the Corps. Eventually, on 8 June, the British evacuated Norway in the face of the German aggression.

Lieutenant Colonel St John Hooley would go on to be promoted, this picture taken as a Colonel, and would eventually become a Major General.

But, while the activity in Norway was going on, the focus of attention was in France where the Germans opened their assault on 10 May. Ernie Man remembered well the frenetic activity that followed the commencement of hostilities:

> At Linenbook we unloaded and set up office, but after a few hours we were told to load up and move to another location, and this was the norm from then on, never staying anywhere for more than 24 hours, moving at all hours of the day and night, sleeping in barns and fields and always under the constant threat of air attack.

Nonetheless, there were no serious problems affecting the RAOC units and the work done, in

preparing them and the logistic system during the so-called phoney war from September 1939 to May 1940, began to work effectively. However, on 15 May it all changed as the Germans broke through the weak French line. By 19 May RAOC units were being withdrawn, and it looked as if those forward of the Base were to be cut off from it before long. Chaos ensued, with stocks still arriving from the UK at the same time as other stocks were being returned. Meanwhile, Ordnance units were also trying to meet demands from formations and

Private Bill Dowle RAOC is second from the left in the middle row of the unit football team in France in 1940. The goalkeeper is Private O'Neill, the linesman Private Johnson and standing at the back to the left of the Sergeant Major is Private Scanlon.

units in contact with the enemy. Order and counter-order prevailed and, for example, both 2 BOD and 3 BAD were told first to embark and then told to go back and re-open the depots.

As it became obvious that the Army was to evacuate, attempts were made to destroy stocks that had to be left. Some were less successful than others. WOI Birch, who was then rather more junior in rank, was one such. He was sent with ten others to destroy equipment that could not be kept and their orders then were to make their own way to the coast and try to escape.

Private Bill Dowle was in 4 BAD at Rennes as the Germans advanced. The depot staff were warned by the CO of the need to evacuate and that lots would be drawn to see which companies should stay. Bill was in 13 Company, and did not win the draw. The HQ and two companies went to Rennes, the rest were issued with rifles and told they were the rearguard. One of his friends bore a letter from Bill telling his parents that at best he would become a POW.

We were still loading lorries when at about 11 o'clock we heard tremendous explosions coming from the direction of Rennes. Shortly afterwards we were summoned back to camp and told that our two units had been bombed. Apparently a refugee train and a troop train had assembled in Rennes station and the French stationmaster had marshalled an ammunition train into the station and passed the word to the Germans who had then bombed it.

WOI Birch.

Bill eventually got back to Weymouth in a ship from St Malo.

George Critchell of 48th Division Ordnance Company made it back to Dunkirk. He describes it as something of a shambles as he and his comrades made their way through the town on foot, having by now abandoned and immobilized their vehicles, to the beach of Malo les Bains where thousands of the BEF had already congregated. After a day and a night on the sands most of George's LAD embarked on the destroyer *Wolsey* and landed at Dover. Ernie Martin was there too. He remembers it clearly:

The beach was crowded with troops and Dunkirk was a pall of smoke in the distance. There was little prospect of getting away as the shipping off shore was under constant air attack. One vessel, the Thames paddle steamer *Crested Eagle*, was on fire and beached near us. It burned all night.

Most Ordnance units escaped on 17 or 18 June, and many, including some of WOI Birch's friends, were on board the *Lancastria* which was bombed. There were 2,000 deaths, of which fifty were RAOC.

It was a disaster but, as a result of Dunkirk, Britain still had the basis of an Army in place from which something might be built, given the right leadership. With the threat of invasion and the huge damage done to morale the focus in Great Britain was on reviving the national spirit and focussing everything on home defence and the building up of the UK base. The country began to resemble an armed camp, and there was a vast increase in war production. For the RAOC, those who had

The *Lancastria* viewed from the destroyer, HMS *Highlander*. Note the people in the water and those walking on the hull.

escaped from France provided an instant reinforcement of skilled manpower. The load on the depots was huge, with five divisions being re-equipped in June and another five in July; although there were many serious deficiencies. People in Chilwell, for example, remember it well, for they had the double experience not simply of taking their share of the returning Army, but of rallying round to supply the re-equipment programme.

Sergeant Major Hall of the ATS remembered Dunkirk survivors arriving in trainloads:

We gave them bacon and eggs and lashings of hot tea and when they'd finished they just fell asleep at the table. Everyone came to building 176 to cook, serve, wash dishes and welcome the soldiers of Dunkirk. The Commanding Officer and the newest recruit rolled up their sleeves and worked side-by-side; our men gave up their cigarettes and chocolate and beds, handed over some of their own clothes and did any odd jobs they could.

We didn't know what tiredness was, and the gratitude of those survivors was wonderful. We weren't going to give them half they deserved but you'd think from the way they looked at the clean white plates and ate their food that they were dining at Buckingham Palace. You can't ever forget it...

It brought home the reality of war, and Chilwell took 7,000 Dunkirk survivors. Then the depot set about building an Army from what was left. Across the country depot facilities had to be expanded and dispersed, and depots and logistic installations were springing up everywhere. Sergeant F Alderman, then a private on his first posting, went to Olympia in London, which was used as an Ordnance depot throughout the war. It was well sited beside the railway at Addison Road, and was a popular posting being right in the centre of London; although that would prove to be a mixed blessing later in the war.

As for CODs, there were just five when the war started: Branston, Didcot, Chilwell, Woolwich and Weedon. However, there was a complete lack of standardization in their layout, organization and procedures. Although they dealt with different commodities, their organization and methods ought to have followed the same basic pattern. Standard methods were derived; largely from the pre-war work undertaken at Chilwell and Didcot. These

Lance Corporal Joseph Shearman RAOC coming ashore at Dover off SS *Skipgate*, aged twenty, with a leg wound, shell shocked and deafened.

procedures formed the basis not only for the CODs but also for all stores depots within the RAOC.

Peacetime procedures were modified and a standard Visidex account was introduced based on the systems and methods developed at Chilwell. OFPs and workshops' stores sections also acted as mini depots and a system of 'DADOS' dumps was established to spread stocks and make access easier for dependent units. Recovery, repair and reconditioning assumed a hitherto unrealized importance and depots were set up in each command purely to deal with returned stores. They were kept separate, quite distinct from 'normal' depots. Packaging was seen as a weakness, an area greatly in need of improvement. Experience showed that depots were packing to suit their own purposes and not to meet the needs of the units for whom stores were destined. Policy was reviewed and packaging procedures brought into line. The employment of officers of the AOER was also of value as they brought commercial practice into the depots from the motor trade. They helped make great improvements in the creation and utilization of storage media and MHE – in the latter case especially the use of fork lift trucks.

Air defence was a major feature of the RAOC workload. Established as a separate Anti-Aircraft Command, its importance was viewed so highly by the Government it was one of the few areas of re-equipment which, before the war, had received relatively lavish attention. There were separate stores and ammunition depots and dedicated RAOC staff and units, and depot stocks were constantly modified to take account of advances in the technology associated with AA guns and ammunition.

Ammunition supply needed a complete overhaul and reorganization. Clearly, providing ammunition for those defending the south of England against a possible invasion was paramount and the three central depots were not best placed to provide this. Consequently a series of small ammunition depots was established in Eastern, South-Eastern and Northern Commands, each planned to hold between 5 and 6,000 tons. But more was needed and further production and storage for the product was required. Therefore in July 1940 two new War Office branches were formed to plan the administration of ammunition and to manage technical matters. It was also felt that a CIOO was needed to coordinate inspections within the commands. So, by July 1940 three branches had been formed in the Ordnance Directorate in the War Office to direct and to organize the future of ammunition services generally. Work was also proceeding to increase ammunition storage, to enhance the capability of CADs Bramley, Longtown and Corsham, the latter being the underground depot that was in its infancy at the outbreak of the war. Additionally, CAD Nesscliffe was created between Shrewsbury and Oswestry. It was the first CAD to be planned and constructed during the war, and work started in 1939, at the commencement of hostilities.

The base load on the RAOC was huge and increasing, as was the load in overseas theatres. From an Army perspective, the Middle East was to be the focus for conflict for the next two years. This was largely due to Winston Churchill who saw the Middle East as a springboard from which attacks could be launched on the Axis powers, and he actively supported the military effort in the theatre. He also had the vision to see a possible American involvement at some stage in the war and realized the Red Sea and Suez Canal could be of enormous value were that to occur. Consequently, he took a huge risk in reinforcing the theatre with men and equipment even at a time when the threat of invasion of the UK was prevalent and before the Battle of Britain was won.

By now the overall strength of the RAOC had increased to 3,294 officers and some 50,000 soldiers, an adequate number to meet most needs at that time, provided they were properly organized and resourced. In the RAOC it was decided that best value could be derived from individuals if they could be given a specialization upon which they could focus. This, it was felt, would make best use of the range of talent available and, for example, storemen were given the suffix 'MT' or 'Technical' or 'Weapons' or 'Ammunition'.

Depot capacity was short of what was required, especially for the increase in technical equipment, as the Army embraced mechanization and the focus it placed on supporting the equipment, as well as the man. Woolwich's inadequacy as a technical stores' depot has already been mentioned. The choice of its successor was at Donnington, near Wellington in Shropshire. Lieutenant Colonel Charles de Wolff undertook the preliminary work to develop the depot and made his first visit in April 1939. There was nothing there other than a single shed. He went at once to the Wellington Rural District Council asking them to provide 1,000 houses for the staff of a depot yet to be designed. After some difficulty coming to terms with the concept they agreed on 500, built with the assistance of the Ministry of Labour. Colonel de Wolff also briefed the staff at Woolwich on the plans, giving them time to adjust to the situation and, in so doing, established a mutual confidence that was to stand him in good stead when hostilities commenced.

In September 1939 the basis of a depot was in place, and stores had started to transfer from Woolwich and be delivered direct from trade. Colonel de Wolff had to leave Donnington in September 1939 for his mobilization appointment in the BEF, but was back by November to find that the process had slowed. His energy at once had the project moving again, but progress was slower than he wished because of difficulties with the builders.

Obviously the Corps' *Gazette* changed to reflect the need for security. The loss of paper supplies from Scandinavia with the fall of Norway also had its impact. Nonetheless, the RAOC continued to produce a healthy monthly journal with updates on the progress of the war and, alongside them, accounts of sporting prowess, even of a dinner in Hong Kong next to a description of disaster in Europe. It also increased in size, despite paper shortages, to reflect the increase in units and the vast increase in RAOC manpower – and they continued to record every posting of all ranks. Security was apparent although it was not difficult to work out where units were. A training unit was 'somewhere in Derby' and it was not hard to recognize the Codon Battalion, especially when its location was given as 'somewhere in Shropshire'.

In Egypt, Churchill's focus for land operations in 1940, 7th Armoured Division was the only operational formation. There were also eight infantry battalions together with the advance elements of 4th Indian Division and the garrisons in the Sudan and in Palestine. This amounted to the equivalent of one armoured and three infantry divisions, but there were virtually no supporting arms or services, and there was a limited base structure and no reserves.

C E de Wolff was eventually promoted to Brigadier to look after the depot he had built.

Planning to support forces in the Middle East was blighted by appalling direction from the War Office. Planning parameters ranged from fifteen divisions for 150 days to nine divisions for ninety days to twenty-three divisions; and all this over a period of a few months. And as for support by the RAOC, some lessons had been learned in operations in the Middle East before the outbreak of the Second World War. However, there was not enough manpower to create organic units for the formations likely to be deployed. And, with the RAOC being low on the manning priority list, it was going to be some time before that situation would be redressed. The peacetime footing upon which the Middle East existed, including accounting for stores and equipment, made preparation for war more complex. And the stocks held in the depots were woefully inadequate for resolving the deficiencies in unit holdings. There was also a policy introduced in the UK, without consultation, to stop production of spares for obsolescent vehicles and equipment. Unfortunately the Middle East, having been low on the priority list, had mostly obsolescent equipment, and therefore suffered badly. It was not an auspicious start.

There were just a few small depots covering the commodity range and serving the two commands, in North Africa and in Palestine. But early in 1940 a fully operative GHQ was formed and with it a DOS was appointed. Colonel W W Richards transferred from his appointment in France and was promoted brigadier. This enthusiastic, energetic, knowledgeable, experienced, far-sighted man was an inspired choice. The task that lay before him was to increase storage accommodation by building new depots and enhancing those already in existence; to increase workshop capacity; to establish a manufacturing capability for a wide range of items, and they ranged from clothing to anti-tank mines. He also had to resolve the issue of provisioning and planning the support of future operations. Finally, he had to create an entire RAOC field force structure to support operational formations. No small task, but under this remarkable man progress too was remarkable.

A BOD and a BOW were established on the Sweet Water Canals at Tel el Kebir, with work commencing early in 1940. A BAD was constructed at Abu Sultan on the Suez Canal just south of Ismailia and an existing dump at El Daba was converted to an AOD. His key problem lay with manpower, and in particular skilled supervisory manpower. Establishments that had been low before the war were now woefully inadequate to meet the demands of the growing force in the Middle East. In March 1940 the theatre had backed an RAOC demand for 116 Officers and 2,267 soldiers, making the point that without them there would be very serious deterioration of units' war equipment in concentration and training, and that any operations would be accompanied by an administrative disaster.

When in May, France fell and then, in June, Italy joined the war any immediate chance of re-equipment or reinforcement disappeared with the loss of equipment and the damage done to the Army in northern France. General Wavell reported to the War Office the equipment situation in the Middle East, focussing on his concerns over tanks and medium anti-aircraft weapons. As serious, but not included in his report, was a woeful shortage of trucks for carrying men and stores. The DOS was instrumental in exploiting every available local resource to resolve this, acquiring 407 vehicles in the space of a few weeks. He also converted a number of Marmon-Harrington tractors into recovery vehicles.

At that time RAOC workshops hardly existed in the Middle East, although there were some RASC workshops, including a Heavy Repair Shop. This was a glaring weakness, and the energy of Brigadier Richards set about building a structure that, by July 1943, would see three major workshops in Egypt and a fourth in Haifa. They were capable not only of repair, but also of manufacture. Typical of the sort of things they provided were moulds and the production of rubber and bakelite items such as tank tyres, grinders and mixers for the paint factory, pistons and piston rings, Soyer stoves, tool boxes and first aid boxes, anything requiring sheet metal work, gun sights, breech mechanisms and tank power traverse components, bivouac shelters, canvas covers and stretchers. Hence they were a major contributor to the supply system, providing locally and saving the long and dangerous trek from the UK.

The staffing levels perhaps best illustrate the increase in capacity of the workshop effort. Number 2 BOW at Tel el Kebir in June 1941 had 1,250 military and 359 civilians. By December 1942 it had risen to 3,050 military and 5,650 civilians. Particularly notable, and one of Brigadier Richards' many successes, was the creation of so many civilian tradesmen drawn from a local population with a relatively low skill base.

Provision was very much a Cinderella at the start of the war, with just one office, in the Ordnance Depot at Abbassia, wherein were employed just two officers and twenty-five clerks of whom some two-thirds were locally engaged civilians. They supported 70,000 troops spread throughout Egypt, Palestine and the Sudan with a range of some 60,000 items. The depot eventually grew into a BOD with three sub-depots; one each for MT, Clothing and General Stores and, as 4 BOD, acquired an ADOS provision and a much-expanded staff.

Towards the end of 1940, 5 BOD began to arrive, forming at Tel el Kebir with the first shed in place by September. The provision branch at 4 BOD undertook the initial stocking, but by March 1941 the new depot had its own ADOS and provision branch as the main body of the depot arrived. By then there was also a full collection of various sub-depots, a Vehicle Depot and a Returned Stores Depot. A Middle East School of Instruction was established there as well, for both civilian and military staff. Prisoner of War tradesmen were especially useful in the RSD for the repair of boots and tentage. 2 Base Workshops and 27 General Hospital were also inside the depot perimeter.

The two depots were given their own separate area of supply, and in theory should have been able to operate freely and separately. However, this was not to prove the case. In many cases advice notes of stores in transit did not arrive, vouchers were mislaid in transit and stores from the UK were simply addressed to the Middle East and could end up anywhere. It was simply impossible to relate receipts to original demands and, despite constant contact between the two ADOS and their staffs, it was impossible to avoid constant and debilitating confusion.

Entrances to the caves at 8 BAD in Egypt.

Ammunition at the outbreak of the war was in very short supply in the Middle East, with just one small sub-depot at the Abbassia Ordnance Depot. Plans were set in train at once to generate sufficient storage for the expected load, based around the doctrine that a BAD should hold 21,000 tons. The first of these was 8 BAD sited in the Tura caves, deep in the Moqhattam Hills just on the east bank of the Nile. They had been used to quarry stone for the Pyramids at Giza, and a number of relics found during construction were passed to the Cairo museum. The BAD opened for business in July 1940, leaving the Abbassia depot empty, but maintaining control over the repair and filling factory there, whose main output was the Mine Contact Anti-Tank, Egyptian Pattern.

Whilst there were storage regulations relating to ammunition and especially the distance between stacks so that it could be stored without risk of propagation, these only applied to storage above ground. There was nothing for storage underground, despite the fact that Corsham, the underground depot in the UK near Bath, had been operating since shortly before the war started. These were issues to be resolved through common sense and experience. Initially planned to hold 15,000 tons instead of the normal 21,000 the eventual stock in 8 BAD would reach 40,000 tons.

Then, later in 1940, 9 BAD was built on the Suez Canal south of Ismailia. This was a traditional depot with rail served storehouses and located on a main artery of sea, rail and road transport. It would prove to be the most effective BAD, holding 90,000 tons. There was also some piecemeal development of ammunition storage east of Suez and in Palestine as well as two AADs, one for Syria and Palestine and the other for the Western Desert Force

The threat in the Middle East up to the end of 1940 came from the Italians. For most of the second half of the year they invaded Egypt and postured around the desert never really

8 BAD, stacking 6" shell; it was a labour intensive task without MHE and pallets.

coming into contact with the British. But on 28 October 1940 the Italians invaded Greece. Comfortable with their ability to resolve the situation on the ground, the Greeks asked for air support, and this first campaign in Greece involved principally the RAF. This was a blessing for it meant Wavell did not have to divert any resources from his planned attack on the Italians in North Africa. There were only some 2,000 soldiers in Greece from a number of regiments and corps, mainly to do with anti-aircraft defence and administration. The RAOC had detachments of an AOD and an AAD outside Athens and a workshop in the town. They served a small dependency, but their presence offered the basis of a support system in the event of any subsequent ground reinforcement.

The Italians were also being attacked from the south. In August 1940 Ordnance Services in East Africa had been considerably enhanced, with the head being upgraded to a DDOS. There was a BOD in Nairobi with AODs at Nanyuki and Mombasa. The South African Mobile Field Force had arrived with its Ordnance support, which worked closely alongside our own. In November 1940 two officers and twenty-two soldiers arrived, and they were to be the last reinforcements of trained UK manpower for nearly eighteen months. This tiny organization was all that was available to support General Cunningham's advance, over large distances, into Abyssinia. By the end of the campaign there were stores and ammunition depots in Kenya, Uganda, Northern Rhodesia, British Somaliland, Italian Somaliland and Ethiopia. Three OFPs, two mobile forward ammunition sections and eight mobile workshops were formed, and because of the length of the LofC one month's supply of stores were grounded at intervals of 200 miles.

In November Wavell opened his North African offensive. Surprise, mobility and speed were the essentials of his plan, and the logistics had to be able to support it. Dumps were established well forward with several days supplies held some thirty miles forward of our own lines, covered only by our patrols. Ordnance Stores were not held in these Field Supply Depots. It was not felt necessary since they would only support operations for a few days, and the spares and equipment would be needed as operations developed and the more elaborate Field Maintenance Centres were established. These contained the full range of workshop capacity, stores and supplies required by the force.

In ten weeks a relatively small force routed the much larger Italian Army. Generally the equipment stood the test, but there were acute shortages of spares, especially for the Infantry Tank. That said, from September the Prime Minister's support for the Middle East theatre began to manifest itself in new equipment shipped out from England. It was a courageous initiative from an England under threat from the attentions of the Luftwaffe, with the Blitz in full swing. F Alderman, working in the depot at Olympia remembered the horror of the air raids and the effect on people at war having to worry about people at home. The RAOC response to this was to post in Londoners to run the depot so they could be near their families.

West Africa was not considered to be under threat. British interests there concerned four countries – Gambia, Sierra Leone, Gold Coast and Nigeria. It was not until the end of 1940 that the GHQ West Africa Command was established, with an ADOS as the senior Ordnance officer. This was because of the threat posed from French interests in North Africa following the defeat of France and the creation of the Vichy puppet state. The Corps assumed full responsibility for supply of Ordnance stores, equipment and ammunition for the Royal West African Frontier Force. They were faced with geographical difficulties, the inadequacy of local labour, the climate, the widespread prevalence of such things as rust, woolly bear, Teredo worm, fungus and mildew, and the distance from the UK base, all of which conspired to affect the degree of support that could be provided.

Following consideration of the best way to provide support it was decided to put a BOD and a BAD in each country, with the small number of RAOC officers and soldiers spread amongst them. As local support began to be effective a West African Army Ordnance Corps was formed.

The WAAOC very
quickly formed a band.

Up until the start of the Blitz bomb disposal had been the responsibility of the RAOC. However, the bombing campaign of the autumn of 1940 stretched the capability of IOOs and AEs to the point where they could no longer cope with the load. There was a need to create, quickly, an organization that could dispose not only of unexploded enemy bombs, but also our own unexploded anti-aircraft shell. Specialist teams were trained, and the task was given to the Royal Engineers because so many of the bombs were buried and the REs already owned and operated the plant needed to get at them. It was the start of a wrangle over responsibility that would go on for years to come.

Meanwhile, in North Africa the ADOS Cyrenaica Area, Lieutenant Colonel C H Cooper, was busy clearing up after the Italian defeat. They had large stocks, especially of ammunition, in the Western Desert, but there was no transport to backload the stores into Egypt. However, 9th Australian Division was nearby and they were able to make very effective use of this bonanza of 'goodies' on their doorstep. In particular, having obtained an Italian weapon they simply appeared at the dump, run by RAOC, to match the ammunition to it. The Italian stores' depot at Benghazi held a wide range of MT stores for the many captured vehicles now being operated by the British and the Allies. Consequently, the ADOS set up an ad hoc static Ordnance Field Park just south of Benghazi from which to supply the forward troops.

The equipment that arrived in the Middle East in September 1940 was sufficient to bring units up to their war establishment, but was insufficient to constitute reserves. However it is important to note the amount of work undertaken by the RAOC in making use of whatever was to hand to plug a capability gap. Tanks had to be modified for the desert, especially with air filters; recovery vehicles had to be created, based on modified local tractors and cranes as there were no military recovery vehicles in North Africa; production was instituted for local pattern water tankers with a 160 gallon tank mounted on a 15cwt GS Morris Truck; local manufacture of 3,000 sun compasses was undertaken; 90,000 anti-tank mines were designed and manufactured and a BOW was established in Alexandria, 150 miles forward of the main base area, for the repair of tanks and guns.

The operation brought home an important lesson about Ordnance stores. They differ from rations, fuel and ammunition in having a large range for a small volume and weight; and their use is hard to predict. However, without say, a fuel pump, the truck cannot deliver the ammunition; without a firing pin the gun cannot fire it; and without spares the tank cannot be an effective weapons' platform in a mobile all-arms battle. A rapid and flexible distribution system was required to ensure that Ordnance stores were attributed their true priority and were properly targeted where they were most needed. Too often were they to prove the 'Cinderella' of the logistic system.

In the United Kingdom the Standing Committee on Army Organization had become concerned about the breakdown of responsibility between the staff and the QMG's department. Accordingly, they advocated the appointment of a Director General of Army Equipment whose task was to coordinate the activities of all the branches with a responsibility for Army equipment. This was a reflection of the huge increase in the work involved in maintaining Army mechanical and electrical equipment. It was the last step in a series of moves that presaged the creation of an equipment maintenance corps as a separate entity. It was one of a series of changes in the structure of the War Office logistic branches, including the staff branches of the QMG; a seemingly perpetual sea of change when one might have thought some stability in a time of crisis might realize some real benefits.

And decisions were also being made about depots. Whilst Donnington and Chilwell were doing sterling work with Technical and MT stores respectively it had become clear that another depot had to be built. This was partly because of the massive increase in equipment, and also because of the need to have something in place to provide the additional support that would be needed for a second front. The depot had to be located in the south of England and laid out in such a way as to permit rapid movement of stores. The opportunity was taken to build a depot to suit the conditions of modern war,

Taken in June 1944, this photograph shows the then Brigadier G W Palmer commanding a depot that he had built and which was now supporting an invasion.

including the risks associated with carpet-bombing. It had to be rail served and have good road access. A place in the country was the choice and Bicester was born. It was divided into two parts, Arncott and Graven Hill and was to take MT, small arms, armament stores, RE stores and signals equipment. All the sheds were to be rail served, and the Bicester Military Railway came into being in the very early phases of the building programme. In January 1941 Colonel G W Palmer was made the designate commandant and took on the planning of the layout, location and construction. Given the rural nature of the location, local staff were hard to recruit and the depot would be principally staffed by military. Heavy lift sheds were built, to be followed by a workshops and by the time all the planning was complete 3.25 million square feet of covered accommodation would be available, with more

to follow. Approval was given to the plans in May 1941, and Treasury sanction followed in June. Work started at once to build the depot and the first issue of stores was made in August 1942.

Meanwhile, the Germans now entered the Eastern Mediterranean scene. Hitler dispatched Rommel and the Afrika Korps to the North African desert and also ordered the invasion of Greece in order to repair the damage done by the Italian defeat at the hands of the Greeks. This time the Greeks asked for a full range of support and on 5 March 1941 Army units began moving north across the Mediterranean from Egypt. The logistic plan was to hold ninety days' supply of Ordnance stores and ammunition, and seventy days' worth had been received by 6 April. The staff of the German Embassy watched the whole deployment. The situation was ridiculous, with the British commander having been told to adopt a low profile and remain incognito, whilst the German defence attaché stood at the dockyard gate and counted the soldiers as they disembarked. Seven field supply depots were established in the forward areas, each holding seven days' stock of essential commodities.

Colonel Douglas White was the DDOS and, as was so often the case, his headquarters was static and under resourced. This was another case where the storage accommodation was less than satisfactory, as much for its separation into widely dispersed sub-depots as the actual physical inadequacy of the buildings – that is where there were buildings. The COME, Colonel J F X Miller, saw no point in setting up a BOW, and concentrated instead on maximizing the output of LADs and formation workshops.

The system was working reasonably well by the time the Germans invaded on 6 April 1941, but there was a major explosion in Piraeus Harbour when bombs hit a ship containing ammunition for the Greek Army. It destroyed the berthing facilities, fifteen rail wagons disintegrated and a lighter carrying 100 tons of British ammunition exploded. Clearly, local German agents had been active and the Luftwaffe knew the precise targets.

The nature of the terrain made it virtually impossible to operate a conventional LofC, and formations had to exist with stocks carried and repairs undertaken by their formation RAOC units. In any event, the Germans very quickly determined complete air superiority. From the outset the war in Greece was one of withdrawal. Once more RAOC soldiers were faced with the ritual of destroying anything that might be of value to the enemy. Ammunition is always one of those commodities, and is harder to destroy in bulk than popular myth would have it. Major W P Dixon, who commanded 4 AAD sent the greater part of his unit of some sixty souls off to the dockside while he personally supervised the depot's destruction, both ammunition and vehicles, before making his own escape.

Colonel White was placed in command of one of the evacuation areas, and personally oversaw the departure of some 18,000 men, some by sea and others by road to another evacuation point. He himself was, as one might expect, the last to leave after a number of adventures that finished with him reaching the good ship *Thursland Castle* by rowing boat and sailing for Egypt, where he eventually arrived safely.

The invasion of Crete by the Germans followed three weeks after their success in Greece, and once more they prevailed. The defence of Crete was in the hands of a New Zealander, General Freyburg, with the equivalent of some six brigades. However, they lacked mobility and some had suffered attrition in Greece and had little time to recover. The RAOC had a small depot on the island for the full range of commodities, less ammunition for which there was a small depot on its own.

The numbers to be supported were well in excess of holdings, and, yet again, transport was not made available to transport stocks where they were needed. Once more the loading of ships was an issue, in this case for stocks being sent from Egypt. Weapons and their associated stores were often separated in transit. For example, nineteen Vickers machine guns arrived without tripods and could not be used, yet they had surely been issued as complete weapons when they left Egypt. There was clearly not a properly established relationship between the Movements Staff of the Royal Engineers and the RAOC at the port of embarkation.

Much of the work in the Ordnance depot involved salvage of weapons and equipment that had been brought back from Greece and just dumped. Captain Casdagli and a team of men made an excellent job of preparing large quantities of equipment for re-issue, thereby offsetting some of the shortages in depot fit stock.

The capacity for repair was limited by shortage of repair equipment, so much having been left in Greece, and by German air superiority. The need to operate in carefully camouflaged areas further inhibited effectiveness. This was also true of the LADs and there were serious limits imposed on their effectiveness. Nonetheless, they did all they could, and one example is the experience of the 102 (Northumberland Hussars) Regiment RHA whose commanding officer was clear that he would never have got his regiment's vehicles out of Greece without the support of the LAD. Lieutenant A L Taylor RAOC, commanding the LAD, ensured the unit Bren gun was taken with it to Crete where it was used to great effect. He went on to command HQ Troop of the Regiment until 20 May 1942 when he was killed. His was a fine example, and his loss was deeply felt.

RAOC casualties in Greece and Crete were thirty-eight officers and 750 soldiers killed, wounded or missing. The number would have been smaller had it not been for the fact that a number of the evacuees from Greece, rather than be taken to Egypt, were dropped off on Crete where they languished with little to do until the end. Critically, there was a high per centage of experienced warrant officers and senior NCOs, and their loss was to be felt when building up the logistic support for future battles in the Middle East.

Replacing them would be difficult, and the problems of manning the hugely expanded RAOC were presenting enormous difficulties and conflicts. For officers, Colonel L E Cutforth returned to AG9 in the middle of 1941 to take control. The Records Office had never quite recovered from its move up to Leicester in the middle of 1940. It was suffering from under staffing and there was a huge backlog of work. Something needed to be done quickly, and Colonel Dyson, a trained chartered accountant, was given the task of restoring efficiency. He was given additional staff and did what was asked of him.

German intervention in the spring of 1941 in North Africa was first felt with attacks on Tobruk and Benghazi and on the shipping between them. Consequently, the use of Benghazi as a port was denied to the British and, to compensate, field supply depots were set up. Two were placed on the inland route and two on the coast road. However, they were static, and with no transport to move them they would be sacrificed to any enemy fortunate enough to gain access to them.

In April 1941 Rommel moved into Cyrenaica with the advanced elements of the Afrika Korps. The balance would arrive in May. Logistically light with a fiery, far-sighted commander, they were an experienced team with good weapons and great confidence in their leader. They were clearly going to be a problem and proved it by driving the British out of Cyrenaica within a month. Only Tobruk held, and would continue to do so until November of that year when it would be relieved after the longest siege in British military history. It was a major weakness for Rommel as it denied him the use of the port and was to remain a thorn in his left flank for the whole of the summer and into the autumn of 1941.

The Allies withdrew to the Egyptian border with Libya. The 4th Indian Division, just back from Eritrea, was on the right against the coast and the 7th Armoured Division on its left, inland. Operation BATTLEAXE on 15 June 1941 was the first of a series of attempts to redress the balance against the Germans. It failed for a number of reasons, including operations in Crete, which were going on at the same time. However, losses in tanks and a poor forward repair policy were also major contributors. The improvised nature of British recovery vehicles did not compare favourably with those of the Germans, specifically designed for the task. Then Churchill decided to replace Wavell in the Middle East with Auchinleck

In the UK there were demands for men for new units to meet new commitments. However, a ceiling was placed on RAOC manpower, and depots were reluctant to lose experienced men as they themselves were expanding and needed all the help they could find. A mobilization centre was established at Arnold, near Nottingham, where units formed up, received their equipment and trained in their role before moving off to join their parent formation. Later a separate centre purely for OFPs was set up at Kegworth.

On 22 June 1941 an event took place that was to have a seismic impact on the future conduct of the war. Before dawn a German barrage of huge intensity announced the end of the Russo-German accord, and preceded the advance of German armies into Russia. The second front had opened, and it was to prove one of the key strategic errors that would see the death of the German Reich. Importantly, in the short term, it meant that there would be no German reinforcement of the Afrika Korps – Rommel was on his own and would have to manage within his existing resources

By 1941 the issue of the RAOC's combatant status was coming to a head. It was not clear why one supply corps, the RASC, was combatant and the other not, and it was perfectly obvious that the RAOC was fighting along with everyone else – if the casualty figures from Greece alone were to mean anything. Furthermore, non-combatant status had for years denied the RAOC places at the Staff College which was a major detraction, not only from the education of RAOC officers, but also for the Army in general where senior staff officers were woefully ill-educated about the logistic implications of some of their decisions although that had already been addressed with the attendance early in 1941 of RAOC officers at Staff College. A situation that seemed such an obvious anomaly to so many throughout the Army was redressed on 22 October 1941 by Army Order 179, conferring combatant status on the Royal Army Ordnance Corps.

At the same time a new specialization was introduced onto the Corps, that of Regimental Dutyman; instructors in military training for employment in training establishments and in units for continuation training. It is unclear whether this was a direct result of the move to combatant status, but it created a 'trade' that was to be a feature of RAOC life, with one or two interruptions, to the end. The 'Rubber Duck' had arrived and was here to stay.

In July 1941 two RAOC officers and four NCOs were sent to Washington to join the British Army Staff at the Embassy. It was the start of a close liaison with the Americans that was to see the RAOC element in the US swell as the streams of equipment began to make their way across the Atlantic – and this even before America joined the war as a protagonist.

The hiatus of lost and missing stores in the Middle East was finally resolved. The creation of 2 BOD in Palestine had so confused further the already confused situation existing between 4 and 5 BODs that a Central Provision Office was established. The provision elements of all three depots were housed at Mena, some eight miles west of Cairo. In theory there should have been forty-eight officers and 300 RAOC clerks, although that number was never reached. Additionally, many LEC had to be dismissed from the existing provision offices and replacements recruited locally, which incurred a considerable training penalty.

Then, on 18 November, the British launched Operation CRUSADER. It was an attack by 8th Army, as the Western Desert Force was now known, comprising two corps together with additional units. It followed a four-month period of intensive training and administrative planning. The British were well ordered and well supported, with good equipment and the logistics to sustain it. The railhead was pushed well forward. Forward bases were established and they supplied Field Maintenance Centres, which were set up to cater for the way in which the battle ebbed and flowed. These were large logistic installations containing not only the fuel, ammunition and food normally associated with dumps, but also Ordnance stores, and RAOC units were formed to handle these stocks. The fluid nature of the desert battle meant these FMCs were often exposed. Number 50 FMC, supporting 13 Corps, was overrun by the enemy, who eventually moved on having caused very little damage, and failing to spot the petrol stocks of which they could have made very good use. Number 62 FMC was so far out on a limb that the Corps Commander moved 22 Guards Brigade out to protect it, so valuable were its stocks. The positioning of 4 AAD at Dhekeila, south-west of Alexandria, gave a forward ammunition

Sergeant W Savage RAOC was an accomplished artist and left many sketches of Ordnance units, offering a unique picture of life at the time. Here he offers 'Glimpses of an OFP'.

re-supply capability, and 18,000 tons would be positioned there just prior to the Battle of Alamein in October the following year.

Neither had Brigadier Richards been idle in developing a field force structure. Each armoured brigade, Army tank brigade and support group had an OFP, Light Repair Section and Recovery Section. The HQ and the Divisional Section of the OFP were with the armoured division and there was a divisional workshop. Infantry divisions each had an OFP and workshops, and they were capable of breaking down to a brigade level of support should that be necessary. Brigade and regimental workshops were deployed with AA units. Corps and army troops requirements were provided from GHQ Troops Workshops and LofC Recovery Sections, but there was, as yet, no Corps Troops OFP. There were also FADs, Mobile Communications Repair Sections, a Mobile Ammunition Laboratory, a Vehicle and Stores Convoy Unit, the RAOC element of the Tank Delivery Squadron, Railhead and Port Ordnance staff. It was a model for the future.

The Vehicle and Stores Convoy Unit was created specifically to provide a means of delivering Ordnance stores with transport resources under the guiding hand of Ordnance staff. It was a clear lesson learned from earlier conflicts where everything had been ad hoc, with a serious impact of operational capability. The unit even provided landing ground detachments that lived on airfields to handle the most urgently required stores, those being air freighted or parachuted forward. Stocks were moved forward as far and fast as possible. They were even sent into Tobruk by sea in anticipation of the raising of the siege so they would be in position when the armies advancing beyond the city needed them.

There was no Armoured Corps OFP, and a squadron of 7 RTR was invited to act as a tank delivery squadron. It was the forerunner of the Armoured Replacement Group that developed later during the war and was to be a feature of armoured replacement during the Cold War period in Germany with the British Army of the Rhine

In the early stages of the attack, 30 Corps Rear Headquarters was overrun. The DDOS found sanctuary for a short while with the DDOS 13 Corps, and returned to 30 Corps when the problem was resolved. The ADOS, Lieutenant Colonel McEwan was not quite so lucky. On 24 November his vehicle broke down and he was captured with a number of others with whom he remained in the same locality for twenty-four hours. He noted that, whilst Italian officers were present, it was German NCOs who seemed to be in charge. The next day the fourteen officer prisoners and about 280 soldier prisoners were moved to Halfaya Pass where he took careful note of the enemy strength and position. The next morning, 26 November, he noticed that a considerable number of the enemy had left and as senior officer present took it upon himself to begin thinking about an escape. He organized the prisoners into eight groups of about thirty-five men each and they departed that evening, each group keeping in touch as best they could with the others. After a long march they arrived at a railhead where the ADOS handed over a couple of Germans they had collected and moved on to rejoin HQ 30 Corps.

Everywhere administrative units moved all over the desert on their various tasks. During the day they had to be on the alert for enemy air attack, and stayed widely dispersed, but at night they concentrated for defence and for security. Concentrating in this way meant they could also centralize and control maintenance, rest the soldiers and recuperate generally.

Tobruk was taken in November and, by 8 December, HQ 13 Corps was in the city with the siege being raised fully on 11 December. However, as eyes in London were focussing on events in the Western Desert and the impact of CRUSADER, another seismic event in the conduct of the war took place.

On 7 December 1941 the Japanese bombed Pearl Harbor. The conflict was now global, and America was directly involved. The crushing blow inflicted on the Americans in this, the first external attack on the American mainland in the nation's history, was paralleled for the British when, on 10 December, the two battleships, *Repulse* and *Prince of Wales*, that had been sent to maintain control of the area off Singapore and Malaya were sunk by Japanese air attack. Japanese forces had landed on the coast of Malaya on 8 December north of Khota Baru and were also advancing over the Thai border and had already overrun airfields, thus denying the two capital ships the air cover that might have protected them.

John McNamara was there:

> ...we had a rude shock when the Japs landed at Khota Baru. The senior officers said it would be impossible for them to advance through the jungle, but they soon proved to be wrong. By Christmas 1941 we were preparing to retreat and by January we were on our way back to previously prepared positions, eventually arriving back in Singapore. We had no Navy, no Air Force and the 15" naval guns were facing the wrong way, except for one which they had managed to turn round.

Hong Kong was also attacked and by 10 December Japanese columns were well advanced into the colony. Here the main depot was in Queen's Road on the harbour front and there were several ammunition stores. Additionally, RAOC held most of the units' mobilization equipment rather than the units themselves. Given the length of the LofC from the UK, a great deal was done to obtain general stores from the local economy. As well as a Hong Kong presence there had been the other units in Shanghai and Tientsin, but they had been withdrawn, to Singapore, early in 1940, with the Japanese occupation of much of China.

Hong Kong and Singapore had both been badly under-resourced. They were not seen to be under threat and good manpower had been removed to bolster up RAOC effort in what were then perceived to be more important theatres. Suddenly, both colonies were faced with a considerable workload due to mobilization and reinforcement. In the case of Singapore, there was also a requirement to dump stocks in the Malay Peninsula to provide as much forward logistic support as possible to troops fighting there.

Hong Kong eventually fell on 25 December 1941 after a bloody battle in which RAOC soldiers were heavily involved. Throughout the battle the Corps in Hong Kong continued to undertake its tasks of supply and repair, distributing stocks to forward units, redeploying dumps and stores in the face of enemy advances, or repairing what they could. The ammunition store at Shouson Hill was twice evacuated, and the soldiers returned both times to make issues, only giving up as part of the general capitulation of the garrison on Christmas Day. The workshop at Shouson Hill was still operating until 19 December whereupon work became impossible and the soldiers joined in field operations. RAOC soldiers were involved, as were others, in the many firefights that developed all over the colony, and suffered accordingly. For example, at the Ridge Depot, around 22 December 1941 some fifty RAOC soldiers were left and many were either killed, or died of wounds. Some were killed seeking to escape; the remainder were captured alive and then killed by the Japanese. The ADMS managed to get into the area a few days later to search for wounded. He found the RAOC party had been bound hand and foot with telephone wire and then were either bayoneted or shot.

When the casualty figures were assessed late in January 1942 it was found that there were ten RAOC officers and eighty-nine soldiers left of the fifteen officers and 139 present at the time of the Japanese invasion. Thirty-three per cent had been killed, the highest per centage dead of any unit in the colony. A sad statistic but proof, if ever proof were needed, that this newly 'combatant' corps was very much a part of the Army it existed to serve. Theirs was an example of gallantry and sacrifice in the highest traditions of the British Army.

While all this was going on CRUSADER was still under way, and in the Western Desert repair of armoured vehicles was a major issue. By 12 December 30 Corps had some 530 vehicle casualties, with 456 having been recovered. Repairs to 230 tanks had been completed and a further fifty were under

...d despite the German
...d Italian attempts to
...event it, convoys of
...pplies from Great Britain
...pt Malta going...

...and it only took a few
...mple pleasures to keep
...e smile on tired faces.

repair. One inhibiting fact was the inaccessibility of both major and minor assemblies on British tanks, which made their repair complex and time consuming. This was not something that affected the American Grant tanks, nor those used by the Germans, and it had a deleterious effect on turnaround times, critical to returning fit tanks to the battle and to placing assemblies into the repair loop.

Repair and recovery in the armoured battle were paramount and the DDOS was implementing a policy of repair as far forward as possible, and giving it his own personal supervision. From 23 December the DDOS was given a definite allotment of third line transport for the move of stores, and rail capacity as well. This was vital because of the length of time being taken to inload Tobruk and turn what was now known as 500 AOD into a properly functioning forward supply base. Shortages of fuel had their effect on the capacity of third line transport available, and meanwhile 503 AWD was working as hard as it could to turn round as much as possible, as fast as possible.

So it was 1942 began. Germany was occupying much of Europe, there had been the defeats in Greece and Crete, Rommel had been initially successful in Libya and the counter-stroke, CRUSADER, was stalling, although Tobruk had been relieved, Hong Kong had fallen, the Malay Peninsula was on its way to being occupied, Singapore was under threat and the sinking of the two capital ships in the Straits of Malacca had been a huge blow. There were some bright spots – Malta was one, where defence of the island had been successful, and its use as a base had meant that in the last quarter of 1941 only one third of the Axis supplies destined for North Africa had got through, and this had an impact on the outcome of the CRUSADER operation.

From the RAOC point of view in Malta the significant achievement had been the awarding of the George Cross to the two IOOs on the island, Captain R L Jephson-Jones and Lieutenant W M Eastman, for their work in 1940 in disposing of several hundred enemy unexploded bombs. Then, from the end of 1940, the task fell to the RE due to the split

Captain R L Jephson-Jones (right)
and Lieutenant W M Eastman would
wait until the end of the war to
receive their George Crosses.

of responsibility agreed earlier as a result of the effects of the Blitz in England.

Churchill was under pressure. So far he had failed to produce the victory that was needed to restore morale in the UK population and demonstrate the nation's ability to win through. But the Americans were now in the war and therein lay the salvation, therein lay the opportunity to turn the tide. However, he needed a victory, and the fourth calendar year of the war was not off to an auspicious start.

Early in the New Year 1st Armoured Division came out from England and took over from 7th Armoured Division in 13 Corps. It was sent into action completely untrained for desert warfare and with its OFP and workshops not having trained with the Division in England. The stores for the OFP did not travel with the unit, and it had to be scaled as quickly as possible from the Egyptian base. It moved forward to its area of operations with the stores still in their packing cases. Sorting was done in the forward areas, and was going on at the same time as the flood of high priority demands came in from units in contact with the enemy. Logistic planning was simply still not a factor in the minds of so many.

By the beginning of February the CRUSADER battles had stalled. Both sides were exhausted and needed time to reconfigure their fighting forces and address key logistic issues, especially the Axis armies who had lost a great deal of their shipping, carrying vital stores, towards the end of 1941. They both held on to the Gazala Line, east of the Gebel el Akhdar, and remained stable on that front until the end of May 1942. Apart from the recovery of Tobruk it was far from the conclusive victory Churchill either wanted or needed. One of the key lessons drawn by the administrative services from the CRUSADER operation was the crucial need for them to have communications. Controlling dumps and railheads, re-distributing stores to meet changing priorities, coping with re-grouping, controlling forward repair – all suffered for the lack of any logistic radio communications.

Colonel George Dawson MBE took over the Records Office in 1942 and was in charge of it until 1946.

In the Far East there was chaos in Malaya. The defence of the peninsula was in the hands of 3 Indian Corps with two Indian Divisions and an Australian Division. Its second and third line ammunition was in the hands of the IAOC, and requests for replenishment were sent back to Singapore Island. Daily ammunition expenditure returns were never received, but from the outset there was signal after signal for more and more trainloads of ammunition. Such was the congestion in the forward areas that many were returned, and there was the ridiculous situation of full trains heading south passing trains heading north filled with the same commodities.

When Kuala Lumpur had to be evacuated new storage sites were established at Johore, but no sooner were they opened than the withdrawal to Singapore Island took place. By the end of January 1942 the last troops to get across the causeway saw the bridge blown behind them. Little had been done to prepare the Island for an attack from the north. It was a naval base and attack was expected from the sea; and that was the way the big guns pointed. To an attack from the land from an enemy with air and sea superiority, it was an easy target.

On 4 February reinforcements arrived in the shape of 18th Division. It was a forlorn hope that they could do anything and they were effectively being delivered straight to their deaths or to a prison camp which, in many cases, would lead to death. Among them were seventeen officers and 400 soldiers of the RAOC, which doubled the Corps' strength on the island.

Many of the troops on Singapore were administrative and had little training in weapon handling or in combat operations, even in tactics at the lowest level. However, like their counterparts in Hong Kong, RAOC soldiers were in the very thick of everything with the battle raging close around them on a small area like Singapore Island. For example, when one of the two Bofors anti-aircraft guns in the Alexandra depot was abandoned by its crew, it was taken over by RAOC soldiers who, somewhat inaccurately, but with great gusto, made their contribution to keeping enemy aircraft at bay.

Eventually, however, it became too much. On the evening of 13 February 1942 the officers and men of the workshop branch, some 200 of them, were ordered to evacuate, which they did only to be captured later on Sumatra. That same evening orders were received to burn the depot, which was done relatively successfully although it appears the Japanese may subsequently have recovered some materiel from the ruins. The soldiers were formed into five companies and sent forward under command of 1 Malaya Brigade to hold the line held by elements of the Loyals, the Leicesters and the Malay Regiment. Despite being badly under strength there was no further withdrawal, but on 15 February, around the time CRUSADER ground to a halt in Libya, General Percival, the commander on Singapore, signed the surrender.

John McNamara was there:

> The Japs were very jittery. As instructed we piled our rifles and Lewis guns and stacked the ammo. They then searched us and marched us through the city to Changi Village, to the silent gaze of the native population, who were busy waving Jap flags. As far as I know the casualties in our company were our Company Commander, Major Ortiger, and Corporal Alexander and several wounded. No shortage of tea, but the Japs turned down our request for razor blades. After a few weeks our beards became acutely embarrassing to them as few of them could grow anything approaching a decent beard. Result – an issue of razor blades and a stern warning to us to shave daily.

From the beginning the Japanese made it clear that anyone trying to escape would be shot. John McNamara explained the difficulty – that it was the duty of soldiers to try to escape. He told the story of Private E Fletcher RAOC who made an attempt:

> He was caught, faced a firing party and was shot. The entire battalion was detailed to attend, but the order was amended, and in fact only our officers were present.

All but one of the RAOC families were recorded as having been evacuated. Not all of them returned to the UK, Australia and South Africa seeming to be better alternatives to some. For those arriving in the UK, with little more than the clothes they stood in, the RAOC association provided support. Clearly, they were all concerned about their loved ones at the mercy of the Japanese. Rather oddly, and wholly inaccurately, a letter was reproduced in the Corps' *Gazette* which may have given them some comfort – albeit misplaced. It was an extract from a letter passed to the *Cambridge Independent Press and Chronicle* by a Doctor Hayman having been received by his daughter, the wife of an Army *chaplain* missing in Singapore. A lady friend of hers in Northampton had written the letter:

> An officer of the Argyle and Sutherland Highlanders has just escaped and a friend of ours has seen him. He says the prisoners in Singapore are well treated on the whole, and that the Japanese General in charge of them is a Christian gentleman – a Roman Catholic who was educated at Oxford. I do think the fact that they are in charge of a Christian General with an English education does make an enormous difference to our anxiety, and I hope you will find strong hope in it.

The reality, it would appear, would be somewhat different. A dangerous article in a regimental magazine, well intentioned but unwise.

In India Ordnance depots and workshops had been designed to meet the needs of a peacetime garrison and any minor operations on the North-West Frontier. Defence in the east was considered unnecessary as the jungles and hills of Assam were viewed as being a sufficient barrier to any invader. However, the

Brigadier W H McN Verschoyle-Campbell OBE MC, who was appointed DOS Indian Army on 28 October 1936.

Japanese action in Malaya had given the lie to any such view, and there was now a clear threat from Burma, to the east of India, but the lie of the land, the rivers and the roads did not lend themselves to effective logistic support of forces fighting in that part of the sub-continent. For the RAOC, there had been talk of amalgamating the Corps with the IAOC, but it had come to nothing. There was, therefore, no central coordination of effort between the two. There were some exchanges, and in 1939 the DOS IAOC had been an RAOC officer, Brigadier W McN Verschoyle-Campbell.

In the early days of the campaign the Japanese Navy dominated the Bay of Bengal. Coastal sites were, therefore, not available for storage locations. Consequently, support had to be provided from depots that were too far west, but which could be replenished through the ports at Karachi and Bombay.

In East Africa an independent command was formed to act as a base from which 11th East African Division could be mobilized, supplied, sent to Burma and be replenished while there.

On 20 April a man died of an illness in the UK. His name was Captain Roger Goodeve. The letter from his sergeant spoke volumes about a man whose name would grace no history book but perhaps represented what was good about officers in the RAOC, and what was strong about the relationship between the officers and that engine room of the British Army, the Sergeants' Mess. Sergeant Flanagan of 6 Guards Armoured Brigade Ordnance Company wrote to Roger Goodeve's wife:

> …let you know how sorry all his 'boys' are at the loss of their 'skipper', and to tender their deepest sympathy. For my part I was his head 'boy'… I would have written before but honestly could not find the words to express my feeling…we both learned to depend on each other… . I will convey your good wishes to everyone but 'goodbye' – no! as he is always with me and always will be…

Captain Roger Goodeve RAOC.

On 6 May 1942 British troops landed on Madagascar with a view to preventing any subsequent attempt at occupation by the Japanese. There was no opposition and an OBD was established as the nucleus of a stores depot and an ammunition depot. Eventually the capital was taken and an AOD established, to be supported from the East Africa base. Subsequently, the invasion force was withdrawn for service elsewhere and the occupation was continued by troops drawn from East and South Africa.

If in the Far East it had been a disastrous start to the year, in the Middle East there was relative

operational calm until 26 May 1942, but with frenetic activity in building the administrative tail to support future operations. In the end it was the Germans who attacked first on the Gazala Line. This should have been turned to British advantage as they were in a sound logistic situation and in a better position to fight a defensive battle. The Gazala Line was heavily mined and strengthened to a degree never before attempted. However, the aim was to protect Tobruk, in order for it to act as a logistic base to support advances into Tripolitania. Unfortunately the three divisions in the

It was a difficult time, and on 3 March 1943 the King and Queen visited Chilwell. Here they are talking with SQMS Bamber ATS.

RAOC mechanics in the desert in 1942. Messrs Coughlan, Carrie and Kendall brewing up at Kassala.

line were stretched and large sections of the obstacles were not covered by fire and, hence, were less effective.

The concept was that known defensive risks were taken assuming Rommel could be defeated if he attacked, and that the British would then move into the assault with their logistic stocks well forward. The mood of confidence was assisted by the arrival of American Grant tanks and British 6-pounder anti-tank guns, which redressed the imbalance in firepower. However, firepower was not the key problem if not backed by tactical awareness, and British commanders had failed to learn the lessons of CRUSADER, that undue dispersion leads to defeat in detail by an enemy able to concentrate his forces at critical points. Even when Rommel found himself overstretched and at risk of being trapped in the eastern minefields, British reaction was too slow and the Germans held a defensive position until sufficient supplies arrived for them to breach the minefield. By 12 June British armour had lost the battle and was down to just fifty cruiser and twenty infantry tanks. They abandoned the Gazala position on 12 June, leaving Tobruk exposed to the full weight of the Afrika Korps – and it fell to the Germans on 21 June, handing Rommel a huge moral victory and the massive logistic stocks held in the port, especially fuel. It was another body blow to Churchill, and would lead ultimately to the replacement of Auchinleck by Alexander and the arrival in the Western Desert of Montgomery to command the 8th Army.

The impact on Ordnance units stationed in Tobruk when it fell varied. 500 AOD was a dispersed, well laid out depot, parts of which were in caves, staffed by some 400 RAOC officers and men. It carried large stocks of assemblies for MT and tanks, as the repair policy was limited to assembly change forward. Everything requiring more work was backloaded to the base. The DOS had convinced the Army Commander of the wisdom of this decision in order to: avoid dispersing skilled military in penny packets, compensate for the lack of handling and repair facilities in field workshops, eliminate interruptions by enemy action, centralize the spares for complex repair and avoid the dispersion necessary in forward workshops.

When the decision was taken to move off the Gazala position 500 AOD dispatched controlled stores and other important items back to the rear and then set about destroying as much as possible. Colonel T G Gore, the RAOC commander, was captured and escaped in 1943 from an Italian POW camp. The main body of 503 AOW was captured with its equipment, and almost the whole of 501 AOD, commanded by Major Bromley and laid out on both sides of the Tobruk-Derna road, was taken.

The 8th Army withdrew onto the El Alamein line, and in so doing caused DDOS(P), Brigadier H C Whittaker, rather alarmingly to find himself forward of Army Rear HQ and consequently GHQ decided to move the Central provision Office to Haifa. It was a bad decision. They were not too out of place where they were and in no more danger than anyone else at the time. The move to Haifa incurred huge problems with the retraining of staff, loss of documents and a diminution in service at a critical time. This was further compounded in August, just two months later when the whole thing was moved again, this time to Tel Aviv.

Just before all this happened, the first sheds of a new ammunition depot were built, in July, at Kineton, a Warwickshire village lying between Warwick and Banbury. It was another phase in the expansion of UK

87

Brigadier H C Whittaker CBE.

storage capacity for munitions.

It was also in August, on the12th, that Montgomery assumed command of 8th Army. Within just two weeks of his arrival he had made the difference that thwarted Rommel's attempt, at the end of August, at Alam Halfa to repeat his success at Gazala.

Having won his first victory Montgomery then set about planning the next confrontation with the Germans in pursuit of his directive, quite simply to evict Rommel from North Africa. However, he was always under pressure from Churchill to go early, in September, for the Prime Minister needed a victory to prop up the nation's morale and to secure his own political position. Montgomery, determined to wait until he was satisfied everything was in place and the necessary training had been done, had the strength of character to resist the pressure, and was supported by Alexander. He eventually launched his assault from the Alamein line with a bombardment that opened at 2140 Cairo time on 23 October 1943.

Private K I Tuddenham RAOC was on a mission when it happened:

I was sent with a station car to Tel el Kebir to pick up an urgent load with the work ticket stamped 'No Speed Limit'. It was tank air cleaners, and even the seat beside me was full. These I took to Mena with RMP help and high speed only to be told to go on to Alexandria where I was met by an officer who told me to go on to Corps (author's note: probably 30 Corps). I went on until I was stopped by a soldier and passed on to another group of officers who told me the air cleaners were wanted by the Flail Tanks who were on the other side of a mine field. As it was now dark and the vehicle I had was fitted with brake lights I must go at walking pace (no braking allowed). An officer went on foot in front of me waving left or right until we reached a row of tanks where the air cleaners were unloaded. It seems that when the tanks are used the dust they make quickly clogs the air cleaners. Once more back through the minefield to Corps where I was told to sleep in the car. Sleep became impossible as the guns started. It was the start of El Alamein.

It seems perhaps incongruous, but as Montgomery was building his logistic resources to support his plan for the Battle of Alamein, the Army decided to undertake a major shift in its logistic organization and create 'a single equipment management corps', to be known as the Corps of Royal Electrical and Mechanical Engineers. There was a committee, chaired by Sir William Beveridge, who would become famous in connection with the post-war social services legislation, and it reported in August 1941 and February 1942. The key recommendation for the RAOC, in the February report, was that the Army should follow the Royal Navy model and have a single branch, in this case a corps, of electrical and mechanical engineers. Further more his view was that electrical and mechanical engineers should be given their appropriate place and influence in the Army.

This was followed by the Sinclair-Weeks Committee reporting also in February 1942, which recommended that the transfer should take place from RASC to RAOC of all responsibility for provision, storage, and issue of motor vehicles and spares. It also confirmed the Beveridge recommendation that responsibility for the whole of the Army's equipment should be transferred from RE, RASC and RAOC to a single Corps. A further recommendation was that, for the time being, artificers of the RAC, RE, and R Signals should remain with their units to assist with user maintenance.

In fact the report did not create a single equipment management corps for the Army, since R Signals retained responsibility for unit repair of communications equipment and RE held on to their own workshops for the repair and maintenance of plant. It left the RAOC as a supply corps, but only responsible for part of the supply of stores to the Army. The RASC still held on to responsibility for fuel, food and fodder as well as a range of other commodities. The formation of REME was a start to the creation of a well-focussed, clearly structured, properly organized logistic system, but it fell short of the mark. The fatal mistake was to relate the Army's activity to that of the Royal Navy without fully examining the supply aspects of repair in land operations. On a ship, always fully loaded and ready for war, even in peacetime, it worked. In an open, confused, mobile land battle it had much less chance of success. It was a model produced by an intellectual with no logistic knowledge and it did not begin to address the real issues of supply and maintenance of armies on the modern battlefield. At the working level for this particular reorganization the relationship between REME and the RAOC, on responsibility for policy on spares, was not clarified and would lead to confusion and conflicting priorities.

A Royal Warrant dated 19 May 1942, and notified in special Army Orders numbers 70 and 71 of 1942, authorized the formation of REME. Some sixty per cent of the RAOC moved to REME, dropping the Corps from 152,000 men to around 75,000. REME was formed on 1 October 1942, twenty-two days before Montgomery launched his assault at Alamein. However, the creation of the new Corps was phased and with the minimum of disruption at unit level where the existing system was well understood. It therefore required no real change to the administrative plans then in their final phase in the build up to Montgomery's famous battle.

One of the keys to his success was the logistic backing that was in place and, thanks to Brigadier, by now Major General, Richards' far-sightedness, properly balanced to meet the Army's needs. The old central OFP organization was now a thing of the past. It was broken down on a formation basis to an Army Troops OFP, Corps Troops OFPs and Divisional OFPs. Initially the plan was that they would also supply spares to workshops, but with the formation of REME there was a policy of giving each workshop its own Stores Section. It was a structure honed in the experience of desert warfare and would be adapted to the rest of the Army – and in broad terms survive in principle to form the basis of much of the logistic support system put in place by the RLC when it formed fifty years later.

The Vehicle and Stores Convoy Unit in particular was a great success. Arguably it broke the rule that transport is best pooled and allocated centrally to meet priorities. However, the net effect of pooling transport resources was often that urgent Ordnance stores were denied transport by staff officers who failed to understand their significance, with priority often given to the 'easier' commodities such as ammunition and food.

Units were formally created to deal with ammunition and stores at railheads, roadheads and ports and in field maintenance centres. What was in 1942 standard practice in the Middle East became general practice throughout the Army. They were to become Maintenance Areas and Ordnance Maintenance Companies. Vehicle depots were still blistered on to OFPs and BODs, but with the transfer of responsibility for vehicle supply from the RASC and a single focus for the task now vested in the Corps, the concept began to emerge of a separate vehicle organization. It all worked, with lessons learned along the way that would stand the Army in good stead for the inevitable invasion of fortress Europe.

After El Alamein, the Central Provision office moved from Tel Aviv to Cairo as it was thought necessary for it to be close to the policy makers in order to ensure the supply of equipment was right for the latest operational plans. At last the realization that logisticians, making their contribution at an early stage in planning, resolved many of the problems before they occurred.

As this was happening the first inloads of ammunition were delivered to CAD Kineton in the UK. Within a year the depot would be holding 80,000 tons.

El Alamein was a stunning success. Montgomery gave Churchill his victory. The first part of his mission to eject Rommel from North Africa was complete and nothing would now be able to prevent him fulfilling it. And as he was pursuing Rommel along the North African coast an Anglo-American convoy of 500 ships with a naval escort of 350 warships arrived off the coast of French North Africa and American and British troops landed in French Morocco and Algiers. Resistance was slight and by 11 November 1942 they had occupied the ports of Casablanca and Bougie. 1942 was proving to be a much better year than might first have been envisaged.

Chapter Five

An End in Sight
1943 – August 1945

This is not the end. It is not even the beginning of the end, but it is perhaps the end of the beginning.
Winston S Churchill, November 1942, after Alamein

There was no doubt but that the tide had turned. On 1 January 1943 the news came that the siege of Leningrad was over. Then on 31 January the information was released that one field marshal, sixteen generals and the entire 6th German Army, or what was left of it, had capitulated and been made prisoner at Stalingrad. Coupled with the news from North Africa and the naval victories of the Americans in the Pacific, there was a feeling that events were moving the Allies' way despite the hold the Japanese had on the ground in China, Burma, the Malay Peninsula and the islands of south-east Asia.

In Europe 1942 had seen a focus on an air campaign to damage German industry, dent morale and destroy communications. The Americans bombed by day and the British by night. On 30 May the first 1,000-bomber raid was mounted by the RAF on Cologne. Apart from some raids on the coast of France there had been no land force activity.

The impetus was switching to the Allies, to the twenty-six nations who, just a year earlier on 1 January 1942, had signed a pact in Washington to the effect that they would use all the resources at their disposal to defeat the Axis, and that none of them would act independently with regard to any of the Axis powers.

In North Africa in November 1942 Operation TORCH, an invasion of French North Africa by an Allied force, had proved successful. It had been in many ways a landmark. It was the first operation on such a scale involving both the Americans and the British under a single Supreme Allied Commander – General Dwight D Eisenhower. It was truly a combined operation with the Supreme Commander in overall charge of sea, land and air forces, with command being exercised through an integrated Allied Forces Headquarters.

It was an operation planned and executed in something of a hurry, with only two months from conception to execution. It was born of the realization and acceptance by the Americans that, success in the Pacific notwithstanding, the defeat of Germany on mainland Europe would have to take priority. They felt initially that everything else was a diversion of resources. It was not a view shared by the British, who felt that diversionary operations in Europe, even on the fringes, drew essential German forces from France and also relieved pressure on the Russians. This debate eventually went with the

British view, but was the reason for the late start on and, hence, short duration of the planning for TORCH.

The outline plan was that task forces would land at three points on the coast – Casablanca, Oran and Algiers. Two of these landings were American and the third was largely British. From the British perspective the operation benefited hugely from the focus over the previous two years on Combined Operations training. One shortcoming, however, was that whilst the staff of 1st Army and its subordinate formations had trained together, they lacked an HQ in theatre to oversee operations and, perhaps most importantly, provide a link with the UK base on a whole range of issues that need not concern the fighting formations.

The AFHQ was perhaps the substitute, but had weaknesses that meant it did not fill the full role. It only began to form up some two months before the operation and in its original design was to be fully integrated. Every branch had to comprise British and American servicemen in virtually equal measure. However, whilst this might have been sensible for operations and intelligence staff, it created huge problems for the RAOC since the responsibilities for different aspects of logistics in the US Army differed from those in the British Army. One significant example was that whilst the British had just separated Maintenance and Supply by forming the Corps of REME, the Americans retained the functions of both supply and repair under one single structure.

The RAOC's position was not improved by the lack of a senior guiding hand. The DDOS for the AFHQ was not approved and put in place until just a few days before the 1st Army sailed. He found a plan in whose formulation he had no hand, run by a branch in whose design and manning he had played no part, despite the difficulties being presented by the combined HQ concept. Brigadier W E C Pickhall was not, however, a man to be put off by a few structural problems. His main attribute, apart from his extensive knowledge, was that his personality fitted him admirably to work with the Americans and he quickly won their trust and support.

It was just as well, for it was to the American HQ at Cheltenham he was sent in order to provide them with assistance. Not only were they not in need of any assistance, he would have been, in any event, unable to give it since he knew nothing of their system. When he eventually managed to get hold of the DDOS in 1st Army it was to find there would be no one in direct control of the AFHQ RAOC element that had been formed for the operation and that DDOS 1st Army would be too busy concentrating on his operational responsibilities to do so. Brigadier Pickhall took over the AFHQ element and started to build a support service for Ordnance staffs on the operational HQs. On arrival in North Africa AFHQ was in an hotel in the centre of Algiers. Almost inevitably the British Ordnance Branch was several miles away in another location. There was no transport and everything achieved by the RAOC HQ staffs during the campaign was in spite of the system and not because of it.

One decision was that there was to be central provision for both 1st and 8th Armies and DDOS(P) Middle East would be responsible for the whole Mediterranean theatre. As stocks in the North African depots were whittled down to support the effort in Sicily and Italy they were removed from the central provision system. However, Persia (Iran), Iraq and East Africa were also brought under the central provision office wing; and a scales office was embedded in it with the crucial task of preparing spares schedules, collating wastage experience and preparing standard Middle East scales The number of items being controlled by the Central Provision Office was by now 402,000, compared with the 60,000 at the commencement of the war.

An interesting, and far-sighted, aspect of the Ordnance plan developed by 1st Army was the creation of Ordnance Beach Detachments to provide immediate support to the landing forces. Five were created for the operation, each comprising six officers and 110 men. All the members of these units were specially chosen and given a high level of specific training not just in Ordnance matters but also in military skills. Their role was to supply both stores and ammunition across the beach.

The stores they were to manage had been scaled to eliminate everything that was not deemed operationally essential. The lack of MHE was also taken into account in the packing. Cases were made

Establishments were not always manned. Here are the five officers of 12 Ordnance Beach Detachment in 1943: Captains J D W Lindley, W G Greig and R Snook, Second Lieutenant A Kirk, Lieutenant F J Thompson.

of wood and given rope handles in order to make handling as easy as possible. Contents lists were prepared and everything was done to facilitate ease and speed of issue under the conditions that were likely to prevail in amphibious operations.

Indeed, packaging had been a subject that had received a great deal of attention since the early part of the war. General Williams was clear that poor packaging would have an adverse effect and at the point where it was least welcome, in the area of operations where facilities would not be anything like as good as those in the base depots. He was also conscious that the packaging would have to deal with a range of differing climates, and the stores' final destination could not be predicted with any certainty. Cartons formed the basis of the system and the carton unit was based on the minimum quantity that would be issued by an OFP. It was the forerunner to the Primary Packaged Quantity, or PPQ

Poor packaging creates waste wherever and whenever it occurs.

Landing reserves were held to re-supply the Beach Detachments, organized on a brigade structure and in theory capable of sustaining the formation for one month's operations. By then a BOD structure should be in place to sustain operations as the fighting troops moved inland. Once the full RAOC structure was in place it would comprise two BODs, two BADs, eight OFPs, one Ordnance railhead company, nine mobile laundries, one base hospital laundry and, perhaps incongruously as this is being written in the twenty-first century, two officers' shops.

It was not a wholly sound concept, for it scattered the Ordnance effort across the theatre and failed to take advantage of the centralization of provision and control and the use of the two BODs as a single warehousing

This example in 557 BOD in Italy shows how it should be done.

Another of Sergeant Savage's pictures showing the various aspects of a laundry at work.

facility albeit located, for security, in different places. As it was the two BODs were treated as co-equal and independent. The idea was that the structure would make maximum use of the available port facilities. As it was, diversion of shipping at short notice and the effects of poor communications meant that the available resources in the theatre could not be targeted and focussed on the problem areas and consequently support to the end user suffered.

In late 1942 the first stage of Operation TORCH had involved a move on Tunis, followed by a withdrawal under pressure to a defensive line that the Allies were able to hold just short of their initial objectives. It was during this time that the Army had lived off its landing reserves, of which a plentiful

Brigadier T H Clarke.

supply had been arranged. There were eighteen brigade sets in the initial landings and then a further ten in the follow up. However, the landings were virtually unopposed and this allowed the DDOS of 1st Army, Brigadier T H Clarke, to move his OBDs to more suitable locations and to sustain units that had arrived in the theatre and were awaiting the establishment of a normal system of supply.

Ammunition re-supply initially worked well in what was essentially a war of movement covering a relatively wide area. However, the loads were excessive, since the establishment of a BAD was based on handling 21,000 tons and this was often exceeded, sometimes reaching 75,000 tons. There were other problems associated with the handling of ammunition in field storage conditions, poor labour support and inadequate and insufficient MHE. However, despite this, units in the field received effective ammunition support. A system of roadside storage was implemented, and was effective given the air superiority the Allies achieved shortly after landing. Further forward problems were created by a poorly managed dumping programme over which there was little control. The result was a poor overview of stocks throughout the theatre, leading to over provision of some natures simply because Ordnance staffs did not know what they had.

Spares support suffered somewhat from the scaling down to the bare essentials, but certainly proved its effectiveness in the early days. The main problem lay with a shortage of vehicles. The initial landings had insufficient to deal with the distances encountered on operations. There was also some loss due to a relatively high traffic accident rate. Furthermore, the enemy had good airfields that gave them better support for their air forces than the Allies had in the temporary landing fields they were using. Consequently, they had local air superiority in the early stages of the operation and were able to inflict damage on vehicles on the move. The solution was to obtain additional vehicles locally, pending the arrival of follow up scales. However, the OFPs were scaled to support the standardized range with which the Army had deployed, and support for the range of non-standard substitutes presented difficulties. Regarding spares support for the repair effort, as the campaign developed one clear lesson was confirmation of the need to provide a stores section for REME workshops. Providing spares from 'convenient' OFPs and OBDs was never going to deliver the immediacy of support required, and in any event was too restrictive on the deployment of both the REME workshops and the Ordnance supply units.

The second stage of the operation ran through from the turn of the year to the end of March 1943. During this period both Armies spent time building up their forces and, in any event, any military operations they might wish to have conducted would have been hampered by the appalling weather that inflicted itself on that part of North Africa during this period. It was in January that the Central Provision Office in the Middle East moved back to Mena having already made several moves around Egypt and Palestine in the previous year. However, Mena proved an impossible location for staff and travel so it moved back into Cairo within a few weeks. One day it would get to stand still. One day the staffs forcing these decisions would understand the practical difficulties they caused and the impact on supply support for the Army by this constant and quite unnecessary shuffling of logistic staff. Just as the build up for the final phases of the war in North Africa was getting underway the organization responsible for part of that build up was being messed about.

Nonetheless, all was ready on time and the final stage of the operation occupied the six weeks from the beginning of April to the middle of May. By then the Allies had built their strength, the 8th Army had arrived in strength, and there had been some regrouping to focus the right forces in the right place. In early May the final assault on Tunis took place and on 12 May the city fell and 250,000 prisoners were taken.

While this was all going on the UK base was working hard to gear up not only to support the active theatres overseas, but also to prepare for an invasion of fortress Europe, whenever and wherever that might be. There were setbacks in building and construction of warehousing, alignment of processes and training, but progress continued to be made. Private Murdoch, however, was involved in what was almost certainly the first Donnington fire, in January 1943:

> It was a Saturday night and I was seated alone in hut 48 A Coy. G Camp when I decided to clean my greatcoat buttons and cap badge ready for church parade on Sunday. Having completed the task I was about to sit down when the door of hut 48 opened and a gruff voice ordered me to go to HQ parade ground with my greatcoat and steel helmet. The order was obeyed and all personnel who obeyed were put into groups and told to report to Building 1, which was situated inside the Depot. We were told this building was on fire and that we were required to remove any flammable stores from the building if possible.
>
> The fire was caused by an electrical fault igniting some flammable liquid stored in the paint store. The depot fire brigade was containing the fire when an order was given to open the door on the windward side of the building. This action allowed the fire to flare up and the flames reached to the roof which was lined with Canadian baseboard which ignited. The fire travelled very quickly across the roof aided by the wind entering from the open door. The burning baseboard soon fell from the roof and we were able to put out the fire. With the flames and fire out we stood down and were allowed to return to camp.
>
> Before leaving however we had an announcement to say we would be excused from Church parade on Sunday.

Meanwhile, the RAOC *Gazette* had opened the year in a format very much smaller than had been the case up to now due to severe paper rationing. The editor was determined to retain that part of the *Gazette* devoted to unit news as it fostered esprit de corps. However, he did ask units to submit their articles every second month. To make space for this the type font was reduced in order to squeeze more information into a small space, but it challenged those whose reading eyesight was less than perfect. The *Gazette* was to be shared with REME for the time being as they had not had the opportunity to set up their own magazine. In March it was this sharing and the space it occupied that meant soldier postings would no longer be included. However, the *Gazette* had, late in 1942, started to print lists of prisoners of war and this was now a regular and helpful feature, and despite the rationing of paper was a feature that would continue.

This sharing policy, incidentally, also included the Corps' band, which would continue to support REME units until such time as their own band could be resourced.

The turn of the year also saw the announcement that the acceptance of combatant status for the RAOC had changed officers' dress, and the blue gorget patches worn by senior officers would be replaced with red, mirroring the rest of the Army.

While the campaign in North Africa had been going on work had also started on planning Operation HUSKY. This was to be an invasion of Europe through Italy, attacking the 'soft underbelly' so favoured by Winston Churchill. It was felt to be a necessary strategic move which would maintain the momentum of the successes in North Africa and carry on applying the pressure in the Germans, diverting their strength from France and Russia.

A planning HQ was established in Algiers in January 1943, but with the commanders focussed on winning the war in North Africa there was no one to lend a guiding hand to the planners. The original concept was for two task forces to land in Sicily as a launching pad into Italy. There was to be an American one in the west and a British one in the east, commanded by Generals Patton and Montgomery respectively with the 7th American and 8th British Armies. General Alexander was to be the Army Group commander. However, once Montgomery began to take a serious interest in the plan it was not to be long before it was changed. His concern lay principally with the dispersion of forces and as a result of his intervention the landings of both task forces were concentrated in the south-east of the island. However, the lateness of much of the planning and the sudden switch of location for the landings presented their problems for the RAOC planners. DOS 13 Corps, Colonel W Grimsdale, was the officer responsible for planning the Corps' support to the Eastern Task Force. He did so in a virtual information vacuum, making scaling of the initial reserves very hard work.

There was a conflict of opinion as to the level of stores to be held in Sicily. On the one hand it could be said that once the island became a stepping stone to Italy no stocks would be required and therefore not too much should be tied up there. However, DOS MEF was determined that a small AOD was required in order to ensure that there was sufficient provision to meet the unexpected. OBDs had to be trained, and, as an opposed landing was expected, the training would have to be of the highest order, while maintaining the secrecy that was paramount if surprise was to be achieved. Early stores' convoys comprised principally ammunition as well as the beach reserves and the initial landing stocks for the AOD.

Essentially simple in concept, the plan was complicated by the diverse sources from which the fighting formations were to be drawn. Two beach groups were formed in the UK to accompany the Canadian Division, one was formed in North Africa and four more came from further east in the Middle East. It was also unfortunate that Headquarters 15th Army Group chose to shed its logistics staff, other than a few advisors, in order to focus on its operational role, for a complex plan requires close direction and the logistics of this plan were far from simple.

By contrast, 8th Army maintained the system it had built up of an administrative spearhead. This was an advanced base headquarters that moved forward with the army opening up ports and logistic installations. The team that had opened up Tunis brought its skills to Sicily.

In the Far East the Japanese continued their inexorable advance up through Burma towards India. Most of the support requirements were met by the IAOC and there was little involvement by the RAOC in the running of depots and installations, although the Corps was represented on the staff. It would perhaps be worth laying one ghost: that of the forgotten Army, with 14th Army, believing itself to be very much the poor relation. This would be to deny the really quite large volume of stores dispatched from the UK; stores that could be ill afforded. The intolerable delay in them reaching the end user was to do with the handling process in India through double handling and the intricacies of the Indian distribution system.

However, there were soldiers from the RAOC suffering in the Far East; those who had been taken prisoner during the early Japanese invasions of Hong Kong and Singapore. Ron Mould was one of the Singapore prisoners:

> In March 1943 I moved to Siam where we were told there were POW camps more like Butlins, but this turned out to be far from the truth and the reality was that we were to be slave labour to build what was to become known as the 'Railway of Death'. I was by this time attached to the RASC and about forty of us were left in Kanburi to form a party to drive rations up the line. So, in 1943 I found myself driving a Nissan truck.

John McNamara was also involved with the railway:

> Next the railroad. Parties started leaving for Thailand early in 1943 and I left with a force in February. 'You will like it up there' said the Japs. The journey took five days and nights by train, packed into the trucks so tightly that you just could not move. Most uncomfortable. After detraining at Bampong we marched twenty miles or so to a staging camp, and then on to the first and my only jungle camp. The work was hard, the rations meagre. Generally, the tasks were tree-felling, bridging, dynamiting and tunnelling. While the weather held things were not too bad, but with the monsoon came the several epidemics that were to take their toll. Cholera was the worst and claimed on average ten lives daily. On returning to camp each evening we would dig graves and bury them. The Japs took fright and deserted us, not returning for some weeks. Sensible people.

In April 1943 a key event took place when the British and American joint planning staff was formed to plan the invasion of Europe through France and into the heart of Germany. It was the decision of the Combined Chiefs of Staff Committee. However, even prior to that the likely tasks for the RAOC in an invasion of Europe were being studied. Major General Williams, the Controller of Stores, had decreed that the whole system for the supply of Ordnance stores to fighting formations should be revised. The scenario was a landing on a narrow shoreline, with no ports and under continuous enemy fire – the worst possible circumstances. It studied everything from unit organizations to the methods of packing most suited to beach operations and subsequent activity inland.

Speed was to be the key. Speed in getting stores ashore, speed in moving them across the beaches, speed in sorting and stacking and speed in the making of issues. A special kind of box was developed for the packing and pre-cartoning of stores, constructed in such a way as to be used as a bin without unpacking the cartons.

On 22 June 1943 a man died, and the story did not emerge until January 1979. His name was Lance Corporal Irvine Roberts and he was just another RAOC soldier – one of so many. In 1978 his brother Cyril, who had no idea of the manner of his death, attended a lecture given by John Marsh in Sheffield Cathedral. John had spent time in charge of a Japanese prison camp called Kanu 1. While there he had witnessed the courage of a young man from Sheffield and so had decided to dedicate his lecture to him. Irvine had joined the RAOC aged twenty-four on the outbreak of war, went to Europe, was

Lance Corporal Irvine Roberts RAOC.

evacuated from Dunkirk and then sent to the Far East. Singapore had fallen after his troopship left South Africa and he, with his fellow passengers, fell straight into the hands of the waiting Japanese. Conditions in the camp to which he was eventually sent were appalling. The hopeless dysentery cases were held in a low tent – many were so weak and emaciated they could only stare with uncomplaining resignation, hiccough ceaselessly and slip into a merciful coma before death. But Irvine emerged as an inspiring volunteer helper. His own condition was precarious, but he never spared himself. He exhibited immense courage, matched only by his faith as a Christian. He never talked about it, he just did it; he lived it. He volunteered to look after the 'death tent', knowing he would follow those he helped to die with dignity in such ghastly circumstances. He was twenty-seven when he died and he truly laid his life down for others. Just another RAOC soldier.

The invasion of Sicily took place on 9 July 1943, and the whole island was in Allied hands by 17 August. Thereafter, it became the launching platform for the invasion of Italy, a task for which a number of plans were developed. Regardless of the eventual outcome of the operational plan, the geography of the country was almost certain to cause problems. Any advance up the length of Italy would have to use the eastern and western coastal strips, with the Apennine ridge running up the middle. There would have to be two lines of communication.

It was eventually agreed that General Mark Clark's 5th US Army would land at Salerno and move up the western coastal line, whilst General Montgomery's 8th Army would land on the 'toe' of Italy. It is not uncommon to have a major reshuffle at critical times, due to uninformed staff decisions. In this case, and just prior to the landings, 30 Corps and two of its divisions were to return to the UK. It was decided that all their fit vehicles would be exchanged for any unfit vehicles held in 13 Corps, which would be part of the invasion of Italy. This 'simple' idea caused chaos, and had to be managed by the small RAOC contingent in Sicily. It was the presence of 557 AOD, placed there by a far-sighted DOS for just this sort of eventuality, which allowed the problem to be handled effectively. The vehicles themselves were handled by a woefully under strength Vehicle Company, even when reinforced by the vehicle sub-park of 1st Canadian Division.

It is a little known fact that the RAOC had its own Officer Cadet Training Unit. It was at Foremark Hall, a country estate near Derby, and was busying itself with turning out young officers to help build the new units that were supporting formations across the Army; teaching them to be officers who could take their place in command or in technical roles in the field force and in base units at home and abroad. Officer Cadet Tom Bretherton was one who endured an intensive course:

…covering a broad range. In addition to Ordnance procedure we had many physical activities,

The staff of the Officer Cadet Training Unit at Foremark Hall, commanded by Lieutenant Colonel K MacIver-Grierson DSO MC RAOC.

drill, weaponry, battle tactics and so on. It was stressed that although the RAOC was an administrative arm it was a combatant corps.

Clearly this was an issue close to the surface following the decision on combatant status just a few months earlier.

> The passing out parade of my course, in August 1943, was taken by the top RAOC officer at that time, Major General Williams, who told us that our performance was as good as anything he had seen during a recent visit to West Point – a comment that was nice to hear but, maybe, a little difficult to believe! It was a pleasure to us to have the Corps' Band present.

Foremark Hall was one of a number of training establishments thrown up by the need to man a corps that had grown from 30,000 in 1939 to 98,000 in 1943, even taking account of the 'loss' to REME in October 1942. In addition to the OCTU there was a unit to train officers for direct entry commissions and training battalions for new intakes of soldiers. There was also a school with branches running officers' war courses, specialist stores training, military training courses and ammunition courses for IOOs and AEs

On 9 September the US 5th Army invaded Italy across the Salerno beaches and, as part of it, went 10 British Corps, with its full RAOC support package. The Germans, despite the surrender of their Axis allies, defended strongly and the Salerno landings were powerfully opposed. Corporal A Craven was part of 8 Ordnance Beach Detachment supporting 56th London Division in what he described as 'the chaos' of the landings. Space was extremely tight in the confined area, and he found himself issuing ammunition to 25-pounder guns that were firing from behind them – the OBD was forward of the gun positions.

Also on 9 September, in a separate and hastily arranged operation, 1st Airborne Division was landed by the Royal Navy at the huge Italian port of Taranto, to be shortly followed by the capture of Brindisi. It took with it its OFP commanded by Captain C C Chidgey. By mid September the Germans had abandoned Salerno, and Montgomery took a logistic risk by switching his main operational effort from the toe to the heel of Italy in order to take pressure of the US 5th Army. The switch was made

successfully with the DDOS involved from the outset to ensure that the transfer of stocks was undertaken in a timely and effective manner. However, overall control was not as tight as one might have wished. The overall responsibility lay with AFHQ still in Algiers, meeting requirements from its North African resources and directly from the UK and USA. The British also had their extensive support base in the Middle East, but Algiers and Cairo are 2,300 miles from each other. Communications were not easy and, with British forces split between 10 Corps with the US 5th Army and those in 8th Army, it was never going to be an ideal logistic support situation. The lack of strong administrative support staff in 15th Army Group, who had gone 'lean' in order to become more effective, did not help, and indeed proved a hindrance.

Captain, later Major, C C 'Bill' Chidgey.

The capitulation of the Italians was not something Hitler was prepared to accept, and Field Marshal Kesselring was ordered to hold a line as far south in Italy as he could in order to stem the Allied advance. He chose the 'Winter Line', a series of natural defensive positions running from Cassino in the west to the River Sangro in the east. This played exactly into Alexander's hands since it contained large German forces a long way from where they might be useful, either in Russia or in France. By the end of 1943 Alexander was halted on the Winter Line with an Army equivalent in strength to that of the enemy he faced.

In India there were changes in the command and control. The Quebec conference in August 1943 had agreed that command would pass to a new south-east Asia Command and it was to be Anglo-American. The Supreme Allied Commander was to be Vice Admiral Lord Louis Mountbatten. One of his first tasks was to re-establish control of the Bay of Bengal and once that was achieved it was possible to form an Indian base for the direct support of operations in the east. This time also coincided with a visit from the Controller of Ordnance Stores. Major General Williams was concerned about two key issues – the lack of contact between field commands and the base due to limitations on visits, and the delay experienced in getting stocks into the hands of the end user in the fighting formations. He was well received and General Sir Claude Auchinleck offered him the opportunity to address a large gathering of officers in Delhi in order to tell them what he considered the important issues. Drawing on the lessons of North Africa and Europe, Major General Williams stressed the need for keeping senior Ordnance officers fully in the operational picture in order that they might more effectively predict the likely support requirements. He also stressed that, in his view, whilst it was perfectly reasonable to disperse ammunition, clothing, tentage and accommodation stores, other general stores, MT spares and warlike stores must be concentrated and their distribution centrally controlled. It was in the area of MT spares that the RAOC could help most, with Major General Williams return to England being swiftly followed by the dispatch of two experienced officers to lend their knowledge to the gradually developing base to support operations to the east.

At about the end of 1943, 11th Army Group, a British headquarters coming directly under Lord Louis Mountbatten, was set up. 11th Army Group had its own Ordnance directorate, whereas previously all Ordnance services in the theatre had come under the DOS GHQ India Command. About the same time the Eastern Army of India Command was resisting the Japanese assault on the Assam-Burma frontier and it was split in two, one half of it to become the famous 14th Army which itself later came under command of 11th Army Group.

The same Quebec Conference was also the time when Churchill and Roosevelt showed Stalin the plans for the second front. The briefing included an indication of the beaches to be used and the timing – late May or early June 1944.

Back in Italy it was obvious that the logistic support situation now had to be addressed in order to align it to the operational plans that would be needed to achieve a breakthrough. AFHQ appointed a DCAO, Major General Roberts, with an HQ that was christened FLAMBO, a code name rather than an acronym. From 24 October 1943 FLAMBO took over all logistic support activities for both the British and American armies in Italy and, in so doing, paved the way for the move of AFHQ from North Africa to the Italian mainland. They took over at a time when, since August, more and more shipping had been bringing stocks from the UK and the US. The long lead times meant that priorities had changed by the time they arrived and the relevance of the items they contained had often to be questioned. Italian ports were not ready for use, those in North Africa were full and Sicily often had to be used as a staging post, which led to delay and confusion. Urgent items were lifted from the island to the mainland by a daily courier service, courtesy of the RAF, and this did a great deal to alleviate the situation.

The 8th Army, on the east coast of Italy, maintained its links with its bases in the Middle East. This allowed for a far better and more focussed service than that which could be provided to the rest of the Allied force spread between Italy, Sicily and North Africa. However, its vehicles were in a parlous state and returning equipment for base repair to Cairo simply did not make practical sense. The problem was addressed by ordering 1,200 engines from the UK and USA, but with little regard for how they were to be stored and managed once they arrived.

A depot, 500 AOD, was opened in Bari in October 1943. It was easier for the RAOC on the east coast as a number of unopposed landings had opened the way north. However, stocking it was a major problem as scaling for a depot that was 1,500 miles from its source of supply in the Cairo area was never going to be easy. The work of the depot was also affected, and the RAOC sustained casualties when the port, on the night of 2/3 December, and then again a few weeks later, was bombed by German aircraft that got through and destroyed ammunition ships berthed there. Another lesson relearned – ammunition should have a separate port or at the very least separated berths.

The spares situation was so worrying that the DOS Middle East decided to send two officers to review and report back on what might be done. Accordingly Colonel Reynolds and Lieutenant Colonel Band sought permission from 8th Army HQ to visit. Inherently suspicious of any visitors, and when they received a signal requesting staff clearance for Reynolds and Band, headquarters 8th Army responded by wishing to know '…number of players, weight of instruments and proposed programme'. Protesting that he was not a man to blow his own trumpet Colonel Reynolds eventually made it and was able to make some headway in remedying the situation. The general policy adopted by 8th Army anyway was to hold stocks forward, and it was the replenishment of those forward stocks that was the key to success.

One major feature of the logistic support provided by the RAOC was the creation of Port Ordnance Detachments and Port Ammunition Detachments. They sorted, identified, and directed consignments arriving at the various ports supporting the 8th Army. The requirement for these small units, commanded by a junior officer, had been proved time and again during the North African campaign, and they had a major impact on the speed and accuracy with which Ordnance stores were delivered by possessing a depth of knowledge that could not be expected of the Royal Engineers' movements staff.

On the down side there was difficulty with the supply of stores by air. The quantities arriving were erratic and hard to predict. This was almost entirely due to the fact that the Air Force used the air transport capacity to meet its own needs to the detriment of the ground forces. Priorities were never properly allocated and, whilst operations were not halted for want of Ordnance stores, there is no doubt that the situation could have been significantly improved with a proper allocation of resources.

At the end of December 1943 General Montgomery relinquished command of the 8th Army to take over 21st Army Group and to prepare for the invasion of Europe through France and into Germany. All other theatres and activities were to be subordinated to the effort to defeat Germany. A sense of urgency filled the air, for the invasion was now just five months away. Commanders were put in place that would be instrumental in the planning and in seeing it through. Brigadier J G Denniston took on the appointment of DOS 21st Army Group, joining Colonel L E Cutforth who was already holding down the appointment of DDOS. Their planning for Normandy took account of all that had been learned in the five successful opposed landings that had taken place in the Middle East.

As Montgomery left Italy it was decided, with the Army held on a German Winter line that was appearing impregnable, to outflank the line by landing to its north at Anzio. The landing was unopposed, but the advance of the Allied Army north from the beachhead, was pedestrian, giving the Germans the chance to react. The result was a beachhead that was never enlarged, but neither was it ever beaten back. It was to be four months before the pressure was relieved with the turning of the Winter Line, coordinated with a breakout from Anzio.

Logistic support for the Anzio operation was not well planned. Maintaining a force over a beach for any length of time is difficult and this one was made more complex by the fact that the forces were mixed, British and American, and their systems were so widely divergent. Whilst it may have been possible to cope with this on a larger front, in the confined space of the Anzio beachhead it presented innumerable difficulties. To try and resolve logistic issues 5th US Army was placed in overall charge of administration, but did so with an HQ that was woefully short of British representation. Not for the first time, and certainly not for the last, the RAOC was under-represented, with no Ordnance staff officer being appointed until four days after the landings had taken place. Eventually there was a DADOS, but with no clerks and no transport.

Landing reserves were scaled in a hurry, and did not reflect the likely requirements; there were, for example, insufficient blankets and stretchers. The ammunition section of the first OBD was left off the shipping and arrived some time after the ammunition it was destined to handle. There were no reconnaissance parties sent in early so sites were poorly allocated and laid out. The OFP for 1st Division was left off the shipping and arrived several days later, leading to acute spares shortages in the early part of the operation. Despite this inauspicious start the operation was eventually to be well sustained. Units indented on 557 BOD south of Naples, and the requisite stores were loaded onto lorries which were driven in the afternoon onto LSTs. These would then sail during the night, the lorries would drive off them to the appropriate stores unit and, having delivered the stocks, would pick up the indents for the following day and return by the same route. Soldiers from the RAOC went as escorts with these vehicles to make sure they arrived at the right destination.

But Italy, with the rest, was now a sideshow. It was the invasion of France that mattered and the RAOC involvement was to be huge. Major General Williams gave a newspaper interview a few days after the landings on 6 June 1944, explaining what it had all involved. The reporter's story was as follows:

There had been no precedents to guide him. No friendly port was available, equipped with modern machinery for handling heavy tanks and guns. 'From whatever angle we viewed the problem it was fantastic', said General Williams. 'The needs were inelastic; the variety of articles fantastic. And through it all there was the need for speed. Our men must land from barges on the open beaches, and they must have sufficiently heavy weapons to hold them and push on. We learned a lot at Norway when we landed there.'

Afterwards General Williams went to Africa, Syria, Iraq, Sicily and Italy. Each successful landing taught something. He had only recently returned from America, where he studied other aspects of the problem. Today General Williams controls a variety of goods unequalled in the history of the world. He has 750,000 different articles in his stores. Every one is indexed. He knows just where they are: how many of each he has. 'Their value'? he said. 'No one knows; no one will ever know. But hundreds—thousands—of millions of pounds.' They are stored all over the country, in factories, halls, houses, in the open. Among these things are Britain's greatest secrets – the surprises which Mr Churchill said we hoped to give the Germans. Ordnance Services know them all. 'You see', said General Williams, 'we had to order them.' But even then, these things are so hush-hush and the security measures so strict that no one man knows about them all. It would not be fair to the man.

The method of supply to the troops had to be reorganized from A to Z. Since speed of supply was essential, RAOC men rehearsed Tuesday's landing on replica beaches prepared in England. 'The problem was to get the stores ashore with our men', General Williams explained, 'and the first principle was that anyone should be able to find anything that was wanted at a moment's notice in the most difficult conditions.'

Stores went ashore in categories. First the Ordnance Beach Detachments with Landing Reserves – a sort of austerity supply – guns, wireless sets, clothing, medical supplies; spares for everything essential; spare dynamos to replace those damaged by water, electrical distributors, screws, nuts, bolts, gun parts, and, of course, ammunition.

'We packed the small stores in special boxes', said General Williams. 'None of them weighed more than 100lb as they had to be carried by hand. Everything contained in the boxes was in cartons, labelled and marked. Boxes were watertight, numbered, and identically packed. To assist identification in the dark, letters and figures were raised, like Braille. And everything was catalogued, so that one knew exactly what was in each box and how much was left after stores were drawn.'

Where possible related components were kept together, but in these Landing Reserves spares had to be mixed. 'Picnic boxes', the General called them. I saw some of the catalogues. On one page were details of: Cars: 2-seater 4-wheeled Austin. Among the items listed were insulating washers, anti-rattle springs, distribution drive spindles. The list was a marvel of ingenuity. As each item was drawn from the box, it was checked off, so that the storekeeper could tell exactly at any moment what every box contained. Next to the Landing Reserves come the Beach Packs—available for brigades and divisions and necessarily with a far wider range of requirements. Then there were Divisional Ordnance Field Depots, where the stores are contained in lorries, fitted with bins, packed in this country, ready to go wherever the troops are: the Mobile Ordnance Field Depots, and, lastly, the Advanced Ordnance Depots – an organization catering for the needs of the troops down to tiny details. If an unexpected article is required, the indent is sent back to England and it is flown over. 'But', said General Williams, 'that is by no means the whole story: in fact only a small part of it. We are getting repair factories out there for ammunition; base industrial gas units where we can make acetylene gas for the Royal Engineers and REME, and oxygen for the RAMC; base laundries and baths.'

And the packing of this vast shop ? I (author's note: the reporter) asked.

General Williams smiled. 'We began last August', he said. 'RAOC, civilians (men and women), ATS – anybody we could get. We have worked day and night ever since. Fourteen hours a day, seven days a week, in hundreds of depots all over England, Scotland and Wales. All leave was stopped long before the rest of the Army had its leave stopped. Some RAOC officers have had no leave for over nine months. We are still packing.'

It was truly a magnificent effort, and the RAOC had indeed come a long way during this war, and it was with the lessons learned over the preceding few years and the greater involvement of RAOC representatives in staff appointments that the ground was to be laid for the planning that coped with the logistic demands of the Normandy landings. The story Major General Williams had to tell the reporter really got under way as the planning entered its detailed phase, at the beginning of 1944.

Brigadier Denniston and Colonel Cutforth oversaw the preparation of staff tables and the revision of scales. Vehicle and major assembly wastage rates were collated and shipping tables were calculated. The RAOC ORBAT to support the invasion force and those units designated to accompany assaulting formations were briefed. While all this was going on the soldiers who were to be deployed were undergoing rigorous military training and the depots were selecting and packing the designated stores. And at different levels there were different planning imperatives: the Army Group was looking at the period D+17 to D+70 with all the vagaries that time frame imposed. In 2nd Army they were concerned with D-Day to D+17.

DOS had decided from the outset that priority had to be given to regimental training. Men had to be as robust as soldiers, as they were technically sound. At the same time the depots were busy with the preparation of landing reserve sets and beach maintenance packs. The volume grew as the invasion grew nearer. An indication of the load was given when the War Minister announced that in the two months leading up to D-Day the Ordnance depots had issued 12,000 armoured fighting vehicles, 60,000 lorries and 2,000,000 spare parts.

Shipping space was, as ever, a problem and priorities had to be allocated. The key was to ensure that sufficient was ashore in the early phases of the landings to sustain the fighting formations. Arranging the loads was complicated by the need to give six weeks notice of requirements at a time when plans were being adjusted within these time frames. And it was essential to ensure that the stores did not arrive on the beaches in advance of the units designated to handle them.

The Army as a whole had very little idea of the detailed work being undertaken to ensure that their every need was met once the invasion commenced. No matter how hard the preparatory work and no matter how detailed the planning, the RAOC would be judged not on its successes, which would be taken for granted, but on its failures. It would be judged by its customers for the service it gave them, irrespective of how the service was delivered. And unknown to many was that in parallel with all this work, planning was also under way for Operation RANKIN, to be put into effect should Germany suddenly capitulate.

Meanwhile, in the Far East, having survived working on the railways in Burma and Thailand John McNamara was on the move again:

> Early in 1944 the camp was cleared and we returned to Singapore, to Changi. This time were housed in the civilian gaol. Not bad at all. Running water, a roof over our heads and electric light. After the war it was described many times as 'infamous'. Nonsense. We still had lice though, but the bugs ousted the fleas, which were generally more unpleasant.

In India and Burma there were armies who sought to drive the Japanese out of south-east Asia and free John McNamara and the many others like him. To support these armies DOS 11th Army Group became responsible for the entire administrative load of Ordnance services in South-East Asia Command. During the interim period before this happened 14th Army had its own Advance Ordnance Depots and had been complete in itself; there was no separate LofC organization and all service installations came under direct command of the Army. It was an unwieldy arrangement, as 14th Army at this stage was undoubtedly the biggest single Army of the whole war.

It was only by a skilful combination of air, road, rail and sea transport that it was possible to get the required tonnages forward. It was quite possible that a store would have to be moved by each of these methods in turn before it finally reached its destination. The main Ordnance installations were four AODs and these were spaced more or less along what might be called the frontier fringe between Assam and Burma proper. Staffing of these installations was principally by IAOC officers and soldiers with a sprinkling of RAOC. The main RAOC representation was on the staff of the various headquarters.

These AODs had a difficult task. Many of the forces they served had retreated in the face of Japanese advances over long distances. They were ill-equipped and, due to the low priority which the war in the East had at that stage, it was only by more than a little improvisation, in many cases, that formations were given the wherewithal to hold out against continued Japanese attacks. To set up an AOD usually required a major surgical operation over thick jungle-covered ground. Choice of site was restricted to the fact that it had to be near a railhead and railheads usually chose to finish in what was then mostly swamp and jungle. Mosquitoes abounded, and it was usual in some seasons to have 60 to 80 per cent of the total unit strength down with malaria at one time. As time went on this was partly overcome by draining the swamps where the mosquitoes bred. Soon after 11th Army Group took over, a separate LofC organization was set up. Thereafter 14th Army could look ahead, instead of peering over its shoulder and attempting to supervise supplies over a long and tortuous LofC.

In Italy the coming of spring in 1944 saw the commencement of the final advance on Rome. Just prior to that, on 18 March 1944, Vesuvius erupted and plans had to be made to evacuate the sub depot at Portici, although in the end it was not proved to be necessary. However, everything was covered with a layer of grey ash that blocked roads and railways and blocked drains, started fires and caused roofs to collapse under the strain. It was an anxious time in 16 BAD as a river of lava flowed, seemingly unstoppable, towards the depot stocks. The hand of God was present that day for at the last moment, and for no apparent reason, the lava stream turned and took a route that led away from the ammunition.

In fact, erupting volcanoes were less of a

**Vesuvius erupts,
but the lava flow missed
the Ordnance Depots.**

problem than light fingered locals who saw some elements of the ammunition as a useful source of supply to compensate for shortages elsewhere. The primary cartridges for mortar bombs were shotgun cartridges by another name and could be far better deployed shooting the local wildlife to provide food than any value they might have helping to slaughter the King's enemies. Similarly, the cloth from breech loading artillery rounds was a valuable source of calico for local women and, as for the copper that could be accumulated from the driving bands of shells and the brass from cartridge cases, it was as manna from heaven.

It was in April 1944 that the Corps' *Gazette* published the new rates for widows' pensions. A private soldier's wife would receive 22s 6d (£32) per week, rising to 30s 0d (£42) for the wife of a WOI. A major's wife received £140 (£3,850) a year, equating to 33s 0d (£45) a week

On the advance north through Italy the frontages were narrow on both sides of the country with the broad sweep of the Apennine Mountains running up the spine of Italy. This created a concentration of units and nationalities on a narrow front, which complicated re-supply. Not only did individual nations among the Allies have their own way of undertaking replenishment, but also the UK logistic units themselves were differently configured and had different procedures depending on whether they came from the UK or the Middle East. Switching the 8th Army from the eastern to the western approach up through Italy further complicated matters.

To meet the challenges the RAOC units were reorganized. Divisional OFPs were scaled to support only divisional troops. There were Corps and Army troops as well, with the Army troops OFP also holding the Army reserves of controlled stores. REME workshops by now had their own RAOC stores sections attached.

The concept of an Ordnance Maintenance Company had been approved, with the task of holding stores at railheads, road heads and in maintenance areas. These units replaced the somewhat haphazard, ad hoc arrangements that had existed in the past for this important task. Ordnance Stores Convoy Units also proved to be essential, as they had proved to be in North Africa. Stores were delivered by these units from the base areas by road, rail and air and taken to forward distribution sites. Here they were picked up and moved forward to the demanding units. The same process in reverse saw demands for urgent stores returned to the base area. The speed of response created by this process meant the forward RAOC units were burdened with far lighter loads, knowing their urgent demands could be met swiftly and accurately. This reduced the size of RAOC units forward with the Army, and permitted reinforcement of the base, where manpower was in short supply.

These were fundamental lessons being learned 'on the hoof', and as fast as they were being learned they were being passed across to the United Kingdom and were being included in the preparation and planning for D-Day. 21st Army Group had delegated responsibility for opening the assault to 2nd British Army and the Ordnance appreciation was based around the units to be deployed, the support structure being made available in the shape of RAOC units and the realities of supporting the fighting formations as they established themselves and then moved out from the beachhead. Key in this was the acceptance that heavy opposition would be a factor, but that with the short sea journey full use could be made of a UK base that was now well stocked. Finally, but perhaps most important of all, was the vast air and naval superiority enjoyed by the Allies, and their massive transport resources. Taking these factors into account the Ordnance plan was based on the assumption that 2nd Army formations on D-Day and D+1 would survive with what they brought ashore at first line and with the Ordnance beach detachments affiliated to the assaulting formations. An additional ammunition company was placed under command of the assaulting corps to ensure adequacy of supply. Similarly, divisions landing on and immediately after D-Day would be responsible for their own OFPs. Then, between D+2 and D+8, sufficient stores should be landed to sustain everyone landing up to D+12 with first line stores, based on the assumption that each landing reserve contained sufficient to support a brigade operating at intense rates. From D+9 onwards landing reserves and beach maintenance packs would be directed to an AOD which, by then, would be established with a view to making issues from D+17, the day on which 21st Army Group would be firm on the continent and would assume responsibility for the overall supply situation. And there would be two LofC terminals set up on the beaches. So, broadly speaking the various forward Ordnance units would sustain the invasion for the first two weeks until it was expected that a full AOD and BAD structure would be set up and from which they could draw.

Based on the plan drawn from the appreciation the build up had involved preparation of the base units, field force units and other small units that were to accompany the invading formations. The initial assault was to be made by 1 and 30 Corps, and the DDsOS of each were charged with ensuring sustainment up to D+1. Their ORBAT was supplemented by them having placed under their control a number of Ordnance Beach Detachments, Ordnance Ammunition Detachments, Port Ordnance Detachments and Port Ammunition Detachments. The assault was to be carried out on a frontage of three divisions, and they were to be supported each by a Beach Sub Area, which meant concentrating the relevant Ordnance Beach organizations into the relevant sub area.

One of the units involved in these preparations was 59th Division Ordnance Sub Park at Donnington. WOII Les Forshaw, then a Lance Corporal, was a member. The unit grew until it had a strength of seventy, including a couple of cooks and a few REME. They moved to Sandown Park in Tunbridge Wells to join 12 Corps with 43rd and 53rd Divisions. He remembers the unit being equipped with 4x4 Ford trucks and a Coles Crane, a battery charging truck and a water bowser, and

Lance Corporal Les Forshaw is on the right of the picture, with Private Colin Moorcroft in Tunbridge Wells.

that they had trained, were well equipped and ready for war. Prior to the invasion the unit was re-titled 159 Infantry Ordnance Sub Park, and was organized into an HQ, a No. 2 section for detail and bulk store trucks and a No. 3 section for supplying and ferrying vehicles to divisional units in Kent. WOII Forshaw believed that the concept for a mobile stores unit operating well forward, arose out of the lessons learned from the need to cut out the long supply chains experienced in the Western Desert and, of course, he was right.

Also within the 21st Army Group ORBAT there were four AODs, numbers 14,15,16 and 17; and it was No. 17 that was designated to be the first ashore, supported by the Stores Company of 16 AOD, and it would have to operate with BMPs. This meant re-training the soldiers with the appropriate skills for the task, skills that were different from normal work in an AOD. The concept was exercised under field conditions and whilst it taught many valuable low level lessons there was one key message from the outcome. BMPs were structured on a formation basis, but they could not be stacked and issued as such in the confines of a beach under fire. Far better to pool them and stack by equipment and vehicle being supported across the formations, and it was in this way they were organized.

The BADs went through a similar process, but 17 BAD was broken down by companies and they were attached, from February onwards, to the beach groups to which they would provide intimate support. Smaller units, the OBDs, PODs and PADs together with the OFPs and the Ordnance Maintenance Companies went into France with the assaulting formations. Combat troops in every sense of the word, they were to go in with Marines,

Commandos and Infantry to provide the essential immediate support they would all require.

There were units in need of support that did not fit neatly into a formation that required Ordnance support, for example on the LofC, and to meet their requirements Forward Trailer Sections were created. For LofC units it was No. 14 Forward Trailer Section, carrying spares specific to that collection of units and their range of equipment. No. 15 Forward Trailer Section met the special requirements of three tank brigades, whilst 16 FTS was scaled for the special requirements of the Canadian Corps and was intended later to support 1st Canadian Army. Finally, 17 FTS met the requirements of the Guards Armoured Division and 11th Armoured Division with their Sherman Tanks, and 15th Division. This FTS held additional spares as a means of ensuring the armour could be kept on the move during the pursuit.

The OFP organization that the FTS supplemented was quite comprehensive. There were four corps OFPs, ten divisional OFPs, and nine independent brigade OFPs. Support in the division was broken down into two parts. The divisional OFP that always accompanied the division was a small unit scaled to meet the division's immediate requirements. However, the corps troop's organization was broken down into the Corps Troops OFP and a number of divisional sub-parks. These were scaled to provide backing for each division in the corps. When a division was moved from one corps to another it took with it its sub-park.

The target date for the completion of all invasion plans, known as Y-Day, was 31 May 1944. By then everything that was to be loaded had to be loaded. As Y-Day approached there was a crisis with the waterproofing on a range of vehicles and some equipments. A new process had to be worked out and applied, and the date of the invasion was at risk if it could not be done in time. Once again the RAOC met the challenge, resolved the problem and achieved the Y-Day deadline.

At the beginning of May 1944 the Rear HQ of 2nd Army moved to Fort Purbrook near Portsmouth. The Ordnance appreciation was published and staff officers could see how their efforts had come together to ensure the support of the invasion. On 13 May 16, and 17 AODs moved to their concentration areas and continued training until the move to their marshalling areas on D+8. By 31 May everything was in place – they were ready to go.

In the early hours of 6 June 1944 all the planning came together as the invasion was mounted. It was a momentous occasion, and rather took the gloss off the entry of 5th US Army into Rome and the fall of the city two days earlier on 4 June. Content as they were that they had done all they could, the

A typical trailer section, in this case near Bayeux. Sergeant Savage gives a good idea of the size of the undertaking, and the large trailers.

Ordnance staffs at 21st Army Group anxiously awaited the SITREPs that would tell them how the initial contact with the enemy was working out. It was something of a relief for them to find out that the Ordnance casualties were lighter than anticipated and that Ordnance units appeared, broadly, to be in place and functioning. But no plan ever really survives first contact with the enemy and local adjustments had to be made to take account of the weather and enemy action. It was here that the training, both as soldiers and as tradesmen, was to bear fruit.

To begin with, weather delayed the landing of the first Ordnance units by some two to three hours, and recce parties that had been assigned the task of finding sites for more advanced dumps could not get forward until D+1 since the forward troops had not cleared the area. So, since the ground for the siting of the Beach Sub Area Ordnance Dumps could not be captured in time for them to set up, initial sites had to be established just behind the beaches. It was congested and they were under constant enemy fire.

Perhaps some idea of the improvisation that was occasionally necessary might be gained by examining the fate of 11 OBD and half of 44 Ammunition Company that were to be part of the early fighting in 101 Beach Sub Area, at the western end of the landing beaches. They were scheduled to land on the first tide and set up four sector stores dumps in the gardens of the houses some fifty yards off the beach. They had to be ready to issue ammunition within four hours of landing, and during this time they had to secure themselves following the landing, ferry the ammunition across the beach, clear the site of mines and assemble their stacks; and do so under fire. The ammunition was in four LCTs, two of which would land two hours into the landings, and the second two at four hours.

It was an uneventful crossing, LCTs carrying 200 tons of ammunition, twenty tons of engineer stores, five 3-ton trucks and an anti-tank platoon, a medical jeep and with about thirty-five soldiers crammed in. Feeding was basic, but given the twists and turns caused by the swell in the Channel there was not too much interest in eating. Sitting off the French coast early in the morning they were able to watch the bombardment by the Royal Navy of the shore defences, and then see the assault troops going in.

Then as they moved on towards the beach they began to experience sporadic enemy shellfire. The two landing craft containing twenty-nine officers and men from 44 Ammunition Company and 11 OBD ground onto a landing on Queen White and Queen Red beaches at precisely H+120 minutes. The sight that greeted them was one bordering on chaos. All the exits were jammed with tanks and moving vehicles was, to all intents and purposes, impossible. With mortar and light machine-gun fire from snipers, added to the shellfire now that they were ashore, they were faced with little choice but to dig in at the back of the beach and to wait for instructions. Their wait lasted only an hour, and they whiled away their time watching with some satisfaction the preferred method, developed that morning, of dealing with the snipers. It involved a 105-mm shell fired directly over open sites from a self-propelled artillery gun straight into the sniper's position. One shot was usually sufficient.

Eventually the Ordnance party got off the beach and split to go to the first two sector dumps and almost immediately took their first casualties as a Bren gun carrier hit a mine and wounded a number of men, one of them seriously. On arrival at the dumps the process of mine clearing was undertaken at once to clear an area in which to start work. In one of the sites, the garden of a large villa, twenty Teller anti-tank mines were discovered and lifted, one in five of them having been booby-trapped.

The first ammunition arrived at H+270, the other two parties for the next two sector stores dumps having beached just thirty minutes beforehand. One of their landing craft had been hit in the engine room and was abandoned, but the men moved off to prepare the other two storage sites for the stores and ammunition that would follow. Almost as fast as the dumps were cleared, stocks began to arrive, as did demands for units already calling out for replenishment. In particular demand was the 105-mm ammunition for the self-propelled artillery – it was being consumed very rapidly indeed; and the guns were only half a mile from the dump. The distances between the four dumps were only 400 yards, insufficient even for ammunition storage safety distances.

Landings later that day, on the second tide, were less successful due to deteriorating weather, and in one incident a sergeant from 12 OBD was drowned. It was also obvious by the time the second wave arrived that the original deployment plan could not be followed as fighting was still going on and there were enemy troops still active. This meant cramming more into the existing stores dumps, and expanding the areas allotted to them. Dexterous use of a bulldozer or two was called for, but in the end space was made.

There was still some threat from snipers, but perhaps the greatest danger came from enthusiastic Royal Naval gunners. Manning 20-mm anti-aircraft cannon, but with no aircraft to shoot at, they would take on anything that moved in the houses behind the beach. The lie of the land was such that cannon shots fired at upstairs windows in these houses, and over flying, crossed the stores' dumps at about head height. The 20-mm round carries an HE filling, and aside from the risk to life and limb of these things flying about, there was also some danger associated with the stacks of ammunition in the dumps being hit by an HE round; or being set fire to by the tracer.

As it happened the only serious fire was on D+2, when a lone aircraft managed to sneak through and drop a single bomb on an RASC petroleum installation that was sited rather too near an ammunition dump. Burning petrol flooded through the dump and accounted for 450 tons of ammunition before burning itself out. For his courage in seeking to prevent the spread of the flames Sergeant McGowan of 44 Company was awarded the George Medal. Together with Sergeant Alden and Captain Thompson and others they were literally breaking down 105-mm boxes with their bare hands in order to move the ammunition; and at the height of the fire 105-mm shells were exploding at the rate of about ten per minute and scattering shrapnel to a distance of 200 yards around the dump. Indeed, it was one of these shells exploding that cost Captain Thompson his life, and it is a surprise that of the 100 or so men involved in fighting the fire, more were not injured.

The stores elements of 11 OBD had a far more eventful crossing. Their craft was shelled as it arrived 700 yards from its beaching point. One of the landing craft was hit, with the engine room catching fire and it had to be flooded in order to extinguish the flames. The second landing craft also caught fire and had to be abandoned, whilst the third, having survived the odd near miss, detonated a mine on beaching and broke its back.

Eventually the OBD got ashore in reasonable order, only to come under intense enemy rifle and machine-gun fire. Leaving the soldiers dug in the officers went forward to recce the dump sites. When they got back they found their soldiers had not taken cover as ordered but were helping fill in the ruts caused by tanks moving up the beach in order to make it easier for others to follow. Gathering everyone together the officers led the way back up to the dump sites, to find one of them under intense mortar fire and heavily mined. The Sappers declared themselves unable or unwilling to clear the site, so the OBD's own mine clearing team set about the task, assisted by the rest of the detachment prodding with their bayonets to uncover the location of the mines. Between them they cleared eighty mines before stocks began to arrive and they got started on their proper job.

One thing was clear – the training for war they had undertaken prior to the landings proved to have been essential. Mine clearing, neutralization of booby-traps, clearing of enemy equipment, neutralization of snipers and the clearing of elements of the enemy bypassed by the advancing troops were just some of the tasks, in addition to their RAOC duties, that they were called upon to undertake.

As the armies advanced inland they were followed by Ordnance parties recceing sites for larger dumps to be established away from the beaches. On D+2 and D+3 parties from 17 BAD, 1 OMC and the Canadian Ordnance Company landed. One recce party, however, never made it. Staff Sergeant Ken Lloyd was part of the recce team for 17 AOD, in his case representing 17 Vehicle Company:

. . .we were on our way from Gosport to Gold Beach when our landing craft was torpedoed at night. The OC, Lt Col Holman, and several other senior officers and other ranks were all lost.

Just part of 17 Vehicle Company would take up quite a large area, as shown in Sergeant Savage's sketch.

The CO, me, Colonel Gore, and Private Jack Whitehead were the only survivors. Much reorganization was necessary and Major Sumpter became Lieutenant Colonel as OC.

Despite the grievous loss of key officers and NCOs, others stepped into the breech and the depot was established and running on time. Reserve vehicles began to arrive on D+7 and beach maintenance packs on D+8 as the initial stock for 17 AOD. Between 15 and 30 June this depot, with its new leadership in place, handled 20,000 tons of stores; something like 1,300 tons a day. 15 BAD opened on D+14 and 12 BAD landed on D+18. Over 7,000 tons of ammunition a day was brought across the beaches to support the fighting formations inland and to build the reserves.

Laundries and bath units began to arrive, moving inland to provide a laundry service mainly for hospitals, but they would also launder personal items when time and resources permitted. The bath units were a huge morale booster, offering every soldier the chance of a shower at least once a week. Industrial gas units also made their way across the beaches.

Other familiar names were also moving ashore. Sergeant Alderman, last encountered in the Ordnance depot in Olympia came ashore as part of a forward maintenance unit. Officer Cadet Bretherton from Foremark Hall OCTU was by now a junior officer:

I joined 30 Corps Ordnance Field Park, a unit of about 120 men including clerks, storemen, drivers, fitters, cooks, orderlies etc, headed by a major with three other officers. During the first half of 1944 the emphasis was on obtaining the stores that we would hold to support 30 Corps, and at the same time, getting all the vehicles and equipment that we ourselves needed as a mobile unit, including such

Staff Sergeant Ken Lloyd RAOC, a Private soldier at Normandy, with the photograph taken when he ended his war, still a Private at that stage, with 17 Vehicle Company in Hamburg.

12 BAD held its stocks by the roadside. Sergeant Savage shows a lack of camouflage netting which would appear to indicate that the air threat was not considered a problem.

1 Base Laundry at Vaucelles, after Sergeant Savage.

items as a water truck battery charger, cranes etc.

Shortly after D-Day COD Donnington was beset with demands for additional anti-aircraft weapons to combat the V1 flying bomb menace that had been visited on London. COD Greenford, being in the London area, was prone to attacks by these weapons and, in August 1944, one landed as a squad of ATS were marching through the depot. There were fifty-seven casualties, of which seven had to be hospitalized.

30 Corps OFP disembarked at Arromanches on D+20, the divisional OFPs having arrived earlier. There followed several weeks in a very crowded beachhead. Every field seemed to be occupied by a unit of some kind or other, vehicles and tents hugging the hedgerows, covered by camouflage netting.

Lieutenant Tom Bretherton again:

There was a lot of movement in the area, including the collection of supplies. We returned to the landing area to pick up shipments that had come in for us. The quartermasters of the combat units came for their requirements, guided by a maze of company signs and emblems, and usually placed on the verges of the roads. There was a danger in placing these signs as the Germans had buried mines along the roadsides. The sappers had to clear them, and then place a line of white tape to indicate clearance, but this was not always complete and the white tape sometimes got removed. Movement was difficult as the roads had been severely damaged by battle and some of them were simply new routes across land covered by army track i.e. heavy wire mesh. Sometimes it took hours to go a few miles, such were the traffic queues. We often had to visit other units in the supply line to get urgent items, sometimes US units, who were very helpful.

The OFPs were transported to France in LSTs and all vehicles had been modified by waterproofing measures such as ducting the exhausts to a higher position in case we had to land in high water. On arrival at Arromanches I noticed that among all the destruction there was just one building standing in the beach area. (On revisiting the place many years later I was intrigued to find the area seemingly full of old buildings – an indication of how imaginatively the French had rebuilt in an attractive old style.)

The smell of death, mainly from dead cattle, hit us as soon as we landed and stayed with us all the time we were in the bridgehead. It was not unusual to drive along a road and find a ridge ahead formed by the backbone of a cow. So much – living creatures as well as inanimate objects – had been crushed in the bombardments. I cannot imagine what the local people went through. Not many civilians were in evidence and the only things we could buy locally were lettuces and Camembert cheese, perhaps also sometimes Calvados, which was very potent! We had been issued with specially printed French money, at the rate of 200 francs to the pound. At times there was widespread enteritis among the troops, no doubt caused by so much rotting matter lying around.

Much of our equipment and many of our vehicles were of US origin. There was a lot of ack-ack activity at night time, notwithstanding the superiority of the allied air forces. The Ordnance supply system worked well. Instruction books relevant to campaign conditions were received by the OFP soon after arrival in Normandy. Each case arriving from the UK showed the degree of urgency, in accordance with a given code. More generally, the whole OVERLORD operation was remarkable for its organization, bearing in mind that these were pre-computer days. We were always kept supplied with food and fuel, and there was even a weekly laundry system.

By D+17 the receipt of stores into the beach sub areas had virtually ceased and everything was moving forward into 17 AOD and 17 BAD. The final clearing out of the OBDs allowed the manpower to be re-distributed to reinforce the depots and speed their workload. Key in this was the creation of a returned stores capability for the repair, refurbishing and re-issue of battle winning equipment. This was in addition to a returned stores depot that had been operated by 1 OMC from D+7, but this had

The sorting area of 3 SD of 17 AOD on D+24.

been principally concerned with the collection of unaccompanied AFG1098 and for captured enemy equipment being returned to the UK for examination and assessment.

Demand for replenishment was by a process known as close theatre maintenance. Demands were flown from Normandy to RAF Northholt in West London where a motorcycle would take them to COD Greenford nearby. Here there was an indent-clearing centre which redirected indents, again via dispatch rider, to the appropriate depot for the item. In an ideal world most of them would have been routed to COD Basing. This was formed from a converted part of the CAD at Bramley, whose location in the central south of England made it ideal for supplying armies operating in France. There were the inevitable stocking problems, chiefly caused by changes of priority, but this was compensated by the location being so ideally placed to provide support to 21st Army Group. The original plan was that it would hold maintenance stocks only, but this was swiftly revised to allow the depot to make up deficiencies in unit equipments. It was also given the task of assembling and storing the clothing and general stores for nineteen landing reserves and eighteen beach maintenance packs. From D-Day to the end of the war in Europe COD Basing met 220,000 indents from 21st Army Group.

Once selected at the depot of choice under the close theatre maintenance system the items would be sent to a main base stores transit depot, based at Micheldever in Hampshire, which had the task of collating these demands into formation packs with appropriate identification, whereupon they were sent to the docks for dispatch by the Ordnance ship to the beaches. This ship was a small coaster, staffed entirely by RAOC personnel responsible for ensuring the highest priority stores were not shut out on loading and were offloaded and sent first to their destination; and then ensuring that the rest of the load arrived at its intended destination.

WOII Forshaw also moved across the channel, but some time after the initial landings:

In late June 1944 we vacated our billets in the town (Tunbridge Wells) and after collecting some 6-pounder anti tank guns to be towed by the bulk trucks the unit moved to the London docks and loaded onto a liberty ship.

At about the same time Alan Midgley was having problems on two fronts. It was D+23 and he was supposed to drive a 15cwt Ford truck ashore to join 16 Stores Transit Sub-Depot and it wouldn't start. It wasn't helped by the fact that he had developed raging toothache on the crossing. Regarding the truck:

I arranged for the derricks to load it onto the tank landing craft and my colleague, also with a 15cwt truck, in front of me to tow me off the TLC. As no extension of the exhaust pipe was fitted the operation was dependent upon keeping the throttle wide open to stop the sea water running back into the engine. As luck would have it a jetty, part of the Mulberry Harbour, was in service so that the towing vehicle was able to land on the jetty and pull my vehicle up the hill at Arromanches.

At that point he got his truck started, and then had to deal with the tooth. He managed to make himself the first patient in a newly arrived dental unit and had it taken out there and then.

One of the early hindrances to progress in breaking out from the beachhead was that Caen, due for capture on the first day, held out and was eventually assaulted on 9 July. The assault was the baptism of fire for 59th Division, which was being supported by WOII Forshaw and 59th Division OSP. The Division later attacked south-east from Caen. The OSP was constantly on the move as a result, '...experiencing the devastation of war and the accompanying nauseating smell of death'.

Eventually 59th Division was broken up and 159 OSP was attached to the Polish Armoured Division in the Canadian Army. The OSP would remain with the Poles until their war ended on the north German plain, at Osnabrück.

The breakout from the beachhead came at the end of July. On 25 July when the US Army broke out of its beachhead at St Lô it drove south towards the River Loire. A German armoured group sought to cut off this move but was contained by stubborn US resistance and was destroyed largely by fighter ground attack from the RAF and the USAAF. Elements of the US 1st and 3rd Armies swung north from the Loire, whilst the British and Canadian armies moved south, and trapped all the German armour in the Normandy area in a pocket near Falaise. However, as the German army inside the pocket was being destroyed, the jaws were held open by the two divisions of II SS Panzer Corps – the 9th SS Pz (Hohenstaufen) Division and the 10th SS Pz (Frundsberg) Division. They were eventually to escape to the north-east, the only complete formations, albeit badly battered, to be able to escape the carnage. What was left of the German Army in Normandy began to flee, back towards Belgium, Holland and Germany, hotly pursued by an Allied army that now scented victory.

In anticipation of the breakout from the Normandy beachhead, 15 AOD was brought into an already overcrowded Rear Maintenance Area. The overcrowding had its advantages, in that the short distances meant that demands could be met swiftly, but there was nonetheless a sense of relief when the breakout did come and there was room to breath as 2nd Army moved forward in the direction of Falaise.

These were major events, but, elsewhere, minor events were taking place that had major impact on individuals. Private C Sayer had been captured at the fall of Singapore and had spent most of his imprisonment since February 1942 building the Burma railway. However, in June 1944 the Japanese had begun to draft prisoners back to Japan and he was selected.

July 4th the dilapidated Japanese

Also in the RMA was 3 Sub-Depot, seen here in bad weather. Note the POWs in the background, being put to work.

merchantman Hofuka Maru, a converted troopship, was slowly steaming from Singapore with its human cargo of 1,200 British prisoners of war. Glad were they to leave behind the two years of hell they had spent as prisoners in Burma and Siam, where the graves of so many of their comrades were constant reminders of the terrific toll of life taken in the construction of the Bam Pong Mulmein railroad.

The effect of the breakout from Normandy and the pursuit was to increase very swiftly the space taken up by the RMA; and the 2nd Army road head was moved forward to the area of Falaise. However, the major problem from the outset was the shortage of transport to deliver stores forward. And soon the shortages of transport were to be exacerbated by the difficulties of delivering fuel forward as the advance gained momentum and began to sweep east towards the German border and north-east to the Belgian and Dutch borders.

One of the advantages and the disadvantages of the time spent within the relatively narrow confines of the beachhead was that the LofC was short. Whilst this had allowed for a speedy service, which had pleased everybody, this close proximity of Ordnance support and the relative lack of movement by fighting formations, at least over any great distance, meant they had the opportunity to stockpile reserves that they thought they might need. However, once they were on the move they had no means of carrying it and much of it was left behind. Of course, it had been issued from Ordnance stocks, and so therefore was no longer an asset, and before it could become an asset it had to be brought back into Ordnance hands, inspected and put to stock. A waste of time and resources, and a clear demonstration of a weakness in the overall system of stock control due to lack of visibility of stocks held forward of Ordnance accounting units.

The DOS 21st Army Group, who had taken responsibility for control of the theatre Ordnance effort on 13 July, decided that supporting the advance with an AOD on the Seine was not an effective use of resources. Instead, he intended to use OFPs well stocked and well forward. There were also pools of controlled stores held with 1 and 4 OMCs. Two FTS were to be held in reserve and FMA packs of clothing and other fast moving stores were fed forward regularly, whether requested or not. And in reserve was 15 AOD, waiting to form the nucleus of an advanced base once a suitable port was captured.

At the outset of the operation it had been decided that the vehicle companies of the AODs would remain under the command of their respective COOs. However, when the breakout took place this was no longer practical as the stores side of the AODs increased greatly along with the vehicle holdings of the vehicle parks. Consequently, control of the vehicle parks was vested in a COO who would control all their activity centrally; and this command of the combined vehicle parks remained in place. It was a sound move, for the turnover experienced was five times greater than that anticipated. As soon as the breakout was achieved nominated AVPs moved up with their formations, and other AVPs set up along the LofC. The speed of the advance when it came imposed a huge strain on these vehicle units and they absorbed any spare manpower, including reinforcements, trying to keep the advanced parks filled so that demands for vehicles could be met as swiftly as possible.

The vehicle problem was one among many, and was huge. There were 700 different types ranging from a folding airborne motorcycle to a tank transporter, seventy feet long. They included armoured cars, flame-thrower tanks, mobile cranes, surgeries, telephone exchanges, printing shops, pigeon vans, office trucks, and many, many more. The average stock grew to 45,000 and required 150 miles of hard standing. It was a similar situation in the United Kingdom, where the expansion had brought proportionately the same problem. The vehicle organization had gone through many gyrations in the process of taking a worldwide holding that had been 44,000 in September 1939 and had increased to 1,403,000 by the end of the war. For the Normandy operation the Chilwell sub depots that had been created to cope with the load, prepared 34,000 assemblies for shipment together with 8,000 tons of

An 'A' Vehicle Park, one of many vehicle parks for a whole range of vehicles.

tank tracks. By August 1945 the organization would comprise 190 separate premises on both covered and open sites and its stocks would include nearly 250,000 major assemblies, 750,000 covers and tubes and 150,000 tons of tank track.

To ensure a good flow of ammunition once the break out came it was decided to base 3 BAD on the Seine once the Army had got that far, keeping 17 BAD free to leapfrog when the length of the LofC justified it. There was a third BAD, held in reserve in the UK in case it was needed.

Mobile laundries, hospital laundries, industrial gas units; even officers' shops – they all moved up the line in support of the advancing armies. Everything that could be put in place was in place and the message from the records of the time was clear; no one would run short. Their customer, the word being used even in 1944, would want for nothing he needed to destroy the enemy.

Lieutenant Bretherton and the rest of 30 Corps OFP followed the pursuit:

When the Allies broke out of the bridgehead the army movements across France, Belgium and Holland were rapid and Ordnance formations were involved in a lot of changes of units and individuals between the various corps as we moved forward. One feature of the advance from Normandy was the need for constant convoys by RAOC units which included stores trucks,

No 1 Base Industrial Gas Unit following the advance.

Local labour had to be employed to cope with the workload, like these clerks at 14 AOD on D+100...

vehicles for issue, guns, etc. We had to move fast, day or night, and usually found the roads passable. The problem was to keep the convoys intact, not to lose any stragglers and to ensure that there was enough clearance under bridges for high vehicles such as mobile cranes. The use of dispatch riders to help do this was a great advantage. There was hardly any civilian traffic but, of course, a great many military vehicles of all kinds.

During the war we operated the Ordnance procedures as they were set out for us, without much thought as to how they had developed. On reflection, in view of the size of the army in wartime, several times that of pre-war days, there must have been an immense effort in the period leading up to the war to devise and install a system that could cope with such an increase in scale. I was told that Major General Williams was the officer mainly responsible for this and had burned much midnight oil working on it. This seems to me an important part of RAOC history.

Another outstanding RAOC officer, who was my CO for a short time before I was posted to 30 Corps OFP, was Brigadier R V Blundell. He was ADOS of the 3rd Infantry Division and a Lieutenant Colonel at that time. A regular soldier, he had been an instructor at Foremark Hall and later served in the Korean War, being awarded the CBE. I met him many years later, by chance, when we were both living in the Isle of Wight and we became friends. Brigadier Blundell joined the army at Hilsea Barracks, Portsmouth as a bugle boy in the inter-war period and had the distinction of holding every rank in the army up to brigadier. I was told that his achievements were held up to new recruits as an example of the possible!

However, the speed of movement of the Allied armies was too fast for the logistics. Paris was liberated on 25 August and Brussels on 3 September. Everywhere, the Germans were in turmoil, retreating headlong before an apparently unstoppable Allied advance. Air superiority, command of the sea, unlimited supplies; the Allies had it all, the war would be over by Christmas, or so it seemed.

But, there was a dilemma, and its root lay in the logistic problems being created by the lack of a port on the channel coast. The difficulty was that whilst much of the German army had indeed been in headlong retreat, there were pockets of brave, well-led men holding out on the French coast in places like Boulogne, Calais and Dunkirk, denying the Allies the use of the ports and, with every mile they

...and as well as local labour, POWs were put to good use, here working with a Pioneer.

drove, their problems became worse.

It was 450 miles to Cherbourg, the only workable port, and a little less to the landing beaches. Supplying four huge armies over those distances was a nightmare. The lack of infrastructure, such as railways and pipelines meant that everything had to be carried by truck, of which there was a frustrating shortage. The British had left an entire army corps west of the Seine just in order to use its vehicles for the move of supplies. Adding to the transport problem was the fact that men were tired, and so was their equipment. Such had been the speed of advance that there had been no time for rest or for maintenance, and the toll was beginning to tell.

However, overshadowing everything was the shortage of gasoline. One million gallons a day were required; a fraction of that was getting through. In Belgium, as the enemy fled before it, an entire US Corps ground to a halt for four days, and Patton's views, as his US 3rd Army, heading for the Saar, stopped for want of fuel, are well known: '...my men can eat their belts, but my tanks have gotta have gas.'

There was a famous directive that Montgomery issued to the British 30 Corps commander: 'Horrocks, take Antwerp, Monty.' It has been held up as a model directive, making the objective clear, but without interfering in the commander's means of executing it. Regrettably, in the interests of brevity, it failed to mention that taking Antwerp, and then for it to be used as a port, meant also taking the north bank of the Scheldt, thereby controlling entry to the port.

Major General Roberts, commanding the 11th Armoured Division, rolled into the city and captured it, and its docks, complete, on 4 September, the Germans having failed to blow them up. However, by not striking north and taking bridgeheads over the Albert Canal, the British committed one of the great miscalculations of the war. Everyone was concentrating on crossing the Rhine and getting on into Germany, and simply failed to take the time properly to consider all the implications of making Antwerp a useable port, despite the logistic problems they were facing. Failure of judgement and foresight at the strategic level was translated into lack of impetus at the operational and tactical level. Tired, as they were, 11th Armoured Division could and should have carried on and finished the job. Horrocks was to say later that it simply hadn't crossed his mind – he was too focussed on the need to get across the Rhine, and this despite the impact that lack of logistic support was already having on his own formation's activities.

As Antwerp was taken Major John Wykes was following up just behind the Guards Armoured Division and went away to their west and into Antwerp as it was liberated. However the Germans did hit back, with missiles:

Adverse weather in the Channel would also inhibit the operation of the Mulberry harbour, further limiting the flow of supplies.

Through the V1 and V2 bombardment we lost several Ordnance Sections, and my Sergeant Chief Clerk was killed by a shell through the office window. I had only just left the office and rushed back for him to die while I was holding him.

Private George Grimes was with 16 Forward Trailer Section, tasked with the support of the Canadians. One of the V1s in Antwerp, he remembers, killed four and wounded four more of his unit.

The shortages of supplies led to a re-awakening of the debate that had taken place in England while the invasion was being planned: whether to advance on a broad front, driving all before them in a steady move into Germany, or to select key thrusts and drive on a narrow front, or perhaps series of fronts, like rapiers into the heart of the Fatherland. Montgomery favoured the narrow approach, and formed the view that all fronts except one should go onto the defensive and one single solid thrust should be directed at the Ruhr with the aim of breaking through the Siegfried Line, knocking out Germany's main power base, the Ruhr, and driving on to Berlin. He envisaged forty-two divisions, of which twenty were armoured.

Eisenhower could not agree to the scheme for a number of reasons. In no particular order: he doubted the wisdom of the strategy; he was concerned that a thrust of the sort recommended by Montgomery could well run out of steam and be cut off if it encountered unexpected resistance; and with so much having been put into it his capacity for recovering the situation would be limited.

There were also the political considerations. Such a move would mean placing large US formations under Montgomery's command. Not only that, but the British could be seen to be 'grabbing the glory' in a war in which the US had invested so much. Neither of these two features would sit easily with the American public or their politicians. Consequently, Eisenhower rejected Montgomery's proposals. However, as the broad front strategy came to a halt for want of supplies, another problem loomed: V2 rockets launched from northern Holland had begun falling on London on 8 September. Something needed to be done about them.

Montgomery met Eisenhower at Brussels Airport on 10 September and proposed to him a variation of the narrow front theme. He suggested laying a carpet of airborne troops over the main waterways in Holland to provide a corridor through which ground forces would advance, crossing the Nieder Rhine at Arnhem and fanning out into the plains of northern Europe to remove the V2 sites, free the port of Antwerp, outflank the Siegfried Line, take out the Ruhr and drive for Berlin.

Eisenhower agreed to the plan for several reasons. He was under pressure to use the very experienced and highly trained 1st Allied Airborne Army. At present it was sitting, very frustrated, in England, as the pace of the Allied advance through Europe caused airborne operation after operation to be cancelled as the reasons for them vanished under the tracks of the advancing land armies. If successful it could revitalize the gradually slowing push towards the Ruhr. And, finally, he now had the imperative of trying to do something about the V2 rockets.

His agreement, however, was tempered. Montgomery would receive no priority for logistic support, and once at Arnhem he was to await an assessment of the new situation before 'breaking out'. There was to be no mad uncoordinated dash onto the north German plain. Montgomery was unhappy with the limitations, but nonetheless seized the opportunity to demonstrate the validity of his vision.

The operation was to be code named MARKET GARDEN. MARKET was the airborne carpet and three airborne divisions were to pave the way. The 101st US Airborne Division, the Screaming Eagles, was to land north of Eindhoven, the 82nd Airborne Division, the All American, was to land around Nijmegen and 1st British Airborne Division was to land at Arnhem. Their task was to capture a range of bridges over the waterways to allow the armour of the British 2nd Army, spearheaded by 30 Corps, to drive up the road and on into the open plains beyond the water obstacles. This part of the operation was code named GARDEN

However, on 4 September Hitler recalled von Rundstedt to retake command of the German armies

Lieutenant Colonel Gerry Mobbs RAOC was the ADOS of 1st Airborne Division. He would be wounded on the last night of the battle and taken prisoner.

in the west. He had sacked the Field Marshal some two months earlier following a series of disagreements regarding the best way to halt and then stem the Allied advance. Recalled to Hitler's headquarters at the end of August von Rundstedt had been appalled at the situation he saw, with the Russians holding in the east a front more than 1,400 miles long from Finland to Romania, whilst in the west division after division had been destroyed.

Von Rundstedt proceeded westwards to relieve Model, the third change of command since 2 July. On the same day, in Wannsee near Berlin, Colonel General Kurt Student, the father of German Airborne Forces, was brought out of the obscurity into which he had descended following the appalling losses suffered by German airborne soldiers in taking Crete. He was ordered to found a new Army: First Parachute Army. It was a force that didn't exist, and would comprise troops scattered all over Germany. They were mostly green recruits, although there were some seasoned units. There were some 10,000 men with no artillery, transport, armour or staff. However, his task was to hold a gigantic hole between Antwerp and Maastricht, holding a line along the Albert Canal. He was ordered to rush his forces to Holland, and to pick up weapons and equipment at railheads of destination. To move his whole force would take four days; remarkable in itself. However, his best units would be on the Albert Canal within twenty-four hours.

Model's last order before von Rundstedt took over would prove to be significant. *Obergruppenführer*, or Lieutenant General, Willi Bittrich, commander of II SS Panzer Corps, having escaped the Falaise Pocket in July, seeking orders, visited him. He was ordered to take his two battered armoured divisions, the 9th and the 10th, north into Holland for refit. Model chose a quiet spot, some seventy-five miles behind the front, near Arnhem.

In Holland, things were changing. The headlong retreat was slowing, order was being brought to the chaos as loyal senior officers began to draw together the shambles that was heading north and east. Equipment began to arrive from Germany; fresh troops began to appear on the scene. The door that had been open to the Allies was about to slam shut in their faces, and logistics were the cause of it; not the work of the logisticians, but the lack of attention paid to their needs and to the relevance of opening key ports to shorten the LofC.

On 17 September, just seven days after the meeting at Brussels airport, the Allies launched the largest airborne attack in history. Some 35,000 men were to drop over three days up to sixty-five miles, in the case of the British, behind enemy lines. That part of Holland was a RMA for the Germans in Europe, and the troops were not of the best. However, with Student and others denying 30 Corps an easy drive up their corridor, and the 9th and 10th SS available to make life very difficult indeed in both Arnhem and Nijmegen it was an operation that did not go according to plan.

In Arnhem itself, the distance from the dropping and landing zones to the objective, poor communications, the presence of much stiffer than expected German resistance, and some appalling command and control decisions saw only 700 of the 10,000 British reach the Arnhem Bridge, the remainder being hemmed into a defensive pocket six miles to the west at Oosterbeek. The RAOC element consisted of twenty-seven officers and men from 1st Airborne Division HQ RAOC and its OFP. This included a detachment of six men who went to the bridge. Commanded by Captain Bernard Manley his task was to:

…commandeer any useable vehicle I could find. The intention was to create a vehicle park.

Instead he and his men ended up defending the bridge with the rest of the airborne soldiers who

Captain Bernard Manley RAOC.

made it that far, in a battle that has become a legend.

The fighting was hard and relentless, with no quarter sought or given. Private Ted Mordecai was one of the bridge party and one short story from him exemplifies this. Ted and his staff sergeant, Harry Walker, were on watch when they saw movement at the top of the embankment to their front. Slowly, two German soldiers emerged from different parts of the high ground, and a little way apart. Quite what they were up to was not certain, and they did not appear to know there were British soldiers about. Agreeing that Walker would take the one on the right, who was behind a tree, and that Mordecai would attend to the other one behind a bush, they raised their Sten guns and fired:

Private Ted Mordecai RAOC.

Harry dropped his man almost immediately and mine came down the bank on his hands and knees screaming out with pain and fear. I gave him another short burst and he stopped screaming and rolled down the bank to lie perfectly still at the foot of it.

Eventually, the whole bridge party was taken prisoner, but lived to tell the tale. Ted, a weapons storeman, was the last soldier manning a machine gun at the bridge, right until late in the last evening. Lieutenant Colonel John Frost, who commanded 2nd Parachute Battalion at the bridge would always, and justifiably, pay compliments to his beloved 2nd Battalion. Yet he was the first to acknowledge that the defence was conducted by soldiers drawn from many regiments and corps, but with one thing in common: they were all airborne soldiers and that made them indistinguishable, one from the other, each trained, above all else, as a fighting soldier. They were, regardless of parent cap-badge, a breed apart.

The same was true of the OFP parked in the DAA in Oosterbeek. Four would die before the battle was over, and only one, Corporal Freddy Grantham, has a known grave. Four more would escape as the division evacuated the area after nine days intense fighting; the rest were captured and some wounded. The ADOS, Lieutenant Colonel Gerry Mobbs was one of those wounded, as was Major C C (Bill) Chidgey who commanded the OFP. When asked how an officer with the initials 'C C' came to be called 'Bill', Major Chidgey was wont to reply, occasionally sternly: '…if your names were Cecil Cyril, you'd be called Bill too!'

Further down the corridor the sea tail of the Airborne Division included as part of it the balance of

A group of soldiers from the Airborne OFP. Corporal Freddie Grantham RAOC is circled.

the Airborne OFP. They only ever got as far as Nijmegen, arriving just in time to help those who had got safely back across the river, before returning whence they came. Sergeant 'Chopper' Collins remembered: 'We saw Reg Plowman (a sergeant from the OFP who managed to cross the river) walking through Nijmegen, so we

The Sea Tail of 1st Airborne Division OFP just north of Eindhoven during one of the many halts on the corridor. The unit tactical sign '89' is clearly visible on vehicles.

picked him up and gave him a lift back to England.'

Perhaps we can leave the last word on Arnhem to Bill Chidgey: 'I'm still very upset at the loss, at that late stage, of the fine men of our little unit who had performed so well throughout the operation.'

During the Arnhem battle Private Sayer was still on his converted troopship suffering appalling conditions, impossible food, dreadful heat, ghastly sanitation and illness spreading faster and faster among the prisoners. Ninety-six had already died and the ship was anchored in a cove at a Philippine Island and Private Sayer was cleaning the latrines on deck when American aircraft attacked the convoy of which they were a part. Many of the prisoners were killed or went down with the ship, but Private Sayer was blown over the side into the water.

> The shore was some seven miles away and meeting one other fellow we decided to try and stick together and try to get into the jungle. After swimming some six hours we were quite close to the beach and could see Japanese soldiers waiting to 'welcome' us, so we altered course and swam parallel to the shore.

Filipinos, who were very friendly and spoke English, found him and his friend naked. They were given clothes and fed, and then were handed over to the Filipino police who were, despite being under the nominal control of the Japanese, guerrillas. They found themselves among friends.

Following Arnhem there was a settling down in the west as the Armies sought to recover from the failed airborne drops and planned what to do next. The obvious choice was a crossing of the Rhine, but before anything could be done winter had set in and the Allies found themselves repelling Hitler's offensive in the Ardennes aimed at taking Antwerp, splitting the Allies and destroying what was by then developing into a major logistic base and port of entry since its capture in November. Its significance was huge, with its massive capacity outstripping the total throughput of the other channel ports combined. And, of course, it shortened massively the LofC to the armies in the north, making far better use of transport and reducing greatly the fuel requirement for the re-supply loop.

Those not involved in repelling the German advance spent the winter largely stationary, refitting and preparing for what would be the crossing of the Rhine in the spring of 1945. Private Murdoch, whom we last saw at the fire in Donnington, was one such:

> Our unit, the 31st Tank Brigade Ordnance Field Park, was stationed in Eindhoven, and was billeted in the school room of the church and convent. Someone

Sergeant Savage drew 15 ABOD as he saw it.

The graph shows the huge difference the opening of Antwerp, shown as the light coloured peaks on the right, made to the logistic capacity of the Channel and North Sea ports.

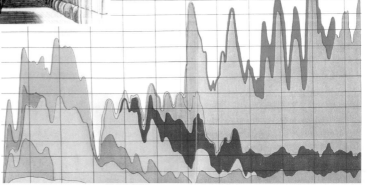

Above: Once Antwerp was taken as much use as possible was made of accommodation as well served as possible by road and rail, as with 2 GS Depot…

…although conditions were not always of the best, largely due to the weather…

…as Major Parnaby and Brigadier R R M Mayhew discovered…

…although some of the field storage was good, as here in 3 TSD of 17 AOD…

...and there was some excellent accommodation as with this shed being prepared for inloading...

mentioned that the bells of the church had been stolen by the Germans. The bells were found at a place called Tilburg and brought back to Eindhoven. The bells were put into place and it was decided to ring them on New Year's Eve but a fault was discovered so the ringing of the bells was postponed. When the fault was rectified the bells were rung and the public celebrated.

...whilst HQ RAOC 21st Army Group found somewhere nice in Antwerp for the winter...

There was another celebration in the United Kingdom with the dedication of a new church at CAD Nesscliffe on 7 January 1945. It was very much an extension of an existing Nissen hut church, which fell far short of what the people stationed at Nesscliffe felt was necessary. The materials were sourced from places about which it is probably best not to ask; the workers were drawn from the talent found in the depot, from a private clerk who carried out the excellent plasterwork to a junior commander who executed the attractive pulpit fall. Building had commenced in the spring of 1944 and the eventual result was a tower with an oak cross and stained glass window as the major features, with external doors in oak with hand wrought metal fittings. There were beautiful gothic arches inside and the walls were all panelled. It was truly a labour of love. On 27 May 1945 it played home to the BBC morning service.

By now, Private Sayer was well ensconced with his new-found friends in the Philippines. He had been put in touch with American officers on clandestine operations to help the guerrillas in their war against the Japanese and was now commissioned as an assistant regimental supply officer. His regiment was a force of

16 Forward Trailer Section had, by December, reached a position at Tilburg in Holland.

31 Tank Brigade OFP in Eindhoven, having sorted out the bells.

four Americans, 250 Filipinos, who were all ex-regular scouts, and himself. 'I had now acquired a pair of shoes and a .45 revolver and had been given a squad of men.' He saw to their feeding and to their equipping, using equipment delivered by the Americans, and joined them as they raided and gathered intelligence about the Japanese. Bridges were destroyed, lorries sabotaged and convoys ambushed. He was nearly caught once when the group he was with were betrayed, but they escaped, one of them by jumping over a 100 foot cliff, yet remaining unhurt.

His last adventure was at the end of January:

We were ordered from Bataan to Zambales as the Americans were effecting another landing there. The guerrillas were to take the airstrip at Aglas. It was a long march over the mountains, but everybody was in high spirits and the march was made without incident. On arrival we found other guerrilla units there and at night the airstrip was attacked. By morning some 300 Japanese had been killed, the remainder fled to the hills, and thirty Japanese bombers were destroyed. That morning the American invasion force landed to be met by ...instead of bullets handshakes.

Within a few days he had been recovered by the Americans and, after being clothed more sensibly and well fed, Private Sayer made his way via Leyte, New Guinea, San Francisco, Chicago and New York back to England.

The last great obstacle in Europe was the Rhine, as much a symbol as it was a major river to cross. The assault was planned to involve 12 and 30 Corps. It was a major effort for which there was a great deal of rehearsal; and those activities kept the RAOC busy enough. Then there were the preparations for the crossing itself, and it was a satisfied DDOS who was told just before D-Day for the operation that both 12 and 30 Corps were satisfied that all their requirements had been met.

By 20 March the concentration of troops for the Rhine crossing began. The RAOC had provided all the camouflage equipment necessary to maintain secrecy. A smoke screen was also laid, assessed to be the biggest ever, and again the RAOC ensured that all the stores required were in place. Finally, as the day, 23 March 1945, approached, reserves of stores, vehicles and equipment were moved closer to the riverbank. It was a repeat in miniature of D-Day in Normandy, even down to the involvement of the Royal Navy and 6th Airborne Division. And as soon as the bridgehead was secured and bridges built, the stores, having been brought well forward, began to flow over to support the fighting troops. And then it began, the final drive into the heart of Germany, with every mobile Ordnance unit taking its place in the huge columns of vehicles heading towards Berlin.

There was the usual plethora of requests out of the ordinary. It appeared at one stage that 11th Armoured Division would grind to a halt for want of fan belts for its new, and rather specialized, tanks. The DDOS of 8th Corps was told he had just forty-eight hours before the division stopped. There was nothing in the theatre, but they were sourced from the home base, flown out and issued to 11th Armoured Division OFP in time to be fitted so that 11th Armoured Division could continue unhindered with its advance to the Elbe.

Arnhem was taken at last, by the Canadians, swinging round from the east to take the town very much as the German Army had in 1940. Just to the south-east, on the Groesebeek Heights near Nijmegen, where the US 82nd Airborne Division had fought a hard battle during Operation MARKET GARDEN, was George Grimes with 16 FTS. He could hear the artillery fire from Arnhem as the Canadians sought to liberate it. He remembers: '...the gliders and decomposing bodies were all around when we arrived in our location.'

V1s continued to cause problems in the UK. One of the last three to launch from Holland struck a building in COD Greenford. The bomb flew over the depot, carried on for 200 yards, turned and came back before striking and destroying Building 413. There were 100 casualties, including fourteen killed. On 5 April 1945 the 1,000,000th indent passed through the indent clearing section at COD Greenford.

Odd things happened from time to time. The DDOS of 8th Corps found a factory where components were being made for Germany's fledgling atomic weapons programme. Members of the RAOC also found ammunition for Germany's largest gun – the guns themselves having been found earlier and captured by the Russians. The IOO of 8 Corps was ambushed in the Munster Forest while seeking out a German ammunition depot of which he had been told. He was rescued by the timely arrival of a British platoon on patrol in the area.

One enterprising young officer commanding 35 Mobile Laundry and Bath Unit undertook a recce of the town ahead and found the Germans had evacuated, so he brought the unit in and set it up in time to be waiting for the infantry as they came to 'liberate' the town. Grins all round as they realized not only had they been 'had' but also there was a clean change of clothes and a shower thrown in as a bargain.

But then came the discovery that was to leave its mark on everyone associated with it. The forward elements of the British Army entered Bergen Belsen and found the death camp. It was a cesspit of filth and disease, with 100,000 bodies unburied and in various stages of decomposition. DDOS 8 Corps had already earmarked an MBLU to be working on the first day. Then within days the bath sections of 304, 106, 305 and 310 MBLUs came to join in. At once the local units of the RAOC were tasked with resolving the clothing problem, but search as they might they could find nothing suitable in the service inventory. The problem was eventually solved by means of a 'levy' on the local population. The sanitation and the cleanliness they brought were really welcome, and the response they received from the inmates helped in many ways to assuage the horror they felt at what they had found.

There had been a risk as 2nd Army raced across Germany that the LofC would stretch, as it had done the previous year, beyond breaking point. It was clear that in such a case the normal transport allocated for Ordnance stores would simply not be available. By mid-April orders were given to ground all the stocks in Corps Ordnance sub-parks, the Army Troops OFP and 17 FTS. This released a large number of vehicles and trailers, which were added to reserve vehicles from 2nd Army Vehicle Park to form RAOC Transport Columns. Thus were the operational needs of the forward troops met, by the RAOC taking on its own initiative the resolution of its transport difficulties. As a consequence, the advance never faltered for the want of Ordnance stores.

The Allies halted on the Elbe, and in accordance with the Yalta agreement, the Russians took Berlin on 8 May, Field Marshal Montgomery having taken the surrender of all German forces in the west on 4 May. It was finished, and yet it had only just begun, for as everyone else relaxed in the aftermath of

WOII Forshaw, still a Lance Corporal at this stage, ended his war at Oldenburg in Germany. Here he is pictured with Colin Moorcroft, centre, and Ted Roberts, left.

the war the RAOC set about clearing up the mess and balancing the books. Their job was never done; and there was still a war in the Far East, to say nothing of the clear up in the Middle East and in Italy and elsewhere. It was all in a day's work.

A small, yet significant, part of the clear up was that undertaken in the Channel Islands – the only part of the United Kingdom to have been occupied by the Germans. Major F M H Sargent was the officer commanding 135 Ordnance Unit based on Jersey.

…may think it strange that we destroyed so much of the enemy's equipment at that time, but we were under orders to eliminate Germany's war potential…when we arrived on the Island there was a strong bitter hatred and resentment of the Germans and anything connected with them.

In fact the role of the Ordnance unit was primarily to supply the British forces on the Island, and only as a secondary role to collect, store, sort and dispose of German equipment. However, the enormity of the clearance task soon became apparent. The unit collected in 10,000 rifles and bayonets, 750 heavy and light machine guns, 150 mortars and flame throwers, 130 radio transmitters and receivers, fifty-nine searchlights with their generators and tens of tons of other equipment. to say nothing of heavy guns and ammunition. 'Collecting and disposing of the ammunition was the most dangerous job' remembered Major Sargent. 'There were nearly 30,000 tons in all ranging from rifle ammunition to shells of a calibre in excess of eight inches.'

Getting rid of the guns was a major problem and many were tipped over the edge of the cliffs and into the sea; a spectacular sight. 'We had all sorts of problems with their disposal, and there were no preconceived ideas of how to deal with things. We just worked everything out on the spot.'

In the Far East, May also saw the success of the push south through Burma by General Slim's 14th Army as Rangoon fell to his forces. It had been a model campaign, with many new and innovative logistic lessons being learned. As the Army advanced it would have been impossible to maintain it wholly by a ground LofC. Indeed, complete formations worked independently of any overland LofC and it was only by clever use of air transport, carefully coordinated with Supply Services, that the right stores could be placed in the right place at the right time. In the final stages of the campaign in 1945, when the Army was pushing on from Mandalay to Rangoon, a complete system of air supply was laid on. Ordnance and Ammunition Depots were set up as near as possible to groups of airfields. Formations demanded their requirements by air and were supplied by air. This worked successfully, and the quantity of stores flown was only reduced when the port of Rangoon was captured and alternative, and arguably more normal, methods of supply could be used.

During the battle for Burma, Ordnance depots in the theatre issued between 200,000 and 250,000 items every month. Between 1 January 1944 and the recovery of Rangoon, 190,000 tons of stores were received from India by sea, rail and inland water transport. One hundred and twenty-five thousand miles of cable, for field communications, and 200,000 battle batteries were issued. One depot dispatched over 1,000 outboard motors for use on the Chindwin River to ferry stores forward to support the advance. Replacement vehicles were necessary at the rate of between 3,000 to 5,000 a month. In most cases, the vehicles travelled from Bombay to Calcutta by rail and then forward another

850 miles by rail. They were then moved forward by vehicle companies. About 1,000 armoured vehicles were issued and a further 1,000 replacement engines. Tank engines, weighing over three tons, had to be flown by air direct to forward air strips. Over 19,000 new or repaired vehicle engines were issued in the last twelve months. Another 24,000 engines were back loaded to the base for repair and overhaul. Huge quantities of tropical clothing were required monthly; socks, 210,000 pairs; boots, 90,000 pairs; underclothing, 180,000 sets; towels, 200,000; and battle dress, 200,000 suits. Over 2 million rounds of small arms ammunition were issued to units and formations between January 1944 and the fall of Rangoon. During the same period 2.1 million hand grenades were required and over 1.9 million rounds of gun ammunition. The ammunition depots handled on average 15,500 tons of ammunition per month.

Everywhere the Japanese were falling back, with the Americans capturing island after island in the Pacific. However, the war was not over, and soldiers, exhausted from the stresses of the war in Europe, found themselves under notice to move to Burma to continue fighting. It was not a happy prospect with preparations in hand for the invasion of the Malay Peninsula. Then, on 6 August the first atomic bomb was dropped on Hiroshima killing 80,000 people. The second bomb followed it three days later, on Nagasaki. Coupled with a Russian invasion into Manchuria on 8 August the Japanese had no choice but to surrender. Entry onto the Malay Peninsula was unopposed. The Second World War was ended.

There was one final act in the Far East that remains a small but significant part of RAOC history. Mountbatten's instructions on the taking of the Japanese surrender were that their counterparts should take officers' swords in surrender. Lieutenant General Koji was head of the Japanese supply services in the Imperial Japanese Army for the 'Southern Regions', and the task should have fallen to Brigadier John Cape, who was DOS Allied Forces SEAC. However, Koji was ill and Brigadier Cape had other duties, so he delegated the task to Lieutenant Colonel Cecil Thomas who was the ADOS of 20th Indian Division and, hence, the senior Ordnance officer in what was then French Indo-China, where Koji was based. The sword is a masterpiece of the Japanese sword makers' art, created in 1429. It is part of the Corps' heritage and is held in trust in the museum of the Royal Logistic Corps.

One of the great achievements of the war was the creation of a vast and complex organization in the UK base to support the efforts of the fighting troops, largely abroad. They had to have systems in place that would support vast armies fighting expeditionary operations in a number of theatres, each with their own peculiar requirements. That it succeeded is a testament to the quality of those involved in its construction and its operation, and to the vision of those who led the RAOC through this huge expansion and the responsibility that came with it.

In the Field Army there was a new approach. The RAOC had combatant status; its soldiers were as well trained as others and able to hold their own militarily, and at the same time they excelled as tradesmen. The events of the Second World War and the effect they had on the RAOC set the seal for its standards and its successes in the post war era.

Lieutenant General Koji's sword

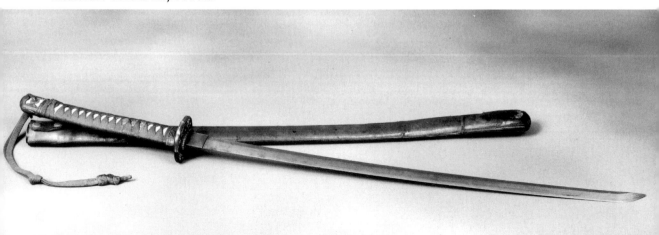

Chapter Six

Cold War, Expeditionary War, Colonial War

September 1945 – 1962

. . .an iron curtain has descended across the continent.   *Winston S Churchill 5 March 1946*

With the end of the war in Europe there was an imperative to hold a general election. The national government had been in power for ten years and if nothing else there was a constitutional demand for the country to express its views. The Labour Party in particular was anxious to test the mettle it had developed during the war years. Even so, they must have been surprised at the landslide they achieved in the election on 5 July 1945, with 393 seats to the Conservatives' 213. The surprise was made even greater by the popularity that Winston Churchill continued to enjoy. However, his success as a wartime leader was not sufficient to overcome the memory of an electorate that retained fresh in its mind the dead hand of a pre-war Conservative government lead by Neville Chamberlain.

Clement Attlee's new government entered power beset by problems, despite its desire to implement a welfare state, to

At the end of 1945 Hilsea had been one of the first depots and barracks the Americans handed back.

introduce nationalization, to minimize unemployment and to perpetuate an openly cooperative foreign policy. It had to contend with horrendous economic problems with the disappearance of many of the country's overseas markets, a shortcoming compounded by the loss during the war of so much of the merchant fleet. Furthermore, the diminution in the nation's capital wealth would inhibit the investment needed to get manufacturing industry back on track and the prospects for regeneration of trade, on which the country depended so heavily, were, in a war-ravaged world, not encouraging. A further blow was struck by the ending of Lend-Lease with the USA, immediately on the cessation of hostilities on the Continent.

One of the objectives of many of the new Labour MPs was to see a rapid reduction in the size of the Armed Forces. Setting aside the Party's natural antipathy to large standing forces, there was a clear need to get men and women out of uniform and turned to productive work in rebuilding the economy, and to do so as fast as possible. This sentiment was in keeping with the views of most servicemen, but reality was to strike, and certainly at the RAOC. The Corps was holding the vast proportion of the stocks of equipment and stores, spread throughout the UK and overseas in places as far apart as Burma and Benghazi, East and West Africa, Libya and the Lebanon, Austria and Germany. Some was going to be needed to support garrisons that would be retained in the post-war world, and yet more was to be returned for disposal.

Attlee, however, had been a member of the wartime cabinet and, despite the views of many in his Party, was conscious of the responsibilities the United Kingdom had to shoulder as a result of the part it had played in the global conflict. Forces had to be found to ensure that both Japan and Germany abided by their surrender agreements, Austria had to be

The ATS, seen here celebrating Christmas, had been a fantastic asset during the war years, and would continue to be so, providing a much needed and greatly respected source of highly competent technical workers.

occupied, especially given the Russian interest, Greece had to be helped, and there were responsibilities in Palestine. The Japanese presence in south-east Asia had to be liquidated, the Empire needed policing and the sea and air lanes that would make all this possible had to remain open. These were daunting tasks for a nation in such post-war disarray.

One thing was clear, with almost every soldier, barring a few pre-war regulars, wanting to return home as a civilian, there would not be enough in an all-volunteer force to come anywhere near close to meeting these commitments. At the same time, as the rest of the army sought to civilianize itself, the RAOC had to receive their unwanted stores, which arrived generally in poor order, sort them, render accounts and either re-distribute or dispose of the stock. To handle all this the RAOC had a strength in 1945 of 8,000 officers, 130,000 male and 24,000 female soldiers, the latter being ATS. Highly trained and, by 1945, very experienced, they would have been a major asset in undertaking the gargantuan task that faced the RAOC. Regrettably, however, the RAOC was to be managed no differently from any other arm or service when it came to discharge. In the first year following the end of the war the Corps' strength reduced by 60 per cent and those who were left were swamped with work. Fortunately, not all those who had served in the war wished to leave, some who left found civilian life unattractive and returned – and some specialists were forcibly retained.

Montgomery's proposed solution to the overall manning problem, when he replaced Alanbrooke as CIGS in July 1946, was to introduce National Service, with a service period of eighteen months. There was a deal of opposition from the Labour and Liberal Parties, but with Tory support a bill was passed on 1 April 1947 that would see young men called up for one year only with effect from 1949. It was designed to produce an Army of 305,000, and ex-National Servicemen who had a six-year reserve liability would flesh out the Territorial Army. The man at the Corps' helm during this period of massive change was Major General Sir Leslie Williams KBE, CB, MC, who was both Controller of Ordnance Stores and Director of Warlike Stores. But as Montgomery moved in as CIGS, Major General W W Richards followed General Williams in managing a supply system that circumnavigated the globe

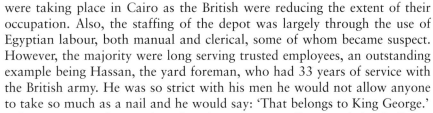

Meanwhile, those left, awaiting discharge were posted to the far-flung reaches of the Empire. Lieutenant Tom Bretherton, whom we last met pursuing a retreating German army from Normandy with 30 Corps OFP, found himself in the Middle East:

Lieutenant Tom Bretherton RAOC.

At the end of the war I was posted to 4 AOD at Abbassia in Cairo, which also included a sub-depot in the caves of Tura, on the east bank of the Nile a few miles south of Cairo. The latter was an unusual site for an Ordnance depot. The stone from Tura had been quarried since antiquity and had been used for the casing of the pyramids of Memphis. After a few weeks at a desk in these caves I was sent to Abyssinia to take charge of the small arms depot, which consisted of some massive buildings filled with various types of small arms, a REME armourer's workshop and shooting range, carpenters' shop, dispatch bays and offices. Security was particularly important because of the nature of the stocks as well as the fact that disturbances were taking place in Cairo as the British were reducing the extent of their occupation. Also, the staffing of the depot was largely through the use of Egyptian labour, both manual and clerical, some of whom became suspect. However, the majority were long serving trusted employees, an outstanding example being Hassan, the yard foreman, who had 33 years of service with the British army. He was so strict with his men he would not allow anyone to take so much as a nail and he would say: 'That belongs to King George.'

In contrast to the wartime situation, when supplies were being built up, my time in Egypt was concerned with the disposal of stores to various destinations, including 5 AOD in the desert at Tel el Kebir. This enormous depot had serious security problems despite elaborate barbed wire perimeters. It was said that thieves were capable of disarming and taking away landmines set around the perimeter. The nearby village was reckoned to have a mass of ordnance stores and was referred to as 6 AOD.

Regarding Hassan, I should add that he was a strict Muslim, and headman of his village. He daily performed ceremonial ablutions in his office and every Friday lunch break he would lead his staff in prayer on a spare piece of land just outside the depot. He had a good influence and we had little disciplinary trouble. The most difficult time was during the month of Ramadan when the prohibition of eating and drinking between sunrise and sunset caused some bad temper and the occasional fight.

Private Parkes also found himself in the Middle East. He was:

...moved to No. 3 MLBU when the orderly room clerk left for demob. We were billeted in Aeronautical Buildings, an old Italian Air force building,

Hassan.

along with other RAOC units – HQ staff and 613 Ammunition Clearance Team. The latter was a swashbuckling unit that departed for the desert on working days in trucks displaying red flags and accompanied by several truckloads of German POWs. They travelled to the desert where the POWs, stretched out in a line, walked over the old battlefields collecting unexploded ammunition. This was placed in piles, packed with explosive and blown up.

No. 3 MLBU was not mobile as the wheels of the laundry unit had been stolen and had not been replaced. It was situated in the remains of an old seaplane hanger on the edge of the harbour. We did all the washing for the 1st Infantry Division and, as a peacetime extra, the unit employed about twenty young local women to sort and pack laundry and to iron and starch KD and other items. We had our KD starched and ironed and we were undoubtedly the smartest unit in Tripoli. The 1st Battalion Coldstream Guards was also based in Tripoli, and their CO complained that it was not right for men of the 3rd Mobile Laundry to walk around off duty looking smarter than guardsmen, so that practice had to cease.

Further East, India was a major headache. Attlee knew it had to go and had to have its independence. He knew it was a drain on resources he simply could not sustain. The severance was swift, almost brutal. Mountbatten was appointed Viceroy at the end of March 1947 with a deadline from Attlee that power was to be transferred by the middle of 1948 at the latest. Having failed to negotiate a solution with the factions after two months, Mountbatten reached the conclusion that partition was the only sensible solution. By the end of 1947 there were only thirty British combat units left in the sub continent, and one outcome of the India withdrawal was an influx of high grade officers from the Indian Army Ordnance Corps, and other Indian Army corps and regiments, into the RAOC. Whilst this was of benefit to officer manning, the situation regarding soldiers would not be resolved until Montgomery's plan for National Service became a reality.

Sergeant Donald Bye was swept up in all this, and departed from India along with everyone else as part of the British exodus. He was one of a little known part of the RAOC, the Army Kinema Section, forerunners of the Army Kinema Corporation and its successors with which so many post-Second World War soldiers are familiar. Its basic training unit was at 20th Century Fox and units were established all over the world, including India. They ran a mix of mobile and static cinemas. The mobile units in India where Donald was posted were mounted in a 15cwt Chevrolet or Ford with its own generator and a coach-built body. It carried two16-mm projectors, a screen and spare parts, all in custom built cupboards. A mix of training and entertainment films were shown and not all the venues were conventional: 'I remember one of my shows entailed a sixty mile journey along rough tracks to an Indian Army stud farm.'

Further east Singapore was reoccupied and most of the pre-1942 logistic installations were still in good

Sergeant Donald Bye was part of this Army Kinema Section Unit. He is standing in the middle row third from the left. The picture was taken at Jubbulpore on 1 December 1946, and the officer commanding was Captain N G Dunbar RAOC.

order, having been used by the Japanese for their original purpose. Certainly this was the case for the Alexandra site, and it was reoccupied by 223 (Indian) BOD together with elements of 221 (Indian) BOD. By December 1945 the first issues were being made and depot expansion was being organized not just on the Alexandra site but also at warehouses across the Island. Towards the end of 1945 443 BAD was established on the site of the original ammunition depot at Kranji, and 221 Vehicle Company arrived to set up a vehicle installation that would eventually become 221 BVD, located on the outskirts of Johore Baru. Hong Kong was taken back, and Japan had to be occupied. In the latter case there was a Commonwealth and Indian Division and the Ordnance support was a mixture of British, Indian, Australian and New Zealand Ordnance installations.

The Middle East was a major commitment, with a headquarters in Cairo and covering an area from Iraq to Tripolitania, from Cyprus to East Africa. The major operational commitment was Palestine. By the end of 1945 there were two divisions, 1st Infantry in the north of the country and 6th Airborne in the south, deployed on active operations to curb the excesses of the Jewish terrorist groups seeking to establish the state of Israel. It was an intensely frustrating internal security operation that tied down large numbers of soldiers for long periods of time. At the heart of the problem lay the League of Nations' mandate given to the British in 1920 with the task of administering Palestine in order to establish a national home for the Jews. The British interpreted this as the Jews being entitled to set up home in Palestine. The Jews took the alternative view, that it was the promise of a national, independent Jewish state in Palestine.

Brigadier G A N Swiney would eventually become a Major General.

The task facing the DOS Middle East, Brigadier G A N Swiney, was to provide operational support for troops deployed in Palestine, whilst at the same time coping with the vast stocks left over from the war in the Middle East. He was, on the one hand, receiving stocks from disbanding units or those returning home, on the other disposing of those and depot stocks. He was also supporting garrison units stationed in the area and supporting troops deployed in Palestine. The size of his depot problem alone is an indication of the task he faced. One sub-depot had some 2 million cases in open storage, and not in good order with most of the boxes themselves either broken already or falling to pieces when moved. It was not uncommon for items to have between twenty and thirty different locations, and some had over 100. There were 2,000 miles of coconut matting, 17,000 tons of springs for American vehicles and the line of spares for Ford vehicles extended for a mile.

As these depots and sub depots were rationalized everything focussed on 5 BOD at Tel el Kebir, which was to be the main stores depot in the region. Unhappily, as everything closed up in Egypt, the civilian staff did not transfer to the discomforts of its desert location and the manning of the depot was left, almost entirely, to British soldiers. This at a time of demobilization presented serious problems to the depot commander. Not untypical was the arbitrary cut of 500 posts he suffered in October 1946.

In the midst of this, thought was being given in the UK to establishing a logistic base in Kenya to support the Indian Ocean and the Middle East, thereby rendering Tel el Kebir superfluous. The reason lay with the view beginning to firm up that it would be necessary to evacuate Egypt some time in the late forties and something had to be in place to service the region. A site in the bush some sixty miles west of Mombasa was chosen, a place called McKinnon Road, and planning was set in train for a capacity of 200,000 tons of warlike stores, most of which would come from Egypt, but there would also be a rationalization of other storage throughout the eastern part of Africa.

Nearer to home there were commitments in Greece and in Austria, in Italy and in France. The clearance task was huge, Italy alone generating in the first year 100,000 tons returned to the UK or

Ordnance Depot Austria.

sent to other theatres, to say nothing of the vast tonnages disposed of locally. At the same time local support had to be provided to those units designated to occupy, or remain in, the countries. In the case of Italy, for example, this would be July 1947, France mid-1948 and for Austria 1955, and there was also the massive task of occupying and rebuilding Germany. Initially the prognosis for a fair and equable settlement in Germany had been good. Zones of Occupation were established, but were expected only to remain in place until elections could be organized, following a final version of a peace treaty. Following that the country would be re-united, albeit with limitations imposed on its industrial output and its political structure to prevent any return to the militarism of the thirties and the forties.

The western Allies entered Berlin on 7 July 1945, some ten weeks after it had fallen to the Russian onslaught. The RAOC presence was initially 37 Port Ordnance Detachment, moving into a location in Streitstrasse in Spandau in the north-west of the city, with the ammunition depot initially being the Zitadelle, an old fortification in the centre of the Bezirk near its town hall. Lieutenant Colonel J C Timmins commanded the RAOC elements in the city.

The United Kingdom was a particular problem. It was divided into one command based on its function – Anti-Aircraft Command – and five based on geography, plus an independent Northern Ireland District. Its depots were full of vast tonnages of stores, and given the relatively rapid end of the war coupled with long lead times for the production of military equipment, more and more continued to pour in from the factories as they wound up war production and sought to clear their premises of now unwanted stocks. To this were added huge quantities being sent back by units in the UK and depots overseas as the Army, and the other two services, came to terms with the rapid run down of the Armed Forces. By the end of 1945 there were 85 million tons of stores in both open and covered storage, spread throughout twelve central depots. Clearing up the mess was a huge task, with added impetus given by the fact that of the covered storage being used some 14 million square feet had been requisitioned during the war and had to be returned as soon as possible to its original owners. It was thirty-seven per cent of the total covered storage available, and it was cleared and handed back by the end of 1946 – quite remarkable.

There was a particular issue with MT spares, which pre-war had been the purview of the newly created COD Chilwell. However, by 1941 this had stretched to include three other depots: Feltham, Bicester and Derby controlled from HQ MT organization based at Chilwell and run by Major General G W Palmer, its first post-war commander. Stocks of MT spares were held in 150 different locations throughout the UK. One feature of the MT organization was that in storage it did not differentiate between spares and complete vehicles, although there was some 'vertical' separation in the depots themselves. Depot stock in1945 was assessed at 240,000 vehicles with a census showing global stocks of over 1.4 million, huge numbers of which were of American origin from the Lend-Lease programme.

Technical stores were spread throughout the country, focussed on Bicester, Old Dalby, Greenford and Weedon, with provisioning based at Donnington, the latter having been the main pre-war technical stores depot. The vast bulk of the general stores range made them difficult and time-consuming to handle. They were stocked in a wide range of depots, including one at Thatcham taken back from American use in 1946.

National Service soldiers prepare ammunition for demolition at Trawsfynnyd. Private Baldwin is half way into the pit, wearing the glasses.

Ammunition was, as in overseas theatres, a major headache. Shortly after the end of the war there were some 2 million tons distributed throughout the five CADs at Corsham, Bramley, Longtown, Nesscliffe and Kineton, a dozen ASDs, which were all field storage sites and a range of command ammunition depots. By the middle of 1946 there was strong pressure to clear the ASDs as they occupied sites of natural beauty, such as the Savernake Forest, and in many cases were stacked along roads rendering them unusable by the public. Mercifully, Brigadier V O Lonsdale, who had directed the ammunition build-up during the war, was to stay at the War Office as DDOS (Ammunition) until early 1949. His task was to turn through 180 degrees that which he had so assiduously put in place.

His job was made more difficult by the large quantities of ammunition, much of it coming in from overseas, that required inspection and subsequently overhaul and repackaging or disposal. He too was beset by the problems of the outflow of skilled manpower to civilian life. Neither was he helped by the situation in the depots. They only had a capacity of 700,000 tons against the 2 million being held, and storage space aside there were difficulties at each one. For example, the capacity and potential for expansion of CAD Bramley, which was built in the First World War, was limited by ammunition storage regulations as it had a main railway line running through it and therefore could not hold very much modern, high risk ammunition. CAD Corsham was underground storage, which presented operating difficulties and CAD Nesscliffe, built during the Second World War, lay in the Severn valley and was prone to flooding. In Kineton there were problems of subsidence in some storehouses due to the inadequacy of some of the, albeit rushed, wartime construction work.

The disposal of surplus and unserviceable stocks was a major headache. To cope with the load Lieutenant Colonel J Farmoor was given the task of setting up an Explosives Disposal Unit at Trawsfynnyd in North Wales, with a detachment at the military port of Cairnryan. Between the middle of 1945 and 1949 it would dispose of over 1 million tons by demolition or breakdown. However the bulk would go by sea-dumping through Cairnryan and Barry in South Wales. This included some 100,000 tons of chemical warfare shells that had been held given the possibility that the Germans might have resorted to the use of chemical weapons. This was a clear sea-dumping task; a task that had to be undertaken in such a way as to ensure there was no chance of any of these shells reappearing at a later date. It was done by filling seventeen old cargo ships with the stock for disposal, sailing them into mid Atlantic and scuttling them.

On 2 January 1946 there was an incident in the Savernake Forest in Wiltshire, the site of one of the field storage ASDs, which brought home to everyone the risks they faced in seeking to clear up the explosive detritus left over from the war. The story of what happened that day is drawn directly from Major General Phelps' history of the RAOC, and evokes the horror and the scale of events:

Private Anthony Baldwin was one of the early members of the EDU.

It was a cold winter's afternoon, and with the light beginning to fade in Savernake Forest, a handful of half-frozen men of the RAOC, assisted by RPC and RASC, were completing the loading of a train with American and German ammunition. In the same siding stood another train of ninety-six wagons, loaded with British ammunition. Suddenly there was a blinding flash and a heavy detonation, and two railway wagons and a three-ton lorry literally disappeared. Fire, the terror of all ammunition personnel, swept around the yard, and more wagons burst into flames. The few men working on the site were rapidly reinforced by the unit's remaining personnel and the Army Fire Brigade, all under the direction of the Officer Commanding the depot, Major K A Briggs, RAOC. All were activated by the fear of the fire spreading to the remaining loaded wagons: one thousand tons of explosives were liable to detonate. But the first explosion had severed the line leading out of the siding so that all remaining wagons were effectively bottled up within the siding. With all working at high pressure in the gathering dark, a multiplicity of actions took place in quick succession. Full wagons were uncoupled and pulled out of danger, burning wagons were extinguished, fire breaks were made by manually pushing wagons up or down the line, the injured were rescued from under burning wagons and full lorries of ammunition were driven out of harm's way. The force of the initial explosion had started fires in wagons many yards away. 5.5-inch shell in some of these detonated with a tremendous roar, and in doing so started more fires. Cordite in other wagons 'flashed off', again spreading fire. The darkness was

intensified by the glare of the burning cartridges, and the flash of detonating shell; and to add to the men's difficulties the water tanks soon ran dry. Where there was water it froze in the hoses if far enough away from the heat.

Eight men had already been killed and six others injured, but, mindful that nearby houses were at risk, the remaining personnel worked on in an inferno of bursting heavy calibre shell, and exploding cartridges and mines. During this period two heavy explosions occurred, each of them hurling debris up to a radius of half a mile. Some 500 5.5 inch shell detonated in this period and over 10,000 25-pounder cartridges blazed. Pieces of railway wagons, axles, couplings, railway track, cartridge cases, concrete, and timber were falling almost

Damaged ammunition in dangerous condition lay everywhere.

continuously on the sidings and adjacent countryside. In all twenty-nine railway wagons and their contents detonated. Ten of them completely disappeared, and of thirteen more only the smallest

fragments were found. Of two three-ton lorries, only the gearbox of one was found. Blast from the explosions was so powerful that a man was lifted two hundred yards by it, landed in a field, and got up amazed but unhurt!

The cold light of the following morning revealed two huge craters, one 75 ft by 30 ft by 14 ft deep and one 90 ft by 40 ft by 20 ft deep. The remains of

And yet more of the devastation caused by the Savernake explosion.

Staff Sergeant S G Rogerson GC RAOC.

lorries, thousands of 5.5 in shell, 25-pounder cartridges, anti-tank mines, detonators, packages, telegraph poles etc were strewn over a large area. It was miraculous that many further casualties did not occur in the operations to contain the spread of the explosions.

Courage on the day was recognized with Major Briggs and Staff Sergeant S G Rogerson being awarded the highest order for gallantry when not in the face of the enemy, the George Cross. George Medals went to Sergeant D A Key RAOC, Sergeant J H Matthews RPC, an MBE for Gallantry for Warrant Officer F W Goodman RAOC and BEMs for Gallantry to Corporal A J Adams, and to Privates F Barnett, D Gallagher and J W Prendergast, all of the RAOC; and to Driver A J Baker RASC. The award of the US Bronze Star further acknowledged Major Briggs' courage. The decorations aside, one last legacy was that the incident would feature large in the mind of any ATO seeking to manage a field storage location as an example he would not wish to see replicated.

In the UK there was a need to re-supply the Army. Clearly, the central depots were the main sources of supply, however there were a range of command depots spread throughout the country to provide the close-in support. Principally this involved clothing and general stores, but small stocks of MT and technical stores were also provided.

AA Command was broken down into five regions and, as the Army began to demobilize, the regular soldiers and units of the command were transferred into the TA. That left the Corps with the task of storing and maintaining the guns, equipment and ammunition of the Command in readiness for its mobilization. The Ordnance support was a network of depots based on the geographical regions and some thirty or so small ammunition depots positioned within reach of the gun sites. It was a complex effort to manage given the dispersed nature of the Ordnance installations, and very manpower intensive.

In Eastern Europe, in the immediate post-war years, the Russians were tightening their grip on the small nations, rendering them mere satellites of the Soviet Empire and pursuing the classic Russian foreign policy of amassing buffer states on its borders as part of the defence in depth of Mother Russia. As a first step, Russia denied any chance of any of these countries benefiting from Marshall Aid, the massive economic support programme generated by the US for the rebuilding of Europe's war-torn countries. It was becoming clear that the Russians had designs on expansion of influence, and where necessary by military means. Relationships with her former allies in the defeat of Hitler were deteriorating. The huge commitment that would be the defence of Western Europe was beginning to become a reality. No longer was it simply a question of clearing up from the Second World War; it was becoming clear that preparations would have to be made for the Third World War.

It all amounted to a tremendous load for the RAOC as it tried to resolve its own issues of organization, structure, manning and procedures whilst at the same time supporting an Army, parts of which were drawing down and other parts of which were building up. Yet throughout all this, the life of the Corps as a living entity went on. It went on socially and regimentally, but perhaps nowhere was it more obvious than in Army and Corps sport, which began to grow almost before the demands of the recent war had ceased.

In 1946 a Corps' Sports Association was created, bringing a sense of form and structure to RAOC sport and announcing by its formation that it was something the Ordnance Corps would be taking seriously. Reports on cricket, football, rugby, shooting, fencing, boxing, cross-country and other sports began to appear routinely in the *Gazette*.

Major T A Hatfield won the foil in the Army Fencing Championships held at Olympia. Lieutenant

G B Saunders of 6 Battalion at Chilwell was working his way through Corps, Army and County cross-country so spectacularly well that he would be selected for the national team and be placed a very creditable fifth in his first international.

Immediately after the war it had been decided that there was value in selected RAOC officers attending management sciences training in order to assimilate techniques being developed in the commercial world for application in RAOC installations. It was a tacit acceptance of the industrial nature of much of the RAOC's work and the relationship there would have to be between commerce and the Corps if best value was to be derived from its efforts. The first course was for seventeen officers at Nottingham University, but it was not felt to be particularly satisfactory. The second, at the Manchester University Institute of Science and Technology was much more so and thereafter there was an annual course of one year's duration held there. Shorter courses for the broader church of officers were also developed at the RAOC School, lasting four weeks. Thus the principles of modern management and its techniques were spread throughout the RAOC.

There was also a great deal of work under way to develop cost accounting or management accounting, the names would vary, in the central and other main depots of the RAOC. Whilst the methods developed were far from perfect they were all directed at improving the management of the system and to obtaining management information that would allow yet further improvements. More and more the RAOC was being run like a commercial business and as such was pioneering the way in which the rest of the Army would follow in the decades to come.

During 1947 there was some relief from paper rationing and the RAOC *Gazette* was able to resume something like its old pre-war shape and size. This was certainly the case for the type font, thereby making it easier on the eye for the older soldier. A key manifestation of the change was the appearance of the Corps badge in colour on the front cover. It was also decided to institute an RAOC museum and the call went out for exhibits to be sent to Feltham where it was to be based. There was also a move to create the post of an Honorary Chaplain to the Corps. A former Colonel, O P Joke, had been ordained in 1946 and there was an attempt to create the position for him. However, there was no precedent, and since the creation of such a post would assume a lineage, and there appeared to be none, it was not looked on with favour and the initiative was not pursued. The Corps was also hard at work trying to set up new branches of the RAOC Association since large parts of the UK were not properly represented and, in the immediate post-war era, it was felt that much could be gained by a drive to remedy that. A Corps diary was produced for 1948, and a refillable case with the diary would set one back 16s 6d (£20) in the UK and 10s 0d (£12) overseas; and the Officers' Club Dinner cost 15s 0d (£18) for members and £1 10s 0d (£36) for non-members.

In 1947 the RAOC took account of the Beddington Committee's 1946 report where the high error rate in manual transactions using the Visidex accounting system was noted. Chilwell was chosen as the test depot for a new system of machine accounting. A 4-Register National Cash Register was introduced, multiplying the number of transactions posted by a factor of five and considerably improving the accuracy. There were also considerable staff savings. As a result of the success demonstrated by this trial, similar machines were installed at Bicester, Branston, Didcot and Chilwell. It was a far from perfect system and there were still elements of the process, particularly provision, that were manpower intensive but it was a great deal better than its manual predecessor.

Headquarters 21st Army Group had, at the end of the war, established its HQ in a small market town, Bad Oyenhausen, near Minden on the north German plain. However, it was by now a peacetime HQ, and accordingly changed its name to British Army of the Rhine on 25 August 1948. Its role was to manage a ravaged Germany with hundreds of thousands of displaced persons, through a network of corps districts. Each of the commanders, in addition to his military role, was charged with restoring order and supporting, in whatever way he could, the stabilization of the civilian community. Apart from 2nd Division the field army that had invaded Germany had been disbanded. By the end of 1947 the BAOR organization comprised, in addition to its one operational division, the four static headquarters of Hamburg District, Hanover District, British Troops Berlin and 41 (Hook of Holland) Garrison in the Netherlands. The main port of entry for all British logistic effort was Hamburg where 15 Advanced Base Ordnance Depot had opened in December 1945. It had two sub depots and the HQ in Glinde, near Hamburg, with a third sub depot and the RSG near Hanover. It was renamed 15 Base Ordnance Depot in December 1946, and acquired a fourth sub depot to handle reserves and this was located in Mönchengladbach.

The BOD operated out to only two 'forward' organizations: 50 Ordnance Depot at Brackwede near Bielefeld and 2nd Division's Ordnance Depot at Viersen, the latter also having a Mönchengladbach detachment. Both the depots had been formed from the divisional OFPs that had supported the field army during the war. Both depots retained the ability to field an OFP capability when necessary, but their primary function was to provide transit for stocks dispatched by the BOD to the various Brigade Ordnance Officers.

Out of the massive vehicle operation that had been a feature of the latter stages of the war in Europe would emerge two units, 16 and 17 Vehicle Companies that would provide the focus for vehicle handling for the long-term future in Germany. The size of the problem they faced is perhaps illustrated by the fact that in 1946 17 Company occupied, for vehicle storage, seventy-five miles of the Bremen-Hamburg-Lübeck autobahn; something over 50,000 assorted types, including A Vehicles.

Private Tom Edwards, seen here on the right of the picture with his two friends, Scottie Findlay, seated, and Pete Bladen, was typical of the thousands of young men called up to serve in the post war period – in his case it was in Hamburg.

But if the collection, disposal and re-issue, where necessary, of stores and vehicles were a problem, they were dwarfed, if not in volume then in complexity and risk, by the difficulties presented by ammunition. Not only did the ammunition organization have to cope with returns from the British and their allies who had used British equipment, but also with German stocks in their former depots. There was also the question of stray ammunition lying around everywhere, German, British and American, posing a perpetual danger to soldier and civilian alike.

At the war's end the major part of this task was handled by 3 BAD. An article in the Corps' *Gazette* described the depot:

> The headquarters was at Liebenau, just south of Hamburg, occupying what was once the German Eibia Propellant Factory, built at tremendous speed shortly before the war by the German Reich, and completed by the summer of 1939. This massive war installation was constructed in the midst of the virgin forest and bearing in mind the danger of air bombing, all buildings were built partially underground, and perfectly camouflaged. The flat roofs of the buildings and storehouses were covered with a layer of earth, and pine trees planted. No trace of the buildings can be suspected from the air, and in fact the factory escaped bombing throughout the war. The depot was designed to be, and in fact is, completely self-maintained. Three power stations were erected for steam production. Steam turbines supply heat for all the offices, storehouses and the whole heating and cooking system.

Sergeant Bill Sharman RAOC.

The outstations of 3 BAD were 154 ASD at Wulfen, 254 ASD at Bracht, 554 ASD at Walsrode and 854 ASD at Boostedt. The capacity totalled 107,000 tons, and during the first two and a half years following the cessation of hostilities 120,000 tons of British ammunition would be collected in, sorted, inspected and repacked, or disposed of as necessary. This figure, however, was dwarfed by the 600,000 tons of German ammunition that would pass through the depot for disposal. This, of course, also came at a time when the requirement for the large number of highly skilled officers and tradesmen in the RAOC ammunition world was at its highest and coincided with the time when the Army was running down its manpower in the euphoric post-war rush to return to civilian life.

The disposal task fell to specially organized units known as Enemy Ammunition Depot Clearance Units. Comprising around 120 men each, their composition changed over quite a short time to reflect the disappearance of so much of the Corps' skilled manpower. It was not long before other-arms soldiers were being drafted in to act as ammunition storemen, and civilians began to be employed for the smaller handling tasks. There was even a programme to train 100 Danish soldiers so they could take on the task of ammunition clearance in their own country.

The clearance task was not easy, for the German ammunition was, perforce, in a parlous state. Where there was storage it was inadequate and often damaged by bombing or shellfire. In many cases the ammunition sites had been raided by desperate German civilians seeking resources for shelter and the useful metals associated with ammunition that could be used to barter for food. Driving bands were removed, packing materials destroyed or taken and the whole situation was one of disarray. It was not helped by the weather in that first post-war winter, which was amongst the hardest in living memory. Snow turned to slush, mud was at once liquid and then frozen, stacks were bound together – immovable in many cases until the onset of spring would free them from the icy grip that bound them, resolutely, together. Nonetheless, by Easter 1946 the bulk of collections from field storage sites had been finished and half the disposal task had been completed.

However, it was a dangerous task and the Savernake Forest was not to prove the only incident of note, and of tragedy, in the handling of unwanted ammunition. Sergeant Bill Sharman was a member of No. 28 EADCU sent to 76 Depot Control Company (Mine Control) at Hänigsen, between Hanover and Celle. The company had seven mines under its control.

These mines had been used to store various Ordnance stores, a few mainly ammunition and component parts of ammunition which was, of course, our province. (The mine) contained smoke/chemical shells which were taken by train under escort to be dumped at sea. There was also Black Powder and a vast quantity of propellant in various sizes. Our job was to dispose of these, the Black Powder/Gun Powder by controlled explosions; the propellant by burning. Everything was going well until June 18th 1946 when at 1030 am the contents of the mine exploded with considerable force unfortunately killing all the workers underground. I was most fortunate because I went down to inspect almost every day after the morning break 1000 am to 1015 am. Another two or three minutes and I would not have been writing this. …The newspapers were rather over the top. It was a big bang (not quite atomic) and as it happened 2,000 feet underground no one knew how long it burned and it certainly couldn't have raced to a surface depot.

In January 1947 a third division was added to the force levels in Palestine, adding to the burden on the British Army and the British economy, and DOS MELF and his long-suffering soldiers. However, given the less intense nature of internal security operations it eventually transpired that the task of supporting the third division lay well within the capacity of the two AODs, one AAD and a vehicle group that provided the Ordnance support in the theatre. .

Shortly afterwards the British government decided to refer the issue of Palestine to the newly formed United Nations to seek a resolution. It was a convoluted process and it was 29 November before they passed a resolution to form a Jewish state. It was reduced in size from the UN partition committee's recommendation, but nonetheless made Israel a reality. It would see the United Kingdom released from its obligations as a mandate power on 15 May 1948.

The middle of 1947 saw the disposal tasks of ammunition in Germany reduced to the point where the ammunition organization was able to return to the peacetime activity of such things as unit inspections, and this they commenced in August with the formation of an ammunition inspectorate. Initially there were detachments covering the whole of the British sector, although the number would reduce over time as the task lessened and as the deployment of the British Army in Germany stabilized around its evolving peacetime roles and cold-war stance.

In December 1947 negotiations between France, Great Britain, Russia and the US over Germany's future broke down and there was a real fear that the Russians might attempt to force a solution by dint of arms. Discussions began immediately in the West and by March 1948 the Brussels Treaty had been signed. Britain, France, Belgium, the Netherlands and Luxembourg formed the Western European Union. It was meant as a clear indication to the USA that the Europeans were prepared to take some responsibility for their own defence. It had its own Commanders-in-Chief Committee, or CiCC. Discussion about a north Atlantic alliance began, although in these early stages neither the British nor the Americans had any intention of committing forces to be stationed permanently on the continent.

It was about this time that a re-examination had been undertaken into the means of vehicle supply for Germany. This was partly due to the proximity of Hamburg to the Russian Zone and the increased tension was seen to pose a threat to vehicle stocks in the event of hostilities. There was also the perhaps more practical issue of a major part of a key Autobahn being used as a rather large car park, albeit by now only thirty miles long. The plan arrived at was to place a depot for fit vehicle stock safely west of the Rhine at Mönchengladbach, and this task was to be undertaken by 17 Vehicle Company. Further east, 16 Vehicle Company would become a returned vehicle park in its existing location at Oldenburg. A small vehicle handling capability would be retained in the port of Hamburg.

Conditions of service were an important issue at the time and efforts were made to retain those who wished to follow an Army career and to offer an attractive package to those wishing to join. Four-man barrack rooms were being developed with modern furniture and spread throughout the Army as fast as the necessary accommodation stores could be provided.

A feature of RAOC life was the wide range of TA formations and units that were developed to support an Army seeking to readjust itself to a world it probably did not understand, and with which it was trying to come to terms. One such was 264 Scottish Beach Brigade, the one and only beach group in the RAOC, comprising 50th and 51st Beach Ordnance Companies, stores landing sections and ammunition landing sections.

It was considered an important task given the vital part played by beach groups in all theatres of war, particularly during the Normandy landings. A case perhaps demonstrating the preservation of a structure to support a war that had been fought and would never be fought again.

One other small piece of RAOC history was the demise of its OCTU at Foremark Hall, near Derby. The Hall was sold and became Repton Preparatory School.

From the very beginning of 1948 the tensions between the western Allies and the Russians were growing stronger and stronger. There was a clear political imperative among the Russian hierarchy to force the United Kingdom, France and the United States out of Berlin and back west of the border between their zones in Germany and the Soviet sector. Progressively during the course of the early part of the year travel along the land corridor that passed through the Soviet Sector to the city was made more and more difficult. The strain was heavy on the RAOC resources, to say nothing of the rest of the Army, in managing the plethora of post-war tasks that were coming its way; many of them, like supporting Berlin from afar, that were unexpected and not planned for.

The strain on resources was made more acute when the Army Council, in March 1948, had to cope with a reduction in budgeted manpower from 534,000 to 345,000, with the distinct possibility of yet further reductions. One outcome of this was that the Prime Minister was eventually convinced that the period of National Service had to be extended from a year to eighteen months.

On 26 February 1948 the Black Watch left Karachi, to be followed on 28 February by the 1st Battalion the Somerset Light Infantry from Bombay. India now belonged firmly, and overtly, to the Indians.

Also in February 1948 there was a communist coup in Czechoslovakia. This was followed by the crisis over Berlin and the starting of the Berlin Blockade in July 1948. There was also clear pressure from the Soviets on the Norwegians, tantamount to bullying, for them not to join the WEU. Pressure was building, internally and externally, for a clear US involvement in something transatlantic to curb and, if necessary, counter Soviet aggression. The pressure, it seemed, was endless and increasing.

The title of Controller of Ordnance Stores ceased to be used when the Army adopted the American Chief of Staff system and there was a reversion to the pre-war title of the head of the Corps as the Director of Ordnance Services. In order to avoid confusion with the three other DsOS in BAOR, MELF and south-east Asia it was suggested that the head of the Corps should be Director General, which would have brought him into line with his Royal Naval and Royal Air Force equivalents. However, the suggestion fell upon deaf ears, for the time being at least.

On the technical front, there was a stirring in the wind that would have a profound effect on the management of assets in the years to come. Work underway at Manchester University and Harvard was seeing the birth of an electrical means of undertaking massive calculation and managing vast stocks by keeping track of items by their number. The computer age was dawning, but for the time being it was just that – a dawn. There was still some time to go before the mist gave way to the light that would offer the logistic world its greatest challenge since mechanization.

The RAOC's HQ, together with the school, having moved to Middleton Stoney near Bicester during the war and subsequently, in 1946, to Matthew Barracks Tidworth, settled in Deepcut. The Regimental Depot had moved to Feltham in 1946, and would remain there until 1955 before it too settled in Deepcut.

One particular issue at the time involving training would tax brains for many years to come and never really see a satisfactory solution – the responsibility for the policy for ammunition training. At this early stage after the war it was placed with Commander Training Establishment. However, the technical content and the fast changing nature of the ammunition world meant that DDOS Ammunition at the War Office had to be closely involved in course design and

The first OOs course.

technical matters. It would be 1950 before this was resolved and the Ammunition School policy was separated out from the rest of the Corps' training organization under the direct control of the ammunition specialists. One of the issues with AE training was the length of the course at twenty-six weeks. In January 1947 there were 150 AEs under training at Bramley, and only one was a regular

Private J Forster was the first National Serviceman enlisted into the RAOC.

soldier. It was a huge commitment in training time for a very small return in time employed at trade.

The first of the six-month Ordnance Officers' courses, which would become in the post-war years, beloved of so many, commenced in January 1948. It replaced the former, pre-war one-year long course, and in particular removed the IOO qualification as one of the results of passing the course. Some of the attendees went on to become senior officers in the RAOC, such as Norman Speller, Len Phelps and Roy Darkin, all of whom would become major generals, two to become DOS, and in Ken Bangham and John Smith there were two depot commandants.

The introduction of National Service in 1948 had a major effect on the RAOC's training organization. The result was four battalions, Nos. 2 and 3 at Deepcut and Hilsea respectively, and 4 Battalion for technical training also at Deepcut with 5 Battalion at Gosport to train enlisted boys. It was the start of an interlude of some fourteen years in which the schoolboys of the country were turned into young men with an introduction to adult life provided by the Armed Forces. On 4 March 1948 the first intake of National Servicemen arrived at 1 (Selection) Training Battalion RAOC, and by 6 o'clock on that first evening over 450 had been processed. From reports at the time it seems every effort was made to make them welcome, with good accommodation and good reception facilities. The cynic would probably say they would do that anyway, with the press and public watching. Nonetheless, it does seem there was a genuine attempt to make a sobering experience as pleasant as possible.

It was to be the start of a period that would have an effect, however, not just on the individuals who joined, but also on the Army and on the society to which they returned, and very shortly there were to be a couple of examples of the selflessness that marked so much of the National Service contribution to the Army and to society. At Trawsfynnd where the Explosives Disposal Unit was destroying unwanted stocks, there was a fire in a lorry carrying ammunition. Private D E Bron, standing by his own vehicle, saw what was happening, leapt into the driving seat of the stricken vehicle and drove it some 400

And they were all entering a new world, one that would have a profound effect on many of them.

to 500 yards (sic) out of the ammunition area into a stream where he began to fight the fire. For his courage he was awarded the British Empire Medal for gallantry. Later that same year, in Germany, four soldiers saw a six year-old German child drowning in a lake, and his sister who went to his rescue was also in difficulties with both children sinking below the surface of the water. Staff Sergeant F M Hines, and Privates W Ashford, A Cuttle and R T Hankinson, in a nearby field, heard the screams of other children and rushed to the scene. Fully clothed in battle order the four of them, at least two of whom could not swim, leapt into the water to rescue the children. The pond, it transpired, was twelve feet deep and it was with considerable difficulty, and only after other soldiers had formed a human chain, that the two children were rescued, safe and sound.

National Servicemen also brought with them a sense of independence. Perhaps it came from knowing they had limited time to serve and that strength of character was not a barrier to progress. However, the regular permanent staff were more than capable of holding their own, as witness the outcome of Lance Corporal Len Parkes' 'interaction' with his drill instructor.

After completing one drill movement I became uncomfortably aware that I was facing the opposite way to the rest of the squad. He approached me and said quietly 'what do you think you are doing, lad?' I thought I could see a way out and replied: 'You made a mistake, Staff. You said squad will advance, left turn and advance meant turning to the right.'

He replied: 'Listen lad, you always obey the last order. If I say to you 'Fly to the moon, right turn' you turn to the right; you do not fly to the moon.'

Regimentally, sport was going from strength to strength. At Hilsea 3 Training Battalion was sweeping the football honours, appearing in no less than six finals in the 1948 season. Lance Corporal A Howard, stationed at Nesscliffe, won the light heavyweight title in the Army Boxing Championships. Among the 4 Battalion footballers was Corporal Norman Rucker of Manchester City, Corporal Steve Brereton of Everton and Corporal John Barnwell of Arsenal. From Didcot 14 Battalion took the Company Cup at Bisley as well as the Juniors Cup, coming ahead of some famous names amongst the Infantry. In hockey Chilwell won the Bari Cup, the RAOC's internal tournament, and Corsham took the juniors competition in the Richards Cup. Feltham became the Army tug-of-war champions and would go on to the tug-of-war at the Royal Tournament, which they would win. The heavy and the light teams at Feltham were trained by Mr W McCabe, who, despite having ceased to work in the depot, continued in his retirement to coach the teams. They went on to win the inter-services at both weights, pulling the Royal Marines and the RAF in a comprehensive victory. It was a team that was aged under twenty-one and composed almost entirely of National Service soldiers who took on and beat teams largely composed of older, regular servicemen.

May 1948 saw the end of the British occupation of Palestine, and the short notice placed a strain on the RAOC as the Corps units in the theatre sought to backload their stocks and close down their depots. The withdrawal was phased over five months, with the ammunition actually having to be shifted in the February. However, in the north units remained until July, and Major George Crooks and his 30 Ordnance Ammunition Company provided close support for them. By 1 July everything was out.

Meanwhile, down in East Africa there was already a cloud over the concept of the Ordnance depot at McKinnon Road. It was obvious that Egypt was not now going to be the subject of a precipitate evacuation, even supposing that the stocks in the depots could be put in a fit state for a move to Kenya. Question marks began to appear over the whole McKinnon Road concept. Nonetheless, construction proceeded, despite the realization that the paucity of rail communications raised doubts as to whether a depot of the planned size could be operated from this site.

In June 1948 the murder of three rubber estate managers in northern Malaya by Communist terrorists sparked off the emergency that was to see the British Army involved in counter insurgency operations on the peninsula for many years to come. There were attacks on a range of civilian installations all targeted at terrorizing the civilian population and damaging local economies. The security forces were strengthened, and the RAOC managed the logistic support of operations in Malaya from Singapore.

As this was happening the Russians finally cut the land corridor by rail and by road to Berlin, as well as all canal traffic. The western Allies refused to accept this flagrant transgression of their rights of access and unanimously agreed to sustain the city and all its needs by air. The Berlin Blockade had begun. Operation PLAINFARE commenced, controlled by a joint British and American organization called the Combined Airlift Task Force. Clearly, it was to be a Herculean task, and the RAOC in Berlin and in Germany was heavily involved in all its aspects. There were, however, no major changes to the RAOC ORBAT in Germany to deal with the situation, save the addition of one parachute heavy drop company to rig any airdrop loads that might be required. The problem was absorbed; the work went on.

By September 1948 the move of 17 Vehicle Company into its new depot accommodation in Mönchengladbach was complete. The first commanding officer in a location that would become familiar to thousands of post-war RAOC officers and soldiers was Lieutenant Colonel V J Thornton. Within a few short months, by January 1949, the huge size of both 16 and 17 Companies was acknowledged and they were designated battalions, paving the way for the vehicle parks to become companies as part of the battalion command structure. In the ammunition world, the volume of work had reduced to the point where 854 ASD at Boostedt, with its relatively small capacity of 6,500 tons, could be closed.

On 29 November at the Annual General Meeting of the RAOC Memorial Fund it was agreed to move the Corps' war memorial from Hilsea to Deepcut. It was also decided to alter the memorial so that it would commemorate, additionally, those who lost their lives during the 1939-1945 War. The plan called for the removal of the existing plaque, containing the names of the fallen in the 1914-1918 War, and placing it in St Barbara's Church, Hilsea. The memorial would then be erected on its new site at Deepcut. A new plaque would be provided for the memorial acknowledging that it commemorated the victims of both World Wars. Their names would be inscribed on bronze plaques set in a new wall behind the memorial.

The RAOC war memorial would be unveiled in its new location on 6 November 1949 by the QMG, General Sir Sydney Kirkman KCB KBE MC.

To achieve this, and because of charity law related to the funding of memorials, it was necessary to raise a fund to cover those elements of the memorial that did not relate to the First War. It required £2,500 (£54,000) to be raised. A rate was suggested for subscriptions ranging from £2 2s 0d (£45) for major generals, 4s 0d (£4.50) for warrant officers and 1s 0d (£1.10) for private soldiers. The plan was to see the work completed by Remembrance Day 1949.

The North Atlantic Treaty was signed on 4 April 1949. NATO was born and twelve nations formed its first members: Belgium, Canada, Denmark, France, Iceland, Italy, Luxembourg, the Netherlands, Norway, Portugal, the United Kingdom and the United States. Interestingly, one of the former Axis powers gained membership at the first pass. Italy was seen to have emerged from its dark age; the Germans, perhaps understandably, were not yet in a position to do so. The Russians immediately countered with the formation of the Warsaw Pact, coordinating all Communist forces under Russian control. It was, however, a quite different organization to the consensus-driven cooperative structure that was NATO.

A further development in 1949 was the drafting of a provisional constitution as a precursor for a democratic federal constitution for western Germany. The Basic Law, as it is still known, became active on 24 May 1949 and with a new, elected, Federal government in place, the Allied Military Governors were replaced by High Commissioners. The military-political changes wrought in Western and Eastern Europe changed the focus for the British Army and adjusted its posture to defend against a potential incursion, not to say an invasion, from the east.

In June 1949 two things happened at opposite ends of the spectrum of reality. The Army Council ruled that compulsory contributions to regular army bands would not, in future, be levied from officers. Instead the Army Council would assume responsibility for the maintenance of bands by means of an annual grant towards expenses and the additional pay of bandsmen. Unfortunately the grant was only £240 (£4,600) a year and was not sufficient to cover the expenses which, for the RAOC band, were £700 (£13,500). Whilst there was income from outside engagements, an Army Council Instruction restricted the level of earnings from this source to just £150 (£3,000) a year. Whilst not in a position to order officers to continue their payments, the DOS expressed the wish that they would continue to support the band by leaving the existing standing orders unchanged. History does not record the response to his plea.

Then the Soviet Army, which had been occupying Korea, north of the 38th Parallel, withdrew, following an agreement with the United States. The Americans simultaneously withdrew from the south. However, the victory of Mao Tse-tung's Communist army over the Nationalist forces of Chiang Kai-shek in October 1949 changed the politico/military balance in the region. It also produced what was considered to be a threat to Hong Kong, reoccupied at the end of August 1945, and led to the force levels there being doubled and established as a two-brigade division with supporting arms. This posed serious problems for the RAOC. Stocks were low and it was not uncommon for stores to be issued directly from arriving ships to demanding units; and a new depot was built, to be opened by November 1950. However, as 1949 came to an end, the British faced a large Communist army across a short border in a small country.

Also in 1949, in a quite different environment, DOS MELF had reduced his installations in the Middle East from a post war collection of four BODs, one BAD and a vehicle group to one command depot, a BAD and a vehicle company, with 5 BOD reduced to a disposals and mobilization role. He also planted a baobab tree in the McKinnon Road depot, commemorating the fact that building had progressed to the point where there was capacity to manage an AOD from the site. There was some hope, expressed by cynics, that the depot might grow to maturity before the tree which had a potential life span, given proper care and attention, of some 400 years. Alas, it was not to be, for just as tension was beginning to build in the Far East on the Korean peninsula, the ADOS East Africa recorded his view that the installation was a white elephant and the concept for its use fundamentally flawed.

On 1 August 1949 the Berlin airlift ended, the Russians having realized that the weight of logistic effort thrown by the western Allies at the problem was not going to be ameliorated until communications were returned to normal. During the thirteen months of the blockade some 2,225,000 tons of commodities of every conceivable type had been pushed through to the city. It had been a major effort, had cost a number of lives and had cemented a relationship between the western Allies and the citizens of Berlin that was to endure for many, many years. Now it was over there was one thing less to do in what had become a very crowded year.

In the United Kingdom there was a crystallization of a trend that had been under way in the RAOC since the early pre-war visits to the USA when Corps' officers had gone to learn about the concept of time and motion study that was being used in the American motor industry and to assess its value in managing the inventory. A Central Depot Planning Officer was created within the DOS Directorate at the War Office. An RAOC manual of work study practice was produced, limited at that stage to motion, or method, study because of the use of time studies in civil industry for wage fixing purposes. This was abhorrent to trade unions and viewed as counterproductive for the Army. Method study wings were formally established within the planning branches of the larger depots, with central planning branches being formed at HQs ammunition and vehicle organizations. Formal training started with Planning and Work Study courses for officers at the RAOC Officers' School, and for warrant officers and clerical officers at COD Chilwell.

It was about this time that a new tradesmen's badge saw the light of day, to recognize the special tasks, together with the required training, undertaken by AEs. They were granted the minimum rank of corporal on successful completion of their training, and also won the right to wear a special badge denoting their trade as something apart – something different from the recognition of the standard 'A' trade badge. There had been a competition for the design, and none had been considered suitable. Eventually Major Leonard Phelps, himself an IOO, was given a weekend to come up with an acceptable design. He took his inspiration from a box of Elizabeth Arden ladies' face powder, and the result was the first three-coloured trade badge to be worn by soldiers in the British Army. Its design has remained unchanged ever since.

Feeling had developed that the organization for managing vehicles and MT spares through the same systems and controlled together from Chilwell was not an effective way of doing business. There had been some small changes of structure in 1946, but the first significant changes were made in time to be implemented in 1950. The commandant at Chilwell took complete responsibility for the control of spares, whilst a newly found commandant took over a brand new vehicle organization. It was the separation of functions that had survived the test of war and supported the Army globally. It was doubtless sound to break it up in this way, but perhaps there ought to be some concern that change was instituted for the sake of change.

In Malaya it was becoming obvious that the Communist insurgency was not going to be easily put down. There had been some early successes against the CTs, but it was obvious from the intelligence picture that they were simply regrouping north of the Malayan border with a view to causing yet more trouble as soon as they were ready. Consequently, force levels were increased in the peninsula, by two brigades and an armoured car regiment. Their principal task was to see to the implementation of the Briggs plan. This was the idea of the director of operations at the time, General Briggs, and involved the setting up of villages which the inhabitants themselves could be trained to defend, thereby denying CTs the sustainment they would normally expect from villages they could dominate.

One might have been forgiven for holding the view that so much was happening in so many parts of the world that it would be nice to have some peace and quiet to plan and to resolve many of the residual problems left from the war. However, there were little lights in the darkness, and the dawning of 1950 saw an unexpected and pleasant surprise for the OC of the RSD at Tidworth when the following letter appeared one day in the post:

Commission Tripartite pour la Restitution de L'or Monetaire
155, rue de la Lot,
Bruxelles.

Dear Commanding Officer,   1st Jan 1950.

Exactly ten years ago today I arrived at your Depot straight from Dunkirk. Like many others I had had a tough time and I was furious and ashamed at having been thrown out of France. Moreover, I was so tired that I could hardly move.

The hospitality which was extended to me and to the other members of my party can only be described as wonderful. I have never been received or looked after so well at any time anywhere before or since then. I was given a room with everything that could be desired in it and I slept for about twenty-four hours – after which I was given what was certainly the most enjoyable meal I have had in my life. All these things did me a world of good both morally and physically.

I remember wondering how the room could have been prepared and made available in the way it had been. It was only later that I discovered that all the officers of the depot had slept in chairs in the Mess that night to make room for the refugees that we were.

I thought that I would like to tell you that I am one of those who have not forgotten and to say thank you again.

Yours sincerely,

JOHN A. WATSON (Colonel)

On 29 March 1950 3 Training Battalion's football team stepped out onto the pitch of an Aldershot stadium packed to capacity to watch the Army football final against 64 Training Regiment RA. The game was played in the presence of His Majesty King George VI, the RAOC's Colonel-in-Chief. It was a great moment when the King handed the

The winning 3 Battalion team.

winners' cup to Private J M Beale, Hilsea having taken the game two goals to one. Sport, again, offering a prospect of sanity, bringing fun to soldiering in a world that some might think had gone mad, and the RAOC was excelling across the Army.

Later in 1950, as part of a reorganization of HQ DOS, the DDOS (Ammunition) moved out of London to set up the headquarters of ammunition organization RAOC at Feltham, co-located with the

On 29 March 1950 the King presented the Army Football Cup to Private J M Beale RAOC of 3 Training Battalion, Hilsea, the team captain.

regimental depot. This left the training and staff duties elements of the HQ in London, together with control of the stores and depots, including stock levels in ammunition depots. The move to an ammunition organization, following the model of the MT organization, also saw responsibility for B wing at the school at Bramley wrested from the training organization and placed with the new ammunition organization. The wing was renamed and the Army School of Ammunition was born. The move was sound, for it brought the responsibility for storage, inspection, repair and administration under one HQ. It came in time for the RAOC to be able to focus its ammunition expertise on the problems it would face with the development of new high capacity ammunition, more complex storage regulations and the advent of guided weapons. It was also in place in time to meet the run-down in the fifties of ammunition stocks and the massive inspection, preparation and disposal tasks that were to come the Corps' way, to say nothing of depot closures towards the end of the decade.

The task they faced initially was massive to say the least. Some 45 per cent of ammunition in the UK ammunition depots required some form of repair. In AA Command, out of a holding of some

60,000 tons of 3.7-inch AA ammunition, 56,000 tons required modification. Most of the ammunition was still of wartime manufacture, made for early expenditure, not years in storage; much of it had been returned from war theatres; all of it had had years of often poor storage. Ammunition repair process buildings were entirely inappropriate for the massive task faced, and the training of technical staffs had to be enhanced to ensure that the IOOs emerged as efficient workshops managers, and the AEs as efficient repair operatives and supervisors. It was a massive job, and the funding was not going to be easy to find.

By the middle of 1950 Kim Il Sung, the North Korean leader, had deduced from a number of official American pronouncements that they would raise no objections if he marched his Army south and took over the whole peninsula. He moved south across the 38th Parallel on 25 June 1950, taking everyone by surprise. The UN Security Council met and passed a resolution inviting members to '...furnish such assistance to the Republic of Korea as may be necessary to repel the armed attack and to restore international peace and security in the area.' By 1 August the US had three divisions, some 47,000 men, in South Korea. They formed the US 8th Army under Lieutenant General Walton Walker with General Douglas MacArthur as the coalition commander.

The British were split, with the military hierarchy, conscious of its overstretched resources arguing against any serious involvement or commitment. Politically, however, the government felt they had to show solidarity with the Americans and so dispatched 27 Brigade from Hong Kong, with just two battalions. Initially, very few RAOC were sent with this very lightweight brigade, on the basis that the Americans would service all its needs and because of its peacetime role in Hong Kong it had not required integrated field force RAOC support. Furthermore, it was only to be an interim contribution, awaiting the arrival of 29 Brigade from the UK. However, it should have been obvious that the support arrangements were not a realistic option, pure practicality apart there was the experience of the recent World War to show that the kind of close in logistic support required by the British contribution, even at this early stage, could only be provided by a British logistic system. They were deployed with a 'pack' of Ordnance stores and ammunition, with just seven men to manage it, and Lieutenant Colonel J A Mockford, CRAOC Hong Kong, went as a liaison officer to the US HQ. Needless to say, it was not long before the weaknesses in the arrangements manifested themselves, with added weight being given by the decision that 27 Brigade was to remain in Korea along with 29 Brigade when it arrived. Consequently, an Ordnance package was put together at very short notice indeed on the insistence of the DOS FARELF, Brigadier G H C Heron. As a result, at the end of August 1948, the Gurkha Infantry Brigade OFP was withdrawn from Malaya, reinforced with volunteers from the base installations in Singapore, completely re-equipped and renamed 27 Infantry Brigade OFP. Commanded by Major Jack Guscott, the advance party arrived in Korea on 1 September to be followed by the main body on 29 September. Jack would later marry the Swedish nurse who cared for him after he was shot in the neck by a negligent discharge from an American guard. Finally, Captain Keith Hind and his Stores Section from 11 Infantry Workshops REME reached Pusan from Hong Kong on 6 September. Swift and positive reaction at all levels in the RAOC in the Far East had resolved a potentially impossible situation for the Brigade. There were huge problems associated with storage, particularly security, and a great deal of hard work was needed to resolve issues with the Americans and the Koreans to say nothing of internal difficulties within the British system, but at least 27 Brigade now had someone to do it for them, and had a system in place to support them in battle.

Then 29 Brigade followed 27 Brigade, coming by sea from the UK with three battalions. Support was from 45 Field Regiment RA and the 8th Hussars with their Centurion main battle tanks. The Royal Marines sent 41 Commando. However, 29 Brigade arrived with its full RAOC support package, including an OFP and a stores section for 10 Infantry Workshops REME.

Following a landing at Inchon, behind North Korean lines, and a spirited attack from the Pusan perimeter in the south, Seoul was recaptured on 28 September and MacArthur was authorized by the US Chiefs of Staff to move beyond the 38th Parallel to ensure the destruction of the North Korean armed forces. This was a move against the better judgement of many in the UN, not least the Russians. MacArthur was, therefore, only authorized to make his move over the Parallel within strict geographical and military limitations, with particular concern being felt at possible Chinese reaction. One limitation was that only South Korean forces could be used.

On 23 September 1950 the Soviets exploded their first nuclear bomb. It coincided with the final defeat in China of Chiang Kai-shek's army by the Communist forces of Mao Tse-tung, and suddenly there were Communists gaining ascendancy and demonstrating power all over the world. The North Atlantic Treaty had been signed in April 1949, although it was not to be until June 1950 that the first operational headquarters, to be known as SHAPE, was set up, and by then the Korean War had started. It was a world in turmoil, and into it moved NATO's first Supreme Allied Commander, General Eisenhower, and Montgomery moved to his headquarters near Paris to be his deputy. So far as the RAOC was concerned the initial impact of this was to adapt its structure to meet the needs of a newly configured army in Germany. The British Army of the Rhine would have to restructure from a force of two divisions to one initially of seven, although eventually only four materialized. The existing re-supply system, drawn in through Hamburg, would have to swing round to a LofC reaching back to the UK through Antwerp, supporting an Army designed to fight the Russians at short notice. The commitment was now permanent and would, at its height, involve a force of 77,000 soldiers.

On 28 September 27 Brigade in Korea was christened a Commonwealth Brigade with the arrival of a battalion of the Royal Australian Regiment to reinforce it.

The outbreak of war in Korea, the formation of NATO and the threatening noises from Communists throughout the world led to a revision of the defence budget. A three-year programme was announced in September 1950 that would cost £3.5 billion (£67 billion). After negotiating with the Americans over authorization for the use of nuclear weapons Attlee increased this yet further to £4.7 billion (£89 billion) thereby doubling pre-Korean war spending. At fourteen per cent of national

Sport, with shooting pre-eminent, was a binding force for retention. Here, B Company of 1 Training Battalion are winners of the Army Rifle Association Company Match. RSM Charles Knockles, who was to be a mainstay of RAOC shooting for many years, is seated on the left of the group.

income it was a crippling amount, especially in a country so ravaged by the effects of the Second World War. The Army was to receive one third of this and from it was to form ten active divisions, with four in Germany, and twelve for the Territorial Army, of which one would be armoured and another airborne. There was also to be a re-equipment programme.

These increases were so swingeing that Attlee, having won an election in 1950 with a heavily reduced majority from his 1945 landslide, felt he had to go to the country again. This time he was defeated and a Conservative government came to power. Militarily they were faced with the fact that the position of the two Alliances in Europe meant focussing the defence of the realm on maintaining an Army in Germany sufficient, in concert with allies, to deter, and if necessary defeat, an invasion from the east. By June 1951 1 (GB) Corps, based in Bad Oyenhausen, had been configured with three

A dishevelled Boer War memorial that would find a happier home at Deepcut.

divisions: 2nd Infantry, 7th Armoured and 11th Armoured. For the RAOC, this meant the creation of an RAOC ORBAT to support the concept of operations, units that were both organic to the formations and part of the LofC This involved an OFP for each division as well as corps troops. There was also organic support for an AA Group in Germany. In March 1952 6th Armoured Division was moved to Germany, bringing its OFP and Ordnance staff with it.

As part of the increased defence expenditure, and in order to retain soldiers and attract recruits into the Army, there was a review of pay and allowances sufficiently significant, so it was hoped, to make a difference; although some adjustment was, in any event, long overdue. The pay of a private soldier on entry rose from £1 8s 0d (£27) a week to £2 9s 0d (£48). An unmarried sergeant on £6 6 0d (£120) a week earned 3s 6d (£3.50) more than a second lieutenant, and many would consider that inadequate recompense for keeping young officers out of trouble. It should be borne in mind that this was pocket money only. There were no food and accommodation charges and married men received an extra marriage allowance. This was also the pay review that saw the introduction of specialist pay for soldiers and qualification pay, which became irreverently known as 'Qually Lolly', for officers up to the rank of major who had completed a long technical course.

In the midst of all this there surfaced an issue of great concern to the RAOC. It was discovered that the oldest known memorial to the fallen of the Corps, that to the AOC and AOD in the Boer War, modelled on Private 'Mick' Barry, was falling into disrepair and was the subject of attack by vandals. It was positioned in Francis Street in Woolwich near the old home of the RAOC at Red Barracks, and easily accessible to those who might wish to do it harm. After discussions with the town council it was agreed that a better home would be at Deepcut in the care of the RAOC. The move was completed by the middle of 1950, with the cost being met from RAOC funds.

In Korea MacArthur chose not to hear the

Lance Corporal Peter Lindsay RAOC was a national serviceman with a background in design and commercial art. Serving in 4 Battalion, his sketch of Deepcut in 1951 shows the memorial firmly and properly in place at the bottom of the parade ground, where it remains to this day.

limitations placed on any advance north, certainly not the military ones. By the end of October the US 24th Division together with the Commonwealth 27 Brigade was on the Manchurian border. The OFP, put together at such short notice, was close in behind it near to Pyongyang, having made the 400-mile journey along the less than adequate Korean roads in twenty-five days. The OFPs of both the British brigades were finding the stretched LofC difficult to manage. The railways were virtually useless, and it appears that the RASC support was too stretched to allow any transport to be made available for the delivery of Ordnance stores. It was an old problem, an old interface issue, raising its head again in time of war when units' needs were most pressing, and re-learning yet again a lesson of so many previous wars. The RAOC circumvented the problem by arranging for units to collect directly from the forward base following a 200 hundred-mile drive south to Taegu. This base unit was 4 Ordnance Composite Depot, an ad hoc unit drawn primarily from COD Didcot with the ASD from CAD Bramley. It had arrived in Pusan with 29 Brigade, the formation it was scaled to support, on 5 November. It comprised fourteen officers and 327 soldiers, with some forty-five per cent of its manpower being made up by reservists. Many of these men had been out of the service for up to four years and the skill fade, both military and technical, was significant. It set up as three sub-depots and an ASD, and was in position up country at Taegu by 20 November, with some elements, such as port handling, left in Pusan. The problems it faced setting up and operating in difficult country were exacerbated by the unexpected adding of 27 Brigade to its dependency with the decision that it was to remain in theatre.

Much of the support for Korea was to come from Singapore where the RAOC was hard pressed to support the fight against the CTs. Depots that had already been weakened by manpower reductions were further weakened by the creation of the units that were sent to Korea and by the individual reinforcements sent out to 'top up' under-strength units. Furthermore, the demands placed by Korea greatly outstretched the capacity of the Ordnance installations, with perhaps some inflation built in to compensate for the one month re-supply time from Singapore to Pusan. The supply of stores to Korea was almost entirely by sea with the possibility of any airlift so remote as to be unworthy of consideration. Ammunition was a case in point where the consumption in Korea meant that 443 BAD stretched its 6,000-ton limit to hold 20,000 tons.

The impact of all this activity in Malaya was that the RAOC simply did not have the resources to provide the service that units fighting the insurgency would normally expect. There were no excuses made, no one stopped trying, but it was all just too much. Something had to give and it was Malaya that suffered until such time as activity in Korea wound down and some normalcy could be brought to supply activity.

The North Korean Army had collapsed, but there had already been counterattacks by the Chinese on the 6th ROK Division on the Yalu River. The UN Forces held there and were in the process of organizing local elections when, on 27 November, the Chinese attacked. There were 300,000 of them against a UN Army of 205,000. The 8th Army was in the west and the centre with four US and four Korean divisions, two British brigades and one Turkish. There was then a gap of fifty miles to the east before encountering 10 US Corps with five divisions and the British command group – arraigned against fourteen Chinese divisions.

The Chinese swept through, and after weeks of fierce fighting a line was established all the way back down, some seventy-five miles, south of the 38th Parallel. The new commander of 8th US army, General Matthew B Ridgeway, famed for his actions commanding 82nd Airborne Division in the Second World War, took a firm grip, restored morale, counterattacked and, by the end of March, was back on the 38th Parallel. However, the close proximity of the Chinese advance to 4 OCD had thrown up real concerns about its position and the vulnerability of its stocks. On 5 January 1951 the depot received orders to withdraw to Japan, to the Australian manned British Commonwealth Occupation Force BOD at Kure. There was no time to make detailed plans for back loading with everyone working all hours to move stocks and Taegu was cleared by 22 January, apart from some small quantities of ammunition which were to be left behind. It took two months to straighten things out in Japan. Problems were faced with the storage accommodation that could be made available and the mess that had to be sorted from the bottleneck that had formed in Pusan slowing everything down. Matters were further complicated by the arrival in Japan of the four months' automatic issue from the UK and Singapore and the loss in the move of account card cabinets which meant the loss of all the issues' experience for their time up to then in Korea.

However, despite the difficulties, balance was being achieved. The forward base was in Japan with advanced elements in the southern part of Korea, holding stocks across the range at about thirty days' of supply. There was also a MLBU, with the bath section attached to 29 Brigade and the laundry in Pusan, and the two brigades had their integrated RAOC support of an OFP and stores sections with the workshops. The system had settled down and was working well by April when the Chinese counterattacked hard and once more the UN forces were pushed south. The British 29 Brigade, which now included a Belgian battalion, was hammered. The Gloucesters were destroyed on the Imjin River, with only 169 of the 850 men escaping to the south. It was an epic defence that rightly has its place in the annals of our history.

The poor infrastructure of roads and railways presented huge problems for the logistics organizations overall in meeting the needs of the British dependency. However, not only had they to compete with the conditions for use of road and rail, they also had to compete with the armies of the other nations involved, as they too struggled to sustain their forces. The winter of 1950 was appalling, with temperatures in some cases dropping to as low as minus twenty degrees Fahrenheit. Clothing was inappropriate, inadequate and insufficient for the conditions and once more in the annals of British Army history the press waged a campaign of behalf of the soldier to redress the problem. This redressing, however, added yet more burdens to an already overstretched RAOC organization as it sought not only to receive and issue arriving stocks of new clothing, but also to repair and refurbish unit returns as the seasons changed.

The British took into use a number of Willys Jeeps, obtaining them from the Americans. The US also provided spares – a necessary task since the British had just sold off their own stocks from COD Chilwell as part of a post-war clear out of unwanted inventory. There was some concern at the rate of issue of these spares, the consumption of which seemed to bear no relationship to the size of the fleet being supported. A check of registration numbers and an on-site inspection soon revealed the cause: there were an additional 200 vehicles being supported, the 'working surplus' having been obtained by acquisitive British soldiers from those vehicles abandoned by American and other US forces on the retreat back into South Korea.

The fighting in Korea continued around the 38th Parallel until June when, with the line moderately stable and no further advantage to be gained in any direction, both sides began the pursuit of peace through negotiation. However, fighting, in conditions not entirely dissimilar to those on the western front in an earlier war, was to continue for another two years. There was some movement for the Ordnance units as they sought to find the best location to serve their dependency. There was also the issue of manning, and the under-resourcing of Ordnance manpower seems to have been a perennial problem, surfacing as an issue in most campaigns throughout history. Supplements arranged locally were, and continue to this day to be, an apparent solution, although the lack of expertise in these 'pressed' men is often more of a disadvantage than the apparent value their numbers would appear to add. At this stage in the Korean War 29 OFP found itself staffed with men from the RA, RE, REME, RUR and 8 RIH.

In the spring and summer of 1951 the Commonwealth contribution was increased to a division of three brigades with the arrival of a Canadian brigade, and 27 Brigade was renamed 28 Commonwealth Brigade. The first CRAOC, Lieutenant Colonel M F McLean, swiftly divisionalized the support being provided to the brigades by pulling together the two OFPs into a single unit. Captain Douglas Mendham had just taken over 29 OFP when it happened, and wondered at his luck; or the lack of it.

The first Commonwealth OFP.

In Japan the Ordnance depot establishment was amended to include the Canadian static element. Then, in December 1951, it was decided to close the BCOF BOD in Japan and to provide Ordnance support to Australian forces in the theatre from 4 Commonwealth Ordnance depot, which was the appropriately renamed 4 OCD.

Yet more benefits were added in August 1951 to the serviceman's remuneration package, again targeted at retention. Pensions were increased significantly and a 'terminal grant' was introduced to boost it yet further.

In Germany the implications for the RAOC of the change of posture and the swinging of the LofC from Hamburg, as the port of entry, to Antwerp were huge. Part of this involved the move and restructuring of 15 BOD as an ABOD, which began to gather pace in mid 1951. Colonel Alan Fernyhough assumed the post of Commandant in May 1952, his predecessor having done most of the planning. One of the key priorities of the plans for the move was to shift forward ammunition reserve stocks west of the Rhine. As a consequence 3 BAD was moved from Liebenau to Bracht. A new unit, 454 FAD was formed, occupying the accommodation at Liebenau, vacated by 3 BAD.

In East Africa McKinnon Road's lengthy illness finally got the better of it and euthanasia was deemed the kindest solution to an installation that really had been a solution looking for a problem. It was closed in September, with the AOD that had been based there being abandoned and all support for East Africa Command was centred on Nairobi.

Life in Egypt began, at this stage, to become difficult. There had been since 1948, following the debacle of the defeat of the Arab League armies by the fledgling Israeli Army, a 'Free Officers Movement' led by a colonel in the Egyptian Army, one Gamal Abdel Nasser.

In Germany, in December, HQ BAOR became HQ Northern Army Group, and took on yet more responsibility that would impact on the life of the RAOC.

There had been a Materials Handling Experimental Unit in the RAOC since the end of the war. Established to investigate improved ways of storing and handling the whole commodity range, it moved to Deepcut where, it was felt, it would be closer to the centre of the Corps' technical life by being near the RAOC School.

In the Middle East the trigger that really created the complications was the British reaction to the Iranian takeover of the Abadan Oil Refinery following a nationalization of the Anglo-Iranian Oil Company – which was to do nothing. This perceived weakness spurred King Farouk to renege in 1952 on the Anglo-

Sergeant Brackenbridge, Car Commander, and Lance Corporal Graham were part of the RAOC's own commitment to defending 5 BOD.

Egyptian Treaty. Faced with the Nationalist Republican threats to his monarchy it seemed to him a sensible way to court popularity. What it meant to the British was, inter alia, a withdrawal of almost all locally employed labour. The effect on RAOC units was instant, with the constant reductions in numbers of military and the drive to civilianization, wherever possible, entire functions were savagely affected. To compensate labour was imported from Cyprus, East Africa, Mauritius and the Seychelles. Infantry battalions and artillery batteries were positioned inside 5 BOD at Tel el Kebir, and forays were made to bump away occasional Egyptian attacks on the perimeter.

Then in 1953 it was decided to dismiss all Egyptian police in the Canal Zone, it having been discovered that they had been responsible for coordinating a number of terrorist attacks on soldiers and their families. In the resulting rebellion the British Army killed a considerable number of them. This led to an orgy of rioting in major cities, with the vengeful mobs directing their efforts not just against the British, but also against King Farouk, the excesses of whose lifestyle had made him terribly unpopular and offered a focus for the Nationalist movement led by Colonel Nasser.

Soldiers, like Corporal Ron Davis, would spend the whole of an eighteen month tour in tented accommodation.

In July his Free Officers Movement led a rebellion that ousted the young King and brought the Colonel to power. Immediate negotiations followed seeking to establish the future of a British Army presence in Egypt. It was unlikely to be prolonged, for the new Republican government clearly wished to see the back of what it viewed as an army of occupation. However, these early negotiations broke down and harassment of British troops and installations started once more. One outcome was the transfer of HQ MELF to Cyprus.

After four years the National Service army had settled down and had brought benefits as well as disadvantages. The principal disadvantage lay in the huge training burden it imposed on the Army, with a relatively poor return in time, given the short period of the National Service commitment. On the plus side it brought together a huge range of talented people from all walks of life who made a great contribution in many ways to the life of the RAOC. Nowhere was this more apparent than in Army sport. The Charlton brothers would both eventually represent the Corps at football, as would Bert Trautman, the Manchester City goalkeeper. At Feltham the Corps bred a tug-of-war team of national standard and almost entirely composed of National Servicemen, and 4 Training Battalion at Deepcut was the Corps' boxing battalion.

Lance Corporal Henry Cooper was part of the battalion from 1952 to 1954. It was a battalion team that could as easily have been the England team. Sir Henry Cooper:

Captain George Eastlake, later Major Eastlake, was our CO. He earmarked all the London boxers and would convince them that joining the RAOC was a good idea. It was near London so they

Lance Corporal Henry Cooper
RAOC

The winning national tug-of-war team for the 1953 National Championship, with Mr McCabe seated in the front row…

could get into town twice a week to box in the London clubs, and they could get home easily at weekends.

Henry was already the ABA light-heavyweight champion when he joined the Army, and had represented his country at the Olympic games. 'I got back from Helsinki on the Sunday and found myself in the Army on Thursday – bit of a culture shock really.' Even more of a shock was when, shortly after arrival, he was marched in to the Sergeant Major's office, for what reason he could not begin to imagine. The Sergeant Major was at his desk, wearing his forage cap with the peak tight down over his face, which was largely hidden. However, as he got to see more, Henry's mind went back to a time six months earlier when his London club was boxing against a Liverpool club and he had knocked out his opponent, Kavanagh by name, in the second round. The reason for this interview was that Sergeant Major Kavanagh wished to renew his acquaintance with the young Cooper.

Lance Corporal Cooper was part of a powerful group of RAOC boxers, men such as George Whelan and Joe Erskine. Many of them were already ABA champions at their weight, or would go on to be when they left the Army. They gained great benefit from being in such a team as they were given plenty of time to train although they were not excused all military duties and training. Parades and the like still had to be undertaken, and with 4 Battalion being a driving battalion Henry learned to drive a three-ton truck. However, standards in the team were high and expectations were just as high.

> There were eleven bouts in an Army boxing match and so long as we won 11-0 or 10-1 we were OK. Win by 9-2 and we were all on orders the next day, inquiring into why we had done so badly. There wasn't a battalion that could beat us, Guards, Paras, the lot – they knew there was no point getting into the ring.

It wasn't just boxing of course, for many units in those days had more than one sporting string to their bow. For example, while 4 Battalion's boxers were cutting a swathe through the Army, its motorcycle team was winning the Army Motorcycle Championship, and its attendant Gort Trophy, which had been presented by Lord Gort who had commanded the BEF in France in 1939. Feltham's domination of tug-of-war reached its pinnacle when Mr McCabe achieved his life-long ambition of winning the national

…and in more active mode as he encouraged the 1952 team to greater and greater heights.

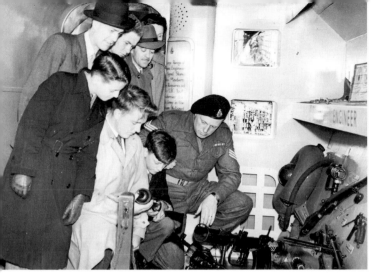

There were other ways than sport to heighten awareness of the Corps. Here Sergeant F Clarke is part of the RAOC Mobile Display Team in 1952.

catchweight competition. His team's success came at the AAA Championships at Haringey Arena in the presence of Her Majesty the Queen. He also trained a team to win the 100 Stone contest in the same tournament, both trophies previously having been held by Wimpey's London Airport Sports Club. It was the first time the Sovereign had attended an AAA championship for twenty-seven years and it was a happy coincidence that she was able to watch her Corps and its young soldiers achieve such an impressive victory.

In September 1952 the advance party of 15 ABOD under Major F S Goodwin moved onto its new site in Belgium. However, the circumstances were not of the best. Personal accommodation was nothing more than a tract of land surrounding the moat of a disused fort. So far as technical accommodation was concerned there were fences and some hard standing and covered storage ranging from not very much at all to almost finished, but not quite complete. It was not an auspicious start to two months of gargantuan effort. The move was completed by November 1952 with 1, 2 and 3 Sub-depots, 5 (Stores Transit) Sub-Depot and 6 (Reserves) Sub-depot in Belgium. Some elements were to remain in Germany: the General Stores and Clothing RSG and the Tentage and Camp Equipment Group of 4 Sub Depot at Hanover; and Rhine Sub-depot, comprising the indigenous MT and Technical Stores Sub Depot in Mönchengladbach, and the MT and Technical Stores RSG in Viersen. In most cases direct supply from the UK was the normal procedure. Apart from having a transit role for stores from UK, the depots in the advanced base were concerned largely with the holding of war reserves, although sub-depots in Germany remained fully active.

A new and additional major ammunition unit, 5 BAD, was raised in the early months of 1952 with the task solely of holding reserve stocks in the Advanced Base. It became the first RAOC unit to move into Belgium, with the advance party arriving at Tielen in mid March. Stocking up started in April, and

And in the midst of it all the sporting ethic remained. Wherever Charles Knockles (one left of centre) or Geoffrey Worsdell (centre) were stationed shooting flourished. When they were together, as here with the 17 Battalion 1952 rifle and LMG teams, ...well...

all elements of the BAD had arrived by early June. This placed the configuration of the ammunition support in western Europe with 3 BAD at Bracht, 5 BAD at Tielen, both lieutenant colonels' commands, and 154 FAD at Wulfen, commanded by a major.

Early in 1953 there was an almost complete change of the top structure in Malaya. General Sir Gerald Templar arrived in February; there was a new commissioner of police and a new head of intelligence. Templar's force levels were raised to twenty-eight battalions, one of which was from Fiji, two of the Kings African Rifles and seven from Malaya, as well as Australians and New Zealanders. There was a change of emphasis in the type of counter insurgency operations, with formations remaining for considerable periods in one area to ensure the Communist threat had been eradicated and that villagers could support and fend for themselves. It was a long-term strategy aimed at building communities that could be self-sustaining and that would resist the Communists politically and, where necessary, militarily. At any one time there were never more than 5,000 CTs, and despite the advantages they gained from the terrain and the difficulties it imposed on the security forces the weight against them would prove too much and the number of operations they could undertake, and the effectiveness of those operations, began to wane.

Life in Malaya was something of an adventure, and everyone played his or her own part in the war on terrorism. For example, RAOC officers took their turn as officer commanding one of the various night trains, all of which carried a guard. This was due to the fact that in 1950 there were 360 attacks by terrorists, including fifty-nine derailments causing nineteen deaths and in 1951 attacks went up by nearly 100, with eighty-one derailments and eighteen deaths. In one of the worst derailments, in which two passengers were killed and five injured, Major W H Clarke of the Ordnance Directorate, HQ Malaya was OC Troops. He explained:

I will never forget that journey. The train carried 600 passengers, according to a local paper, and was derailed after the armoured pilot train, which runs a couple of miles ahead, had passed. An Indian passenger said: 'I felt a crash as two of the carriages in front collided. Men, women and children screamed amid the firing which continued for fifteen minutes.'

Shortly after this Major Clarke and an Indian walked by the carriages, calming the passengers, and gradually the commotion died down and order was restored.

As in most post war theatres there was a considerable load on the RAOC in meeting the wide range of EOD tasks. Captain G Prosser's experience, while perhaps not unique was, well, at least different. He was sent out to destroy nearly 1,500 pounds of gelignite, located in a disused tin mine deep in the jungle. Carrying full equipment, including a carbine, together with the necessary explosives, he set out from Kuala Lumpur, flying to Kuantan on the East Coast and thence by road to Chukai in a Land-Rover escorted by an armoured car. He then went twenty miles up river, during the night, in a police motor launch with an escort of a dozen policemen armed with rifles and Bren guns. When he started this last stage of his journey the river was sixty yards wide, but it quickly narrowed to twenty yards, whereupon the density of crocodiles intensified. There were floating logs, sandbars and shallows, and for the last few miles two men walked most of the way, helping to keep the craft moving. When the party disembarked there remained a six-mile march along a disused trail through the

Malay ORs in
several orders
of dress.

Private Ahmad Bin Kassim, a Malay OR at 223 BOD.

jungle to the mine. This was heavily overgrown, and all members of the escort kept a constant lookout for terrorists. All the gelignite was in a magazine and in a dangerous condition. Some of it had exuded nitro glycerine and the task took several hours. They got back to the river by early afternoon and returned to Chukai by daylight. Just another day in the life of…

One feature of RAOC life not fully appreciated in places like Malaya was the fact the Corps recruited locals to serve in its ranks. They wore the RAOC badge with every bit as much pride as the next man, and were almost universally exemplary in the conduct of their duties. Lieutenant A C Smith wrote:

When you disembark from a troopship in Singapore, you may be surprised to find that your driver, proudly wearing his Corps badge, is Malay. He is one of the 250 or so Malay Other Ranks of 223 BOD. Few people, who have not served in Malaya, know of this small, but efficient, body that performs all duties of Ordnance. They are recruited from all parts of Malaya and after three months basic training they report at the BOD, very smart and, like all locally enlisted troops, proud to wear British uniform. At this stage the RAOC School plays its part, and in a comparatively short time, clerks, drivers, shoemakers, crane operators, textile re-fitters and the like emerge from its classrooms. The Malays add a touch of colour to the Corps in Singapore. Their Regimental Mufti revives some of the pre-war splendour of military uniforms, and whether on duty at an RAOC Officers' Mess Ball or celebrating one of the numerous Muslim festivals, the MORs, in their Regimental Mufti, are always a centre of attraction. This colourful uniform is really the Malay's national costume with the colour modified to suit the Corps, and with the addition of the Corps badge in the hat (Songkok). This uniform is not a free issue but is paid for by the men themselves. Promotion is encouraged and some of the older NCOs are pre-war soldiers with extensive service and experience. One such is SQMS Scully, the senior MOR of 223 BOD.

SQMS Scully, the senior MOR.

Just as the Malayan situation was looking promising another colonial disturbance emerged in Kenya where Jomo Kenyatta had subverted the Kikuyu tribe into rejecting the Government. His aim was to take power and to see Europeans and Asians ejected from the country. The main political arm of the

The RAOC had been properly represented at the King's funeral. Here the Processional Detachment is learning to get it absolutely right at the RAOC Training Centre.

movement was the Kenyan African Union, and there was a paramilitary arm called Mau Mau. It would be four years before the rebellion was brought under control, and it would occupy 10,000 troops in so doing.

By April 1953 the situation in Kenya had become sufficiently pressing to warrant the deployment of 39 Brigade to help in the battle against the insurrection. By October it had been joined by 49 Brigade. Both brigades had their OFPs for direct support, and there were the static Ordnance units, including a BOD with purpose built accommodation and a command ammunition depot. As was the case with so many internal security operations, the RAOC played its part in the military operations as well as its normal role. Lieutenants Tony Camfield and Mike Callan each commanded platoons of RAOC and RASC soldiers that formed part of the Nairobi Internal Security Battalion, and 'bags' of terrorists resulted from time to time from their activities.

In June 1953, following her accession to the throne, Her Majesty Queen Elizabeth II confirmed that as sovereign she would continue in the role her father had assumed as the Duke of York and subsequently throughout his reign – to be the RAOC Colonel-in-Chief. To mark the decision it was decided that Her Majesty should be invited to approve a portrait. Funding to support it would come from across the Corps, and subscriptions were sought from officers and soldiers alike. At her coronation on 2 June 1953 six officers and 160 soldiers of the RAOC were part of the 'Street Lining Contingent' in London in the area around both sides of Marble Arch from Cumberland Gate and extending into Oxford Street. The Contingent Commander was Lieutenant Colonel E A Horsey OBE.

The Armistice in Korea was signed on 27 July 1953, by which time British casualties were 793 killed with 2,878 wounded and missing.

In Germany the Ordnance position was being trialled to support the military posture being developed for the Cold War. The RAOC element of the 3rd Line LofC support was formed by the creation of the 1 (GB) Corps Ordnance Maintenance Park, but only for the duration of a major exercise. It comprised a stores company, an ammunition company, a vehicle company and an industrial gas platoon, found from other RAOC units in Germany and the UK. However, the outcome was not the creation of a much-needed RAOC structure on the LofC, but a deferred decision that would mean continued reliance on an ad hoc solution in war.

Early 1954 saw a number of small developments. The new rifle to replace the bolt action Lee Enfield was paraded in the Corps' *Gazette* with graphic descriptions of how much better it would be. Shooting was in any event a major force in Corps' sport led by notable figures like Geoffrey Worsdell and Charlie Knockles. And it wasn't just in the regular Army that the Corps did so well. In the Airborne Division, 16 Parachute Brigade OFP, a TA unit, had won the annual unit shooting competition in 1953.

The pay of regular soldiers was increased yet further as a retention measure, even at a time when the Army was to lose some 11,000 men in yet another of the seemingly endless round of manpower reductions. And there was an announcement that a team from 17 Battalion in CAD Nesscliffe had won a basketball championship, describing the sport very quaintly as 'something developed in the USA in 1891'. The author hoped it would be a sport of which more might be seen. How little he knew.

The Vine Hunt outside the Officers' Mess at CAD Bramley.

The question of depot accounting also reared its head once more. Conscious that systems were developing elsewhere in the world, visits to Canada and the USA by Major General Lancelot Cutforth resulted in a study on upgrading existing systems to take advantage of improvements in technology that were, by then, already having their effect across the Atlantic. Once more Chilwell was chosen as the test bed for experiments and trials with the new system. The outcome was a more powerful NCR, this time with thirteen registers, and a much more comprehensive view of the account. Processing and provision were greatly simplified and a much more effective system of stores management, especially of Dues In[1] and Dues Out[2], was possible. To give an indication of the size of the task, conversion to the new system at COD Chilwell involved the balancing and audit of some 80,000 account cards, 100,000 dues in cards and 6,000 dues out cards: the heading up of the new account cards by typewriter and the entry of opening balances on the new account cards. A time study showed that the process would take twenty minutes per item, and there were some 200,000 items to be transferred. The task required the setting up of a conversion unit of forty people.

However, despite the effort involved and the need to maintain a service to the Army while all this was going in, the result of the trial was a huge improvement in efficiency. In the end it was all worth it.

The working party that was studying and introducing these changes had also been tasked with introducing punched card techniques in order to provide analyses of information for provisioning and for management purposes and to produce issue vouchers for certain types of stores. The contract was awarded to IBM Ltd. The machines were introduced, into COD Chilwell in 1957 and then later into Branston, Didcot and Donnington, as part of Provision, Control and Accounts Branches.

The Commonwealth Division in Korea was reduced at the end of 1954 to brigade strength. HQ RAOC was disbanded, and the OFP reformed as an independent brigade OFP. Then, the first half of 1955 witnessed even greater attrition. The Korea Sub Depot of the BAD was disbanded and the BAD reduced to a major's command. The FOD in Pusan disappeared and the Forward Ordnance Maintenance Company was reduced to platoon strength. The drawdown would continue until July 1956, when the Commonwealth Force was further reduced to a battalion. From then on the maintenance of the Commonwealth Forces in Korea, now re-named the Commonwealth Contingent Korea, became the responsibility of HQ FARELF, with Inchon in Korea receiving its supplies direct from Singapore.

Korea had been an experience; a supply experience and soldiering experience. It was the custom at the time for RAOC subalterns to spend time with the infantry once they had been inducted into the Corps. This was in part due to the fact that there were no real posts in the Corps of any merit for officers below the rank of captain, but the spin-off in experience not just of leadership, but also teeth arm supply problems, was considered hugely valuable. Sometimes, however, it was experience that came at a price. Geoffrey White and John Lock were attached to the Middlesex Regiment and went with the Regiment, each commanding a platoon, to Korea. They were killed in action. Their Commanding Officer wrote to the DOS:

> Each fell leading his platoon. Geoffrey White was directing his men on the objective, which they had captured, when he was hit by machine gun fire. John Lock was wounded in an attack, but undaunted led his men on again, only to be killed – two very gallant young officers.

October 1954 saw the presentation of a jewelled brooch to Her Majesty the Queen, from the officers of the RAOC. It was the first of a series of brooches that the Corps would present to her.

In Germany 1 (GB) corps was re-titled 1 (Br) Corps and moved into Bielefeld. The first of what would be many an article from Corps HQ appeared in the Corps' *Gazette* in February 1955.

Boys' training had been at Haslar in Portsmouth, but it became overcrowded so they transferred to Blackdown as a company in 1 Training Battalion. One feature of boys' training at the time was the formation drill team they developed and which appeared for a few years at all major military events. It would not survive the pressures on manpower, but it was for a while a wonderful piece of public relations for the RAOC and for the junior entry of soldiers in preparation for adult service

During 1954 negotiations had commenced again with the Egyptians, with the assistance and connivance of the Americans keen on pursuing peace in the Middle East. The outcome was an agreement for a complete British evacuation by the middle of 1956, subject to some installations in the Canal Zone being kept in working order up until mid-1963 in case they might be required for strategic deployment. This imposed a huge load on the RAOC, for the agreement saw the retention of 5 BOD, 9 BAD and the BVD in much reduced roles with the rest of the RAOC units closing down and being withdrawn to the UK. The drawdown was to be spread over a lengthy period and this would preclude the dumping of stocks. Instead, there could be a measured programme of returns, and sale of those items not required. For 5 BOD, the task was rendered worse by having to remain working to service a dependency of 30,000 that would remain, declining gradually in size, until the end of the British presence.

On the other hand 10 BOD was faced with the quite different task of disposing of its 158,000 tons of stores and preparing the depot operating areas to be passed into the stewardship of the Egyptian Army. Stocks would either be used to support units remaining, directly or via 5 BOD, or they would be returned to the UK or, where it made sense, disposed of locally.

The end of 1954 saw the end of Anti-Aircraft Command. Almost a military institution, it had been overtaken by events. Harold Macmillan, then the Minister of Defence, made the announcement in the House on 1 December, pointing out that the advent of missiles and long-range high-flying aircraft had rendered anti-aircraft defence with guns almost futile, and the Government had to make savings. Some gun regiments would be retained, in the field force where they would still be of use, but the rest, almost entirely TA, would either be re-roled or disbanded. As part of the same package of cost-cutting measures, he also announced that the second battalions of some infantry regiments, battalions that had formed as recently as 1951, would also be cut. The same series of announcements informed the nation that the 3rd Division would return from Egypt and be stationed in Eastern Command. Any one of these initiatives would have meant a higher workload for the RAOC both at home and overseas and there would be no additional resources to cope with it. For all three to come together was, well – difficult to say the least.

There was one small acknowledgment of the problems faced by the support services generally. The Army estimates for 1955 made reference to the difficulties of supply in the nuclear age and for the need to invest in vehicles with the ability to operate off road, and aircraft with a short take-off and landing capability. Regrettably, the announcement focussed on the means of distribution, and made no mention of the communications and IT infrastructure that would be required actually to manage the assets.

In Hong Kong a simple, but moving, ceremony took place as a memorial was

Sub-Conductor Brown lays a wreath at the Sai Wan War Memorial, Hong Kong.

unveiled to those killed in the Japanese invasion or who subsequently died in captivity. It records the names of the fifty-one officers and men of No. 6 Section of the RAOC who died and who have no known grave. Another fourteen, including the ADOS, Lieutenant Colonel R A P McPherson, lie buried in the cemetery. The original plan had been, due to shortage of space, to allow just one RAOC representative at the unveiling in keeping with the allocation to other Corps. However, such had been the contribution of the RAOC to the defence of Hong Kong, and such had been their sacrifice, this was raised to four. The warrant officer in charge of the Union Jack was SQMS L Munsey who had served with No. 6 Section, had fought with them and had spent the war as a prisoner of the Japanese. Lieutenant Colonel J E Jackson, Major L T H Phelps and Sub-Conductor K Jackson were the other members of the RAOC party.

In May 1955 Germany realized its post-war dream, becoming a sovereign nation. It had finally been judged politically to have emerged from the ashes of the Second World War. In Berlin this was the year in which the rank of the senior RAOC officer was downgraded to major, and in which two locally important moves were made, of stores to Alexander Barracks and ammunition to Ruhleben.

One of the ideas General Cutforth had brought back from his visit to the USA in 1954 was that a new form of electronic information management, called a computer, might have some relevance to stores accounting. Others were also interested, and consequently a meeting took place on 30 June 1955 involving the Treasury, the War Office and the Ministry of Defence, the outcome of which was to ask General Cutforth, by then the DOA, to set up a working party to investigate the use of automated data processing for Ordnance stores. He was not slow off the mark and the first meeting took place on 7 October 1955 with, alarmingly, the Treasury in the chair.

On 27 July the British left Austria, one thing less to support, and then on 3 October left the Sudan. This was a slightly more emotional moment for it severed a link with the Crown that went back over half a century. Memories of the stories of the siege of Khartoum and the death of Gordon may well have passed through some minds as officers and senior NCOs sipped cocktails beneath the Mahdi's tree and the band of the Royal Leicestershire Regiment played.

Just as the tide was turning in Kenya problems arose in Cyprus. The Army Council must have given thanks that the seemingly perennial problems in the colonies occurred sequentially for, had they materialized simultaneously, the Army would simply have been swamped. In Cyprus the problem stemmed from the desire for union with Greece. There was a word for it: enosis. It actually started in 1950 when a priest called Michael Mouskos was made Archbishop of the Cypriot Orthodox Church and took the name Makarios. While in Athens he had met a somewhat disgruntled Greek Cypriot colonel called George Grivas and between them in 1951 they began planning how they might convince a British government that enosis was a good idea. Grivas moved to Cyprus in November 1954 and began the construction of a terrorist movement called EOKA, the National Organization of Cypriot Fighters. Makarios preferred political action, but understood the need for some military activity from which he could spawn an effective basis for negotiation. He agreed to the start of a campaign on 31 March 1955, limited to attacks purely to damage British military infrastructure. However, this was bound to escalate, and the first British soldier was killed by a grenade attack in October 1955, shortly after the arrival of reinforcements on the island in the shape of two RM Commandos and two infantry battalions. There were other murders, and three altogether were of RAOC soldiers. By the end of the year Army strength had risen to 12,000 with an additional 2,000 RAF.

At the end of the year, 9 BOD in Egypt was handed over to contractors and just thirty days later, at the beginning of 1956, the empty site at 10 BOD was handed over. The two depots relocated to the UK, probably the first time there was a complete move of an RAOC unit, with disbandment and trickle posting having been the norm, in peacetime, up until then. The closure of MELF units on such a scale had a significant effect of the RAOC Gazette, and the loss of sales was so keenly felt that a rise was

Lance Corporal Duncan Edwards RAOC, who died in the 1958 Manchester United air crash.

felt to be necessary in the subscription paid by officers, rising to 12s 0d (£9.50) a year. There would appear to have been some reluctance to pay, given the reminders that appeared regularly in the Gazette for the return of the standing order forms.

Rugby featured in the Corps' news early in 1956. It was noted that one Peter Jackson, who had played for the Corps in 1949/50 and had gone on to play for Coventry was awarded an England Cap against Wales. And a name appeared that would resonate rugby throughout the Corps for many years to come. Sergeant Norman Bruce of 1 Regular Training Battalion represented the Army against Oxford University. There were other examples of RAOC soldiers playing at Army level: in football there were Private Trevor Smith of 15 Battalion and Birmingham City; Lance Corporal A Biggs of 15 Company and Bristol Rovers; and Lance Corporal D Edwards of 117 Coy and Manchester United; and in hockey, Sergeant M J Bedford. Duncan Edwards would later be killed in the infamous air crash at Munich Airport in 1958 that resulted in the tragic loss of Manchester United players.

In January five more battalions arrived in Cyprus, together with the armoured cars of the Royal Horse Guards (The Blues). The 17,000 troops were organized into four brigades and, at the same time, there was an increase in the number of RAF helicopters. Their arrival coincided with the arrival from Egypt of GHQ MELF, and accommodation, especially for families, proved a real problem. For the families the keen anticipation of a move away from the restrictions on life in the Canal Zone was soon dissipated by the security situation in Cyprus, to say nothing of the temporary and inadequate nature of the quarters in places like Berengaria Village and Limassol. The huge increase in manpower and commitments at the turn of 1956 warranted an increase in the RAOC commitment and a reorganization and strengthening of the units on the island. 146 Vehicle Depot, commanded by Major L W Rosher, and 301 Ammunition Depot, commanded by Captain Peter MacDonald, were formed as independent units from sub-depots of 625 Ordnance Depot, and 238 Army Vehicle Park joined them later. Specialist units included 4 Mobile Laundry and Bath Unit, and the GHQ Printing Press. 625 Ordnance Depot grew from a major's command and was taken over in September 1955 by Lieutenant Colonel C R Cowan. The pressure on RAOC soldiers was particularly acute as the unrest in the civil population meant that few, if any, could be trusted to work in the depots. The need for depot-trained and experienced soldiers was acute, and fortunately there was a good source of them from the military manpower in the UK base depots.

In 1956 there was an attempt at a negotiated solution, but Grivas disobeyed Makarios' instructions to desist from military activity during the negotiations and nineteen bombs went off. Makarios was very angry, but refused to condemn the bombings. The outcome was his exile to the Seychelles in March. Terrorist attacks continued, and Captain Peter Lane RAOC, aged thirty-one, was the fourteenth victim in a series of assassinations. Two killers, who had been working nearby in some scaffolding, shot him in the back of the head and escaped into a crowd from which no witnesses could subsequently be found. He had only been on the island for three months, staying with his wife, Barbara, and their nine-week old daughter in the Nicosia Palace Hotel. Another death was that of Private Isbell, shot in similar circumstances, although this time accompanied by two friends. He was just nineteen years old.

A particular role that placed a doubly heavy load on one section of the RAOC community in Cyprus was the bomb disposal task, undertaken in addition to the heavy load of inspection, repair, redeployment and issue of ammunition. The bomb disposal tasks included large amounts of stray ammunition in addition to improvised explosives devices, pipe bombs and the like. Over 4,300 bomb explosions were investigated. 4,688 unexploded devices were dealt with, and there were just less than 3,000 recoveries of arms, ammunition and explosives. The RAOC casualty list included the deaths of two AEs. When Sergeant R Kilby, the first to be killed, met his death he had dealt with forty-nine unexploded bombs, and investigated twenty-three further incidents. On this occasion, early on 31 July he had accompanied a police patrol to Sinda Village, where there was evidence of homemade mines having been planted. His search revealed two, which he safely defused. A third, which was buried beside the village well, detonated as he attempted to deal with it. Then, Staff Sergeant J A Culkin died dealing with an explosive device in Limassol on 25 September 1955. Rather more successful was the neutralization of the bomb that an EOKA sympathizer on the staff of Government House had placed underneath Field Marshal Harding's bed. Despite the risks, and the golden rule that a man's life is worth more than the preservation of property, the IOO on this task, perhaps conscious of the high profile of the intended target, neutralized the device and was able to find sufficient forensic evidence to pursue the potential assassin. It is worthy of note that 1 Ammunition Disposal Unit, specially created for the task, was the first formed RAOC unit to undertake bomb disposal duties.

In March 1956 the last British teeth arm units left Egypt by troopship, leaving the remnants of the RAOC to tidy up the aftermath before themselves departing. It was the end of a seventy-four year occupation, and it coincided with the withdrawal of the small Ordnance presence in the Sudan; a purely coincidental move. At the same time there was a change in Germany, when 11th Armoured Division was re-titled 4th Armoured Division and reorganized. There was an inevitable adjustment and re-scaling exercise for the RAOC, the loss of the Mobile Laundry and Bath Units from the divisional ORBAT, and all MLBCs were disbanded. Just to give a taste of the implications for the RAOC of such reorganizations, apparently trivial in their implications, 95,000 line items of MT and Technical Stores were being held in 15 ABOD. As a result of this revise, 47,000 items had to be out-scaled and 23,000 new items had to be brought in. And before that task was completed, the next revise, with yet further changes had been received.

To reinforce the emphasis on work study techniques, the planning branches in depots and RAOC HQs were re-named as Planning and Work Study Branches. At the same time formal training in these subjects was centralized with courses being run at the RAOC School.

The anti-terrorist campaign on Cyprus carried on, but in July that year came the announcement that Nasser was to nationalize the Suez Canal and many eyes turned in that direction. However, that did not make the problems of Cyprus go away, and the situation was not helped by the need to divert resources to the Suez issue. The build up for the operation just added yet more to the load on the RAOC units on the island.

By this time East Africa Command comprised only Kenya, Uganda and Tanganyika and it seemed likely that British soldiers would be present only as advisors. Consequently, it was planned that by June 1957 all Ordnance units in the Command would disband, or be re-allocated and that any stocks would be passed to a newly constituted East Africa Land Force organization, in which the total RAOC representation would be one officer and eight soldiers. The East African Army Ordnance Corps would disband. There were a few problems that delayed the outcome, but by late 1957, the EAAOC was no more and most of the stocks and accommodation had been handed over to EALF, with a few sheds being retained in British hands for a clearing up operation by the few RAOC soldiers remaining and for the AEs remaining purely for stock inspection and repair.

Still in July, the Commonwealth Brigade in Korea reduced to one battalion. Further rundowns would continue, followed finally by the close of the base in Japan at the end of 1956.

While the strains of post war Nationalist rumblings were being dealt with across the globe there had been some fundamental decisions taken by first Churchill's and then Eden's governments that were to have long term implications for the Army and consequently the RAOC. The first of these lay with the commitment to maintain on the soil of continental Europe a force under the command of SACEUR that would equate to the fighting power of four divisions and a tactical air force, commensurate with the size of force then currently being maintained. This numbered, in those days, 80,000 servicemen. Furthermore, they also undertook not to withdraw or reduce these forces, were the majority of members of the Alliance not to be in favour with such a move. There was a sound political reason for this: it would help persuade the French, Belgians and Dutch that German rearmament and membership of the Alliance was an acceptable proposal.

Eden inherited these expensive commitments when he came to power in 1955. Almost his first act was to seek ways in which he could reduce the economic burden they caused. As foreign secretary he had been instrumental in building the Central Treaty Organization, born out of the Baghdad pact of January 1955 between Iraq and Turkey, and the South-East Asia Treaty Organization. He saw structures such as these as a means of spreading the military commitment and precluding the need for large overseas British garrisons.

However, as the last British troops left Egypt with the Egyptians having agreed to the preservation of former military installations being managed by a British company, there was no alliance in place that would guarantee Britain's use of its former bases in an emergency; nor would Nasser countenance it. Thus it was that, just six weeks after the last soldier had left Egypt, Eden invited the Chiefs of Staff to prepare plans to execute a return. This was caused by Nasser's declaration of nationalization of the Suez Canal as a means of raising money to fund the building of the Aswan Dam on the Nile, alternative sources of funding, such as a loan, having been denied to him.

The French and the British had agreed that if other means of resolving the issue failed, with its attendant risks to the right of passage for their shipping through the Canal, then they would invade with a view to occupying the Canal and if necessary to topple Nasser from power. However, there were shortcomings to the concept, not the least of which was military. There was no plan in place for such an operation; there was no strategic air or sealift available and there was simply no capability to provide the logistic support that would be required for such an operation. The net effect, caused almost entirely by this last factor, was the call up of 23,000 reservists, 2,451 of whom were RAOC. It also meant the retention of a further 560 regular soldiers beyond their planned run-out date, and this was in addition to 500 officers and soldiers diverted from their parent units throughout the RAOC to provide individual reinforcements. Captain Mike Callan, then the adjutant at HQ RAOC 3rd Division, recorded the frenetic activity at all levels as the build up for the operation got under way:

> We worked eighteen hours a day for the first six weeks. The demands from units seemed to be insatiable. At the same time we were mobilizing 3 Division OFP and 4 Mobile Laundry and Bath Company (an Army Emergency Reserve Unit) as well as units of other arms and services. Yet there was a great sense of purpose and if items were available, we got what we needed.

General Keightley, C-in-C MELF in Cyprus, was to command the operation using II Corps HQ from Germany; and the French would also be subordinated to MELF. With the use of 10th Armoured Division from Libya being denied due to the objections of King Idris, and the number of tanks available from the UK being limited, together with the shipping to lift them, limitations were being imposed on the flexibility of commanders from the outset.

The operational headquarters, II Corps, had no logistic representation to undertake planning, and this was a weakness that would last for several weeks. Then, as logistic planning got under way, there were continual changes of ORBAT that made the task for the RAOC of scaling the force very difficult indeed. Furthermore, the decision to prepare under peacetime conditions imposed bureaucratic delay. Further complications would derive from the control of strategic shipping and airlift being in the hands of the Ministry of Transport, and their focus was on economy and not operational capability. There was no military movements representation at the ports so loading was uncoordinated and not related to operational need. Just about everything that militated against effective logistic support was in place.

RAOC soldiers disembarking from the SS *Empire Fowey*.

The RAOC was faced with the task of scaling and then stocking the operation, including the vexed and inevitable task of bringing units up to entitlement. At the same time it had to provide training facilities to compensate for the skill fade in the reservists, many of whom had been in civilian life for many years. In addition to the organic units in 3rd Division, the major formation involved in the operation, the military component at COD Bicester, would find 521 ABOD, Bramley produced 10 BAD and 201 Vehicle Battalion formed up at Chilwell. This was recognition of the fact that a forward base would be required to support field force units moving into the hinterland to support their formations and that it would have to be run based on depot procedures and not those in use in the field force. This could only be achieved using trained military manpower from the base depots.

The plan first conceived was to advance with an armoured column to Cairo and then from there to break out to Port Said, to Ismalia and to Suez. If Nasser failed to accept the proposals on the future of the Canal the invasion would commence on 15 September, with the assumption that the operation would last only eight days. In the event the shortage of amphibious landing craft limited the planners to an assault on Port Said to be followed by a rapid advance along the Canal. Politically, Eisenhower, with an election

They would find themselves working under the sort of conditions to be found in 521 ABOD.

looming, was left with little choice but to oppose the operation, whilst the French and the Israelis worked together to ensure British commitment. They concocted a plan that saw the Israelis invading and the French and the British interposing themselves as peacemakers and using that as a guise to occupy the Canal Zone.

The operation began on 29 October with an Israeli parachute drop on the Mitla Pass and by the time the Franco-British drop took place on 5 November they had conquered the Sinai. Among those dropping with 16 Parachute Brigade was the BOO, Captain H M Ritchie, and Captain Peter Jobson, holding the same post in the Commando Brigade, came ashore with the Marines at Port Said. However, it was only a matter of days, following some sporadic fighting, that international political pressure, orchestrated principally by the USA, but also involving the Russians, forced a ceasefire on a very frustrated British Army. Those who had landed were just getting up a head of steam and had to stop, and many of them never even landed. This, of course, made the whole thing more galling for reservists who had been called up against their will and then found themselves kicking their heels with nothing to do.

The shipment of stores and ammunition had seen just over 26,000 tons arrive off the north coast of Egypt in forty-seven ships. Just under 1,000 tons had been offloaded and unscrambling the mess that was left on the ships to maintain a force that had been going to war, but was now going nowhere except home, was to prove a nightmare. The load would fall upon 3rd Division's field force units as there had not been time to land any but the smallest advance elements of the forward base units from the central depots. The proximity of Cyprus with its Ordnance installations proved most helpful.

Eventually, with its OFP still sitting in Malta, 3rd Division, minus a brigade, disembarked at Port Said on 10 November and relieved 16 Parachute Brigade and the Commando Brigades who had been the British element of the initial assault force. They were sent back to Cyprus and, on 21 November, UN forces began to arrive. They were without any accommodation or camp stores and so the Government authorized the sale of stores available from AF G1098 equipment from a general hospital that had been landed, together with other Ordnance stores. The UN's arrival saw the commencement of the Franco-British withdrawal and by 14 December all RAOC units had departed.

Macmillan came to power, replacing Eden in January 1957. His achievement of leading the nation followed ministerial posts as Minister of Defence, Foreign Secretary and Chancellor. His experience coupled with the Suez fiasco convinced him that the size of the Armed Forces needed to be reduced, and this would have to include the abolition of National Service. Coincident with this decision came a report by the Inspector RAOC, Major General G O Crawford, pointing out the economies, including the closure of several civilian clothing depots, which would result were a cash grant to be given to departing servicemen rather the physical issue of a 'demob' suit. Actually, it was rather more a complete set of clothing than just a suit, comprising, as well as the suit itself, a mackintosh, one pair of shoes, a shirt and separate collar, two pairs of socks, a hat, collar studs and cuff links. Its cost was £12 17s 0d (£187)

The Prime Minister also declared that an airmobile strategic reserve would replace the need for major overseas bases and the added power of new tactical nuclear weapons would offer the potential for conventional force reductions. The Defence White paper that year ended National Service in 1959 bringing force levels for all three Services from 690,000, with 300,000 National Servicemen, to an all-regular force of 375,000 by the end of 1962. The Army Council sought to set the Army's slice of this at 200,000, but Duncan Sandys, the Minister of Defence, felt that this was not a number to which the Army could recruit. Accordingly, the figure was set at 165,000 of which the allocation to the RAOC was 11,554 all ranks. It would prove to be insufficient to meet the tasks imposed upon the Army.

It also brought problems for the RAOC. For some years since the war there had been a thrust by some elements in the MOD to civilianize wherever possible RAOC posts. In some quarters this thrust extended to a concept of complete civilianization on the Royal Naval model. The DOS, Major General

Lancelot Cutforth, in warning of the danger to the military supply system, was successful in gaining agreement to two basic principles: that the RAOC would remain a military Corps, although it would have a civilian component to assist, principally, base depots; and that control across Ordnance Services would remain military. Seven criteria were established as a basis for Ord 1 to assess the RAOC structure as part of new Army ceiling. These principles were that it was necessary to retain military control, balance off home and overseas postings, ensure training for war and a nucleus on which to expand on mobilization, ensure appropriate training for officers filling senior posts, provide for emergencies short of mobilization, provide a balanced career structure and to ensure commissioning prospects for soldiers.

As ever, it was logistics that got in the way, and in this case it would impact on the concept of a Strategic Airmobile reserve. There simply was not enough strategic air transport in the RAF fleet to meet the requirement. And even as the size of the fleet increased the problems in the Middle East, many of them caused by Nasser, made the diplomatic clearance for overflying very difficult. Consequently, despite the Prime Minister's wishes, to be able to meet Britain's commitments east of Suez meant the creation of new bases in places like Kenya, Aden and the Persian Gulf as well as Malaya. For the RAOC, it offered the opportunity to standardize on a structure and a scaling policy that would provide three OFPs and three stores sections that could deploy with any of the three brigade groups making up the reserve. The success of this concept was proven on a number of occasions when OFPs deployed with brigades other than those to which they were affiliated.

The planned reduction saw the Army's seventy-seven infantry battalions reducing to sixty; thirty RAC regiments became twenty-three; and the RA lost twenty regiments in addition to the fourteen that had vanished with the disappearance of Anti-Aircraft Command. Not least of the problems was the difficulty of amalgamating many famous regiments, as household names disappeared from the ORBAT. The importance of the Army having its own air arm was recognized in the acceptance of the need for an Army Air Corps whose formation was authorized.

As part of the overall rundown that the Army had been experiencing throughout the fifties, the CADs at Buckingham and Nesscliffe were earmarked for closure, the former in 1957 and the latter in 1959. Buckingham returned to civilian use, the land having been requisitioned, and Nesscliffe became a training area to be used in the future by generations of soldiers. Some indication of the size of the task can be gained from the fact that over 100,000 tons of ammunition had to be moved, including 7,000 tons of chemical warfare ammunition; 2,000 acres had to be cleared and declared free from explosives; and seventy-eight miles of railway track had to be lifted.

Aden had been a coaling station on the trade route to India. Early in 1957 the need for a base in the Middle East that lay beyond Egypt saw the formation of HQ British Forces Arabian Peninsula. Two RAOC units were formed to support the new HQ: a small Composite Ordnance Depot commanded by Major B Wilmshurst and a stores section, commanded by Captain Tony Camfield, for the workshop. Subsequently an Ordnance detachment was set up in Bahrain, serviced directly from Aden.

February 1957 saw the first report by the ADP working Party, advising that it felt computerization of the Ordnance range of stores to be feasible. Furthermore, it would, in addition to producing staff and financial savings, give ever increased speed, greater accuracy and improved provisioning. Importantly, it was judged that it would not prejudice the supply of MT spares in war. The report sought permission to prepare a detailed specification and to seek tenders from manufacturers for an ADP system, with Chilwell again selected as the test bed. Approval to proceed was given in June 1957 and a sub-committee of the Working Party was set up to prepare a specification for the manufacturers.

Later in 1957 a major addition was made to the Army's ORBAT with the reformation of the Army Air Corps. Whilst the third line support for spares was to remain with the RAF, second line support fell to Army units. It was the start of an association between the RAOC and the AAC, and the wearing of the powder-blue beret, which would last for the remainder of the Corps' life. It also imposed a training and organizational burden as RAOC soldiers learned to come to grips with the alien procedures and processes used by the RAF. It would, however, be two years before the first DADOS (Air), Major Lance Brett, joined the AAC organization.

On 14 March in Cyprus Grivas agreed to suspend military operations if Makarios were released. This was eventually agreed, although he was not to return to the island. However, the campaign against EOKA was virtually over.

Boy soldiers were re-titled Junior Leaders and RAOC and REME were both to be taught at Deepcut.

On Independence Day in Malaya on 31 August 1957 the number of terrorist incidents from the Communist insurgents had fallen markedly. The campaign, waged by the Malayan Army, would continue for another three years, by which time what remained of the Communist hierarchy had taken refuge over the Thai border. It was the end of a most successful anti-terrorist campaign thanks largely to the determination of British governments to see the thing through and to the resilience of the Malayans without whose support, inevitably, success would not have been possible.

Independence for Malaya, coupled with the clear end in sight of the emergency, meant changes for the RAOC. There was no longer any need for the larger installations in the Far East and with stringent manpower cuts being imposed across the Army something had to give. Consequently, 7 FOD on the Malayan peninsula was handed over to the new Federation army for them to use. The major formation was 17th Gurkha Division and the OFPs of 28 and 63 Brigades took on a greater load to compensate, aided by 3 BOD resorting to some detailed issues direct to units. With all this, wherever Colonel Geoffrey Worsdell was posted shooting excelled, as witness the plethora of trophies won under his tutelage by HQ FARELF.

Another of Lance Corporal Peter Lindsay's etchings, this time of Red Barracks at Woolwich.

The specification for the Chilwell computer was approved in November, and from then on the War Office assumed executive responsibility for evaluation of the tenders, with the advice and assistance of the Treasury, whose hand it appears to have been hard to remove from the controls. The Ordnance Directorate would take the lead in processing the study.

On 31 December 1957 the RAOC finally said goodbye to Woolwich, with the closure of TSSD Woolwich. It was the end of an association that had spanned the centuries and a matter of great regret for many an officer and soldier as the Corps said farewell to its homes in the Arsenal and the Dockyard.

In Cyprus it had proved difficult to find a political solution to the problems and the Turks insisted that if independence were to be granted then the island should be partitioned. In March 1958 Grivas renewed action with a bombing campaign and the murder of a Special Branch officer, much to Makarios' disapproval. There were further negotiations. The outcome was a reduction in the size of the British-retained sovereign base areas and an acceptance by Makarios of self-determination rather than enosis. This created a rift between him and Grivas that never healed, but the campaign of terror was over and Makarios returned to the island and to power on 1 March 1959. Grivas was flown out by the Greek air force thirteen days later to Greece, and awarded the rank of general in his retirement.

On 11 April 1958 Her Majesty the Queen paid a visit to the RAOC and was welcomed to its home at

Her Majesty the Queen is greeted at the start of her visit by Major General Sir Leslie Williams.

Blackdown. She was accompanied by her husband, His Royal Highness the Duke of Edinburgh.

Sergeant Norman Bruce played his first game for Scotland, against the French at Murrayfield; and there was reference to one Lance Corporal R Charlton RAOC appearing on the short list for the England team to play in the 1958 World Cup in Sweden.

There was a major upheaval in the organization of the Field Army with the introduction of a brigade group structure. It meant that brigades were to be self-sufficient, and that involved the creation of Brigade OFPs, and they would have to be born in large part from the existing divisional OFPs. The greatest impact was in Germany where the quantity of OFPs doubled instantaneously, and the re-scaling and re-equipping exercise was huge. While this internal Corps restructuring was going on, support had to continue to be provided to an Army that was itself restructuring. The disbandment in the UK of AA Command resulted in the disappearance of the RA Anti-Aircraft Group in Germany and the creation of a Field Artillery Group and 7th Armoured Division was reformed to 5th Infantry Division.

The Middle East was in turmoil. King Hussein of Jordan, friend of the UK and a graduate of the RMA Sandhurst, faced a rebellion in his own country and saw his cousin King Feisal of Iraq murdered along with a senior pro-British statesman. The deployment of 16 Parachute Brigade into Amman helped to restore order and they were back out again by the end of October. It was a tiny operation, but a good example of the constant drain on RAOC resources at a time when elsewhere consolidation was the order of the day. Major H J Pike was the OC 16 Parachute Brigade OFP. He flew in his advance element, brought the rest in by sea and proceeded to establish a forward operating base that swiftly began to assume the proportions of a mini depot. There was also a DADOS HQ British Forces Jordan, Major K J Wright, as well as an ad hoc Port Ordnance Section commanded by Captain T Bentham, and a small detachment of two ammunition storemen. In addition to their Ordnance task the soldiers of the OFP were required to take their place in the defence scheme of the Amman airfield, alongside the parachute battalions. For this role 'Pikeforce' was formed from the OFP, other RAOC personnel present, the REME workshops and RASC personnel, under the command of Major Pike.

Then came an Ammunition Platoon and a Port Ordnance Section, the former for Amman and the latter for Aqaba. The balance of the RAOC LofC units, a Vehicle Transit and Servicing Platoon, a Port Ammunition Section and a Bath Section all arrived. The Vehicle Transit and Servicing Platoon and the Port Ammunition Section were located in Aqaba, while the Bath Section moved up to Amman where, despite difficulties of water supply, it made a welcome difference to the well being of soldiers. Contracts for laundry, tailoring, oxygen, distilled water, electrolyte, the re-treading of tyres, to name just some of the services that had to be provided, were let. And everything was in place just in time for the decision to be taken to withdraw. And, of course, the RAOC was among the last to leave having cleared up the mess; not the least of their tasks being to satisfy the Command Secretary that the books were straight.

During this period the size of the Ordnance commitment in Aden increased several fold. Captain Jerrie Hulme was the adjutant and recalled often how hard worked they all were to meet their commitments. Yet another drain on diminishing resources, but the service carried on anyway.

And in Iraq a small, but perhaps significant event took place as the British finally left after forty years. It was not anticipated that they would return, and there was no foreseeable reason why they should.

A DOS Evaluation Committee, with its Treasury representative, examining the installation of a computer to manage depot stocks reported in December 1958. It proposed that ADP be installed at COD Chilwell and that, of three systems from which the final choice was to be made, an IBM 7070 installation was preferred. The report laid out in detail what tasks it considered the computer should assume initially and, as follow-up tasks, how the load should progressively be assumed, the initial preparatory action required and the additional personnel needed. It ended with the recommendation that, following the successful implementation at Chilwell, a similar system embodying the same make and type of computer should be installed at COD Donnington. An ADP Unit had already been set up at Chilwell on 6 August 1958, with the officer in charge one Lieutenant Colonel J J Wise RAOC. It was faced with the gargantuan task of rewriting all Chilwell's procedures to suit the new age. It was a major piece of work, and went largely unnoticed by the RAOC at large; and certainly by the rest of the Army.

In 1959, a decision was made to station part of the UK Strategic Reserve in Kenya. It thus became necessary completely to re-think the logistic organization required in Kenya to maintain the UK force. For the RAOC, this resulted in the re-establishment of much the same range of services as had previously existed, although the new units were smaller. Beginning with the establishment of 305 Ammunition Depot at Gilgil in June 1959, RAOC support was rapidly built up so that by the autumn of that year the main units in Kenya were: 541 Ordnance Depot, 305 Ammunition Depot, 24 OFP, and stores sections attached to two REME workshops.

In that same year there was yet more re-organization in Germany. To begin with there were adjustments in the ammunition support arrangements. The reserve ammunition holding task being undertaken by 5 BAD was taken over by 3 BAD, resulting in the disbandment of 5 BAD. In order, to improve the arrangements for the forward tactical holding of ammunition, 1 (Br) Corps Ammunition Company was formed at Sennelager and the Stores Company that was the basis of the OMP in war was combined with 50 Ordnance Depot to become the Forward Stores Depot Münster. And then a new Corps Stores Company was established in June 1959, along with 1 Guided Weapons Company as a part of Corps Troops in 1960. Forming up at Mönchengladbach it went to reside in Wulfen. Its formation was a natural result of the introduction of guided missile regiments into the ORBAT. The first commander of 1 GW Company was Major Bill Baker. He had prepared for the task with an arduous two years in the United States studying the Corporal missile. At the same time a review of supply methods and stock levels allowed the size and shape of 15 ABOD to be reduced. It all amounted to a great deal of very hard work.

The introduction of guided missiles and the much more technical nature of the work carried out by RAOC ammunition personnel, to say nothing of the increasing load in the disposal of improvised explosive devices, had let to a review of status and role. Some three years earlier the decision had been taken to award the right to wear the AE badge to sergeants and above. Prior to that the wearing of trade badges of any sort had been restricted to corporals and below. Now the trade was to be renamed to Ammunition Technician, and IOOs became Ammunition Technical Officers.

In 1959 the two principal concerns in the Corps appear to have been the introduction, and therefore management, of guided weapons and the advent of Automated Data Processing. Both formed the main subject areas for the 1959 DOS Study Period.

And in July 1959 ADP was very much in the minds of the DOS evaluation committee that had recommended the IBM solution. Shortly before they had published their report at the turn of the year there had been a late submission. Consequently, they had been reconvened and, much to their delight, had to go through the whole evaluation process again. The cause of their problem was a British Company, EMI Ltd. However, they found that the EMI system had 8,000 words of core store as compared with the 5,000 words of the IBM, was faster, more powerful and cheaper than the IBM 7070, and so they opted for the EMIDEC system, with forecast staff savings of some £280,000 (£3.8 million) a year. It further recommended that the Donnington configuration also be based on the EMIDEC 2400, to ensure standardization and to provide an insurance against equipment failure at either site.

In Cyprus the agreement that saw the end of the EOKA campaign also saw the creation of the Sovereign Base areas and the withdrawal of RAOC to sit within them. Then a further re-organization of RAOC units on Cyprus took place in January 1961 when a single unit, Ordnance Depot Cyprus, was formed from the separate units then existing on the island. Later that same year GHQ MELF disbanded, and was replaced by a much smaller HQ Near East Land Forces. One outcome was the downgrading of the Headquarters' DOS post and Brigadier John Sheffield handed over to Colonel Len Coates in January 1962. During that same month the outcome of a study into ammunition storage in the UK was announced. It had been known for some years that there was an over-capacity in the base depots and that one of them would have to go. The choice was obvious. With the limitations imposed by underground storage on the holding of high charge-weight ratio munitions and guided weapons Corsham was no longer sustainable. It would close by 1964.

There were other changes caused by the reduction in the Army and the amounts of stores and equipment it was expected to hold. All the stores depots – Bicester, Branston, Chilwell, Didcot and Donnington, with their sub-depots regardless of the type of store they held – were brought together in a new organization, Stores Organization RAOC. This meant the demise of the MT Organization RAOC that had seen Chilwell and all its achievements through the war and the immediate post-war years, and of General Stores Organization. Major General Hooley formed HQ Stores Organization at Chilwell in September 1959, but in the following month the HQ moved to Milton, near Didcot. The Ammunition Organization remained autonomous, as did the Vehicle Organization, which had gained its independence in 1957.

However, on a much larger scale, by 1959 it had become clear that the allocations of manpower to the RAOC in the 1957 restructuring into a regular force would have to be amended if the strength of the Army was to be contained within the overall total of 165,000. A study by the Quartermaster General's department concluded that, given a one-third reduction in the tonnages of stock held in the RAOC Central Depots, it was possible to accept a 20 per cent cut of 2,311 all ranks in the RAOC's military manpower. Rather than be led by the inevitable, the DOS decided to present the QMG with the options that would best suit the Corps. He set up a working party to offer a range of options that would meet the requirements imposed by the cuts. It began its work towards the end of 1959 with just two assumptions: that 90 per cent of any savings would come out of the base, and just 10 per cent from overseas; and that abandoned sites should be those with the worst storage accommodation. Ammunition and vehicles were less of a problem than other commodities. Corsham was already earmarked to close, and the Vehicle Organization RAOC had been formed in 1957 on the back of a reorganization that had rationalized the structure into five central depots. The problem lay with those depots holding clothing and general stores where four CODs, Branston, Didcot, Chilwell and Donnington, had provisioning roles and one, Bicester, did not. As a result it was difficult to find a post war task for Bicester, despite the fact it had 3 million square feet of the best storage accommodation. The storage accommodation in the five CODs comprised 12.5 million square feet of permanent space. Given the reduction of one-third in tonnages that the QMG had accepted there would only be a need for 9 million square feet, equating to a reduction of one COD. An adjustment of this size would have huge manpower implications not only for uniformed, but also civilian manpower.

The recommendations of the working party were:
To remove MT and Technical stores and vehicles from Bicester.
To move all the clothing stocks from Branston and Didcot into Bicester.
To close Branston and Didcot, including the Didcot sub-depots at Thatcham and Longtown.

The exercise was to be called Operation NETTLERASH.

The risk in the plan was the increase that would be required in COD Bicester of 1,300 civilian posts in an area where poor civilian recruitment potential had always affected the depot and had led to the formation of four battalions of National Servicemen to run it.

1960 was yet another good sporting year for the RAOC. On this occasion it was 29 Company from CAD Kineton who won the Army Football Association Challenge Cup in front of 5,000 spectators in the Aldershot stadium, and in the presence of the Duke of Gloucester. This victory was in addition to the large number of local and district successes, and the strength of Corps football was further underpinned by having eight players in the Army Squad, three of them from 29 Company. Private Jim Lloyd of 3 Battalion at Hilsea boxed at international level and represented England in the Rome Olympics in 1960, winning the bronze medal at welterweight, in addition to many other boxing honours, both national and Army he had won in his time with the Corps. In cycling Private McGinnes of 4 Trade Training Battalion was a force to be reckoned with. He won as an individual and at District, Army, and Inter-services level, as well as a member of a number of teams at each of these levels.

However, it was also a year in which to record a sad loss. On 1 July Major General Sir Basil Hill KCB, CB, DSO died in the eightieth year of his life. He was an example to all, a fine and experienced soldier who had served in many theatres of war and who he had also been capped at rugby nine times for his country. He was a sportsman, a soldier and a gentleman and he left his mark on the Corps he loved.

On Thursday 17 November 23817975 Private Henry McGannity reported for duty at 1 Training Battalion with the distinction of being the last National Serviceman to be called up to serve in the Corps. It was the beginning of the end of an era in RAOC and Army history.

Private Henry McGannity was the last National Serviceman to join the RAOC.

In December 1960 the Regimental Depot moved to Hilsea Barracks. This followed the disbandment of 3 Training Battalion and with the purpose of providing rattle accommodation for the rebuild at Deepcut. Its stay there was to be determined by the length of time of the rebuild, and would not be long.

In June 1961 President Kassem of Iraq laid claim to Kuwait as being a province of his country and suggested he might take it over. There was a defence agreement between Kuwait and the UK upon which the ink was barely dry and the Emir of Kuwait immediately called upon the British to honour it. This they did with a mix of troops already in the Gulf and 24 Brigade from Kenya to command the operation. The RAOC Advance Party was already in place in the shape of a platoon, commanded by Lieutenant John Woodford, that was paying a visit to Bahrain. Captain Dickie Pratt's small unit in

Bahrain loaded a couple of LSTs with stores and sent John and his men off with something to prime the Ordnance support. They were swiftly backed up as the 24 Brigade Ordnance units began to arrive and soon there was a stable Ordnance footprint in the country. There was one major bonus in that the need for strategic movement of major assets was offset by the pre-positioning of armour in Kuwait allowing the 3rd Carabiniers to fly out and be in position swiftly. In the end, the presence of the British in the country deterred the Iraqis from pursuing their claim and calm returned once more.

The Army Rifle Championship was won in 1961 for the first time by the RAOC by Captain David Carpenter of 17 Battalion. His victory saw him awarded the Queens' Medal as well as the Army Rifle Association Gold Jewel and the Watkin Cup.

In September 1961 the War Office gave approval to the DOS' plans to shave his manpower by the range of depot rationalizations he had proposed, allowing him to fight the battle of retrenchment on ground of his own choosing. It was a masterly piece of management skill, and allowed the Army to benefit from the fact that the professional made the decisions that would see the run down occur with the minimum impact on the service the RAOC could provide. He had already started work and the transfer of stocks from Longtown, Thatcham and Didcot was already under way. It was judged that road was the best means of effecting the re-distribution and 65 Heavy GT Company RASC was allocated to the task. The Company moved into Bicester on 14 August 1961 and commenced work two days later.

The Adjutant, Captain P Moran with RSM F Hall, outside the barrack gate as Hilsea closed in 1962.

On 28 February 1962 14 Battalion from COD Didcot, even as the depot was beginning to wind down, beat the Irish Guards by nine bouts to two to take the Army Inter-Unit Boxing Championship. It was the Corps' first victory at this level in boxing since those halcyon days in 1952-54 when 4 Battalion, led by the Cooper brothers, had so successfully dominated Army boxing.

The RAOC left Hilsea Barracks on 31 March 1962. It had provided the Corps with a home for over forty years when the Headquarters had moved from Red Barracks at Woolwich. Another sad occasion as a place with which the Corps had so many links, so many memories, was left vacant. But a new barracks had been built at Deepcut, at the bottom of the hill, and it was time to move on. On the same day the ADP Unit at Chilwell became the ADP Installation.

On 11 April 1962 the Corps retained the Army Football Cup. This time it was 6 Battalion at Chilwell that took the honours, beating 6 Training Battalion RASC by two goals to one. And Ordnance Depot Cyprus won, for the second year, the Army Life Saving Championships, together with a number of local sports trophies on the Island.

In Germany, in May 1962, the Corps Vehicle Company was formed. This placed four companies and the Corps Distribution Point under CRAOC Corps Troops, together with the technical responsibility for seven workshop stores sections. He also had to provide support to Corps and Army Troops from the Rhine to the East German frontier.

On 2 June railway engine number 45505 was dismantled for scrap. The engine was one of the 'Patriot' class, built at the London Midland and Scottish Crewe Works in 1932. There were fifty-two engines of this class and this one, on completion, bore the number 5949 until 1934, when it was renumbered 5505. For the first fifteen years of its life the engine had no name but, in 1947, under the policy of the

LMS Railway to name some locomotives after Regiments and Corps, No. 5505 received the name 'The Royal Army Ordnance Corps,' and Corps crests presented by the RAOC were mounted over the nameplates. After nationalization in 1948, all engines of British Railways were renumbered and 5505 became 45505, retaining its name. During the latter part of the Second World War and following it, most of the 'Patriot' class engines received certain modifications, including the fitting of a larger boiler. But 45505 was not modified and remained as built until withdrawn from service.

The officers' mess at Gatcombe House, Hilsea; another etching by Peter Lindsay.

The MHEU moved from Deepcut to Bicester. It had been found that, although Deepcut offered a depth of technical knowledge and experience, the functions of a trials unit, which it essentially was, meant that location in a major depot was of greater value.

The Depot disbanded at the end of March 1962, its role being assumed by 1 Battalion at Deepcut and it then became the Depot and Training Battalion RAOC. In celebration of what was to be its final departure from Hilsea Barracks the RAOC Band and the Corps of Drums of the Junior Leaders Battalion RAOC Beat Retreat on the barracks square on the evening of 15 March. The officers' mess then held a last function, a cocktail party, in Gatcombe House, a mess in which was vested so much of the Corps' history.

In late 1962 HQ NEARELF became HQ Cyprus District, still located at Episkopi, and RAOC representation on the new HQ was reduced to a DADOS with the commandant of the Ordnance Depot, a colonel, located some forty miles away in the Dhekelia SBA, becoming Head of Service. Such arrangements are never satisfactory and impossible for the major filling the DADOS appointment, who finds himself stuck firmly between two masters.

National service soldiers would perform to the highest standards, as witness the bearing and turnout of this group from CAD Buckingham marching through the town on 10 June 1954. Sergeant Keith Moss provided the picture, and is at the front of the rear file wearing glasses. A National Service sergeant, he put up his third stripe after just eleven months.

Sergeant M H Perkins RAOC, outside his place of work in Dettingen Barracks, Blackdown.

The end of 1962 saw the end of a period of intense activity across the Army, and one that had placed a great strain of the RAOC as it sought to provide a service in so many disparate ways, and under so many different circumstances. It was also the end of National Service, an episode that had made its mark on the Corps. It remains, however, a fact that the RAOC could not have undertaken the work demanded of it in the seventeen post-war years to 1962 had it not been for its National Service soldiers. By the time the last one left, a total of 97,313 young men had seen service with the RAOC. They had exhibited courage and died in the service of the Crown, they had brought technical skills and sporting achievement, and they had left their mark on the RAOC – as the RAOC had left its mark on them. SQMS B H Knapp, reporting on an operation in Cyprus in 1955 spoke with pride and affection of his National Service squad:

….to my surprise there wasn't a single 'tick'. The word 'operation' made them forget their 'Group', and for the first time their conversation was enthusiastic about something other than the end of their time…The whole operation lasted thirteen days, they were thirteen days that caused me to revise my opinion of the National Serviceman …The lads stood up to the long, long hours with just as much verve and spirit as any regular and had the supreme satisfaction of one of the Commanding Officers of the Marines come and personally thank them for 'doing such an astonishingly good job under such conditions'.

For generations to come many of those, then, young men would look back on their time in the RAOC, and speak of it with affection. Perhaps Sergeant Michael Perkins summed it for most of them:

I returned to my humble job as a trainee with a major insurance group. It was a long time before – in civilian life – I had responsibilities on a level with those I had carried in the Army. All I have left…a single item of kit I have so carefully looked after. If it won't get me on another 252 I will confess to being in probably improper possession of Hangers Coat Wooden 1. It is stamped with the number I will never forget: 2293691.

Notes

[1] Dues In: stock due in to a depot from a supplier, ordered but not yet received.
[2] Dues Out: items requested by units but for which there is no stock available to meet the demand.

Chapter Seven

Changing Times 1963 – 1972

There is a certain relief in change, even though it be from bad to worse…it is often a comfort to shift one's position and be bruised in a new place.   *Washington Irving, 1824*

As National Service ended, and a new Army composed entirely of regulars began to take shape, the country was superficially in good economic order. Wages in the previous decade under a Conservative government, led for the last six years by Harold Macmillan, had risen by an average of seventy-two per cent, whilst prices had gone up by a much lower forty-five per cent. Consumers found more on which to spend their money, and had more on which to spend it. The last vestiges of rationing had disappeared and there was an increase in house building. The Prime Minister was heard, famously, to say the country had never had it so good. It was the year in which a bound twelve month's worth of the RAOC *Gazette* would set the purchaser back £2 7s 6d (£30) and a ticket for the HQ RAOC Officers' Mess Ball cost £2 10s 0d (£31) with a bottle of subsidised champagne at 10s (£7). The Regular Forces Employment Association was telling of jobs as a butler for £17 0s 0d (£215) per week, a court bailiff for £14 0s 0d (£175) per week or a stores supervisor at £1,000 (£12,500) a year. A Hillman Minx for the family cost £475 (£5,600) ex works; and it came with a heater and windscreen washers included. Never, indeed, had it been so good.

However this all masked an underlying malaise; that successive Tory chancellors had failed to find a permanent solution to the problem of controlling inflation while at the same time stimulating economic growth and maintaining a favourable balance of trade. When Harold Wilson's government, with its tiny majority of four, came into power in October 1964 it would inherit a balance of payments deficit of £800 million (£9,600 million), and that would dominate politics in the time of the Labour Government. It would certainly affect the Army, for it was to herald a decade of change upon change caused by cuts in funding brought on by the parlous situation that was the reality of the country's economic situation.

Prior to that, the first of the many studies that were to plague the organization and manning of the forces over the succeeding few years had been undertaken in 1962 by Lieutenant General Sir Archibald Nye. Whilst the study was to examine the organization of the War Office it was charged specifically, as part of its remit, with looking at that part of the organization that made policy for the formulation of requirements for equipment. In particular it was to examine the number of senior officers with a view to removing those who were purely involved in the administration of the process rather than the technical content.

Germany remained the Army's most important deployment, and the structure and organization of BAOR was affected by the decision in the early sixties to opt for a posture of forward deployment. This was largely due to the fact that Germany was now an independent nation and part of the NATO alliance and was developing its Navy, Army and Air Force. The old concept of withdrawal to the Rhine offering up large tracts of German territory to advancing Russians, did not sit comfortably with having German soldiers as equal partners in the defence of their own country.

For the RAOC this made the new Advanced Base in Belgium something of an anachronism just as it had been built and brought into use. Instead, the RAOC was faced once more with the prospect of holding stocks east of the Rhine to support Armies that would now be operating much further east. It was also a time when the drive for greater efficiency would lead to a reduction in the number of RAOC store holding units in Europe. As a result the Forward Ordnance Depot at Münster and a number of other depots for accommodation stores and the like were formed into 15 ABOD (Forward) and based at Münster. The moves reduced the DOS BAOR's span of command from fifteen to twelve. However, for the commandant of 15 ABOD it meant a command that was geographically widely spread with storage conditions ranging from some very basic pre-war accommodation to the modern buildings at, say, Viersen near Mönchengladbach.

The end of 1962 had seen a rebellion in Brunei against the Sultan, supported from across the border by the Indonesian government. Dr Sukarno, the Communist leader of Indonesia, objected to the inclusion of Sarawak and North Borneo into the Federation of Malaysia, due to come into existence in September 1963. In effect, it was an excuse to divert the attention of the Indonesian people from the domestic difficulties they were experiencing – difficulties entirely due to mismanagement by Dr Sukarno. The dispatch of four battalions from Singapore, one of them a Royal Marine Commando, put down the rebellion in very short order, although five marines were killed.

In March of 1963 another study was launched that was to have a fundamental effect on the RAOC and on its sister Corps, the RASC. It was led by General Sir Roderick McLeod. Since the end of the Korean War there had been a constant drive to decrease the size of the Armed Forces. Inevitably, there was a disproportionate attack on the logistic services whenever this happened in order to preserve as far as possible teeth arm numbers in both units and individuals. The nine years of these cuts had meant that a root and branch examination of the logistic services was required to address the perceived anomalies in the roles and responsibilities of the various Corps involved in providing logistic support to the Army and to the other two services where appropriate. Probably it was a review long overdue, for the split of various responsibilities had evolved over the years as a result of convenience, internecine regimental strife, vested interest and government interference. An examination of the requirements and

a proper allocation of resources, focussed on the efficient and economic provision of logistic support, were long overdue. It would be interesting to see how close the McLeod team would come to an effective solution. Dealing with the Nye examination of the structure, roles and organization of the higher echelons of the RAOC whilst at the same time coping with a detailed examination of the same aspects of its operational and regimental structure was something of a load for DOS' staff as they sought, at the same time, to ensure that the Army continued to be properly supplied.

As if to emphasize this, at the end of December 1962 trouble had flared once more in Cyprus, with Greek Cypriots attacking Turkish Cypriot areas, the Turks having resisted attempts by the Greeks to regard the island as a single unified state. Because of the threat to British service families living outside the Sovereign Base areas, the Commonwealth

On 12 March 1963 Major General H J C Hildreth CBE was presented with a cigarette box by the Lord Mayor of Portsmouth to mark forty years association of the RAOC with Portsmouth; from 1921 to 1961.

Secretary, Duncan Sandys, convinced the Turkish and the Greek authorities to accept a peacekeeping force drawn from the Cyprus garrison.

Malta, in the meantime, had been granted its independence on 20 May 1963, with Prince Philip, the Duke of Edinburgh, officiating at the ceremony. It was an emotional occasion, but also marked the start of a deterioration of relationships that would eventually lead to a withdrawal of the British some nine years later in 1972. In the meantime, Malta was responsible for the small British outstation in Libya at Benghazi; Tripoli having closed on 31 March 1963. There was also a small detachment of 10 Vehicle Company at El Adem where they maintained a pre-positioned squadron of Centurion tanks.

On 14 March 1963 the final parade of 14 Battalion took place at Vauxhall Barracks, Didcot, as the last regular unit to be stationed there for some time. The barracks as soldiers' accommodation would fall into temporary disuse, but the quarters would continue to be used, primarily for people working at Bicester. It was seen as the end of an association going back to the RAOC's arrival there in 1915, but it was a premature judgement as the barracks would go on to be used for other purposes associated with the RAOC for the rest of the Corps' existence.

Battledress ceased to be official uniform on 1 April that year with the advent of the new barathea service dress for soldiers. Apart from being the end of something of an era bearing in mind the numbers of British and foreign troops that had worn it in peace and in war, it also presented a problem of issuing the new and withdrawing the old from right across the Army, territorial and regular. It was no small task.

The job of emptying CAD Corsham was completed by June 1963, one year earlier than scheduled. This had been another major undertaking, conditioning and redistributing the considerable stocks in the Army's last underground depot. Underground storage had always presented problems and there were some limitations from the start of the types and natures of ammunition that could be stored below ground. However, technological advances had changed the design of high explosive ammunition such that the walls were thinner and they contained a greater proportion of explosive. This made them much more likely to propagate a detonation in the event of an accident and consequently imposed more stringent storage criteria. These criteria imposed regulations that did not sit comfortably with the limitations of underground storage and, as a means of holding ammunition, the concept no longer made economic or practical sense.

The Federation of Malaysia came into being on 16 September 1963. The initial thoughts had been that it would comprise the eleven Malay states, the three territories in Borneo, and Singapore. There were, however, some surprises in store for the new Federation. The Sultan of Borneo decided at the last minute to keep his country out of the new structure and a few weeks beforehand Singapore decided on a unilateral declaration of independence. Then, considering itself an independent state, it freely surrendered that status to become a part of the Federation of Malaysia.

However, not everyone approved of the new structure and accusations of some form of neo-colonialism were levelled at the Federation. The Indonesians had, despite the suppression of the Borneo rebellion, carried on causing trouble with cross-border incidents, although in January 1964 a ceasefire was brokered by the United Nations. Unfortunately, it was short lived and by February the Indonesian army was openly conducting operations across the border and assisting insurgents in any way it could. Major General W C Walker, commanding 17th Gurkha Division, was on the spot to contain the incursion, proof if proof were needed that forces on the spot can often be more effective than those flown from half way across the world. He was there with his initial deployment very early indeed. The planning, such as it was, in the early days of the deployment was undertaken at short notice, and for the RAOC it meant a number of reiterations of soldier establishments and stores scalings before a force could be assembled to meet the requirement. And, of course, it all had to come from within the limited FARELF resources.

By great good fortune, when the news of the initial deployment came through the DDOS FARELF and his staff were engaged in a curry lunch in 3 BOD, so he was surrounded by his O Group. Placing curry and gin and tonics to one side they set about working out the requirements to provide first and second line support for a force of two battalions operating in jungle 800 miles from Singapore. By the following morning it was a five-battalion force with a HQ and an armoured car squadron. However, by the time the build-up for the larger force was planned the immediate support required by the two battalions was packed and loaded, and an LST with first line scaling of spares and a selected range of forecast requirements sailed on the Monday afternoon. Captain Tony Camfield took with him twenty clerks and storemen from the base installations in Singapore, mainly 3 BOD.

By 5 January 1963 there were eight RAOC officers and 100 soldiers deployed, and they were re-titled 99 OFP with Major H C S Chilman in command. This was because of 99 Brigade's role as an internal security brigade and the proximity of base installations from which it could be re-supplied. Consequently, 99 Brigade did not have an OFP in Malaya, hence the need to form one for Borneo from manpower poached from Singapore's base installations. Up until then, and before the unit was established on land, Captain Camfield had operated a unique OFP detachment, with stores laid out on the tank decks of the LST, and issues made 'over the side' to units ashore using a motley collection of inshore craft for delivery. Some demands were passed by Aldis lamp! Issues were maintained even during the period stocks were being transferred ashore and this three day 'lying off' period was a particularly arduous one for "Camfield Force". It meant seventy-two hours hard going without rest.

The build-up continued with 10 Infantry Workshops being flown in with Captain John Battersby and his Stores Section; 21 Air Maintenance Platoon under Major R J Hoy deployed with 3 AASO. Captains Robin Bowden and Ray Thornton were both BOOs with their own brigades. The logistic support for forces operating in Borneo eventually evolved onto the classic pattern of FMAs containing a mix of logistic units feeding stocks to units deployed forward. Support from Singapore into the FMAs was by sea with a mix of LSTs and small, hired ships.

When 3 Commando Brigade joined the force in April 1963 it too was without second line support and so 98 OFP was formed; again by bleeding base units, with Major Dick Owen in command. After some difficulty setting up an ammunition point, despite the prevarications of the local port authority, the small unit soon settled down to providing support to units in the western area of operations. However, one thing that was to plague the service the RAOC was able to provide, was the insistence on stringent cost control and full peacetime accounting measures. Further difficulties were imposed by the insistence of the Command Secretary that he be based in Singapore and not forward with the brigades where the decisions needed to be made. Consequently, spending authority could take up

Every form of local transport, including boats and trucks, was used.

to a month from an organization that was detached by time and distance and unaware of the local imperatives. That said, there was a good relationship in HQ FARELF with the Secretariat, as evinced by the high local purchase expenditure for which there had been no budgetary provision. The Command Secretary, alive to the operational impact of unnecessary shortages, turned a 'professional' eye to the expenditure. However, the problems caused by his mal-location were proof, if proof were needed, that civil secretariat representatives have to be deployed forward; and early.

Much the same was true of some of the logistic effort. The DADOS of the central brigade acted as the RAOC adviser to the operational staff, and the BOO, who was an ATO, acted as OC Ammunition Inspectorate Borneo. However, much of the logistic control continued to be exercised by HQ FARELF whose staff were remote from the scene and out of touch with detailed operational developments. Logistic crises arose because of lack of a detailed knowledge of the operational policy of Force HQ. Eventually a CRAOC was established on the divisional HQ once 17th Division was fully up and running, and the forward deployment and forward decision making made a huge difference.

In the initial deployment, and with a lack of an RAOC hierarchy on the spot, little thought had been given to the location of logistic units. No allowance had been made for expansion when siting and so when new commitments had been added, new locations had to be used. The western OFP ended up spread over some thirteen miles, with the consequent wasteful use of manpower, and the difficulties of control and security. There was also something of a lack of discipline by demanding units. Quantities of material requested were often inflated and the rates of wastage, particularly of clothing, personal equipment and battle batteries, were high. The wastage of airdrop equipment was also high, owing to a poor recovery rate, and parachutes not recovered within four days developed black spot and were rendered useless. The CRAOC, Colonel L G Dally believed that some of the problems were caused by anxious brigade staff who over-insured, coupled with the tendency of unit quartermasters to hoard. An early grip by a properly constituted RAOC HQ would have seen off many of these problems, but, as had so often proved the case, it was too small and late in being established.

Much of the local purchase effort was concentrated on Hong Kong, as a major source of supply for most requirements. The CRAOC, from December 1962, Lieutenant Colonel Bob Allen, was closely involved in this, as he and his staff were preparing roulement battalions from the Hong Kong garrison to deploy to Borneo.

One casualty of the Borneo campaign was Sergeant Thackeray of the RAOC, attached as an Auster pilot to 656 Light Aircraft Squadron AAC, who was wounded on his first flight over West Sarawak. He was taking an RAF padre on a series of visits as well as dropping mail to some isolated detachments. One of those was quite close to the Indonesian border and he came within range of light weapons, whereupon he was hit by small arms fire. Both he and the padre were wounded and with some difficulty Sergeant Thackeray managed to land his Auster on a helicopter landing-site from which he and the padre were evacuated, by helicopter. Sergeant Thackeray survived his ordeal, but the padre, regrettably, succumbed to his wounds.

The end of National Service had brought with it yet another review, this time of training and of the training organization and standards, conducted by Brigadier R V Blundell. In essence not a huge amount changed. Of course there were revisions to take account of technological developments, for example in such trades as photography and ammunition, and the growing EOD requirement had its impact on ATO and AT training. However one major shift was the creation of the Vehicle Specialist trade introduced in 1963. It combined into one trade the former trades of storemen (vehicles), drivers (specialist), drivers (AFV) and certain drivers (B vehicles). From 1963 the vehicle depots were to benefit from having one trade that specialized in the work of, and was restricted to employment in, those depots. It produced a breed of men who could service, maintain and drive every vehicle in the British Army.

Of course changes in technology and advances in methods would inevitably mean the end of some trades. For example, following the introduction of a new army boot with an integrally moulded sole, the DMS boot, the requirement for the trade of shoemaker vanished and shoemakers were invited to re-muster to another trade, or take discharge. Similarly, following a decision that future supplies of industrial gases in operations could be met by bottled gas as a normal supply item, the Corps's industrial gas manufacturing units became obsolete, and the trade of industrial gas operator vanished.

Sport continued to be an important part of RAOC life, pursued at Corps and unit level. It had been a good season for the rugby players with the RAOC winning all its key inter-Corps matches. 28 Company RAOC from CAD Bramley got to the final of the Army cup, but were pipped at the post by the Welsh Guards. The score line told the story of a hard fought game, with the Guardsmen winning by just nine points to six. And there was a deal of international representation, with Captain Norman Bruce still playing for Scotland and several others at Army and Combined Services level.

It had been a good year for 28 Company for, as well as their success in rugby, their hockey team won their local district championships and took the prestigious Bari Cup, the RAOC's own hockey championship, for the fourth year in succession.

On 1 June 1963 a new RAOC flag was introduced. This was because the Blue Ensign with the Corps' Badge in the fly was liable to cause confusion as the design was too close to that of the Blue Ensign with the Arms of the Board of Ordnance in the fly, flown by ships on War Office, Royal Artillery or Royal Army Ordnance Corps business. It was decided to reintroduce, with some modifications, the Corps Flag of 1923, which had been designed by Captain A R Valon, OBE MC, an Ordnance Mechanical Engineer, who later became a major general and the Colonel Commandant of REME. The flag was to be more in keeping with normal regimental flag design, comprising seven red diagonal stripes running down from left to right from the flagstaff, on a dark navy blue background. Superimposed in the centre was the RAOC badge in full heraldic tinctures. The flag would be six feet by four feet and the stripes one and three-quarter inches wide.

July 1963 saw one of those little tasks that came the RAOC's way, but which went largely unreported and certainly unheralded by the world outside. Major Tom Bentham and Sergeant Len Shute must have been mildly concerned at the scene that greeted them on the island of Jeddah, where they had been dispatched at the request of the Commander Land Forces Persian Gulf. A large quantity of Italian

The Blue Ensign that was to be replaced.

The original 1923 flag upon which the new one would be modelled.

artillery ammunition had exploded, creating a mass of rubble and scattering unexploded projectiles near and far. The island was used as a prison and before mopping-up operations could be started about 100 prisoners had to be moved to the mainland. This done, Major Bentham and Sergeant Shute destroyed by demolition some 200 shells that were readily accessible, but it was evident that many more were buried under the rubble. Back came the prisoners. Under the closest possible supervision tons of rubble were turned over piece-by-piece, and eventually a further 650 shells were brought to light and blown up. During the course of these operations some 650lb of bulk explosive and 3,500 feet of detonating cord were used. They received their plaudits from CILSA, and anyone who has served in the Middle East in July will know how debilitating the heat would have been in what was a considerable clearance task.

In September 1963 the workload of the CRAOC 1 (Br) Corps troops had at last been acknowledged as being excessive and it was not something that could simply be resolved by tinkering with the existing organization. Something fairly radical was required and it came with the formation of 1 (Br) Corps Ordnance Maintenance Park to relieve him of a great deal of his operational responsibility. Lieutenant Colonel E J Bruen took command in Bielefeld of a unit that comprised the Corps Ammunition Company at Sennelager, the Corps Vehicle Company at Osnabruck and the Corps Stores Company in Bielefeld. It was a long overdue addition to the third line support capability of the RAOC in supporting 1 British Corps.

The new flag.

On 1 October 1963 a major event came with the opening of the first computer centre for the RAOC at COD Chilwell, known as an Automated Data Processing Installation. It had been four years in gestation and its successful delivery was thanks to the hard work of Colonel Alan Pettifor and overseen by the Commandant at Chilwell, Brigadier Edward Ranson. He was known to many as Ranji, an officer who had joined the Army in 1925 as a boy soldier, had risen to the rank of Brigadier and who would go on to complete forty-eight years in the service of the Crown. The opening of the installation had been announced in the births column of the local newspaper as: 'ORD, *prematurely to Emmy née Decker, wife of M T Ord a daughter Ivy. Absent friends please note.*' 'Ivy' was a play on words, signifying Issue Voucher, and it did not pass notice that the day of the advertisement was Friday 13 September.

The cost of the machinery was £500,000 (£6.2 million), with the building in which it was housed costing £100,000 (£1.25 million). It could perform 40,000 simple transactions a second and print 300 lines of text a minute. It would work sixteen hours a day seven days a week and in the course of a single day was expected to handle 10,000 input transactions a minute of up to 138 different types.

When Mr Joseph Godber, the Secretary of State for War pressed the button to set the machine running he turned to the DOS, Major General Hildreth, and the Commander Base Organization, Major General Payne, and asked 'what have I started?' Unknowingly, probably, he had just started a revolution in inventory management in which the RAOC was already in the lead in both the military and commercial logistic arenas. The sadness is that subsequent treasury parsimony and

Major General Payne.

mismanagement by influences outside the Corps meant that over the years the Army was to trail in an area in which it had once led the country. The Army gave the world logistics; such a pity it would in the future need the world to give it back in order to perform to the best possible standards.

In Singapore 28 Commonwealth Brigade OFP was the smallest unit in the formation and when faced with the annual sports competition they knew their chances of bringing back medals against much stronger opposition, especially from the Australians and the New Zealanders, were slim. So they decided to recall a Corps heritage and concentrate on something they knew they were good at, to whit tug-of-war, to emulate the standards set in Feltham during the post-war years. After some hard training they did precisely that and at the end of the sports day the cup for the event returned with them to grace the silver cupboard in the OFP orderly room.

By the turn of the year, the garrison peacekeeping force in Cyprus had been successful in containing the fighting in Nicosia, but had been unable to deal with the wider trouble spreading across the island. Consequently, in February 1964 the strategic reserve, a full division, was deployed from the United Kingdom. This preceded by just one month acceptance by the United Nations that it should assume responsibility for peacekeeping on the island. The division put on its powder blue beret and gradually thinned out as other contingents arrived from contributing nations. The United Nations force, UNFICYP, was to consist of approximately 6,000 men drawn from seven countries with the task of maintaining peace while a mediator appointed by the UN sought to find a solution.

Logistic support was to come very largely from the British and was to follow British procedures. This presented the odd difficulty from time to time, with 'odd' the operative word, with the added complication of having to retrain each contingent as it changed over every six months. Tentage and accommodation stores, vehicles, fuel, rations, common user ammunition and stationery were among the ranges of items provided, and to recover the costs from the UN a unique form of cash accounting needed to be introduced, and the contingents held to it so that HMG did not sustain a loss. Initial support for the operation came from Ordnance Depot Cyprus and the Assault Detachment of 1 OFP, and forward with UNFICYP was an RAOC major with a BOO at HQ Nicosia Zone and 16 Parachute OFP giving organic support. There was also a detachment from the Stores Section attached to 3 Infantry Workshops; and the Bath Section of 1 OFP. Then on 6 May 1964 a small team that eventually became known as the Ordnance Detachment Cyprus replaced the Parachute OFP. Inevitably, food became the single most complex factor with dietary tastes and culinary aspirations having to be satisfied from Canada to Finland via Ireland; and in Finland between the north and south of the country. Eventually the solution was for seven different ration scales with special foods having to be sourced from Germany, the Netherlands and Scandinavia. The Bakery too was stretched given the different tastes of, for example, Austrians and Swedes for bread; and the standard British loaf was not popular with any of the foreign contingents.

The UN intervention provided a timely relief, for trouble was also brewing in Aden, with terrorist acts in the port being combined with guerrilla incidents up-country, born of a movement that saw integration of Aden with its hinterland, the Yemen, as a legitimate political objective. In Aden itself a bomb was thrown at a group of government ministers resulting in the declaration of a state of emergency and the closing of the border with Yemen. The situation was not helped by a declaration of Alec Douglas-Home's government, in its dying days, that Aden would grant, by 1968, independence to the federation of rulers that had been formed in 1963 in the area around Aden – a shaky political structure to say the least. However, the down side of this independence, from the local point of view, was the declared intention to retain a base in Aden.

In the United Kingdom the NETTLERASH programme finally ground to an end with the stocks in Didcot and Branston all moved to Bicester and the depots closed, and Thatcham, also emptied of Stores Organization stocks and handed over to DDOS Southern Command for use as a Command depot. Didcot was handed to the Central Electricity Generating Board for the construction of a coal-fuelled power station that now dominates the Oxfordshire skyline – and that of neighbouring counties. Didcot had been a depot constructed in 1915 with the internal transportation process dependent upon horse transport; this not simply for the movement of stores, but also for the administration of the depot. At the end there were still two horses in use for such tasks as refuse collection, coal distribution and grass cutting – Goliath and Lottery. Both were found good homes for a peaceful retirement.

When it ended, Operation NETTLERASH had proved to be one of the biggest physical reorganizations undertaken by the RAOC in the post-war era. Many thousands of tons of stores were transferred into the retention depots, and some 3,000 military and civilian posts saved in the whole process. It goes without saying that it was carried out while service to the Army, quite a lot of which was on operations, remained undiminished.

There was a plea in the Corps' *Gazette* for November for more members of the RAOC to invest their pay in a monthly copy. The price was one shilling (£0.62) per month and equated to the purchase price of five cigarettes or two cups of tea. It was a plea to be often repeated and would remain so until something imaginative could be done to improve the position.

To resolve an insurgency in the Radfan, an area of mountains about sixty miles north of Aden, the British moved in 39 Brigade HQ to command the operation to quieten the tribesmen in the area. Rising to a strength of six battalions the force, after some really quite aggressive action, completed its task. The RAOC support available at the time came from the CRAOC and his staff, and an Ordnance Depot in Aden that had good war reserves and stockpiles of pre-positioned stores, and it had an outstation in Bahrain. Demands for units up country came via a convoluted arrangement that had unit QMs taking over the counter issues directly from the depots and passing them forward. It soon became clear that this would not be sufficient and that effective 2nd Line support would need to be provided. Accordingly, Major Harry Mitchell's 24 OFP arrived very quickly indeed from Kenya and became operational on 20 May 1964. Further additions came with 17 Parachute Heavy Drop Platoon, 24 Air Maintenance Section and a Stores Section serving 633 Squadron AAC workshops. 17 Para Heavy Drop Platoon arrived in Aden with the main element of 3rd Para Battalion Group; but as there seemed no possibility of an airborne assault with a heavy drop commitment, Captain D E J Evans, the Heavy Drop Platoon commander, asked that the Platoon be allowed to operate as infantry. The Commanding Officer of 3rd Parachute Battalion, Lieutenant Colonel Tony Farrar-Hockley, agreed and overnight they became 3 Platoon, A Company, 3 Para.

The Ordnance units that came with 3 Para were from the small garrison in Bahrain, a residue of the earlier deployment that had been left in place following the potential invasion of Kuwait by Iraq in 1961. They left behind in Bahrain the small Ordnance Depot and a Malkara[1] platoon.

17 Parachute Heavy Drop Platoon RAOC operating as 3 Platoon A company 3rd Battalion The Parachute Regiment

Major John Elliot GM RAOC.

The arrival of the OFP and its dispatch to Thurmia, meant that stocks could be held forward, re-supply times were greatly shortened and a more 'traditional' arrangement with which units could more easily identify was in place. This was further enhanced as more and more transport became available, and as the airstrip at Thurmia was enhanced to take Beverley aircraft.

To protect Aden as a base, 24 Brigade was moved into Little Aden by the end of the year, catching up with its OFP. Unhappiness with this arrangement was allowed to fester and then when the Labour Government came to power in October 1964 there was the realization that Wilson would be less keen to retain a base in the area and that encouragement for a withdrawal might be provided by an overt and effective campaign of terrorism. This inevitably produced, inter alia, a spate of IEDs with extensive and courageous work being undertaken by Major John Elliot and his team. The result was the award of a George Medal to Major Elliott for his individual contribution in personally neutralizing over 150 IEDs. His successor, Major G C Browlee would go on a couple of years later also to be awarded a GM for services of a similar nature and at a similar level of activity.

In March 1964 the agreement was announced for optional mess dress to be worn in the Sergeants' Mess. It was to comprise No. 1 dress trousers with black shoes, and there was the option of a red cummerbund beneath the jacket to offset the semi formal shirt with turned down collar. Miniature medals would also be worn on the jacket which was to be similar to the officers' version, but without epaulettes or buttons. It was to be lined in scarlet with blue cuffs of the same material edged with Russian lace. The cost was £14 0s 0d (£175), and the agreement received a mixed reception. Some were delighted, but others were of the view that sergeants' mess formal functions were fewer and far between in the early sixties and the expense was not warranted.

While all this was going on the McLeod Committee had completed its work swiftly, some might say with indecent haste, and, on 22 April 1964, its findings were announced in Parliament. In simple terms the McLeod report broke the logistic services down into three functions: Supply, Transport and Maintenance. These would be formed on cap-badge lines with RAOC remaining as the Supply Corps of the Army and hence taking responsibility for the provision and supply of rations, POL (including the operation of pipelines), miscellaneous chemicals and disinfectants, RE transportation stores, boat stores, and signals project stores. It would have responsibility for the Barrack Services and would sponsor the Army Fire Services and NAAFI - EFI, the latter being the field force element of NAAFI. The McLeod Committee had also recommended that the RAOC should take over the Royal Engineers' stores organization, but a decision on this was deferred.

There was also an issue over the redeployment of Staff Clerks from the RASC. Originally thinking they were best employed in the Royal Signals the McCleod Committee had recommended this as a course of action. However, the traditional route for Staff Clerks to commissioning was Barrack Services and this was a sufficiently powerful driver to have them follow the barracks world into the RAOC.

The move, it was decided, was to be in three phases. The first, the takeover of the responsibilities of RASC units, was complete by July of 1964, just three months from the publication of McLeod's findings. The rest, the transfer of individuals by cap badge and the absorption of RASC depots into the

RAOC base organization and the refining of the ORBAT to support operations, would take a little longer. It is perhaps worth noting that there were operations under way in Aden, Cyprus and Borneo as the reorganization was being implemented and the restructuring had to be undertaken in operational theatres in addition to everything else that was going on.

As an example of what this meant on the ground, perhaps events in Aden will serve to illustrate. The Royal Air Force became the single service managers for rations, petroleum, oils and lubricants with ground and aviation fuels being supplied direct to units under contract by the Shell Oil Company. The problems of ration supply were not, however, entirely lifted from Ordnance shoulders as the DDOS and his staff had to initiate and negotiate such matters as the provision of boneless meat to make possible up-country distribution by polar-packs and to ease the task of final preparation in the field. The RAOC also sponsored a scheme for the preparation and supply of ready-to-cook fresh vegetables to forward troops and outstations. When terrorist attacks and walkout by staff crippled the main oil refinery in the territory, the RAOC, with RE support, took over and operated for several critical months the vast installation and the distribution network. The main customers included RAF Khormaksar, then said to be the busiest airfield in the world, and all the shipping then bunkering in Aden Port. Barrack services for RN and RAF units increased the RAOC's responsibilities in the Command with units and dependents extended from South Africa through Central and East Africa to the Gulf.

The reorganization went ahead, and the service never faltered. There had been recognition of the increased work and responsibilities, however, before the McLeod reorganization, with the upgrading of many RAOC posts in Aden, so at least the Corps had that satisfaction with a colonel DDOS heading up the RAOC representation.

On the evening of Wednesday, 6 May, the Pipes and Drums of 52 Stores Company RAOC (TA), formerly 12 Stores Company, beat Retreat on the esplanade of Edinburgh Castle. Colonel J L Lamb OBE, TD, TA, Deputy Inspector of Reserve Army Units RAOC, took the salute at the march past. The idea of having a pipe band with an RAOC (TA) unit originated, in the summer of 1957, in the minds of Lieutenant Colonel I J Lamb, and Captain L A M MacDonald, the Commanding Officer and

The RAOC TA Pipe Band on the Esplanade at Edinburgh Castle.

Adjutant respectively of 12 General Stores Company RAOC (TA) and an 'unofficial' band was formed. The funds to equip it were raised by private subscription, together with support from the officers, warrant officers, sergeants and soldiers of the unit. By June 1958 the Band had been officially recognized and thus 12 GS Company, became the first RAOC unit to have its own pipes and drums. Following consultation with the Lord Lyon King of Arms, the Chief of the Clan Lament and the Representative Colonel Commandant of the RAOC, it was agreed by the War Office Dress Committee that the appropriate tartan to be worn by the pipers was, in view of the surname of the then Commanding Officer, that of the Clan Lament to which those of the surname 'Lamb' belong.

A new issue of regulations for the storage and handling of ammunition was due to be produced. Brigadier (Retd) Alan Fernyhough, as the retired officer responsible for pamphlets, was involved with HMSO in its production. Never an officer to be tampered with, he was famous for his remarks in the address he used to give to Young Officer's Courses at the School of Ordnance. It would open with the words: 'I am here to tell you about the creeping paralysis of civilianization.' HMSO, being an entirely civilian organization was, therefore, never likely to be given anything other than short shrift, so when he received another of the interminable phone calls about this pamphlet Alan Fernyhough was in no mood for trifles. The question was one of the cover and the colour it should be. The rather terse response was that he didn't give a '...tinker's cuss' what colour it was as long as it could be READ. The result was a pamphlet that, on production, had a cover in a rather fetching, and instantly recognizable, shade of deep red.

Norman Bruce.

A posting to the Far East, to an OFP, meant that Norman Bruce's appearance for Scotland against England in the Calcutta Cup in 1964 would be his last. Scotland won, for the first time since 1950, by fifteen points to six, with three of the points coming from a try by Norman. Having first played for his country in 1958, he had won thirty-one caps, and his Army and Combined Services appearances were by then beyond counting. His last appearance for the RAOC before moving off saw him lead the team to winning the Palestine Cup against REME for the seventh year in succession.

In Germany as a result of McLeod the roles and responsibilities of the RAOC increased markedly, taking on a number of field force units such as 49 Supply Company as well as base installations such as supply depots, barrack services, petroleum depots, Army fire brigades and some static RASC HQs, together with responsibility for Staff Clerks throughout the Command. It was a massive task, while at the same time continuing to provide a service that meant the rest of the Army did not know the amalgamation was taking place.

It also meant the RAOC taking on the static RASC headquarters in Celle, Osnabruck and Dortmund giving a total of five CRAOCs in addition to those in the divisions. Clearly this was too many, but initially they were all to be left in place to help oversee the changes.

Operationally, in Germany, it had been the role of the RASC to establish and run the Replenishment Points, the large third line grounded dumps of stores and supplies that fed forward to the divisions in 1 (Br) Corps in war. Under the reorganization 49 Supply Company, whose task this had been, logically moved to be part of the COMP thereby placing responsibility for fuel and rations with the CO. Hence, one organization now had complete responsibility for, and control of, all materiel and supplies at third line. Renamed as Replenishment Parks, the COMP was tasked with forming one for each of the four divisions and one for Corps troops, each holding 5,000 tons of stores and combat supplies. The COMP was a significant command, almost 1,500 strong in war, with only two RP companies, 49 Company and the Ammunition company, existing in peace, and the others coming as reinforcements from the UK. The Vehicle Company and Stores Company did not use the RP re-supply route to move their stocks but instead went straight through to OFPs and Stores Sections.

Significantly, despite its importance to the sustainability of 1 (Br) Corps and its divisions, the COMP had virtually no communications capability with which to control its vast and disparate empire. To help offset this the replenishment regime was altered. Instead of each RP being tied to a division they were pulled further back in the 1 (Br) Corps area and brought closer together. Stocking policy was more broadly based and to meet individual formation needs a series of transport exchange points were set up further forward from which divisions could draw their specific needs.

Elsewhere, the Territorial Army, it was realized, was impossible to equip effectively. Most of the stores that were assigned to achieve mobilization were of Second World War origin. They were out of date, of limited use and far too expensive to replace. The practicalities of using the TA as a force of eleven divisions were far removed from reality. The outcome of a study into the future and roles of the Reserve Army led to an amalgamation of the individual element and the fixed unit part of the volunteer reserve army into the oddly entitled Territorial and Army Volunteer Reserve. The units particularly vulnerable to the axe were those with a heavy equipment liability, such as armour and artillery. They were also among the hardest to recruit. Despite opposition from the more senior echelons of the TA what emerged was a leaner and more effective reserve army, and one whose equipment was affordable.

In the spirit of delivering the benefits of yet further reorganization to the Army, General Nye's committee published its report. It was a wide-ranging study affecting most parts of the organization of a War Office that had been amalgamated in July and August 1964 into a single unified Ministry of Defence that had itself formed in the April. For the RAOC there were some far-reaching changes. The Army Board accepted Nye's recommendation that the QMG's department should consist of a Directorate of Army Logistic Plans and Operations under a VQMG, and a Directorate of Army Maintenance under a DQMG which was to be responsible for the Q policy for materiel. The telling blow was that Service Directors should leave the Army Department, which is what the War Office had become in the new MOD structure, and hand over to the Q Staff their responsibility for major policy. What this meant was that Q staff policy, which was policy that directly impacted on the roles and responsibilities of the RAOC, was now the responsibility of staff officers with a general background and no real knowledge of logistics. In order to compensate for this, the 'expertise' of the Services was to be provided by having a number of staff-trained Service officers integrated into the Q Staff'. However, the crucial, and most damaging, aspect of this restructuring was that it removed from the DOS the responsibility for provision policy. Despite Major General John Hildreth's best efforts the decision stood and the new structure was put in place with the links from the Department of Army Maintenance direct onto the provision officers of the major depots, the Ammunition Organization and the Vehicle Organization. The DOS was all but excluded from the loop as the Brigadier (Ordnance Provision) and four of the five Provision Branches (Ord 8, 13, 17, and 21) were removed from his directorate to become part of the new structure. The DOS was left with one Provision Branch (Ord 7) for coordination purposes. At the same time the Ordnance Directorate ceased to be a part of the War Office in the sense that it was not transferred to the newly formed Ministry of Defence. In its place a Headquarters DOS was established in First Avenue House in High Holborn.

Meanwhile, within the RAOC, the DOS was to be responsible for the detailed implementation of 'Q' policies, in whose formulation he had no direct hand, and for the efficiency of the Corps.

As if there were not enough reorganization the Services were beset by the stated need for rationalization. It was perceived that there were a number of commodities, such as food, fuel, weapons, ammunition and utility and load-carrying vehicles that were common to the three Services.

It was sensible, so ran the logic, to capitalize on the unification of the three Services within a single MOD and make one of them responsible for supply of such items to all three. Splendid at first sight, but the reality was that only about 8 per cent of commodities were common and their supply and management in the individual Services were on a different foundation. For example, the priority afforded road sweeper spares in the Army, where they simply kept the roads clean, was different from the RAF where rubbish on a runway kept aircraft on the ground and had serious operational consequences. As to the language, that too was different. For example, MT in the Army meant Motor Transport; in the Royal Navy and the Royal Air Force it was Mechanical Transport and the arguments over which to use were still raging in committees in the MOD at the turn of the millennium, some thirty-five years later. However, at least it explained why, when the RAOC took over responsibility for MT on behalf of all three Services, bicycles pitched up at RAOC depots as part of the transfer of stock. Two months into the problem and the arrival of a RAF liaison officer at Chilwell went a long way to solving many of the difficulties.

There were also a number of small incidents and events resulting from the policy of rationalization, many of them largely unreported. One such was the handover of logistic support for Gibraltar to the Royal Navy. Hence, an association with the RAOC in its various forms that had existed since 1704 was severed

Logic, of course, would naturally lead to the view that the Service with the larger requirement would take on the lead role for the commodities in question, and certainly that had been the case with MT. However, logic took no account of the need, for example, to preserve the career structures of supply staff in the other two Services. The key changes involved Accommodation Stores, which went to the RAF, and Rations, including Operational Ration Packs, which went to the Royal Navy. This single-service management was restricted only to the primary provision of stocks. Distribution to users remained very much a single Service issue. It is to be wondered what it all really achieved, coming together with all the other studies raging simultaneously, to say nothing of the support requirements for an Army conducting operations and reorganizations at the same time, all with equipment and supply implications. It was a series of studies that members of the RAOC could have done without – or at least postponed.

Actually, among all the studies undertaken, that conducted by the Cooper Brothers into the use of costing in the Supply and Repair Services did actually add value and provided useful confirmation of initiatives for which the RAOC had been seeking approval for some time. This would see the introduction of work measurement and costing into RAOC installations to help provide management information as an aid to decision making. At about the same time the outcome of the Wilson-Smith Committee investigation into the extent to which the RAOC could be civilianized went in favour of the Corps and saw no further scope for civilianization on top of that already happening. Welcome news indeed, but the time expended on the supporting staff work, especially given all that was going on, was disproportionate.

On 1 September 1964 the ADPI at Bicester became operational, although it would not be officially opened until December of the same year. It had benefited hugely from the pioneering work undertaken at Chilwell. It was forecast that the system would cost £606,000 (£7.25 million), and would save some 375 posts, valued at £268,000 (£3.25 million) per year.

It had originally been intended to computerize the stocks at Bicester and Branston, but Branston was no longer to be one of the main depots. It was decided that a project to computerize Bicester's stocks could only be of added value if it included ammunition. Work began in earnest in 1964.

The year was marked by a special retirement; that of WOI (Sub-Conductor) Gladys Warden BEM, who completed her twenty-two years service, all of it with the RAOC, with her marriage to Staff Sergeant Isaac of the REME. She was only the second woman to be accorded the title, the other being WOI

(Sub-Conductor) Frankie Hardwick. The DOS, Major General Sir John Hildreth viewed her service as so special he wrote, unusually for a retirement such as this, to thank her for her years with the RAOC.

At the same time there was a crucial decision in the War Office that the only way to manage stock volumes on operations, especially of fuel and of ammunition, would be to introduce modern palletized techniques together with the means of handling them, into the forward areas. Consequently, work was put in hand to develop the concept and the means. It was work that would involve the RAOC's Materials Handling Experimental and Packaging Unit and the Military Engineering Experimental Establishment.

On 30 September 1964 the gates of COD Didcot finally closed. The site was taken over by the Central Electricity Generating Board, and eventually a new coal-fired power station was built there. Vauxhall Barracks was retained and housed a number of organizations over the years to come.

In Germany a small decision was taken that would have a long-term effect for the RAOC. A need was identified to store vehicles forward for some spearhead units that might have to be deployed at short notice. Consequently, an old railway coach repair yard at Recklinghausen was taken over, and what would eventually be the site of a forward vehicle depot for 17 BVD came to life.

Then, at the end of 1964, the situation in Borneo escalated, requiring a further deployment with a major threat being identified in the area of Kuching, the outcome of which was a reinforcement bid to the UK. The essence of the problem was that Indonesian activity in Sarawak was becoming too much for the single brigade deployed there and it required the creation of an additional brigade sector. The staff selected 3 Commando Brigade for the task and it

WOI Sub-Conductor Gladys Warden.

moved there with 3 Commando Brigade OFP in January 1965. The OFP had been raised from volunteers in UK in March 1964 after the Brigade had been obliged to leave its original OFP in Kuching. The new OFP differed in that the soldiers had all completed the All Arms Commando course and wore the green beret, just like the rest of Commando Forces. It was to be a brief stay as HQ 3 Commando Brigade were relieved in February by HQ 19 Brigade, and the OFP withdrew by air and sea between 24 and 26 February 1965 to be replaced by its 19 Brigade counterpart. The original static OFPs, something of an oxymoron, had elevated to the status of OMPs, and the working arrangement between them and the brigade OFPs was never entirely satisfactorily resolved.

What did work well, however, was the management of ammunition. It was no easy task, with large stocks held forward in the patrol bases in awful conditions and requiring constant inspection. Damage from airdrops was also a major problem, especially of 105-mm artillery ammunition, requiring a local demolition programme. And there were a high number of ammunition accidents, almost all errors of drill. However, they required the prompt attendance of an ATO and threw into disarray any pre-planned inspection and disposal programme. Struggling manfully with all this, and clearly enjoying themselves, were young ATOs, fresh out of Bramley; including David Botting, Tony Smith and Freddie Cantrell.

Ammunition trained personnel were also busy on the mainland of Malaysia, where insurgents were quite regularly placing IEDs. Although the Federation of Malaysia was responsible now for its own defence, it possessed no real anti-IED capability, so it fell to RAOC ATOs and ATs to go to its assistance. The result was three George Medals. Captain Tom Judge acquired his for clearing a device underneath the Malacca Club by stopping the timer just minutes before it was due to complete the circuit. Subsequent investigation also showed that an anti-handling arrangement of bared wired in very close proximity had come within cigarette paper thickness of connecting.

During the night of 28 October 1965 Captain Mike Hall and SQMS B J C Reid earned their GMs. They were faced with a device which was number twenty-five in a series of similar devices. Determined to work out what it was, for the safety and benefit of others, they set about dismantling it. It was in a biscuit tin, so was hard to penetrate gently. Seven pounds of TNT, two grenades, some incendiary material, three anti-handling devices, a timer and four hours later the whole thing was in pieces – safe.

Much more quietly, the RAOC had left Kenya on 31 March 1965 with the Kenyan Army taking over those RAOC installations it required for its own purposes. It was a peaceful and orderly departure, Lieutenant Colonel Gerry Landy being the last CRAOC.

On 26 February 1965 the RAOC's oldest Ordnance Depot, at Weedon, closed. It was a dull, chilly afternoon, redolent in many ways of the sense of loss both in the RAOC and the local community. When the buildings had been erected in 1803 the country had been under threat of invasion from Napoleon at a time when it was considered prudent to build an arsenal in the centre of the country, where an alternative seat of government would also be made for King George III and his ministers. Since that day the depot had seen service in many more wars and had supported the Army through them all. Its closure was a cause of great sadness for many.

On 10 May 1965 Her Majesty the Queen was able to pay a visit to an RAOC installation, and in this case COD Bicester was fortunate to be chosen. The sun shone and there was an air of great festivity

Mrs Davey closes up for the last time at Weedon. It was a sad day for many.

The Queen pays a visit to Bicester on 10 May 1965.

about the place. Her Majesty, of course, visited as the RAOC's Colonel-in-Chief, but took the opportunity to review those members of other Corps who made their contribution to the working of the depot: R Signals, RCT and RPC. She was accompanied by His Royal Highness the Duke of Edinburgh, and despite the work involved in preparing for and executing a Royal visit, the depot continued to function supporting the Army. Indeed, the rest of the Army would never know the visit was taking place.

On 15 July 1965, 345 officers and 2,300 soldiers transferred from the RASC to the RAOC. They included 87 per cent of officers and 99 per cent of soldiers as voluntary transferees. The two Corps marked this historic reorganization with an exchange of mess silver. On Monday 13 December 1965, in the HQ RAOC Officers' Mess, Major General W J Potter, the Transport Officer-in-Chief, presented on behalf of the Royal Corps of Transport a silver model of a pre-1939 Mark X horse-drawn GS wagon together with its pair of light draught horses and drivers. On behalf of the RAOC General McVittie presented to the RCT a silver rose bowl.

It had been some seventy years since Lord Kitchener had voiced his view that there should be but one supply corps for the Army instead of the two that existed at the time. That presupposed that in the days of a Corps dedicated to maintenance there would be but one of those as well. However, despite the advances, McLeod was only able to go so far without bumping up against the difficulties imposed by what was at once the British Army's greatest strength and its greatest weakness: the regimental system. Cap badge warfare was prevalent throughout the study. Thus it was that the Royal Engineers retained responsibility for supply of engineer material and the RAMC for medical stores. And the new Royal Corps of Transport retained far too great a hold on the delivery of combat supplies. Similarly, in maintenance the Royal Signals, for example, retained responsibility for repair of some signals equipment, and the Royal Engineers for engineer equipment.

In Germany in June 1965 a Belgian ammunition train caught fire in a cutting near Minden. The train had been stopped and four of the wagons uncoupled, but the fire increased and two of the wagons exploded, scattering ammunition over a wide area. The SATO in charge of No. 3 Detachment of the BAOR Ammunition Inspectorate, Major C W Smith, and his second in command, Captain Peter

Istead, found a third wagon with its wooden end on fire, the surrounding area covered with burning propellant, exploded shells and a number of dangerously hot 90-millimetre shells which might have detonated at any moment. Major Smith and Captain Istead arranged for water to be played on the third, burning wagon and then, gaining access to it, managed to move its explosive contents away from the still burning end. They then uncoupled the third and fourth wagons, each containing about ten tons of 90-millimetre ammunition, and moved them about sixty yards farther down the track. Having thus prevented a further major explosion they set about dealing with the other ammunition which lay in and around the first two, still burning, wagons. This was a long and hazardous operation, taking some twelve hours from about nine in the evening until about nine-thirty the next morning by which time all the ammunition had been cleared. Both officers were awarded the GM.

By 1965 the store holding capacity of the RAOC in the UK had been reduced to three main depots: Bicester, Chilwell and Donnington – all controlled by Stores Organization. Ammunition was held in just three depots, Bramley, Kineton and Longtown, and the Ammunition Organization also controlled the Army School of Ammunition and the Armaments Research and Development Unit. It also assumed responsibility for a number of ex Ministry of Supply depots holding ammunition, but the volumes were small and the dispersion made their management complex and inefficient. By now it was clear that there was no longer a need for separate Stores and Ammunition Organizations and a study was set in train to merge them. This happened on 1 April 1966 when HQ Base Organization came into being, based at Didcot, the home of Stores Organization, in Vauxhall Barracks. One key aspect of the reorganization was that responsibility for storage of ammunition was separated off from technical control and a brigadier was appointed to set and maintain technical standards. He was the Chief Inspector of Land Service Ammunition.

The Vehicle Organization went through similar trials. It had started the decade with five vehicle depots, but the reduction of vehicle stocks, which had started in 1957, went on inexorably during the early sixties. Between 1960 and 1964, the stock levels of vehicles fell from 52,219 to 24,913. Annual receipts and issues fell from 67,201 to 49,902. Further closures were inevitable, and in 1965 it was decided that CVD Marchington would have to go. Rationalization had its impact on the progress of closure as the true liability was worked out. However, there would be no stopping it. A major advance in 1965, that was to simplify the management of vehicles and spell the death knell of more depots, was the incorporation of the global vehicle census onto the COD Chilwell computer.

Throughout 1965 disturbances had been going on in Aden, and on 1 September the speaker of the Aden Parliament was assassinated, causing Harold Wilson to suspend the Aden Constitution. Then, in February 1966, the United Kingdom confirmed that it no longer intended to maintain a base in Aden after the granting of independence to the Federation, planned for 1968, on the stated grounds that the British were not going to stay anywhere they were not wanted. This followed a year that had seen 286 terrorist incidents, leading to 237 casualties. However, any idea that a declaration of a total withdrawal would lead to a lessening of trouble was ill founded. Indeed, it intensified the internal struggle between those aspiring to post-colonial power and led to 480 terrorist incidents in 1966. Of the 573 casualties that emanated from this, five of the dead and 218 of the wounded were British servicemen.

However, with the early warning having been given and mindful of the short notice requirements that would come the way of the RAOC, the DDOS, Colonel Neil Barclay, decided to take the initiative and set about planning the RAOC redeployment into the two depots in the Gulf that were to remain to support deployments in and to the Middle East, one in Bahrain and the other in Sharja.

In August 1966 Colonel E H Hancock assumed the appointment of DDOS MEC in Aden for what would be the last year of the British occupation. Despite all the careful planning he was faced with the reality of having to maintain a full supply service to the forces left in Aden while transferring stocks to the Gulf, and having to take full responsibility for POL supply after the closure of the Aden refinery which would take place some five months before the end of occupation. Maintenance of soldiers under operational conditions, with troops widely scattered in most adverse conditions of terrain and climate, meant, effectively, supporting in excess of two brigades worth. This had to be done with establishments that had been written for the support of one brigade and was no easy task. It was not helped by the hostility created among the locally employed civilians who, although they worked in the depot and drew their pay, were hardly acting in the best interests of the Crown. As Colonel Hancock took over the Stores Sub-Depot Aden held 72,000 item headings, the Vehicle Sub-depot had 1,100 vehicles, and the Ammunition Sub-depot held over 5,000 tons. All this had to be used up, redeployed worldwide, or disposed of by October 1967. There was an added complication with 'B' vehicles, since units remaining in Aden until final withdrawal would have to abandon most of them as they left. The DDOS therefore arranged to change over the holdings of those units so that they would leave behind only the oldest vehicles.

In Hong Kong, Lieutenant Colonel J L Laurenzen had moved up from his post as CRAOC Borneo to inherit the task overseen by his predecessor of developing a new Ordnance Depot at Kai Tak, the work on which was completed and the depot handed over to the Army in April 1966. The move from Kowloon Tong to Kai Tak was fully pre-planned using critical path analysis, probably its first use by the Army. All aspects were analysed in detail, vehicle loads were calculated, and from that information detailed timetables for the move of each section were assessed. The results of the critical path analysis were tabulated, programmed and fed into an IBM 1620 computer at Hong Kong University. The computer printout of earliest and latest acceptable times for starting and finishing each component of the analysis gave the total time necessary for the move as fifty-seven working days. The move started at the end of May and was completed in mid August, five days ahead of schedule. Over 4,600 tons of stores were moved in just over 3,000 vehicle loads, and as it happened Army units in Hong Kong were scarcely aware that the move was in progress, as a normal supply service was maintained throughout. The new depot, complete with military living accommodation, was opened on 2 September 1966.

The NATO term Explosive Ordnance Disposal was introduced to replace Bomb Disposal, although the more familiar name continued to be used for some time to come.

At Deepcut the Depot and Training Battalion was split into a Regimental Depot and a separate Trade Training School, and a department for centralized administration was formed under an Administrative Commandant.

The RAF became the single service managers of Accommodation Stores, and in so doing deprived Bicester of a large part of its stockholding, placing yet another cloud over any justification for a computer especially for the depot. In any case, the concept was about to be overtaken by events. Until that time all items in the inventory, irrespective of operational importance or monetary value, received the same provision attention and treatment, with each item being reviewed annually. All previous history of each item received the same credence, irrespective of its age, within the review period. Scant attention was paid to the economics of ordering, that is balancing the costs to order, the costs to hold, and the price 'breaks' applicable to differing quantities ordered. Materiel was stored in part number order within VAOS section order. Frequently required items were stored amidst slow moving items, making binning on receipt and selection for issue, slower and more costly than need be. It was the job of Lieutenant Colonel Bob Stronach, the officer in charge of provision research at Chilwell, to examine how the provision and warehousing tasks could be re-shaped by effectively combining the new statistical techniques with the power and speed of computer processing.

The Pareto Principle, applied to the value of an inventory, indicated that some ninety per cent of the value of the materiel was contained in ten per cent of the stock items. This appeared to offer benefit if more of management's time and effort were to be devoted to the ten per cent. It was also felt that the use of mathematical techniques such as regression analysis, exponential smoothing of demand histories, and economic order formulae would give much greater exactitude and subtlety to the calculating of re-order quantities. The flaw in the reasoning, of course, was that something relatively cheap could keep a vital piece of equipment out of operation. The focus was on economy, not capability, demonstrating yet again the dead hand of the Treasury's accountants and their influence over defence decisions that would ultimately affect operational posture. Nonetheless, the logic of economy lay at the basis of the development of the second-generation computer system, originally intended to replace the ICL 2400's at Chilwell and Donnington in 1975.

August 1966 saw the official end of confrontation in Borneo, with the Bangkok Accord having been signed in June and then ratified on 11 August. When at its most intense there had been 17,000 servicemen involved in operations. These included Australians and New Zealanders from the Commonwealth Brigade in Singapore. Casualties had included 114 killed and 181 wounded from among the Commonwealth soldiers involved. Lieutenant Colonel Gordon Dennison was the CRAOC at the time, and recalled how, with the talks having gone on for months, he was, in June, given just twenty-four hours to produce plans for the backloading of all Ordnance stores in the theatre. Inevitably it was done, and the actual work commenced in July, with the first local sale in September. An RSG was set up based on the two OMPs, but inevitably the pace of withdrawal overtook their capacity to handle and move the stores; and the ammunition inspection load was particularly heavy. However, in the couple of months either side of Christmas it was all done and the last RAOC unit packed its bags and left in February 1967

The end of confrontation also heralded a major reduction in defence expenditure to £2 billion (£23 billion) per year. It was largely to be funded by significant cuts, to include a far as possible those stationed east of Suez – of which both Aden and Borneo were a part. The Gurkhas were to find a cut of 5,000 down to 10,000 whilst in the rest of the Army 15,000 were to be shaved off the Army's strength, bringing it down to 181,000 and heading for 166,000 by 1971. This initial cut meant the loss of four armoured and four artillery regiments and eight battalions of infantry.

Within six months of these draconian cuts more pain was to follow. Complete withdrawal from Singapore and from the Persian Gulf was to be effected by 1971, and the Gurkhas were to become a Hong Kong based force of just 6,000. The nation's defences were to focus on Europe. No 'out-of-area' capability was to be retained, and as if to emphasize the point the Royal Navy was to be stripped of its aircraft carriers. But not everything was in decline. In Europe two new, small units were forming up. No. 2 GM Platoon moved to 154 FAD at Wulfen, in support of 36 Heavy Air Defence Regiment, becoming operational on 26 February 1967. Another platoon, 3 Platoon, meanwhile remained in the UK in support of the UK Training Battery and supported the conversion of 37 Heavy Air Defence Regiment to Thunderbird II.[2]

By the end of 1966 the reorganization of the Q Empire resulting from the Nye Report was two years old. The vision had been of a generalist staff supported by a few staff trained logistics corps officers in the hope that they might add a touch of reality to policy making. In fact, only one lieutenant colonel's post was annotated to be filled by RAOC. The reality, however, was that there were eighty-two logistic corps officers and civil servants against just eight generalists and only sixteen of the ninety had attended Staff College. Ninety per cent of those dealing with materiel were either RAOC, ex RAOC filling retired officer posts or civil servants with an Ordnance Services background.

The Nye structure was not proving a great success. There was huge duplication of effort as the DOS tried to stay in a loop from which he was excluded, but in which he needed to be involved. And when the Army was represented on committees in the newly formed MOD there were two Army representatives for every Naval and Air Force representative, one from the DQMG and the other from DOS. By now most of the recommendations of Nye and all the other studies of the early sixties had been implemented and were being made to work.

The balance of Ordnance support needed to be changed in the UK commands, and the reorganization plan submitted by the DOS was approved by the Standing Committee on Army Organization in 1966. It would begin in Western Command in 1967. For Barrack Services the primary requirement was seen to be the Married Quarters Exchange Shop, holding a range of portable items in frequent demand, and giving an over-the-counter service. Barrack Stores were to be replaced by Ordnance Support Units to be located only alongside major concentrations of troops. The Command Depots were to be replaced by a lesser number of Regional Depots basically to hold training pools and mobilization reserve stocks. In addition to the traditional tasks of the previous Barrack Stores, the OSUs would act as distribution points for stores sent from CODs direct to units and for unit returns; hold and issue to married quarters miscellaneous chemicals and disinfectants; hold a very limited stock of items such as batteries, tyres and tubes, to meet urgent demands; provide minor refurbishing facilities; act as a returned stores transit point; and hold pools of vehicles and materiel for annual training camps. With the exception of one range, Army Forms and Publications, the Regional Depots would no longer be in the normal supply chain.

Security was, of course, always a problem in Ordnance depots, with pilferage a constant headache for commandant and security officer alike. Imagine the concern in one major Ordnance depot in the United Kingdom when it was noted that the locally employed gardener-cum-handyman was being allowed to pass in and out of the depot gate with barrow-loads of rubbish without producing a gate pass and without being searched. Although suspicious of a leg-pull, the Depot Security Officer decided to put up an umbrella and ordered that the wheelbarrow be searched every time it left the depot. His orders were faithfully carried out for several weeks with negative results. Shortly afterwards the gardener-cum-handyman who, like most of his kind, was of advanced years, retired. Time passed. A new G-cum-H was appointed and at the same time the depot stocktaking team submitted its annual report. It revealed a deficiency of seventy wheelbarrows.

On 1 January 1967 there was a major change in the method of proving ammunition as fit for service. With stockpiles held at readiness for forces ready for very short notice the old systems of confirming the effectiveness of ammunition by proving components was seen to be wasteful, inefficient and, in terms of confirming combat capability, ineffective. It had taken some working up, and it had been taken as high as the Army Board, but Complete Round Proof became a reality with the formation of a Complete Round Proof Assessment Team. DOS was given charge of it and he located it at CILSA. Having given authority for conventional ammunition CRP the Army Board further directed the institution of a similar system should be considered for guided weapons. It would happen three years later with the formation of a Missile Proof Assessment Team. This systematic approach to the condition and performance of ammunition followed on from the setting up of the Reliability Focus in CILSA's HQ at Didcot.

Storage of ammunition was also a problem. Given the increased use of ammunition with a high ratio between the amount of explosive in shells and the thickness of the shell casing, the very thing that had caused the closure of Corsham, safety distances became much more taxing. The storage at Bramley was nowhere near good enough to cope with these advances and it was clear that it would have to be evacuated. Plans were put in hand for a rebuild at Kineton and the relocation of other stocks to Longtown,

As part of an Army wide review of the reserve forces the RAOC HQ AER became Central Volunteer HQ RAOC.

A major step forward in the development of new ADP systems for inventory control in the Army came with the setting up, on 1 April 1967, of the Inventory Systems Development Wing, under a brigadier, at HQ Base Organization at Didcot.

In one of the many post-McLeod adjustments the number of static HQs in Germany was reduced. CRAOC 1 (Br) Corps Troops vanished and his duties were re-distributed among the other static

CRAOCs. They were renamed: Celle as Corps Troops (East), Osnabrück as Corps Troops (Central) and Dortmund as Corps Troops (West). Elsewhere in Germany the Armoured Delivery Squadron vacated the heated 'A' vehicle storage accommodation which it had been occupying within the North Parks perimeter of Ayrshire Barracks, Mönchengladbach. This provided an opportunity for 17 RVD to concentrate itself mainly into North Parks, with 'A' Sub Depot moving into the excellent, and now vacant, heated accommodation. The accommodation in South Parks was handed over to a number of units, with 15 BOD acquiring some space there while, to make way for a new Autobahn, two buildings in South Parks were dismantled and re-assembled in North Parks. Apart from heavy 'A' vehicles, all other vehicles were stored in the open at 17 RVD.

The Arab-Israeli war exacerbated the situation in Aden, further polarizing positions with increased tension following assertions that the British had assisted the Israelis. Whilst manifestly untrue it did nothing to help George Brown, the Foreign Secretary, in seeking a peaceful resolution to the Aden problem by getting Egypt on side. There was also extreme discontent in the Federation Army at prospects for their future once independence was granted. This was not helped when an Arab replaced the British Commander and a mutiny exploded. The Federation Army, and the police, turned on the British, alongside whom they had fought. The British eventually redeemed the situation although on 20 June 1967, during the period of a hand-over between the Royal Northumberland Fusiliers and the Argyll and Sutherland Highlanders, twenty British officers and men were killed by terrorists in Crater. Later the Argylls re-took the area with the characteristically aggressive, and now famous, intervention of Lieutenant Colonel Colin Mitchell. However, from then until November, the British effectively stood back and allowed the warring factions to fight it out and, as a precaution, evacuated all families in mid 1967. In the run up to this the RAOC had finally to close down its operation, while maintaining support to the troops as they prepared to leave. Key in this effort was the management of fuel no longer available from local resources without expert, trained help. The lesson is clear, denuding the ORBAT and placing reliance on civilian contractors or host nation support is undertaken with risk. It has to be weighed in the balance, as does the disbanding of logistic units on the basis that the commercial world will provide. The DDOS's problems were made worse when, from early June 1967, the Egyptian/Israeli war closed the Suez Canal, with virtually no stores arriving by sea.

Planning for the withdrawal was made difficult by constant changes in plan, and the retention of much of the planning detail for security reasons. Nonetheless, the idea was to scale down as much as possible, to hold stocks forward in units and to collapse the Ordnance support as the number and the deployment of operational units reduced. It was successful and no unit suffered operationally for want of any vital stores or supplies. As a withdrawal, as an evacuation, it was a model of its kind.

Eventually, the 3,500 remaining men in Aden were taken off by a naval task force between 24 and 29 November 1967. The British had suffered forty-four killed and 325 wounded in the last year of their occupation of Aden, and the Army element of the British presence in the region was reduced to 900 split between Sharja and Bahrain.

In Malta the defence review meant a drawdown and planning was put in hand to effect a major rationalization in 1969. However, one immediate reaction was to see responsibility for the foothold left in Libya transferred to Cyprus.

In July 1967 came the overt attempt by communists in Hong Kong, outwith the control of their masters in Peking, to destabilize the colony and evict the colonial power. The outcome was a major campaign of bombing using IEDs, some 5,700 being laid in the succeeding two and a half months. A superhuman effort was required by ATOs and ATs supporting the Royal Hong Kong Police to contain it, with several hundred devices a day appearing over a period of a few months. Captain Peter Hewlett's small command was reinforced from Singapore and from the UK on emergency tours. There was humour as well as tragedy in the work. For example, there was the AT who attended a device on a rubbish tip only to see it running away from him as he approached and the rat in the box woke up to what was going on. Mercifully, most of the devices were filled with gunpowder rather than high explosive, so most of the injuries were relatively slight. The only death was Sergeant Workman who fell off Lion Rock while trying to clear a device. The SAT, WOI Stan Woods sustained two sets of injuries. On the first occasion he was run over by a Chinese motorist while kneeling to dismantle a device set on a traffic island in the middle of Queen's Road. On the second occasion the device was in a glass jar and exploded as he approached, knocking him backwards and flaying him with powdered glass. He recovered, but thereafter anyone who shared an office with Stan was treated to the sight of him scratching his forearms as yet another bit of the glass worked its way to the surface and popped up as a lump on his skin. What he said as he found each one does not bear repeating, but reflected on the birthright and origins of the unknown gentleman who had laid the IED. For their work during the campaign both Peter Hewlett and Stan Woods were awarded the MBE, and a BEM went to Sergeant D L Birch. It is also worthy of note that the death of Sergeant Workman was recognized by the Hong Kong Chamber of Commerce, headed by a Mr Herries. A most generous cash grant was made to Mrs Workman and an endowment was settled on her, the income from which would allow her to see her children through to the end of their education at the age of eighteen without her having to worry about money. It was a generous settlement, almost beyond belief – but was greatly appreciated, not just by Mrs Workman but by Sergeant Workman's fellow EOD operators – largely because someone was saying 'thank you' when so often success or effort went unnoticed outside the RAOC.

The campaign eventually ended when the Chinese authorities in Peking grew impatient with the clique in Hong Kong who were acting very much to their own agenda and were not in tune with Chinese policy for the colony. They were invited to Peking for guidance and advice, and were never seen again in Hong Kong.

Towards the end of 1967 Sergeant Gordon Webster was stationed at 3 BAD, and had recently married. However, the significance of his presence at this time in the RAOC was the culmination of 100 years of service to the Corps in its various forms. Great grandfather Edmund served in the Corps of Armourers from 1 October 1867 to 1892. Grandfather Webster, the first armourer to be commissioned, served from 1888 to 1920 and he was succeeded by his sons, Edmund Thomas, 1915 to 1936, and Claude Vivian, 1921 to 1958. Edmund Thomas was succeeded by his son, Frank, and he became a captain and Claude Vivian by his son, Gordon, then at 3 BAD and who had joined in 1957. There was another son who also reached the rank of sergeant. It was a magnificent record of service.

On 1 October 1967 the Deepcut Garrison Church of St Michael and All Angels was rededicated the Garrison Church of St Barbara by the senior chaplain, Reverend D S Coey MA BD CF during the Matins Service. The RAOC Staff Band, under the direction of Captain Ray Mitchell LRAM ARCM played in the church on that day. The change of name was agreed by the Chaplain General in view of the fact that Deepcut, and not Hilsea, was now the spiritual home of the RAOC. A number of articles from the old garrison church at Hilsea, including the pulpit, organ and stained glass windows and all memorials connected with the RAOC, were removed and positioned in the new St Barbara's at Deepcut.

ISDW set up a study group in October 1967 to examine the problems likely to be met in establishing what then came to be known as a Central Inventory Control Point. A critical path analysis was drawn up to direct and control the study

The end of 1967 brought with it the agreement to form a third line RAOC unit for operations other than those on the central front in Germany. When the concept of a mobile strategic reserve had been developed, Ordnance units were only provided up to second line, intrinsic to the formation. This was fine so long as there were depots close enough to likely areas of operation to provide the necessary depth of support. However, the extensive programme of withdrawals being undertaken from overseas theatres and bases meant this could no longer be guaranteed. There was also a need to provide support for the ACE mobile force operating with NATO, but away from the central front. Thus it was 10 Ordnance Maintenance Park came into being. It comprised 47 and 48 Companies, both former RASC units that had retained their original numbers. One was essentially a bulk petroleum company and the other a supply company. Their role was to hold reserves of combat supplies, complete equipments, clothing and other Ordnance materiel; holding and delivering by pipeline POL products for both the Army and the RAF; bakery and laundry; local procurement of Ordnance materials and services; and providing an OFP type service for units in the FMA. It formed up at Perham Down in February 1968.

At the same time another unit was also formed, 3rd Division Airhead Company. This was to replace a gap in organic support for the Strategic Reserve, particularly at the divisional airhead where the company's job was to provide a transit facility. It was also to provide an OFP type service to divisional troops for combat supplies and spares; and to hold reserves of combat supplies. It was to operate for a trial period with four officers and ninety soldiers.

Meanwhile, economies were to affect Britain's airborne capability, with 16 Parachute Brigade reducing to two parachuting battalions. This had its effect on the logistic support requirement and consolidating the Transport squadron, the OFP and the REME workshop into a single battalion structure would achieve the necessary economies and provide a better service. The battalion was established on a trial basis.

The year 1968 emerged as unique in the annals of British military history. It was the first since 1660 in which the Army was not involved on some form of active operation, and the only one since the Second World War in which a soldier had not been killed on active duty. It was a unique distinction that has prevailed until the present day.

At the beginning of the year, on 1 January, the DOS resolved a major issue that had been taxing the tempers of many since McLeod – the titles for warrant officers in the RAOC. From that date there were to be just two to cover all RAOC trades except regimental duties. They were to be Conductor and Staff Sergeant Major, instead of the four that had resulted from the transfers from RASC. These two titles would preserve the two appointments which had existed for many years in both RASC and RAOC and which had many historical associations. There was, therefore, no break with tradition. Conductors and Staff Sergeant Majors were to be known as 'Conductors', and 'Staff Sergeant Majors Class 2' and Sub-Conductors became 'Staff Sergeant Majors.' This was designed to put an end to the habit that had crept into the lingua franca of the RAOC of referring to warrant officers as 'WOI Smith' or 'WOII Jones' and would see these important men referred to by their proper titles: Conductor, SSM, RSM, SQMS, RQMS and CSM.

The RAOC continued to do well in sport, with 16 Parachute OFP taking the Army Minor Units Cross-Country championship. Other units also put their heart into entering and in many cases winning, just about anything going. One example is 17 RVD at Mönchengladbach in Germany. The soccer team won the Rhine Area Minor Units Challenge Cup, the DOS BAOR Cup and the North Rhine Inter-Service League Championship, Division 2. They also won the BAOR Minor Units Challenge Cup. Their hockey team led the Rhine Area Multi-Services League, were runners-up in the Rhine Area Minor Units championship and were strong challengers for the DOS BAOR Cup. At basketball the unit team won the Rhine Area Minor Units Championship, reached the semi-final of the BAOR Minor Units Championship and the strong-arm squad won the Rhine Area 88-stone Tug-of-War Championship. Indoors, the table tennis team won the Rhine Area Joint Services League, Division 2. The small-bore marksmen came near to mopping up everything in sight – they won the Rhine Area Challenge Cup and silver spoons and the RAOC League. In the Army Rifle League their A team won Division 1, their ladies team Division 2 and their B team Division 3. For good measure they were

The RAOC Methuen Team Winners 1968. Sitting far left Corporal Alan Glasby; third from left Captain David Carpenter; third from the right Staff Sergeant Mick Coldrick and in the back row on the right Major Charlie Nockles.   Many of the great names of RAOC shooting in one picture.

runners-up for the Baker and Home Cups and in the BAOR Minor Units Championship. And, in case all this sporting activity brought a crop of injuries, 17 RVD had on hand a first aid party who themselves won the Rhine Area Minor Units First Aid Competition. The military strength of the unit was just 200 and they were not unique. Similar performances could be found throughout the RAOC.

Shooting had been a strength in the RAOC going back many years, and in 1968 the Corps set a new standard for achievement in the sport. For the first time it took the Methuen Cup at Bisley. It achieved a score of 1,003 points, and to put that into perspective it was a record for the event, and a score of such magnitude that it was expected to stand for many years to come. Those taking part included Captain David Carpenter, Sergeant Mick Coldrick and Corporal Alan Glasby – names that were associated with Corps shooting over a considerable period of time. It was a fitting end to the uniformed career of Major Charles Knockles MBE, who, after a legendary shooting career in the Army had acted as treasurer and secretary of the RAOC team since 1960. Mercifully, he would be taking a Retired Officer appointment at Deepcut and so would be able to continue holding the team together as he had done for so many years.

RAOC shooting prowess was not confined to the regular element. At the National Rifle Association and the Territorial Army Rifle Association meets, held concurrently at Bisley, the RAOC T&AVR teams had conspicuous successes. They were winners of the TARA Falling Plate competition, the Volongdis LMG Pairs match and the Hamilton Leigh competition.

In April 1968 the CRAOC in London District appeared for the first time on parade, mounted as a member of the Staff of the Major General, as the GOC London District is known. The reasons went back a number of years when the CRAOC was required to join the major administrative inspections of the Household Division; the only Service head to be so invited. For a number of years this meant the Major General taking part in parades attended by his staff, all mounted, with CRAOC standing at the edge of the parade ground. Discussions took place, mostly it appears in the bar of the Army and Navy Club, and ended with the then CRAOC, Lieutenant Colonel Trevor Vaughan-Griffith, proposing to the Brigade Major and the Chief of Staff that CRAOC should attend the parade mounted. The Major General agreed, subject to CRAOC being able to ride properly. Equitation courses took place, but before he could undertake a parade Trevor Vaughan-Griffiths was posted. His replacement had one month to sort out his equitation, and Lieutenant Colonel Ian Crompton's only abiding memory was to avoid Mondays when both instructors and horses were less than well tempered following the weekend.

A later incumbent of the post, here Lieutenant Colonel Christopher Pittam is pictured in all his finery on 10 April 1970.

Nonetheless, he made his first parade mounted on Monarch, a grey, and with a Royal Blue saddle cloth and the RAOC badge resplendent upon it. Then it was decided instead of simply wearing No.1 dress ceremonial, he should be properly dressed in a frock coat and wearing the same embellishments as the rest of the staff. He was so attired by July of 1968 for an inspection of the 1st Battalion the Scots Guards in Edinburgh. CRAOC London District was to remain annotated a mounted post, and all those posted in to the appointment either rode or had to learn.

By the middle of the year a change had taken place in the organization of RAOC support to 1 (Br) Corps. The COMP had become unwieldy and given the two re-supply routes used for C Sups and materiel it made sense to re-package the responsibilities. Consequently, CRAOC Corps Troops (West) assumed responsibility for the vehicle and stores companies. This left the COMP responsible for 44 RP Company, formerly the ammunition company, and 49 RP Company in peace, reinforced by four other RP companies in war. Internally, there was some reorganization in the companies to tailor them to their role. In peace 44 Company ran Depot 90, the ammunition depot in Sennelager, and 49 Company managed a series of wholly unsatisfactory fuel dumps all over Germany where reserve stocks were held in cans. A great deal of time was spent on visits to track down the 'leakers' and remove them. Usually, and inconveniently, they were at the bottom of the stacks.

There was also a major reorganization of 36 and 37 Heavy Air Defence Regiments to form a new enhanced 36 Heavy Air Defence Regiment with two large batteries, each supported by a GM Platoon RAOC. However, it was not until 1970 that 3 GM Platoon moved to BAOR to join 2 Platoon at Wulfen.

The middle of 1968 also saw the move of CILSA from the Ammunition Organization to HQ DOS. This reflected more sensibly its role and responsibilities for global ammunition management, rather than storage, and roles in EOD and acting as the Ammunition Reliability Focus. It was a paper move, the organization remaining at Vauxhall Barracks in Didcot.

The work on palletizing stocks for forward areas had shown that, apart from heavy or awkward loads, a high proportion of the materiel could be palletized or packaged for handling by forklift equipment.

Furthermore, it could be done within NATO standard dimensions of a unit load of a 40' x 48' base x 62' high, and with an upper weight limit of 4,000lb. Combat supplies were the obvious target commodity since they were required daily in war in large quantities. However, the work did not stop there for it was shown that there were many other Ordnance stores to be delivered forward on pallets, and Engineer stores as well. These included bulky and awkward equipment such as barbed wire, tank track and bogie wheels.

The lack of a suitable cross-country forklift truck was also a problem, especially since there was no civilian equivalent. The result of a great deal of work was the trial in 1968 of the Eager Beaver, and its release into service the following year to RE, RCT and RAOC units.

The huge amount of work that had to be done to establish unit loads of the many commodities, including ammunition, fell to the MHPEU. It devised, trialled and promulgated a large number of unit load specifications, which were configurations of stores on a pallet that could be described as a standard requirement and the unit would see value in it being delivered when needed without requiring the unit to demand each of the individual items in the pallet. It had a particular application with ammunition, especially artillery ammunition. But here safety factors and the need for adequate protection made the working out of pallet loads a most difficult exercise. In particular the requirement, for speed and efficiency in battle, to have 'balanced' loads of shells, fuzes, cartridges and primers on one pallet generally raised the hazard rating of the pallet with serious implications on storage in the UK and BAOR. It also raised the probability of a higher rate of deterioration of the pallet's contents, which needed to be taken account of in the storage, proof and inspection cycles. The end product was a system of packaging

An Eager Beaver shifting simulated ammunition; this one on Exercise BOLD GANNET in Denmark in1984.

design and handling that had many natures of ammunition, and certainly the most important ones, coming from the factory already packaged and held together on pallets for front line operational use. It transformed ammunition handling throughout the ammunition supply chain from the factory to the end user.

The ISDW study into the development of a CICP reported in 1968. It was accepted as the basis on which the CICP should be planned and developed and there were two main objectives, one of method and one of organization. The improvements in method included the division of the inventory into three categories based upon the cost and operational importance of an item, thus replacing the five traditional commodity divisions. Significant here was the fact that the high value/high cost part of the range was also to include those items that were considered operationally important. It was a start, but division of the inventory based largely on cost would create problems in the future when increasingly high technology weapon platforms would complicate hugely any decision on what was and was not vital since it could not be judged on cost alone. Combat capability had to be the arbiter; the question was how to judge it.

There was a restructuring on the command arrangements in the United Kingdom with the formation of HQ Army Strategic Command to take control of the increasingly large Army commitment to a mobile strategic capability.

Planning and Work Study had been developing in the RAOC throughout the sixties, but it was still regarded with hostility by the unions on behalf of the civilians in RAOC installations. However, in

1968 the MOD accepted a study report that recommended the fullest possible use of work measurement throughout the RAOC. It coincided with the arrival of Critical Path Analysis into the suite of tools available for Work Study Practitioners. It was a technique that would be put to great use throughout the RAOC in the years to come.

In the early part of the year there was a rationalization of Ordnance units in Singapore with the creation of ammunition and vehicle sub-depots in 3 BOD. This allowed the closure of 221 BVD and 443 BAD as an efficiency measure and as a precursor to the run-down. With the ending of base repair in Singapore in 1968, it had already been possible to reduce the holdings of 3 BOD from 240,000 items to 180,000 and by a series of rationalization and realism measures was down 65,000 by 1 April 1979. One such, for example, was to route all Hong Kong demands through Singapore rather than directly to the UK in order to use up unwanted stocks.

There was also rationalization in Malta where the RAF took responsibility for all logistic services. They took over the ammunition depot and the fire service, whilst the laundry was sold to a civilian contractor, lock, stock and barrel or perhaps it should have been wash basket. Further rationalizations were to take place in mid 1970, aimed at concentrating the remaining RAOC support in one place and to provide 'rattle' accommodation for a series of moves on the Island.

The trial of 3rd Division Airhead Company had, in the past year, proved the validity of the concept. Consequently, the Airhead Ordnance Company became an integral part of the RAOC organic support of 3rd Division, with Major E H Brown in command. The unit was fully established on a permanent basis on 28 October 1969. In April that year the existence of 16 Para Logistic Regiment was confirmed; no longer a trial, but a reality. The other role carried out by RAOC in support of airborne forces was undertaken by 16 Para Heavy Drop Company. It was formed at the same time as the brigade, to take over the role which up to then had been carried out by Air Maintenance Platoons since 1946. Its role was the preparation of heavy equipment for dropping by air. It would rig the loads and ensure they were correctly transferred to and loaded on the aircraft. They were also responsible for collecting used heavy drop parachutes from dropping zones.

On 17 April 1969, in what might have appeared at first sight as a minor operation in support of the civil power, the Prince Of Wales' Own Regiment of Yorkshire was deployed into the province of Ulster at short notice following a series of riots and latterly some bombings. At the time RAOC support in the Province was an Ordnance Depot at Kinnegar, a vehicle depot at Long Kesh, a supply depot at Lisburn and an ammunition depot on the coast at Ballykinler. The EOD capability comprised the ATO and WOII who were the Ammunition Inspectorate in Northern Ireland.

In May 1969 the first store shed was completed in Dulmen and handed over to the RAOC. It was the first of many that would see a new depot on the site in just a few years. By August of that year all the pre-stocked unit equipments[3] held in Belgium had been moved to Dulmen. Following this, in recognition of its changing status, 15 ADOD was re-titled on 1 August 1969 as 15 BOD. It was no longer 'advanced'.

From 1968 the inevitable downward trend in vehicle storage requirements had continued. Stocks were down to only 18,140 and receipts and issues were to fall to just over 37,000 by the end of 1969. It was clear that more CVDs would have to be closed, and plans were made in 1969 to close CVD Feltham by March 1971, and CVD Irvine by May 1972.

With regard to controlling the RAOC's massive inventory it had become clear that even the smallest under or over provision of stocks in the high value end of the range could have prohibitive consequences. Clear determination was needed of entitlement, usage, wastage and, eventually, disposal. It was also clear that these were issues in which there was significant interest from all over the MOD. Consequently a team was set up at ISDW drawing together, inter alia, REME, finance, Q policy and the general staff to develop a system that could achieve this. It was called Project VESPER, the acronym meaning Vehicles, Equipments, Spare Parts & Economic Repair, and did not include ammunition. The technicalities of maintenance and recording of ammunition meant that something quite different was required.

The RAOC continued to make an impression at unit level in sport, and in some of the more exacting ones. The Parachute Brigade OFP won the Army cross-country championships. The outcome was the result of a concerted effort by a team of one junior officer and a group of junior NCOs and private soldiers, with self motivation a key constituent of the build up of training for the events that led to eventual victory. Similarly in boxing where 16 BVD in BAOR beat HQ 4 Guards Brigade to take the minor units championship for the theatre. Boxing success also occurred in the Far East where, at the Training Centre, Singapore, Corporal Bob Lockwood, an Ammunition Technician of 443 BAD, won the Far East Land Forces middle weight championship on points, from Corporal Baird of 29 Commando Light Regiment, Royal Artillery. Brigadier Roy Darkin, late of the RAOC, presented him with the championship belt, one that had been won only once before by an RAOC soldier: Private D Lane of 3 BOD in 1956. It had been

Corporal Alan Glasby being fêted as the winner of the Queen's Medal.

competed for since the 1930s when it had been presented, originally, by the Maharaja Kumar of Tikari as a trophy for the All-India championship.

Then, in July, Corporal Alan Glasby won the Queen's Medal at Bisley; the only other member of the RAOC to have done so being Major David Carpenter. And in addition to the Queen's Medal, Corporal Glasby won the Roupell Cup and the Whitehead Cup and was a member of the Army Eight.

Once again a Territorial made his contribution to the sporting name of the Corps. Captain Guy Ackers was British and English Short Range Small Bore Champion for 1969. More than 500 competitors entered the qualifying round and more than 300 passed to the eliminating round. The twenty highest scorers shot in the final in which Captain Ackers scored 399 out of 400 points. The Chairman of the National Small Bore Rifle Association made the presentation of the *News of the World* Challenge Cup, Badge and Gold Medal for the British Championship and The Royal Society of St George Trophy and Badge for the English Championship.

Sporting prowess, as a contribution to overall fitness and team effort, has always been ranked highly in the Army, and rightly so. Proof that it was effective in enhancing professional performance is perhaps evinced by the prowess of 16 Parachute Brigade Heavy Drop Company in winning the Parachute Brigade Weapons competition. This was an event where every company in the brigade put in a platoon strength team to compete in a wide range of infantry skills. It was a competition in which

16 Parachute Brigade Heavy Drop Company, winners of the Parachute Brigade Weapons Competition.

there was intense rivalry between the companies of the Parachute Regiment, for reputations were at stake. The competition had always been regarded as the forte of the infantryman, with RAOC soldiers as incidental outsiders. It was a rude awakening when the officers and men of the Heavy Drop Company, showed that they were soldiers first and tradesmen second as they became the overall winners and were awarded the Evelyn Woods Cup, a trophy dating back to 1898

The implementation of the Somerville Plan brought major changes both to the level of stocks in BAOR and to their deployment. In August 1969 17 RVD was renamed as 17 Base Vehicle Depot, its task being to hold 'A', 'C' and unfit 'B' vehicles at Mönchengladbach, and fit 'B' vehicles, pre-stocked unit equipment and WMR at Recklinghausen. Coincident with this arrangement was the integration of 16 BVD into the Ordnance Depot Antwerp with responsibility for fit 'B' vehicles and pre-stocked unit equipments. Two years later 17 BVD, then commanded by Lieutenant Colonel Ronnie Bateson, underwent further major change, when A, B, C and the Returned Vehicle Sub Depots were amalgamated to form 17 BVD Sub Depot (Main) at Mönchengladbach and 17 BVD Sub Depot (Forward) at Recklinghausen. In the UK CVD Marchington closed.

Also in August 1969 the running sore that was the Irish troubles began to weep once more. Disturbances in Londonderry and Belfast were precipitated by the Northern Ireland Civil Rights Association, with the situation compounded by the adverse reaction of the Unionists led by men such as Ian Paisley. The Royal Ulster Constabulary sought to intervene, but this simply generated friction with an already hostile Republican population and it soon became clear that the situation was beyond the capability of the RUC to cope. Neither did the resident 39 Brigade, with two battalions of infantry and an armoured car regiment, have the strength to provide the required level of support to the civil power. By the end of the year the one battalion of the PWO deployed in April to provide immediate support had risen to ten battalions. By now the brigade was not simply there to offer a barrier between factions, or to support the police, but to combat the Irish Republican Army, which had arisen from the ashes of earlier conflicts to take advantage of Catholic disaffection and the tumultuous civil order situation.

The strain on the RAOC was considerable. With an establishment designed to support a small and static brigade it suddenly found itself at the centre of a major counter insurgency operation. Perhaps worst affected were Barracks Services, so often the unsung heroes of the Corps. Suddenly they had to find, at very short notice, accommodation stores for eight major units going in to a range of generally empty and unsuitable factory sites and mills that had fallen into disuse and were verging on derelict.

This was to say nothing of the expansion in all other areas of supply. Particularly pressing was anti-riot equipment; never stored in any quantity because it was never considered likely to be needed. The riots in 1969 showed how different it was to be, with even simple things like the ancient skill of stone throwing developed into an art form by the use of well cut paving slabs.

The costs of material and the associated packaging was increasing, at a rate some judged to be alarming. Handling it better and packaging properly, without waste, were becoming more and more critical to the effective management of stores. Consequently the MHEU was re-titled to the Materials Handling and Packaging Experimental Unit and took the development and trialling of packaging under its wing.

At the end of 1969 the replacement in Libya of King Idris by the revolutionary government of the flamboyant Colonel Gaddafi saw the end of the British presence in the country. The detachment in El Adem and the bases left in Tobruk and Benghazi were packed up and on their way by 31 March 1970. Major Philip Bomford was working at the time in Q Maintenance in the MOD in London, with one of his tasks being custodian of the packs of training stores dotted around the world, one of which was Libya. Almost as soon as the departure was forced on the UK, the Army Training branch in the Ministry were inviting him to go to Canada to examine the training area at Suffield, near Medicine

Hat in the centre of Canada and deep in the prairie. It was an area where all weapons could fire live over the enormous ranges out there and after costing it as an option he went back to set it up, using as a start point the training packs from Libya. The advance party would move in 1972 and the outcome would be the British Army Training Unit Suffield. It was to prove a mammoth boost to the realism of battle group training and would boast its own static OFP, and, subsequently, Ordnance Company.

The end of 1969 also brought with it a culmination of a great deal of work in inventory management, work that would provide a springboard for the future, that would see the birth of new systems that would take the RAOC into and beyond the next decade. A new computer building had been completed at Bicester, and the computer equipment for the first phase of the project had been delivered in the form of an ICL 1906F with 64K store and two massive fixed disks for holding stock data. Feasibility studies of the use of computers in 15 BOD and the OFPs in BAOR had been completed, and their findings confirmed both by HQ BAOR and the Ministry of Defence. Feasibility studies into the use of computers in RAOC in Hong Kong and Cyprus had been authorized and were about to start. Project VESPER was under way. ADP procedures for new management systems for ammunition and for low value material had been completed and programming of the Clothing, General Stores and Ammunition ranges was in hand. Work on the conversion of the Chilwell and Donnington ranges to the new computer system was under way. Proposals for a Secondary Depot System had been circulated and a successful trial had been carried out in the Command Ordnance Depot in Northern Ireland.

There had also been considerable advances in computer technology, bringing many benefits in the management of the stores range and the delivery of information better to manage the inventory. One example was the ability to enter instructions or data directly by means of magnetic tape encoders rather than punched cards. It was at the RAOC's instigation that magnetic tape encoders were first used in 1969, and in so doing pioneered their use in Government.

At this time most store holding units at the secondary level were supported direct from the CODs, and the level of work did not necessarily warrant a computer installation. To obviate this and to provide them with the benefits of ADP it was decided that all scalings of stores in and out of the secondary depot and all provision action would be undertaken by the CICP.

January 1970 saw Hong Kong established as a separate military base directly dependent on the UK with no further links with a rapidly running down Singapore. It became the home of the Gurkhas and the Gurkha LofC back to Nepal. It also took command of forces remaining in Brunei. The increased workload saw the introduction of an ADOS appointment at colonel rank, with Colonel Bob Allen being the first incumbent, having been CRAOC less than six years earlier. There is an old saying, among the cynics, that to be posted to Hong Kong you had to have been there once before, so maybe it was true after all.

In conjunction the depot commander's rank was increased to lieutenant colonel. The Gurkha LofC existed to maintain the Gurkha recruiting in Nepal and to tranship trained soldiers to join their regiments and to permit the move of families. It employed a DADOS who, despite the apparent serenity of his role, was kept busy not simply managing the logistics but also managing the frequent senior visitors who felt compelled to 'come and have a look'.

The Ulster Defence Regiment was formed on 1 April 1970, to replace the Special B Constabulary with its reputation for Republican oppression. Initially it consisted of seven battalions, later eleven. It was simply not possible to make any pre-provision in anticipation of its formation, and the new requirement posed such problems as the supply of uniforms, particularly woollen pullovers and combat dress. At the time the old olive drab combat kit was being phased out across the Army and the new disruptive pattern material combat dress was being introduced in step. To take on the additional and unexpected commitment of the newly formed 8,000 strong force, in addition to everything else, was a considerable challenge. It was only eventually achieved by pillaging clothing and equipment that should have gone to regular units elsewhere in the Army.

The year was marked by extensive and increasing rioting and violence in Northern Ireland. In May 1970 a section of 321 EOD Unit was deployed to the province to support the small EOD capability in the inspectorate, which by then had been involved in investigating some thirty explosions and had neutralized three IEDs. It was planned that it should be there for six months.

In June the general election went the way of Edward Heath's Conservative opposition party, and Lord Peter Carrington became the Secretary of State for Defence. One of the Conservative's early decisions was to retain, despite the strictures of their predecessors' defence review of the late sixties, a presence in Singapore after the run out of the base, due in 1971. This fitted with the Australian and New Zealand policy of leaving something there and so some protracted negotiations saw the formation of a Commonwealth Force, ANZUK, comprising units of all three services from Australia, New Zealand and the UK, with the major component being 28 Commonwealth Brigade. This was welcome news to the RAOC and not just because it preserved a really good posting. It would make any subsequent run-down easier since some stocks from the old regime would have to remain, thereby offering a phased approach. However, by then the number of items being held by 3 BOD, now very much a composite depot, were down to 21,000, a reduction of 220,000 in two years, and yet availability to meet demand at unit level was never compromised.

Ordnance support for the ANZUK force was complicated by the fact that the Australians and the New Zealanders operated on pre-McLeod lines as opposed to the functionally based British so 'workarounds' were necessary; and not difficult. The Ordnance effort was based on the Australian 5 BOD, and the commander of the ANZUK Ordnance Depot for most of its short life was Lieutenant Colonel John Gregan RAOC. The new depot benefited greatly from the run down of 3 BOD for both stores and staff.

In Germany, some clever staff work by Brigadier Norman Speller, DDOS 1 (Br) Corps and Brigadier John Stanyer, DOS BAOR saw the old COMP based in one barracks, Barker Barracks in Paderborn, and had planning under way to add a third company whose peacetime role would be to operate a new ammunition depot being planned for Pombsen, about twenty miles south of Paderborn. A new approach required a new name and on 1 October 1970 Lieutenant Colonel Keith Berresford took command of 1 (Br) Corps Combat Supplies Battalion.

By the middle of the year the General Stores range of stores had been moved from Antwerp, and the contents of the Forward Stores Depot in Münster had been moved in to Dulmen. With its reduced relevance the depot in Belgium had ceased to be a part of the Advanced Base and on 1 April 1970 had been renamed British Forces Antwerp. The rump of 15 ABOD (Rear), 16 Base Vehicle Depot and 40 Supplies and Petrol Depot came together to form Ordnance Depot Antwerp, a composite depot that would support British forces in Belgium and act as a reinforcement depot for some units deploying in the rear areas.

In June there was a move, approved by the Treasury, to create an Inventory Control Point at Viersen in Germany to provide ADP support for the management of the inventory on the Continent. Approval was also given to install a mobile computer on a trial basis into an OFP in Germany.

Reduced global commitments were causing reviews of manpower in the Central Depots in the UK. In Chilwell there was a portent of things to come, as reduced dependencies forced the closure of the MT Sub Depot at Derby. It was no longer necessary for MT stores to go into an 'MT' depot for the flexibility offered by the computer at Bicester meant they could go where space and need best suited. In this case large numbers of tyres and tubes were consigned to Bicester, whilst track and bogie wheels were sent to Donnington.

The UK storage reorganization, approved in 1966 and started in 1967, came to an end. Nine OSUs were now in place: Burscough, Old Dalby, Thetford, Colchester, Feltham, Woolwich, Ashford, Aldershot and Tidworth. The four Regional Depots were located at Thatcham, Hereford, Catterick and Stirling. The reorganization had brought about considerable economies, both in stock levels and in accommodation.

In December the second section of 321 EOD Unit, commanded by Captain David Hodgens, was stood up for deployment to Northern Ireland. The bombing activity had increased beyond the capability already there, and the planned six month deployment of just one reinforcement section was looking decidedly shaky. They moved to Omagh to support 8 Infantry Brigade.

Early in 1971 the situation in Northern Ireland took a new twist. A child was run over in the Bogside in Londonderry by a scout car and the subsequent province wide riots saw the introduction of a third brigade, initially a roulement brigade, to supplement 8 and 39 Brigades in Londonderry and Belfast respectively. It was 16 Parachute Brigade and was sent to occupy an old shirt factory in Lurgan, arriving in early February, thus setting in place a three-brigade structure that would remain throughout the continued life of the RAOC. There were already the two EOD teams with the two permanent brigades and another was deployed at short notice, again from the shadow[4] 321 EOD Unit, drawn in this case from the Western Command Ammunition Inspectorate detachments in Liverpool and Hereford with drivers from Donnington. There were five men in an EOD team, a captain, a WOII and a senior NCO together with the two drivers; Captain Frank Steer, WOII Alec Jackson and Sergeant Pete Sanders were the operators, and while some of the drivers came and went Private 'Geordie' Hindle would prove to be a mainstay of the team, providing a large part of the 'glue' that held it together. They were equipped with a Land-Rover and arrived on the day four BBC TV engineers were killed by a mine as they drove up to repair a radio mast on Brougher Mountain in the west of the Province.

Major George Styles was the SATO. Realizing how ill-equipped the new team was he handed £5 (£42) to the team leader and told him to go to Woolworths to buy his team's equipment; and to 'be sure to bring back the change'. Such was the state of the art in those early days. Reliable information says that the list of purchases included three pairs of paper underpants – in case of emergency.

There had also been the death by shooting of the first British soldier to die in this phase of the troubles and this was further compounded in March by the kidnap and murder of three young Royal Highland Fusiliers, two of them twin brothers, in the north-east of Belfast at Ligoniel. By the end of March there had been 395 EOD incidents.

In Germany, in June 1971, work started on the new ammunition depot at Pombsen. It was to offer a significant increase in the volume of ammunition the British could hold east of the Rhine. Also, at Wulfen, a new company HQ was established to look after the two GM platoons with the Heavy Air Defence Regiment. 7 GM Company was born and was treated as a battery like any other in the regiment, with the Company/'Battery' Commander flying a Battery Commander's pennant.

It was about this time that a badge was introduced for ATOs to wear on the right sleeve. Ammunition Technicians were heard to make unkind remarks about the blank space in the middle.

Internment without trial was introduced in Ulster in the summer and the first arrests were made on 9 August 1971, some 326 out of a list of 520 who had been identified by the RUC. Violence escalated with the number of terrorist incidents doubling. Then in September came the first ATO casualty when Captain David Stewardson was killed in the village of Castle Robin attempting to gain access to a well-constructed IED made of solid plywood. The type was subsequently opened and found to have two micro switch anti-disturbance switches built in to it. It was purely an anti personnel weapon, and had claimed the IRA's first EOD victim.

With all that was going on there was a deal of overstretch. Here soldiers of 3 Division Airhead Ordnance Company are operating as infantry in Cyprus with 1st Battalion the Prince of Wales' Own Regiment of Yorkshire; which meant they were not available for their 'proper' job.

Barely had the RAOC reorganization in the UK settled down than the Stainforth Committee on Army reorganization recommended the formation of a HQ United Kingdom Land Forces located at Wilton in Wiltshire, and the disbandment of the five Commands. The chain of command would be directly to ten Districts with Northern Ireland retaining its special status in reporting directly to the Ministry of Defence. The loss of the Commands cost the RAOC four brigadier appointments, with the DDsOS of the commands being replaced by a single one star appointment at Wilton, the Chief Ordnance Officer. The Districts had CsRAOC, with the rank, lieutenant colonel or colonel, dependent on the size of the District.

The impact on the recently settled RAOC structure in the UK was to see the conversion of three of the Regional Depots, Hereford, Catterick and Stirling, being converted to OSUs. Thatcham remained as the one UKLF Ordnance Depot. War reserves and training stores remained in place at the three new OSUs, but accounting for them was centralized at Thatcham.

More new ammunition storage was also to be built in the UK. The Army Board approved the plans to rebuild CAD Kineton in two phases, one for each of the two sub-depots, and to close CAD Bramley. New technology in the design and construction of explosive store houses meant they would occupy a much smaller area and provide much more efficient density of storage. There was a small downside to this plan in that there had only recently been a new build in Bramley for a GM repair facility and plans had been laid for a permanent Army School of Ammunition to replace the wooden huts beloved of so many generations of ammunition trained personnel in the RAOC. These plans would need to be revisited. The cost of the Kineton rebuild was placed at £15 million (£120 million) with phase one to be complete by 1979 and no date having been given for phase two.

And this is what the storehouses would look like when they were finished.

Perhaps as a logical follow-on from the success of the logistic battalion concept in the parachute brigade, although not necessarily linked, the Commandant General Royal Marines, in 1971 put forward proposals for forming a Commando Logistic Regiment. It would combine the Commando Transport Squadron, the Commando OFP and the Commando Workshops into one unit. It formed up at Plymouth in early 1972 with Lieutenant Colonel Ray Thornton RAOC, as its Commanding Officer. The OFP, originally formed for Borneo, became the Ordnance Squadron, designed to hold on wheels a two-months scaling of aircraft, MT, and technical spares, and some naval stores, to meet the many needs of the brigade. It also had to provide a combat supplies troop to undertake stock control in the brigade maintenance area and DPs, the bulk breaking of fresh rations, and a local purchase capability. The Ordnance Squadron also provided two permanent assault detachments, one for each of 41st and 45th Commando Groups, the latter having a specialist role in arctic and mountain warfare.

In Singapore, on 1 September 1971, 3 BOD finally closed its doors. That which could be re-distributed was re-distributed, that which could be sold was sold. Depots that had been British were now Singaporean and in many cases were full of surplus stores that the enterprising Singaporeans would either use or sell. On 28 September 1971 Brigadier Bill Eccles, the last DOS FARELF, boarded his aircraft for the long journey home, leaving behind the rump that was ANZUK.

On 20 October 1971 Major George Styles, the SATO in Northern Ireland, controlled an operation in which Captains Alan Clouter and Roger Mendham neutralized a large and complex IED at the Europa Hotel. The render safe procedure took seven hours. Two days later another even more complex bomb was laid in the same place. This time it took nine hours to clear. There were two outcomes. One was a George Cross for George Styles, the fifth awarded to the RAOC since 1940, and George Medals to Alan Clouter and Roger Mendham. The second was that the Europa Hotel undertook to fund the Felix tie that would thereafter be worn by anyone having served a tour undertaking EOD work in Northern Ireland.

There are several stories alluding to the creation of the name 'Felix' used in connection with EOD operators, the most popular being associated with cats and their nine lives. The reality is far removed from that. Radio voice procedure at the time required different branches of the Army to have an appointment title for use in radio traffic. The infantry, for example, were called Foxhound, the Artillery Sheldrake and the RAOC was Rickshaw. It meant that the person speaking was the most senior representative of that discipline available, and could be of any rank. The realization that the ATO needed his own appointment title came with an attempt by HQ 39 Brigade to speak to the operator on a particular job and who was trying to identify himself by spelling the acronym ATO phonetically over the radio. His difficulties were made worse by the fact he had never really taken the phonetic alphabet seriously and was trying to spell it as 'apple', 'tom', 'olive'. Fortunately, he was well known and the watch keeper simply said: 'For God's sake Kevin, speak in clear.' Captain Kevin Goad was delighted to oblige, but his difficulty set in train a move to create an ATO appointment title.

The call from the Royal Signals to discuss this had come to Major Styles in September 1971 shortly after the death of David Stewardson the first ATO to be killed by an IED in Ulster. His death had affected EOD operators throughout the Province and George felt a need to lift morale. Consequently, in response to the question of a name he responded over the telephone: 'Phoenix'. He had a picture in his mind of an EOD Phoenix rising from the ashes of David's death. Either the line was bad, or he was misheard, or he was misunderstood; but the

Felix, the cartoon character, was the brainchild of the then Staff Sergeant Brian Shepherd.

Royal Signals NCO wrote down 'Felix' – and a legend, a name, a cartoon character, and a huge boost for morale, was born. When a design for the tie was sought Captain Alan Clouter, then the Northern Ireland Inspectorate ATO, found inspiration in the Lisburn NAAFI where he saw a tin of Felix cat food and sent the label to the Europa Hotel as the basis for the design of the cat's head.

David's death also sparked a conversation in Alan Clouter's office that went something along the lines of 'if he hadn't had to walk up to it he'd still be alive'. From that came the idea that a robot might be used to deliver to the IED a disruptive device based on the Sweetman Perforator, a Second World War weapon used to neutralize enemy sea mines. The result was a developmental process at FVRDE and RARDE that went through a series of gestations resulting in Wheelbarrow, the well-known tracked robot, appearing on the streets within the year. Capable of delivering a range of anti-IED weapons in addition to the original perforator, it was a major boost in the fight against the bomber and came into service following the deaths of a number of ATOs and ATs caused largely by the fact that they had been forced, for lack of any alternative, 'to walk up to it'.

ANZUK Ordnance Depot officially came into being on 1 November 1971, being mainly located in the old Naval base in the north of Singapore Island, near the Straits of Johore. It was a composite depot having stores, vehicles and ammunition sub-depots. It was responsible for the provision and supply of Ordnance materiel to ANZUK and visiting national units; the de-munitioning and re-munitioning of ANZUK ships; the provision of missile test facilities and ammunition proof facilities for RMN and Singapore Armed Forces respectively and the operation of a forward Ordnance detachment to support ANZUK's 28 Infantry Brigade in the field. Details for the technical procedures and operational methods to be adopted by this tri-national Ordnance unit were worked out earlier in 1971 by a local committee, on which Colonel Peter Bower represented the RAOC's interests. The outcome was that the stores and vehicles elements worked on RAOC procedures, and the ammunition sub-depot worked to British procedures and standards. It was a great deal of hard work for a concept that would founder on the rocks of political moves even then under way in the UK and Australia.

In Malta in December a festering disagreement with Dom Mintoff, the Labour Prime Minister, exploded when he demanded a payment for the use of the Malta bases. Failure to pay would mean a departure at once. The British were not inclined to pay and so 14 January 1972 was fixed as the date for departure; which left very little time to prepare and to pack. In the end the commander British Forces Malta decided the families would leave by the due date, but the rest would leave when ready.

The role and organization of 10 Ordnance Maintenance Park, to say nothing of its name, had been the subject of review for some time. The current configuration did not reflect its task and consequently it was changed. The unit became 10 Ordnance Support Battalion, with 48 Company restructuring as the RAOC AMF(L) Company to replace a previously ad hoc unit and 47 Company configured to support the 10,000 strong United Kingdom Mobile Force (Land) with its optional roles on either the southern or northern flank of NATO. The new battalion was located mainly at Prince Maurice Barracks, Devizes, and comprised the original two regular companies and two shadow companies that were to be made available from the UK Base Depots for exercises and operations. The two regular companies were composite, providing a wide range of support, with such things as ammunition, vehicles, stores and petroleum platoons, with 47 Company having a Local Resources Platoon of two sections. Posting to the local resources world was highly prized by the soldiers and young officers fortunate enough to be chosen. They would be deployed in peace to support exercises all over the world and it was a wonderful environment for independence of action and learning the business of logistics right at the consumer interface, to say nothing of seeing the world from the Caribbean to the Equator, Nepal to South America, southern to northern Europe.

On Sunday 30 January 1972 there was to be a NICRA march in Londonderry. The 1st Battalion of the Parachute Regiment was deployed, a riot ensued and in the violence that followed thirteen civilians were killed and the same number wounded. It was a day that has lived on in the legends of the troubles as 'Bloody Sunday'. One outcome was the resignation of Brian Faulkner's Ulster Government and its replacement by direct rule from Westminster. William Whitelaw was to be the first Secretary of State.

At about the same time the importance of the EOD task was recognized by the upgrading of the

211

senior ammunition post from major to lieutenant colonel; from SATO to CATO. Important, however, was the accompanying change in the reporting chain. CATO worked to the General Staff chain of command, thus removing from the CRAOC the oversight he had previously had for EOD. It was a long overdue switch since the CRAOC was not necessarily an ATO and hence not in a strong position to brief on EOD matters.

In Malta the Ordnance Depot finally closed on 23 March 1972, having accepted and disposed of the residue of departing units while at the same time continuing to support those who needed Ordnance support right up until the last minute. It was a task the RAOC was becoming used to with similar events happening all over the world as overseas commitments drew down.

The original plan for inventory management for the RAOC had been for a CICP to control the whole of the RAOC inventory to be housed at Bicester, which would have meant closing and transferring all the provisioning organizations at Chilwell and Donnington to the Oxfordshire depot. However, by 1970 such progress had been made in data communication that it was possible to leave them in place. On the surface their concentration at Bicester would appear to have been the most efficient solution, but the disruption would have been huge. In a sense the first great lesson of the computer age was being taught, in that location is less important than the ability to transfer and manage timely and accurate information.

Brigadier Jimmy Roycroft.

The CICP was formed at Bicester on 1 April 1972. It had been brought forward from its original target date of 1975 because of the condition of the Chilwell computers which badly needed replacing and would not have lasted the additional three years. It was ultimately to take over the provision, control and accounting responsibilities from CODs Bicester, Chilwell and Donnington, the Chief Ammunition Control Officer's Branch of HQ Base Organization and the CADs at Bramley, Longtown and Kineton, as well as the Chief Provision and Control Officer's Branch of HQ Vehicle Organization and the CVDs Ashchurch, Hilton and Ludgershall. A brigadier, the Controller CICP, ran it and the first incumbent was Brigadier Jimmy Roycroft.

The CICP's ADP Division would operate the main computer installation at Bicester, the subsidiary installations at Chilwell and Donnington, and the data links to the other central depots, ICPs overseas and other service computers in the UK. It would also carry out initial programming, maintenance and exploitation tasks on the system's suites of programmes. There would be an issues, finance and control division with responsibility for all stock control in central depots, for estimates and the long term equipment programme, for management statistics and for stock control of war reserves and stocks earmarked for special tasks. An equipment division would be responsible for the two high-cost and operationally important ranges: ammunition and vehicles/equipment, with control of the UK stocks of those commodities. A stores division, formed from the three commodity branches located at Bicester, Chilwell and Donnington, would be responsible for the provision of all the lower cost and value stores, whilst a technical records division would identify all demands not recognizable from indices of part numbers and publish and issue appropriate indices to RAOC units and other users worldwide.

It was a hugely complex undertaking, and would take two years to settle into the posture that had been envisaged for it. In concept it was farsighted and imaginative. That it would never be exploited to its full potential was a fault not of the vision or of those who tried to apply it, but the paucity of communications links and the differing requirements of the other two services.

To man and operate the Pombsen Depot in Germany, by now half way to completion, 43 RP Company formed up under Major Clem Hellis and further north the last shed was completed at Dulmen, although it would be another year before the barracks were finished and the site was properly ready for occupation. However, the stores sites at Hanover and Glinde were emptied and their contents deposited in Viersen and Dulmen.

The summer of 1972 saw one of the more spectacular EOD tasks when a threat was received that there was a bomb on the liner, the *QE2*. By now EOD work in Northern Ireland, built on the wide experience from earlier colonial bombing campaigns, had made the RAOC a centre of global excellence in the rendering safe of IEDs. Courses were being run at the School of Ammunition for operators from all over the world. On 18 May CILSA received a call to say that a blackmailer had claimed seven bombs had been planted on the liner, by then one and a half days from New York en route to Southampton. A parachute trained ATO or AT was required to go in as part of a team to uncover and then render safe the IEDs. The choice was made for Captain Bob Williams, the EOD instructor at the School of Ammunition, to undertake the task. He was not a trained military parachutist, but had undertaken privately a number of free fall descents. The other three who jumped were trained parachutists and whilst they had skills that might assist once any device was found, their principal task was to get Captain Williams onto the ship from the sea, into which they were to descend.

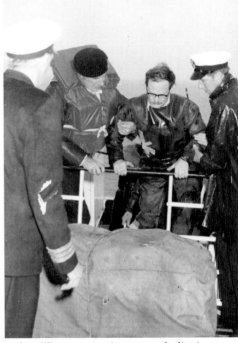

Bob Williams mustering as much dignity as he can performing the difficult task of boarding the *QE2* from the sea. Any bomb they might find was going to be simple by comparison.

Conditions were awful and under normal circumstances a drop would not have been considered possible, but after several runs the team eventually made it. A search of the ship, however, revealed nothing and it was realized that a time consuming and successful hoax had been perpetrated. One outcome, though, was the formation of a parachute-trained section for 321 EOD Unit. Bob Williams received an MBE for his efforts.

Major Robert Williams MBE on the left of the group, with the captain of the *QE2* and the special forces soldiers with whom he made the parachute descent.

Operation MOTORMAN began in Ulster at 0400 hours on 31 July 1972. It was mainly aimed at clearing the 'no-go' areas in Londonderry, and the removal of roadblocks that had been established in the city. To mount it there was a heavy troop reinforcement into Northern Ireland, and the shipping in through Lough Foyle of heavy earth-moving equipment. The secrecy of the planning was necessarily such that the CRAOC did not receive notice of extra supply or accommodation requirements until just before the event. Some eleven battalions were deployed for the operation. Whilst the load that fell on the RAOC in Ulster was considerable, perhaps the more difficult was that falling to the lot of HQ DOS in London. There it was the unenviable job of the DDOS, Brigadier Mike Callan, and of Ord 2 to calculate the POL and food items likely to be required, without knowing either the exact size of the force or the duration of the operation. A new CRAOC took post in August 1972, and as if to give him early warning of his potential problems, five days later a bomb, estimated to contain between 300 and 400 pounds of HE, exploded in a post office in the married quarters area in Lisanelly Barracks, Omagh, severely damaging four quarters and making twelve uninhabitable. A rapid reaction was required from the RAOC, in particular from Barracks (West) to avoid a drop in the married families' morale. The crisis was dealt with by furnishing and using some empty quarters and by moving families in with neighbours while the damaged quarters were refurbished. Bombs had become part and parcel of life in Northern Ireland, and in the field of bomb disposal the Corps was by now deeply committed. The whole saga was typical of the short notice, highly intense work the RAOC undertook almost as routine; while still carrying on with its normal, and essential, tasks.

By the end of 1971 some 250 acres of the old Minden Barracks area at Deepcut had been reclaimed, landscaped and transformed into a functional building complex, and the major event of 1971 was the move of HQ Training Centre, the School of Ordnance and the Regimental Depot out of the assortment rattle accommodation they had been occupying for a large part of the previous decade into the new, purpose-built accommodation. Her Majesty the Queen opened the new training centre on 9 June 1972. Prior to an extensive tour of the facilities and the opportunity to meet a large number of soldiers and families Her Majesty officially began proceedings with a short speech:

It was in 1958 that I last visited you here in Blackdown. Since then there have been many changes. Perhaps the most significant is the increasingly professional approach to soldiering that exists in the Army today. This professionalism has been demonstrated in many campaign theatres since 1958, in Cyprus, Malaya and Borneo. As your Colonel-in-Chief, I am indeed proud of the way in which you have carried out your tasks, sometimes under most difficult conditions. Day after day men of the Royal Army Ordnance Corps in Northern Ireland are putting their lives at risk by defusing the terrorists' bombs. My thoughts and prayers are with the people there, and I am sure that there can be few of them who would withhold their admiration from those brave men who risk, and sometimes lose, their lives in the attempt to protect innocent members of the civilian population.

The Royal Army Ordnance Corps has also made significant strides in the use of modern industrial and management techniques, and where necessary adapted them to the military task. To train the modern soldier, a sophisticated organization is required. In order to provide accommodation for this organization. Blackdown Barracks as it exists now, was designed and built. I hope it will prove to be, not only efficient, but also a pleasant environment in which to train, study and relax.

I wish you well in these new barracks, and I am sure that success in your important role will do much to enhance the proud record that has already been created. It gives me much pleasure to declare Blackdown Barracks open.

Also in June 1972, following the funeral of Major Bernard Calladene, killed on EOD duties in Northern Ireland, the RAOC *Gazette* published a *Tribute to Courageous Men*. It was a quote from the address given by the Reverend R L Parsonage, Assistant Chaplain General of Northern Command as a tribute to Bernard Calladene and others who had lost their lives, and to those officers and soldiers whose duty it was, and remains, to perform the task of disposal of bombs:

Among those present, (at the service) some will be wondering how they would bear such grief if it happened to them. Others will rightly wonder, and even marvel, that such bravery of the sort that is before us can really be; whereby a man seems so willingly and unceremoniously to walk literally in the valley of the shadow of death doing simply what his job and duty requires of him. Spontaneous acts of bravery are one thing, but a conscious calculated rendezvous with the unknown must be another.

In the context of this setting we may well see what men are capable of at both ends of the scale. At the one end, that viciousness, that callous disregard for anything and everybody in the furtherance of personal or community ends in terms of what they want. At the other end, that matter-of-fact performance of duty which turns out to be as near to selflessness as anything can be.

In 1972 came the first top-level reorganization that would affect those alterations made in the sixties as a result of the Nye report. The responsibility for Q Staff policy for rations, POL, Barrack Services and Fire transferred to the DOS. At the same time, the rump of Q (Maintenance)[5] and Q (Clothing and General Stores) were merged into a new staff directorate, soon to be renamed as the Directorate of Clothing and Textiles (DCT), under a staff trained RAOC Brigadier

Prominent among those who contributed greatly to the performance of the HQ DOS during these momentous years of change and great activity was Colonel R Hill, WRAC. 'Billie' Hill had begun her long association with the RAOC in the War Office in 1945. By the time of her retirement in 1972, she had worked for ten Directors of Ordnance Services, with practically all her service being in Ord 2. Billie Hill became known and respected throughout the Army for her immense expertise in equipment matters and war reserves, and no operation was mounted in the post war years without her being intimately involved in its planning. As a lieutenant colonel and later as a colonel she had managed her branch with consummate skill, and her final promotion in 1965 and the award of the OBE were well-earned tributes to her qualities and abilities.

Colonel Hill was, in fact, the last serving member of a band of ATS and WRAC officers who, during the Second World War and for many years thereafter, gave most loyal service to the RAOC. They included Majors Pauline Shilton and Joyce Morris in Ord 9, Majors Sheila Howe and Joyce Robinson in Ord 13, Captains Dorothy Adams and Christine Lee and Majors Margaret Beale and Anne Grayson in Ord 2, and in HQs and depots outside the War Office/Ministry of Defence, Majors Pam Partridge, Brenda Bass, Sheila Colmer, Liz Galloway and Gwen Prosser. It is of more than passing interest that in the early eighties it would be decided that WRAC officers could serve in the RAOC on equal terms with their male colleagues and be controlled, administered and managed by AG9. Few seemed to have remembered that it had all been done before!

It was only a little while later that approval was given for the Felix tie to be worn by those who had undertaken EOD duties with 321 EOD Unit. It became the badge of office of those who had done this work in the Province, and was on a green base with the head of Felix, the cat, and the red hand of Ulster equally interspersed in a pattern. It cost £1.25 (£10).

When HQ Base Organization had formed in 1966, the Vehicle Organization, still controlling five CVDS, had remained independent, and directly responsible to the DOS. But by 1972 it had shrunk in size to a HQ and three CVDs, at Ashchurch, Hilton and Ludgershall, and both its autonomy and the rank of its commander were in doubt. Scope, it seemed, for another study and another restructuring. To RAOC officers and soldiers serving out with the Army and trying to provide the best possible service it seemed never-ending.

As the end of 1972 approached it had been a decade of constant change in the provision of materiel support to the field army in Germany and in the UK. Each brigade now had an OFP, each REME workshop a stores section. Some Signals, Artillery and Engineer regiments now had small stores sections in their attached workshops and those that didn't have workshops acquired FAMTO and FATSO[6] sergeants to operate their accounts. Portable bins, called Thomas Bins, fitted into 3 and 10-ton GS vehicles provided much more storage space for small items than their predecessors and hence the carrying capacity of mobile units had been greatly increased. HIAB[7] cranes appeared mounted on lorries, and Eager Beaver cross-country forklift trucks brought a new dimension to handling stocks in the field.

For combat supplies there was now a C Sups Platoon commanded by a captain attached to every transport squadron. Commanded by the CRAOC, they lived with the Divisional Regiment RCT and accounted for the C Sups that the regiment distributed. At divisional headquarters the CRAOC had a DADOS C Sups on his staff, but on exercise and on operations he deployed with HQ RCT. It was unnecessarily convoluted, and stemmed directly from the cap badge focus that the McLeod report had foundered on – and was still some way from Lord Kitchener's entirely appropriate aspiration.

Welcome though some of the new arrangements were, the materiel re-supply system in forward areas lacked any form of communications whatsoever and nothing was forecast for RAOC Field Force units. Those that had a radio, and some did, had acquired them by means that were... well... unconventional. The lack of a link through BRUIN, the operational trunk communications telephone system operated by divisional and corps signal regiments, meant that officers and warrant officers went on exercise with their pockets full of coins. The yellow telephone booths of the Deutsches Bundespost were well used and were known as the 'ten pfennig BRUIN'. Without them the re-supply of materiel would have been much less effective, and it goes without saying that the 'system' did not allow for the reclaiming of telephone calls from public call boxes. There was not a computer to be seen in forward units in direct contact with the customer and provision and accounting continued on the well tried Kalamazoo[8] manual system where 'breaking PAF' meant old fashioned 'steam driven' action by technical clerks to replenish stocks and ensure the continued sustainability of materiel re-supply – and at all times in all weathers.

The RAOC *Gazette* had a monthly column by an anonymous officer or retired officer in the RAOC called 'Observations by the Checker' where snippets of gossip could be uncovered and where the author could exercise the acerbic wit that seemed to be a pre-requisite for selection for the job. In June 1964, when the decade of 'death by studies' was starting there appeared the checker's report of a conversation he had overheard between two senior officers. He was sufficiently circumspect not to record who they were, and he placed it under a heading 'Thought for the Month':

> In the climate of a small regular army and a manpower crisis, it is always the services – and that means the Corps primarily – which suffer most. It all stems from the Charcittian conception that the services are a useless appendage – a tail, which if lopped off will in some mysterious fashion sharpen the teeth. This is, of course, biologically indefensible, but is a theory that dies hard. In fact the services are not a tail but the viscera of a fighting animal and if they fail then for all its teeth and claws the animal will succumb.

Perhaps it would have been better entitled 'Thought for the Decade' and thereafter. There was still much to be done.

Notes

[1] Malkara: a large anti-tank missile fired from a light armoured vehicle.

[2] Thunderbird: a high altitude anti-aircraft missile.

[3] Equipment held in packs for reinforcing units to collect prior to deployment.

[4] Shadow Unit: formed of officers and soldiers with a day-to-day task in the UK Base with a secondary role to deploy on operations when needed. In this case the HQ of 321 EOD unit was drawn from Didcot and the section from the different Command Ammunition Inspectorates.

[5] Maintenance in this context means maintenance of re-supply, not maintenance of equipment as in repair and maintenance.

[6] FAMTO and FATSO were stores held at first line for the repair of motor transport and technical equipments

[7] HIAB was the trade name for a lorry-mounted crane.

[8] Kalamazoo was the trade name for the binders that held the account cards.

Chapter Eight

Save, Save, Save – Save the Falklands 1973 – 1982

We could have saved sixpence. We have saved five pence – but at what cost?

Samuel Becket, All That Fall 1957

In 1973 the Army Board was faced with difficult decisions. To maintain the strength of the Armed Forces some 43,000 recruits were required, yet only 26,000 a year were joining. The best prediction was that an Army of 135,000 could be sustained against an establishment of 152,000. Two studies were set in hand to examine the future size and shape of the Army, looking towards the end of the decade, and they were initiated in the light of an arbitrary cut of £350 million (£2.5 billion) in defence expenditure.

But whilst the Army Board might be perplexed, life at regimental duty went on unfettered by the budgetary concerns of its masters. It was only a small event, but down in the West Country the Ordnance Squadron of the Commando Logistic Regiment won the Commando Logistic Regiment Log Race. The outline of the event is fairly obvious, with groups of marines and attached Army personnel running huge distances carrying very heavy weights in the form of logs, one per group. It was introduced as a annual competition and the Ordnance Squadron would go on to win for many more years to come.

Private Omar Salem, a storeman at CAD Bramley, won the Army Individual Badminton Championship for the second year in succession. He retained his title by beating the Dorset champion, a Royal Signals Sergeant, in two straight sets. Omar, who was born in Singapore, had joined the Army Department Police out there in 1966 when he had already shown prowess at badminton by taking the Singapore Combined Schools championship and the Singapore Youth championship. He was selected to play for the Combined Services against the English County champions, Surrey, as the only Army representative in the team, the remainder being RAF.

Senior officers in the RAOC, cognisant of the need to improve the conduct of logistic business, whether or not it was required by defence reviews or unplanned cuts already had a number of initiatives under way examining the support profile and how well it suited the Army's requirements. Of major importance was the development of a 'one base' concept. After the Second World War the UK provided the logistic base for a raft of garrisons across the world, in some of which brush fire wars or internal security operations took place. In Europe, BAOR was clearly important, but it was benign, held many of its own reserves on the Continent and did not require the same focus.

However, the withdrawal from virtually all the UK's overseas garrison commitments and the creation of what amounted virtually to a 'one-on-one' situation meant that some reconsideration of the means of providing logistic support was required. Instrumental in the decision-making was the advance in computerization, which meant it was not necessary to store in a warehouse nearby so long as the transport arrangements were in place to overcome any concerns about the location of stocks. Fortunately the study coincided with a massive increase in the size and number, and hence capability, of the commercial cross-channel ferry fleet due to the growth in the volume of trade with Europe and increases in tourism. This would allow more to be held in the UK with a high degree of certainty that stocks could be transported on time to BAOR.

Late in 1972 there had been a change in the organization for the ammunition inspectorate in the UK with the formation of 1 Ammunition Inspection and Disposal Unit created by the amalgamation of the Ammunition Inspectorates of Northern, Southern and Western Commands and of Scotland. The HQ of the new unit was in Old Sarum Barracks, Salisbury, with Lieutenant Colonel Alan Yardley having the dual roles of Commanding Officer and of CATO HQ UKLF. The unit was deployed with SATO East at Hounslow, with detachments at Ashford, Colchester and Nottingham; SATO North at Catterick with detachments at Liverpool and Edinburgh; and SATO West at Hereford. Almost from its inception the unit was hard at work on EOD and IED tasks. Early in 1973 a bomb campaign was waged against prominent members of the Jewish community in the UK and then on 8 March 1973 the IRA detonated car bombs in London, at New Scotland Yard, the Old Bailey, and in the vicinity of Horseferry House, the Home Office Building in Horseferry Road. During that day there were fifty-one calls to suspected car bombs, but only four proved to be real bomb incidents. The detachment of No. 1 AIDU deployed in London for a joint Metropolitan Police/RAOC operation found some difficulty in getting around, since a rail strike that day had greatly increased the numbers of cars parked throughout the capital. That factor did, however, save Horseferry House from damage since, with Horseferry Road filled with cars, the bombers had been forced to park the car holding the bomb around the nearest corner, in Dean Stanley Street.

Later that year, on 17 September 1973, Captain Ron Wilkinson, an ATO from the Hereford Detachment was seriously injured while attempting to neutralize a bomb that terrorists had placed in a street in Edgbaston, Birmingham. He died six days later of his wounds, the first ATO to be killed on mainland Britain undertaking EOD duties.

Then again in 1973, there was a further car bomb incident at Wormwood Scrubs prison in London, and a most serious incident involving a fifty pound bomb which detonated in a servicemen's weekend chartered coach on the M62 motorway, killing twelve, some of whom were dependants. The work seemed never ending for the AIDU, and many ATOs and ATs became quite expert at the occasionally grisly task of sifting through the detritus following an explosion for intelligence and forensic evidence.

The power of the computers being introduced into the RAOC lay in the structure being put in place for their deployment throughout the Corps. The primary level was to be the main depots in the United Kingdom, with their stocks controlled directly by the Bicester computer in the Central Inventory Control Point. Secondary depots were the main depot complexes in the theatres. Hence Hong Kong and BAOR were both considered 'secondary' and known as Inventory Control Points, to be joined later by Berlin for that range of its holdings not purchased locally off the Berlin budget funded by Germany. Their stock levels were controlled by the CICP and that included not simply replenishment, but also instructions to return stock or dispose of it in some way when it was not being used. The concept also allowed for a third level of computerization, the Tertiary Depot. These were the OFPs and Stores Sections holding inventory in direct support of the consuming units. This would be in place once a suitable field force computer system could be developed and deployed. Their stock levels also would be controlled by the CICP through the ICP. The first moves towards this all-encompassing structure had been made with the installation of the second-generation computer at Bicester in 1971/72.

The CICP itself was officially opened on 16 April 1973, the culmination of about 1,000 man-years of systems analysis and programming by ISDW. The CICP itself comprised the Provision, Control and Accounts departments of the three CODs and of HQ Vehicle Organization and the Ammunition Control Cell of HQ Base Organization. The responsibility for the functions had been taken over from COD Bicester on 1 April 1972, and from COD Chilwell on 3 July. The Ammunition Control Branch had moved from HQ Base Organization to the CICP on 6 October 1972 to form the Ammunition Branch of Control Division. However, technical problems delayed the assumption of the role from COD Donnington until early 1973. Once complete this placed all the accounting for the Army's entire materiel stocks, and those Army originated stores used by the other two Services, within one organization based at Bicester with its CICP outstations at Donnington and Chilwell. This replaced the previous system where each depot had only undertaken provisioning and stock control for those items held in its own sheds.

The key issue was that the computer could keep track of the location of any stock item irrespective of where it was stored. Consequently, there was no longer any necessity to store items of the same or similar type in one discrete location, a feature that would allow major changes in the way stocks were held in the UK and abroad. Furthermore, the computer's capacity to store massive quantities of data and to process it at great speed made possible fundamental changes to three important functions. Provision reviews at all levels in the system were now a continuous process. Recommendations based on the actual consumption of items could be made on their retention in stock in a particular storage area or unit, or their disposal by sale or by return to another depot. And it was possible now to highlight uneconomic holdings of high cost and low usage items.

From the outset, the introduction of the system, even though not fully deployed, made a significant difference in volumes of stock being held and the amount of space required in which to store it. As an example, the RAOC Stores Section supporting the very large base repair facility in Germany at 37 (Rhine) Workshops REME held 53,400 stock items with an average availability of ninety-one per cent. Within two years of the CICP taking control the number of stock items had fallen to 15,600, a reduction of seventy-one per cent, whilst the average availability of items stocked remained undiminished. Even without the imposition of a defence review the RAOC was, by dint of its own efforts, making considerable inroads into the savings that would be demanded of it simply by the introduction and efficient use of modern management practices.

The introduction of System Two, as it was known, was not, however, without its difficulties. Technical problems, mostly associated with 'head crashes' in the hardware, created great difficulties. Unfortunately, one of the equipments affected was the recently introduced Chieftain tank which was experiencing teething troubles that demanded a high spares usage and this raised the issue of inventory control to a very high level. It even arrived on the agenda of the Army Board. The outcome, however, was a swift decision, and money made available, to replace the inadequate discs with something more suitable for the task and System Two was up and running more swiftly than might otherwise have been the case.

But the work did not stop there. With System Two in operation, ISDW, as the RAOC's think tank on IT, continued in existence under Brigadier P K Goozee, firstly to carry out exploitation of System Two, including a special system for managing guided missiles, the secondary and tertiary depot supply support systems, and the VESPER project; and secondly to plan and implement the third generation computer system, expected to be installed around 1980/81. VESPER was planned to become an all-embracing computerized management system, controlling, accounting and advising on a multitude of aspects concerning vehicles, weapons and many of the other more expensive items in the inventory. Then in October 1973 the staff of ISDW, the programming group of the CICP, and an increment for planned new tasks, were joined together to form the Computer Systems Development Wing.

Meanwhile, in Germany a small explosion resulting from the press of a button by General Sir Harry Tuzo, the C-in-C BAOR, ripped a piece of magnetic tape from a plaque marking the opening of the ICP in BAOR. For months previously the staff had been working furiously to get the account in line with the CICP, so that every UK sourced item in Germany had a record that was replicated. Because the overall concept for computerization of the inventory assumed a tertiary level of IT infrastructure at the level of OFPs and Stores Sections the ICP was given the task of setting up the Tertiary Depot system in Germany. The aspiration was that the introduction of the system would reduce tertiary units response times to requests for stores that they did not have on hand; it would allow the OFPs to operate a stockage support system for units they served; it would provide better control and accounting systems for the OFPs and Stores Sections; it would provide a rapid means of 'cross-servicing' where items required by one unit could be provided by another local unit rather than going back all the way through the system and it would reduce clerical tasks at unit level thereby offering staff savings. The computer selected for the task was the MAC 16, a rugged configuration with a core store of 24K, which seemed an awful lot at the time, and exchangeable disk storage, which was mounted in two containers, each carried on a 4-ton flatbed truck. It was called TAIS, meaning Transportable ADP Inventory System.

Elsewhere in the RAOC life carried on as normal, if normal it ever was. SQMS R Morris, nearing the end of his twenty-two years' service, offered a view of life in a BAOR OFP. It was not that different to any other RAOC unit in the Field Army:

The average strength is normally about eighty six men; this allows for postings in and out, with the inevitable gaps, and the occasional welfare or sick cases which fast become a liability in such a small unit. The barracks and OFP locations vary immensely as they are influenced not only by the availability of buildings and storehouses, but also by the number, size and geographic allocation of those units whom they exist to serve. All the BAOR OFPs are constantly busy, both supplying stores and. carrying out their military role as soldiers with a part to play within BAOR and NATO. They also find time to participate in the normal sports: football, rugby, cricket and hockey, as well as canoeing, sailing, boxing and golf. No joke, this last one; we have an Army golf links within half-an-hour's drive!

The contenders in the BAOR minor unit boxing champions in 1971 and 1972 have included several OFPs, two of which were very successful in I972 and 1973. Another BAOR OFP won the 1972 'Parashot' competition very convincingly.

The Corps has also been well placed in BAOR tennis and cricket. My OFP is, at present, second in the Garrison hockey league, provides five players for the Divisional RAOC side and two for the RAOC BAOR team. Our rugby team is, with little amendment, the Divisional RAOC side and it provides four players for the RAOC BAOR fifteen. However, life is not all sport. To elaborate on this: During the past two years my OFP has been involved in, at different times I hasten to add, the following activities:

Providing personnel, stores and vehicles for the Administrative Base Unit in Larzac in the south of France, about seventy kilometres from the Mediterranean; very nice for those who wish to obtain a good suntan and enjoy excellent French cooking, not forgetting the wine. Providing personnel for the British Army Training Unit at Suffield in Canada. Only two were lucky enough to go there, unfortunately, but neither of them wanted to be relieved at the half way mark. One of them even brought back a wife! In addition to local commitments providing a bath section, complete with personnel, for an adventure training exercise in Northern Italy; a very nice independent command for a Regimental Duties Corporal, Skiing courses in Bavaria and at the Special Training Centre, Silberhutte, in the Harz Mountains. Over twenty soldiers had this experience. Sailing courses at the British Weser Yacht Club on the River Weser. These courses are done in civilian clothes and are quite popular during the sunnier season. We actually obtained two 'C' helmsmen from these courses. Organizing and thoroughly enjoying an adventure training exercise in Norway; canoeing, sailing and trekking with our own canoes, sailing dinghy and aching feet. Only a lucky eight soldiers, but there will be more. Participation by the whole of the members of the OFP in a three and a half week summer camp at Mumau, in Bavaria, to remove cobwebs. We caught up on physical efficiency tests, classified personnel on their personal weapons and revised basic military skills. Despite a very fun training programme, a lot of sightseeing and beer tasting took place. Another camp is planned for the coming year. Training for and completing, successfully, the Nijmegen Marches as a unit team in 1972, it took place in one of the hottest periods on record.

You will notice that I have made little mention of the more mundane pursuits: exercises which in the same period have taken up more than four months of our working year; training periods in barracks which have resulted in a fair crop of Regimental Proficiency Certificates and a satisfactory number of trade classification upgradings. These still happen and will continue to happen both for the benefit of the individuals requiring the qualification and the benefit of the OFP which will gain, we hope, by increased efficiency.

Another little sideline is our attempt to cover ourselves in glory both on the ranges and on the athletic field. The results of the 1972 RAOC BAOR rifle meeting speak far louder than I can say, and the BAOR athletic meeting of 1971 is my witness here. We did not do so well in 1972 although our sister OFP won the 100-stone Tug-of-War and were runners-up in the 88-stone version.

We also manage to lead a reasonable social life, and this in spite of being in a small village, more isolated than most barracks in BAOR. The barracks contain a unit cinema, a well finished WRVS club, a NAAFI and a well-run Junior Ranks Club that is going from strength to strength. This is in addition to Officers' and Sergeants' Messes that are considered as the 'core' of the Corps in our Division. Aside from these amenities, the village is very friendly, and those who attempt to speak German are sure of a hearty welcome from the locals. The local Schutzenverein is also very pleased to compete against budding Annie Oakleys and always make us welcome at their dances or Schutzenfests. This last, of course, applies to most OFPs in the northern end of Germany, especially those in the country districts.

Over the last year, something I almost forgot to mention, we also managed to issue approximately 50,000 items of stores, so it wasn't all beer and skittles.

It was pretty much par for the course; life was far from dull.

In June 1973, twenty-one years after its foundation, 3 BAPD was awarded the freedom of the newly created municipality of Gemeinde Bruggen formed from the amalgamation of the towns of Bracht and Bruggen. It was the first time such an honour had been bestowed in Germany on a unit of the British Army. It was a singular honour and attracted the highest representation from the RAOC, with the DOS, Major General Leonard Phelps attending in person. The day of the parade coincided with the publication of the Birthday Honours List for that year, in which General Phelps had been awarded the CB. Word of this leaked out to the Germans and the DOS spent large parts of his day trying to explain to bemused Germans precisely what one had to do to Command a Bath.

But just to show that hard work and hard play achieved results across the board, the top three places in the finals of the Army Music Group and Singer competition, held in the BBC Playhouse Theatre, London, on 26 April, were gained by units and individuals of the RAOC. The competition had been initiated as a result of a suggestion by Harry Secombe. He was convinced that there was musical talent in the Army which should be brought to the attention of a wider audience and, perhaps, as a result of the publicity, achieve even greater heights of fame nationally. It was a competition that had been run since 1968.

In July the new ammunition depot in Germany, at Pombsen, near Paderborn, was finished two years ahead of schedule and would be opened September. The new stores depot at Dulmen also opened in the same period and this allowed 15 ABOD fully to be concentrated upon just two sites – Viersen and Dulmen. This put forward a great deal of the ammunition and PUEs for reinforcing units coming into

BAOR during a period of emergency. With the opening of Tower Barracks at Dulmen on 2 April 1974 the move into the depot would be complete with the arrival of the RAOC trade training wing established for those soldiers stationed in Europe who required trade upgrading.

Branston, which since the completion of Operation NETTLERASH had been holding ex-Ministry of Supply stores and stocks for the Royal Ordnance Factories, was finally closed as an Ordnance site in the middle of 1973.

It was in 1973 that 17 BVD in Mönchengladbach won the ICI Challenge Trophy. This was a shooting competition open to every unit in the Army, and taking it for the RAOC was no mean feat. One of the members of the team was Captain Graham Macdonald, who was a world renowned judo referee who had himself achieved 3rd Dan Master Grade as a black belt in Japanese judo. He was of sufficient standing in the sport that when stationed in Japan where he had been a member of the Kure City ten-man judo team and, having studied with the 9th Dan Ogata Hisato, had been offered a place at the Tokyo Kyodan for special training. He declined a career at the very top of the sport to return on posting after his Japan tour. In his spare time he had also managed to acquire a private pilot's licence.

In the same year, and for the first time since its inception, a unit of the RAOC took the Army Minor Units Cricket Cup competition. The Central Ammunition Depot team from Bramley won the final match and the cup by defeating the Infantry Junior Leaders Battalion from Oswestry, at Aldershot on 7 September 1973. It was Lance Corporal Knight who did the damage for Bramley, ably supported by Corporal Lindsay.

The George Cross had, by this time in the RAOC's history, been awarded to a member of the Corps on five occasions, and the George Medal on fifty occasions. Thus it was that on 19 October, at Deepcut, two holders of the George Cross and thirty-five holders of the George Medal attended a reunion dinner. It was arranged on the instigation of the DOS who felt some recognition was required of the gallantry that had been shown not only in Northern Ireland, at that time very much in the headlines, but in other campaigns and in other events throughout the world. Among those present were a number of retired RAOC officers and soldiers, namely: Brigadier R L I Jones GC, Major T W Downing GM, Major P S Easterby GM, Major T A L Judge GM, Lieutenant J Search GM. WOI P E S Gurney GM, Sergeant K Telford GM, Sergeant E P Thorner GM. Sergeant F G Giblett GM, Sergeant J T Proudlock GM, and Private A Hilton GM.

Squash had always been popular in the RAOC, and the Corps' team had always done well. However, in the early seventies it entered a new era with the growing talent of Corporal 'Robbie' Robinson beginning to make itself felt. In the course of fourteen days he became RAOC Soldier Champion, RAOC Open Champion and Army Soldier Champion, and was runner-up in the Army Open competition. It was the start of a period when the RAOC team would come to dominate Army squash, and Corporal Robinson, who one day would become Lieutenant Colonel Robinson, would be leading the way.

An event took place on 5 March 1974 relating to the RAOC involvement in EOD and IED work. A reception was held at the Henry VIII Wine Cellar, beneath the Ministry of Defence Main Building, at which Major General Norman Speller took receipt from Garrards, the crown jewellers, of two identical silver centrepieces one of which would go to the Corps Headquarters Officers' Mess at Deepcut and the other to the Sergeants' Mess at CAD Kineton. A large part of the cost had been contributed by a number of organizations and individuals who wanted to express appreciation for the lives and property saved by the efforts of the ATOs and ATs engaged in bomb disposal. The names of only some of the donors are recorded on the plinths of the pieces since, for security reasons, some wished to remain anonymous. Many distinguished people, including the Deputy Chief

223

St George slaying
his dragon.

Constable of the Royal Ulster Constabulary, and representatives and individuals who had associated themselves with the centrepieces, previous CILSAs, and a large sprinkling of ATOs and ATs, attended the reception. In creating the design, the modeller explained that he was trying to:

> ...suggest the anonymity of the warrior and his loneliness. Also... tried to underline the ultimate moment of solitary face-to-face confrontation with a bomb – looking down the throat of the dragon.

Major General Norman Speller.

On the plinth were mounted three badges: the RAOC badge and on either side, the badges worn by Ammunition Technical Officers and Ammunition Technicians on their uniform sleeves. Countersunk in the base of each was a plate bearing the simple inscription: FELIX.

The placing of one of the centrepieces at Kineton had presaged the move, on 13 May 1974, of the Army School of Ammunition, as it closed down at Bramley after fifty-two years and re-opened as an independent unit in newly built premises at CAD Kineton. A small explosive device, initiated by Colonel R L Jones, Commandant of the CAD, revealed a brass plaque, embedded in stone and bearing an inscription commemorating the event and the school's re-opening at Kineton. During its life the school at Bramley had trained some 50,000 students from home and abroad and had witnessed many changes during that time. When it opened only conventional ammunition existed, and the technical information was contained in two volumes which placed together measured just two inches thick. By 1974, conventional natures had become more numerous and more complicated, whilst guided missiles and a growing bomb disposal commitment had been added. By the time the school moved, four feet of shelving were required to hold the necessary regulations and pamphlets. In 1922 the chief instructor had been a major, and only two instructors were required. Fifty-two years later the chief instructor, who was also the commandant, was a lieutenant colonel, and there were thirty-three instructors. It was roughly the same size when it officially reopened on its new site on 1 July 1974 at CAD Kineton.

The school had much to teach with the growing complexity of conventional ammunition, more and more sophisticated guided weapons, nuclear artillery in the shape of Lance, for which the school ran all the NATO training, and EOD/IED. In the latter case the beginning of the seventies had seen a significant increase in the cleverness with which terrorists were manufacturing their 'infernal machines' to use the quaint legal term for IEDs. From the small and clever little bombs with their tilt switches and other anti-handling devices they moved on to larger and larger bombs and by the middle of the decade 1,000 lbs of explosive was not an unusual size. The laying of them was becoming more and more cunning, designed to counter the gradually increasing sophistication of the ATO's tools and to draw him to his death in carefully constructed traps, and activity levels were high, with some 2,500 devices being neutralized between March 1972 and March 1977.

Particularly unpleasant was the introduction by the IRA in 1973 of the blast incendiary. This involved strapping a gallon or so of petrol to a high explosive device, the detonation of which would create a fine spray of petrol filling an area which would then be ignited by the flash of the HE detonation. The effect on buildings was wholly destructive, as the pressure created by the exploding petrol would bring most buildings to the ground. The effect of the burning petrol on human flesh defies description.

The distribution of 321 EOD Unit sections was on the basis of one section of a captain ATO and two ATs, with supporting elements, for each of the three brigades in the province. This could be supplemented where necessary by teams from the Ammunition Inspectorate in Headquarters Northern

Ireland and the Ammunition Sub Depot at Ballykinler. But it would be wrong to assume that the RAOC's involvement in Northern Ireland was only in the high profile area of EOD. Many of the regiments serving over there in an infantry role, such as Artillery and Engineers, took with them their workshop together with the RAOC stores section for them to perform also in an infantry role. Witness the task of Corporal P A Swainstone providing close protection for the Secretary of State for Northern Ireland, Merlyn Rees MP, on his visit to the Gunner regiment with which Corporal Swainstone was normally stationed in Germany.

On 1 July 1974, because of the reduction in stock holdings, 17 BVD ceased to exist as an independent unit, and became a sub depot of 15 BOD which as a result changed its title to 15 Composite Ordnance Depot.

Later in July, on the 15th, Archbishop Makarios was swept from power in Cyprus by a coup d'état that emanated from the Greek community. The cause had been his agreement to dispatch back to Greece some 650 regular Greek officers who had been serving with the Cyprus National Guard and the Greek national contingent on the island. This destabilized the delicate political balance between the Turkish and the Greek communities. Within five days, on 20 July, the Turkish Army had invaded Cyprus to ensure the safety of the Turkish community. The eventual outcome was to be a divided island with the Greek Federal Republic of Cyprus in the south and the Turkish Federated State in the north.

As the crisis hit, 19 Brigade was deployed from the United Kingdom with additional support elements from 10 Ordnance Support Battalion and 16 Parachute Heavy Drop Company. On Cyprus itself the local RAOC contingent, commanded by Lieutenant Colonel R W Bromham, was kept busy. Its first priority was to provide accommodation within the SBAs for the service families whose homes were among the local community. They were, de facto, British refugees. Once again Barracks Services were to the fore providing additional accommodation stores and obtaining what they could from local resources to provide basic facilities for the affected families, while the Supply Depot saw to the issue of COMPO with which to feed them. The Bath Unit from 10 Ordnance Support Battalion was deployed, led by Sergeant Biddle, for the purpose of providing bathing facilities to the 8,500 Turkish refugees that packed out the Western SBA. In the end only fifty a day used it, and the section spent most of its time trying to prevent the Turks from purloining bits of equipment for other purposes, such as furnishings for impromptu coffee shops. The refugees' requirement for tentage, food and other necessities of life were all met by the RAOC at very short notice. By the end of the emergency some ninety RAOC reinforcements and 508 Company RPC from COD Bicester would be deployed to support the local garrison.

It was at about this time that the QMG set about resolving two of the anomalies left over from the McLeod study; the issue of the RAOC taking on responsibility for engineer stores held at the RE Stores Depot Long Marston and medical stores at the RAMC Supply Depot at Ludgershall. Naturally, it was in the hope of finding savings, in this case by bringing both organizations within the RAOC's CICP for accounting and provision, and that it might be possible to close down the two depots if room could be found for their stocks within the CODs. It is to be hoped that there was also some aspiration to move towards Lord Kitchener's vision, all those years ago, for a truly single supply corps in the Army.

It would not have caused the slightest problem for the RAOC in taking over the supply responsibility for engineer stores: the stocks could have been accommodated in COD Donnington where a range of engineer equipment already existed. There were, however, objections from the Royal Engineers on the spurious grounds that RE Services' contracts for material such as hard core for road building could not be handled by RAOC; and that the stores held at Long Marston were critical to RE functions and responsibilities and could not be delegated. With regard to medical stores, which included drugs that required special storage and expertise, the DOS had reservations about taking on such a specialized commitment. However, he did offer storage space at Donnington, and computer support for the RAMC in running their depot there. In the event, the whole concept, both for the RE and the RAMC was dropped. The excuses, for that was all they were, for not implementing the concepts were spurious. The initiative foundered on the same rock as so many other initiatives for sensible and obvious rationalization: the tribalism inherent in the regimental system. The final decision had far more to do with protecting careers within the other two Corps than with concern for ensuring a robust and properly focussed supply system for the Army.

In recognition of its emerging role the MH&PEU was re-titled the Materials Handling and Trials Unit. Still stationed at Bicester, it remained an independent unit controlled by HQ DOS.

The emergency in Cyprus had been relatively short-lived. By October 1974 most of the reinforcing units had returned whence they came. However, the work did not stop there. There was the task of returning and renovating all the camp and accommodation stores and redistributing back the stores to the homes outside the SBAs that had been evacuated at the start of the crisis. It was a major effort that absorbed the attentions of the local RAOC staff for many months after the reinforcements had returned home.

In Germany 3 BAD placed itself on the sporting map by winning BAOR Minor Units Rugby, beating HQ 4th Division by 42 – 0. Most of the scoring was done by 'Digger' Denholm playing at fly half and kicking a number of drop goals and scoring a try and Paddy MacCarthy both scoring and converting. The team went on to meet the Duke of Wellington's Regiment in the Army Finals in Aldershot, but were unable to repeat their Germany success and were runners up. Nonetheless, the team had undergone a fantastic season and had made their mark and that of the RAOC on Army rugby.

At the beginning of 1975, 12 OFP began the trial that was to introduce TAIS into those Field Army units that were to become tertiary depots. Unfortunately it was not successful. The reasons were entirely technical, with the computer itself not being sufficiently robust to withstand field conditions. Furthermore, when mounted in its container on the flatbed lorry the load was deemed to be overweight and hence unsafe. The tertiary depot concept had to be shelved while viable alternatives were found.

It was also the time when Hong Kong became an ICP. The installation began on January 1975 and was complete by May. Hong Kong had, since the demise of FARELF, been the centre of logistic support for the region. This included not just the Hong Kong garrison, but also 28 Brigade in Singapore, a battalion and a training organization in Brunei and the Gurkha LofC in Nepal. It was a wide and disparate load for a small and isolated garrison, and being tied into the CICP system by becoming an ICP would confer great benefits. It reduced the manpower in the depot by forty and reduced the item headings held from 60,000 to 30,000.

When, in 1974, the Labour Party had defeated the Tories and been returned to power, the political shift and its focus on a socialist agenda brought the almost inevitable defence review early in their

In 1974 a new depot was opened in Kowloon in Hong Kong, improving greatly the service the RAOC could offer to the colony.

term. It commenced in 1975, making the studies of 1973 into size and shape even more relevant. It was, of course, an exercise in saving money; thousands of millions by the end of the decade was the declared aim. The review was, as usual, promoted as a means of adjusting the nations stated responsibilities with a view to making the numbers fit a stated political aspiration without accepting that the reality was likely to be somewhat different. In this case the Armed Forces were committed to the defence of the homeland through a defence posture in Europe and the shedding of any residual global responsibilities. This, of course, in spite of the UK's position as a permanent member of the UN Security Council with all its concomitant responsibilities and political aspirations, regardless of how the latter might be understated.

One inevitable outcome of any review would be a revisiting of the withdrawal from east of Suez that the previous Labour government had instated only to have it overturned by the Tory Government that had been in power in the interim. They would no doubt have been pleased with the Australian decision, taken some two years earlier, to withdraw from the ANZUK force. By the time of the review they had gone, leaving behind only the New Zealanders and the British who were in the process of splitting down the multi-national logistic system into two separate national ones. Ordnance Services Singapore opened for business in the Naval Base on 1 October 1974 on the same day as its counterpart New Zealand Advanced Ordnance Depot. By 1975 it would be closing down.

One benefit of the Defence Review for the RAOC was that it would provide the underpinning funding to allow development of the systems and processes that would see the introduction of better management systems and improved IT. The realization of the benefits to be gained and the imperative to save money caused the QMG to set up a logistic review working party, known as the Strickland working party, to examine the balance of Ordnance stores and vehicle holdings between the UK and the Continent with the aim of reducing manpower, holdings, and, hence, costs in BAOR. It arrived at three recommendations. It required a reduction to be made in the levels of 'B' vehicle holdings in Europe with direct supply from the UK. This was accepted but would have to be balanced with the need to hold a pool of such vehicles to provide 'rattle' for the base overhaul programme that was constantly underway, mostly in 37 (Rhine) Workshops REME.

It also wanted a move further east from Viersen, Mönchengladbach and Antwerp of the PUEs of reinforcing units and suggested Recklinghausen for the vehicles and Dulmen for the stores. It recommended a system of direct supply of Ordnance Stores from the UK. In the latter case, of course, this was just a natural progression of the advances being made in the supply of BAOR resulting from the improvements being introduced by the RAOC with the deployment of its new management systems. That said, there was always some confusion between what was being held as a maintenance stock and what was a war reserve and until that was unravelled there would always be some confusion, the outcome of which was duplication of holdings and consequent overstocking. One small, but complicating, factor was the question of 'A' vehicle spares of whatever complexion. Since they were only ever to be used in Germany it made sense to keep them all over there; and this fitted with the one-base concept since it was built on economy of storage and effort and knowing the location and the consumption point of the item.

The outcome was a saving of 15,000 soldiers across the Army, and a restructuring programme that was supposed to make a more effective contribution to the UK's NATO contribution. In particular a level of command was removed within the Field Army. The brigade headquarters was to go and command of battle groups was to be exercised through task forces direct from divisional HQ. The Task Forces would flex in size and shape to suit the immediate needs of the battle, although they existed in peace as garrison HQs controlling largely those regiments they had commanded in the former brigade structure. They were known as Task Force Alpha through to Hotel, following the phonetic alphabet; with the exception of Task Force Charlie, which, as the former 4 Guards Brigade, was known universally as Task Force Charles.

Where independent 'brigades' were quite obviously required they became field forces, so 16 Parachute Brigade, which lost its parachuting capability as a role no longer required in modern war, became 5 Field Force whilst the UKMF(L) brigade ceased to be provided by 1 Infantry Brigade but by the rather ineptly named 6 Field Force. It was a renaming and restructuring exercise that was greeted by friends and allies with amusement and, among the more professional, incredulity, not to say concern. Heaven can only imagine the satisfaction with which our enemies viewed it. All this was to be in place by 1978.

The restructuring suggested for the RAOC in BAOR to support all this was an exercise in virtual lunacy. It was suggested that the CRAOCs and their HQs in the Divisions be abolished. It envisaged Ordnance support, other than combat supplies for a division, being provided by two platoons, one holding general stores and being incorporated into a Transport Battalion, the other holding MT and technical stores and being part of a Repair Battalion. As a concept the platoon structure proposed was not unsound, but not for an entire division and not without a properly formed and expert staff to control activity and deal with emergencies. The DDOS 1 (Br) Corps, Brigadier Gordon Dennison, was invited by the DGOS to provide an RAOC counter proposal, and was given four principles within which to work. He had to ensure the reinstatement of the divisional CRAOC in order that he might provide the focus of all RAOC activity in a division. In order to demonstrate economies and to reduce administrative overheads the span of command would have to be widened, even if it lead to some loss of flexibility. One RAOC unit was to act as the focus for demands for all material for every unit in the division, except for those items specifically the responsibility of stores sections, and finally combat supplies in peace should be provided through the static supply, petroleum and ammunition depots.

Working within these guidelines Brigadier Dennison brought forth the proposal that within each division there should be a HQ RAOC of much the same strength as before, and a divisional Ordnance Company of six officers and 139 soldiers, subject to the outcome of field trials. The arrangements for 5 Field Force, an independent brigade-size formation, were to be slightly different with it having a DADOS and its own Ordnance unit of a slightly different strength and organization. The static RAOC organization should be altered so that supply depots and barracks units located within divisional areas should become divisional units; the Corps Troops OFP should be re-formed as the 1 (Br) Corps Ordnance Company and there should be no change in the roles of the Combat Supplies Battalion, or of the Corps Stores and Corps Vehicle Companies.

The trials of the Divisional Ordnance Company took place in 4th Division, due to it being the choice for the Wide Horizon series of exercises designed to trial the new structure. Lieutenant Colonel Jerrie Hulme was CRAOC at the time and he formed the ad hoc ADOC by drawing in elements from 6 and 20 OFP. For these exercises the CRAOC was placed in charge of the Divisional RV and located at it. The importance of this was that all material, vehicles and stores coming in to the division had to pass through the RV to the units and it gave the CRAOC a controlling hand in what was very much his end of the business, that of providing material support to his dependency in the division. He also had part of his HQ, controlled by the second-in-command, forward at divisional rear HQ providing advice to the staff. The role also gave him command, as HQ DAA, of the units that tended to cluster in the rear of the division and around the divisional RV and which up to then had been looked after by a rather detached divisional rear headquarters. It amounted to several hundred men and vehicles.

Life in the Army during the seventies and in the logistic world in particular, was really yet more of a case of study upon study, and in March 1975 the Somerville report was produced. General Somerville had been the Vice Quartermaster General to General Sir William Jackson and the QMG had, while still only the designate for the post, and in 1972, discussed with the DOS, Major General Leonard Phelps, some far reaching ideas for the control and organization of the Q Area. The outcome had been the work of the Somerville team. The Commander Base Organization, Major General John Stanyer, had been one of his team of two-star officers, and the only one from the logistics corps. One

Major General John Stanyer.

recommendation received with some relief was that there should be no change to the structure of the logistics corps. This had less to do with QMG's belief that there were too many 'logistic tribes' and more to so with the fact that it was too soon after McLeod to institute yet more major change. The effect of the Yom Kippur war on western economies would mean more cuts, having to do more with less and, therefore, a focus on improved systems was needed rather than changed organizations. However, a new logistic staff structure common to all levels was to be introduced and an integrated logistic headquarters was to be established as part of the QMG's area, located outside London. It was to be called the Logistic Executive (Army).

The outcome of the 1975 Defence Review was very much in line with the Army's belief in the size of force that could be recruited and sustained. However, it did not, of itself, achieve the savings that the Prime Minister required. To do so there would have to be significant savings in civilian staff and these would perforce hit the Q services as they were the largest employers and among those the RAOC was the largest of all. The Army's share of the 30,000 reductions was 11,700. From this the Q services had to absorb 5,400 with 2,720 going to the RAOC. The difficulty lay in the fact that the Defence Review had left the teeth arms in a relatively strong position with more and more complex equipment to improve their capability, and there was more on the way. It had to be managed in the depots, and spares and other resources for the support of theses equipments had to be provided – with a shrinking military and civilian workforce. It could only be achieved by a fundamental review of the depot system and the relationship between stocks held in BAOR and the UK, and the DOS, Major General Norman Speller put in hand a study the name of which was something of a misnomer: FAIR VALUE. One thing was clear from the outset: there was little to be gained in the overseas garrisons and the bulk of the savings would have to come from BAOR and the UK.

The outcome of the Strickland Report had already made inroads into the BAOR workforce. Not only did it allow the closure of one vehicle depot, but also the imminent opening of the new POL depot at Warendorf would make it possible to close the Nienburg Petroleum Depot with net savings. Furthermore, the introduction of bulk refuelling at Warendorf would largely do away with the need for the Arsbeck Petroleum sub depot of 3 BAPD. Once these and other small savings, together with the savings in overseas garrisons, had been taken there was a balance of 1,586 posts to be found within the UK.

The Ordnance structure in the United Kingdom, outside the Field Army, consisted basically of two parts; barracks services and the regional depot structure. It was felt there was little scope for cuts in the former but in the latter case there were some twenty depots with a varied range of tasks staffed by around 2,000 civilians. An earlier study undertaken by the COO, on his own initiative, had identified a restructuring that had reduced the regional depots to four, Stirling, Hessay, Thatcham and Hereford, with some small outstations that were absolutely necessary – for training and the like. This would have saved 800 posts by 1980, but would have needed ministerial approval. The depots were taken out of the chain of supply for barracks stores, and this, coupled with a decision to downscale married quarters to basic items only, took out the need for repair workshops and the many skilled craftsmen who worked in them.

The FAIR VALUE exercise lent weight to the outcome of the COO's study, and a further review of barracks services meant the eventual figure saved was 900 posts leaving just 686 to be found in the UK depots and other installations with their 8,800 civilian staff. However, 1,500 were employed in the CICP and they were needed to manage the extra stocks brought back by the Strickland recommendations. Hence they were largely untouchable, leaving the bulk of the savings to come from the depots themselves.

Bramley had already been earmarked for closure, and the continued existence of Vehicle Organization had been thrown into doubt by the creation of the CICP, so they got the quest for savings off to a good start. HQ Vehicle Organization became HQ Central Vehicle Depots, and reduced in 1974 from a brigadier to a colonel's appointment with the three CVDs being reduced in status to vehicle depots. An examination of the vehicle depots showed them all to be operating at half capacity with a long-term storage plot that really only required two of them. The original decision was to close Ludgershall and Ashchurch in favour of using the third depot at Hilton and re-opening Marchington, closed in 1967 by an earlier review, but just eight miles from Hilton. The decision was overturned when the cost of rebuilding the roads in Hilton to take 'A' vehicles was found to be prohibitive and an increase in sales activity and the global vehicle liability made an Ashchurch-Ludgershall option much more sensible. Consequently, Hilton became the chosen subject of closure and the Marchington idea foundered.

In the Central Depots the requirement for cuts had also been presaged by a DOS economy study, in this case in 1971, which had indicated areas of redundancy in the UK base. For example, one recommendation had been that the Ordnance Stores and Disposals Depot, built up at Branston after the closure of the COD at Branston under NETTLERASH, should be closed and its stocks of textiles transferred to COD Donnington. Approval for the recommendation had been given in 1973, two years before FAIR VALUE.

It had been felt for some time that insufficient use was being made of the height of storehouses, but means of maximizing storage space had not appeared until the sixties. Even then the concepts were just that: concepts under development. They were very expensive and difficult to justify. However, by the early seventies great progress had been made in storage techniques, and the move of the Branston stocks of textiles provided an opportunity for the Chief Planning Officer at COD Donnington, Lieutenant Colonel Norman Green, to apply the new principles of high-rise, narrow aisle storage, using adjustable pallet racking. The official opening of the new textiles store in Building 6 at COD Donnington took place on 17 July, marking the beginning of a new era in warehousing methods that would be taken into use in the RAOC. An indication of the added value of these new methods can be seen from the fact that the old methods of storing the textiles occupied some 220,000 square feet of storage space in stacks that were fourteen feet high. The new high-rise, narrow aisle technique, stacking to a height of twenty-seven feet, made it possible to house the stocks of textiles in about 70,000 square feet of floor space.

However, the major problem was the civilian staff associated with retaining the amount of storage space needed for the inventory. Planners had to remember that FAIR VALUE was not an exercise in improving the efficiency with which the storage cube was managed throughout the RAOC, but an exercise in saving money by reducing civilian staff levels and then to manage as best as possible with what was left, including an increasing workload. In 1975, the storage needed in the Central Ordnance depots was 1.175 million cubic feet. The inventory had been growing by an average of 14,000 stock items per year over the preceding decade as equipment varieties and their complexity increased. This growth was expected to accelerate both in range and in depth at a forecast rate of 30,000 items per year over the coming decade. Furthermore, the introduction of direct supply to BAOR over the full range of the inventory would inevitably increase the depth of stock holdings. Consequently, the estimate was made that by 1980 an increase in storage requirement to 1.4 million cubic metres would arise. This was only marginally less than the combined capacity of the three depots at Bicester, Chilwell and Donnington. However, to make the savings needed in numbers, the only way of achieving it was to remove the staff overheads in one depot, regardless of the impact on the predicted storage liability. One of them had to go – the question was which one? The loss of which one would cause the least damage to the supply system?

The key lay once more in modern, high-rise storage solutions. It was a solution that would require investment, but the balance of advantage would go with the depots most easily able to adapt their structures to the new methods. Without the necessary investment all three CODs would have had to remain open and it would have been impossible to realize the savings demanded.

The low roofed structure of the Chilwell buildings meant that the only combination of two depots that would meet the target was CODs Bicester and Donnington. The proposal was to modernize them and to transfer the Chilwell range of fast moving stocks to Donnington. Bicester would take the rest, and Chilwell would close. The savings would net out at 426 out of the 500 that had been assessed as attainable from the Base Organization. The balance could be found, it was adduced, in the margins of a range of staff adjustments. By October 1975 the Army Board had approved the proposals in principle, allowing them to be discussed with other government departments and the trade unions.

It was not a decision that was universally welcomed. Intensive lobbying took place to switch it and to lose Bicester with its dispersed nature making it hard and expensive to manage and its rural location making staff recruiting difficult. It was a battle that would last to 1978, but the financial case was proven sound, as was the economic logic. After scrutiny at the highest level, which included Parliament, it was agreed, and between 1977 and 1981 Brigadier John Macdonald and then Brigadier Gerry Berragan, the commandants of Chilwell during that period, were left with the unenviable task of keeping the depot closure programme in hand while continuing to support an Army with operational commitments. It says much for them, and for the workforce at Chilwell, that they, and Chilwell, succeeded.

In Singapore the end of 1975 saw the peak of activity in disposing of depot stocks from Ordnance Services Singapore. Most of the ammunition went either to the UK or Hong Kong in a series of moves so successful that they permitted the early handover of the Attap Valley Ammunition Depot to the SAF. Between November 1975 and March 1976 the RFA *Sir Galahad* made five journeys to Hong Kong taking with it stores and vehicles not just from depot stocks, but also from unit holdings. The easy and most economic solution to barracks stores was to leave them in the 1,943 married quarters and include them in the sale to the Singaporean authorities.

The impact of the defence review in Cyprus was to consolidate the disparate parts of the Island's garrison wherever this made sense. It saw the disappearance of HQ NEARELF, and the amalgamation, with a consequent reduction in numbers, of the RAOC staffs of the HQ and the local garrison. HQ RAOC Cyprus was created and the plan was that all the RAOC units would be consolidated into RAF Akrotri in the western SBA. The plan did not survive reality as the custom built supply depot could not be replicated and so had to stay where it was in Dhekelia. However, COMPO and dried goods were found homes to the east thereby pacing the supply depot's stocks in three different locations: Dhekalia, Akrotiri and Limassol. There was also the huge task of relocating stores between the two SBAs, which consumed a great deal of effort, to say nothing of the skills issue, since almost all the civilian labour from the west refused to move to the east; and this included the skilled artisans from the RSD in the western SBA. To obviate the difficulties would cause a repair and refurbishment facility to be retained in the Western SBA. Throughout all this the RAOC in the Cyprus garrison continued to provide support to the UN Force on the island.

The final phase of the rebuilding project at Deepcut, the construction of the new Headquarters Mess, was completed towards the end of 1975. The formal opening took place on 28 November and was performed by the QMG, General Sir William Jackson, who was at that time also a Colonel Commandant of the RAOC.

A major feature of life for the RAOC in Germany was Exercise SNOW QUEEN, an adventure training exercise in Bavaria where soldiers learned to ski, both alpine and langlauf. In January 1976 Private Goodhall of 12 OFP arrived at the RAOC skiing hut at Ofterschwang to find himself the 1,000th soldier to have attended ski training since the hut was opened three years earlier by Lieutenant Colonel David Medd, the then chairman of RAOC skiing. The hut was well equipped with skis and boots and the instructors were all properly qualified products of Army Ski Instructors Courses. The cost was £27 (£120), but by the time messing and accommodation was recovered for the allegedly unsatisfactory living conditions in the Corps' hut this reduced to £15 (£67). The effect of this exercise on the many young men and women who passed through it was to strengthen characters, build fitness and face challenges that for many were new and stimulating. And all for £67 at 2005 prices.

That said, it was a price that might have to rise since 1976 was the year in which inflation reached 26 per cent, which was to present yet further problems to the Treasury in trying to balance the national books. Inevitably this would mean further raids on defence in pursuit of yet more savings and no relief from the constant demands to achieve more with less,

The same year also saw the second erosion of the Nye reorganization with the transfer of DCT to DOS. This placed a general staff responsibility under the guiding hand of the DOS as DCT was involved in all aspects of clothing research as well as primary provision for the Army's range of clothing. It was a fascinating, but often thankless, task as just about every soldier in the army, and at every rank, had their own views on dress and on clothing.

In March 1976 CAD Bramley, whose future existence was in some doubt, was invited to exercise its right to march through Basingstoke with bayonets fixed, colours flying and bands playing. This was in recognition of the granting of the Freedom of the Town some two years earlier. The mayor of Basingstoke asked the mayor of his French twin town, on a visit that week, to take the salute – which he duly did. The picture shows Lieutenant Colonel Cliff Jeffries commanding the parade and leading

Bramley marches past.

the march past. Of special interest, however, is Conductor Eldred, on the right of the picture, as befitted his appointment taking the place of a subaltern officer on parade complete with officers' accoutrements.

It was in 1976 that the groundwork began to upgrade System Two at the CICP and Stores System Three became a gleam in the eye if the IT world. It was essentially a technology update and as such a management opportunity was missed to review and revise the forecasting and procurement functions which had been found wanting with System Two,

Following the trials of 1975 Brigadier Dennison's proposals for the restructuring of Ordnance support to 1 (Br) Corps were largely accepted. The re-structuring was to be done in two phases, the first during 1976 and 1977, and the second during 1978 and 1979. During re-structuring the great problem facing the RAOC would be the usual one of maintaining an acceptable level of service to units while RAOC

Staff Sergeant McGrattan with a group of Vehicle Specialists, showing some of the extraordinary diversity of vehicles these remarkable men were able to handle and manage.

units and units in their dependency were undergoing change, and still maintaining a mobilization capability and meeting a commitment to provide personnel on roulement for service in Northern Ireland and UNFICYP. At the end of the re-structuring, the RAOC in 1 (Br) Corps would be required to maintain the corps at the same level of service but with nearly one fifth less manpower. In the past there had been two OFPs per division: in future there would be one, and it would be called an ADOC.

The first phase commenced almost at once. The outcome was that peacetime functions of HQs RAOC Corps Troops East and Corps Troops West would be taken over by the divisional CRAOCs, and subsequently the two static HQs would be disbanded. CRAOC Corps Troops (Central) was to remain, but he became CRAOC Corps Troops with a deployable operational role. The personnel for the Bath Sections were removed from the establishments of OFPs, but the OFPs retained the commitment to provide a bath service on exercises and in war. The manpower in war was to be provided on a 'shadow' basis from RAOC units in the base; in peace it was an additional burden that would have to be shouldered. Combat Supplies platoons were removed from Brigade Transport Squadrons, and disbanded. They too were to be provided on a 'shadow' basis for operations and some exercises in like manner to the bath sections. It was purely an exercise in money saving. Whilst one might not get too over exited about the rather tenuous means by which a bath might be provided, to denude the division in peace the means of providing control and provision of its food fuel and ammunition was an act which might politely be described as cynical, although other, more powerful, expressions of disbelief might also be worthy of consideration.

On 29 March 1976 the rear party of Ordnance Services Singapore, commanded by Captain F Pickett, left the island and with it went 130 years of association with Singapore. The last RAOC commander in Singapore had been Lieutenant Colonel Colin Rogers.

On 7 April 1976 a major advance in the re-supply of combat fuels in Germany took place with the opening of a new bulk-refuelling depot at Warendorf. Its construction had been made possible by the extension of NATO's Central European Pipeline System into the rear area of 1 (Br) Corps. It allowed the replacement of the old, inefficient, manpower-intensive business of supplying fuel in jerry cans and managing packed stocks in large, and hazardous, dumps throughout Germany although a small packed reserve stock of fuel had still to be retained, for flexibility, and to allow for temporary breakdown at any point in the bulk system. The new system provided for bulk stocks of petroleum, diesel and aviation fuel to be moved forward from Warendorf and other depots and emergency offtake points on the CEPS by RCT road tankers to composite maintenance groups and replenishment parks, where reserve stocks would be built up in fabric tanks, and on to XPs and second line distribution points, where the bulk would be cross-pumped into first line 'pod' vehicles, or in the case of the Army Air Corps into RAF pattern 1,000 gallon refueller vehicles. The establishment and operation of the various fabric tank complexes in the CMGs, RPs, and the RCZ was an RAOC responsibility which fell, predominantly, on RAOC TAVR units

In the second phase of BAOR reorganization it was planned to follow the 'Dennison' model, with selected brigade OFPs, and stores sections attached to field workshops forming into divisional Ordnance companies, with the remaining OFPs and stores sections being disbanded. A slightly smaller Ordnance company would be provided to support the independent 5 Field Force. The 1 (Br) Corps Troops OFP was to be reformed as 1 (Br) Corps Troops Ordnance Company, whilst 7 GM Company would be disbanded and the stores sections attached to various regimental workshops would be reorganized to match the new order of battle.

In the event this second phase of reorganization took place very much sooner and the first to convert was 2nd Armoured Division in September 1976. Lieutenant Colonel Bill Sefton oversaw the creation of Major John Eddison's 2 ADOC, formed from 12 OFP and elements of the stores sections from 6 and 12 Field Workshops REME. Major David Watt's 4 OFP reformed as the 5 Field Force Ordnance Company.

In August there was a major fire at 3 BAPD. The fire started in the early afternoon of a Sunday, on the Bruggen-Swalmen road and, with winds gusting to fifteen knots, it crossed the depot perimeter within twenty minutes. In a further twenty minutes it had reached the traverses of the RAF storage site where only heroic fire fighting by depot military staff and the German fire service stopped it reaching the ammunition. But the wind was too high for the fire to be brought under control and jumping the RAF storage site and igniting the wood beyond, it burned its way across the depot making its exit on the western perimeter into more woodland. During the Sunday night and on into Monday sparks carried on the wind caused many fires in other parts of the depot and there was real concern for the safety of the ammunition stocks. By Monday evening the conflagration was at last brought under control and the danger of calamitous explosion had been averted. That said there was to be a further ten days work by Army and German fire services damping down small outbreaks that continued to flare from time to time.

Some 500 acres of woodland were lost, of which 270 lay within the depot perimeter. About 150 German fire appliances from all over North Rhine Westphalia were deployed into the depot area and almost 2,000 people were eventually engaged in fighting the fire. Throughout it all luck was with 3 BAPD. No one was hurt and no ammunition was lost.

The Depot and Training Battalion, comprising an HQ, an Employment Wing, A Company for Training, B Company the administration of permanent staff and students on employment training, and C Company for the administration of all WRAC personnel, had been in existence in that form since the early seventies. By 1976, however, it was considered unsuitable and the regimental depot was re-formed as a separate unit. The result was an RAOC Training Centre comprising the Regimental Depot, a Training Battalion, the Apprentices College, the School of Ordnance and CVHQ. This was also the time at which all 'B' vehicle drivers' training ceased at Deepcut as the RCT took over Army-wide responsibility for the task. It was to be centred at the Army School of Motor Transport at Leconfield near Hull. There was the usual tribal weeping and gnashing of teeth as this happened, but the reality was the RCT was the Army's corps of drivers and it made perfect sense for them to take on the role. What made far less sense was that the ASMT was woefully under-resourced for the task and the result was a huge waiting list for courses. The outcome was that soldiers were kept hanging around at Blackdown for months awaiting their driving course before they could be posted out to units to the intense frustration of the soldiers themselves, the staff at Deepcut and the units who were impatiently awaiting their arrival.

It was in November 1976 that the formal announcement was made of the decision taken some time previously that CAD Bramley was to close and to do so in less than two years by September 1978. The School of Ammunition, of course, had moved two years earlier, presaging the eventual closure of the depot itself. It was also the month in which, as part of the reorganization that produced the LE(A), CSDW and the ADP Wing of the CICP were brought together to form the Directorate of Supply Computer Services, with Brigadier Laurie Lawrence as its first director.

Following acceptance of the Somerville Report in 1975, the LE(A) opened for business on 7 April 1977 on a site recently vacated by the RAF at Andover in Hampshire. It amalgamated into one establishment the Director of Equipment Management (Army), HQ Transport Officer in Chief (Army), HQ DOS and HQ DEME. HQ Base Organization would be incorporated into HQ DOS once the Commander's tour of duty ended and the same was true for HQ REME Support Group. The RAOC was now reduced to one tied major general's appointment, that of DOS, as were the other two logistic corps with their Head of Corps.

As part of the reorganization the heads of corps were re-titled Directors General, hence DGOS, placing them on a par with their colleagues in the other two Services. A fourth major general at Andover held the post of Chief of Staff of the Logistic Executive with the task of coordinating the work of the Directors General and developing the work of the Logistic Executive. It was a bold attempt to provide an overarching headquarters within the Q area aimed at using the full capability of the three logistics corps in support of the Army and removing the tribalism of cap badges. It was an attempt to develop a QMG solution rather than relying on each of the Corps producing its own solution to meet its own particular needs.

One crucial decision was that the post and role of the DQMG set up over ten years earlier under the Nye reorganization was to go and the equipment management responsibilities were to go to the DGs. Quite where each would sit lay with the level of involvement in the equipment and the RAOC took responsibility, for example, for petroleum equipment and ammunition as well as clothing and textiles, all or which lay firmly within its bailiwick. But there were problems with the 'less obvious' elements of the distribution. In the end DGTM took over responsibility for those equipments that 'puffed or floated'; DGEME assumed the management of those equipments subject to, or closely connected with, base repair during their life cycles; and DGOS assumed responsibility for the rest. It was a split based more around giving each a slice of the cake rather than a logical appraisal of the Army's need or the delivery of the best possible service to the customer. Quite what a corps whose function was

During all this turmoil Captain M T King of Ord 2, one of the departments moving to Andover, decided to take advantage of the relative peace and quiet offered by the joint British and Royal Nepalese Army 1976 expedition and took himself off to climb Everest with some friends.

transport and movements had to do with equipment management in any form remains a mystery until its is viewed from the perspective of fair shares for all and the internecine strife that bedevilled much of the logistic restructuring that had taken place over the lifetime of logistics in the Army. However, whatever structural issues there might have been, the bonus lay in the fact that the equipment manager had full responsibility for the equipment under his care and could make and implement decisions without first having to obtain a Q staff gloss.

So it was that the changes of 1976 and 1977 returned to the RAOC control of practically all the responsibilities which had been taken away in the Nye reorganization and added new ones, and the equipment management system set up in 1964 was virtually dead, although vestiges of it remained within branches of the Logistic Secretariat under the COSLOG. Within the LE(A) the DGOS became responsible to the QMG in two capacities, as a Q Staff Director over the range of materiel allocated to RAOC, and as the Director of the RAOC. Major General Mike Callan, who had succeeded Major General Norman Speller as DOS in October 1976, assumed the new title of DGOS in September 1977. The organization of his headquarters within the LE(A) at the outset essentially consisted of:

Major General Mike Callan.

> A Deputy Director General who was the principal staff officer looking after staff duties, organization, training, and regimental matters. He also had responsibly for a number of things that did not sit easily in the other directorates being formed, such as Food, Fuel, Laundry and Bath.
>
> The Directorate of Supply Management, managing the stores inventory and with the main equipment management responsibilities of the RAOC under its hand. These included B vehicles and a wide range of smaller more individual equipments.
>
> The Directorate of Supply Computer Services, which drew together under one head every aspect for the policy on and provision of computers for the RAOC.
>
> The Directorate of Land Service Ammunition, formed from CILSA but also drawing in the ammunition equipment management responsibilities that had previously lain with a Q Staff department known as Equipment Management 3. At the same time he took under his wing the ammunition provision wing at CICP, thereby assuming technical responsibility for it.
>
> The Directorate of Base Depots formed up in January 1978 from the former Base Organization, consequent upon the retirement of the Commander.

Over quite a short time the headquarters of these directorates moved into Andover, although there were outstations elsewhere in the UK base except, that is, DLSA, which, due to accommodation shortages at Andover, remained in Didcot.

In the midst of all the reorganization a small event may have passed unnoticed when, on 5 June, Colonel Ted Shepherd left CAD Bramley as its last commandant in the rank of colonel, the last in a long line stretching back to the First World War, and left it in the capable hands of Lieutenant Colonel John Elliot who would oversee the rundown and closure. It would be an unhappy task for anyone. Activity was also quite intense at Bicester, where in addition to its role with the CICP changes were always under way to the storage estate pursuant to the many reorganizations that were taking place. In 1977, for example, a commitment to store quantities of composite ration packs on behalf of the RN Victualling Department was finally ended having been undertaken in 1970. There was also a heavy engagement in a number of emergencies. In 1976, following an earthquake disaster in Turkey, it made a massive issue of tentage to house homeless, as part of the British Government's aid programme.

The depot was also honoured around this time with the grant by the town of Bicester, on 15 July 1977, of the Town Charter in recognition of the close association between the town and the COD. In the presence of the Lord Lieutenant of Oxfordshire, and before a parade comprising four guards and a scroll party commanded by Lieutenant Colonel R B Bowden, the town mayor of Bicester, Councillor John Hollis, himself a civilian officer of the COD, presented the scroll conveying the honour. The Representative Colonel Commandant, Major General A R Cornock, received it on behalf of the depot.

Major General A R Cornock

At the same time there was timely recognition of the work undertaken by 321 EOD Unit in Northern Ireland with the award of the Wilkinson Sword of Peace. It was entirely appropriate, given the huge amount of work it had undertaken and the extent to which lives and property had been saved, to say nothing of its own casualties in achieving all this. It should be remembered that this was not an entirely RAOC affair, but involved soldiers from many regiments and corps. There was the infantry that provided the escorts, from a wide range of regiments, the RCT who drove the teams and the Royal Signals who manned the equipment that protected against radio controlled IEDS. The citation said it all:

Eight years ago, 321 EOD Unit RAOC was established in Northern Ireland to counter the terrorist bombing campaign. Its role is of a non-offensive protective nature, in that its actions are aimed solely at preventing loss of life and property. The unit is manned by Ammunition Technical Officers and Ammunition Technicians of the Royal Army Ordnance Corps with a supporting staff of drivers, storemen, signallers and escorts, all on emergency four-month tours from units in UK and BAOR. The Unit has become well known and has received considerable publicity. It is self evident that the operations of the unit have saved human life, and there is no doubt that they have both prevented damage to a vast amount of property and helped to prevent terrorists achieving their aim of totally disrupting the economy and society of Northern Ireland.

Since 1969 to date the unit has dealt with some 24,500 calls of which some 9,500 were to actual terrorist bombs—adding up to 296,000 pounds of explosives. A statistician has estimated that every pound of explosives detonated by terrorists in Northern Ireland causes £1,000 worth of damage. Using this figure it can be estimated that the Unit has prevented about £100 million worth of damage to property in Northern Ireland since 1969. There is no doubt that this saving of property has prevented untold misery in the form of lost homes and loss of places of work. In the words of a former Chief Constable of the RUC it has done much to promote goodwill and friendly relations between the community at large and the Security Forces. It is an indisputable fact that the actions of the EOD operators which can be seen by everyone to be totally peaceful in intent and to have no sectarian bias whatsoever, have created a bond between them and the community.

The next leg of the restructuring was in 3rd Division in September 1977. It moved its headquarters to Soest in Germany to provide the basis of the new 3rd Armoured Division HQ. Lieutenant Colonel David Cornwell moved from the old to the new as CRAOC of the new division. Because the division's brigades were retained in the UK for restructuring as field forces, which required Ordnance companies, 3 ADOC was raised in BAOR in December, from elements of 6 OFP and the stores section of 5 Field Workshops. It was located at Soest, commanded by Major Derek Skinner.

The disbandment of 36 Heavy AD Regiment in 1977 saw the consequent demise of 7 GM Company. The only visible sign of its existence remained in the drill Thunderbird II missiles left gracing the entrances to both 154 FAD and the Army School of Ammunition.

It was at the end of the year, in November, amidst all its other tasks, the RAOC was beset along with the rest of the Army, by Operation BURBERRY, to provide emergency cover across the country during the civilian fire services strike. To accomplish this, Green Goddess fire appliances, being held for a major emergency such as general war, were issued from Home Office depots.

The load was particularly heavily felt by the Army Fire Service, from the Chief Fire Adviser on the staff of the Chief Ordnance Officer at HQ UKLF through to the Fire Advisers of Ordnance Branches at Districts. RAOC static units were called on to provide troops to man some of the fire fighting teams, and in certain cases to control fire fighting activities in defined areas. For example, COD Donnington provided crews to man two Green Goddesses covering a part of Shropshire, whilst HQ COD Bicester controlled fire fighting in a large area of the south Midlands. The Commandant of CAD Kineton, Colonel Keith Berresford was made the military commander for Warwickshire and, for the operation, took command of soldiers from 29 Commando Regiment RA, the HQ and Signal Squadron from 3 Commando Brigade, and with RAOC and RPC soldiers from Kineton itself. By the end of the three-month strike over 407 incidents had been dealt with by the seven Green Goddesses based at Kineton.

Captain Peter Foxton was, at the time, the adjutant at Deepcut. He recalled:

> Over the Christmas period the Training Battalion and Depot had nine fire fighting companies deployed, from Cardiff in the west to Chatham in the east. One was even found by the Corps' Band.

It was about then, at the turn of the year, that the full impact of what was to come hit home at CAD Bramley. On 6 January the redundancy notices were issued to the remaining civilian staff, a large number of whom had worked there for many years and loyally so. The point was yet further made on 7 January when the first steps were undertaken to disassemble St Barbara's Church, a focus for worship in the depot for fifty-two years. It had originally come from the clothing depot at Pimlico, and its next home was to be Didcot; with the exception of the stained glass window and the oak panelling from the sanctuary with its list of names of those killed while undertaking EOD duties. These went to Bramley church where their presence would be a reminder of the part the depot had played in village life for so many years.

Back in Germany the re-structuring of 1st Division, with Lieutenant Colonel Mike Owen as CRAOC, had begun in December 1977 with 11 OFP providing the main element in April 1978 of the new l ADOC. It was located at Soltau, commanded by Major David Harris. In an emotional moment 7 OFP, which had been the last RAOC unit to wear the red jerboa, the Desert Rat insignia of 7 Armoured Brigade, had disbanded earlier. The old Ironside Barracks at Scheuen, near Celle, a home of the RAOC and of the two OFPs for many years, was handed back to the Germans for use by an adjoining Bundeswehr armoured battalion.

The restructuring of 4th Armoured Division followed almost at once, at the beginning 1978 supervised by the CRAOC, Lieutenant Colonel Mike Robinson. The ADOC, commanded by Major Ted Champion, was formed at Detmold on 21 January 1978 from elements of 20 OFP and the Stores Section of 4 Field Workshops. The structure now in place in 1 (Br) Corps mirrored that developed on operations for the divisions of 21st Army Group in 1945, after a number of gestations. It is perhaps worthy of note that events do tend to come round time and again.

Another part of the restructuring plan for Germany had seen the end of HQs RAOC Corps Troops (East) and (West) by the end of 1977. The responsibilities they had for static units and administrative functions should have been taken over by the divisional CRAOCs, but it had proved to be optimistic for it was, inevitably, the RAOC static organization, especially barrack services, that was most heavily committed in the many moves and permutations involved in the overall re-structuring plan for 1 (Br) Corps. Consequently, HQ Corps Troops (West) was retained until April 1978, and HQ Corps Troops (East) until the following year. From 1979, the renamed HQ RAOC Corps Troops (Central) reverted to its old pre-McLeod title of HQ RAOC Corps Troops, and took command of 1 Corps Troops Ordnance Company, the former 1 (Corps Troops) OFP, now re-designated to match the divisional Ordnance companies, but without a workshop stores platoon. It was commanded by Major Graham Cowell and located at Gutersloh. The new CRAOC also took command of the Corps stores company, basically unchanged, and remaining at Richmond Barracks, Bielefeld; the Corps vehicle company, with slightly increased manpower for its essential peacetime role, to be based at Oldenburg; and the supply depot, Bielefeld, together with the barrack stores at Bielefeld and Sennelager. The Combat Supplies Battalion escaped any surgery since the unit had full-sized tasks in operating combat supplies depots within the 1 (Br) Corps area in peace and in its war role already depended to a great extent on reinforcement by regular shadow or T&AVR units.

In the UK the changes were no less draconian. In Phase 1, planned for 1976/77, it was proposed to remove bath sections and combat supplies platoons from OFPs and to disband them; to disband the 3rd Division Airhead Ordnance Company, with its role to be undertaken by a bulk transit platoon which was to be created as part of 10 Ordnance Support Battalion; and to disband 16 Parachute Heavy Drop Company. In Phase 2 the OFPs of both 19 and 24 Brigades and the Ordnance Squadron of the Parachute Logistic Regiment would be disbanded, and Ordnance Companies formed for the three field forces being set up as an integral part of the new UK land forces structure.

When 3rd Division disbanded, the brigades in UK were reformed as 6, 7 and 8 Field Forces, with a restructured 16 Parachute Brigade becoming 6 Field Force and remaining at Aldershot. The Ordnance Company for 6 Field Force was created using manpower made available by the disbandment of 5 Airportable OFP, the Ordnance Squadron of the Parachute Logistic Regiment, and of 16 Para Heavy Drop Company. By the autumn of 1978 the first OC, Major Dan Putt, was pretty much at full complement and had almost one third of his manpower in Northern Ireland, with C Squadron the Life Guards, operating as infantry.

The wreckage that was the tearing apart of an airborne logistic role emanated from the Chiefs of Staff decision that the Army's parachute capability should be reduced to one battalion group, with no dedicated logistic support. But the logistic problems would not go away with the reorganizing zeal of the staff. There remained, for example, the old problem of responsibility for the storage, rigging and recovery of medium stressed platforms, for which there would be a small residual commitment. HQ UKLF carried out a study to see if the role could be undertaken by an existing unit, inevitably without any increase in manpower. Not surprisingly there was no RAOC unit that could take on an additional role of this sort and consequently it went to 47 Air Dispatch Squadron RCT.

16 Parachute Heavy Drop Company held its final parade at Hullavington on 1 September 1978 after a short but eventful existence. It was followed shortly afterwards by the Parachute Logistic Regiment at Aldershot on 10 December 1976. Major General Anthony Farrar-Hockley DSO MBE MC, who had been the brigade commander when the regiment formed in the late sixties, took the salute. It had been in existence for less than ten years, but its passing was mourned by many.

19 Brigade was restructured as 7 Field Force, with a BAOR role. For its Ordnance support 7 Field Force Ordnance Company was formed from 19 OFP and 8 Field Workshops Stores Section in April 1978, with Major Bill Manuel its first OC. 5 Brigade reformed as 8 Field Force, but as its role was home defence as the Commander-in-Chief's reserve, it was only felt necessary for it to have a

The farewell parade of 16 Parachute Logistic Regiment.

Territiorial Army Ordnance Company. There was no continuing role for 24 Brigade OFP, with its history of extensive service in numerous theatres and it ceased all operational commitments on 1 July 1976, performing its final act as one of eight detachments in the Brigade disbandment parade on 8 July. The OFP detachment comprised thirty-four officers and soldiers led by the Officer Commanding, Major Kerry Curtis, and the Chief of the General Staff, General Sir Peter Hunt, took the parade. The Commander in Chief UKLF sent a message:

> During the thirty-six years which you and your predecessors have been with 24 Infantry and Airportable Brigade you have had a proud record of active and arduous service ranging from the War itself, through such varied and exciting theatres as Kenya, Aden, Radfan and more recently Northern Ireland.
>
> It is a record of which to be proud.

421 EOD Unit on parachute training.

In 10 Ordnance Support Battalion, 48 Company's role, as one of the regular companies, in support of the ACE Mobile Force remained unchanged throughout the seventies, and the company was not therefore affected by the defence review. However, 47 Company's role of providing third line support for the UK Mobile Force, now down from a division to one field force at about the size of a pre-review brigade, was much reduced, and both the company and the battalion HQ took a significant share of the military manpower cuts

The value of the parachute capability built into 421 EOD Unit was proven when on 23 May 1978 there was a bomb incident at sea reminiscent of the mid-Atlantic *QE II* incident of the early seventies. The ship involved was the cruise liner *Oriana*, and 421 EOD Unit's Parachute Section flew out to the ship, but did not parachute as by the time they arrived overhead the ship had been thoroughly searched without any device being found. Later that year a call to a North Sea oil rig resulted in personnel and equipment from 1 AIDU being deployed in support of an RN EOD team which had been detailed to deal with the incident.

On 16 May 1978 Her Majesty the Queen visited the RAOC, basing the event around Bicester. It was a very special year for the RAOC, being the diamond jubilee of the Corps' foundation in 1918. Similarly, it was the twenty-fifth anniversary of Her Majesty agreeing to become the RAOC's Colonel-

in-Chief following the death of her father and her own accession to the throne. One of the high points of her visit was to name an Army railway engine 'Conductor', thereby reinforcing, yet again, the high importance attached by the warrant officers of the RAOC, to say nothing of the officers, to having this appointment as part of the fabric of the Corps.

On 30 June 1978 CAD Bramley closed its gates. However, it had been given a new lease of life as the result of a late decision by the Americans to use it as a storage facility for some of the increases they were planning in holdings of PUEs and ammunition for US

Conductor Bradley escorts the Queen...

reinforcements for the central front in Europe. It also meant continued employment for some of the civilian staff as well as requiring a small residual military presence. However, as a depot its contribution to the Corps' activities was past. In its day it had been a major part of the ammunition world, but perhaps an indication of its lessening role was that, when the decision was taken to close

it, the tonnage of ammunition in storage was less than that involved in just one 25-pounder shell refuzing programme during the Second World War.

The middle of 1978 saw the beginning of troubles in the Lebanon that would prevail in that unhappy country until a ceasefire could be arrange in 1990. The UN put a force into the south of the country to try and help restore some semblance of order. The logistic support for the 7,000-man UNIFIL was to come from Cyprus. It was a huge workload, certainly in the early stages since it was, as it remains, traditional for a number of nations to deploy their contribution to a force with virtually nothing, secure in the knowledge that the UN would provide. The load for this inevitably fell on Ordnance Services Cyprus, working to the

...and watches as she 'christens' the engine 'Conductor'

French Logistic Battalion that provided the close logistic support for the UN force. It was fortunate that Sergeant M Spicer of Ordnance Services Cyprus was a fluent French speaker. Once again rations proved to be the most complex issue, with some twenty different scales having to be catered for.

In October 1978 an increase of 4,000 in the planned manpower establishment of the Army was announced. The need for this increase stemmed from a number of factors. First, it had become clear that the reductions in unit establishments that were implemented as part of the restructuring of the Army had some unanticipated adverse effects. Experience of restructured establishments had shown that units had some difficulty in meeting all the demands made of them in peacetime. The small additions to unit establishments that were announced were intended to improve significantly standards of training and readiness. Secondly, a number of enhancements in capability, which were occurring as new equipment entered service, called for additional personnel, including some in support of the other two Services, for example, in providing an artillery battery for Commando Forces. Thirdly, a number of soldiers would have to be deployed to BAOR to take on operational tasks hitherto carried out by some of the armed members of the Mixed Service Organization, a uniformed, civilian force raised after the Second World War, for whom suitable replacements were no longer available as they retired. Finally, a composite unit of battalion size was to be formed in BAOR in order to release an infantry battalion for deployment to the United Kingdom, thus increasing the pool of units available to undertake emergency tours in Northern Ireland and elsewhere.

One of the other outcomes of the defence review of 1975 was the acceptance that a stock of vehicles both at Mönchengladbach and at Antwerp could no longer be justified and, on 31 December 1978, the Vehicle Sub Depot at Mönchengladbach closed its gates, prior to formal disbandment on 31 March 1979. Thus it was that 17 BVD, a unit that had landed across GOLD Beach at Normandy soon after D-Day in 1944, that had advanced to Hamburg by August 1945 and that had, in peace, gone through a number of changes of location and name (17 Vehicle Company, 17 Vehicle Battalion, 17 Reserve Vehicle Depot, 17 Base Vehicle Depot) and had occupied Ayrshire barracks in Mönchengladbach for just over thirty years, was no more. The handover ceremony to the incoming custodian unit was brief and simple, but as the breeze fluttered through the trees was there perhaps the sound of tortured water as if a landing craft were beating ashore against a turbulent sea while under fire? And, in the autumn sunshine, the leaves were gold.

The result of all this was another name change and 15 Composite Ordnance Depot became 15th Ordnance Group. In so doing it took command of the ICP at Viersen, the Ordnance Depot at Viersen, the Forward Stores Depot at Dulmen and, later, 89 Supply Depot. After a year the Forward Vehicle Depot at Recklinghausen joined the group and a short time after that the Viersen units became Ordnance Services Viersen.

With the retirement of the last commander so the existence of Base Organization came to an end, to be succeeded by the Directorate of Base Depots embedded in the LE(A) at Andover. HQ CVD RAOC (UK) had previously moved from Chilwell to Ashchurch with the plan having been for it to move eventually into HQ Base Organization, but the latter's demise precluded that. Instead it remained where it was, eventually to become CVD Ashchurch in 1980.

On 1 May 1979, after a period of considerable restructuring, following on from FAIR VALUE, COD Bicester began to receive stocks on transfer from Chilwell. It involved the move of some 32,000 tons of stores. It was finished by November, and in the

Robbie Robinson in April 1989 with the Army Squash Trophy that he won more times than probably he could count.

meantime Donnington began in the August to receive its consignments, with the transfer having been delayed because Building B1, that was going to take to bulk of the transferred stocks, was not completed on time.

In the general election of April 1979 Margaret Thatcher was swept to power as the country's first woman Prime Minister. The impact on the morale of the Armed Forces was instantaneous. Conscious of the state they were in after a series of paltry pay reviews and faced with the prospect of a staged pay increment that year she instantly made up the annual pay rise to a single payment to be made at once and a subsequent review of Service pay put it onto a much more equable footing.

George Jones :

> I was posted after my initial training in 1941 to Donnington where I worked in Shed 4B...in 1949 I joined a TA RAOC Stores Section...my last duty in 1979 before leaving the TA was to return six 40-mm AA guns to Donnington, to Shed 4B. So there I was ending my Army career in the place I had started it in 1941. I related this to the young female clerk and she seemed quite bewildered – who could blame her?

Proof, if proof were needed, that members of the RAOC made the time to be a part of the community in which they lived, was the award in 1979 of the Wilkinson Sword of Peace to Ordnance Services Hong Kong, the second time in two years it had been won by an RAOC unit. It was granted for the contribution made to bettering the lives of poor people in Hong Kong. It was done by sending what amounted to patrols out into isolated villages, undertaking adventure training with locals, helping disabled children, assisting with local projects and raising impressive sums of money for charity.

3 BAPD, which since 1965 had consisted of both the Ammunition Depot at Bracht and the Petroleum Depot at Arsbeck, lost its petroleum role following the opening of the new Warendorf Petroleum Depot in April 1976 and the introduction of bulk re-fuelling to units of 1 (Br) Corps. It reverted to its old title, 3 Base Ammunition Depot, on 1 April 1979.

1979 was a year that brought two waves of letter bombs in Britain. In the first, in June, fifteen identical devices bearing Northern Ireland stamps were discovered. Fourteen of them functioned or were neutralized in sorting offices in Birmingham whilst the fifteenth injured a postman in Berkshire. The second wave involved a series of explosives devices posted in Belgium just before Christmas, with nine being encountered, of which two exploded and seven were neutralized. December also witnessed the start of an incendiary bomb campaign in North Wales against holiday homes belonging to English owners. All this was in addition to its inspectorate and stray ammunition workload – life in 1 AIDU was far from dull.

Trouble had been a feature of life in Rhodesia since 1965, involving a civil war between the white-dominated colonial government and several African guerrilla movements, principal among them being ZAPU and ZANLA. The situation was eventually resolved at talks in London in 1979, chaired by the Foreign Secretary, Lord Carrington. The result was a truce and an agreement to grant independence to Rhodesia subject to early elections on a one man, one vote basis. To achieve this it was first necessary to effect a ceasefire in order to conduct proper elections. The British Government agreed that Sir Christopher Soames would be sent to Rhodesia to oversee those processes, and in addition to his largely civilian staff a small military force was provided on what became known as Operation AGILA.

The operation was mounted to supervise the ceasefire and to control the integration of some 22,000 guerrillas, who had mostly been based outside Rhodesia, back into the country. As part of the AGILA Force a detachment from 10 Ordnance Support Battalion formed up at South Cerney at the end of November 1979, and left for Rhodesia a week before Christmas. The party of twenty-three, under the command of Major R N Atkins, who also had the role of Force Ordnance Officer, was located at the country's capital, Salisbury. Almost immediately after their arrival stores began to pour in, but even so not quickly enough as the unit found itself having to make issues before all stocks were on the ground. Some hangar space allotted on arrival soon proved inadequate, resulting in the erection of six marquees for use as storehouses. Within a week some 1,260 British personnel and 350,000lb of freight had arrived and approximately 500 men had been kitted up and deployed to the sixteen assembly places and twenty-three RVs to which it had been agreed that members of the Patriotic Front would report.

There was a Local Resources Section under Captain Peter Ball, and it had a difficult time in the initial stages since they were trying to make purchases at the time when all businesses were closing down for the Christmas and New Year holiday periods. Nonetheless, they managed to spend over £1,000,000 (£3,000,000) in the first month. A particular surprise came just as the shops were closing for the New Year break, when the Force Ordnance Officer found that he had been made responsible for feeding the 20,000 Patriotic Front personnel in the sixteen assembly places. Armed with a ration scale, and an intelligence summary of the numbers expected to be moving into each assembly place, he made plans for the procurement and distribution of food. Unfortunately the intelligence assessment turned out, as was so often the case, to be wrong, and by quite some margin. One assembly place to which 250 rations had been sent saw just five

Captain Peter Ball with Corporal Steve Parsons.

members of the Patriotic Front, while another, to which 2,500 rations had gone, took in nearly 6,000.

In addition to the detachment from 10 Ordnance Support Battalion, there were also in Rhodesia, for Operation AGILA, fifteen staff clerks operating in Government House and at HQ of the Ceasefire Monitoring Group, and a NAAFI/EFI detachment of 1 Officer and two NCOs, hastily embodied from NAAFI for the operation. By March 1980 Operation AGILA had been successfully completed, and along with other contingents the RAOC personnel had been withdrawn to their units in the UK.

The late seventies and mid eighties were heady days for RAOC squash, with the Corps fielding an almost unbeatable team. For example, early in 1980 the RAOC entered the Army Inter-Corps squash championship as hot favourites to win for the second year in succession and did not disappoint the forecasters. Determined to retain the title, which they did, a full team was fielded, comprising Staff Sergeants Robbie Robinson from Rheindahlen and David Bradley from Bracht; Major John Woodliffe from Ashchurch; WOI Frank Linnane from Headquarters 1 (Br) Corps; Major Ted Champion from the Apprentices College and Staff Sergeant John Wallis as sixth man.

To maintain RAOC sporting success at the very top of the Army, the 3 BAD rugby team also took the Army Cup, beating the Royal Regiment of Wales in far from ideal weather conditions in the Army stadium at Aldershot. The high winds played havoc with ball handling and conspired to prevent some early scores by the Bracht players who played by far the better rugby. Despite this, the match was nail biting in its tension and the final ten points to nine victory was only secured by a penalty kick in the last minute of the game. It truly was a magnificent victory, breaking the twenty-four year monopoly on the Army Rugby Challenge Cup by the Royal Regiment of Wales, the Welsh Guards and the Duke of Wellington's Regiment. And it was achieved with all the other RAOC sports successes in such things as cross-country, shooting, athletics, to name but a few, when so much else was going on.

47 Company, after a series of changes, had its role in support of the UK Mobile Force recognized in its title in 1980 when it became officially 47 UKMF(L) Company. It would later go on under a further renaming exercise to become 91 Ordnance Company.

There was a welcome change in April 1980 with the alteration of the title of DDOS 1 Corps to Commander Corps RAOC, thus bringing it in line with that of the heads of other supporting arms and services. Brigadier John Skinner, the then DDOS of 1 (Br) Corps, was the first, and indeed the only,

RAOC officer to hold the appointment since, in mid 1981, BAOR changed over to the NATO staff system of nomenclatures. The DOS BAOR then became the Commander Supply BAOR, whilst the CCRAOC became Commander Supply 1 (Br) Corps. The change caused many old, familiar, even historic, titles to become defunct. The ADOS became the SO1(Sup) and, depending on the commodity he managed, the DADOS became an SO2(Sup)(Mat), or SO2(Sup)(POL) and so on. In HQ BAOR the CATO, whose duties involved the control of petroleum as well as ammunition, thenceforth rejoiced in the title of SO1 (Sup)(Ammo, POL & Tech). Nomenclatures in other staff branches were no less lengthy with, for example, the AQMG (Ops) becoming known as the SO1(G1/G4/G5[Plans]). But the main advantage was that NATO allies no longer had to ask the meaning of some of the quainter British mnemonics.

It had been almost a decade since the CICP had been established with the vision of setting up a tertiary system down to RAOC second line units in the Field Army. The first trial having been a failure the concept had been on ice since 1975. Brigadier Bill Whalley, the Commander Supply BAOR was unhappy about this as he could see the many advantages that were possible in the tertiary structure. He put his shoulder behind reinvigorating the system and proved largely successful with the prospect of having something working by the end of 1982 provided work could begin at once – which it did.

In September 1980 the, by then world famous, RAOC EOD training capability at the Army School of Ammunition was further enhanced with the opening of a custom built IED and EOD training facility. Called the Felix Centre, it was a major improvement on some of the rather ad hoc arrangements that had been the vogue beforehand and contributed significantly to the quality of training in this really rather dangerous field of expertise.

By January 1981 there had been a revisiting of structures and titles. It came as no real surprise to most thinking soldiers that the need for brigade levels of command was obvious and they were to be reinstated and the rather nebulous titles allocated to the task and field forces were to go. For example HQ Münster Garrison/Task Force Charlie returned to being the eminently more manageable, and more easily understood, HQ 4 Brigade. As a result the various field force Ordnance companies were also renamed. So, for example, 5 FFOC became 31 Ordnance Company of 5 Ordnance Battalion, but under the operational command of 24 Infantry Brigade; 6 FFOC became 81 Ordnance Company of 10 Ordnance Support Battalion, but remained under the operational command of 1 Infantry Brigade; 7 FFOC became 52 Ordnance Company of 5 Ordnance Battalion, under the operational command of 19 Infantry Brigade; and 8 FFOC became 82 Ordnance Company (V) of 2 Ordnance Battalion, under the operational command of 5 Infantry Brigade.

On 16 March 1981 Brigadier Alan Fernyhough died. Those involved in the changes then being considered at UKLF wondered what he might have said about it all. One thing is certain, he would have said something. With his passing went a font of knowledge, an acerbic wit and a brain that had done so much to educate the inexperienced. In his address at the memorial service the Colonel Commandant, Major General Sir John Hildreth, described the Brigadier in the words of Shakespeare's Julius Caesar, Act III:

Brigadier Alan Fernyhough.

> ...but I am constant as the Northern Star, of whose true, fixed and resting quality there is no fellow in the firmament.

No truer words were ever spoken.

On 10 July 1981, Mr. Philip Goodhart, the Permanent Under Secretary at the Ministry of Defence in a statement on Defence in the House of Commons said of the situation in Northern Ireland:

Of all the invaluable work performed by the Armed Forces in the Province, few tasks are so consistently demanding and dangerous as the work of the RAOC bomb disposal teams. Their levels of technical skill, coupled with ice cool nerves, commanded the highest admiration and respect even among other members of the security forces in the Province, who themselves face the dangers of terrorist attack. Men with the necessary attributes are a rare commodity, and at any one time there' are only about fifty of them in small teams throughout the Province. It is worth mentioning just a few of the cold statistics to bring home the value of the men who stand specifically between society and the bomb. In 1980, Northern Ireland bomb disposal teams were called upon on over one thousand separate occasions, and so far this year the tally has run to over six hundred. Many of these – about half - turn out to be hoaxes or false alarms, but every one must be approached with the same care and thoroughness and makes the same demands of skill and courage.

We were shocked when, on 19 May, a six hundred pound bomb near Newry killed five soldiers. Very few of us, however, even noted in passing that on 3 February this year a bomb disposal team succeeded in neutralizing an exactly similar bomb near Bessbrook in South Armagh, again containing more than six hundred pounds of explosives. Similarly, as recently as 15 June, a van was found on the northern outskirts of Lurgan containing six hundred pounds of explosives in beer kegs and was defuzed by our experts. Alas, only a month or so ago, a senior non-commissioned officer was killed while attempting to defuze a booby-trapped car bomb. He was the seventeenth soldier to be killed on these duties in Northern Ireland. Since 1971, over one hundred decorations and gallantry awards have been made to soldiers working in this area

It is a proud record, one which saw the RAOC suffer among the highest casualties of any regiment or corps that had served in the Province whilst at the same time achieving one of the highest numbers of awards for courage and service.

It was, however, not just in the more high profile world of actually disposing of the bomb that the RAOC was present. They were also there in the background. Experienced ATOs and ATs had been used from the middle seventies to head up a new army organization: the Bomb Intelligence Teams, later to become Weapons Intelligence Sections. This was a unique organization with a headquarters on the main corridor of HQ Northern Ireland and a team in each of the brigades where they provided commanders with intelligence on incidents concerning explosives and weapons. Commanded by an ATO and with the support of Military Police and an Intelligence Corps collator these teams played an important role in the identification of terrorist bomb making techniques and the expert collection of evidence, and would continue to do so throughout the life of the RAOC.

Working closely with the Northern Ireland Forensic Science Laboratory BIT/WIS attended scenes of explosions and finds of explosives and weapons and gave quick feedback on incidents to assist the police in their immediate investigations. Where terrorist suspects in custody appeared to have technical information BIT/WIS could provide expert advice to the investigating officers and occasionally carry out operations to establish the accuracy of the evidence collected. They played an invaluable role in the fight against terrorism and many members of the teams were recognized for their contribution.

In 1981 John Nott, the Secretary of State for Defence, announced yet another defence cut. Driven by the desperate state of the economy and the need to make savings, its greatest impact was on the Royal Navy and the Royal Air Force and re-emphasized the focus of British defence effort on Europe. In particular, therefore, it was the expeditionary capacity that suffered with a loss of amphibious shipping and naval air assets.

Brigadier Gerry Berragan on the left handing Brigadier Brian Barratt the selection of Chieftain spares. The DGOS, Major General Jimmy Brown, casts a watchful eye over things, but, being very short in stature, must have been standing on something.

The autumn of that year saw the last stocks out of Chilwell into Donnington, with the Commandant, Brigadier Gerry Berragan handing to the Commandant of Donnington, Brigadier Brian Barratt, the last item to be transferred. Perhaps there was something of a Freudian symbolism about the items chosen: a selection of Chieftain spares so mounted on a plinth as to be completely useless.

EOD teams were once again deployed on operations in London in October 1981, following a bomb incident in Oxford Street, and dealt with sixteen calls. In the same month two explosive devices were laid in south Wales during a visit of their Royal Highnesses the Prince and Princess of Wales, responsibility being claimed by the 'Welsh Army Workers Revolution'. Both devices were rendered safe.

On 21 November COD Chilwell exercised, for the last time, its right to march through Nottingham with bayonets fixed and drums beating. The RAOC contingent of two companies, commanded by Lieutenant Colonel Tony Ward, marched through the City to St Mary's Church in the old Lace Market. There in a simple but moving ceremony. the banner, which had been presented to the COD by the City on the grant of freedom in 1973, just eight years earlier, was laid up. It was almost the end of an association of some sixty years between the RAOC, with a depot in some form at Chilwell, and the city, although an RAOC presence would still be maintained in the new station by the vehicle division of the Directorate of Supply Management.

The Freedom Scroll is trooped through the ranks as part of the ceremony.

When Sir Christopher Leaver became Lord Mayor of London, on 14 November 1981, the RAOC played a major role in the parade. This occurred because Sir Christopher had done his National Service as an officer in the Corps, and it was on his invitation that the RAOC was to play its part. It was a happy party, with the Representative Colonel Commandant, Major General John Stanyer, the DGOS, Major General Jimmy Brown and the Commander RAOC Training Centre, Brigadier John Turner, taking part firstly in the river procession from Cadogan Pier to the City and then later in the procession through the City in a yellow Rolls Royce and finally as guests at the Mansion House luncheon.

The RAOC Band was, inevitably, conspicuous as it so often was on major

Sir Christopher Laver as a young officer in the RAOC.

events affecting the life of the Corps. There was also a detachment from the Training Battalion and from the Apprentices College. Two tableaux, mounted on floats, depicted the historical aspect of the RAOC's association with the Tower of London, as well as the modern Corps, emphasizing IT and EOD. These were accompanied by a static display near St Paul's Cathedral giving a more varied picture of the Corps' activities. A special RAOC commemorative first-day philatelic cover, organized by HQ RAOC Training Centre, and sold to spectators of the parade, raised over £2,000 for various charities.

The Training Battalion and Apprentices College in the march past.

Another series of studies hit the Army in 1981, and UKLF in particular was beset by study No. 4, the outcome of which had its impact at the end of the year to take effect in 1982. The outline organization of the Corps within UKLF up until then had remained largely unchanged from that which had prevailed throughout the seventies, except for the re-titling that had permeated the Army the previous year. However, study No. 4, saw the removal of seventeen one star posts from the HQ, of which one was the COO, downgraded to a colonel and now known as DCOS (Supply), with Colonel Malcolm Parry-Davies the first incumbent. His new branch, now called G4 (Supply), would suffer significant cuts when it set up in April, not the least of which were the loss of two lieutenant colonel posts. At district level the CRAOC was re-titled Commander Supply, with the DADOS (Barracks) thenceforth assuming the title of SO2 (Supply) (Accommodation Services). As a Corps, however, the one star balance was retained since study No. 4 agreed that, with the TA increasing in size to counterbalance reductions in the regular Army, Commander TA for the RCT, RAOC and REME should be created at brigadier rank. Up until that time RAOC TA sponsored units had been commanded by a colonel operating from Deepcut under the command of the Commander RAOC Training Centre. Under the new organization, the Commander RAOC TA, the first being Brigadier Keith Berresford, set up an independent HQ at the old CAD at Corsham, where the barracks had remained in use as an education centre, with overall responsibility for all RAOC TA units, sponsored and independent.[3]

Lance Corporal Phil Weatherby.

The decade leading up to this change had seen a period of stability for the reserve Army, sponsored units being controlled technically by three regional lieutenant colonels TA, whilst independent units came under their respective district RAOC staff. The stability had seen an effective training regime introduced, leading to a more cohesive and competent TA, very much a part of the one Army to which it belonged with its regular counterpart. Indeed, they took their place in equal share in regular battalions with, for example, TA companies managing POL and heavy lift stores respectively in 10 Ordnance Support Battalion. There was also a significant individual contribution to the life of the Corps with the TA providing two Queen's Medal winners between 1972 and 1980: WOII J Meynell and Sergeant T Haynes; and Staff Sergeant A Crabtree became the best Army driver in 1980 when he won the Advanced Motorists' Cup. Then, in the summer of 1980 at the small arms meeting at Bisley a member of the CVHQ RAOC Shooting Team won the Queen's Medal. Lance Corporal Phil Weatherby, who had been with RAOC TA for four years, had beaten all comers from the Territorial Army – and showed them quite convincingly that non-infantry units were able to beat them at their own game. Lance Corporal Weatherby was also the RAOC rifle champion for the third time at the Corps Small Arms Meeting in May 1980.

There was a renaming exercise for RAOC units to sweep up and regularize unit titles after so many changes. Brigadier John Skinner undertook at the same time a re-evaluation of the RAOC structure in Germany, in the light of the John Nott defence review and taking advantage of the re-titling exercise, to set in place a proper battalion structure that in one fell swoop placed the RAOC on a par with its counterparts in other regiments and corps and at the same time presented more effective support for the dependency. Accordingly, each of the divisional Commanders Supply became COs of Ordnance Battalions, numbered to coincide with the division's number. The Combat Supplies Battalion became 5 Ordnance Battalion, while the purview of CRAOC Corps troops was made into 6 Ordnance Battalion. In the UK 10 Ordnance Support Battalion became 9 Ordnance Battalion. Companies were similarly re-titled, so 47 UKMF(L) Company, for example became 91 Ordnance Company, while the old 48 Company moved to an AMF(L) Logistic Battalion. The rest of 9 Battalion was made up of 92 Company, regular shadow ammunition, 93 Company, TA petroleum, and 94 Company, TA Stores – all with a third line role. It also retained command of the brigade Ordnance Company for the UKMF(L) Brigade, re-titled from 81 Ordnance Company, which it was so briefly, to 90 Ordnance Company.

But despite the cuts and the overstretch people still found the time to play, and play hard, as witness Captain Sarah Watmough competing at Corps level in the salom.

By the end of all these reviews the manpower in Germany as a result of the defence review had reduced overall by thirteen per cent. That of the RAOC had reduced by nineteen per cent. Some things never change.

As part of the devolution of command responsibilities from HQ UKLF proposed by study No. 4, 1 AIDU was placed directly under DLSA for all purposes other than operational tasking within UKLF. Almost concurrently, with the standardization of RAOC unit titles, it became 11 Ordnance Battalion (EOD), with its HQ at Tidworth, where it assumed responsibility for manning and operating the United Kingdom Joint Services EOD Operations Centre

One of the key changes in the staff structure at HQ UKLF resulting from study No. 4 was the assumption by the brigadier ACOS G3 of all responsibility for operational logistics. The ACOS G4, Brigadier Harry Brown, late of the RAOC, who under the previous organization handled G4 operations lost all these responsibilities and was restricted only to dealing with peacetime G4 matters. This was to have implications for the working of the HQ and far sooner than anyone might have thought.

On 31 March 1982, a Wednesday, the closure ceremony for COD Chilwell took place in front of the Garrison Headquarters in the presence of the Lord Lieutenant of Nottinghamshire, the Hon Eve Chetwynd, daughter of the eighth Viscount Chetwynd who had founded the Shell Filling Factory that had originally occupied the site. Also present were the Lord Mayor of Nottingham, the GOC Eastern District, the DGOS, Major General Jimmy Brown, and the last Commandant, Brigadier Gerry Berragan. In his closing speech the Representative Colonel Commandant, Major General Mike Callan, paid tribute to the loyalty and dedication of the depot's employees over the years, and recalled the highlights of Chilwell's history from 1915. After the closure speech a short service of benediction was held. The last post was sounded by a bugler from the RAOC Staff Band, during which the RAOC flag was lowered for the last time. Two minutes later, during the sounding of reveille, the flag of HQ 49 Infantry Brigade, the new tenants of the garrison, was raised. The final act was the formal handing over of the keys of the Chilwell Station by Brigadier Berragan to the Commanding Officer 38 Central Workshops REME, the new Chilwell Station Commander.

So it was that COD Chilwell, built up all those years ago by General Sir Leslie Williams to a peak of excellence during the Second World War; the depot that had kept the Army's vehicles operational throughout that war; the depot that had issued during the five and a half years of that war 30,000,000,000,000 individual items; the depot that had issued yet more and more in the many wars and emergencies of the post world war period – closed.

Two days later the country went to war.

On the night of 1 April and into the morning of 2 April the Argentines invaded the Falkland Islands and South Georgia. The Argentine claim to what they called 'Los Isalas Malvinas' had been a long-standing cause of dispute between the British and Argentinean governments and the post-war rundown of the British presence in the South Atlantic had sent a message of lessening interest in the fate of the islands. What finally confirmed a complete lack of interest in the eyes of the Argentines was the decision, as part of John Nott's defence cuts to cease patrols by the survey ship *Endurance* and the plan to withdraw it from service. For General Leopoldo Galtieri it presented a golden opportunity for he presided over a country with massive economic problems and deepening political unrest. He needed a diversion and thought that the signals he perceived as being sent by the British government coupled with the deep economic problems being faced by Margaret Thatcher's government would preclude a serious British reaction and he would be able to occupy and retain the islands without undue difficulty.

The early warnings that there might be a problem came with a landing in March by a group of Argentines on South Georgia claiming to be scrap merchants in search of waste metals. A party of twenty-two Royal Marines was sent over to South Georgia from the small garrison on the Falkland Islands in order to keep them under surveillance. When the invasion came the small RM contingents on the two islands were quickly overwhelmed, but not before the South Georgia party had taken on and successfully damaged an Argentinean Navy corvette with a Carl Gustav 84-mm shoulder launched anti-tank weapon. Mercifully there were no casualties among the British and the whole garrison was taken prisoner and eventually returned to the United Kingdom.

According to Article 51 of the UN Charter there were clear grounds for an immediate declaration of war. However, the British chose to use diplomatic means to resolve the situation if possible while, at the same time, preparing a task force to recover what they could of the situation. The problem was always going to be force levels, since what the British could lift and sustain over an 8,000-mile LofC was considerably less than the Argentineans, who were very much closer, could put onto the islands. And the British were completely unprepared for what had happened.

The Foreign Secretary, Lord Carrington was visiting the Middle East and the CDS, Admiral Sir Terence Lewin, was in New Zealand. Admiral Sir Henry Leach was First Sea Lord and, although not the Deputy CDS in the absence of Lewin, he got the ear of the Prime Minister convincing her and the Cabinet that the Royal Navy could and should, as the pre-invasion tension mounted, respond with a task force. Three hunter-killer submarines were dispatched almost at once and the First Flotilla under Admiral Sir Sandy Woodward, on exercise in the Atlantic, was also sent south. Many of those in this task force, and many of those who were to follow, had in their possession the redundancy notices ordering them out of the Service as a result of the 1981 John Nott defence review.

Leach saw this affair as a means of vindicating the Royal Navy's role in expeditionary warfare and the continued requirement for a naval air and amphibious capability. He was clear that this was purely a naval matter, and he did so to the extent that the mounting headquarters for all land operations, HQ UKLF, was given no inkling at all of the impending operation. So, when the Argentines invaded, the Prime Minister was able to say with great confidence that a task force would sail immediately, quite confident that large parts of it were already underway or practically ready for sea. But no one, it seems, had told the Army.

At HQ UKLF the staff restructuring that had been put in place at the beginning of the year had left no senior logistician or logistics staff officer between the two DAQMGs in the operations branch and the C-in-C The new system was about to undergo the severest test possible and those two junior officers were about to understand the true meaning of loneliness. On that Friday morning, 2 April 1982, Major Frank Steer RAOC, one of the two DAQMGs in Q Operations in HQ UKLF, was taking a relaxed approach reading the signal from the Joint Intelligence Committee confirming they could foresee no likelihood of an Argentinean invasion of the Falklands. Just at that point his opposite number, Major Peter Hubert of the Queen's Regiment, almost kicked down the office door in his haste with the words:

…we're mounting 3 Brigade[4], can I borrow your staff captain?

It was to be a long loan, and it was the first they had heard of it.

Major Hubert had responsibility for operations outside NATO, whilst Major Steer's 'parish' lay closer to home. However, in an unspoken agreement they immediately set up as a team of two sharing a burden, with Peter leading, that was to keep them fully occupied for the next seventeen weeks.

The land forces, of which the Royal Marines, despite being a part of the Royal Navy, were a part, were held at the standard seven days notice to move. All the plans for outload of their stores and supplies were predicated on them having that amount of time to prepare. However, Margaret Thatcher had announced that a task force would sail on Monday. It was an order that would brook no debate – it had to be done; it would be done.

There had already been an inkling that preparation would have to be complete earlier than anticipated, and on the Friday afternoon staff officers at HQ UKLF were busy trying to work out if, with the weekend looming, they could call in some of the dormant contracts that in war would bring fleets of civilian vehicles to the depot gates for outloading; but this was not a war. With ammunition needing to be outloaded from the RN depot at Glen Douglas in Western Scotland and CAD Kineton in Warwickshire, stores from Bicester, Donnington and the Engineer Depot at Long Marston, medical supplies from Ludgershall and food from Naval depots additional transport significantly in excess of that which could be provided by the regular army was essential. The TA solved the problem. The big tasks lay with the movement of ammunition, and when the COs of TA regiments in Manchester, Liverpool and Birmingham rang in to say they had drill halls full of soldiers who had turned in, without being called, to do anything they could it was as manna from heaven. Regiments were dispatched to Scotland and Warwickshire to await orders on arrival. Plans as to what they would lift and to where, were made as they were en route. Plymouth was the main port of debarkation, and to make the long journeys, especially from Scotland, would put many drivers outside their permitted hours. Police simply tore up the tachographs and helped them on their way with escorts.

In the Ministry of Defence the Army Logistic operations centre, QMG's ops room, was manned and at Bicester the Supply Management operations centre sprang into life, having been informed at 7 am on 2 April that the Commando Brigade was now at seventy-two hours notice to move. It would be good to be able to say that plans were taken down and dusted off, but there were no plans. It would have to be flown by the seat of the pants, but mercifully there were military at every level, in the depots, in the operations centres of the depots, at HQ UKLF and in Andover, with vast experience and a huge collective corporate knowledge and the capacity for twenty-four hour working, seven days a week. With them in place it could not fail. Managing it without them would have been unimaginable – it still is.

Telephones all over the country rang as hard-pressed staff officers in Ordnance Branch in UKLF called in every favour, every friend, everything they needed. Lieutenant Colonel (Retired) Roy Cobb, late of the RAOC, worked miracles with colleagues in ALOC and SPOC. The request for a 5,000 man tented camp, for which there was no provision at all, was greeted by a head lifted from the plan he was working on, and a half smile; the question, '...could we do it?' was greeted by a look that would have frozen mercury. He did, it was there on time to be loaded on the massive container ship *Atlantic Conveyer*. Where from? Best not to ask.

Throughout the country telephone calls were robbing units who were not going of items of equipment that were in short supply in the deploying forces. Night vision equipment, foul weather clothing, AFG1098 – no chain of command permission or agreement; it was a weekend. It was a call straight to the unit, a vehicle would call and it would go – all headed to Plymouth or to the RAF base at Lyneham. The reckoning would come later. They had to sail on Monday and they were going to war. They would sail on Monday as ready for war as could be. Operation CORPORATE was becoming a reality.

The Commando Brigade would take with it all three Commandos, 40, 42 and 45, the latter being specially trained for its NATO role in Norway and hence especially valuable in cold, wet weather conditions. It was to be supplemented by an in-role[5] battalion of the Parachute Regiment, the 3rd Battalion, detached from 5 Brigade. The latter was a poorly equipped formation, the second battalion of which was 2nd Parachute Battalion and the third was 1/7 King Edward's Own Gurkha Rifles. The brigade's role normally was to be the C-in-C UKLF's reserve in Home Defence.

The task force sailed from the UK to follow those Royal Naval elements that had already been at sea when the crisis struck. On board the ships, a part of the Commando Logistic Regiment, was Major Tony Welch's Ordnance Squadron with men spread throughout the ships. He explained:

> The Squadron Headquarters was embarked in RFA *Sir Lancelot*, but transferred to RFA *Sir Galahad* at Ascension Island. During the trip to the South Atlantic plans were drawn up for the support of 3 Commando Brigade, once it had established a beach-head in the Falklands. In essence, the plan was to use two Landing Ships Logistic, the RFAs *Sir Galahad* and *Sir Percival*, to carry two days of combat supplies, each backed up with a further four days supply in RFA *Stromness* and some sixteen days of ammunition for the Brigade in the P&O Car Ferry, MV *Elk*. The LSLs would lie close to the shore and provide direct support to troops on land. Once empty, they would replenish from RFA *Stromness* and MV *Elk*, sheltering in comparative safety outside the Total Exclusion Zone,[6] only coming close inland under the cover of darkness. This plan was thought to provide both flexibility and safety for the vital sinews of war

At that stage he had no idea where precisely the landings would take place.

A crucial link in the LofC to the Falklands was the Ascension Island base, midway between the UK and the objective. Early in the operation a logistic support unit, the British Forces Support Unit, had been set up under naval command. It was an ad hoc unit which, despite efforts to keep strengths to a minimum, grew as the operation progressed, and gathered detachments as the need arose. It eventually operated as a tri-service unit with the RAF having the greatest share of the commitment involving in particular the ground and airborne re-fuelling of long-range transport aircraft.

The first RAOC involvement at Ascension Island followed a request for a petroleum operator trained as a Chemical Laboratory Assistant to carry out tests on stocks of aviation fuel to confirm their fitness for use in RAF aircraft. Corporal Webster and Lance Corporal Williams of 91 Ordnance

Company were flown out to Ascension Island with their portable petroleum test kit on 5 April. A few days later, having satisfied the RAF that the fuel was within specification they returned to the UK.

In effect the BFSU was mainly a tri-Service Airhead Organization but, unlike the normal Army equivalent, it did not initially have a HQ staff or representatives of the various support services. Thus, on 25 April, two Army officers, one of whom was Major Roy Lennox RAOC, were sent out to join the HQ in order to assist the Commander BFSU in running his HQ and to offer any Army expertise he might need. Of a total strength of just under 1,000 at its height, 140 were Army personnel.

By the time the Amphibious Task Force arrived at Ascension Island large quantities of materiel had begun to pour in by air, making it necessary for the Commando Ordnance Squadron to establish a twelve man detachment on the island to expedite the through supply of its materiel. The detachment, which became known as the RAOC Airhead Detachment, took over the whole task of receiving all stores unloaded from aircraft or ships, varying from Seacat missiles to units' G1098 outfits to general stores for all three services to hold, sort, and where necessary to re-pack or re-palletize. Other RAOC personnel serving as part of BFSU included a laundry detachment made up of four soldiers, either supply controllers or supply specialists detailed for this special function, provided by 9 Ordnance Battalion. They were equipped with the standard laundry trailer, of 1939-45 war vintage which, not unexpectedly, broke down on the two occasions on which they tried to use it. Luckily, a disused static laundry was found to exist on the island, was put into working order and enabled the detachment to provide a useful service to the personnel of BFSU. On the island there was also an EFI detachment of seven NAAFI personnel, under the command of WOII Perrot, in civilian life a NAAFI auditor, and it provided shop and club facilities at several locations on the island and was greatly appreciated.

A further RAOC detachment was a Petroleum Operating Section, comprising twelve petroleum operators drawn from RAOC units in BAOR and UK, and commanded by Captain Trevor Couch. The detachment took over and operated a four and a half kilometre aviation fuel pipeline from the coast to the airfield. It had been built by a Troop of 51 Squadron RE in just over a week. The Petroleum Operating Section manned two boost pumps at the shore installing a single boost pump mid way along the line, and at the airhead fuel farm which they took over from the Tactical Supply Wing RAF. The section subsequently developed the fuel farm so that it contained eight 30,000-gallon pillow tanks.

By 14 June, some 5,500 tons of materiel had been handled through Ascension Island, and 12 million gallons of aviation fuel had been consumed. Despite inevitable problems, amongst which were the facts that the organization was ad hoc, and that there had been no rehearsal of the role, those on Ascension Island played a pivotal role in the eventual success of Operation CORPORATE.

The plan had been for naval elements to arrive first in the Falklands and win the air and naval battle in order to achieve local superiority so that landings could take place unmolested. However, this was not achieved. The sinking of the Argentine battleship *Belgrano*, followed by the sinking of the British frigate HMS *Sheffield* and subsequent damage to another British destroyer accompanied by the loss of some Harriers and helicopters in late April and early May had brought home to the government and the country that this was a war and would incur yet more casualties. It also brought home to Sandy Woodward the fragility of his force levels when compared with the Argentines, leading his risk analysis to arrive at the conclusion that he would have to manage a landing without achieving the level of local security he had sought. By 8 May it was clear that a negotiated solution was unlikely and plans began to focus on a landing between 18 and 22 May.

As planning for a landing progressed and more became known about the Argentinean force levels on the islands, estimated at some 10,000 men, it became obvious that more men were needed if a landing was to have any chance of success leading subsequently to victory. One immediate solution was to add 2nd Battalion the Parachute Regiment, the other 'in role' parachute battalion, to the Commando Brigade and the decision was also taken to add 5 Brigade to the force. This presented an immediate problem since two of 5 Brigade's battalions had been detached to the Royal Marines so two more would need to be found to replace them. Then the brigade would need to be trained. Other factors militated against it being the ideal choice. It was light on weapons, had no artillery or armour and, perhaps worst of all, no dedicated regular Army logistic support. It was supposed to live off the land in war, drawing what it needed from the most appropriate place depending on where it was deployed in the UK. It was originally conceived as a garrison force for the islands – there would be no need for it to fight so its logistic and support weapon shortcomings would not be a problem. So ran the logic. As it was, only one battery of artillery could be found instead of the three, one per battalion, that doctrine demanded it should have.

The concept was that Julian Thompson's Commando Brigade could mount the landing, to be joined later by 5 Brigade, at which point Major General Jeremy Moore would take over in the role of divisional commander; although he had no divisional headquarters. It might after all be necessary for 5 Brigade to fight. The landing operation was called Operation SUTTON.

In order to allow time for the amphibious force to concentrate, the window for landing had to be stretched to some time between 19 May and 3 June. While this was happening the opportunity was taken at Ascension Island to reorder the loads on the ships to try and configure the logistic package to meet the likely operational scenario. It was on 20 May that the commanding officers were called aboard HMS *Fearless*, the command ship for the amphibious force, to be given orders that San Carlos water was the chosen place for a landing at a time still to be determined. Once it was ashore the brigade would only exploit as far as it safely could while awaiting the arrival of 5 Brigade which had left Southampton on the liner *Queen Elizabeth II* on 12 May.

Configuring 5 Brigade for its role had presented challenges. Woefully under resourced, it had to be reconstituted and then supported logistically, almost from scratch, and then go to war. For the RAOC its Ordnance Company would need to be created, for the Ordnance Company that was in its ORBAT for general war was TA and the TA was not being called up for this operation. Instead, Major Geoff Thomas' 81 Ordnance Company, awaiting re-titling as 90 Ordnance Company, was to be reconfigured from its primary role supporting 1 Infantry Brigade in the UKMF(L) and a great deal of rescaling was undertaken at short notice. The Company was configured to support infantry, armour and artillery and it would be doing almost none of that in the Falklands save to support an almost entirely infantry dependency in a light role. There was now also a perceived need to provide more depth to the logistic support, partly due to the distance and the realization of the logistic problems and partly due to the increased size of the deployment. Accordingly Major Robin Smith's 91 Ordnance Company found itself suddenly re-roling from supporting the UKMF(L) to supporting, at very short notice, a war in the Falkland Islands. To do this he had to undergo some reorganization dropping his stores platoon and taking on a bakery platoon, laundry platoon and a NAAFI/EFI section. The two companies set sail in *QE II*, MV *Baltic Ferry* and MV *St Edmond*. The number of ships taken up from trade was on the increase.

The RAOC task was not helped by the choice of the two battalions to make up the strength of 5 Brigade, the 2nd Battalion of the Scots and the 1st Battalion of the Welsh Guards, both coming from public duties. This meant that their QM departments had to be realigned from an essentially peacetime posture to one suited to support a battalion at war. If there were serious questions over the choice and suitability of the two battalions, no thought whatsoever was given to the implications for Ordnance support, or any other form of logistic support for that matter. The RAOC was presented with a fait accompli and would simply have to get on with it – which it did.

While 5 Brigade was making its way south, accompanied on the *QE II* by Major General Moore who joined the ship at Ascension Island, the landings commenced in San Carlos water before first light on 21 May 1982. At dawn, *Sir Percival*, *Sir Galahad* and *Stromness* sailed into San Carlos with the amphibious task force to act as floating depots to support the five battalions ashore. They made a faultless landing with none of the anticipated enemy reaction.

Logistic support in depth was provided by MV *Elk*, with its 5,000 tons of ammunition, outside the Sound in the TEZ. The Commando Ordnance Squadron began to unload combat supplies vehicles the moment that anchors were dropped. All went well until about 1430 when Argentine Air Force war planes made themselves felt. *Sir Galahad* took thirteen separate attacks that afternoon and by the evening it was realized that support direct from the ships would not work. Thereafter, the ships would leave the sound during the day and return at night to ferry stocks ashore in order to set up a Brigade Maintenance Area on the beach. This was a Royal Naval decision designed to reduce the target array in the Sound and to secure the safety of the supply ships. It did not impress the Royal Marines who very much wanted their logistic support afloat and to hand.

The decision was taken to establish the BAA in Ajax Bay. It had a good beach but a frontage of only 300 yards and a depth of about 600 yards. Into this tiny area had to fit the Field Hospital, 45 Commando Echelon, Headquarters of the Logistic Regiment, Workshops and Transport Squadrons, the Field Records Office, the Satellite Communications Unit and the Ordnance Squadron with its hundreds of tons of stores and ammunition. There was precious little space available, particularly as part of the area was covered with stone runs; rivers of granite boulders that cascaded down the mountain sides. However, any lingering doubts were dispelled when on 22 May a bomb hit *Sir Galahad* and stopped, embedded and unexploded, some thirty feet from 300 tons of ammunition. *Sir Lancelot* was also hit. The risks were too great. But the nightly forays into the Sound of the supply ships for unloading meant the logistic build up was very slow. In his book on the Falklands War, co-authored by Simon Jenkins, Max Hastings was to write:

> One of the most important and most painful lessons of the war is that peacetime exercises do not test logistics to the full, do not reveal men's utter vulnerability to supply problems on the battlefield.

It also meant that the helicopter and ship-to-shore capacity was fully utilized moving stores and supplies. As a result Julian Thompson had no helicopters to move his troops forward and exploit the successful beachhead he had achieved. The Royal Navy, bearing the brunt of the air attacks, was unhappy at the relative inactivity of the land element and there was considerable pressure from Northwood for him 'to get on with it'. However, he was not to be swayed until he could be sure he had all his logistic resources safe and to hand. Ashore, there was no time or space for the Ordnance Squadron to prepare neat storage layouts or segregated ammunition stacks; they just received stock from the ships and issued to the fighting troops twenty-four hours a day. Then, on 25 May, the Argentine Air Force turned its attention on Ajax Bay. They dropped eight bombs, four of which exploded killing five men and setting alight a stack of ammunition. Luckily, the fire did not spread and the Argentines did not visit again, but it did once more underscore the vulnerability, potentially at least, of the logistic support for the force ashore. Stacks, immobile on the ground, were not nearly so satisfactory, in the view of the Royal Marines, as stocks afloat and mobile.

It was a significant day for the Argentines, 25 May, as it was their Armed Forces day. There was a feeling about the place that they would have to 'do something' even though the attrition against attacking aircraft from Harrier, Rapier, Seacat and Blowpipe was having a serious effect on the morale and capability of the enemy air force. Accordingly they put into the air two Super Etendard carrying between them two of the three remaining Exocets they possessed. Already used with such devastating effect against HMS *Sheffield*, they were after another high price target, ideally one of the two carriers with the naval force, for the loss of either would bring the British assault to an abrupt end. When the British realized what they were facing they threw all the anti-aircraft defences they had into stopping the attack. But there was a chink in the defences and through it the Argentine pilots saw a large signature on their weapons array radar – large enough to be a carrier. The missile launched and struck its target, which turned out to be the *Atlantic Conveyor*, carrying much needed supplies and support

Storage conditions were far from ideal as shown in this picture of Ajax Bay, taken a little later in the war and showing the one Chinook Helicopter to have survived the Argentine Air Force sinking of the *Atlantic Conveyer*.

equipment for the force ashore and afloat.

Mercifully, she had offloaded the 12 extra Harriers she had brought down and they were already on the carriers, as well as one Chinook heavy-lift helicopter. However the other three Chinooks went down with the ship, as did ten Wessex helicopters. It was a major blow and would seriously inhibit the chances of deploying significant forces out of the beachhead and then supporting them. Roy Cobb's tented camp also went down. Roy was on the telephone when Major Steer ventured, not without trepidation, into his office to inform him, once he had put the phone down, that another 5,000 man tented camp was needed.

'What have you done with the last one?' A perfectly proper question.

'I haven't done anything, but the Argentines have sunk it.'

'And I suppose you want another one? Tomorrow?' The pitch of the voice rose a little with the second question.

'End of the week will be fine.' Again, the look that would freeze mercury, but Major Steer left Roy's office with him reaching for the phone, knowing it would be done. And it was, along with a huge amount of other losses from the sinking being made good, by Roy and by other hard pressed Ordnance staffs throughout the UK.

'What about my overtime?' The question floated down the corridor behind the disappearing Major Steer.

'We don't pay overtime...' he muttered to himself knowing that Roy, a retired officer on Civil Service terms and conditions, knew that as well. And the lights burned late into the night along the Ordnance corridor as they had done for many nights before and would continue to do so for many nights to come.

The following day the British began their advance out of the beachhead, commencing with an attack on the Argentine position at Goose Green. Julian Thompson had originally only planned to screen this off to protect his flank as he advanced across the island. However, London was concerned about the length of time the build up had been taking and with the naval losses that were being suffered a victory was needed, and the Argentinean garrison at Goose Green was to provide it. The 2nd Battalion the Parachute Regiment was given the task and, after a battle lasting almost two days in which the CO, 'H' Jones, was killed, prevailed. The Commando Squadron found itself supplying mortar ammunition direct to the mortar base plates and Milan anti-tank missiles to the front line. There were no enemy tanks for them to be fired at, but they made wonderful 'bunker-busters'. Gazelle and Scout helicopters flew into landing sites at Ajax Bay and then direct to the battle, taking great risks and flying with great skill to ensure the forward delivery of the much needed ammunition and the evacuation of casualties.

Then 5 Brigade arrived, on 30 May; and with it came Jeremy Moore to command the force ashore.

On the journey south, a logistic plan had been hatched that all logistic stocks, for both 3 Commando and 5 Infantry Brigades, were to be treated as force assets. Both brigades would be supported from Ajax Bay with materiel remaining on ships as a reserve and to provide some dispersal of assets. 81 and 91 Companies would be commanded by the Commando Logistic Regiment Royal Marines and, apart from a small element ashore, the members of both units would be distributed among the support ships. A new ORBAT was worked out and an unofficial title of 81st/91st Ordnance Company (*QEII*'s Own) was adopted. Robin Smith and Geoff Thomas decided that, with two heads being better than one, they would have joint command of the new organization. At least that was the plan, or so Robin Smith thought:

> During the long voyage south in the comfort of *QEII* there was time to plan and debate a series of logistic concepts to support the inevitable operation to retake the Falkland Islands. Early plans were based on floating maintenance areas comprising store ships manned by RAOC soldiers supplying troops ashore by helicopter or landing craft. News of the vulnerability of shipping to Argentine air attack soon made this concept high risk and a logistic base ashore in San Carlos became the only option. However offloading plans became dependent on the need to protect shipping rather than the logistical needs of the land operation making replenishment planning and the requirement to build up stocks ashore a fraught day-to-day process.

Following the 1975 Defence Review, the Petroleum Platoon of the Commando Ordnance Squadron had been made a Reserve Army unit. This meant that the Squadron had deployed to the Falklands without their petroleum operators and had to make ad hoc arrangements. Members of 81 Ordnance Company, who had deployed with the 2nd Battalion the Parachute Regiment, were given hasty instruction by Sergeant Tarawacki of the Commando Ordnance Squadron and then, commanded by Sergeant Bushell, ran the emergency refuelling site at Port San Carlos for the helicopters and Harriers. At Ajax Bay after only ten minutes of instruction by Sergeant Tarawacki, Private Potter, whose Army engagement ran out the day the task force landed, operated the Brigade's POL point single-handed, almost without sleep, until 5 Infantry Brigade arrived. He received a Mention in Dispatches for his efforts.

However, with the arrival of 91 Company, the first ashore, came the expertise, in its petroleum platoon, to manage the fuel. The supply of petroleum was becoming a nightmare. Few vehicles were taken to the Falklands as it had been rightly assumed the road-less terrain would preclude their use, so very little thought had been given by the staff to POL re-supply. However, the Marines found that their BV206 over-snow vehicles were just as good at crossing the wet, marshy terrain of the Falkland Islands and they were extensively used. They were petrol fuelled vehicles. And there were other, unforeseen, demands on petrol, which the Army called CIVGAS.

Robin Smith was not unduly worried by this since a reserve of packed fuel had been loaded in Southampton and had travelled down with 5 Brigade. At least he wasn't worried until he found that the harbour authorities had left his packed reserve stacked on the dockside in the UK because transport regulations forbade the transportation of packed fuel with other cargo – and no one had bothered to tell him, or anyone else for that matter. Major Robin Smith:

> Every day was a CIVGAS crisis. There had been a woeful underestimation of fuel consumption. Not only were we faced with the increased use of the BV206, but the Rapier, which only ran for two or three hours a day in training were now running 24 hours a day. We tried every workaround we could. We sent UBREs[7] out on mexifloats[8] to tankers in the bay to be filled and when they returned used them to fill jerricans in order to get the fuel out to where it was needed. Subsequently we used Airportable Fuel Containers for the same task, but there were problems with the Avery-Hardoll couplings which suffered badly from the ingress of salt and sand. I had one man permanently stripping and cleaning them, for the Naval Auxilliarymen were paranoiac

Filling jerricans, and then distributing, was a never ending task. Note, in the background, the congested nature of the beach logistic support area.

about damage to their equipment which was also used to refuel helicopters.

Once packed it had to be distributed in order to keep radios and Rapier anti-aircraft systems working twenty-four hours a day. A lot of fuel was needed and it had to be transported to the top of some very steep hills. 91 Company took on this thankless task with a will, discovering fuel where none was meant to be, getting it to the storage tanks and then issuing it day and night.

Robin's men developed a further idea for holding bulk fuel ashore. The plan was that a 10,000 gallon fabric tank would be taken out on a mexifloat, filled and returned to shore. However, no one understood the fluid dynamics that would see a three-quarters full fabric tank roll elegantly into the sea and lie there like some partially submerged whale. Robin Smith had sent his men out to collect the fuel in the fabric tank from an oiler and when they became overdue to return he went in search of them.

> I found this thing in the sea and the early efforts to recover it were proving to no avail. In the end we towed it slowly into Ajax Bay and beached it. What we had planned to take half a day took five, but once it was ashore it proved a most valuable asset.

Aside from POL the provision of other Ordnance stores was not without its problems. The hasty loading of ships in United Kingdom meant that stock was in the wrong order for unloading and much time was lost sorting out the mess. A considerable amount of materiel had to be moved before the combat supplies could be reached. Ashore, operations were hampered by a lack of MHE and the fact that the ground, at the back of the beaches, had been churned into a sea of mud. They also found that all ships carrying the Brigade's equipment and stores had been loaded in accordance with peacetime shipping regulations, so it wasn't just the failure to load packed fuel in the UK that affected the RAOC footprint in the advanced base that was Ajax Bay. No consideration had been given to the order in which stores would be required. As an example, on *Baltic Ferry*, a roll-on/roll-off ferry, all the ammunition had been loaded first and could only be unloaded through the stern door after the removal of hundreds of tons of unit freight, defence stores and equipment. On the *QEII* things were better but only marginally so. It was possible to gain access to each loaded hold only through small doors to each level or via a tortuous route through corridors and staircases.

Robin Smith remembered one of the first lessons he had been taught on joining the RAOC:

> I well remember a lecture on my young officers' course by the Corps' historian Brigadier Alan Fernyhough. He concluded by imploring us to remember one vital piece of advice; to ensure that tents and tent poles sailed on the same ship. In the Falklands this advice was forgotten. Gunners, guns and ammunition were all loaded on different ships under an ill-judged assumption that they would all come together during an unopposed offloading.

By now the advance by the Commando Brigade on Port Stanley had commenced, and this extended the distances from the logistic base at Ajax Bay. To help reduce distances for replenishment the Commando Ordnance Squadron established an FMA at Teal Inlet and stock was moved from Ajax Bay by helicopter and LSLs. Under the shadow of Mount Kent a forward distribution point was set up at Estancia House, and life went on under the shadow of continuing Argentine air attacks.

To the south, the forward units of 5 Brigade had reached the settlement of Fitzroy. Replenishment was by now over a distance of sixty miles, with re-supply being undertaken by LSL, Landing Craft or helicopters. Consequently, it was decided to move the logistic base from Ajax Bay to Fitzroy and Major Tony Welch, was sent forward to prepare for the reception of stock and personnel. He arrived at the settlement just as RFA *Sir Galahad* steamed into the bay at Bluff Cove carrying elements of the Welsh Guards and some 400 tons of ammunition and stores on board. She joined RFA *Sir Tristram* which was also moving supplies forward.

The LSL *Sir Galahad* some thirty minutes after being hit. The ammunition dump being formed by 81 Ordnance Company is in the middle ground.

However, there was no Rapier air defence in place, nor had the Royal Navy any ships in the area to provide protection against air attack. Moreover, 5 Brigade Headquarters was just establishing itself in a shearing shed in Fitzroy and had not been told about the ships so there were no reception arrangements in place. They simply were not expected, and certainly not in broad daylight. The outcome is history. The Argentine Air Force, clearly considered by some not to pose a threat any longer, still had steel in its belly. Two aircraft appeared, flying low over the horizon and within minutes *Sir Tristram* was crippled and *Sir Galahad* was ablaze. All efforts were turned to rescuing the troops and crew on board the ships and to tending the injured. Within an hour, the Argentine planes were back again, this time attacking the troops on the ground. Tony Welch saw it all, but could do no more than find what cover he could:

> Ewen Southby-Tailyour, a Royal Marine Officer, and I took cover under a trailer attached to a farm tractor. We watched the cannon rounds from the attacking aircraft churning up the ground in front of us and it was only after the attack was over we realized we had taken shelter under a petrol tanker.

For the second time in the conflict, logistic plans had to be abandoned and it was back to the drawing board. Although *Sir Galahad* was terribly damaged and eventually scuttled, *Sir Tristram* was less badly hit. The fires on board were extinguished and it was found that the stores in the holds were unaffected. Royal Engineers blew off the damaged rear door to the tank deck and a detachment of 81 Ordnance Company went on board to recover the stores. The bulkhead of the tank deck was still hot to the touch and the wheels of the MHE smoked as they were driven in and out of the hold to remove the materiel and ammunition.

To cope with the new situation it was decided that re-supply would continue from Ajax Bay with just forward detachments remaining at Teal Inlet and Fitzroy. The air attacks on San Carlos Water and Ajax Bay had ceased, but it was clear from the Bluff Cove incident that this local respite could not be guaranteed elsewhere. The long move forward of combat supplies, with helicopters flying hour after hour with under-slung loads, continued with ammunition being delivered direct to gun positions as well as to forward logistic bases. As the guns moved ever closer to Stanley so the ammunition left behind had to be picked up and moved to the new positions. Everyone steeled themselves for the final assault on the little town of Port Stanley.

Sergeant Sharkey, right, and Corporal Stevens, left, working out the next set of underslung loads.

However, the final assaults by the Commando Brigade and 5 Brigade broke the Argentines and they surrendered on 14 June. Supporting troops on operations was no longer a priority. But there would be no rest, for not only was there a need to ensure that people were properly supplied with the essentials of post-war life, there was a now a need for decent accommodation properly equipped, showers, baths, clean clothing, laundry, fresh bread and fresh food.

The supply chain became the reverse of that which had been operating up to this point. Its base was to be in Stanley, based on the liberated Falkland Islands Company offices and the outstations remained at Fitzroy, Teal inlet, Ajax Bay, and across Falkland Sound at Fox Bay. The airfield at Stanley was not in a fit condition to receive transport aircraft, so the first priority was to set up an organization to handle parachute-dropped stores and equipment. The second priority was to achieve some order in the chaos that was Stanley. Filth had to be cleared up so that storage and living areas could be created, piles of ammunition and weapons had to be checked for booby-traps and then made secure. The unloading and loading of ships, which had sailed round from San Carlos Water, had to be co-coordinated and, not least, the thousands of Argentine prisoners of war had to be accommodated, fed and watered.

Just ten days before the surrender, on 4 June, when the war was still in full swing, COD Donnington hosted a visit by the RAOC Colonel-in-Chief, Her Majesty the Queen. Clearly the depot was in full swing supporting the

Members of the Commando Ordnance Squadron celebrating their part in the victory with the Corps flag.

Gone, but not forgotten. A gentle reminder to Her Majesty that not everyone could be at Donnington to greet her, for perfectly understandable reasons. She is flanked by Major General Jimmy Brown, the DGOS, on her left, and Brigadier Keith Berresford.

operation in the South Atlantic, the outcome of which even at what would be seen to be that late stage was still not certain. However, the opportunity to see her Corps at work and to thank people for their efforts was not something to be dismissed lightly, and the Queen had a most enjoyable day; as did the Donningtonians whose morale, already high, was greatly lifted by her interest, care and understanding.

A study was carried out personally by DSCS, Brigadier S H Lawrence MBE, in 1980 and it had revived the TAIS concept. However, any deployment of a field computer system was going to be swept up in the politics surrounding the deployment of field computing with WAVELL, the 'operational' HQ level system being considered for formation headquarters in the Field Army. The key issue was to evaluate whether the system should be operational or administrative. A conference was held in late 1980 at HQ 1 (Br) Corps chaired by the Chief of Staff, and on grounds of cost the administrative solution won the day and the way was clear for its use for logistic systems. The RAOC solution to TAIS, known as COFFER, standing for Computerized Office and Field Force Electronic Record, was deployed in 1982 to 3 Ordnance Battalion with Lieutenant Colonel David Harris, the Commander Supply, being given the first sets. It would ultimately be spread around most second line stores units in the RAOC and be the basis for inventory management at that level for many years to come.

Eventually, the time came for the Commando Ordnance Squadron to leave the Falklands for home with the main body departing on Friday 13 August, smiling, despite the inauspicious nature of the day and date. It was long after the other elements of the invasion force had left, and it would still be a few more weeks before they would be followed by 81 and 91 Companies. The logistic task in the Falklands was handed over to the Falkland Islands Logistic Battalion, a new unit created to support the post-conflict garrison. The supply company was to be the direct descendant of the Ordnance units that served through the war and many of its officers and men were, over the next ten years, to be the same soldiers who had fought in the war, and who had overcome so much to deliver what was needed to allow the infantry to finish their task.

A major part of the clear up was ammunition, British and Argentinean, and it soon became clear that the existing RAOC technical manpower was inadequate for the size of the clearance task. DLSA, Brigadier Charles Smith, visited the Falklands in July and recommended the formation of a composite ammunition company to undertake the task. An advance party of ten ATs, commanded by Conductor Steve Harmon, arrived by air on 1 August, to be followed by the rest, including the Company Commander, Major Peter Courtney-Green, three days later. The company initially comprised fifty-nine men, including a platoon of twenty-five men of the Royal Pioneer Corps. The RAOC element comprised ammunition technicians, supply specialists, supply clerks and MHE operators. On the company's arrival it took under command two ATOs, Captains Geoff Cox and Rick Gill, and four ATs who had sailed with the task force but who had had the misfortune to remain at sea until the surrender. The company became part of the Falkland Islands Logistic Battalion, which then had two RAOC companies, a stores company and the composite ammunition company.

Most of the British ammunition on the islands was in reasonably good condition, although it was widely dispersed in supply ships, at beachheads and in ad hoc dumps. The only real problems were found at abandoned gun positions from which the gunners had been lifted out to fresh positions, leaving behind the ammunition that had been prepared for firing, and at dumps of infantry support weapons ammunition, which had been similarly prepared. There were particular problems with mortar ammunition, 66-mm rockets and guided missiles. In general the Argentines had abandoned their positions more hastily than the British, and it was their ammunition which posed real problems. The types and origins of the ammunition used by the Argentine forces were more varied than would be encountered in the average NATO army. Whilst much of it was made in the Argentine, a great deal had been purchased from a variety of overseas suppliers, including, for example, Italy, Spain, the USA, the UK, France, Israel and the USSR. Some of it had clearly found its way to Argentina by indirect routes: an example was SAM 7 anti-aircraft missiles which were marked in Russian and overprinted in Arabic.

It was found that the problems in Stanley were concentrated at a number of sites around the town, the houses and streets having mostly been cleared by the time of the company's arrival. However, one house was later discovered in which the local resident, a Falkland Islander born and bred, had hidden all the arms, ammunition and explosives he could find, since he was determined to repel another invasion, should one occur, with or without the help of British forces.

Clearing the area around Stanley proved to be frustrating, because as ammunition and explosives were laboriously disposed of more tended to be found, or be brought in from outlying areas. An area of particular difficulty, the racecourse, illustrates some of the problems. Here the Argentines had dug twelve large, deep pits, filled them with ammunition and covered them with camouflage. It had perhaps been a satisfactory arrangement at the time but, as the ground thawed, the pits filled with water, completely submerging all the ammunition in them. Their clearance was an extremely unpleasant job for the men who spent seven weeks doing it under the direction of Staff Sergeant K Burton. Pumping out the water was never completely successful because the surrounding ground was so sodden that the pits would quickly fill up again, and most of the men spent several hours every day with their feet in mud and with water up to their thighs, and, as often as not, exposed to driving rain.

During the six months of its existence the composite ammunition company made large areas safe, established fit stocks of some 3,500 tons of ammunition in properly laid out field storage locations, and back-loaded to the UK some 2,500 tons. The company left the Falklands early in January 1983 after handing over its responsibilities to an Ammunition Platoon of the Logistic Battalion's Stores Company, and was disbanded on arrival in the UK.

The final outcome of the war was a much-enlarged garrison in the Falkland Islands, based around a battalion group with RA, RE, AAC and logistic support. Quite a difference from the handful of Royal Marines that had been the original garrison and something of a departure from a 1974 defence review that had presaged a withdrawal from the UK's overseas commitments.

The RAOC ended the war with new structures in place in the UK base and in Germany, yet another operational commitment to meet in the South Atlantic for which it was to receive no extra manpower and running commitments in Cyprus and Northern Ireland. No lessons were learned from the Falklands War, but huge numbers of old ones were re-learned – and the Army promptly forget them in the post-war euphoria of a job well done and the fiscal difficulties associated with preventing them happening yet again the next time round. And as the RAOC entered, unknowingly, the last ten years of its existence, Roy Cobb began to reconstitute 10,000 men's worth of tentage – and how he had got it in the first place? Still best not to ask.

Notes

[1] Traverse: a protective earth mound or brick wall built round ESHs to prevent propagation in the event of an explosion.

[2] Under the NATO staff system the principal staff branches were G1 for personnel, G2 for intelligence, G3 for operations, G4 for logistics and G5 for civil affairs.

[3] Sponsored TA were units formed of specialist trades, such as Petroleum Operators, who had no evening or weekend training commitment and simply came together for two weeks a year at a central location for training or exercises. Generally, the theory was that their civilian role was the one they filled in the TA and this reduced the technical training requirement. Independent units were of a more general nature, had drill halls and met for several evenings and weekends a year as well as their two weeks annual camp commitment.

[4] 3 Commando Brigade

[5] Equipped and trained for parachuting. Of the three battalions of the Parachute Regiment two were at any one time 'in role'.

[6] A 200 mile zone around the Falklands that Her Majesty's Government had declared off limits to Argentinean Naval elements on pain of interdiction.

[7] Unit Bulk Refuelling Equipment, a mini container or pod mounted on a 4 or 8 ton truck. There were usually two per vehicle giving a total capacity of 3,000 litres of fuel.

[8] A motorized raft used for ship to shore transfers, operated by the RCT.

Chapter Nine

Born Out of War; At War to the End 1983 – 1993

Sand gets in everything . . . eyes, breakfast and rifle   *Kate Adie, BBC Television Journalist 2004*

One of the outcomes of the Falklands War was to give Margaret Thatcher another term as Prime Minister. She won the June 1983 election with 397 seats to the Labour Party's 209. The repelling of the Argentinean invasion had been a hugely popular undertaking and the jingoism it generated had been a great national binding force. National pride had received a huge boost and Britain had shown it could still wield a stick as a great power. However, it was over almost as quickly as it had begun and in the post-war euphoria of victory there was no more public inclination than before the war to maintain massive fleets or large armed forces. With the war a thing of the past, it was not long before the country returned to the familiar domestic nightmares of strikes, economic decline and social discontent.

For the Army there had been no time to stand still, to take a breath. The first changes had begun soon after the war in the South Atlantic came to an end; just one of the many shifts of structure and process through which the RAOC had been forced to work over the years, yet at no time was it allowed to affect the service it gave to the Army.

This time the pressure, the reorganization, was both external and internal. Internally there was a move to reform the RAOC's field force structure into battalions. For example, on 20 July 1943 1st Battalion RAOC had formed at Bramley to man the large ammunition depot located there. In January 1946 it was re-titled Central Ammunition Depot Bramley, and remained in being under that name until it was handed over to the US Army in the mid 1970s. In 1983 the battalion re-formed as 1 Ordnance Battalion, an amalgamation of RAOC units in 1st and 2nd Armoured Divisions, as part of the wider reorganization of 1 (Br) Corps.

A formation parade was held at Soltau, West Germany, with all three companies present. The ceremony was a simple one, with both the Divisional Commander and Commander Supply 1 (Br) Corps present. Brigadier John Skinner, in his address to the battalion, reminded them that the job had not changed significantly, or the way in which it is done. The battalion and company headquarters had still to achieve that delicate blend of encouragement and harassment which was such a successful feature of British Army organization. He made the point that they had now become a battalion and that when they had settled down, grown together and developed that corporate spirit, then that sense of belonging to a battalion would be apparent. He stated that belonging to a battalion or a regiment is so important in Army life that many others envy the spirit it generates. He had summed the importance to the RAOC of the restructuring exercise into battalions, the sense of identity it would bring, not just within the RAOC but in the wider Army of which they were now so much more obviously a part. The symbolism was significant.

The reorganized and renamed units of the RAOC soon began to make their presence felt on the sporting field – Army squash champions, Army badminton champions and BAOR minor-unit football champions all within the first three months. Army sport always had a great bonding effect, and at a time when the country had been focussed on a war and the RAOC had faced in its wake yet further changes, its effect was never more important. Not for nothing was it a feature of Army life on which all good commanders focussed.

However, it was more than just sporting prowess that would emanate from the changes. There was a significant amount of work in restructuring the Ordnance companies and the stores sections to accord with the new battalion structure. It also regularized to a greater extent than hitherto the place of the RAOC within the division, and in particular the role of the Commander Supply, who was now also a Commanding Officer. His role was determined as being in the rear of the division controlling the divisional RV and commanding the plethora of small units that congregated in the DAA. The structure also called into question the division of labour that had emanated from the McLeod report which, although it had sliced up the logistic tasks into functions, had still arrived at a solution based on cap badges. In particular the role of the RAOC and the RCT in the control of combat supplies needed to be reconsidered. However, at this stage it was a step too far in the midst of all the other work generated by the introduction of the RAOC battalion structure.

In the corridors of power in HQ DGOS in Andover things were happening that would lead over time to a radical change in the way the Army conducted its top level business. The beginnings were relatively innocent in that Michael Heseltine, the Secretary of State for Defence, wished to establish a management information system, which he called MINIS, so he could monitor his department and make decisions based on real information. Budget holders were to report personally to him on their stewardship of their area of responsibility. The DGOS was one such and many hands were wrung among hard pressed staff officers faced with the prospect of yet another series of ministerial briefs.

The pressure was further increased with the introduction of a regime of corporate planning, taking a five year look at the way ahead, setting targets and objectives and determining key performance measures and indicators. If the logistic support of the Army was a multi-million pound business then it was to be run like a business. The New Management Strategy was being born and it would be there to stay.

In June 1983 the RAOC hosted the biennial international conference on terrorist devices, involving 250 delegates from thirty-five countries, demonstrating the leading position the RAOC had developed in this work. During the course of the year consultancy advice was requested by, and given to, the governments of Thailand and Bahrain, and to the American element of the multi-national force in the Lebanon in the wake of the bomb that killed 250 US Marines close to Beirut airport. The Army School of Ammunition was also a part of this spread of experience. During the year it would train 154 students from overseas countries.

It was Friday 24 June 1983 when Lieutenant Colonel Bill Burnip, accompanying the DGOS, Major General Bill Whalley, on a tour of BAOR, rang in to Ord 1, DGOS' principal staff branch, to see if anything was going on.

'It's very quiet' was the response. 'You can tell the General the Corps is in safe hands.'

Just ten minutes later, at around 11.00 am Lieutenant Colonel David Furness-Gibbon rang asking where the DGOS could be found.

The Donnington
fire burned with
huge intensity...

'Donnnington's on fire '

'What do you mean on fire?'

'How does fifteen appliances and rising sound?'

It was eventually to rise to twenty-four major appliances and to gut building B6 completely, a storehouse that was a victim of its history. From the end of the Second World War until the mid-seventies depots were run on the concept of detailed ranges of fast-moving stores held in conventional binning and block stacks. Realistic precautions were taken and, measured against a low fire risk, any outbreak would be within the capability of depot staffs and depot fire brigades. There were no major fires during this period and in any event the work in the depots was labour-intensive with staffing at a much higher level than was to be the case in the eighties and nineties. Consequently, more people were available for first aid firefighting and to keep an eye out for the unexpected.

However, the demands of manpower and financial savings led to closures and to the concentration of stocks in smaller areas. Paradoxical really, since the Army's equipment programme was bringing more and more complex equipments into service and the run on of ageing equipment, caused by delays in new equipment and funding restrictions, were creating a significant retention and maintenance problem. The inventory was going up not down. However, the closure programme gave rise to the introduction of adjustable pallet racking, and high density storage became a reality with large amounts of MHE. Because the Donnington buildings had to be redesigned and rebuilt around the existing structures it meant that the unprotected steel pillars that were used for the cranes were also the roof supports. It was this mass of steel, that was not removed during the modernization process due to enormous cost, that came crashing down at the height of the fire, sounding for all the world like large explosions.

...and the
destruction was
complete.

Originally, fire protective practices in the Army had been based upon strict disciplinary measures, with statutory requirements only governing the safety of personnel. Reliance, therefore was placed on the normal range of fire points backed where necessary by an Army Fire Brigade supported by the local authority. The fire risk inherent in HDS was recognized at a very early stage in its introduction, but compartmentalization, one of the key safety measures, had been ruled out for practical reasons whilst other measures in train to ameliorate the risk had not been fully implemented, due to time and the cost requiring a staging of expenditure.

In this case the fire started in the worst possible place, about one metre high in the racking in the centre of the shed. It was at 10.00 am when the shed work force of some twelve military and seventy civilians went to their mid-morning break leaving behind just one warrant officer and three female members of the workforce. At about five minutes past ten one of these women was sitting at a work table in the checking area when she saw flames coming from nearby racking. She ran to a nearby workstation calling out '...fire in the racking'. By nine minutes past ten the depot fire brigade had been informed and they attended, with the immediate assistance of two local area fire brigade units.

The fire plume spread rapidly upwards in a 'V' formation and almost immediately the flames reached the top of the stack. They hit the roof and a tremendous elongation of flame occurred along the top of the racking with rapid fire spread in all directions. The fire was finally brought under control at about 4.00 pm after massive effort by the fire services, but the storehouse and all its contents were completely destroyed.

Fortunately, there was no loss of life or serious injury. However, the stock lost included ranges of mechanical transport spares, technical spares and textiles being held in bulk for the manufacture of ceremonial uniforms, all at an assessed value of £160 million (£320 million). The impact on the Army was very serious for many of the spares were lifetime buys for major equipments and their replacement presented huge problems. In many cases it involved finding sources of supply for spares for out-of-date equipment still in service where the now destroyed lifetime buys had provided a reserve of capability against delays in replacing existing equipments.

Elsewhere better things were happening. For the second year running an RAOC unit in BAOR received the freedom of a German city. On 10 September 1983 members of the Forward Ordnance Depot, Dulmen, exercised their new right to march through the town with swords drawn and bayonets fixed. The ceremony, held in the picturesque market place in Dulmen, brought to a climax a week of Anglo-German celebrations, ranging from a military families' street party to a football match, from formal civil receptions to beating of retreat outside the Rathaus, or town hall, by the RAOC Staff Band and the Pipes and Drums of the 2nd Battalion, 51 Highland Regiment (Volunteers).

There were operational commitments to be considered as well. There were only two units of the British Army on permanent operational duty: 22 SAS Regiment and 11 Ordnance Battalion (EOD), the latter commanded in 1983 by Lieutenant Colonel Graham Cowell. He was responsible to the Home Office, through the Ministry of Defence, for ensuring that EOD operators from all three Services were of a standard suitable to cope with IEDD situations in Great Britain. This was achieved by each of the Battalion Companies, 521, 621 and 721 holding biannual licensing exercises involving, where possible, the civilian police, who were usually the first disciplined force to react to such situations. Historically, licensing exercises began within 1 AIDU with a series of exercises to ensure staff were kept up to the mark. Major Peter Courtney-Green, in the mid-seventies, had realized that to be effective such training should involve the police. He, together with Superintendent Mike

The Director General of Ordnance Services, Major General Bill Whalley, at the Freedom ceremony.

Prunty of Merseyside Police, devised the first of a series of exercises that brought the two organizations together. Subsequent SATOs North, Major Charles Jackman and Major Alan Glasby, further developed the exercise with increasing RN, RAF and RE involvement into what by the early eighties was truly a joint police/armed services exercise. Other units or bodies would contribute; RAVC to advise and demonstrate the use of explosive search dogs; RAMC for real medical cover and casualty simulation; REME for vehicle and wheelbarrow repair; RPC as witnesses and a labour force. The scenario of the exercise was always that of the Great Britain of the day and the police would react as in real life and investigate incidents. Dependent upon the incident and their investigation an EOD team might then be tasked to the scene. It was realistic and effective training and did much to sustain the high level of operational capability required by 11 Ordnance Battalion to fulfil its duty to the nation and the public.

The 'cosmopolitan' nature of the EOD licensing exercises is shown here, with a RN operator working with the police with WOII Alan Proctor RAOC looking on.

Advances were also taking place with the RAOC's IT capability. The replacement was taking place at Bicester of Stores System 2 by Stores System 3, phased over the three year period between 1982 and 1985. The major new function provided by SS3 was SCARAB, a Scales and Related Applicability Base, thereby redeeming a major deficiency of SS2, which had been the lack of a unified scales process. SCARAB provided a capability to issue by scale all NATO stock numbers in that scale. Unfortunately, the capability to work upwards from NSN to scale on line to establish applicability and commonality was not available due to a very significant processing overhead. Furthermore, there continued to be functional deficiencies that had been the result of mainframe capacity constraints in SS1 and SS2. There was, for example, only a small amount of item history data.

At about the same time the RAOC was introducing a classified online network. The development of this, almost in spite of a military communications community that persisted in putting up barriers, addressed in part the central, manual data capture load, and therefore the currency and accuracy of the data, inherent in centralized processing. This network, which attracted a number of acronyms of which ASDN, Army Supply Data Network, was probably the most appropriate, comprised a number of systems. First there was ROLAND which allowed update and enquiry facilities by ammunition depots and RAOC staff branches. Then there was SALOME which provided a similar service for VESPER, which was the system for matching equipment liabilities against the assets actually held and their deployment. Finally, there was RAOC Mail in both a classified and an unclassified version.

Unfortunately, the security regime required depots and HQs in UK and BAOR to have secure processing facilities. This meant separate hardware and secure communications serving each site. A fairly mundane implication of this was the need for establishment action to create suitably vetted posts so that cryptographic equipment could be held and used; all an added complication and an added burden. Management and maintenance of the growing network was carried out at Bicester by a joint DSCS and 2 Signals Brigade team, with the RAOC end being looked after by Lieutenant Colonel Tony Course.

It was throughout this period that COFFER, having proved itself in the 3 Ordnance Battalion trials, was being distributed throughout Ordnance companies and some stores sections attached to REME workshops. As tertiary depots they were now a part of a structured system of IT support that went to the very heart of the RAOC and the repository for its inventory information held on the Bicester mainframe. It was a tremendous advance, but the system still suffered from being demand led and not consumption led. Furthermore, units that held and used large quantities of spares, were still accounting manually for their stocks. Thus whilst the RAOC could see what it was holding in RAOC units, it replaced stock based on the demand pattern from the tertiary depots, not knowing what the quartermasters were actually doing when they received the stock. This could include hoarding and bartering. Once an item went into the unit it was lost to sight and could no longer be managed. This was one link in the IT chain that was still missing, and until that gap was plugged the aspiration of a global warehouse where the RAOC could manage the complete inventory would not be realized. However, the technology to permit that was still a little way off; and there was no sign whatsoever of any communications fit being put in place to allow COFFER to work effectively in deployed field force units, let alone a unit system that could fit in with it. For the present data would be passed in these circumstances either by tapes carried by dispatch riders or, and only in Germany, down a telephone link provided by the German telecommunications authorities into the field location.

On 11 September 1983 6 Ordnance Battalion, based in Germany in Bielefeld and Gütersloh, won the Cambrian March, an annual infantry patrol competition for regular and Territorial Army units. It had been described by *The Times* as the toughest competition of its type in NATO. The 6 Ordnance Battalion team, of nine men, was led by WOII (CSM) D V Jones and they completed the four day test of endurance and military skills ahead of the teeth arm teams. To offer some idea of what this involved, the patrol covered fifty miles of Welsh mountains and moor land, punctuated by various tests in which the team carried out, for example, river crossings, clearance of buildings, flushing out snipers and completing helicopter drills. The competition ended with them carrying the rifles and sixty pounds of equipment they had carried throughout the competition on a six mile run to be followed by an assault course and a falling plate shoot. The weather they endured was reliably reported as the worst for the last ten years of the competition. It was proof yet again that RAOC soldiers with the right training could be better than the best at what the best thought they were best at.

In January 1984 a contract was let for the development of the western site at CAD Kineton on ground over which the Battle of Edgehill had been fought in 1642 during the English Civil War. The build involved the construction of 105 Explosive Storehouses together with all the supporting service and administrative buildings. The ESHs were of a new design which would allow the maximization of storage of high density, high capacity modern ammunition, countering the sort of storage problems that had closed other ammunition depots at places like Bramley, Corsham and Nesscliffe. It was due to be finished by 1987 at which point CAD Kineton would be the most modern and one of the largest ammunition depots in Europe.

On Wednesday 8 February 1984 the evacuation took place of the British Force in the Lebanon, on the first anniversary of its deployment to that war-torn country when its task had been to demonstrate the Government's support for the legitimate government of the Lebanon in the face of a range of insurrectionist groups. Majors Mike Southworth, Stuart Bennet and Frank Steer, all RAOC, filled the DCOS role on a series of four-month tours each. The evacuation was in two parts, with BRITFORLEB redeployed from their base in Hadath, a Beirut suburb, to the RFA *Reliant*, and on Friday 10 February, 518 civilians of twenty-six different nationalities were evacuated from Beirut to RAF Akrotiri, Cyprus. Both operations were successfully carried out with remarkable speed and efficiency and with considerable RAOC involvement. The operation was directed by Colonel Peter Forshaw, late RAOC, DCOS GI/G4/G5 at Headquarters Land Forces Cyprus.

The force moved, complete with all vehicles and equipment, to the port of Jounieh, some fifteen miles north of Beirut, from where three Sea King and three Chinook helicopters then airlifted them, with their equipment, onto *Reliant*. The operation took ten hours and seventy sorties to complete and RAF Phantoms from Cyprus provided air cover. Colonel Forshaw commanded the operation from the *Reliant* and Major Frank Steer RAOC was responsible for the airlift from Jounieh. The Chief of the

Defence Staff, Field Marshal Sir Edwin Bramall sent the following tribute:

> I wish to send you my warmest congratulations. The delicate manoeuvre of extracting our troops safely from such a sensitive environment and the difficult task of loading vehicles and equipment on to RFA *Reliant* has been accomplished with great skill and professionalism.

The second operation, to evacuate the 518 civilians, was conducted in two phases. Initially the evacuees were airlifted by Sea King to the RFA and then taken by Chinook and Wessex helicopters to RAF Akrotiri in Cyprus. Once again air cover was provided by RAF Phantom aircraft from Cyprus. British Forces Cyprus also chartered two ships, the SOL *Georghious* and the SOL *Phyrne*. Each ship had a military evacuation team embarked which were commanded by Major John Wright RAOC and Major Richard Bird RAOC respectively. The SOL *Georghious* was dispatched to Jounieh to take on evacuees but due to a combination of poor weather and

Major Mike Southworth and Staff Sergeant Bob Waller in the mine proofed RAOC Land-Rover with its anti roll bars in Beirut early in 1983.

unfavourable local factors it had to return empty handed. The SOL *Phyrne* remained on standby at Limassol but was not tasked. In a special tribute, the Secretary of State for Defence, the Right Honourable Michael Heseltine MP said:

> I wish to send my warmest congratulations on the safe completion of the evacuation of five hundred and eighteen British and other nationals from Lebanon which followed so closely on the heels of the redeployment of BRITFORLEB from its Hadath base. From a hazardous environment ashore and with little help from the weather you have moved people and equipment in a combined land, sea and air operation without a hitch. The fifty-six deck-landings today on the RFA *Reliant* alone bears testimony to the skill and dedication of all ranks of the Services and RFA crew members involved, a skill I know has been mirrored by those on land in headquarters, airfields and ports. My sincere thanks to you all.

Immediately following this the RAOC was involved in a famine relief operation for Ethiopia, again centred on Cyprus. At very short notice large quantities of water-purifying equipment were issued as well as stores required for air dropping the relief aid. At the same time there was a continuous need to supply defence stores to the military forces deployed in support of the civil police at Greenham Common near Newbury in Berkshire where the presence of American cruise missiles with a nuclear capability had inspired a women's peace movement into permanent protest.

In March 1984 Margaret Thatcher's government was assailed by the impact of a miners' strike led by Arthur Scargill. It had no direct impact on the RAOC in the sense that no soldiers were deployed to counter any activity by the miners, although considerable quantities of accommodation stores were provided for deployed police forces. However, the impact on the economy was severe and would lead to further cuts in public spending that would have their impact on defence. Almost without exception the easy in-year cash regulator was Vote 2K1, the money set aside in the defence budget for vehicle and equipment spares. They were seen as essentially short lead time items and cuts were seen as easy to make, and they could be swingeing. Not only were there spares cuts, but they were accompanied by yet further run-on of ageing equipments, and an increase in the number of variants being supported. For example, in 1976 there had been just nine variants in the A Vehicle fleet. By the mid-eighties it was nineteen, and it was predicted to be twenty-seven by the mid-nineties.

The impact on a vehicle fleet that was growing ever more unserviceable for want of proper maintenance through lack of money for spares went largely ignored, despite the equipment managers' warnings. The lack of an effective forward looking repair policy was a further difficulty, and the outcome for the RAOC, the B Vehicle equipment managers, was a huge amount of work in reprioritising budget spends and managing an ageing and gradually more and more decrepit fleet. The outcome would manifest itself in large numbers of vehicles with low readiness and availability towards the end of the decade for want of effective care and maintenance. It would be a level of availability that was so low it would reach the Army Board agenda.

It was at this time that Captain Robbie Robinson won his third consecutive Army Squash Championship when he defeated Captain Chris Wilson RA, the then Scottish champion, three games to nil. However hard Wilson tried to vary the pace of the game Robinson matched him shot for shot. A very gifted and talented player, Robinson was never extended to the full and he dominated Wilson with a display of power cleverly mixed with a variety of lobs, boasts and delicate drops. In the same tournament Corporal Clark Adam from 9 Ordnance Battalion beat Corporal Pollard, the under-25 Champion, in the Classic Plate to retain his place in the Army team. The RAOC really was a powerhouse of Army, national and international squash.

Later that same year CVD Ashchurch was invited to organize and run the UKLF indoor tug-of-war championships; and of course they participated. There were ten teams, including some very notable performers, such as 4 UDR, the then current Northern Ireland champions and 1982 Army outdoor champions; 40 Field Regiment RA, three times Army outdoor champions and Braemar 1981 and 1982 Inter Services Champions; and the Junior Leaders Regiment RA, the then current UK National Youth Champions. Emulating their forebears from Feltham in the early fifties, and carrying on

The Ashchurch team in training, with Major Bob Reid at the back as the anchor man.

a tradition of tug-of-war in the RAOC, CVD Ashchurch won all three weights: 560 kilos, 640 kilos and catch weight. A wonderful result that was only a foretaste of yet more to come. Ashchurch went on to win two of the Army titles, and came second in the 640 kilo pull. The depot had won, in a period of six weeks, three District, four UKLF, two Army titles and one runner-up. During the three competitions, the Ashchurch teams pulled 127 ends, winning 124 and losing only three.

Throughout the RAOC, units were building on the Corps' leadership and expertise in the use of computers, and had been quick to realize the potential benefits of their use to help with many aspects of their work. Applications for microcomputers were landing increasingly frequently on the desks of the DSCS manned RAOC Small System Group. By the middle of 1984 there had been 138 applications throughout the RAOC for microcomputers, with potential uses including a microcomputer in the stores section in the Hebrides, a system for the Commando Logistic Squadron which they took to all sorts of remote and exotic places, an ICL personal computer with the RAOC in the Falklands, a hand held microcomputer to check stock records in the field so that up to date figures could be readily captured and passed on to the decision makers, and a system to keep account of the costs of running air-conditioning in flats in Hong Kong. The savings attributable to each project averaged £60,000 (£115,000), and this was after the costs of the microcomputers and associated software had been taken into account.

The RAOC was also using turnkey products, largely off the shelf, to improve some of its management processes. One such was the Ammunition Management Area Network and Depot Assistance system, known as AMANDA. This system replaced the limited in-house small system 'Microfix' in the management of ammunition depots. It was introduced and managed through working with a company called Secure Information Systems Limited and was looked after for the RAOC by Lieutenant Colonel Bill Gaskin RAOC who had spent a lifetime in ammunition. Time consuming and laborious tasks such as the management of fraction packs and an algorithm to ensure the issue of the most appropriate stock were significant features of AMANDA.

The year saw the raising of ten District Ordnance companies. They were TA units established to provide Ordnance support to home defence units in general war when there was a real threat of invasion and bombing of the UK mainland.

During the latter part of September and early October the whole Army was heavily involved in Exercise LIONHEART, an amalgam of the annual 1 (Br) Corps Exercise SPEARPOINT and a reinforcement exercise called FULL FLOW. It was the largest exercise mounted by BAOR since the end of the Second World War and all the RAOC's UK depots were involved in the preparation, and in issuing stores and equipment to units taking part.

A TA Petroleum Operator on Exercise LIONHEART assembling a Bulk Fuel Installation while dressed in NBC kit.

The reinforcement phase of the exercise saw over 50,000 soldiers moved across the Channel. This included 500 regular RAOC whose war role lay in Germany although in peace they were individually employed in the UK base in a range of roles. They were joined by 1,300 members of the RAOC TA. For the RAOC the exercise was intended to test the mobilization of depots in Germany and the ability to re-supply 1 (Br) Corps in war. Depots in the rear issued stores to 125 units. They supplied and subsequently received back into stock over 3,000 vehicles. Some 8,000 pallets of simulated ammunition were issued to forward depots by road and by rail, hindered by raids by special forces and simulated chemical attacks.

The SPEARPOINT phase of the exercise was supported by the five in-theatre Ordnance battalions, brought up to full war strength by the reinforcements shipped out from the UK base and by 2 Ordnance Battalion which deployed from York with 2nd Infantry Division. It was a huge commitment and involved a massive planning load. It proved to some extent that the system worked, but the real test could only ever come if it was to be done for real. It is extraordinarily hard to learn deep and meaningful logistic lessons on an exercise where so much has, perforce, to be orchestrated and the next one was not planned to take place for another five years, and that would be a war. However, apart from proving that the new battalion structure worked well, the clear, key lessons showed up a shortage of lift and MHE in RAOC units and installations and at unit level across the Army. There was also a

Vehicles ready for issue to LIONHEART at FVD Recklinghausen.

worrying shortage of bulk fuel lift, a problem that was to go unresolved for many years. It was also noted as a key point that if PTARMIGAN, the new field communications trunk system that had replaced BRUIN in the 1 (Br) Corps area, could link the RAOC IT system together it would improve response times and planning. It would have been a major force multiplier. It would never happen.

The Tory party conference in Brighton that year was marred by an attempt by the IRA on the life of the Prime Minister and members of her Cabinet and their spouses through the detonation of a bomb that had been carefully secreted in the building. A team from 11 Battalion (EOD) was on the scene within minutes and immediately dealt with a second suspect device and in so doing allowed rescue work to process without delay. It had already been a busy year for the Battalion with thirty-four live devices having been neutralized and 552 other IED related incidents having been investigated.

The thrust to civilianization and the constant battles to do more with less, were perennial problems for the RAOC. Michael Heseltine, the Secretary of State for Defence had said that any job being done by servicemen that could be done by a MOD civilian should be civilianized; and any job being done by a MOD civilian that could be contractorized should be contractorized. However, the Corps did have the support of the Army Board for its stance that the supply chain was an end to end process including the

base depots, and that its concept for reinforcing its under-strength operational units in Germany was sound. In the Army Board report on the LEAN LOOK study, which was, *inter alia*, an examination of manning levels related to tasks, whilst accepting the recommended cuts of 202 military and 1,050 civilian posts, they agreed that most non-operational roles were already civilianized. They further agreed that the RAOC Field Force was inadequately manned for its mobilization tasks and that the retention of military manpower in certain RAOC non-field force units was justified. They confirmed that the shadow unit concept was operationally essential and that total civilianization or contractorization

The RAOC Explosive Ordnance Disposal Team at the Brighton bomb scene.

of the UK base and BAOR theatre depots was operationally unacceptable. Would that their advice had been heeded in the years to come.

The miners' strike ended after dragging on for a year. It had been characterized by violent clashes between the police and miners' pickets. However, in the end Margaret Thatcher's determination paid off and the result of the strike was a profound defeat for the miners and the subsequent closure of many more pits. But, the government's troubles were not over, and it was to be plagued by a whole series of white-collar and public service workers strikes reaching out into 1987. Nonetheless, in spite of this the country's economic state was being reversed. North Sea oil played its part with Britain becoming self-sufficient and thus in a unique position of strength in its energy base. Certainly, there was no longer a dependence on coal. And the balance of payments moved into the black, although there was a shift in the basis of productivity in the economy. Manufacturing was less and less important with the focus moving to services and technology.

At the Sovereign's Parade at Sandhurst in May 1985 there was a momentous event when Junior Under Officer David Ruff, to be commissioned that day into the RAOC, was presented by his Sovereign, also his Colonel-

David Ruff receiving the Sword of Honour from his Sovereign who, within a matter of hours, as his commission would be granted at midnight that night, would also be his Colonel-in-Chief.

in-Chief, with the Sword of Honour as the best cadet of his course. It was the first time an officer cadet being commissioned into the RAOC had earned the prized sword. David Ruff would serve on in the RAOC into the RLC and retire as a full colonel after a successful and, in parts, exciting career.

Stores System 3 went live at COD Bicester, without interruption to the supply system in general. It was the largest IT project the RAOC had ever undertaken, or would undertake. For its time it was well advanced, employing the most modern data base and transaction processing techniques. The aspiration was that it would last many years into the future. At the same time a mainframe computer was put into COD Donnington to operate in tandem with the Bicester computer and thereby provide resilience in the system.

The highest honour that a council can confer is that of Honorary Freedom of the Borough and, on 25 January 1984, the council of the Borough of Surrey Heath had unanimously agreed to accord this honour to the Royal Army Ordnance Corps, being mindful of the long and distinguished record of the Corps and the ties between it and the borough. The Local Government Act 1972 requires a special meeting of the council to be called for the purpose of passing the appropriate specific resolution conferring the honorary freedom and such a meeting took place on 23 January 1985 in the presence of Brigadier David Parker, the Commander of the RAOC Training Centre.

The Freedom Parade at Deepcut on 17 May 1985 was one of the most impressive ceremonies to have been held in Blackdown Barracks since they were opened by Her Majesty the Queen in July 1972. The sun shone brightly as the Freedom Scroll was read by the borough chief executive, Mr Michael Orlik. A sword was then presented to the mayor, Councillor John Hall, by the Representative Colonel Commandant, Major General Mike Callan, on behalf of the Corps. An illuminated engrossment of the council's Resolution of 23 January, in the form of a scroll impressed with the Seal of the Council and witnessed by the mayor and the chief executive and town clerk, was presented by the mayor to the Representative Colonel Commandant. The scroll was contained in a walnut casket bearing the arms of the borough and the RAOC badge

Following a trooping of the scroll, the entire parade, consisting of officers and soldiers from the Training Battalion and Depot RAOC and commanded by Lieutenant Colonel 'Baz' Dickson, moved to Camberley where they marched through the streets with bands playing, drums beating and bayonets fixed. Refreshments were then served by the mayor and the General to the thirsty participants, before moving to the Civic Hall where the borough entertained representatives of all ranks of the Corps and their wives to luncheon. On that evening a reception was held for over 100 borough guests in the Headquarters RAOC Officers' Mess, culminating in Beating Retreat by the RAOC Staff Band.

In conjunction with the granting of the freedom, a civic service was held in St Michael's Church, Camberley, on Sunday, 19 May, at which the garrison padre, the Reverend Derek Bailey, participated and the Representative Colonel Commandant read a lesson. From 11 am until 6 pm on that day, Blackdown Barracks opened its gates to the public and about 10,000 people took advantage of the opportunity. On arrival they were faced with an impressive display of all aspects of the RAOC's work.

Towards the end of 1985 changes were made to some RAOC trades. Drivers were amalgamated with the supply specialist, or storeman, trade. It was felt that this would allow greater flexibility of employment within units and improve the promotion prospects for drivers. The new trade would be known as supply specialist, with no reference to driver as a trade, either subsidiary or primary. A further change was made to permit vehicle specialists to fill some MT appointments, to widen employment possibilities and improve promotion prospects. Perhaps the most significant change was that by 7 October 1985 the RAOC Manning and Record Office was to assume responsibility for the management of WRAC members of the supply specialist and supply controller, or technical clerk, trades. Under these new arrangements the RAOC M&RO was to manage WRAC of both trades from the date they completed employment training to the end of their service, whereupon they would revert to WRAC management for discharge. However, during their service, members of both trades were to be posted and promoted on an equal basis with male RAOC soldiers, with the exception that WRAC were not to be permitted to serve in field force and certain other units identified by the Army Board.

A glimpse into a future that would eventually come the way of the RAOC was the move, in December 1985, of relevant staff from the Employment Training School RAOC at Deepcut to conduct clerical training at Worthy Down, although the Army School of Clerical Training was to be under the technical control of Commander RAOC Training Centre. Allied to the move was the implementation of a revised training system for staff clerks which was due to be completed by April 1986. The major changes included the re-introduction of a mandatory Class 2 course and the introduction of a SNCOs' Clerical Duties and Office Management Course for corporals selected for promotion and for sergeants.

At around the same time a review of logistic training had been conducted with the idea of reducing training overheads by amalgamating logistic training establishments. However, it was found not to produce the required savings and, because of the difficulties that would be caused by the loss of either the RCT or RAOC 'Corps' Home' with attendant morale effects, it was decided not to pursue what amounted to a combat service support training regiment concept. Nonetheless, the idea was another harbinger of things to come, as was the bringing together of some, perhaps less contentious, aspects of training when it was decided that there was to be an amalgamation of RCT junior leaders with RAOC apprentices to form the Junior Leaders Regiment RCT/RAOC at Colerne near Bath. The link was to become effective from 5 November 1985 with the first joint intake at Colerne, and the closure of the RAOC Apprentices' College in December 1985. The RAOC Junior Company was to be 88 Ordnance Company and certain key permanent regimental staff appointments were to rotate between RCT and RAOC. The junior leaders would spend three terms at Colerne where they would develop their basic military and leadership skills. They would then report to Blackdown, or Worthy Down in the case of staff clerks, to complete their training as RAOC tradesmen prior to joining their first unit.

As part of the same overall package of re-alignment, HQ RAOC TA was to move from Corsham to Deepcut, with the attendant reduction in rank of the appointment of Commander RAOC TA from brigadier to colonel; with the move taking place in 1986.

History would record that 1985 was one of the quieter years, operationally, experienced by the RAOC for some time. The commitment to Northern Ireland continued while Cyprus was involved in planning for the supply of rations to a UN observer force intended for the Israeli – Syrian border, feeding soldiers from Austria, Canada, Finland and Poland. Accommodation stores were provided from Belize to help with relief work following an earthquake in Mexico and a volcanic eruption in Colombia. And there was the perennial re-supply of the Greenham Common deployment. That apart, little had disturbed the momentum of planned activity. However, that momentum was considerable with the RAOC working hard to meet the demands of units involved in training and other peacetime activities whilst at the same time being heavily committed in continuing to resolve the legacy of scaling problems.

The major training event in that same year had been Exercise BRAVE DEFENDER, involving regular and territorial units in the defence of UK base installations. It was a nationwide exercise, and the ten TA Ordnance companies were all involved, and were tasked with supplying food to the whole of the force deployed on the exercise. The EOD capability was also tested with fifty-one teams deployed and undertaking a range of simulated tasks.

Some research into the history of St Barbara's Church at Deepcut revealed the identity of the artist responsible for the stained glass east windows. They were originally installed in the Portobello Barracks Church, Dublin in 1912 and were moved to Deepcut ten years later. Advice from Dr Michael Wynne, Keeper of Paintings at the National Gallery of Ireland, was that the windows were the work of one Alfred Ernest Child. They were commissioned by the widow of the Reverend Charles O'Reilly who was chaplain to Portobello Barracks in 1887 and 1898 – 99.

Child was born in London in 1875 and, after winning a scholarship to a London art school in 1891, became assistant to Christopher Whall, an eminent stained glass artist. He is reputed to have been Whall's favourite pupil and a design by him for lead glazing was shown at the 1899 Arts and Crafts Society Exhibition. In 1901 he moved to Dublin and began teaching there. In 1903 the An Tur Gloine, or Tower of Glass, opened with Child as manager and his students were soon lining up to fire their glass at his small gas fired kiln. His first commission in Ireland was a two-light annunciation window for Loughrea Cathedral. He was renowned as a neat, punctilious artist and the high standards he set led to his students winning prizes as the best in Europe in the early years of the twentieth century. By 1937 his sight had begun to fail and he died in 1939.

The DGOS, Major General Gerry Berragan, receiving, on 17 January 1986, from ex-Staff Sergeant Sidney Rogerson into the safe keeping of the RAOC Museum the George Cross he was awarded for his activities during the Savernake Forest explosion.

One of the various re-organizations that came about in the mid-eighties was the creation of Continental TA. The idea was that soldiers who had left the Army and settled with their families in Germany might provide a useful source of in-place rapidly deployable TA manpower. Some legal niceties had to be circumvented, not the least of which was the fact that to mobilize the TA required a Queen's Order, the validity of which, for German citizens, was suspect. However, solutions were found and the RAOC contribution was to be 171 (BAOR) Vehicle Platoon (V). The role of the platoon was to support the Forward Vehicle Depot at Recklinghausen, although until April 1987 the unit would be based at Dulmen and concentrate on recruiting and military training.

During the first weekend in May 1986, sixteen potential recruits for the Platoon attended an assessment weekend. They had a variety of backgrounds, some had served as soldiers, some were working on the civilian net and some were dependants but they all had one thing in common; they were keen enthusiastic volunteers. They arrived on the Friday evening and it was soon obvious that a lot of the old skills and talents were still evident in the ex-soldiers. NCO material was soon on show and one recruit's penchant for drill soon produced the platoon's drill instructor. A unit spirit began to gel from the very start with advice being freely given and accepted. Those who were successful at the end of the weekend were attested by Brigadier Peter Istead, Commander Supply BAOR, and Colonel Tony Smith the Commander 15th Ordnance Group. Certainly, it was clear that the formation of a vehicle platoon in Recklinghausen was a viable proposition.

The summer of 1986 also saw another RAOC sporting success in what might be described as a minority sport. The BAOR element of the RAOC Parachute Team, The Cannonballs, made history at the Rhine Army Parachute Championships by taking the open event overall winners' trophy, the only

British military team ever to win the prize. Although the other fifty-five teams who entered produced excellent results in specialist accuracy or relative work performance, the Cannonballs achieved the highest scores in both disciplines. In addition, the team took all the prizes in the BAOR event – some eight major trophies in all. The team was managed and controlled by Major Gary Hawthorne from headquarters AAC 1 (Br) Corps and for this competition comprised WOII John Frew, Sergeant Steve Slater, Sergeant Kurt Ziverts, Corporal Sean Hutchinson and Lance Corporal Graham Pemberton. Sergeant Slater was the individual style champion and Corporal Hutchinson the individual accuracy and overall champion of BAOR.

The Cannonballs parachuting team, with Major General Peter Istead GM, as he was to become, in the centre.

When Sir Christopher Leaver was inaugurated as Lord Mayor of London in 1981, the RAOC, at his request and because of his national service as a subaltern in the RAOC, had not only participated in the parade, but also provided the Guard of Honour. It was from this event that the idea arose of establishing a formal link between the City and the RAOC. It was recommended that the best way to establish such a link would be an affiliation between the Corps and one of the City's ancient Livery Companies, and that this would be a good way of further enhancing the good relationship that existed between the City and the Army, and the Royal Army Ordnance Corps in particular. Consequently, as a result of negotiations carried out by representatives of the City, DGOS and the Colonels Commandant RAOC, an affiliation between the Corps and the Worshipful Company of Gold and Silver Wyre Drawers, one of the City's most ancient livery companies, was proposed. The affiliation received the official approval of Her Majesty the Queen as Colonel-in-Chief of the Royal Army Ordnance Corps and the Court of the Livery of the Worshipful Company of Gold and Silver Wyre Drawers.

Perhaps some explanation of what a livery company is might go some way to understanding the importance of this event for the RAOC. Livery companies at the time numbered ninety-six, and were then, and remain, part of the traditions of the City of London. Most were founded in the Middle Ages as craft guilds to regulate such things as quality and training in the respective trades carried out in the City. Many received their charters from the Sovereign between 1300 AD and 1700 AD. The liverymen had to obtain the Freedom of the City of London before being admitted to the livery. The liverymen had, and retain, the right to elect the Lord Mayor and the Sheriffs of the City. In effect, therefore, it is from the ranks of the liverymen that the government of the City of London is formed.

As for the Gold and Silver Wyre Drawers, the craft went back at least 4,000 years and the earliest 'wire' was made by gilding skins with gold foil, cutting it into strips and winding it round thread. In the fourteenth century the principles of the modern product were established. Essentially, silver was

Major General Jerrie Hulme, in ebullient mood, signs the agreement in the Tower of London with Peter Nathan, the Master of the Gold and Silver Wyre Drawers.

coated with gold, and then drawn through smaller and smaller holes in a die to become fine wire. To make gold thread, the wire was then flattened and spun onto silk or, in modern times, a man-made fibre. Today when silver and gold wire and thread are combined it is known as Morris lace. In embroidery the wire is fashioned into patterns, such as purls, or coiled springs; spangles, or pearl purl, such as is used for borders to badges. Modern methods are sophisticated and, while automated, still require highly skilled operatives; but the craft is essentially the same as in the past. A link was formed that proved itself over the years and was to carry on into the formation of the RLC, bringing mutual benefit to both to the RAOC and the livery.

The pressure continued, from ministers, and the civil servants who briefed them, to civilianize as many military posts as they could in the base, and contract out as many of the supporting functions as they could, despite the advice of the Army Board that had emanated from the LEAN LOOK studies. The senior civil servant in the MOD responsible for civil service manpower and recruiting wrote to senior colleagues with an interest in the issue to affirm that civilianization of as many Army and RAF logistics posts as possible, including the most senior, was a legitimate long-term civil service aim. His stated reason was the financial savings this would accrue, and he proposed an outline manning policy that would see this as a possibility. Clearly, it would also be a major boost to civil service careers. But, in so doing, he failed completely to understand the crucial importance of a flexibly manned supply chain and the need to be able to deploy it right along the LofC within the UK and as far forward in the operational area as necessary. The depots in the UK base were known in those days as static depots, perhaps a term brought in to differentiate them from their mobile, field force counterparts. However, it sent a message that the people in them and the functions they performed were also static, when the reality was quite the opposite. Advanced base areas, usually at ports or airports of entry in the theatre of operations, required to be operated as depots and to act as the forward elements of the UK base depots from which they would draw their resources, including manpower. To restrict the depots within a discrete budgetary area, and having to make savings within that budget, and in a discrete geographical area, concentrated minds on the internal management and structures to the detriment of the resilience of the supply chain, as it has come to be known, as an overall integrated whole, operating, quite literally, from the factory to the foxhole.

Meanwhile, the enduring story of the Webster family and their contribution to the RAOC carried on. On 14 October 1986 Conductor Gordon Webster, whom we last saw as a sergeant at 3 BAD in 1967, was presented with the Meritorious Service medal, by Brigadier John Jackson MBE GM in the Ashchurch Station Warrant Officers' and Sergeants' Mess. It was a special occasion, if only because the obligatory qualifying factor before the candidate can be considered for the award is twenty-seven years continuous exemplary service of the highest order. Those who knew him would have understood, since he was a man who consistently set and maintained very high standards. Conductor Webster followed a long line of service tradition, and 'The Websters' were all distinguished and intensely proud of their long connection with the Corps. It was entirely appropriate that Gordon's father, Major Claude Vivian Webster (Retd), who had enlisted as a boy entrant in 1921, was there to see his son's presentation. The last paragraph of his citation summed it all up:

> Additionally, he has given freely of his own time to unit events and has established close and influential links with the local civilian community. This selfless devotion to the Army and this unit in particular have been and are a continuing example to all ranks.

At Aldershot on Monday 27 October 1986 the RAOC became Army inter-corps hockey champions by beating the RAPC by two goals to nil. It was a thrilling finale to an excellent three day tournament in which a total of ten teams participated. At about the same time the RAOC won the inter-corps squash championships, beating the Army Physical Training Corps. And Captain Robbie Robinson became Combined Services champion – again, while the Cannonballs freefall parachute team repeated their 1985 success by winning all ten trophies in Germany, beating fifty-six other teams and becoming Army champions once more. The tradition of shooting went on, with Alan Glasby, by now a major, taking the Army Small Bore championships for the self-loading and the bolt-action rifle, as well as the Army 'three positions' trophy for the twelfth consecutive year. By now his aggregate of Army shooting championships was twenty-three. He also led the RAOC team that retained the Inter Corps Small Bore Target Rifle championship for the fifth consecutive year. During this competition Sergeant Bill Boxhall became the Army Small Bore Short Range champion with the amazing score of 596 out of a possible 600.

The RAOC Band chose this time to change its headdress. It would be worn by the Band when in full dress, and by RAOC buglers of the Junior Leaders Regiment RCT/RAOC who were converting back to the blue full dress worn in the sixties. The helmet was made as an exact copy of the headdress worn by soldiers of the AOC until 1914. Known as the Home Service Helmet, it was made of cork in a range of standard sizes and covered with dark blue cloth for RA, RE, most infantry and the logistic corps, and with rifle green cloth for Rifle and Light Infantry Regiments. Research in the files of the Royal Army Clothing Department, the predecessors of the Directorate of Clothing and Textiles, turned up the specification for the 1882 model. It was followed with essentially only two differences: it proved impossible to obtain sheet cork as thin as that used 100 years earlier and the helmet was therefore a little bulkier; secondly it was not possible to find a thin facing cloth of suitable texture and barathea was used instead to cover the helmet. The metal fittings were all of gilded brass chosen for its rich depth of colour and, even better, it did not need polishing. On the front of the helmet was the new Corps' pattern of badge, or 'plate' as it was known. The outline design was standard to nearly all regiments and corps who were by tradition entitled to the helmet in full dress. This was an eight pointed, rayed, brass star with the upper point replaced by the crown of the reigning Sovereign. Taking a centre point slightly above the true centre of the star, a laurel wreath surrounded a detachable garter which contained the badge of the regiment or corps. In the

A Junior Leader in full dress.

case of the RAOC this was, of course, the shield taken from the Arms of the Board of Ordnance in nickel silver and set on a black cloth ground. Finally, the RAOC was permitted to add below the garter the Corps' motto on a separate brass label. The result was, therefore, very much like the existing cap badge placed in a star though with rather different proportions.

Displaying yet more versatility, during October 1986, the RAOC was given the honour of guarding Windsor Castle. The guard was provided by the Training Battalion and Depot, 15 Battalion and 16 Battalion, and the RAOC Staff Band also took part in all guard mounts. The preparation started in early 1986 when many additional items of uniform and equipment were ordered from various Ordnance Depots, including the Tower of London. The three units also started their initial selection of manpower, from whom the final guard would be chosen. Plans began to take shape on 29 August when the detachments from Bicester and Donnington arrived at Blackdown to start the last month of preparation. The first two weeks training was conducted by MTIs, but last two weeks of training began in mid September when Colour Sergeant Fagin and his team from the Irish Guards arrived to put the finishing touches to the drill. By the end of September Colour Sergeant Fagin was happy with the standards achieved and the requisite three guards were formed.

Mounting every guard, it was a special time for the Staff Band as it was their first public appearance with their new helmets. Each guard changeover lasted forty minutes and the Staff Band played a selection of music while the sentries were posted. Every mount was watched by large crowds and they always appeared impressed with the turnout and drill of the RAOC soldiers. One old Knight of Windsor, a retired Guards officer, regularly complimented the guard on their performance, saying that the RAOC mounts were considerably better than some of those carried out by Guards battalions. The Royal Family was in residence during the latter stages of the duty and watched at least one guard mount. It was another job out of the ordinary, undertaken with all the skill and dedication of true professionals.

The last round of ammunition left Bramley on 7 February 1987 and the doors finally shut on 28 February 1987. No decision had been made regarding the future use of the site except that the pre-1978 Headquarters building was to remain as a TA centre. What was certain is that the RAOC had no further use for the depot. In the two years before 1978 it had been assumed that after the last wagon of ammunition had been dispatched and the last soldier posted, the depot would close for good. However, the US Department of Defense had expressed an interest in the site for the storage of American Army ammunition and their eventual use of the depot had lasted until mid 1986 when they gave notice that they were terminating the contract.

A large part of the old regimental area had already been sold and houses were now being built on the site of the old quarters near the guard room and on the sports field. Now it was finally all over; a part of the RAOC's history and a happy memory for so many. And Captain Robbie Robinson won the Army Individual Squash championship for the eighth time!

It was by now almost one year to the day after the first RAOC platoon arrived in Colerne as part of the newly formed RCT/RAOC Junior Leaders Regiment. The company of which it formed a part won, in this the first year of the Regiment's existence, the coveted Champion Squadron/Company Cup. It was an award made every term and was the subject of intense rivalry and competition between the four

The Windsor
Castle Guard.

sub-units. There were nine individual events throughout the term and the winning result was conclusive with 88 Ordnance Company taking first place in the assault course, march and shoot, military knowledge, education, drill, sports and swimming competitions. They were runners up in the basic fitness and highway code tests.

Then the Junior Leaders went on to win the 560 kilogram tug-of-war at the Royal Tournament. They were a new team, drawn from that winter's intake, so what had started as scrawny youths in their first few weeks in the Army had turned in a few short months into fit, healthy young athletes. This was largely due to their own efforts, but they were inspired, if that is the right word, by Sergeants Eddie Edwards and Nigel Willis overseen by WOII (CSM) Eric Blunn. It was something of an experience for these young men, performing through the early stages of the competition in the Earls Court arena and then marching in twice on that last day to a packed auditorium to pull the final. They were watched by about 200 members of the regiment, who added to the noise being made generally by the crowd, and by the C-in-C UKLF. Quite a start to their military careers, and one they would remember.

It was about this time that Lance Corporal Phil Hawkins won the Jim Barry trophy. It was a trophy that had been presented to the Army Sailing Association by the parents of Lieutenant Jim Barry who was killed in action at Goose Green while serving with the 2nd Battalion the Parachute Regiment during the Falklands War. They decided to establish a sailing trophy in his memory as he had been a keen and active sailor up to the time of his death. As a result, each year the Army Sailing Association would select a young sailor who had demonstrated outstanding qualities and sailing achievement to receive the award. Phil Hawkins had started sailing in earnest in 1985 when he purchased a Laser dinghy and began competing entirely on his own initiative. He entered the Joint Services Single Handed Championships that year and came ninth. Spurred on by his success he travelled the length and breadth of the country attending a range of open meetings. In 1986 he came seventh in the Joint Service Single Handed Championships and then entered the National qualifying rounds for the European Championships which were held in Switzerland. He came twenty-ninth and was short listed as a reserve for the National Team. Also in 1986, and again on his own initiative, he contacted the skipper of the Army team and became a member. He sailed with *Redcoat*, the Army team boat, regularly throughout the year and was awarded his Army colours. Following that he was pre-selected as part of the Army crew for the European J24 Championships due to be sailed at Capri in 1987. He had made a considerable impact on both the offshore and dinghy sailing scene in a very short period by using his initiative and drive to achieve results.

He was typical of the young men the RAOC was able to produce, and was producing, across the sporting and professional disciplines. This was further demonstrated by FOD Dulmen when, during the early part of 1987 and within an eight-day period, they won the Army Inter Unit Half Marathon, provided the majority of the RAOC team which won the Inter-Corps Cross-Country title and took the BAOR Inter-Unit Marathon Championships.

In June 1987 Margaret Thatcher made history, becoming the first Prime Minister since Lord Liverpool, Prime Minister between 1812 and 1827, to win a third term. She did so on the back of a middle class electorate that was feeling profoundly more and more prosperous and could see no need for a change. Not only that, but the Tories played the national defence card, claiming the country was safe in their hands from outside aggressors. Against this the Labour Party's policy of unilateral nuclear disarmament found little favour. However, over the next three years the seemingly invincible march of Thatcherism, with its thrust to home ownership, share ownership, monetarism and privatization, began to lurch into disarray.

In Spandau prison in Berlin, Rudolf Hess committed suicide. It was 17 August 1987 and it was the end of an era, the passing of the last living link with Adolf Hitler's inner cabinet and the madness that had infected Europe in the thirties and forties. He was aged ninety-three. The immediate result of his death was that the Russians no longer had a reason to enter West Berlin in order to guard the prison on

Her Majesty the Queen at Kineton. Major General Gerry Berragan, the DGOS, is on her left, while Lieutenant Colonel David Braithwaite, responsible for organizing the visit, keeps a watchful eye in the background.

rotation with the British, the Americans and the French. It also presaged an extraordinary period for those stationed in the divided city. By then a man called Mikhail Gorbachev had been in power in Russia for two years and he was already preaching the politics of conciliation; of perestroika. Margaret Thatcher had announced publicly that she could work with him. The winds of change were beginning to blow through Europe, and Berlin would find itself at the centre of it all.

On Thursday 17 December 1987 the DGOS, Major General Gerry Berragan received on behalf of the RAOC the VC awarded to Lieutenant William Raynor for his part in the defence of the Delhi Magazine in 1857 at the outbreak of the Indian Mutiny. Three VCs were awarded for that action, with Conductor John Buckley's by now already at the museum. The third, that won by Lieutenant Forrest, was in the National Army Museum and all three were serving with the Indian Army Ordnance Department at the time.

The Raynor VC had been in the family until the early sixties when it had been sold to an American collector. In November 1987 on hearing that it was coming up for auction at Spinks, Lieutenant Raynor's great grandchildren, William Raynor and Shirley Trollope, were determined that it should not leave the country again. With help of Martin Williams, a family friend, they purchased the medal for £11,130 plus buyer's premium, and gave the RAOC the opportunity to obtain the medal at the auction price. To launch the museum's Raynor VC Appeal Fund, the Raynor great grandchildren generously donated the buyer's premium of over £1,200, with the RAOC left to find the £11,130 balance. The Corps' intention at the time was to raise the money by appeal and it was successful in so doing.

On 24 March 1988 the RAOC was delighted to receive a visit from Her Majesty the Queen, its Colonel-in-Chief, this time to CAD Kineton. On a very windy and blustery day the royal party arrived at 1230 and drove along a route lined by soldiers of 9 Ordnance Battalion to the Parade Square to be received by the Representative Colonel Commandant, Major General Mike Callan, who then presented to Her Majesty the DGOS, Major General Gerry Berragan, the ADC, Brigadier Harry Brown, the Commandant CAD Kineton, Colonel Bill Manuel and the Staff Officer for the Royal Visit, Lieutenant Colonel David Braithwaite. The Royal Guard of Honour was under the command of Major Mike Southworth and was formed from soldiers of COD Bicester, COD Donnington and CAD Kineton. The Queen then toured the depot and the School of Ammunition as well as visiting the messes and meeting a whole range of people, military and civilian. To commemorate her visit in the year which marked the thirty-fifth anniversary of her Colonelcy-in-Chief and the seventieth anniversary of the amalgamation of the Army Ordnance Department and the Army Ordnance Corps to form the Royal Army Ordnance Corps, a gift was made to her of a brooch in the form of an Ammunition Technical Officer's badge.

It was customary for the RAOC to commission a piece of silver to commemorate a Royal occasion and the choice for Her Majesty's visit to Kineton was conceived to accentuate the theme of ammunition with one of the outstanding moments in the history of the Corps by having a replica of the gateway to the Delhi Magazine made as a silver centrepiece. Soon after the decision to go ahead had been made the Corps had acquired the Raynor VC and it was then decided that the centrepiece should commemorate the three members of the Ordnance Department who won the VC in defence of the magazine on 11 May 1857.

There were two identical gateways to the original magazine and they had survived both the effects of the explosion and the ravages of time, although they suffered by then the ignominy of being traffic islands in a busy

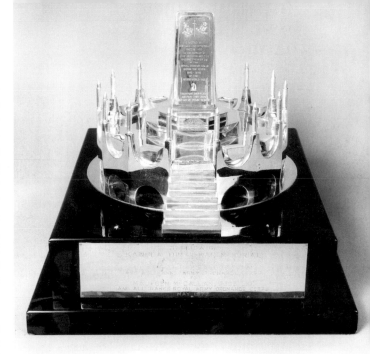

Replica of the gateway to the Delhi Magazine

thoroughfare. In 1922, a tablet had been erected at the top of one of the gateways bearing the names of the defenders of the magazine in order to commemorate their action. It was this gateway that had been copied and, as the tablet on the replica was too small to carry the full commemorative inscription, it was been inscribed 'The Delhi Magazine VC Memorial 11 May 1857'. The plinth bears the following inscription:

In memory of three of the gallant Ordnance Department defenders of the Magazine who were awarded the VC for outstanding valour at the outbreak of the Indian Mutiny: Lieutenant George Forrest VC, Lieutenant William Raynor VC, Conductor John Buckley VC.

The RAOC, of course, had a close association with the metal from which VCs are made. It was held at COD Donnington where it remains to this day. It weighs 22lb 6oz and looks a bit like a lump of

The block of VC metal.

cheese and it is all that remains of the cascabels of two Russian cannon, captured at Sevastopol in the last great battle of the Crimean War. The cascabel, a large knob at the rear end of the cannon, held ropes which were used when the piece was being manhandled as in 'running-out' after firing. The cannons, minus their cascabels, stand proudly outside the Rotunda at Woolwich. They are referred to as Russian cannon although it has been suggested that they could be 'Chinese'. Nationality apart, scientific analysis sponsored by the Tower of London proves that the Donnington metal did really come from one of the Woolwich cannon.

Details of previous custodians are scant. In the nineteenth century it was held by 'The Civil Service' and was considered by some to have come to Donnington from the Weedon Depot. The oldest Stock Record Card in Donnington begins with the first Donnington entry on 11 May 1953 -'25 lbs' and a stocktaking on 23 October 1959 recorded '25½ lbs'. When the one and only subsequent issue was made on 16 February 1970 the description had changed to ounces, and it was for fifty, reducing the block to 358 ounces. That off-cut, sufficient to make about twelve medals, was sent to Messrs Hancocks & Co of London – the Court jewellers who had been responsible for making the medal since its inception. And there it sat, and sits still, awaiting the next recipients. The latest would be awarded to Private Johnson Beharry of the Princess of Wales' Royal Regiment for action in Iraq at the beginning of May 2004.

At Donnington, the newly built shed that was due to replace the building burnt out in the fire of 1983 was to be opened on 25 May 1988. Just one month prior to that, on 25 April 1988, another building in the depot, B1, was gutted by fire. Whilst the cause of the 1983 fire had been unclear, this time the police view was that it was arson by a person or persons unknown. There were actually two fires on this second occasion. The first was discovered at 11.25 am by a soldier working in the building. He raised the alarm and with three others helped to control the fire with fire extinguishers until the AFS arrived to put it out. A newly spent match was found at the rear of the pallets by the seat of the fire, and the police were called to investigate.

Then, at 3.38 that afternoon, as investigations into the first fire were underway, a telephone call was received in the depot fire station operations room from a civilian clerk who was in an office some 100 metres away from Building B1 reporting a plume of smoke belching from the southern corner of the building. At the time people working in the building were unaware of this. However, an eyewitness from the married quarter's area said later:

> All I could see just beyond the bottom of the garden was a vast cloud of black smoke – the height of it was incredible – and within it, a giant fireball.

The AFS were there with two appliances within forty-eight seconds, but, despite their speed of reaction, when they arrived the fire had a firm grip and extinguishing it was beyond their capability. They called for ten pumps and within five minutes the Shropshire fire brigade was on the ground with its first units. In the end twenty-eight appliances were deployed and, despite the best efforts of the fire brigades, some two thirds of the building was destroyed. The repercussions locally were to be serious with great concern being expressed in the community not only about the rather careless loss of two major storehouses in five years, but also the risk to health from the asbestos in the roof of the building which would have been cast for miles in the smoke. It quite rightly was to lead to a major enquiry.

The loss of stores was valued at £167 million (£265 million), with additional costs for lost storage media and the building itself rising to £175 million (£277 million). As with the 1983 fire the RAOC was faced with the massive task of clearing up the mess, replacing lost stock and keeping the Army operating at the same time. The situation was exacerbated because many of the spares lost had formed a part of 'lifetime buys', and would be very difficult to replicate. It would do little to relieve the pressure caused by the poor state into which much of the Army's equipment had deteriorated.

Mercifully, there seemed at the time to be nothing major on the horizon and the mid to late eighties showed a downturn in the pace of operational activity, although deployments to Northern Ireland remained a standard and the Falklands featured high on the list of long unaccompanied tours. Northern Ireland EOD activity increased in 1988, but that only affected a small element of the RAOC's work, albeit a high profile element. A feature was the gradually increasing use by the terrorists of higher technology techniques in the construction of their IEDs with extensive use of radio control and anti-handling devices. There was also a trend towards the use of devices initiated by command wire, and these were particularly difficult to detect. An increase in activity was also experienced on the mainland by 11 Ordnance Battalion (EOD) with over 400 calls being received to tasks involving IEDs in addition to the normal load of 3,000 to 4,000 items of stray ammunition collected annually nationwide. One particularly unpleasant task was Operation ALAMANDA, the rendering safe of 156 fuzed chemical shells left over from First World War and found when clearing the site at Bramley.

An AT on Operation ALAMANDA. It was difficult and dangerous work.

A feature of life was the increasing use of TA, almost always as individuals, to reinforce or to replace regulars. Often it was in the more esoteric trades, like laundry operative, but it spread across all the RAOC's disciplines. It became commonplace, where regulars were in short supply, to ask for a TA replacement with confidence knowing they would fit and before long it would be hard 'to see the join'. Not only was the TA becoming more and more closely integrated with the work of the regular Army, becoming more and more 'one Army', but it was accepting and executing increasingly complex roles. For example, EOD Companies were being raised to help in Home Defence, where a very high level of EOD activity was expected.

It may have been a consequence of the seeming downturn in operational activity, but reports of the time in the mid to late eighties feature a corresponding load of exercises and adventure training expeditions as officers and soldiers took the opportunity to walk, ski, sail, canoe or parachute just about anywhere they could. Reductions in training caused by lack of money for exercises and restrictions in track mileage for tanks made their contribution by reducing the training load and freeing up time for soldiers to undertake expeditions – and they took every advantage of it.

Sport remained high on the agenda as well, with every unit seemingly reporting yet more and more success at a local and at Army level. FOD Dulmen in Germany was just one example. In a season which had spanned an eight month period the Dulmen team remained unbeaten in all major championships, including four coveted Army titles: the Army Minor Unit Relay Championships; the Army Minor Unit Cross-Country Championships; the Army Minor Unit Marathon Championships and the Army Inter-Unit Half Marathon Championships. Never before had any one unit won as many Army cross-country/road racing championships within one season. To illustrate the team's standard, when FOD Dulmen competed in the 1988 Fleet and Crookham pre-London half-Marathon, incorporating the Army Championships and attracting a class field of some 4,000 runners and over 800 military and civilian teams, they convincingly won the Army Championships by some 137 points from the 3rd Battalion the Parachute Regiment and were placed second team overall, just behind Aldershot Farnham and District, the 1986 National Cross-Country Champions. And there were some stunning performances from people like WOI (SSM) Marsh, Sergeant Avery, Corporal Brown, Lance Corporal Downes and Private Burke.

As with so much in the RAOC the TA was playing its part in sporting activities, promoting the RAOC and their part in it. One such unit was 55 Ordnance Company (V). On the weekend of 15 to 17 April 1988 they towed a 25-pounder field gun in aid of the mayor of Hounslow's Charity Appeal. The aims of this mammoth endurance task were to see how

The 55 Ordnance Company team pulling their gun.

many miles they could pull the gun in a twenty-four hour period and thereby raise as much money as possible for worthwhile local causes. The three alternating teams of eight Territorial soldiers from the unit succeeded in achieving an incredible eighty-five miles overall in the allotted time, without the gun stopping. Each soldier personally pulled for nearly thirty miles, much of the time in continuous rain. Some £3,000 (£5,000) was handed over at a reception shortly after the event with the promise of more to come as sponsorship pledges came in.

Gun pulls were clearly the fashion at the time, as 73 Ordnance Company (V) also did one from Southend to Romford in aid of Danielle Gray, a local girl who was suffering from cerebral palsy. The unit's target was to raise £10,000 (£16,000) to assist her parents to raise the necessary £60,000 (£95,000) to take her to the Peto Clinic in Hungary for life saving treatment. They raised £10,313.06 (£16,500).

It would be wrong to think that all this non-operational activity was taking place in relative calm, for everywhere people were being kept extraordinarily busy supporting the Army on a daily basis. Witness activity in 3 Ordnance Battalion in Soest in Germany, commanded by Lieutenant Colonel Peter Foxton. The Battalion supported 3rd Armoured Division, and was involved in the complete re-equipping of the Division, which was the first to receive the Challenger main battle tank, and at the same time was taking on the infantry's new mechanized combat vehicle, Warrior. Other vehicle deployments included the new Land-Rover 90/110 series, concurrent with the new SA80 rifle. During the same period the Battalion provided the technical support for the formation of the Army's twelfth armoured regiment and the mechanization of the first of 6 Armoured Brigade's infantry battalions.

Staff officers were busy too – memories of the eighties focus on manpower cuts and financial stringency, within the all pervading mantra of the approaching NMS, due to be implemented in 1991. Major General Peter Chambers:

It's all I can remember, study upon study and cut upon cut – one merging into the other in a seemingly endless stream.

It was a constant stream of demands to achieve more with less, and at times became intolerable. Between 1982 and 1988 up to eighty studies were undertaken in DGOS' area, examining the role, efficiency and effectiveness of Army Ordnance Services. Importantly, they included the Q IT strategy study, the materials management review strategy study and an enabling study into the structure of the Q area. One very senior officer was heard walking the Ord 1 corridor in Andover after a particularly difficult request for yet more blood letting calling out to no one in particular and everybody in general in great frustration:

…will somebody, just once, please say 'no, we cannot do it' …

Of course no one ever did say 'no'. They knuckled down to the job not knowing what demands would be placed on them. They were just secure in the knowledge that they would make it work, whatever it was. They'd done it before and there was no reason to suggest they would not do so in the future. Too many relied on them getting it right for there to be any contemplation of getting it wrong.

The cuts were a product of the state of the economy as the power of Thatcherite economics began to wane and crumble under the increasing personalization of her term in office. The new management strategy, planned for introduction in April 1991, was considered necessary in order to ensure the accountability and financial probity of commanders in a quest for what the Government considered to be value for money. Its emphasis was to be on outputs, in other words to pay and to have responsibility for the services delivered at the point of delivery, rather than an input based regime. As such it was not a new concept, and indeed much of it was redolent of the control system of the nineteenth century. However, unlike the control system which fell into disuse, largely due to lack of interest by senior military officers, this time it was here to stay. In the meantime the savings regime that was a constant theme carried on. It seemed that no sooner was a budget set, but a cut was imposed seeking the realization of a savings target. But the RAOC was not lax in identifying and implementing savings. For example, between 1982 and 1988 some £137 million (£218 million) was saved in annual running costs, while £421 million (£670 million) was taken in one off savings ranging from such things as packaging improvements to energy saving to stock level savings.

One major change that went unheralded in the rest of the Army was the outcome of a study by the consultants Delloite, Haskins and Sells unto the purchase of spares for in-service vehicles. They recommended the move of this responsibility away from the Procurement Executive to DGOS' area, specifically to the Director of Supply Management. The resultant improvement in efficiency led to a reduction in lead times which accrued savings of £160 million (£254 million).

In May 1989, after a one year delay caused by the second fire, building B55 was opened at COD Donnington, replacing B6 which had burned down in the 1983 fire. By the end of the year it would contain 50,000 pallets of stock held in the most up-to-date storage, all controlled by computer, thereby increasing productivity and reducing the manpower normally required to manage a shed of that size. Along with this rebuild programme, and based on experiences from recent fires, a major programme was under way to improve fire protection in all storehouses throughout the RAOC. The cost of this high profile programme was £120 million (£178 million), and unlike previous attempts to obtain the necessary funds which had encountered difficulties, the centre seemed fully prepared to meet the bill.

As the new shed in Donnington was opening so a vehicle depot was closing. One of the reviews seeking financial savings had concluded that Army vehicle storage was best organized based on the two military depots at Ludgershall in Wiltshire and Ashchurch in Gloucestershire. This meant closing the entirely civilian manned vehicle sub-depot at Hilton in Derbyshire. The rundown of depot stocks started in April and by September it would be empty, with a planned depot closure date of 22 December 1989. Fortunately, with all but a few exceptions, the members of the workforce were able to find alternative work in the local area.

On 17 July that year there were three tragic deaths at CAD Kineton in most unusual circumstances. Sergeant D K Barker, Lance Corporal K T Robinson and Private D B Carson were killed by methane poisoning while engaged in a routine demolition. It appeared that the shape and position of the demolition pit they were using did not permit the normal and rapid dissipation of the gases following a demolition. As the task was completed the three moved forward to clear the pit and were, without any warning, overcome by fumes and died.

1 August 1989 saw 17 Ordnance Battalion in Cyprus, so named following the RAOC's renaming exercise and focus on battalion structures, disbanded. It had been in existence for only two years, but had to go as an ACDS(L) Logistics Review of Cyprus in October 1987 had recommended the formation of a joint Army and RAF supply unit on the Island. The eighteen months of implementation complete, the Joint Supply Unit was born. The Battalion had supported the British forces in Cyprus and those training on the island, and had provided support to the United Nations forces operating in Cyprus, Lebanon and on the Golan Heights. It was a task performed very much to their customers' satisfaction while at the same time managing to make significant savings and stock reductions, thanks partly to COFFER. The new joint unit, however, was to use the RAF unit supply ADP system, which offered even more possibilities for an improved service to customers and yet further reduced stock levels.

A new dimension was entering into the work, and hence the procedures, of the RAOC. Environmental health and safety had arrived to stay and to be developed. With MHE the RAOC led the Army in developing the procedures for its effective use. Now procedures had to be developed for the movement of dangerous or hazardous goods, taking account of differences in roles and implementation dates between the UK, the European Community, NATO and the rest of the world. It was work that was in addition to everything else and for which no resources were made available.

In the Field Army, such things as bulk petroleum handling were a potentially major environmental hazard. The flexible fabric tanks in which the petroleum spirits were stored were robust enough, but a major fuel leak would be very damaging, and the German approach to any environmental damage, caused by any leak, no matter how small, had serious consequences. The petroleum fraternity in the RAOC had developed ways of constructing the fuel farms in such a way that any leak, however small or large, could be contained. There was rarely a problem.

In October 1989 four teams won gold medals in the Cambrian patrol: 2nd Battalion the Parachute Regiment, 2nd Battalion the Royal Regiment of Fusiliers, 1st Battalion the Staffordshire Regiment and the Training Battalion and Depot RAOC, the depot thereby repeating the RAOC's success of previous years. Thirty-one teams entered and the RAOC team was the rank outsider, indeed, many sceptics said they would be lucky to complete the patrol let alone win a medal. They came through because they were fit and well trained, determined to prove that it is not only the 'teeth arms' who took their soldiering seriously. Training for the event was extremely thorough, and from the outset they were clear that the aim should not just be to complete the patrol but to win a gold medal. And that was from the CO and was supported throughout the unit. It was a real feather in the cap of those who took part, and once more showed that with the right training the RAOC soldier was the equal of any. This was a competition primarily aimed at the reconnaissance platoons of infantry battalions, and consequently demanded the very highest standard of physical fitness and basic infantry skills. At the outset it seemed, even to them, a mountain too high to climb. Corporal Jamie Muir was one of the team:

> At first I thought that entering the Cambrian Patrol was another Mickey Mouse idea... We wouldn't have any chance with the training let alone the patrol.

But they did, and at about the same time, 9 Ordnance Battalion became the Combined Services Minor Unit Marathon champions having taken the Army Minor Units athletics earlier in the season, and then went on to be the Army Minor Unit Rugby champions at the end of the 89/90 season. The Training Battalion and Depot also became Army Minor Unit Hockey champions in the 1989 season.

On 9 November 1989, in Berlin, a historical event of seismic proportions took place: the Berlin wall was breached and West Berlin was flooded with people from East Germany. It was an event that was to herald the collapse of Soviet power and end the days of communism as a major world political force. The implications were enormous, the eventual outcome uncertain, but one thing was sure – an invasion of a most unexpected kind took place. For some two thirds of the East German population of 16 million souls the nearest part of West Germany was actually West Berlin and during that first weekend 2 million of them descended on the city. Double parking was an understatement, quadruple was nearer the mark and they were all Trabants. Each new arrival from the East was entitled to DM100 (£52) Bregrüssungsgeld, or 'greeting money'. The banks moved some 200 million Deutschmarks (£100 million) that weekend, and to meet the demand they were sending teams to the main supermarkets, collecting spent money and returning to the bank in order to circulate it through again.

They emptied the supermarkets throughout the city of food. Every shop, no matter how small, was virtually completely de-stocked. Consequently, a huge demand was placed on the Berlin central food markets, which quickly emptied. They sought replenishment from their normal sources of supply, all of which were outside the city in West Germany. Unfortunately, as the re-supply vehicles tried to get down the motorways into the city from the West they encountered massive traffic jams caused by 'wall to wall' Trabants, with their drivers exercising their new-found freedom to travel. It was to be some days before the markets were fully stocked.

The implications for Ordnance Services Berlin were that in order to feed the Berlin garrison it had to broach the blockade stock for the first time since 1948. This was a stockpile of 120 days' rations designed to counter any attempt by the Russians to cut off the city as they had done in the blockade of the late forties. The effect of the fall of the wall was not clear at that stage, and the Russian reaction was still uncertain, but it seemed a risk worth taking. It had to be taken; there was no other way of feeding the garrison.

There was a sense among soldiers generally that their reason for being in Berlin, and in Germany, was no more. Coffee housing around the corridors of the Ordnance Services headquarters building on the Monday morning, just as things were beginning to come into some sort of focus, at least for the short term, Corporal Dennis Williams, the FOWO's clerk, offered a view:

> …marvellous really, we've just been present at the end of World War Three, and not a shot's been fired. Bloody marvellous.

His Commander Supply was part of the group reviewing the events of the previous few days. Lieutenant Colonel Frank Steer answered him:

> …or have we just been present at the end of the First World War…

Neither of the two men had an answer, but it was food for thought.

No matter how historians might view events, however, to politicians and the populations of Western Europe the need for large in-place armed forces and masses of reserves had just vanished. It was not long before the cry on everyone's lips was 'peace dividend'. Almost at once thoughts turned to the cuts that could be made in an Army which, on the face of it, no longer had a serious enemy, and for which the threat of high intensity warfare, for which it had prepared for so many years and for which it was equipped, had disappeared. Studies began to take place at once looking at the future size and shape of the Army, and covetous eyes fell at once upon BAOR, and on the amount tied up globally in the logistics to support a war that would not now be fought.

The reduced logistic footprint that would inevitably result from a smaller support package caused minds to turn towards a review of the logistic services with a clear agenda that included cuts and amalgamations. Thoughts turned even towards Lord Kitchener's vision, now over a century old, for one logistic corps to serve the Army with all its needs. However, there was one thing that might mitigate against it – the Army was now far more equipment intensive than had been the case in his time and the need for a maintenance and repair capability had been something he had been unable to visualize. Even if he had, it was certainly not on the scale that faced late twentieth century armies equipped for high intensity warfare. To offer a feel for the scale of the change the RAOC inventory on the day of its formation in 1918 had comprised some 25,000 items. By 1990 it was some 800,000.

At a meeting at Hedsor Park in 1989 involving QMG, General Sir Edward Jones, and the heads of the Army's logistic corps a concept had emerged of a 'two pillar' structure for logistics – one responsible for combat support and the other for equipment support. This emanated from the findings of the enabling study into the structure of the Q Area, and in a sense was therefore presented as a fait accompli with no alternatives really considered, nor was there time to do so. By the end of the meeting, actually a series of meetings, General Jones considered that there had been a de facto agreement to the principle and resolved to set in train a review of the Army's logistic support organization and systems in peace, transition to war and war with a view to adopting such a structure. It was to start work in January of 1991, and would be headed by Major General Neil Carlier, late of the Royal Engineers. However, in July the government announced the Options for Change round of studies into the size and shape of an Army that would have to cope with a world without a Berlin wall and everything that went with it. It would be conducted in a climate seeking savings and where the RAOC had already seen, in the preceding fifteen years, a reduction in civilian manpower from 20,000 to 11,000 and military manpower from 9,000 to 7,000.

This caused the QMG to bring forward the start of the Logistic Support Review to August 1990, but General Carlier would not be able to join the study team until the originally planned start date of

January 1991. In the meantime, the QMG's deputy, the Director General of Logistic Planning (Army), Major General Geoffrey Field, also of the Royal Engineers, would supervise the work. The team comprised three colonels, one from each of the three principal logistic corps in the QMG's area, the RCT, the RAOC and the REME, and a civil servant. The RAOC team member was Colonel Adrian Lyons MBE. Together they began to develop the thoughts and ideas that had found their origins at Hedsor Park, and had a great deal already formed and in place, with a first draft virtually complete, by the time Major General Carlier arrived to take up the reins. He would have no opportunity to affect the outcome and DGLP(A) had little capacity to influence matters since he was fully involved over the same period with the introduction of NMS, the Options round of work and, from August 1990, a war in the Gulf. The LSR team was left very much to its own devices.

The eventual outcome of Options for Change was a drastic reduction in size, taking the Army down to an overall strength of 116,000 including those in training, with just two divisions, one of them heavily armoured and based in Germany the other lighter and based in the UK, and some specialist brigades. The Army population in Germany would reduce from a peacetime strength of 55,000 to 23,000. The outcome of the LSR would form the basis of the support requirements for this new Army for the nineties and beyond.

Major General David Botting CB CBE.

It fell to 3 Ordnance Battalion, through the medium of 32 Ordnance Company, to conduct the last British Army border patrol along the line that had for so long separated East and West Germany. The patrol was commanded by Lieutenant S McMahan.

In July 1990, Major General David Botting assumed the appointment of DGOS. He had no idea that he was to be the last person to do so. However, with both Options for Change and the LSR about to bite and a war just round the corner, the future of the RAOC was in his hands, as well as the RAOC part of whatever logistic system would support the post Options for Change Army. Most people agreed a better man for the job would be hard to find. In the end, most people were proved right.

Decisions had been made about the size and shape of an Army whose role was still not clear, but whose size was influenced by the fact that there was no foreseeable threat of war. Yet within weeks the country was at war, and potentially high intensity war at that. On 2 August 1990 the Iraqi leader, Saddam Hussein, in a move to create what he considered to be the legitimate nineteenth province of Iraq, invaded Kuwait. The first members of the RAOC to feel the effects of this were Major Alex Boyd and his fellow members of the British Liaison Team in Kuwait. By 4 August both he and WOII Finan were under arrest, and would remain as hostages for another 140 days. WOII Richardson was to join them on 28 August having evaded capture until then when together with Conductor Richardson, who was in Kuwait but not a member of the BLT, he too was arrested.

In the UK the RAOC realized it had to ramp up the supply support, and had no money with which to do so. The cuts and the shortages created by the proliferation of equipment with limited support funding made this task more difficult than it ought to have been. Nonetheless, British servicemen were once more going to war, and everything was going to be done to make sure they went as well supported as possible. Saying 'no' was not an option.

Mercifully, the infrastructure that had been in place to defend Western Europe against invading Russians was still there. Whilst the units were in some cases not suited to expeditionary warfare, at least the resources, the stocks, could be made available. The Ordnance support in BAOR from which the logistic support would be drawn comprised five battalions in the 1 (Br) Corps areas. These included the dedicated divisional battalions, and over time they had developed into a three company structure: two forward companies providing the immediate spares support for the battle groups and the third, or rear, company manning the Divisional Support Areas in war. In peace these 'rear' companies managed the forward storage sites and the supply depots with their stocks of fresh and packed rations. The FStSs were NATO constructed ammunition storage areas, built in the eighties, holding ammunition and stores forward for a European war for which they would now not be needed. In war Commander Supply commanded the DAA, with its plethora of units and bits of units, and ran the divisional RV as well as his three-company battalion and at the same time was the staff officer on the divisional headquarters responsible for supply. Opinion for some time in the RAOC had been that this was too much for one man.

Behind the divisions were the Corps Supply Areas, and 5 and 6 Ordnance battalions respectively were in each of those. There they held bulk stocks of fuel, ammunition, spares and assemblies, and vehicles. They also provided detachments to man the offtake points on the Central European Pipeline System that supplied fuel of all types direct into the 1 (Br) Corps' area. Then there were the forward depots at Warendorf, holding fuel, Wulfen, holding ammunition, Dulmen, holding stores and Recklinghausen, holding vehicles. In war these would have all outloaded their stocks into the forward areas. Reserves were held even further back, west of the Rhine in 15th Ordnance Group clustered around the town of Mönchengladbach on the Dutch border. Even further back holding reinforcement stocks and PUEs was the Ordnance complex at Antwerp.

Then in the United Kingdom was one of the BAOR divisions, the 2nd Division, with its Ordnance battalion. Otherwise there was the AMF(L) Logistic Battalion, the logistic assets of the Commando and Airborne Brigades and 9 Ordnance Battalion. The latter was a real asset, for as the third line battalion supporting the UKMF(L), it had the full range of expertise to support expeditionary operations. And then there were the base depots, mercifully still staffed by enough military to provide a deployable capability if needed, and with the experience to support the forward elements without having to be told what to do.

By 10 August Operation GRANBY, designed to counter Saddam Hussein's invasion of Kuwait, was a reality, although there was still some doubt over who or what would be going. At first it was unquestionably an RAF affair, with some RN units, and the depots swung into action to provide those items for which they had a responsibility where there was commonality of equipment or where single service management was vested in the Army. An RAF deployment also meant Army units, principally Royal Signals and RE, deploying, and they too required support.

A headquarters was established in Riyadh, the capital of Saudi Arabia, with General Sir Peter de la Billière in command. It was to be a small HQ, essentially strategic in nature, using the General's experience as an Arabist and as a man well-known in the region to exercise influence with the Saudi royal family. It was to be called HQ British Forces Middle East. He would also be the liaison with the American commander, General Norman Schwarzkopf. In the UK the operation was to be run from a Joint HQ established at the

Lieutenant Colonel Alan Taylor RAOC.

RAF war HQ at High Wycombe

Regardless of the declared date for GRANBY the ALOC, QMG's operations room, and the SMOC at Bicester were manned and working. SMOC's role was to act as a central focus for all operational issues less ammunition and vehicles. The former was dealt with at SMOC Ammo based at Didcot with DLSA, whilst vehicles were looked after from the LE(A) at Andover by the Equipment Managers. Operations rooms were also set up in the depots, but throughout the RAOC manpower reductions meant that hard decisions needed to be made about twenty-four hour manning and the need to ensure the issues programme was not affected. The shortage of military personnel in the depots was already being felt, and worse was to come in the years ahead.

Consistent under-funding over the years had reduced stocks of MT spares, clothing and NBC equipment to support the early deployment which was from both Germany and the UK. Consequently, the close working relationship developed in peace between the UK and Germany-based depots and the CICP at Bicester and the ICP in Viersen played a huge part in making provision for the deployment. However, even at this early stage the need for good communications and dedicated logistic links was beginning to assume greater and greater importance. And it didn't help that a force configured and equipped to fight a war in Europe needed a different range of support and equipment in order to fight a broadly similar war in the desert.

As hard pressed staffs everywhere worked every hour imaginable to prepare a properly supported

The officers and men of 6 Ordnance Battalion Group.

292

force, rumours would inevitably abound, as one warrant officer in the Ordnance Directorate in HQ BAOR discovered:

> ...at one stage the whole Directorate stood to after a tannoy announcement instructed everyone to open up their operations rooms. Most of us returned from a hurried lunch break having assured our better halves that the 'balloon had gone up' only to discover they had been opened in order to allow access for the cleaners.

One of the difficulties that would inevitably emerge from the fixation over the years that war would only happen on the north German plain was that many of the RAOC's smaller but essential trades had reverted to the TA. There was no Queen's Order for Operation GRANBY and so the TA could not be mobilized which is why, very early on, Major Jim Wilberforce's 91 Ordnance Company in Corsham, near Bath, provided, at very short notice, eight soldiers to be laundry operators, normally a TA role, for a hospital deploying from Germany.

The international community came together through the medium of the UN to condemn the invasion and occupation of Kuwait. However, it was soon obvious that Saddam Hussein was not prepared to listen. On 14 September, in response to a request from President Bush, Britain agreed to commit heavy armoured forces to a force to contain any further Iraqi incursion beyond Kuwait's borders. Operation GRANBY became GRANBY 1, the title GRANBY 2 being reserved for the roulement that would be necessary in a few months time. The following day France committed a 4,000 strong brigade and the Egyptians and Syrians increased the size of their presence in Saudi Arabia.

The British contribution was to be 7 Armoured Brigade, the Desert Rats, from 1st Division comprising two regiments of Challenger MBTs and one infantry battalion mounted in Warrior armoured fighting vehicles. Because a complete formation, in other words a division, was not deploying, infrastructure had to be left behind in Germany to provide support for those not going. This accounted for the decision on the organization and source of the RAOC support. The concept for the deployment was for two Ordnance battalions, one to go forward and provide intimate support to the battle groups and the other to provide the RAOC element of the Forward Mounting Base at the port of entry. As such it was a classic tried and tested logistic posture for an expeditionary operation: a presence at the point of entry and a presence in contact with the fighting elements.

Lieutenant Colonel Alan Taylor's 3 Ordnance Battalion was to provide the HQ and one of the forward companies, 31 Ordnance Company commanded by Major Trevor White, for the forward deployment. From 1 Ordnance Battalion Major Carl Hewitt's 11 Ordnance Company was sent as the other forward company and from 4 Ordnance Battalion 43 Ordnance Company commanded by Major Paul Williamson was sent as the rear company to run the RAOC element of the DSA. The FMB was to be handled by Lieutenant Colonel Tim Murray's 6 Ordnance Battalion and he took with him from his own battalion 62 Ordnance Company commanded by Major Eddie Weeks, to handle bulk spares. From Lieutenant Colonel Roger Mendham's 5 Ordnance Battalion came 51 Ordnance Company to manage petroleum and 53 Ordnance Company for ammunition. Because the food supply system in Germany was from static depots there needed to be a food supply system in the field, so 91 Ordnance Company was thrown in as well, and also took its LRS platoon on the basis that as much support as possible was to come from the local economy – and they were the experts in local procurement; which used to be called pillaging.

In HQ BAOR Lieutenant Colonel Colin Den McKay set about creating a system that would funnel all their requirements into those units that were deploying, diverting stocks by cross-servicing wherever necessary from other units. Working in close cooperation, Lieutenant Colonel Tim Cross, Commander Supply 1st Division, established a Materiel Mounting Centre in Verden in Germany to handle the stocks and direct them to their destination. It would eventually be staffed by eighty-three officers and soldiers from all over Germany, a unit created to meet a need for which there was no manpower provision. And their presence in Verden meant they were away from their parent units in the BAOR base when they were most needed. Peter, yet again, was paying Paul. The re-supply system was paying the price.

A period of intensive training also took place. And given the Iraqi known use of chemical weapons, NBC instructors, hitherto a derided breed of individual, at last found people paying very close attention to what they had to say. There was also an intensive programme of reconnaissance in Saudi Arabia, focussing initially on Al Jubail, the planned PoE. One of the aspects of the PoE noted during the reconnaissance was the lack of infrastructure to provide some of the basic needs of western soldiers. For example, the fixed bakeries in supply depots in Germany were not available locally and so one had to be taken. Consequently, the AMF(L) field bakery, the only mobile bakery in the Army, was added to 91 Ordnance Company. By the end of the war it would have produced over 10 million loaves, to say nothing of a mountain of 'stickies'.

The ammunition outload commenced on 21 September. There was to be sufficient for thirty days plus twelve days reserve stocks. For spares, and after the ICP had scrutinized the BAOR holdings against the anticipated requirement, it was anticipated that something like 28,000 extraordinary demands would be placed on the central depots – 66 per cent on Donnington and the remaining 34 per cent on Bicester. At Donnington alone this meant fitting out twenty-six ISO containers with shelving to take detailed stores. And here was the first portent of the importance of the container, which was to become one of the ubiquitous features of the war. They were used for everything: storage, accommodation, offices and a whole range of other things limited only by soldiers' imagination. The timetable was by now fixed, and the depots had until 14 October to select, prepare and dispatch the stores.

In Germany everyone was focussed on meeting the embarkation timetable. Between 24 September and 15 October Ordnance Depot Antwerp

Just how seriously the NBC threat had to be taken is shown by the reaction of these soldiers who would break off from their breakfast in mid January 1991 following an attack alert.

And training carried on constantly.

Ordnance Company's containers loaded and ready at [Don]nington for shipment to the Gulf.

deployed a team to Bremerhaven on the north German coast to help manage the loading. At the height of the 7 Armoured Brigade deployment two ships a day were leaving the port, whilst over a three day period thirteen trains were offloaded and their contents stowed aboard the waiting vessels.

Lieutenant Tom Lishman's LRS arrived in Al Jubail on 28 September, about to embark on a task that, in sheer size and importance, was well outside the normal scope of this small team's rank, so they got on with it. Within just a few days they obtained local promises, effectively credit, of £1 million, so they could trade. By the time a civil service contracts officer arrived later in the war Tom and his team had spent some £32 million on the local economy, accounting for it in a services' education exercise book. On one occasion, when the force was building up to a division, he was tasked with obtaining 40,000 'chermargues', the scarves worn by the locals in the desert against the ingress of sand. When they arrived, RAOC in Al Jubail was asked for payment for customs duties. When asked why import tax was payable on locally procured items the explanation came that the local businessman had sub-contracted the task to his brother in Bradford.

On 1 October that year, and for the first time, women officers were accepted as fully integrated cap-badged members of the RAOC. There were twenty-five officers permanently employed with the Corps, and every one of them elected to make the

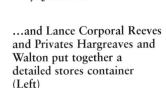

Above: Everyone got stuck in, military and civilian. Here packing Stores for Operation GRANBY are, from left to right, Lyn Carline, Maurene Craggs, Kath Gregory and Beryl Jenkins...

...and Lance Corporal Reeves and Privates Hargreaves and Walton put together a detailed stores container (Left)

transfer. A lunch was arranged in the UK to mark the occasion; but a similar event planned for Germany had to be postponed because of Operation GRANBY. That said, Captain Sarah Watmough, who was to command her rations platoon as part of 91 Ordnance Company, made the UK lunch before she deployed.

The FMB in Al Jubail soon became known as the FMA for the force, with Colonel, shortly to be Brigadier, Martin White as its commander. Late of the RCT, he was the ideal choice for the role, having only a few months earlier relinquished command of the 10,000 strong LSG for the UKMF(L). The LSG's essentially expeditionary nature in its NATO role meant that Colonel White had precisely the right experience to manage the rear logistics for the deployed

Conductor Marv Walden went to the Gulf as the BOWO of 7 Armoured Brigade.

295

force. Naturally, he and his embryonic HQ were in very early, to be followed on 9 October by the pre-advance party of 6 Ordnance Battalion to come under Martin White's command.

They were soon hard at work with the LRS sourcing the huge number of requirements for establishing a camp and a headquarters, from cleaning materials to office machinery to furniture, fridges, freezers and air conditioning units. And then there were the generators to power it all. Initially, the space Lieutenant Colonel Tim Murray was given was woefully inadequate for his needs – history from so many campaigns repeating itself yet again! However, on this occasion he had the LRS under command and he sent them forth to let a contract for an area adequate for his needs with the necessary infrastructure already there, or contracts to put in place what might be missing.

By 10 October 91 Ordnance Company was able to issue rations. The blessing here was that the Meals Ready to Eat provided by the US Marines and upon which our soldiers had hitherto been feeding, could be dispensed with. They were wholly unattractive, and were christened by the soldiers with some equally unattractive names based around the acronym MRE.

It was not to be until 23 October that 6 Ordnance Battalion was complete, by which time it had grown with the addition of a platoon of 63 Vehicle Company, re-titled 63 Vehicle Platoon, and Major Nick Bell's 221 EOD Company from Germany reinforced by elements from 11 Ordnance Battalion (EOD). They brought with them not only their EOD capability, but much needed ammunition expertise. This was no exercise, and for the first time for almost everyone the stock in the ammunition areas was not simulated.

When the powers that be found that Tim Murray had let the contract for his real estate and was about to move in, he was told he couldn't do it. But it was too late, he already had, so he did and thanks to that he was able to place 51, 62 and 91 Companies close by each other along with 63 Vehicle Platoon. A third line Ordnance Battalion was starting to take shape.

The ammunition storage managed by Major Phil Hanlon's 53 Ordnance Company was in two ammunition supply points provided by the US Marines, inevitably some way out of the town. Conditions were far from ideal, with a fine dust invading just about anything that was exposed. It made programmes such as re-fuzing

Containers proved to be a major storage asset, especially those rigged for detailed stores by the military and civilian staff at Donnington.

of artillery shell extremely difficult and quite delicate. And Major Peter Knoll's 51 Ordnance Company was busy in the early stages establishing one bulk fuel installation to serve the FMA and another further forward providing immediate support for the Brigade.

The arrival of 3 Ordnance Battalion was complete by the end of October. They were seeking to get forward to support the Brigade in its training and to do some training themselves. WOII(CSM) Willis of Major Trevor White's 31 Ordnance Company, wrote:

We deployed for Saudi Arabia on 26 October 1990, thus being the first Forward Ordnance Company to deploy to the Gulf. The initial reception on arrival left a lot to be desired and the standard of food, sanitary conditions and accommodation initially were appalling. However, once the vehicles arrived two days later it was all hands to the pumps to get the vehicles ready to deploy in support of 7 Armoured Brigade…

On 6 November 1990 Headquarters 3 Ordnance Battalion deployed to the desert. WOII Willis again:

…my initial impression of the desert was one of awe, it is a sight to behold.

WOI Barry Johnson GC RAOC.

On that day, in the UK, WOI (SSM) Barry Johnson became the sixth, and last, soldier of the RAOC to be awarded the George Cross. WOI Johnson, aged thirty-eight, was cited for his action on 7 October 1989 in the Waterside district of Londonderry. At the time he was serving as an EOD operator with 321 EOD Company RAOC and was tasked to an incident in which a vehicle containing an improvised IRA mortar device was abandoned in the middle of a housing estate and close to one of the city's hospitals. On examination it became clear that the van contained a mortar with a live bomb in each of its six tubes, and was intended for an attack on a security force base in the city. Aware of the immediate and grave danger to civilian lives in the heart of a residential area and in particular to patients in the hospital, he decided against the use of remotely controlled equipment to deal with the bombs, although the use of this equipment would have been the normal practice and would have placed him at much less personal risk. However, he assessed that it posed too great a danger of inadvertently launching one of the bombs during the render safe procedure. He decided to remove the bombs from their firing tubes and to dismantle them by hand. He was fully aware that he might be operating against a clock and the mortar could include anti handling devices.

With the help of an assistant, he carefully moved the firing tubes from the back of the vehicle and placed them on the ground. As the next step was extremely hazardous, WOI Johnson sent his colleague back behind cover and continued the disarming procedure alone. He managed to place the firing tubes in such a manner that if they fired or the bombs detonated, those in the hospital would not be endangered. In the dark and in a bitterly cold drizzle which made the handling of the heavy metal objects more precarious, he proceeded to remove the bombs and to dismantle each in turn. While he was dismantling the last bomb it exploded causing grievous injury to his face, his eyes and his legs. Despite being completely blinded by the high velocity fragments and being thrown across the road by the force of the blast, such was his courage and determination to ensure that the task was completed safely that, though in great pain, he forbade evacuation until he had briefed his assistant on the precise details of the device so that the operation could safely be completed by a replacement operator. He was to spend a long time in hospital recovering from his injuries, and his courage was rightly recognized by the nation's highest award that can be granted for an act of selfless bravery when not in contact with the enemy.

On 7 November a third BFI was opened by 51 Ordnance Company, and by 9 November all three were full and ready to issue fuel. As this was happening a great deal of political activity had culminated in the realization that Saddam Hussein would not listen to reason and that the campaign to hold the Kuwait situation would now have to move onto a more aggressive footing; that of evicting the Iraqis from Kuwait. More forces were needed, and on 10 November a warning order was received in HQ BAOR for Operation GRANBY 1.5, so named because this was a reinforcement of existing forces and not the anticipated roulement. HQ 1st Armoured Division would be going, taking with it 4 Armoured Brigade from 4th Division and taking back its own 7 Armoured Brigade when it arrived in Saudi

Arabia. The choice of brigades was based on the level of training and readiness they had been able to achieve, with exercises by their battle groups at BATUS, the massive training area in central Canada, being high on the list.

This was going to increase the pressures on the system, for those items in short supply for a brigade would now be even harder to resolve and the list would also expand considerably for what was the largest deployment of men and materiel to a desert war since the campaign in the western desert of North Africa fifty years earlier. The RAOC buckled to, and repeated the exercise undertaken only a few short weeks earlier for GRANBY 1.

The RAOC reinforcement was based around the need to run two DSAs for a full divisional deployment. Accordingly, the 3rd Ordnance Battalion Group was given a composite platoon drawn from 13 and 43 Ordnance Companies in Germany which were the rear

Soldiers of 51 Ordnance Company preparing the defences around a new BFI.

companies for 1st and 4th Divisions, plus 90 Ordnance Company from the UK. For 6 Ordnance Battalion there was a second ammunition company, 52 Ordnance Company from 5 Ordnance Battalion. In fact, whilst it was nominally 52 Company, the men were drawn from ammunition units all over Germany. The officer commanding was Major David Newell, the second-in-command of 154 FAD; and the original 52 Company stayed in Germany – so for a while there were two. Other individual reinforcements came from all over the RAOC, and had quickly to be fitted into a team in which, initially, they were strangers. In many cases their tasks in their parent units back in Europe were filled by TA. Eventually, 3 Battalion would have a strength of 570 and 6 Battalion 871. Added to the other small units and the individuals in HQs and about the place, one in

Every service was provided. The soldiers manning this laundry in 22 Field Hospital were almost certainly individual TA volunteers, but were indistinguishable from their regular counterparts.

three of the RAOC was in the Gulf. With the commitments in Northern Ireland, Cyprus, Belize, Canada, Hong Kong and the Falklands, none of which could be seriously tampered with, over 50 per cent of the RAOC's active, available strength was deployed. If this went on for any length of time there was going to be little chance of rotating units and individuals. And as the warning orders were going out for the new nominees, 3 Ordnance Battalion received its first air raid warning, although nothing materialized.

The next warning came during a service to celebrate St Barbara's Day, and it had to be abandoned while the necessary protective action was taken. It was pointed out that:

> St Barbara is the patron saint of those in danger from tempest and explosion...so it was all clear by lunchtime.

Margaret Thatcher's government, or perhaps more accurately the lady herself, was by now deeply unpopular. A downturn in the economy, the raising of interest rates to fifteen per cent and the attempted imposition of a poll tax were just some of the occurrences that contributed to the Tory party realizing that she had probably become a liability, coupled with her ever increasing personalization of her role. Michael Heseltine challenged her in a ballot for the party leadership, effectively for the premiership. She won the ballot, but not sufficiently convincingly to preclude her resignation as Prime Minister and the subsequent selection of John Major for the post, which he assumed on 28 November 1990. It was not an auspicious time with the country at war, and Ronald Reagan, the American President and a friend of Margaret Thatcher, was aghast.

Concern was being felt in the UK at the command and control arrangements for the RAOC in the Gulf. Lieutenant Colonels Taylor and Murray were acting not only as battalion commanders of constantly increasingly large battalion groups, but as staff advisors to their respective commanders. Additionally, Alan Taylor with his responsibility for the DAA was seeing his span of command increase to some 800 vehicles and thousands of men. The original RAOC view that the perceived role of Commander Supply in a division at war was more than one man could handle was becoming a reality; and the same was true in the FMA.

Consequently, when 1st Armoured Division deployed it brought with it Lieutenant Colonel Tim Cross in his staff role as Commander Supply, leaving all the command functions of the division's Ordnance Battalion and the DAA to Alan Taylor. In the FMA Lieutenant Colonel Steve Thornton came in as the SO1 in HQ FMA, and Lieutenant Colonel Brian Mobley went to HQ BFME in Riyadh – both men arriving in mid December. However, there was a battle going on between London and Riyadh, between General Sir Edward Jones and General de la Billière, on the issue of heads of service for the theatre. The Directors General of Transport, Ordnance Services and Electrical and Mechanical Engineering were lobbying the QMG strongly for the deployment of a colonel each to fill the role. There was local opposition to this in Saudi Arabia, but eventually QMG prevailed and a day or two after Christmas Colonel Mike Lake and Colonel Peter Gibson deployed as Commanders Transport and Maintenance respectively, and the DGOS's choice for Commander Supply was Colonel Frank Steer, then serving as the SO1 QMG1 in the MOD. In the event he was the first of the three to arrive.

Lieutenant Colonel Tim Cross RAOC.

They found that the only staff they had was what was already there, which was not even close to being adequate. They were co-located in a single office in which about twelve people had to work, but in which there was only room for six desks; and there was one telephone line between them all. They had to try and build something that might work from whatever they could find without in any way impacting on the battalions in the division or the FMA, and to do so in the face of continued local opposition to them being there in the first place. Colonel Steer quickly determined the overall strategy, telling the officers who were forward to look only forward, and leave him to watch their backs in order to free up as much of their time as possible. To build a small HQ he raided the Battle Casualty Replacement pool despite yet more opposition; how any of the three colonels were expected to achieve anything with no resources whatsoever is hard to imagine – or perhaps they weren't. However, after a while the Supply Cell managed to obtain a couple of junior officer watch keepers to support Brian Mobley and Major Alex Sturdy in Riyadh; and a driver, Corporal Tony Forster, who very quickly became 50 per cent of a two man team as he piloted Commander Supply all over Saudi Arabia.

If the office communications were poor in Riyadh, they were no worse than elsewhere. In the FMA a large office accommodated something like 150 staff working all the logistic functions, and there were only eight telephone lines. This was enough of a nightmare, but there was also the usual issue of operational level logistic communications and the links between consuming units and the sources of supply in the UK and at the FMA. COFFER was the IT solution for the provision of Ordnance Stores, and it was old and unsuited to the environment in which it was operating. It had gone out with the two Forward Companies, and a set had been issued to 6 Ordnance Battalion for use in 62 Ordnance Company. It was not a system that 6 Ordnance Battalion used in Germany, so there was a steep learning curve to be climbed. It was supposed to act as the accounting system for a secondary depot, which was what the FMA's storeholdings were. It was, in effect, a mini-ICP, but this was not a role for which it was either designed or suited.

It was antiquated, and to keep it, and other systems working, an In Theatre support team was deployed by DSCS. This was largely an initiative of Colonel Owen Brady, and it used RAOC Small Systems Group manpower with Lieutenant Colonel Terry Byrd OBE sourcing the special software needed for an IBM PC to talk to the Stores System 3 mainframe and enabling OLIVER and RAOC Mail facilities. OLIVER was a system for on line verification, giving access to the Bicester mainframe to check stock levels and, where necessary, make a demand for the item. It was an extraordinarily valuable tool, but so poor were the land line communications from the Gulf that it was only to be in touch with the Bicester computer for two hours in the whole of the build up to the war and during it, and those were the two hours leading up to midnight on the night the Allies went through the breach in Saddam's defensive berm and into Kuwait. It might as well not have been there.

The DSCS team was led by Captain Nigel Banks, supported by WOI Bob Leat and Acting Sergeant Adrian Conway-Hyde and was tasked with supporting all RAOC systems as well as 'finding and using' any source of data communications in theatre. They were also to provide general IT advice locally if required. One of the many difficulties with COFFER was that that it was really only configured to use fixed land lines and could not operate over PTARMIGAN, the Army's deployable, operational trunk telephone system for use in the field at divisional level. This was despite the clear lesson of Exercise SPEARPOINT from five years earlier of the value that such a capability would provide. There simply was not enough bandwidth, or capacity in layman's terms, and there was a marked lack of the yellow public telephone boxes that had solved the problem in Germany. There was simply no way to transmit COFFER data and Nigel Banks spent untold hours trying to make a link. Despite his best efforts he was unable to do so. This meant that the only way demands could be made was by dumping them onto tapes and taking them by dispatch rider all the way back to Al Jubail for 62 Ordnance Company to transmit them on the forward companies' behalf, and at times that distance was as much as 400 kilometres.

The first thing Alan Taylor said to Commander Supply on his initial visit at the very beginning of January was that he was not receiving replenishment stock from the UK, and stocks were getting low. He had been unable to get an answer as to the reason except to obtain a reassurance that everything he had asked for had been sent. Although he knew he should, he had neither the time nor, if the truth be known, the communications to find the real answer. More than a little research and the reason became clear following a long talk by Commander Supply with COFFER operators in 62 Ordnance Company. It lay in the system. Basically, the mainframe in Bicester was not recognizing the existence of a secondary depot, an ICP, in the Gulf because there hadn't been one there before, and was dumping all its routine demands for replenishment, dealing only with the high priority ones – and, because the demands it was dumping were routine, it wasn't telling anybody. So nothing had been happening.

Supply Branch in the Gulf was asked if they could re-submit the demands to kick the system into action. The reply was short and soldierly, with the advice that those in the UK could '...kick the ...thing themselves'. Very shortly after the problem was identified, however, the UK depots swung into action and the shortfalls were made up. Then the problem moved, for it all arrived in Al Jubail at once and had to be distributed to the forward units – but that was another story.

The arrival of the GRANBY 1.5 reinforcement raised another little issue where the routines of BAOR and the Staff College to which many were working did not quite work in the circumstances then prevailing in the Gulf, and demonstrated yet again that the standard mores had to be implemented with care. Commander Supply caught a chance remark as the issue of training ammunition for an infantry battalion was being discussed. The staff officer remarked that having issued to meet the training liability there were no reserves left. Alarm bells rang, and a very quick and very senior RAOC investigation was undertaken.

It was found that the cause of the problem lay in the fact that the infantry were armed with the new SA80 with its 5.56-mm ammunition. However, it had not been deployed across the Army as yet, and the rest of the forces in the Gulf were armed with the 7.62-mm self loading rifle. Ammunition reserves were based on scales in a document known as the A6606, and the reserve liability for small arms ammunition was only a few rounds per weapon per day. This was based on the fact that in Germany soldiers in the rear areas would fire virtually nothing, whilst those on the front line would consume vast quantities, but per man in a large command this would provide adequate stocks to allow for all that. In the Gulf where only the infantry were armed with the weapon they would chew through the reserve very quickly indeed. In fact, it wasn't a reserve at all.

IT in the Gulf, and its inability to communicate, were perennial problems, a real barrier to progress and a limitation on operational capability.

A swift telephone call to the UK resolved the problem, once a lack of comprehension had been overcome.

'How much have you got?'

A number was given. It was enough.

'Send it.'

'How many days' supply is that?'

'Dunno, just send it, all you've got - and now.'

They did, and it arrived in good time to get well forward and be there when the infantry needed it, but it was an example of how lateral thinking is the key to success, and how easy it is to get into a mind set when everything seems so clear and settled as it had in the days when the two power blocs faced each other across an international boundary.

As 1990 drew to a close the UK contribution to the war in the desert was removed from the US Marine Corps who were destined to punch directly north along the coast to Kuwait City. Instead, the division was to join 7th US Corps as part of the long left hook that would take Saddam's army in the flank and drive into Kuwait City from the west.

This meant the FMA operating an LofC that was 400 kilometres long instead of fifty. That quite simply meant shortening it by setting up a forward logistic base. The road they would use to make this move was built for the oil industry and was less than adequate, barely a two lane highway. It would be shared by the British, American, French and Saudi forces. A small convoy had a turnaround time of thirty-six hours. This was not going to be easy, and there was a clear time line for it to be complete – twenty-one days, and the move would start on 3 January.

In January 1991 it was announced that Ordnance Depot Antwerp, where there had been an RAOC presence since November 1944, and which for so many years had been fundamental to the reinforcement of BAOR, would close by 31 March 1992. It was the start of the Options reductions, but oddly it closed the back door to Germany and the Low Countries through which the rest of BAOR could have withdrawn when it downsized. Now something else or somewhere else would have to be found.

Included in the same package of downsizing measures was the closure of the FVD at Recklinghausen, Ordnance Service Viersen and the ICP BAOR, all of which would be essential in managing a theatre wide drawdown once GRANBY was over. It was a fundamentally flawed staff decision imposed on the RAOC for reasons that remain unclear. On his return from GRANBY 1.5 later in the year, and on hearing of the decision, Brigadier Chris Hammerbeck, Commander of 4 Armoured Brigade, said it was the first time he had been involved in a planned withdrawal when they had closed all the RVs first.

On 7 January the RAOC Band arrived in the Gulf in their secondary role as stretcher bearers and medical assistants. Captain Terry Davis, the Director of Music was allocated with the band to support a second line dressing station working with the Gurkha Transport Regiment

The move up into the desert of the FFMA presented a number of new problems. Water was needed in vast quantities and tankers had to be provided for that as well as reverse osmosis plants. Lack of accommodation was also a problem, and where in Germany plans had been made to use buildings for war, tents had to be used in the desert. The Directorate of Clothing and Textiles used almost all the available supplies of tents on the civilian market, and still it was not enough. Shortages would have to be catered for by improvisation – ISO containers again?

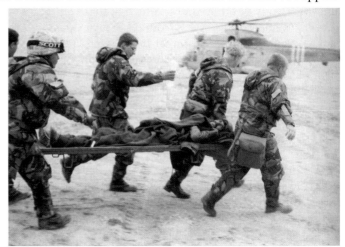

Members of the RAOC Band training in Saudi Arabia for their war role as medical orderlies.

The UN set 15 January as the date for Iraqi withdrawal from Kuwait to commence. They didn't go. On 17 January the RAF and United States Air Force opened the war for the recovery of Kuwait with bombing raids throughout Iraq.

And the Army still managed to run a cross-country championship, and Lance Corporal Dave Neal RAOC of the Commando Ordnance Squadron won it. He was the first RAOC soldier to have done so in twenty years, and only the third since 1945, the other two being 2nd Lieutenant Sanders in 1949 and Captain Darlow in 1971.

At O315 local time 17 January 1991 active service was declared in the Gulf. Shortly after that Brigadier Chris Hammerbeck, Commander 4 Armoured Brigade visited 31 Ordnance Company and in conversation with some of the soldiers said,

> ...logistics are the heart pumping blood to the fingers – the battle groups. Without the heart the fingers don't move.

To soldiers who had already spent weeks in the desert it was heart-warming stuff, and made all the hard work just that bit more worthwhile.

The setting up of the FFMA involved moving 20,000 tons of ammunition, hundreds of vehicles and stores, rations, water and other consumables. Not for the first time in a major modern war, fuel was a critical problem. With the available tankers it was eight days before the stocks in the forward BFIs began to beat the graph, before they actually started to build up reserves rather than just consume everything they were moving in day-to-day maintenance. It was also a problem for the Americans and the two nations decided to cooperate in the construction of a pipeline which, mindful of PLUTO, the Pipeline Under The Ocean of Normandy 1944 fame, was christened, with just a touch of humour, Pipeline Over the Desert, or PLOD. Captain Mike Holmes was to command an ad hoc unit, 511 Pipeline Platoon, to operate the British contribution.

As the FFMA was being inloaded the FMA continued to receive stocks and to try and move them through. The big items, like ammunition, fuel and food were quite easy, but the problem lay with the myriad of spares that were flooding through. The people on the ground and in the division created a whole series of 'workarounds' and, to a large extent, they worked, and the right stocks eventually appear to have got to the right place. However, control was in reality almost impossible and the 'workarounds' should not have been necessary, substituting as they did for a lack of logistic communications and IT throughout the logistic support chain, especially at the point of consumption and the key distribution nodes. Added to that was the need to compensate for under resourcing of the RAOC by employing soldiers from other cap badges, but this was not a success because of the training requirement. The problems in Al Jubail were so similar to those experienced by Major Mears outside Constantinople supporting the Army of the Black Sea some seventy-one years earlier, shortly after the birth of the RAOC, it was frightening.

There was also the inevitable split of priorities for which there was so much historical precedent, with transport set aside for the move of stores being hijacked at the last minute to move ammunition. Important thought it was, if the weapons platform didn't work for lack of spares, the ammunition was useless. On one notable night fifty vehicles that had been set aside to clear the FMA of spares and get them into the division's RVs simply failed to materialize. If ever there was a case for the integration of the supply and distribution functions and organizations, as Lord Kitchener had visualized and as the Ordnance Department Field Train had operated a century and a half earlier, Operation GRANBY proved it yet again.

But, despite the problems, by the eve of battle everything seemed to be in place. So it was that Alan Taylor felt free to celebrate his birthday on 12 February with a dinner in the desert; knowing it was only a matter of hours before they would cross the start line and there was nothing more that could be done. Kate Adie, the BBC journalist, had been part of it all, almost from the beginning, and since the press pack was looked after as one of the many small groups in the DAA, she and 3 Ordnance Battalion got to know each other very well:

> The RAOC and Lieutenant Colonel Alan Taylor introduced me to the practical aspects of Army life in Saudi Arabia: the importance of a shovel, the usefulness of Woolite and the necessity of driving in circles.
>
> 'I like gardening,' I said, on being presented with the shovel. 'We had a trench and a latrine in mind,' said the RAOC.

31 Ordnance Company ready to go. Note the dispersion, and the freedom from the need for camouflage resulting from total air domination.

'What's Woolite?' I asked.

'There are two thousand lads in this unit,' came the reply. 'You are a) the only woman, and b) the only person ignorant of cold water laundering.'

'Why have we packed up everything, driven for four hours and arrived back at our starting-point?'

'Useful practice,' replied the colonel, looking at the knackered media unit trickling into camp from several directions. 'Now I know how many of you are going to get lost when we actually go to war.'

However, the eve-of-battle dinner was unforgettable: trestle tables with candles stuck onto can-tops, and the sound of a lone piper in the desert as we all stood under the stars, contemplating war.

She was highly respected by the soldiers as easily the most professional journalist there. It would seem the respect was mutual. And within a few days of leaving the table that night that is what they were doing – going to war.

The following day they began to move forward into the positions they would be occupying just prior to the opening of the ground war as their launch pad into Kuwait. To give an example, just part of the size of a DAA move, a new Divisional RV was needed, and emptying the old one took almost 100 8-tonne vehicles. It was a huge problem, and there was as much or more in the FMA waiting for transport to take it up the line. More proof that effective communications and IT to control Ordnance Stores was an absolute necessity and a clear force multiplier, along with an effective distribution system equipped with sufficient transport resources.

On 18 February PLOD began pumping fuel at the rate of 90,000 litres per hour and 53 Ordnance Company received its 100,000th pallet of ammunition, with more still on the way. All the units were in the forward areas, it was all ready, and time began to hang heavily. Alan Taylor went round at Stand To and spoke to the soldiers about what they thought. His diary recorded the moment:

They were all quiet and reflective, but really apart from the uncertainty we all feel at the moment they want to go in. They are impatient to get started with what will eventually take us back to our homes...we don't know what is going to happen, a bit frightened but mainly because of the

An ammunition field storage area

uncertainty. We just don't know what we are going to encounter in the breach or beyond the breach...

The attack was launched at 0400 on 24 February 1991, and the first RAOC unit to cross into Iraq was 31 Ordnance Company at 1610 on 25 February in close support of 4 Armoured Brigade. Not far behind was 11 Ordnance Company supporting 7 Armoured Brigade. Having gone through the breach they would swing to the east heading straight for Kuwait City as 1st Armoured Division pursued its role as flank guard for 7th US Corps. In theory they were faced by up to six Iraqi divisions, and to counter this they were to use pace and speed to get, and then remain, inside the enemy's decision cycle. Stores sections with REME workshops, combat supplies platoons with transport regiments full of ammunition and packed fuel, Ordnance Companies carrying everything they could all pouring through with the brigades they were supporting. For replenishment to be successful under these conditions stocks of all commodities had to be well forward in the battle groups, and the support had to be close behind to provide immediate replenishment to match consumption. Loaded, and with supplies that would keep the division operating for a week, they drove east, to be there when they were needed. WOII (CSM) N A Willis of 31 Ordnance Company recorded his impressions:

> The impact and speed of the ground offensive took me by surprise; no one had anticipated resistance to be so light or the battle groups to move so quickly. We were virtually on the move constantly, the majority of halts being no longer than four hours, I could hear the battle groups fighting only six kilometres in front of us, and minutes later we would drive through the recently taken objectives as the brigade motored on to its next objective.

The pace of the advance and the relative ease with which victory was achieved presented its own problems. Dumps of stock, especially ammunition, were there for when they were needed, but they were not required. With transport fully loaded and heading forward there was no thought of collecting it, and when this was all over someone was going to have to come back and clear it all up. It would be something the RAOC would have to come to terms with.

At 8.00 am local time on 18 February a ceasefire was declared. It was over. 3 Ordnance Battalion ended its war thirty kilometres north of Kuwait City, and started looking at the clear up and the time when they might be going home. One important part of the service that was suddenly needed again was EFI, and stocks were brought forward as quickly as possible. Normal life was to resume, and the six officers and sixty-four soldiers of the EFI who were deployed in the Gulf began once more to bring smiles to the faces of tired soldiers.

When it was all over Major General David Botting, the DGOS, wrote to all members of the RAOC through the medium of the RAOC *Gazette*:

Colonel Frank Steer MBE, Commander Supply BFME, visiting RAOC units north of Kuwait City shortly after the ceasefire. The point to note is the intensely black sky at midday caused by the smoke from burning oil wells becoming trapped under the overcast cloud and oil percolating down mixed in with the rain. It was time for the soldiers to go home.

Now that the Gulf war is over, albeit we are still involved in the massive logistic return operation, I thought it would be appropriate to write a foreword to this issue of the Corps' *Gazette*. First, on behalf of all members of the Corps, I wish to pass on our deepest sympathy to the family and friends of Sergeant Phillips and Private Fogerty, who tragically died during Op Granby. Not only will we remember them as friends, but also for so proudly serving the Nation, the Army and the Royal Army Ordnance Corps.

All of you can be equally proud of your achievements in support of this complex operation. Logistically, it has been the largest mounted since the D-Day landings. More than a third of the Corps has been deployed to the Gulf and most of the remaining civilian and military staffs, to greater or lesser degrees, have been directly involved in one way or another. In addition, we are indebted to the valuable service provided by members of the TA and EFI.

Op Granby was a 'logistic triumph' and the 'logistic support was outstanding'. Not my words but those of other senior officers who have expressed their congratulations to us all and some of their letters have been circulated to you. In addition, the general public and the Government are full of admiration and praise for the totally professional manner in which you have all carried out your work in support of Op Granby. I wish to add my gratitude and thanks to you all.

But as fast as the troops were coming home, so more were going out. Someone had to clear up the mess, to get all the unused stock back to Germany and the UK ready for whatever might come next. It was a massive problem, and Lieutenant Colonel Malcolm Wood's 5 Ordnance Battalion was chosen for the task, arriving in March 1991. As they arrived, an invited team of Colonel Brian Allen, Lieutenant Colonel Bob Cannons, Lieutenant Colonel Colin Den McKay and Lieutenant Colonel Norman Callaghan arrived to decide how it could best be sensibly done. Coming from the base and from the depots they knew the problems their fellow soldiers were facing, and they knew the problems that would surface in the depots. The instructions they gave reduced by a considerable amount the time it would take 5 Ordnance Battalion to clear up and come home. The main part of the load, and it was huge, would fall on Donnington which, at that stage, was starting to cope with the stores returning from Germany as part of the drawdown and was still maintaining the Army at the same time. And no additional resources were provided to help.

The speed with which the politicians wanted to bring home those who had fought in the war, for purely political reasons, meant that equipment was more or less dumped for someone else to clear up. Commander Supply was especially worried about the safety of the returned ammunition and requested the immediate provision of a real expert to handle the ammunition areas. Lieutenant Colonel Alan Glasby was sent out, and a better choice would have been hard to imagine. After his first visit to the ammunition sites to see the size of the task he saw Colonel Steer, by now located in Al Jubail, who said he would be up there himself to have a look at the problem the next day. Alan Glasby, quite forcefully said that was not a good idea and he needed a week to sort things out. When asked why, Alan said simply:

'Two words.'

'Which are?' said the Colonel, himself an ATO, expecting something old fashioned, Anglo-Saxon and soldierly.

'Savernake Forest' was the reply

It was ghastly, it raised the ghosts of the past, and it required great technical skill and judgement to sort out; but it was just a part of the huge task that faced 5 Ordnance Battalion. In the end they did so well that they were back home by July that year. However, it reinforced the lesson learned so often before that when there is a deployment the recovery phase needs to be planned from the outset. As an indication of scale COD Donnington took back 3,000 containers; 2,000 vehicles were returned to RAOC depots and, of the 74,000 tons of ammunition deployed, 48,000 tons was returned with most of it being in need of refurbishment. These were mammoth tasks. However, when the RAOC soldiers eventually returned home they were faced with the redundancies emanating from Options for Change and the resulting decreases in manpower. It was a repeat of the past. At the time the workload was increasing the skilled and highly talented manpower was decreasing

They were also faced with the outcome of the LSR which was going to bring about the most fundamental change to the organization of logistic support for the Army for decades; some would argue for over a century. And it was to have major impact for the RAOC. It was the first overall study of Army logistics in over twenty years. There had been studies in the

Just part of the load of containers and stores 5 Ordnance Battalion had to get back to the UK...

interim into some features of the task, but the recommendations had in many cases not been fully implemented and as a result much of the change they postulated had not taken place. This had led to Army logistics management falling behind and failing to keep place with the rapid advance of logistic practices and procedures in the civilian world, and in which the Army had once led the field. The most disturbing area of difference was in communications, the level of management information and IT, where the Army was woefully lacking, as the very recent exercise in the Gulf had demonstrated so clearly – yet again.

The LSR formed the view that the way forward was to develop organizations to match the functions they are expected to perform. It saw the removal of unnecessary interfaces with

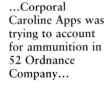

...Corporal Caroline Apps was trying to account for ammunition in 52 Ordnance Company...

...and as for the vehicles...

...whilst Sergeant Steve Williams of the AMF(L) Supply Company tried to get to grips with 80,00 jerry cans.

overlapping authority and blurring of responsibility. The LSR team saw two broad functions emerging, which came as no real surprise given the outcome of Hedsor Park. One would be support for combat forces, consisting of functions directly supporting the maintenance of forces at combat readiness and in combat. It was Kitchener's vision realized. However, the equipment intensive nature of modern armies meant that in order for logistics to work this support function had to be complementary to the support of equipment, its maintenance and availability.

The Service Support function was destined to draw together under one organization all those disciplines that existed in the Army that provided service support. Supply, the business of the RAOC, would be integrated with Transport, Pioneers, Catering and Postal and Courier. It would provide a single supply and distribution organization which would mirror best commercial practice. Catering would be linked with the supply of food, the labour force that worked with the depots and with field force units would become part of the same whole and mail distribution would be part of the overall Army distributing system.

All this was very laudable, but then it all began to get confused with the Cap Badge issue, when what was needed were systems and processes properly resourced with a staff structure in place to control and direct a modern logistic organization. However, the outcome of the study would see the end of the RAOC as a separate corps, together with the RCT, the RPC, the ACC and the Postal and Courier Branch of the RE. It was to happen in April 1993, less than two years ahead. The Equipment Support organization, based around REME, which was not to lose its identity despite its change in focus, would form up a year earlier, taking under its wing those elements of the RAOC involved in managing spares and vehicles.

The number of IEDs used by terrorists in Northern Ireland in 1991 had been the highest since 1978. Some 1,700 incidents involving 9,000 kilograms of explosives were attended by 321 EOD Company. However, they were better equipped for the task with a new remotely controlled EOD robot and a new bomb suit for personal protection. At the same time, on the mainland, 11 EOD Battalion had dealt with over 100 PIRA incendiary devices, and also had work to do to counter the work of animal rights activists and Welsh Nationalists. This was in addition to the 3,000 or so conventional stray ammunition tasks they had to cope with.

The beginning of the financial year for 1991/1992 saw the live introduction of the New Management Strategy. One of its key features was to organize budgets so that they became the responsibility of the user of the service they were there to provide for. The effect on DGOS' budget was significant, reducing it from something in the order of £5 million to £1.5 million. This was due to the redistribution of responsibility resulting from the new budgetary regime. For example, the responsibility for purchasing POL had hitherto lain with DGOS. Now it lay with the Commanders-in-Chief of the front line

A remotely controlled Wheelbarrow.

Wheelbarrows at the scene of an explosion in Ulster on 16 October 1987, precluding the need to 'walk up to it'.

commands and accordingly the money was placed in their budgets to the detriment of DGOS.

From April until July 1991, the Commando Ordnance Squadron deployed with 3 Commando Brigade Royal Marines as part of Operation HAVEN. The task was to provide support to the UK/Netherlands Amphibious Force deployed to act as a protective barrier between the Kurds and Saddam's armed forces. It was a multinational operation mounted to help save some 600,000 Kurdish refugees who had fled into mountains in Northern Iraq after their unsuccessful rebellion against Saddam Hussein's armies. As mountain troops, the role of 3 Commando Brigade Royal Marines was military, to confront and pursue the remnants of Iraqi northern divisions, rather than being directly humanitarian. The Ordnance Squadron was tasked with supporting the Commando Brigade in a tactical role as well as providing some humanitarian relief to the Kurdish refugees. The squadron had elements deployed in Turkey from Iskenderum on the Turkish Mediterranean coast, to Diyabakir Airfield 400 miles inland, to Silopi on the Iraqi border. In Iraq the squadron deployed in Zakho and Sersenk, with representatives detached to Commando units.

Sometimes, however, the walk was necessary, perhaps because Wheelbarrow could not get there or, as in this case, the control cables on an earlier model had become entangled forcing Captain Tony Laceby to approach the device and render it safe manually.

A dedication ceremony for an EOD memorial was held at CAD Kineton on Sunday 23 June 1991. The memorial was erected to the memory of the twenty-three RAOC EOD operators who had lost their lives since 1945. The service of dedication was conducted in heavy rain by the

Sergeant Dave Lang, Chief Clerk of the Commando Ordnance Squadron on Operation HAVEN, working in the BAA at Silopi in 42 degrees of heat.

Lance Corporal 'Gaz' Hayes at the BMA at Semank.

Chaplain General, the Reverend James Harkness. Major General Peter lstead OBE GM, and WOI Barry Johnson GC read the lessons. The DGOS and numerous ATOs and ATs, past and present, attended as did many relatives of the deceased, although not all could be traced and contacted. In his address the Chaplain General struck a chord:

'We claim responsibility.' In these three words are summed up the evil intent of those who, for whatever reason, make murder and destruction a way of life. By these three words they stand condemned out of their own lips by all civilized and reasonable men and women. And yet these words haunt our world and impact on the lives of all those who are trying to go about their ordinary and lawful business.

At the forefront of those who attempt to counter this evil in our society stand those who serve in Explosive Ordnance Disposal Units, better known to us as 'Bomb Disposal'. It is these men of all ranks, and especially those whose names are recorded here on this memorial, that we have come to remember and honour today. In doing so we are acknowledging a debt to them which can never be fully expressed in words, and to whom the greatest tribute is the security and safety which encompasses our daily lives, because we know that they are always ready to act to save lives and protect property. How easily we take all that for granted allowing it to be regarded merely as a function, as a duty; and as a skill to which we have a right. And, bombarded by the visual images presented by the media, we too easily make it all impersonal protecting ourselves

The EOD Memorial.

from the human dimension so that the man in the 'bomb suit' ceases to be one of us. But you know that that is not true. For behind the complex equipment and inside the 'bomb suit' with its seeming anonymity, there is a living human being.

The cost of the memorial construction was raised by personal and unit donations and from commercial concerns associated with EOD or the RAOC. The Worshipful Company of Gold and Silver Wyre Drawers was notably generous. In addition, many of those involved with the building and furnishing of the memorial gave their services free or at a much reduced prices.

In the middle of 1991 the QIT strategy study, which had been carried out by the leading commercial consultants, Touche Ross, reported. It endorsed, by and large, the plans the RAOC had for the way ahead for IT in managing supply. Where gaps were identified, they were mainly in REME. However, regardless of how well or how not so well individual components were performing, a major plank of the QITS study recommendations was the need for a reorganization of the QMG's management of IT. This saw the removal of DSCS from the DGOS, hence his losing control of his own IT systems development and the formation of a Directorate of Logistic Information Systems reporting direct into QMG. The RAOC Small Systems Groups would move to the new directorate in due course and the rest of the manpower came from all over the QMG's area, bringing together all the disparate IT functions. The RAOC was the biggest net contributor, which meant DGOS was the biggest net loser. However, the outcome of the study meant the positioning of a major logistic resource directly under the hand of the QMG and acknowledged the responsibility of the staff to deliver logistic resources that met the needs of the Army as a whole.

The first director was Brigadier James Nurton OBE, MC, late of the Scots Guards, with two late-RAOC officers, Colonel Alan Pollard, as Chief of Staff, and Colonel Terry Byrd OBE as Director of Customer Support. The latter effectively became DSCS and was responsible for all RAOC supply systems. However, as if that were not enough, he also had the additional burden of transport, pioneer and postal systems as well as a thing called QP24, which was the deployable HQ G4 function recommended by QITS, but which would never see the light of day.

On 1 December 1991 there was a service of dedication for three new stained glass windows at St Barbara's Church at Deepcut. The first was provided by the Normandy Veterans Association in memory of those killed during the campaign. As a centrepiece it had the French and German Star, with representations of the landings in the background. BAOR also had one, funded by subscriptions from within the theatre, it displayed the BAOR Shield surrounded by displays representing life in Germany. The third came from the RAOC Training Centre with the Book of Knowledge, the Torches of Learning and the Sword of Wisdom surrounded by scenes typical of the life of the establishment. The windows were a nice memorial that would provide a constant memory of the association of the ninety-one year old church with the seventy-three year old RAOC.

The following day those WRAC soldiers serving in RAOC trades followed the officers, and were badged RAOC. It had been a long time coming, but the women had worked with the RAOC for so many years, and made such a contribution, it was right, fitting and appropriate that they should join the family of the Corps. Throughout the RAOC all over the world ceremonies were held to mark the importance of the occasion.

In Viersen on 20 December 1991 the ICP carried out the final computer runs in the run-up to its eventual closure on 31 March 1992. In the preceding five months all its accounts had been transferred to the UK, with all its technical and operational roles having ceased. It had been in Germany since 1973 as part of the CICP/ICP system that operated not just to BAOR, but also to Berlin and Hong Kong. But that was now over, as was so much throughout Germany and the Low Countries as 1992 became the year of 'lasts' and closures as so many units fell under the combined axes of Options for Change and the LSR. It was an emotional time for many, and not just soldiers of the RAOC. Many of the locally employed civilians who had served so loyally for so long were also cast side and for many their association with RAOC units had been less a job and more a way of life. For some it was to prove devastating.

The key in much of what was happening was to remain professional throughout, and to ensure that whatever was taken forward into the new Corps was the very best the RAOC had to offer. That required close attention to maintenance of standards, and in every facet of the life of the RAOC. An example was the band, which on 27 March 1992 underwent its quinquennial review. As its name implies, this is a five yearly inspection by the Army School of Music at Kneller Hall. Suffice it to say they were awarded a grading of outstanding, the first such award to any Army band for over five years. It reflected huge credit on an outstanding Director of Music, Captain Steve Smith, and it made the point that everyone, the band included, was going to go with their heads and tails firmly up.

The Directors General and Directors of the Forming Corps of the RLC knew that if the new Corps was to get off to the best possible start it would need their combined efforts. Consequently, on 9 September 1991 they met in the first of a series of meetings that saw them christened the Famous Five. They spawned a number of sub groups to cover every aspect of life in the new Corps including uniforms, badges, charitable funding, trade structures and so on. They were determined to get it right, to hand on the very best they could to the fledgling RLC. Within the RAOC the DGOS was determined to mark the last year of the RAOC with a programme of parades and functions intended to be a celebration of the Corps and its activities. It was, he hoped, to culminate in a visit by the Queen to her Corps.

In this spirit the RAOC *Gazette*, under its devoted editor Lieutenant Colonel (Retd) Bill Masterton, for this, the last year of the RAOC, was full of involvement in sport at unit, Army and Combined Services level, in exercises, thereby keeping up the standards, and in adventure training, to more and more exotic places. The Army, at senior level, may well have been pondering its future, but at regimental duty, where it really mattered; people were just getting on with the job and thoroughly enjoying life.

Private Mick Barry cast an approving eye over the band as it marched off his square, pleased to see that standards had not slipped – not one jot.

One of the key lessons from the Gulf War, and upon which many fastened, as some sort of Holy Grail that would solve all the problems, was to be able to track assets in transit, to know where they were. A system entitled Visibility In Transit Asset Logging, or VITAL was introduced to fill a missing link in distribution management, with the operation in Bosnia as the focus. A major feature was speed of development with a pilot being deployed to Bosnia in just over six months. Shop floor data capture was necessary in depots, using bar coding, to enable the packing of an issued item into its initial container to be captured. Workarounds had to be made in existing, and ailing, depot systems. VITAL was linked to SS3 to reduce data capture and improve data currency. Interfaces were also designed to allow consignments delivered direct ex-trade to be tracked. The project enjoyed high level patronage from QMG personally and during the key early stages considerable effort was provided by Brigadier Kevin Goad, the commandant of COD Bicester, to ensure that the pilot could be proven and the pipeline to Bosnia properly tracked. It would add value, but would not compensate for the prevailing lack of IT and communications at unit level and in the area of operations generally that would permit effective management by the RAOC of a 'virtual' warehouse; a clear force multiplier.

Staff clerks had existed in the British Army since 1890 when a need for professional clerical support in military headquarters was identified. By the end of the Second World War they were employed throughout the Army from the War Office to the front line, and were badged RASC. They transferred to the RAOC under the McLeod reorganization in 1965, and although their time with the Corps was short they brought to it their very high profile and great goodwill as they served across the Army wearing the RAOC badge. However, in the early nineties, as part of an MOD wide review under options for change, the management services of the Army were brought together into a single Adjutant General's Corps. This included such organizations as the Royal Army Pay Corps and the Royal Army Educational Corps. Swept up with this were the staff clerks of the RAOC, and, despite a hard fight to retain them, on 6 April 1992 they transferred to the AGC. It was as if the move of the School of Clerical Training in 1985 to Worthy Down had been a portent of the future, for Worthy Down was to be the home of the AGC.

It was a sad parting for the staff clerks had made a great contribution, serving in many of the world's trouble spots in embassies and being among the first to deploy, with their commanders, on operations. They were all dined out of the Corps with either the DGOS or his senior local formation representative attending the dinner in order properly to say goodbye and thank you. The dinners were all subsidised from RAOC funds. During their all too brief tenure of twenty-seven years with the RAOC some 130 had been commissioned, and at the time of the transfer, five were lieutenant colonels. They had earned an OBE, eighteen MBEs and 118 BEMs, and seven had been Mentioned in Dispatches. They were going to be sorely missed, and with their departure went fourteen per cent of the RAOC's manpower.

However, this was just one of a series of fundamental changes that was to take place affecting the RAOC. At a strategic level, the first phase of the LSR reorganization of the QMG's responsibilities also took place on 6 April 1992. This was to affect the RAOC in three ways. Firstly at Andover, the Director General Equipment Support (Army) came into being. It combined the existing DGEME, the Director Support Planning (Army) from QMG's London staff, most of the Director of Supply Management (Army)'s equipment management organization from DGOS' area, elements from the Engineer in Chief's department and, finally, most of the finance division from the LE(A). Secondly, DSM(A)'s vehicle spares division and technical equipments division would transfer and become DGES(A)'s responsibility, with DSM(A) himself becoming Director of Equipment Support 5. He would be the principal supply manager within DGES(A), responsible for B vehicle management, as well as certain other technical ranges, a budget spend of some £80 million and responsibility for policy on DGES(A)'s spares budget of some £250 million. However, DES 5's staff retained their RAOC cap badges, since the RLC, of which they were to become a part, was not to see the light of day for another year. Thirdly, throughout the chain of command an equipment support staff was to be created to mirror the organization at LE(A).

The theory was that the reorganization would bring together all those responsible for the support of equipment in the Army. It therefore combined the equipment manager, supply manager, engineering support, finance and contract staffs into a single focus of responsibility. However, an important principle was that this reorganization of responsibility would not divide the existing material supply system. From 5 April 1993 this was to be the responsibility of the Director General Logistic Support (Army), and in the meantime the existing logistic corps would continue to make it work; as they always had. Whatever the aspiration, if the process at the front end was not completely clear to QMs and RQMSs, it would fail and the acid test of that would only come when the system was tested – and tested on operations. Meanwhile, as an interim measure, at Andover a Directorate of Supply was established to cover the intervening year, with Colonel Kieran O'Kelly as its director

At an operational level, in BAOR some sense was at last percolating through. After some serious lobbying and a lot of hard work by the Commander Supply, Brigadier David Harris, it was accepted that some RAOC presence was needed in the base area during drawdown to receive, sort and dispose of unwanted stocks and send back to the UK that which was required for retention. So it was that just a few weeks before Hilsea Barracks was due to close it was decided to leave it open. In Mönchengladbach Ayrshire Barracks, the former home of 17 Vehicle Battalion in all its various guises, was kept alive to handle the vehicles; a necessary role with all the vehicle parks in Antwerp and Recklinghausen having been closed already. Lieutenant Colonel Steve Owen became both the last Commanding Officer of Ordnance Services Viersen and the first, and only, Commanding Officer of the Theatre Drawdown Unit. Mercifully, the two ME29 computers that had been in the ICP had not been disposed of when it closed and they could be retained in order to account for the stocks that would be acquired and then distributed by the TDU. Lieutenant Colonel Owen had a unique command:

> As the rest of BAOR underwent Options for Change, Ordnance Services Viersen reroled as the Theatre Drawdown Unit BAOR on 1 April 1992, setting up business in the technical accommodation in Hilsea Bks Viersen and in North Park Mönchengladbach. TDU accounted for and processed stores, equipment and vehicles no longer required by units closing down under Options for Change in Germany. During its life TDU saved MOD some £36,000,000 in stock replacement costs. TDU was a hard working unit, always focussed on supporting units closing or amalgamating whilst striving for the avoidance of waste. Its unique role meant high profile visitors including CINC BAOR, DGOS, AUS(Q) and QMG who were all suitable impressed with the purpose and efficiency of the unit. Although only destined for a short existence it nevertheless enjoyed a full regimental life and had notable success in sporting, military and adventure training activities.

It has to be a source of wonder what would have been done had it not been for the foresight that made the TDU a reality.

Clarity was beginning to emerge from the work being undertaken to make the recommendations of the LSR a reality, as they affected Logistic Support as opposed to Equipment Support. By April 1992 important news on structures and organizations was made public. RAOC soldiers were to be members of the Royal Logistic Corps in April 1993. HRH the Princess Royal had agreed to be the Colonel-in-Chief of the new Corps with the Duke of Gloucester and Duchess of Kent the Deputy Colonels-in-Chief. The professional head of the Corps was to be DG Log Sp (A), and the RAOC was delighted with the announcement that the first incumbent was to be Major General David Burden CB CBE, an RAOC officer. The other good news was that the new Corps' home was to be Blackdown, with Headquarters RLC TA to be established at Grantham, at that time the home of the RCT's TA.

Major General David Burden CB CBE, late of the RAOC and selected to be the first head of the Royal Logistic Corps and the Director General of Logistic Support (Army).

Support for the Field Army would also see significant changes. At 4th Line, in BAOR, it was planned to have two new battalions created from the remaining depots, at Wulfen, Warendorf, Dulmen and Bracht. Their organization was to be geared primarily to their operational role. The new 3rd Line unit for the Germany-based 1st (UK) Armoured Division was to be an amalgam of 5 and 6 Ordnance Battalions, whilst for the UK-based 3rd (UK) Division, 9 Ordnance Battalion would continue to exist with a slight change of title and some minor enhancements. At 2nd Line, both 1st (UK) Armoured Division and 3rd (UK) Division would each be supported by two new units which combined Supply and Transport functions, to be called Close and General Support Regiments. Close Support would provide re-supply of all commodities to brigade units, giving the user one point of contact for combat re-supply. General Support would be geared principally to artillery re-supply with much of its modus operandi based on the lessons from Operation GRANBY, tempered by the requirements of Options for Change and the recommendations of the LSR. Terminology would change in a number of ways, one of which was the decision that the RLC would be a mounted corps, so companies and battalions would become squadrons and regiments.

It was eventually agreed that much of the trade structure of the existing corps would remain largely unchanged, as would the main planks of the individual training organizations, until the RLC had settled down. Much of this work was undertaken by the Famous Five.

In the meantime, the Junior Leaders Regiment at Colerne closed and RAOC Junior Leader training was moved to Bovington where they trained alongside Royal Armoured Corps Junior Leaders. This would eventually be the same for RLC juniors prior to a planned move to Harrogate a year or so later.

But there would still be a Corps left behind. The many thousands who had served in the RAOC still required their regimental 'home'; and there was the money accrued by the RAOC in its benevolent fund from the one day's pay scheme which had to be looked after. It was decided that the heritage of the RAOC was to be managed by a board of trustees, and this included the RAOC's funds held in trust. The Officers' Club was to remain, and it would hold an annual dinner. The RAOC Association would also hold an annual gathering and dinner in April each year, and an RAOC Sunday also emerged as a feature in Deepcut involving a church service and a lunch to which wives and families were welcome. The RAOC *Gazette* was to continue, but in very much reduced form, and very much less frequent, as a newsletter to keep old comrades in touch with events and, where necessary, each other. The good news was that, for the time being at least, Her Majesty the Queen would continue to be Patron of the RAOC Trust.

That year, the final year of the RAOC's existence, yet another RAOC unit was awarded the Wilkinson Sword of Peace. In this case it was due to a link between the Training Battalion and Depot that went back over the preceding twenty-two years with the White Lodge Centre in Chertsey. It was a home for children with cerebral palsy and other serious illnesses, and over the period of the association some £67,000 had been raised to support the centre.

Then, just when it was all going quiet and there should have been some time to reflect and reorganize, and get things off to a good start, Her Majesty's government decided it needed to become involved in the Balkans. It was to be a NATO operation, and each of the nations involved would be taking with it a National Support Element. The joy of being the HQ of the UK NSE fell to 5 Ordnance Battalion, not long returned from clearing up the mess that had been left in the Gulf following the end of the war. They would be commanding a number of units, but from their own they would be taking a bulk petroleum capability from 51 Ordnance Company. The RAOC representation would be filled in large part by 31 Ordnance Company, with an EFI detachment attached to it. Lieutenant Colonel Malcolm Wood MBE, about to depart on his second deployment in command, could have been forgiven for wondering if was something he'd said. His re-badging into the RLC would be done on operations.

The result of this was that the amalgamation of 5 Ordnance Battalion with 6 Ordnance Battalion to form a third line regiment of the RLC had to be brought forward, to November 1992. The new unit, commanded by Lieutenant Colonel Trevor White MBE was to be called, for the time being, 5/6 Ordnance Battalion and he would command the whole thing from his HQ in Bielefeld. He would take under command the remaining companies of 5 and 6 Battalions, as well as the supply depots at Hohne, Dortmund and Munster, which had previously been the responsibility of 1 and 3 Ordnance Battalions. It was not a small task.

In September 1992 321 EOD Company celebrated its twenty-first birthday. The statistics reflected an impressive record of service. Soldiers serving with the company had recovered 200,000 kilograms of explosive, disarmed 4,700 devices and had become the most decorated unit in the Army in peacetime with more than 270 awards for bravery. The price, however, had been hard to bear. Twenty officers

Her Majesty the Queen, and it is clear from her demeanour that this event is a celebration of success and a positive view of the future and not regret for a passing. She is accompanied by the DGOS, Major General David Botting CB CBE.

and soldiers had been killed and a further twenty-two injured in pursuit of their duties in the company.

On 19 March 1993 her Majesty the Queen visited her Corps for the last time, at Deepcut. The Army at the time was deployed on nineteen operations worldwide, and, as well as supplying materiel support to them, the RAOC was deployed on some as well. These included Bosnia, Western Sahara and the Turkish/Iraq border. The visit was organized by the Chief of Staff of the Training Centre, Lieutenant Colonel Ron Gray, ably assisted by WOII (CSM) Mike Robinson. The Guard of Honour was drawn from all over the Corps, and the standard used on the parade, which was commanded by Captain Nick Wilkes, was carried by Lieutenant McMahon. It would be laid up in just a few short days in St Barbara's Church, on the penultimate day of the RAOC's existence. The Guard was joined in the march past by a collection of RAOC Association Banners, with Major General Mike Callan at their head. Her Majesty toured the barracks, saw displays and talked to people. She was reminded of the courage displayed by so many when she met five highly decorated members of the RAOC: Major Nelson Gunson MBE GM; WOI (Retd) Peter Gurney GM and Bar; Lieutenant Colonel Alan Glasby OBE GM; Major Kevin Callaghan GM QGM; WOI (SSM) Barry Johnson GC and Major (Retd) Mick Coldrick MBE GM.

She then attended a reception, enjoyed lunch in the officers' mess and, finally, unveiled a sculpture near the front door of the officers' mess to mark the seventy-five years that she and her father had been Colonels-in-Chief of the RAOC. Then she left, and her Corps prepared to step into a new future just a few days hence.

Major General David Burden, the first head of the RLC:

As I briefed the new Colonel-in-Chief in the mess at Deepcut on the morning of Monday 5 April 1993, I realized that the day was a watershed in military history. And yet an hour later, standing on the saluting dais with the Princess Royal watching the old Corps flags lower and the new one rise on a sun drenched parade ground that had been subject to a violent storm minutes before, there was a great sense of continuity. Joining the new Royal Logistic Corps was the regimental strength of the Royal Corps of Transport, the infantry skills and artisan ingenuity of the Royal Pioneer Corps, the determination and imagination to deliver in all circumstances of the Army Catering Corps and the morale-boosting role of the unsung heroes of the Postal and Courier Branch of the Royal Engineers. Much would be different including flags, uniforms, cap badges, regimental marches and unit titles; but so much would be familiar.

The Corps' home was well known and to me and many others. Familiar buildings, sights, artefacts and heritage remained. Crucially at Deepcut and elsewhere, after the heady mixture of sadness and celebration of the day, the basic worldwide framework would be familiar, well tried and recently

A highly decorated group flanking their Sovereign.

Before she left the Queen unveiled a memorial to the RAOC, positioned outside the Headquarters Officers' Mess.

successfully tested on a major operation. The RAOC supply system and its umbilical cord from depot to the front line, was in place and delivering to its dependency at home and overseas. At its head were a number of senior officers who would take their knowledge, their management skills and their soldiers into the RLC. With such tried experience the new Corps could not fail. Indeed, in many respects, the RLC would prove to be a continuum of the RAOC in the late twentieth century. That was no cause for a sleepless night!

It was a future supporting an Army that would be adapting to the changes brought about by a new world order, by the fall of the wall; the collapse of a super power, Russia, and the potential rise of another, China; the rise of a plethora of small nationalist states, some of them unstable; a global terrorist conflict; mass migration; and global organized crime. It would be an Army that would have the single, integrated supply and distribution service it had long been denied. A soldier of the RAOC from 1918 would, in many respects, recognize much with which he would be familiar: the Arms of the Board of Ordnance at the centre of the RLC cap badge; an attitude of service and commitment in sustaining the Army and a level of professionalism that allowed RLC soldiers to compete with the best in the Army, and be capable of winning on just about every score. It was a proud heritage, and it would carry on. The warrior would continue to receive his arms. Saying 'no' was still not an option.

The RLC Cap Badge, with the Ordnance Shield at its heart.

Appendix A

The Conductor

Conductor from Conducere, to conduct. One who leads, guides or escorts - *Concise Oxford Dictionary*

The earliest record of the office of Conductor is contained in the Statute of Westminster 1327 when Edward. III decreed that the wages of Conductors of Soldiers from the Shires to places of assembly would no longer be a charge upon the Shire.

During the siege of Boulogne in 1544 historical records mention the Conductor of Ordnance. Then, a Royal Warrant dated 20 January 1642 addressed to one Sir John Haydon, Lieutenant General of the Ordnance, concerning a Train of Artillery to be formed for service overseas listed three Conductors; John Kerbye to be in charge of draught horses, Christopher Jones to be in charge of the ammunition and William Anderson to be in charge of the fire workers. In 1683 Charles II issued Instructions for Our Principal Engineer which included mention of the provision of Conductors to see to the 'conducting of trenches and mines'. It is recorded that the Conductors wore red cloaks.

In 1689 a train for service in Ireland included a Chief Conductor who was paid four shillings (£23.00) a day. Further varieties of Conductor were recorded for a train established for service in Flanders in 1691. Included were Conductors of Stores, a Conductor Plumber, Conductors of Woolpacks and Conductors of Horses. At the capture of Newfoundland in 1762, Lieutenant General Amherst's force included a Conductor and Clerk of Stores. In a book dated 1776, entitled *The Military Guide for Young Officers* by Thomas Simes Esq, is written:

Conductors are assistants to the Commissary of the Stores, to receive or deliver out stores to the Army, to attend at the magazines by turns when in garrison and to look after the ammunition wagons in the field; they bring their accounts every night to the Commissary and are immediately under his command.

A Royal Warrant of 1 February 1812 detailing the establishment for a field train includes Conductors first and second class, and notes that for allowances and prize money they were to receive half of that given to a Subaltern Officer. Early records of Woolwich Arsenal give the information that in 1808 one Charles Sargent was a Conductor at the age of sixteen. He served at Corunna with Sir John Moore and was pensioned in 1818 at the early age of twenty six years. He lived on to draw a pension until 1886.

Wellington had strong views about the importance of logistics and the Board of Ordnance, early in the nineteenth century, included some 150 Conductors. For the Crimean War of 1854 records show that a siege train was hurriedly formed which included a number of Conductors of Stores. The Land Transport Corps was reorganized in 1856 and included Conductors in the establishment and in 1860, Conductors accompanied officers of the Military Store Department to New Zealand.

By Royal Warrant of 11 January 1879 a class of warrant officer was constituted to be denominated Conductors of Supplies and Conductors of Stores. Their position was to be inferior to that of all commissioned officers but superior to that of all non-commissioned officers. It was at this point that it became a military appointment for soldiers in the rank of warrant officer. The title of Conductor of Supplies was abolished in 1892 and replaced by Staff Sergeant Major 1st Class. Sub-Conductor was introduced in 1896.

After the McLeod reorganization in 1965 there were four warrant officers 1st Class appointments in the RAOC, namely Conductor, Sub-Conductor, Staff Sergeant Major 1st Class and Staff Sergeant Major. These appointments were rationaliszd to Conductor and Staff Sergeant Major in a letter referenced Ord/1/BR/2150(DOS) dated 14 November 1967. The letter acknowledged that Conductors and Staff Sergeant Majors 1st class held a special position in the Army and the titles had long historical tradition. However, it was confusing to have both, but there was a wish to continue our traditions. Conductor was originally the senior appointment in both the Army Service Corps and the Ordnance Store Corps and so it was decided that all Conductors and SSMs 1st Class should adopt the title Conductor and Staff Sergeant Majors and Sub Conductors should take the title Staff Sergeant Major. The new titles took effect on 1 January 1968

Conductor is a prestigious appointment, awarded to the best of the RAOC's warrant officers, and to hold it is a matter of honour. The incumbent is senior to all other warrant officers and junior to all commissioned officers in the whole of the Army. He attends the sergeants' mess, but is no longer a member. As a mark of his importance whenever the Colonel-in-Chief paid a visit to the RAOC she was always greeted by the Head of the Corps accompanied by the senior Conductor. The Conductor's status permits him to wear an officer's accoutrements and to take the place of a subaltern officer on parade,

It is an appointment that transferred to the RLC on its formation and it is to be hoped they work actively to retain it. A measure of its significance is contained in a letter from General Sir Michael Gow of the Scots Guards who, when commanding 4 Guards Brigade, wrote to the editor of the *Gazette*:

In the Foot Guards, a Regimental Sergeant Major is always referred to as 'The Sergeant Major' and never as 'Mister'. It is thus quite clear that the holder of this appointment is unique – that there is only one such person in a battalion, and the other warrant officers are called 'Quartermaster Sergeants' (for the RQMS), 'Company Sergeant Major' and so on.

It is, or should be, well known throughout the Army that the Senior Warrant Officer rank is held by your Corps, and that is the Conductor. This ancient title can be traced back to 1327, and it must be a source of pride to any Warrant Officer who is privileged to hold this rank and appointment. Yet it distresses me that a Conductor is referred to as 'Mister' and not by his proper title. Had I been remaining in my present appointment I would have no hesitation in directing that my BOWO and Chief Clerk should be addressed properly, and trust that this letter will be received favourably in influential and authoritative circles in the Royal Army Ordnance Corps so that this error is put right.

Appendix B

What Do They All Mean

Names of Some RAOC Installations
From the RAOC Gazette January 1948

Bicester: The earliest record is the Domesday Book when in 1130 it was called 'Bernecestre' and later in 1219 it was called 'Burnecestre'. The first element is from Old English 'byrgen', a burial ground, of ancient British origin, similar to the tumuli on Salisbury Plain. Later the Romans built a road across it, 'Akeman Street'. The origin of Akeman is obscure but the old name of Bath in 973 was 'Acemannes ceaster'. The Romans also built a 'castra' on the burial ground and this word was rendered in Old English as 'caester', meaning 'a city or walled town, originally one that had been a Roman Station', so the meaning of Bicester is 'A Roman Station on a British burial ground'.

Bramley: Was called 'Brumelai' in the Domesday Book and later in 1160 'Bromelege'. It is from Old English 'brom-leah' meaning 'a clearing in the forest overgrown with broom'.

Chilwell: This is identical with 'Childwall' in Lancashire. It was originally 'Childeuuelle' in the Domesday Book, meaning 'the stream of the children'. The reason for the name is obscure.

Derby: Derby was called 'Deoraby' in the Anglo-Saxon Chronicle in 917, but later in 1000 'Nornworthog'. This name seems to have been dropped for, in the Domesday Book, it is called 'Derby'. It is from Old Scandinavian 'dinraby', ' the By or village where the deer were seen'. It is interesting to note that 'Normanton' just outside means 'the town of the Norwegians'.

Corsham: It was called 'Cosesham' in 1001 and 'Corseham' in the Domesday Book. It probably means, Cossa's or Cusa's homestead, but this derivation is not absolutely clear.

Donnington: It was called 'Dunniton' in 1180, and by 1303 'Donynton'. The origin is very similar to Donnington in Berkshire, which was originally 'Dunnan Straettun', which meant 'The town on Fosse Way belonging to Dunn'. In this case however the 'town' is near Watling Street, called 'Waeclingastreat' in Old English, and meant 'the road to Watlingceaster' or 'St. Albans'.

Feltham: It has been called that since 969 and means 'the ham or village in the field'.

Greenford: Was called 'et Grenan fords' in 845 and as 'Greneford Magna' in 1254. It means 'Greentord'. Greenford minor or 'Little Greenford' is now called Pedvale or 'Pear tree valley'.

Kineton: Known as 'Cyntun' in 969 and 'Quinton' in the Domesday Book, it is from the Old English 'cyne-tun' or Royal Manor.

Appendix C

Ordnance Department Awards

Victoria Cross

18 June 1858   Lieutenants G FORREST, W RAYNOR and J BUCKLEY of the Bengal Ordnance Department for the defence of the Magazine at Delhi on 11 May 1857 during the Indian Mutiny

25 February 1862   Conductor J MILLER of the Bengal Ordnance Department for rescuing a wounded officer under fire on 28 October 1857 during the Indian Mutiny

George Cross

24 December 1940   Captain R L JEPHSON-JONES and Lieutenant W M EASTMAN for bomb disposal work between June and November 1940, on the island of Malta

11 October 1946   Major K A BIGGS and Staff Sergeant S G ROGERSON for limiting the effects of an explosion at a railhead in an ammunition depot at Savernake, Wiltshire on 2 January 1946

11 January 1972   Major S G STYLES for defusing two large terrorist bombs at the Europa Hotel, Belfast

6 November 1990   WOI B JOHNSON for dismantling a terrorist mortar device in Londonderry despite being badly injured in the process

George Medal

17 December 1940   Captain R CHALKLEY – Bomb Disposal

17 December 1940   Captain D A S MARTIN – Explosive clearance, Gibraltar

22 July 1941	Captain F V PLATEL, Staff Sergeant THORNER and Staff Sergeant I TELFORD – Limiting effects of explosion in cave gallery used for ammunition storage at Massara, Nr Cairo, Egypt
26 September 1943	Captain T W DOWNING – Reducing danger after an ammunition accident on the SS 'Craster' in Belfast Lough, Northern Ireland
23 December 1943	Lieutenant J SEARCH – Preventing an explosion in a petrol fire on the quay at Syracuse, Italy
28 July 1944	Major R W H BEATON and Major W WHITTLES – Limiting effects of an explosion at an ammunition depot, Bitonto, Italy
15 September 1944	Sergeant F W PEARCE – Grenade incident at HQ Training Establishment Battle Camp, Bradgate Park, Ashby-de-la-Zouch
10 November 1944	Major G C G PEPPER and Sergeant J S McGOWAN – Preventing an explosion after an air raid at the petrol and ammunition dump at La Brache d'Hermanville, France
15 March 1946	Captain M F SMITH – Saving life after an explosion at an enemy ammunition dump on Erns/Jade Canal, Ernden, Germany
11 October 1946	Sergeant D A KAY – Limiting effects of explosion at an ammunition depot at Savernake, Wiltshire
26 June 1947	Sub Conductor E R ROBSON – preventing an explosion at a Japanese ammunition depot at Zyathwye, South Burma
2 July 1948	Staff Sergeant K W NASH – Saving life after explosion in ammunition repair workshop, Saxelby, Leicestershire
31 July 1951	Captain R V HARLEY (R Sussex Regt att RAOC pending transfer) and Private GIBBONS – Saving life after explosion in a storehouse, Hampstead Norris, Berkshire
23 April 1954	Private A HILTON – A non-swimmer who rescued two soldiers from a vehicle which crashed into a river in winter
12 March 1957	Sergeant A T TAYLOR – Bomb disposal – Terrorism – Famagusta, Cyprus
19 June 1957	Captain G PROSSER – Bomb disposal – Terrorism – Belfast docks, Northern Ireland
23 July 1957	Sergeant J T PROUDLOCK – Bomb disposal – Terrorism – Nicosia, Cyprus
14 July 1959	Staff Sergeant F G GIBLETT – Bomb Disposal – Terrorism – Larnaca area, Cyprus
7 August 1959	Major W C HARRISON MBE – Bomb Disposal – Terrorism – Athelussa, Cyprus
7 February 1964	Major W MUSSON and Conductor S BRAZIER – Disposal of grenades on building site in Aldershot, Hants
19 February 1965	Major P S EASTERBY MBE – Bomb Disposal – Terrorism – Nicosia, Cyprus

27 August 1965	Captain T A L JUDGE – Bomb Disposal – Terrorism – Malacca, Malaysia
1 February 1966	Major C W SMITH and Captain P W E ISTEAD – Limiting effects of an ammunition train explosion, Minden Niedersachsen, West Germany
18 March 1966	Captain M HALL and Conductor B REID – Bomb Disposal – Terrorism – Malacca, Malaysia
25 March 1966	Major J F ELLIOTT – Bomb Disposal – Terrorism – Aden
20 February 1968	Major G C BROWNLEE – Bomb Disposal – Terrorism – Aden

Terrorist Bomb Disposal – Northern Ireland Post 1971

15 February 1972	Captain D MARKHAM Captain A J CLOUTER SQMS T J GREEN
3 October 1972	Captain R F MENDHAM Sergeant R E DEDMAN
20 February 1973	SQMS P M DANDY SQMS M J MITCHELL
1 May 1973	WOII J M COLDRICK Captain H D McCORMACK Captain M F STACEY WOII C B TENNANT
24 July 1973	WOI P E S GURNEY (1)
18 September 1973	Sergeant K CALLAGHAN (2) WOI F H ELDRED Captain J N GUNSON
18 December 1973	Captain C FIELD Major M W NEWCOMBE
19 March 1974	Staff Sergeant A V GLASBY (3) Lieutenant Colonel M H MacKENZIE-ORR OBE
18 June 1974	Staff Sergeant A G GRIFFIN Major J A JACKSON MBE WOII D OLDHAM
25 March 1975	Lieutenant Colonel J M GAFF
11 January 1977	Staff Sergeant R J BRUCE
12 December 1977	WOII K F A ADAMS
19 September 1978	Staff Sergeant G GOODRUM
21 April 1980	Staff Sergeant J A ANDERSON

11 November 1986	Major M J DAVISON MBE
12 April 1988	WOII P M HURRY
31 October 1989	Staff Sergeant M G KNOX
14 May 1991	Major K MOLLISON
5 November 1991	Major M BLATHERWICK MBE
27 October 1992	Captain J L A EARLEY QGM (2) WOII D A DUFFY BEM

Bibliography

Barnett, Correlli, *Britain and Her Army*, Cassell & Co., 1970

Carver, Field Marshall Lord, GCB CBE DSO MC, *Britain's Army in the 20th Century*, Macmillan, in association with the Imperial War Museum, 1998

Chandler, David, and others, *The Oxford History of the British Army*, Oxford University Press, 1994

Fernyhough, Brigadier A H, CBE MC, *History of the Royal Army Ordnance Corps 1920 – 1945*, Royal Army Ordnance Corps

Forbes , Major General A, CB CMG, *A History of the Army Ordnance Services,* The Medici Society, 1929

Haslam, Captain M J, RAOC, *The Chilwell Story*, RAOC Gazette1982

Hastings, Max and Jenkins, Simon, *The Battle for the Falklands*, Pan Books, 1997

Horrocks, Lieutenant General Sir Brian KCB, KBE, DSO, MC LLD (Hon), *A Full Life*, Collins, 1960

Kennett, Brigadier B B, CBE and Tatman, Colonel J A, *Craftsmen of the Army*, Leo Cooper, 1970

Lawton, E R and Sackett, Major M W, *Bicester Military Railway*, Oxford Publishing Co., 1992

Liddel Hart, B H, *History of the Second World War*, MacMillan, 1970

Lowe, Norman, *Modern British History*, Palgrave, 1984

Morgan, Kenneth O, *The Oxford History of Britain*, Oxford University Press, 1999

Mowat, Charles Loch, *Britain Between the Wars 1919-1940*, Methuen & Co., 1955

Phelps, Major General L T H, *A History of the Royal Army Ordnance Corps 1945 – 1982*, The Royal Army Ordnance Corps

Sharpe, L C, *The Field Train Department of the Board of Ordnance 1793 to 1859*, L C Sharpe, 1993

Shaw, Brevet Lieutenant Colonel G C, RAOC, *Supply in Modern War*, Faber & Faber Ltd., 1938

Steer, Frank, *Arnhem – The Fight to Sustain*, Pen & Sword, 2000

– *Arnhem – The Landing Grounds and Oosterbeek*, Pen & Sword, 2001

– *Arnhem – The Bridge*, Pen & Sword, 2002

Official Military Publications:

The Administrative History of the Operations of 21st Army Group on the Continent of Europe

Regimental Publications:

The RAOC *Gazette* 1918- 1993

21 Army Group Ordnance, Major J Lee-Richardson RAOC (Printed and published in Germany 1946)

A Logistician's War - A History of RAOC Operations on Op GRANBY, Major S N Addy RAOC

Unpublished Sources:

Reminiscences of ADOS Staff HQ 48 Division collected by Major George Critchell

Uncle Charlie related by C H Eyles

50 Years of Bicester and Bicester Garrison 1942 - 1992

Chilwell 1939 - 1945

Assorted papers provided by retired and serving officers and soldiers

Other Sources

The RLC Museum, Deepcut, Hampshire

The World Wide Web

Index

Anti-Aircraft Command, 160, 167
Antwerp, 116, 120, 121, 122, 152, 242, 291, 294, 302
Anzio, 100
Apps, Corporal Caroline, 307
Aqaba, 169
Arab league, 152
Arab-Israeli war, 197
Arborfield, 62
Archangel, 18
Argentine Air Force, 259
Argyle and Sutherland Highlanders, 85, 197
Army Air Corps (AAC), 167, 168, 262
Army and Navy Club, 201
Army Catering Corps (ACC), 308, 316
Army Officers Emergency Reserve (AOER), 59, 71
Army Ordnance Corps (AOC), 8, 9, 10, 11, 12, 15, 16
Army Ordnance Department, 8, 12
Army Physical Training Corps, 279
Army School of Ammunition, 146
Army School of Music, Kneller Hall, 312
Army Service Corps (ASC), 13, 15
Arncott, 77
Arnhem, 117, 120, 124
Arnold, 79
Arques, 15
Arras, 66
Arromanches, 112
Arsbeck, 229, 243
Arsenal FC, 142
Artillery College, Woolwich, 20
Ascension Island, 252, 254
Ashchurch, 212, 215, 230, 242, 244, 271, 279, 287
Ashford, 40, 208, 219
Ashford, Private W, 141
Asser, Major J W, 22-30, 62
Aswan Dam, 164
Atatürk, 18
Atkins, Major R N, 243
Atlantic Conveyer, 252, 255, 256
Attlee, Clement, 127-8, 130, 149
Auchinleck, Field Marshal Sir Claude, 79, 87, 99
Audruicq, 15
Austen, Mrs, 48
Austen, Sub-Conductor, 48

Austria, 56
Auxiliary Territorial Service (ATS), 63, 70, 86, 128, 215
Avery, Sergeant, 285
Ayrshire Barracks, 197, 242, 314

B

Bad Oyenhausen, 136, 149
Baghdad pact, 164
Baghdad, 29
Bahrain, 167, 172, 184, 193, 197
Bailey, Reverend Derek, 275
Baird, Corporal, 204
Baker, Driver A J, 135
Baker, Major Bill, 170
Baker, Major General J, 52
Baldwin, Private Anthony, 133
Balkans, 315
Ball, Captain Peter, 244
Ballincollog, 21
Ballykinler, 203, 225
Baltic Ferry, 258
Bamber, SQMS, 86
Band, Lieutenant Colonel, 100
Bangham, Ken, 141
Bangkok Accord, 195
Banks, Captain Nigel, 300
Barclay, Colonel Neil, 193
Bari, 99
Barker Barracks, 207
Barker, Sergeant D K, 287
Barnett, Private F, 135
Barnwell, 142
Barratt, Brigadier Brian, 247
Barrett, Private, 50
Barry, 133
Barry, Lieutenant Jim, 281
Basing, 111
Basingstoke, 232
Basra, 21
Bass, Major Brenda, 215
Bataan, 123
Bateson, Lieutenant Colonel Ronnie, 205
Battersby, Captain John, 179
Beale, Private J M, 146
Beale, Major Margaret, 215
Beddington Committee, 136
Bedford, Sergeant M J, 162

British Somaliland, 75
Bromham, Lieutenant Colonel R W, 225
Bromley, Major, 87
Bron, Private D E, 141
Brown, Major E H, 203
Brown, George, 197
Brown, Brigadier Harry, 249, 282
Brown, Major General Jimmy, 247, 250, 261
Brown, Corporal, 285
Brown, Sub-Conductor, 160
Brownlee, Major G C, 185
Bruce, Sergeant, later Captain Norman, 162, 169, 181, 187
Bruce, Captain, 27
Bruen, Lieutenant Colonel E J, 182
Bruggen, 222
Brunei, 177, 206, 226
Brüning, Chancellor, 41
Buckingham Palace, 55
Buckingham, 167, 174
Buckley, Conductor John, 282, 283
Bulford, 47
Burden, Major General David, 314, 316
Burke, Private, 285
Burma, 90, 103, 125
Burma railway 'Railway of Death', 96, 103, 112
Burnip, Lieutenant Colonel Bill, 265
Burscough, 25, 208
Burton, Staff Sergeant K, 262
Bushell, Sergeant, 257
Butler, Lieutenant G E, 46
Bye, Sergeant Donald, 130
Byrd, Lieutenant Colonel, later Colonel Terry, 300, 311

C

Caen, 112
Cairnryan, 133
Cairo, 30, 50, 80, 89, 94, 98, 99, 129, 165
Calais, 115
Calcutta, 125
Calladene, Major Bernard, 214-15
Callaghan, Major Kevin, 316
Callaghan, Lieutenant Colonel Norman, 306
Callan, Lieutenant, later Major General, 158, 164, 214, 236, 250, 274, 282, 316
Camberley, 275
Cambrian patrol, 288

Cameron, Colonel D C, 37-8
Cameron Highlanders, 57
Camfield, Lieutenant, later Captain Tony, 158, 167, 179
Canada, 299
Canadian Amy, 112
Cannons, Lieutenant Colonel Bob, 306
Cantrell, Captain Freddie, 190
Cape, Brigadier John, 126
Carlier, Major General Neil, 289
Carline, Lyn, 295
Carpenter, Captain, later Major David, 173, 200, 204
Carrington, Lord Peter, 207, 243. 250
Carson, Private D B, 287
Casablanca, 89, 91
Casdagli, Captain, 78
Cassino, 98
Catterick, 40, 46, 208, 209, 218
Celle, 187, 197
Central Electricity Generating Board, 184, 190
Central Treaty Organization, 164
Chamberlain, Neville, 56, 58, 60, 63, 67, 127
Chambers, Major General Peter, 286
Champion, Major Ted, 238, 244
Chanak, 29
Changi gaol, 103
Changi Village, 85
Chapman, Sergeant, 62
Charlton brothers, 153
Charlton, Lance Corporal R, 169
Chatham, 4, 40
Cheltenham, 91
Chetwynd, Hon. Eve, 249
Chiang Kai-shek, 144, 148
Chidgey, Captain, later Major C C 'Bill', 98, 119, 120
Child, Alfred Ernest, 276
Chilman, Major H C S, 179
Chilwell, 19, 31, 40, 47, 48, 49, 52, 57, 70, 71, 76, 113, 132, 136, 142, 145, 151, 159, 165, 170, 171, 182, 189, 193, 195, 206, 212, 220, 231, 242, 247, 249-50
China, 30, 33, 90
Chittening, 22
Chukai, 156
Church of St Michael and All Angels, 198
Churchill, Winston, 56, 63, 68, 71, 79, 84, 87,

Middleton Stoney, 140
Midgley, Alan, 111
Military College of Science, 38
Miller, Colonel J F X, 77
Milton, 171
Minden Barracks, 214
Minden, 192
miners' strike, 274
Ministry of Defence (MOD), 189, 203, 205, 206, 209, 273, 278, 299-300, 313
Ministry of Supply, 52-3
Mintoff, Dom, 211
Mitchell, Lieutenant Colonel Colin, 197
Mitchell, Conductor, 50
Mitchell, Major Harry, 184
Mitchell, Mrs, 44
Mitchell, Captain Ray, 198
Mobbs, Lieutenant Colonel Gerry, 119
Mobley, Lieutenant Colonel Brian, 299, 300
Mockford, Lieutenant Colonel J A, 147
Mockford, Staff Sergeant, 50
Model, 118
Mombasa, 75, 131
Monarch, 201
Mönchengladbach, 137, 143, 155, 170, 177, 197, 199, 205, 223, 242, 291, 314
Mons, Battle of, 13
Montgomerie-Massingberd, Sir Archibald, 46
Montgomery, General, later Field Marshal Bernard, 87, 88, 89, 95, 98, 100, 116, 117, 124, 129, 130, 148
Moorcroft, Private Colin, 105, 125
Moore, Major General Jeremy, 254, 256
Morris, Major Joyce, 215
Morris, SQMS R, 221
Morris, Lieutenant Colonel Temple, 67
Moss, Sergeant Keith, 174
Mosul, 29
Motor Traders' Association, 62
Mould, Ron, 96
Mount Everest, 27, 235
Mountbatten, Vice Admiral Lord Louis, 99, 126, 130
Muir, Corporal Jamie, 288
Mukden Incident, 43
Mulberry harbour, 116
Munich air crash, 162
Munsey, SQMS L, 161

Münster, 28, 177, 207, 315
Murdoch, Private, 94, 120
Murray, Lieutenant Colonel Tim, 293, 296, 299
Mussolini, Benito, 41
MV *Baltic Ferry*, 254
MV *Elk*, 252, 255
MV *St Edmond*, 254

N

NAAFI, 185, 210, 244, 253
Nagasaki, 126
Nairobi, 75, 152
Nairobi Internal Security Battalion, 158
Namsos, 68
Nantes, 64, 65
Nanyuki, 64, 75
Napoleonic Wars, 5
Narvik, 68
Nasser, Colonel Gamel Abdel, 152, 153, 163, 164, 167
Nathan, Peter, 278
National Army Museum, 282
National Cash Register accounting system, 49
National Government, 41
national miners' strike, 35
National Service, 129, 140, 141-2, 166, 175, 176, 180, 247
Neal, Lance Corporal David, 302
Nesscliffe, 122, 133, 142, 158, 167, 269
Netheravon, 47
Neuralia, 43
New Scotland Yard, 219
Newbury, 62, 63
Newby, Sub-Conductor Bill, 21
Newby, Tom, 21-2
Newell, Major David, 298
Newry, 246
Nicosia, 183
Nienburg Petroleum Deport, 229
Nigeria, 75
Nijmegen, 119
Nippes, 28
Normandy Veterans Association, 311
North Africa, 99
North America campaign, 5
North Atlantic Treaty Organization (NATO), 143, 148, 176, 194, 199, 202, 227, 233, 245, 251, 252, 268, 287, 291, 295

Richards, Colonel (later Major General) W W, 65-6, 73, 81, 89, 129
Richardson, Conductor, 290
Richardson, Mrs, 44
Richardson, WOII, 290
Richmond Barracks, 239
Ridge Depot, 82
Ridgeway, General Matthew B, 150
Ritchie, Captain H M, 166
Riyadh, 291, 300
Roberts, Cyril, 96
Roberts, Lance Corporal Irvine, 96-7
Roberts, Major General, 99, 116
Roberts, Ted, 125
Robinson, Captain, 48
Robinson, Major Joyce, 215
Robinson, Lance Corporal K T, 287
Robinson, Lieutenant Colonel Mike, 238
Robinson, WOII (CSM) Mike, 316
Robinson, Corporal, later Lieutenant Colonel 'Robbie', 223, 244, 271, 279, 280
Robinson, Mrs, 48
Rogers, Lieutenant Colonel Colin, 233
Rogerson, Staff Sergeant S G, 135
Rogerson, Staff Sergeant Sidney, 276
Rome, 103, 106
Rommel, Field Marshal Erwin, 77, 79, 83, 87, 88, 89
Roosevelt, Franklin D, 99
Rootes, (Lord) W E, 59
Rotterdam, 41
Royal Air Force (RAF), 19, 23, 53, 54, 63, 90, 99, 112, 142, 167, 168, 186, 189, 194, 199, 234, 235, 246, 252, 253, 268, 269, 278, 287, 292, 302
    Akrotiri, 231, 269
    Khormaksar, 186
    Northolt, 111
Royal Armoured Corps (RAC), 167, 315
Royal Army Clothing Department, 44
Royal Army Educational Corps(RAEC), 313
Royal Army Medical Corps (RAMC), 54, 102, 192, 225, 226
Royal Army Ordnance Corps (RAOC), 4, 5, 8, 9, 10, 11, 16, 17, 18
    Aid Society, 22
    Anti-Aircraft Command, 42
    Apprentices' College, 275

Association, 36, 58, 315
Association Banners, 316
badge, 157, 181, 275
band, 37, 60, 95, 98, 144, 238, 247, 250, 267, 275, 279, 280, 302, 312
bandmaster, 50
birth, 16
cap badge, 313
Charitable Fund, 22
combatant status, 79
D-Day casualties, 107
Felix tie, 210, 215
first National Serviceman, 141
flag, 181, 250, 260, 316
Gazette, 22, 23, 25, 27-8, 35, 38, 42, 43, 54, 57, 58, 59, 62, 67, 72, 85, 94-5, 104, 135, 136, 137, 158, 159, 161-2, 176, 184, 214, 216, 306, 312, 315
in Iraq, 305
march, 26, 45, 67
Memorial Fund, 143
Mobile Display Team, 155
motto, 27
Officer Cadet Training Unit, 97
Officers' Club, 20, 66, 136, 315
Officers' Mess Ball, 157
Officers' School, 145
Old Comrades Association, 36
organization, 38-40
patron saint, 26
Polo Team, 44
Records Office, 26
reorganization, 88
School, 26, 136, 163
sport, 36-7, 43-4, 46, 50-1, 54, 57, 62, 135-6, 142, 146, 148, 153-5, 158, 162, 169, 172, 173, 181, 187, 199-200, 204-5, 218, 221, 223, 226, 232, 244, 249, 265, 271, 277, 279, 280-1, 285-6, 302
Sports Association, 135
Sua Tela Tonanti, 45
Sunday, 315
TA Pipe Band, 186
The Cannonballs freefall parachute team, 277, 279
training centre, 234
Trust, 315
war memorial, 143

Y

Z